GUIDING LEARNING WITH TECHNOLOGY

Niess, Lee, and Kajder

GUIDING LEARNING WITH TECHNOLOGY

Margaret Niess
Professor of Science and
Mathematics Education
Oregon State University

John Lee
Associate Professor of
Middle Grades and Social
Studies Education
North Carolina State Univeristy

Sara Kajder
Assistant Professor of
English Education
Virginia Tech

BICENTENNIAL
BICENTENNIAL
1807
WILEY
2007
BICENTENNIAL
BICENTENNIAL

John Wiley & Sons, Inc.

VICE PRESIDENT AND PUBLISHER	Jay O'Callaghan
ACQUISITIONS EDITOR	Robert Johnston
PRODUCTION MANAGER	Dorothy Sinclair
MARKETING MANAGER	Emily Streutker
DESIGNER	Kevin Murphy
ILLUSTRATION EDITOR	Sandra Rigby
PHOTO EDITOR	Hilary Newman
MEDIA EDITOR	Lynn Pearlman
EDITORIAL ASSISTANT	Eileen McKeever
PRODUCTION MANAGEMENT SERVICES	Ingrao Associates
PHOTO CREDIT	©Andersen Ross/Digital Vision/Getty Images
BICENTENNIAL LOGO DESIGN	Richard J. Pacifico

This book was set in 10.5/12 Slimbach Med by Prepare and printed and bound by Courier Kendallville. The cover was printed by Courier Kendallville.

This book is printed on acid free paper. ∞

To order books or for customer service please call 1-800-CALL WILEY (225-5945).
ISBN 978-0471-65388-2

Printed in the United States of America

10 9 8 7 6 5 4 3 2 1

Brief Contents

Contents

Guiding Learning with Technology by Margaret Niess, John Lee, and Sara Kajder

Preface

Who dares to teach must never cease to learn.
—*John Cotton Dana*

Remember the Year 2000 problem—the Y2K problem or the millennium bug? Although widely advertised, no significant computer failures occurred when the clocks rolled over into 2000. Was the lack of significant failures a result of *preparation* or was the problem overstated? Certainly the concern led to significant examinations, revisions, and improvements in the computer systems in *preparation* for rolling into 2000.

With the arrival of the twenty-first century, significant challenges emerged for the education of future citizens. Will *all* students, regardless of their personal characteristics, backgrounds, or physical challenges, have opportunities to learn the knowledge, skills, judgment, and wisdom for becoming productive citizens in the twenty-first century? Will they be educated for living and working in a society significantly influenced by constantly emerging technological advances? Will the existence, versatility, and power of information and communications technologies make it possible and necessary to reexamine the curriculum they should learn and how they can best learn it? Will the technologies be used well or poorly in the process of educating *all* future citizens? These concerns are perhaps every bit as critical as the concerns were with the potential millennium bug. The question is, How will education respond to these concerns?

Teachers are keys for assuring educational reform that adequately prepares students to meet the challenges of the twenty-first century! However, they cannot simply teach as they were taught and what they were taught. As teachers, they must *continue learning*. They must also be *prepared*! They must consistently engage in learning about the new and emerging technologies. They must consistently focus on learning how to teach both *about* and *with* the new and emerging technologies. They must learn and become active participants in curriculum and instruction revision. This learning is initiated in their teacher preparation programs. In fact, teacher preparation programs are currently challenged to establish the foundation on which their graduates are poised and committed to continued learning.

Guiding Learning with Technology is intended to support the entire teacher preparation program preparing those of you who are or who will be teachers in the twenty-first century. It is designed to help you guide students in learning with multiple information and communications technologies—both the existing and the emerging technologies. The overarching goal for this book is to challenge your thinking in ways that stimulate your interest, preparation, and continued learning in guiding students as they learn with technology.

The focus, then, of this book is on preparing you for teaching your content where you develop a strong integrated knowledge base about the technology, about teaching your content with technology, and about incorporating sound teaching and learning practices with technologies as integral learning tools. This book is about helping you develop a technological pedagogical content knowledge (TPCK) that will support you as you continue to learn about teaching with technology throughout your career in teaching.

Book Content

Guiding Learning with Technology is divided into three main parts. Part I (Chapters 1–4) sets the stage for your preparation to guide learning with technology. The first chapter introduces the concept of technological pedagogical content knowledge (TPCK) and its importance for teaching your subject matter at your intended grade level. The second chapter illustrates and discusses the National Educational Technology Standards for Teachers (NETS·T) and how they can guide your development of TPCK. The third and fourth chapters focus on students, namely, the current understandings about how students learn followed by the current National Educational Technology Standards for Students (NETS·S).

The second part (Chapters 5–10) is designed to engage you in learning, unlearning, and relearning with and about some of the key information and communications technologies for teaching in the twenty-first century. Each chapter is focused around a technology capability and how those capabilities can be integrated with teaching multiple subjects and grade levels. Specially, the Student Technology Standards and how you might guide students' learning about and with the specific technology are the focus in each chapter.

- *Writing and Word Processing* (Chapter 5) explores the importance of all teachers' involvement in guiding students in learning to use word processing as they communicate in writing.

- *Spreadsheets* (Chapter 6) establishes your knowledge about spreadsheets while also demonstrating how spreadsheets can support students in learning in multiple subject areas to use them as productivity, communications, research, and problem-solving and decision-making tools.

- *The Internet and Databases* (Chapter 7) connects database technologies with the Internet, showing how you can guide student learning both with and about these technologies. A specific emphasis in this chapter deals with guiding students' learning about social, ethical, and human issues when using the Internet while learning to use them as productivity, communications, research, and problem-solving and decision-making tools.

- *Multimedia and Media Literacy* (Chapter 8) discusses a twenty-first-century view of literacy, a literacy that recognizes the importance of using multiple medias in developing ideas and in becoming multimedia authors as a means of learning. This chapter discusses the multimedia design process for integrating media such as concept mapping software, presentation software, and movie or video software development while incorporating these multimedia in learning language arts, mathematics, science, and social studies.

- *Hypermedia and Web Authoring* (Chapter 9) expands the idea of multimedia to authoring Web hypermedia. A particular emphasis in this chapter is on authoring nonsequential media and developing electronic portfolios that display growth in learning as well as the result of learning.

- *Responding to Emerging Technologies* (Chapter 10) is the chapter that recognizes that information and communications technologies keep evolving and emerging. The focus of the chapter is on helping you develop an open attitude toward an active pursuit of the advances in emerging technologies, looking for ways that you might use them to support your students' learning. The technologies that are discussed serve only as examples to engage your thinking about potential changes in the curriculum you teach and tools that you might use to engage your students in an active learning environment. Ultimately, your considerations toward emerging technology tools must be directed toward providing students with *tools for thinking and learning* in the twenty-first century.

The third part (Chapters 11–13) is directed toward your pedagogical preparation for guiding students in learning with technology. This part of the book focuses on teaching with technologies, integrating the various strategies in your classroom designs and lessons, implementation, and assessment of instruction with technology as an integral component of the curriculum and instruction.

- *Models and Strategies for Technology-Infused Lessons* (Chapter 11) focuses your attention on the development of a repertoire of various instructional models and teaching strategies for teaching with technology. No one strategy is best in every instructional case. As recommended in the NETS for teachers, having a set of generic models and strategies that are multipurpose in application will assist you in developing technology-infused lessons. The ideas in this chapter are linked to the lesson ideas that are developed in Chapters 5–10.

- *Designing, Implementing, and Reflecting on Instruction with Technology* (Chapter 12) is devoted to an examination of the questions and challenges for expanding and enhancing your thinking and decision-making skills throughout the three stages of a teacher's thinking when teaching with technology: planning prior to teaching; monitoring and regulating while teaching; assessing and revising after teaching. These challenges focus the development of your ability to integrate your knowledge of the content you plan to teach, your knowledge of teaching and student learning, and your knowledge of the technology.

- *Assessing Learning with Technology* (Chapter 13) directs your attention to assessing subject matter content knowledge, technological content knowledge, and the knowledge of how students process their understandings of the subject matter content with the technology. This chapter is focused on helping you appreciate and gain an understanding of how technology can be used to enrich the evidence of student learning.

Key Features of This Text

Guiding Learning with Technology is a unique resource designed to be useful to you throughout your teacher preparation program as well to support you when you enter the classroom as a licensed teacher who never *ceases to learn*. Five key features highlight the usefulness of the text:

1. *Snapshot of Learning and Teaching with Technology.* Each chapter begins with a classroom problem, situation, or example to set the stage for the emphasis in the chapter. These snapshots are intended to provide you with the realities of teaching with technology, with a focus toward the particular chapters in which they appear. They demonstrate effective classroom practices and illustrate the vital role that you play as the teacher in guiding students' learning with technology.

2. *In the Classroom* activities highlight ideas for teaching with technologies in ways to guide students in meeting important objectives as identified by the National Educational Technology Standards for Students (NETS·S) and the content area standards in language arts, mathematics, science, or social studies. These activities are designed to be used with your students when you are in your practicum or student teaching as well as when you are a licensed teacher.

3. *Technology Links* are provided throughout the text. These links are accessed through the publisher's website (www.wiley.com/college/niess) as a means of providing you with the most up-to-date links. The links are identified individually throughout the text and collectively in the Technology Links matrix provided in Part IV of this book along with descriptions of the topic for the link.

4. *End-of-the-Chapter Activities and References.* Each chapter concludes with:

   - Practice Problems that provide opportunities to guide your learning about the ideas in the chapter;

   - In the Classroom Activities that encourage you to integrate your developing understandings as you observe and work with students and teachers in actual classrooms;

   - Assessing Student Learning with and about Technology where you are challenged to consider the issue of assessing students' learning in a technology-enhanced learning environment;

   - E-Portfolio Activities that provide ideas for developing an electronic portfolio as a demonstration of your developing understandings;

   - Reflection and Discussion challenges for continuing the dialogue about the chapter ideas; and

   - Annotated Resources for you to use as you think about and develop your knowledge and skills with the chapter ideas.

5. Standards, Links, and Matrices are included in Part IV as appendices. This information is offered to support you as you investigate the ideas and focus your continued learning. Among the items in this part are the following:

   - NETS student standards,

   - NETS teacher standards,

   - Matrix linking the Interstate New Teacher Assessment and Support Consortium (INTASC) 10 principles with the NETS teacher standards providing a framework for linking the essential knowledge, skills, and abilities of new teachers as they begin their first teaching positions with guidelines for teaching with technology,

- Sample of aligning the English/language arts standards with the NETS student standards to demonstrate the integration of technology in learning specific content,
- Website links to multiple curriculum area professional organizations,
- Matrix that summarizes the In the Classroom activities throughout the text,
- Matrix that summarizes the Technology Links throughout the text,
- Glossary of terms and their use in the various chapters of the text, and
- A comprehensive reference list.

For instructors: (Available at www.wiley.com/college/niess.)

Instructor's Manual: Designed to help instructor's maximize student learning, the Instructor's Manual presents the authors' teaching philosophy, contains sample syllabi and chapter outlines as well as ideas for in-class discussion, and ideas for in-class and out-of-class activities.

Test Bank: The Test Bank is a comprehensive testing package that allows instructors to tailor examinations to chapter objectives, learning skills and content. It includes traditional types of questions (i.e., true-false, multiple-choice, matching, and short answer), as well as open-ended essay questions.

PowerPoint slides: The PowerPoint slides aid professors in visually presenting the key concepts found in each chapter of the text. Intended as a lecture guide, the PowerPoint slides present material in a concise format that enables easy note-taking.

The Wiley Faculty Network: The Wiley Faculty Network (WFN) is a faculty-to-faculty network promoting professional development and training. The WFN facilitates the exchange of best practices, connects teachers with technology, and helps to enhance instructional efficiency and effectiveness. The WFN provides training and professional development with online seminars, peer-to-peer exchanges of experiences and ideas, personalized consulting and sharing of resources. For more information on the Wiley Faculty Network, please contact your local Wiley representative. Go to www.WhereFacultyConnect.com, or call 1-866-4FACULTY.

For students:

The Book Companion Site: (www.wiley.com/college/niess) will contain support material that will help students develop an understanding of course concepts and teaching methodologies and strategies. Some of the resources available are listed below.

Study Guide: The Study Guide includes pre- and post-chapter assessment questions including true-false, multiple-choice, short answer and essay.

Web Resources and Technology Links: This resource provides links to major websites cited in the chapter text as well as other web resources for students.

Links to National and State Standards

Acknowledgments

This book could never have been completed without the thousands of students over our many years of guiding both preservice and in-service teachers to teach with technology. Their enthusiasm and questions have energized us as we have explored multiple technologies and considered how these technologies might be used as learning tools in multiple content areas. Of course, no thanks will be complete without recognizing the many K–12 students we have taught in language arts, mathematics, science, and social studies over the years. They helped us understand the importance of *learning with students* as we guided their explorations with the technologies toward the development of essential knowledge and skills in the various subject areas. Their excitement and exploratory behavior energized us in challenging *old ways of learning* and motivated us in the design and implementation of a *twenty-first-century model of learning and teaching*—a model that relies on the interconnection and intersection of the content, pedagogy (teaching and student learning), and technology. Thanks to all of them, we have and will continue to learn in order to be better prepared to teach about guiding learning with technology.

MN, JL, and SK

Reviewers

We are also very grateful for the feedback and suggestions provided by the many reviewers and wish to express our gratitude to each of them. Their constructive suggestions and innovative ideas strengthened our work:

Cynthia Alexander, Cerritos College; Savilla Banister, Bowling Green State University; Ken Berry, California State University, Northridge; Carl Beyer, Concordia University, River Forest; Timothy Brannan, Central Michigan University; Ray Braswell, Auburn University; Mary Bucy, Western Oregon University; Randal Carlson, Georgia Southern University; Gwen Chandler, Florida Community College; Li-Ling Chen, California State University, Hayward; Zeni Colorado, Emporia State University;

Victoria Costa, California State University, Fullerton; John Curry, Brigham Young University, Idaho; Lisa Dallas, Eastern Illinois University; Lee Davidson, Andrews University; Vanessa Dennen, Florida State University; Keith Dils, King's College; Judy Donovan, Indiana University Northwest; April Flood, Eastern Illinois University; William Gibbs, Duquesne University; Rick Gibson, Friends University; David Gilman, Indiana State University; Tim Green, California State University, Fullerton; Joan Hanor, California State University, San Marcos; Diane Haun, Hillsborough Community College; Ellen Hoffman, Eastern Michigan University; Terry Holcomb, University of North Texas; Ann Igoe, Arizona State University, Tempe; Bill Ison, University of Texas, Arlington; Brenda Jacobsen, Idaho State University, Pocatello; Toni Jones, Eastern Michigan University; Jessica Kahn, Chestnut Hill College; Bernadette Kelley, Florida A&M University; Cindy Kovalik, Kent State University; Paulina Kuforiji, Columbus State University; Sean Lancaster, Grand Valley State University; Robert Legutko, Desales University; Jon Margerum-Leys, Eastern Michigan University; Luis Martinez-Perez, Florida International University; Diane McGrath, Kansas State University; David McMullen, Bradley University; Donna Miley, Indiana Purdue University, Indianapolis; Michael Mills, Delaware Technical Community College; Melissa Nail, Indiana State University; Jim Neale, Georgia Southwestern State University; Brian Newberry, California State University, San Bernadino; Thanh Nguyen, Bridgewater State College; Charles Notar, Jacksonville State University; Ray Ostrander, Andrews University; Kiran Padmaraju, Eastern Illinois University; Tatyana Pashnyak, Bainbridge Junior College; Carole Polney, Dowling College; Cindy Rich, Eastern Illinois University; Richard Riedl, Appalachian State University; Jill Rooker, University of Central Oklahoma; Cindy Ross, Bowling Green State University; Shannon Scanlon, Henry Ford Community College; Peter Schrader, California Polytechnic State University Pomona; Ralph Shibley, University of Rio Grande; Barry Sponder, Central Connecticut State University; Herbert Steffy , Heidelberg College; Peter Terry, Bluffton College; Andrew Topper, Grand Valley State University; Janet Walker, Indiana University of Pennsylvania; Minjuan Wang, San Diego State University; Lih-Ching Chen Wang, Cleveland State University; Jana Willis, University of Houston, Clear Lake; John Wilson, Indiana University, Bloomington; Locord Wilson, Jackson State University; Sara Wolf, Auburn University; Alan Young, Brigham Young University, Idaho; Linda Young, Indiana University, South Bend; Mingyuan Zhang, Central Michigan University; Connie Zimmer, Arkansas Tech University.

PART I

Preparing Teachers to Guide Learning with Technology in the Twenty-first Century

If we teach today as we taught yesterday, then we rob our children of tomorrow.

—*John Dewey*

The twenty-first century marks a shift in what society expects and needs from its future citizens. Teachers are expected to prepare their students for a world that is and will become different from the world in which they were prepared. If teacher preparation methods courses continue as they have been, focused on the teaching strategies and classroom management, planning for instruction, and assessment of learning developed from the directions of the twentieth century, they will most certainly rob the children of tomorrow. With the integration of technologies as tools for learning, the preparation of teachers must evolve toward preparing preservice teachers to teach in ways that help them to guide their students in learning with appropriate technologies. Today in the twenty-first century, teacher preparation methods courses must assume the task of guiding preservice teachers toward the abilities, strategies, and ways of thinking for teaching *today and tomorrow*.

Part I of this book introduces the foundation for preparing teachers to guide learning with technology. These four chapters frame the remaining parts of the book by introducing technological pedagogical content knowledge (TPCK), the National Educational Technology Standards for Students (NETS·S), and Technology Standards for Teachers (NETS·T). These standards must be integrated with the more recent curriculum content standards for the variety of subject matter that students are engaged in learning in the twenty-first century if the teachers are to be prepared for *guiding the children of their tomorrow*. To adequately prepare students for living, learning, and working in the twenty-first century, you, as their teacher, must be prepared to enable your students to learn differently than how you learned.

CHAPTER 1

Teaching in the Twenty-first Century

Bob Daemmrich/The Image Works

Introduction

What is the first word that comes to your mind when you hear the word *technology*? Computers? Internet? These responses are typical of most people who automatically think about computer-based, electronic technologies. Yet, the word *technology* actually refers to any device or systematic technique that improves the quality of life.

Chiappetta and Koballa (2002) describe technology as tools invented by humankind to make work easier and life better. Certainly, computer-based, electronic technologies can be included, but as highlighted in the Snapshot of the Introduction to Technology for Preservice Teachers, technology is far more than computers and the Internet. Fire was an early invention supporting humans by providing warmth, food, and even a mechanism for clearing areas. Wheels helped humans transport materials as well as themselves. Hammers, axes, and nails supported humans in accomplishing building tasks. Pens and pencils afforded easier communication of ideas. Of course with the invention of the printing press, written materials were more rapidly available for a broader range of people throughout the whole world. Trains, cars, and planes were all technological inventions that made travel of distances easier and more reliable. Telegraphs, telephones, and television enhanced communication capabilities. More recently, the invention of the computer has significantly changed how people work and communicate.

Yes, computer and electronic technologies will likely saturate people's lives, work, and communication in the twenty-first century. Technological innovation over the past 50 years has significantly affected both work and communication. These innovations signal a cycle of evolving improvements and enhancements. As soon as you buy a computer, that computer is quickly outdated by one with more memory, faster speed, and increased capabilities.

Think about the impact of computer-based technologies on education. The memory size of computers available for educational use over the past 25 years provides an example of the enhanced capabilities in computer technologies. In the early 1980s memory for computers typically available in education was described in terms of kilobytes (1024 bytes or 1 kilobyte, abbreviated as 1K or 1 KB), with computer disks of a size of 4K expanding to 16K in as little as a year, increasing the amount of storage by four. By the 1990s, though, classroom computers were available with memory described in megabytes (one million bytes, displayed as 1 MB or 1000K). In essence, then, people were able to store 1000 times more information than with the previous data storage devices. Today, memory sizes are more often described in terms of gigabytes (displayed as 1 GB, 1000 MB, 1,000,000 K, or 1,000,000,000 bytes). The future is coming even faster with a measurement bigger than a gigabyte.

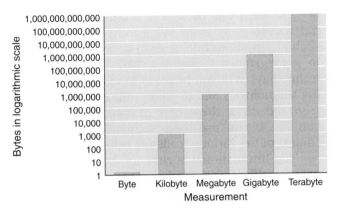 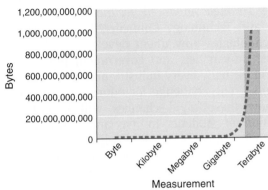

FIGURE 1.1   Increase of computer memory measurements.

The terabyte (or 1000 gigabytes) may soon replace the measurement for hard drive space for computers.

Figure 1.1 gives you an idea of the sharp increase over the past 20 years of the common computer memory size measurements. The first graph displays the growth using a logarithmic scale showing a steep slope (or increase). However, the second graph provides a clearer picture about how a move to terabytes simply dwarfs the measurement increases over the past 20 years.

Another way to look at this increase is to consider what the computer devices were able to hold. In the 1980s computer disks comfortably stored a short paper, yet the typical educational computer storage devices of today can store entire books and movies. A similar change has been observed for the speed of computer processors. In the 1980s the speed was measured in hertz, yet now it is more typically expressed in megahertz and even gigahertz. Will a terahertz be the more common measurement soon?

With this astounding rate of change, schools now maintain a broad range of electronic technologies for teacher and student use. Not only will you find various computer generations in the schools, you are likely to find many different applications that provide capabilities for new ways of thinking about teaching and learning.

In the 1980s computer users needed to know some form of programming to use the educational applications. Students worked with programming languages such as Logo, BASIC, and Pascal to explore computer technologies. With the emergence of word processors, spreadsheets, graphics tools, and databases, the dependence on programming quickly diminished. The newer applications required less computer technical ability and far more artistic ability. With this shift computers became viewed more as productivity tools than programming tools.

Of course, the emergence of the Internet in the 1990s demanded another change. Educators needed to shift their thinking about electronic, computer-based technologies toward communication and information tools. A similar momentum was evident in the capabilities of the Internet. The Internet initially offered capabilities for users to communicate via text but quickly expanded to include audio, graphics, and motion for the communication. In reality the emergence of information and communication technology with the Internet was perhaps as significant a change to humans as the printing press was over 500 years ago.

With electronic technologies, change is a constant. For example, when the World Wide Web was first introduced in the late 1980s, if you wanted to make a Web page you had to program in hypertext markup language (HTML). Within a decade, advanced Web authoring applications have enabled users to design pages using simple interfaces without any HTML programming. Now people create Web pages or sites with ease and comfort. Look at the rapid development and popularization of weblogs (or blogs). Blogs are an example of the rapid change associated with electronic technologies. Blogs are basically "memos to the world" and have made such an impact on society that Webster's dictionary quickly added the word to its compilation of English language words (normally at least 20 years of common use is required before such an addition). Not only does change happen with electronic technologies, but also it appears to be happening at an increasing rate.

The questions that teachers now must ask as they confront the various evolving electronic technologies are centered within the notion of the "value added" to the teaching and learning experiences. As new electronic technologies emerge, whether you, as a teacher, incorporate these technologies depends on your response to important educational concerns.

Donald L. Evans, U.S. secretary of commerce, noted in *2020 Visions: Transforming Education and Training Through Advanced Technologies* (National Science and Technology Council, 2002), "Powerful new technologies now under development by U.S. business, universities, and government promise to transform virtually every industry and many human endeavors." The challenge for educators is to consider how these rapid changes will impact the preparation of students to live and work in the twenty-first century. Yet, as Rod Paige, U.S. secretary of education, reminisced in a letter dated September 9, 2002, in that same publication, "We still educate our students based on an agricultural timetable, in an industrial setting, yet tell students they live in a digital age." Learning to learn with these electronic, computer-based technologies has become an important skill for the future. The job of teachers today is to scaffold students' learning so that their students are prepared to participate in society in their future — a future that must grapple with the impact of ever-emerging electronic technological changes.

You are preparing to teach in the twenty-first century. While you are perhaps best described as a *digital immigrant*, your students are more appropriately described as *digital natives* (Prensky, 2001). What will you need to know and how will you need to know it to take advantage of the emergence of electronic, computer-based technologies in ways that are more appropriate for your students' futures? Will you only be prepared to teach as you were taught? Will you take advantage of new electronic technologies? Has your subject matter content changed with the impact of these technologies? Will your students need to learn this content in a different way, using different learning tools? What must you learn about such electronic technologies in order to be prepared to guide students' learning both *with* and *about* technology? Will you be ready to respond to advancing technologies and to guide your students to learn *with* and *about* these new technologies? And, will you be able to use these technologies within the context of the various academic subjects?

The International Society for Technology in Education (ISTE, 2000) challenges teachers in the twenty-first century to be prepared to use technology as "an integral component or tool for learning and communications within the context of the academic subject areas." How will your knowledge base for teaching and learning *with* and *about* technology be different from that required of teachers in the past to meet this challenge?

CHAPTER LEARNING OBJECTIVES

After reading this chapter, you should be able to:

1. Differentiate between *technology* and *computers*.
2. Detail the knowledge a teacher needs to guide learning *with* and *about* technology.
3. Describe how teachers' pedagogical content knowledge (PCK) develops.
4. Explain technological pedagogical content knowledge (TPCK) as the knowledge teachers need for teaching their content with and about technology.
5. Illustrate the pedagogical reasoning used in preparing to teach with technology.

Snapshot of the Introduction to Technology for Preservice Teachers

On the first day of the Introduction to Technology for Teachers class, Professor Chavez began with a challenge to her students.

Professor Chavez: So you want to teach? What do you want to teach?
Karen: Prekindergarten to second grade.
Tony: Elementary.
Trevor: Science at middle school.
Sharon: Math at high school.
Aaron: Social studies.
Susan: Language arts.

One by one the students responded, with the elementary preservice teachers indicating the grades they hoped to teach and the secondary preservice teachers indicating the subjects they planned to teach.

Professor Chavez: Great! We have a nice diversity of levels and subject areas you want to teach. Now, I wonder what you need to know in order to teach these subjects and levels. Let's gather a list of your ideas.
Melissa: Well, for sure I need to know the subject I plan to teach. I'm planning on teaching

mathematics so I better know mathematics!

Professor Chavez: I agree! I sure wouldn't want you teaching mathematics if you did not know mathematics! Of course, I could ask you how much mathematics you need to know to teach it. How about you elementary pre-service teachers? Is just knowing arithmetic good enough for you?

After challenging students about the amount of subject matter knowledge they needed for teaching, Professor Chavez asked them to identify what else they needed to know in order to teach. As students offered ideas, Professor Chavez recorded the ideas on the whiteboard.

What do teachers need to know?
- Content
- How to teach
- How to evaluate what students have learned
- Classroom management
- School law
- Ways to encourage student learning
- Teaching with technology

One student suggested "teaching with technology." So Professor Chavez shifted the discussion to gather students' ideas about their understanding of technology, referring the students to their electronic personal computers (tablet PCs) for this discussion.

Professor Chavez: You each have an electronic tablet at your desk. Turn the power on and you will see that I have you all set up to respond to my questions by writing your ideas on the tablet. When you have completed your ideas on teaching with technology, send your ideas to my station. I am all set up to receive all of your ideas.

After the students completed sending her their ideas, she asked them how this method of gathering student input was different from the previous strategy where she called on individual students.

Jeremy: Well, for one, now you are getting information from each of us. Before, you just called on a few of the students. Some students were not necessarily participating in the discussion. Of course I was!

Professor Chavez: Good! You are right. Each of you sent me your ideas electronically so I can gather all of your ideas for the discussion.

Let's check out your ideas. For now, I'm going to show you three of the responses to my question of what you mean by technology for classrooms. I won't show who sent the ideas but I will select three that seem to summarize the ideas.

What is common to each of these lists [pointing to the projected version]?

Student 1	Student 2	Student 3
Computers	Computers	Pen
Calculators	Electronic tablets	Pencil
Electronic tablets	Internet	Overhead
	Electronic books	Books
	Word processor	Computer
	Spreadsheet Digital cameras,	Electronic tablet PCs
	DVD	Digital camera

Karen: Computers and these electronic tablets! Isn't that what you mean by technology? I sure don't see why Student 3 has pen, pencil, and books as technologies. They are certainly used in the classroom but they aren't really technologies. Electronic tablet PCs are technology and use writing tools like pens and pencils but the writing is different!

Professor Chavez: I suspect that is what most of you think, too. Right?

Class: Right!

Professor Chavez: But in reality the word "technology" is not as restricted as you have portrayed it. Technology is as old as humanity itself because it refers to human inventions. Pens and pencils are human inventions! Technological inventions have accompanied and sometimes driven human progress and changes in civilizations for thousands of years. Major technological developments over the course of human history have changed the way humans have lived in such dramatic ways that understanding these technological developments mimics human progress. Of course, in this discussion, I restricted your thinking to technologies used in classrooms.

Joseph: So Student 3 is right—pens and pencils are technologies used in classrooms?

Professor Chavez: Yes they are. Remember that classrooms have been around for a long time—longer than pens and pencils. But pens and pencils aren't immediately recognized as technologies. As you can see, Student 2 focused on a broader array of electronic technologies than Student 1 did. You are all right [displaying a frequency listing of all the responses the class submitted]. All the items you recorded are technologies useful in classrooms but most of your ideas fall into the category of electronic technologies.

Today, with the rapid change in electronic technologies, when people use the word "technology" they are actually referring to electronic technologies. And you are absolutely correct; you do need to learn about teaching with these technologies. In fact I just demonstrated one way of teaching with technology using electronic tablets as a means of engaging the entire class in the discussion.

Knowledge for Teaching in the Twenty-first Century

Today's teachers are asked to prepare students "to live, learn, and work successfully in an increasingly complex and information-rich society" (ISTE, 2000, p. 2). This growing recognition highlights that learning must incorporate computer-based, electronic technologies *and* that learning to use these technologies must not be separated from learning and communicating in the context of the different subject areas. The question is, What do you, as a future teacher, need to learn and know in preparation for meeting the demands of a teaching career that will be marked by a curriculum that increasingly incorporates electronic technology tools for teaching and learning?

Teachers' Knowledge

Two hundred years ago, teachers simply needed to complete the class or level that they planned to teach. A reading teacher needed to be able to read. A writing teacher needed to be able to write. An arithmetic teacher needed to be able to compute with whole numbers, fractions, and decimals. But the level at which the teachers needed to know and understand the subjects was determined by the grade they planned to teach. An elementary teacher needed an elementary education. A teacher planning to teach addition, subtraction, multiplication, and division of whole numbers was not necessarily required to have knowledge of these operations with fractions.

By 1986, Lee Shulman, then president of the American Educational Research Association, challenged educators to recognize that the preparation of future teachers must be focused on more than simply knowing the subject to be taught. Shulman proposed a more in-depth look at what teachers must know in order to teach, highlighting that future teachers need to be prepared to transform that subject matter content through teaching strategies which make that knowledge accessible to learners. To teach, teachers need to be able to integrate multiple domains of knowledge: knowledge about subject matter, learners, pedagogy, curriculum, and schools. He added that teachers needed to develop a kind of content not previously identified, namely, pedagogical content knowledge, or PCK.

From Shulman's research-based perspective on what it means to teach, what must you do to prepare to teach with technology? To think about that question, first think about three key knowledge bases outlined in a pedagogical content knowledge for teaching with technology: subject matter content, teaching and learning, and technology. Then consider their intersections: pedagogical content knowledge and technological pedagogical content knowledge.

Subject Matter Content Knowledge

Certainly, you have a well-developed knowledge of the subject(s) that you plan to teach. You have and will continue to develop this knowledge through classes aimed at the accumulation of knowledge in the discipline. You have learned your subject(s) through many years with a focus on learning the content (rather than on teaching the content) — at the elementary level, at the secondary level, and even at the college level. Your initial content knowledge assumes basic skills and broad general knowledge of your subject disciplines along with knowledge of inquiry in the specific disciplines. Here are some questions for challenging your understanding about how you know the content of the subject matter you plan to teach:

- What are the major themes or ideas in your content discipline?

- Does your content discipline rely on specific processes for developing the key themes or ideas?

- How much of what you know is dependent on the way you learned your subject(s)?

- Do you think in terms of your content by the chapters in a textbook or do you think in terms of your content as an integrated whole?

- Does your knowledge of this discipline represent an integration of the concepts and processes that connect them?

Knowledge of Teaching and Learning

You also must focus on the development of knowledge about both teaching and learning. This knowledge is an integration of knowledge about learners, pedagogy and creating learning environments, curriculum, and assessment. In preparing to teach, you must learn how students learn and develop. You must learn how to develop and provide learning opportunities to support their intellectual, social, and personal development. You must learn to design and plan for instructional opportunities that meet the needs of diverse learners. You must develop a solid understanding of a variety of instructional strategies to encourage your students' development of critical thinking and problem-solving skills. You must learn about individual and group motivation and how to design a learning environment that encourages positive social interactions and active engagement in learning. You must learn how to plan instruction based on knowledge of a variety of subjects along with the school, community, and curriculum goals. You must learn about formal and informal, traditional and alternative assessment strategies to evaluate and document your students' growth in knowledge. You must learn to use reflection to support an on-going evaluation of your own growth in knowledge as a professional educator. Your knowledge of teaching and learning began when you were a student as you observed and participated in learning. However, this knowledge of teaching and learning was focused on how you learned. Your knowledge of teaching and learning must now develop and focus on guiding a variety of students in a variety of ways—expanding to see your subject matter content and your students from the eyes of a teacher.

Technology Knowledge

In preparation for teaching in the twenty-first century, you will need a well-developed knowledge of technology. This knowledge includes a solid basic understanding of technology operations and concepts. This knowledge includes proficient use of technology that is more than keyboarding and using electronic e-mail or accessing the Internet. This knowledge includes an understanding of social, ethical, and human issues related to technology. This knowledge includes the use of technology as a productivity tool, as a communication tool, as a research tool, and as a problem-solving and decision-making tool (ISTE, 2000). Now more than ever you need to consider teaching and learning your subject using various technologies as tools for learning even if you have not previously experienced learning your subject with various technologies. But what technologies do you need to know and understand how to use as learning tools? Word processing, spreadsheets, databases, presentation software, and other multimedia software all offer capabilities to serve as productivity, communication, research, and problem-solving and decision-making tools. And by integrating them with Internet capabilities, the possibilities are extended. In addition, plenty of different technologies and technology applications are available for the various content areas. As you prepare to teach, you definitely need to expand your knowledge of the basic operations and concepts of more and more technologies. Your knowledge of technology will expand in a similar way that your knowledge of your subject matter has. As your knowledge grows and matures, you will develop a more integrated knowledge of concepts and processes with electronic technologies.

Pedagogical Content Knowledge

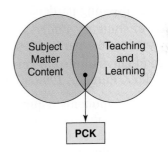

Shulman characterized pedagogical content knowledge, or PCK, as knowledge of

> the most regularly taught topics in one's subject area, the most useful forms of representation of those ideas, the most powerful analogies, illustrations, examples, explanations, and demonstrations . . . including an understanding of what makes the learning of specific concepts easy or difficult: the concepts and preconceptions that students of different ages and backgrounds bring with them to the learning. (1986, p. 9)

PCK results from the integration of your knowledge of subject matter content with a pedagogical knowledge of teaching and learning. As you think about particular ideas in your content, you may find that you are also thinking about how you might help students understand these ideas. For example, what do students understand about triangles? Does a triangle include the space inside? Models help students visualize, so you might have them arrange themselves to form a triangle, each child holding a point of the triangle. Then you can guide their thinking about the points and perimeter of the triangle. Children's preconceptions present teachers with significant challenges in explaining concepts. When they turn on a flashlight, they see light at the flashlight bulb and then see the light reflected on the wall. Often their preconception is that the light "jumped" from one to the other. Yet, they need to learn that in actuality the light travels between the flashlight and wall even if they cannot see it. How would you challenge their preconception that light just simply appears rather than is invisible as it travels? The specialized knowledge of a teacher is to think of the content as to how the concept might be taught in a way that students develop accurate conceptions. This knowledge is PCK, the integration of subject matter content knowledge with knowledge of teaching and learning.

Grossman (1989, 1990) proposed four central components of PCK for consideration of the types of knowledge for development in the teacher preparation program:

(a) an overarching conception of what it means to teach a particular subject;

(b) knowledge of instructional strategies and representations for teaching particular topics;

(c) knowledge of students' understandings, thinking, and learning in a particular subject;

(d) knowledge of curriculum and curriculum materials (Borko & Putnam, 1996, p. 690).

Each of these components requires a consideration of both subject matter content knowledge and pedagogical knowledge of teaching and learning. However, the knowledge represented by the overlap of the two domains of knowledge is essential for teaching that results in a translation of the ideas in a form understandable by students.

Pedagogical Content Knowledge for Teaching with Technology

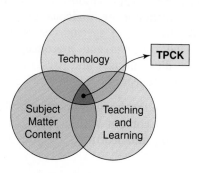

Although knowledge of subject matter content, knowledge of technology, and knowledge of teaching and learning are essential for teachers who plan to teach with technology, the intersection of these three knowledge bases is critical and arguably a more essential knowledge for a teacher in the twenty-first century. The integration of the three domains of knowledge (subject matter content, teaching and learning, and technology) emphasizes the growth and development teachers need for teaching with technology, a specialized PCK — a pedagogical content knowledge for teaching with technology or a technological pedagogical content knowledge (TPCK) (Margerum-Leys & Marx, 2002; Mishra & Koehler, 2006; Niess, 2005a; Pierson, 2001; Zhao, 2003).

TPCK for teaching with technology means that as teachers think about particular subject matter concepts, they are concurrently considering how they might teach the important ideas embodied in the concepts in such a way that the technology places the concept in a form understandable by their students. Niess (2005) adapted Grossman's four central components of PCK as a way to think about the development of TPCK in the teacher preparation program:

(a) an overarching conception of what it means to teach a particular subject *integrating technology* in the learning;

(b) knowledge of instructional strategies and representations for teaching particular topics *with technology*;

(c) knowledge of students' understandings, thinking, and learning *with technology* in a particular subject;

(d) knowledge of curriculum and curriculum materials that *integrate technology with learning in the subject area*.

Elementary teachers often use themes as a way of connecting various content areas. For example, a theme of imagination provides the framework for a multidisciplinary unit for grades 3–5 (O'Hara & McMahon, 2002). How can you incorporate this theme in the various subject matter content areas you might teach in grade 3? How can you incorporate technology as you think about this unit? In the Classroom 1.1 outlines some ideas similar to those that O'Hara and McMahon suggested for this theme. In each area, the teacher has envisioned how technology might be used as a tool for the learning activities. This type of thinking is at the heart of technological pedagogical content knowledge — the intersection and integration of thoughts about engaging students in learning subject matter content with technology.

Another example of TPCK is displayed in the Snapshot of the Introduction to Technology for Preservice Teachers. In this case Professor Chavez'

In the Classroom 1.1

IMAGINE THIS!

TECHNOLOGY OBJECTIVE: **NETS•S I, III, IV, V**

- Concept mapping software, Internet, word processors, and drawing software: Technology as a productivity, communication, and research tool.
- Develop skill with multiple technologies.

CONTENT OBJECTIVE: **Language arts:** Explore the art of storytelling and the role that imagination plays.
Social studies: Explore the role of culture in imagination.
Science: Explore the special characteristics of real versus imaginary animals.
Mathematics: Explore drawing to scale.

GRADE LEVEL: 3–5

PROBLEM: Walt Disney's work is a model of how imagination makes use of technology to encourage everyone to dream. How can a theme of imagination be used in learning in various content areas?

Consider these ideas for teaching different subjects with technology (O'Hara & McMahon, 2002).

Content Area	Instructional Strategies	Technology
Language arts: Examine the art of storytelling and the role that imagination plays.	• Have children recount their favorite Disney story. • What are the characteristics of the story that make it a favorite? • Gather the ideas, describing the role of imagination in their creation. • Present created stories to the class and discuss how the technology supported their imagination for telling the story.	• Use concept mapping software (Kidspiration or Inspiration) to tell a story.
Social studies: Explore the role of culture in imagination.	• In groups, discuss how imagination surfaces within the cultural characteristics of each of the Disney "lands."	• Students use websites such as Wikipedia and the Virtual Magic Kingdom to explore the imaginative features and characteristics that make the amusement park unique.
Science: Explore the special characteristics of real versus imaginary animals.	• Watch and read Disney stories. • List as many animals as possible that are in the stories. • Small groups: Identify the characteristics of real-life animals and compare this list with a list of the characteristics of the imagined animals in the Disney stories. • How do the characteristics differ?	• Using a drawing application to create an imaginary animal that has characteristics of real animals. Use a word processor to explain the characteristics and their combination that makes the animal imaginary.
Mathematics: Explore drawing to scale.	• Collect pictures of imaginary animals in the Disney stories in the science unit. • Identify key points on a favorite picture of an animal.	• Using a drawing application with grid mode, map the points and connect the points to draw a smaller version of the picture.

content was her knowledge of education. She was integrating that content (importance of engaging all students in class discussions to maximize learning of all students) with her knowledge of teaching and learning (strategies for engaging students in classes) with her knowledge of technology (electronic tablets and personal computers). In essence, then, Professor Chavez was introducing the notion of learning with technologies through the students' own learning experiences to help engage them in the development of their TPCK, a knowledge base for teachers who will teach in the twenty-first century.

Pedagogical Reasoning with TPCK

In each content area, knowledge of integrating technology in teaching that subject includes both concepts and processes. With TPCK teachers merge the three knowledge bases as they reason to transform the content, as they know it, into content meaningful for their students. They use a reasoning processing to connect multiple concepts. This pedagogical reasoning process begins with comprehension of the subject matter and continues with new comprehension after reflection on instruction. The transformation of knowledge into a form accessible by the learners is at the center of this self-perpetuating process. The transformation process models five important subprocesses: preparation, representation, selection, adaptation, and tailoring (Wilson, Shulman, & Richert, 1987).

* *Preparation* requires an examination and critical interpretation of the knowledge of the subject matter. In this first step, teachers winnow and reconceptualize their subject matter knowledge for pedagogical consideration.

* *Representation* entails the repackaging of subject matter in a manner that is suitable for instruction. These repackaged ideas include analogies, metaphors, stories, or any number of other representations.

* *Selection* is engagement in the activity of selecting appropriate educational strategies. These strategies accommodate some characteristics to facilitate learning specific subject matter content.

* *Adaptation* includes the alteration of subject matter to fit the characteristics of specific students. Considerations of students' prior knowledge and the pedagogical objectives for a lesson influence this adaptation.

* *Tailoring* results in a special configuration of subject matter for students with individual needs.

How are these subprocesses involved in the pedagogical reasoning processes in which a teacher engages to incorporate technology in the classroom instruction? Consider this example of how a social studies teacher might use pedagogical reasoning while planning lessons to make use of digital historical resources.

Brian teaches eleventh-grade United States history. He discovered the Library of Congress' online digital collection called American Memory several years ago and has been interested in providing his students with an opportunity to work with some of the primary sources available on the website. As a new school year approached, Brian decided to incorporate the sources in his class. He remembered a collection at American Memory on religious petitions that had been presented to the state of Virginia government during and just after the American Revolution and thought this topic would be interesting for his students to investigate. Technology Link 1.1 shows how you can access this online collection.

Technology Link 1.1

*A*ccess to the online religious petitions collection at the American Memory resource is available by using the **Memory** link at this book's website.

www.wiley.com/college/niess

A number of issues immediately confronted Brian. Several of them required that he apply various domains of his teacher knowledge. For example, Brian had to decide how students would access the electronic resources. He had to determine how students' work with the documents would fit in the curriculum. He also had to take into account the state standards guiding his instruction. Once these considerations and other general matters had been addressed, Brian began to think about the more specific and detailed processes relating to subject matter content. He had already rationalized the content in terms of relevance, particularly given the consistency of the national debates about the role of religion in American life and government. Now, Brian needed to reason through the actual activities that he wanted his students to complete. Although he might not have systematically considered the five subprocesses for transforming his subject matter knowledge into the instructional pedagogy he planned to use, Brian did informally consider each aspect of the model.

Brian sat down at his computer and searched the religious petitions collection at the American

Memory website. He was immediately struck by the complexity of the site and realized that it was essential that he provide significant guidance for students as they worked through the site. This initial decision resulted from Brian's belief that many authentic historical resources need to be adapted for student use. While browsing the site Brian realized he would need to formalize his ideas about the topic (in the context of the curriculum) before spending too much time searching for documents. Almost immediately, Brian found a secondary resource linked from the front page of the collection titled "Religion and the Founding of the American Republic." From this resource Brian learned that some people in Virginia in the late 1700s were debating the appropriateness of the Virginia state government funding charitable religious activities. Given that the issue of government support of religious activities is still being debated today, Brian decided to make this issue his content focus. Before going to the site, Brian wanted to help his students understand the historical roots of America's current church-versus-state debates. His reasoning toward the specific topic of government-funded religious activity in eighteenth-century Virginia provides an example of how you will need to integrate your content knowledge with your knowledge of teaching and learning.

With a relevant and meaningful topic determined, Brian was ready to consider how the online resources might be tailored and adapted for use in his class. Brian identified some secondary resources on religion and their founding to provide a brief description and a small image of one petition written by an unnamed Baptist in 1785. This petition was signed by more people than any other petition addressing the issue of tax support for churches and represented a good example of what Brian wanted his students to learn. This specific document thus became the central focus of the activity. Brian decided to have his students closely read and analyze the document. These decisions are examples of how Brian selected a resource and a pedagogical approach for utilizing the resource.

Despite his excitement about finding the resource, Brian was not pleased with the quality of the image because it was very hard to read. He accessed the full American Memory collection of religious petitions site hoping to find a better image, one that his students could read. He did find a higher quality image, but the process of locating the document image was not so easy. He did have the date of the petition and the collection of petitions was organized by date (as well as by geographic location). Unfortunately, the date of the petition did not appear on the full list of petition dates. Instead of giving up, Brian

began to browse though other petitions hoping that it was either misfiled or the reference in the secondary resource was incorrect. The date listed in the secondary resource was November 27, 1785, so Brian first looked for petitions dated November 27 on other years. He found nothing, so he decided to look at other documents in November 1785 that started with November 2_. This approach solved the puzzle. The petition was actually produced November 2, 1785.

With access to a higher quality image, Brian began to consider how his students might use the document. Two immediate questions confronted him, though. First, he had to determine whether his students would be able to make sense of the language of the document. Second, assuming students would read the document, he had to determine whether his students should read it on the computer or in print copy. The answer to the first question was rooted in Brian's assessment of his students' abilities. He determined that his students needed some help making sense of the document. Brian worried that his students might not understand the language of the petition and they might not be able to read the handwriting of the author. Since no transcription was provided, Brian decided reading the document might be an interesting task for the class as a whole. He constructed a short assignment in which each student in his class would take a small portion of the document (one or two sentences) and transcribe it from the original eighteenth-century handwriting to a word-processed text. The individual pieces of text were to be stitched together to form a fully transcribed file. Brian figured that this whole process would only take about 15 minutes, leaving enough time for the students to directly access the document image on the Web. So he decided to schedule time in the computer lab.

Brian's next task was to set up students' work on the computer in such a way that would maximize their time and exposure to the document. He did not want students spending excessive time stumbling through Web pages. Brian decided it would be worthwhile to direct his students through a short series of steps that supported them in navigating the document. He reasoned that this exercise, if repeated, could lead his students to develop a sense of comfort with the American Memory site and this understanding would facilitate future use of documents in the class.

The directions were simple and purposeful. First, Brian directed his students to type in the Web address, http://memory.loc.gov. Once the site was displayed, he directed his students to click on the link Browse. He then asked them to select the time period of 1700–1790 in the box labeled Browse

Collections by Time Period. A list of collections appeared and Brian instructed students to select *Religious Petitions, Virginia ~ 1764–1802*. Although there are a number of ways to reach the collection, this approach utilized a time reference Brian thought might be useful to guide the students in their consideration of the petitions.

After a brief overview of the collection, Brian guided his students through a few additional steps that resulted in the document being displayed on their screens. Brian passed out the transcribed copy of the document and proceeded with the lesson. In this lesson, Brian's students analyzed a document to determine the author's intent, the tone of the language, the context, and the general content.

Much of this work was removed from technological considerations, but the technology did enable Brian and his students to not only find the document, but to see a facsimile of the original. The actual effect on students at seeing the document image was difficult to measure in quantifiable assessment terms, but the impressions that students had when viewing and reading original source materials were extremely positive. Seeing the handwritten petition was a powerful experience for them, grounding what can sometimes be cold and calculated analytical historical work in an empathetic real-world context. Students were encouraged to imagine the author sitting at a desk penning the petition, or maybe a group of citizens gathered around a table reading it by candlelight. These experiences put students in touch with history and aided in not only historical understanding but also historical sensibility.

Brian, too, experienced great satisfaction designing and implementing a lesson that more accurately translated his perception of these historical events in a manner accessible to his students. Through this process Brian used pedagogical reasoning as he integrated what he knew about history (the subject matter) with what he knew about teaching and learning (learners, pedagogy, schools, and curriculum) and about technology (searching the Web and using word processing) — a pedagogical content knowledge for teaching with technology.

creased technological access to information, future citizens need to know how to process that information, how to analyze and use that information, and basically how to use that information to learn.

The significant shifts in the impact of electronic technologies have focused attention on looking at the knowledge that teachers need to know to teach in this new century. Besides knowing their subject(s) and knowing about teaching and learning, teachers need to know about technology. It is now recognized that teachers need to have a pedagogical content knowledge, that is, knowledge of

> the most regularly taught topics in one's subject area, the most useful forms of representation of those ideas, the most powerful analogies, illustrations, examples, explanations, and demonstrations... including an understanding of what makes the learning of specific concepts easy or difficult: the concepts and preconceptions that students of different ages and backgrounds bring with them to the learning. (Shulman, 1986, p. 9)

Teachers need to incorporate a pedagogical reasoning that integrates what they know about their subject with what they know about technology and what they know about teaching and learning as they redesign their curriculum and instruction in a manner that supports students to construct how they view and are able to use the knowledge they are learning. For technology to become an integral component or tool for learning, teachers must also, however, develop an overarching conception of their subject matter with respect to technology and what it means to teach and learn with technology—a technological pedagogical content knowledge, or TPCK.

As a preservice teacher your task will be to learn about different technologies, but more importantly to learn how to learn with these different technologies. This understanding does not automatically happen by learning how the technology works. This understanding requires that you think about what you plan to teach and that you look for ways that technology supports that subject, with careful attention to the ways that your students learn and can use the technology as a tool for their own learning.

Summing It Up

Both what and how American citizens learn and are taught has changed over the past century. From the Agricultural Age to the Industrial Age to the Information Age, America has needed its citizens to have an expanded education, an education that best prepared them to be able to participate in different careers in support of the particular age. Now, with in-

End-of-the-Chapter Activities and References

PRACTICE PROBLEMS

1. What are the important concepts of your primary subject matter discipline? Create a concept map showing how these concepts are interrelated.

2. Select a major theme in your content area that might be used at the level you plan to teach. Outline ways that various technologies might be used in this theme.

3. Conduct a Web search to identify lesson ideas that incorporate specific technologies in the lesson to support the students' learning. How is the technology used? Is it a productivity tool, a communication tool, a research tool, or a problem-solving and decision-making tool?

4. Access the Memory link described in Technology Link 1.1 to search the online religious petition collection to find the petition that Brian found for his students. What instructions would you design to guide students in finding that document?

IN THE CLASSROOM ACTIVITIES

5. With permission to observe a classroom activity, ask the teacher for the objectives that are planned for the activity. Focus your observations on two or three specific students during the activity. Interview the students individually after the lesson. How did they describe what they learned? Did they learn what the teacher wanted them to learn?

6. Ask to observe a class where the students (at the subject and level that you are looking forward to teach) will be using technology in their classroom activity. Ask the students what they are learning and what they think the purpose is for the use of the technology. Ask the teacher the same question. Use their responses to answer the following: How is the technology being used? How were the students prepared to use the technology?

ASSESSING STUDENT LEARNING WITH AND ABOUT TECHNOLOGY

7. Ask the teacher in a class that you observed how he or she assesses the students' understanding gained when they use technology in learning. Do the students have access to the technology to demonstrate how they know and understand what they were taught? How does assessing students with access to the technology differ from assessing them without access to the technology?

E-PORTFOLIO ACTIVITIES

8. Collect a variety of student artifacts that show how students use technology in classes that you hope to teach. Find an example of each of these uses of technology: a productivity tool, a com-

munication tool, a research tool, and a problem-solving and decision-making tool. Prepare a word-processed description of the ways that students can use technology to support their learning, using the artifacts as supporting evidence.

9. Prepare a description of your understanding of *technology*. From your perspective, identify five major technology inventions that have influenced civilization. Explain their influence.

10. Prepare a description of your understanding of technologies for the classroom. From your perspective, identify five major technology inventions that have influenced what and how students learn.

REFLECTION AND DISCUSSION

11. Think about the primary subject that you hope to teach. How did you learn what you know in that subject area? Identify concepts or ideas which you learned that are probably no longer considered as important. Explain why you think those ideas are no longer important.

12. Read the article by Niess (2005) that describes student teacher experiences in teaching with technology in the development of their TPCK. Explain your understanding of a pedagogical content knowledge for teaching with and about technology (TPCK).

Annotated Resources

Grimmett, P., & MacKinnon, A. M. (1992). Craft knowledge and the education of teachers. In G. Grant (Ed.), *Review of research in education* (pp. 385–456). Washington, DC: American Educational Research Association.
Grimmett and MacKinnon suggest that teachers must develop specific pedagogical learner knowledge. A primary element in pedagogical learner knowledge should be, according to Grimmet and MacKinnon, the manner in which individual learners reason and think. The authors also consider the recognition of the problems individuals have learning, knowledge about how individuals best learn, and learner motivations as a part of pedagogical learner knowledge.

Gudmundsdottir, S. (1991). Pedagogical models of subject matter. In J. Brophy (Ed.), *Advances in research on teaching: Vol. 2* (pp. 265–304).
Gudmundsdottir finds that teachers with considerable experience (dubbed experts) have a better developed pedagogical content knowledge base than do novice or beginning teachers. This difference, for Gudmundsdottir, is connected to the expert teachers' ability to see the big picture relating to curriculum. Additionally, expert teachers have a wide variety of teaching methods at their command. Gudmundsdottir attributed the beginning teacher's scarcity of pedagogical content knowledge to the lack of emphasis in most teacher education programs on getting students to think about the subject matter in pedagogical terms.

International Society for Technology in Education. (2000). *National educational technology standards for students: Connecting curriculum and technology*. Eugene, OR: ISTE.
This document describes six technology standards for students and provides curriculum examples and scenarios for a variety of classroom levels and subject matters.

Margerum-Leys, J., & Marx, R. W. (2002). Teacher knowledge of educational technology: A study of student teacher/mentor teacher pairs. *Journal of Educational Computing Research, 26*(4), 427–462.
This article describes the nature and sharing of teacher knowledge of technology in a student teacher/mentor teacher pair.

Niess, M. L. (2005). Preparing teachers to teach science and mathematics with technology: Developing a technology pedagogical content knowledge. *Teaching and Teacher Education, 21*, 509–523.
This article describes how science and mathematics preservice teachers develop their TPCK through the work in their teacher preparation program. Student teachers' view of the integration of technology and the nature of their discipline (science or mathematics) are identified as important aspects of the development of TPCK, highlighting the importance of breadth and depth of knowledge the discipline.

O'Hara, S., & McMahon, M. (2002). Imagination. In Hannah, L. , Menchaca, M., & McVicker, B. (Eds.), *Multidisciplinary Units for Grades 3–5*, Eugene, OR: ISTE.
This multidisciplinary unit provides ideas for integrating technology with various content within the theme of *imagination*.

Wilson, S. M., Shulman, L. S., & Richert A. E. (1987). '150 different ways' of knowing: Representations of knowledge in teaching. In J. Calderhead (Ed.), *Exploring teachers' thinking* (pp. 104–124). London: Cassell.
This article clarifies the pedagogical thinking involved in pedagogical content knowledge. The authors describe a model of pedagogical reasoning and action, which includes six components: comprehension, transformation, instruction, evaluation, reflections, and new comprehension. They report that a linear relationship exists among these components of pedagogical subject matter and continues with new comprehension after reflection on instruction. At the center of this self-perpetuating process is the transformation of knowledge.

CHAPTER 2

Technology Standards for Teachers

Michael Newman/PhotoEdit

Introduction

As American education matured over a 500-year period, what future citizens needed to know and be able to do has become more than how to read, write, and do simple arithmetic. With the advances, expectations for teachers' knowledge also has increased. Many more teachers were needed as the number of students attending school for longer periods increased, and these teachers needed an improved education for dealing with the more diverse student populations as well as the broader subject matter content.

What emerged by the early twentieth century was the recognition that teachers needed to be prepared to implement new teaching and learning practices. Yes, teachers needed to know more than just the subject matter. They needed to know both the art and science of teaching—the pedagogy. By the middle of the twentieth century, the responsibility for the quality of the teacher workforce in public schools had predominately shifted from local county control of the 1800s to the state level. State-level organizations were specifically identified to monitor the quality of the teacher workforce.

By the end of the twentieth century, the expectations for a teacher included at least a bachelor degree in an appropriate discipline along with appropriate teacher preparation coursework and supervised student teaching. College and university programs were designed and approved as meeting state teacher preparation regulations. Many of these teacher preparation programs were accredited not only by the appropriate state teacher licensing agency but also by a professional organization, the National Council for Accreditation of Teacher Education (NCATE), an organization focused on promoting national standards for both the initial preparation and continued professional development of teachers.

With the emergence of the Information Age in the twenty-first century, access to technology has affected what teachers need to know and be able to do to teach children born in this more digital age. What do these teachers need to know and be able to do to teach these children? How must they be prepared to teach in schools in a digital age? Is the development of their knowledge of content and knowledge of teaching and learning (pedagogy) adequate? Is there any reason to consider their knowledge of technology along with their knowledge of the content and knowledge of teaching and learning? How must teachers be prepared to integrate their knowledge of technology with their pedagogical content knowledge (PCK), that is, their technological pedagogical content knowledge (TPCK)? Just what does it mean to develop a TPCK for teaching in the twenty-first century?

Under the influence of a society heavily invested in information and communication technologies, several professional organizations oriented the teacher licensing agencies toward a consideration of what teachers should know and be able to do with technology. The National Council for the Accreditation of Teacher Education (NCATE) requires a commitment to technology by its accredited teacher preparation programs. This commitment to technology is expressed in their expectation that preservice teachers develop a PCK for facilitating "students' learning of the subject matter through presentation of the content in clear and meaningful ways and through the integration of technology" (NCATE, 2003, p. 15).

In concert with NCATE and the impact of technology on designing an education in an increasingly complex and information-rich society, the International Society for Technology in Education (ISTE) developed a set of teacher standards to guide college and university faculty in preparing teachers with the knowledge and ability to scaffold their students' learning with technology: the *National Educational Technology Standards for Teachers: Preparing Teachers to Use Technology* (NETS·T; ISTE, 2002). What do these technology standards expect of all teachers? How do these standards support the development of a pedagogical content knowledge for teaching with technology (TPCK)? Is a requirement to teach with technology during the student teaching experience needed to address these standards in the initial teacher preparation program?

Although NCATE standards focused on both the initial teacher preparation and the continuing professional development of teachers, another professional organization, the Interstate New Teacher Assessment and Support Consortium (INTASC), provided a framework that specifically addressed the essential knowledge, skills, and abilities of new teachers as they begin their first teaching positions. Their 10 principles described what a beginning teacher must be able to do to teach regardless of subject or grade level. These principles presented an effective beginning teacher as a professional who is able to integrate content knowledge with pedagogical understanding to assure that all students learn (INTASC, 1993). With the influence of technology on education, though, the INTASC principles have provided yet another framework linked to the NETS·T standards in describing the knowledge, skills, and abilities new teachers need in order to be prepared for teaching with technology in the twenty-first century.

CHAPTER LEARNING OBJECTIVES

After reading this chapter, you should be able to:

1. Discuss the development of a pedagogical content knowledge for teaching with technology (TPCK).

2. Describe the importance of strategic thinking as a skill for teaching subject matter content with technology.

3. Use the National Educational Technology Standards for Teachers (NETS·T) to describe fundamental concepts, knowledge, skills, and attitudes for applying technology in educational settings.

4. Explain how the various standards [NETS·T technology standards for teachers, the National Council for Accreditation of Teacher Education (NCATE) guidelines, and the Interstate New Teacher Assessment and Support Consortium (INTASC) 10 principles] provide direction for preparing beginning teachers for teaching in the twenty-first century.

Snapshot of Student Teaching with Technology

Student teachers in a one-year, graduate science and mathematics teacher preparation program were prepared throughout their program to integrate technology in student teaching at the middle and high school levels. These student teachers planned their lessons with the help of the teacher preparation program faculty, including their university supervisors and their cooperating teachers in their practice teaching schools.

To assure that the student teachers could plan for and implement lessons where their students had hands-on access to technology, the student teaching program provided classroom sets of Calculator Based

Learning (CBL) or Calculator Based Ranger (CBR) equipment to be checked out as needed. Each of these technologies allowed the collection of real-time data. The CBL is a handheld, battery-powered instrument that accepts a variety of sensors, including microphone, motion (distance, velocity, acceleration), pH, temperature, and light intensity. For example, with the temperature and the pH probes, students can collect the temperatures and pH of the water in a stream at various locations to investigate their hypotheses about why fish are unable to survive in particular portions of that stream. The CBR is a handheld, battery-powered instrument that collects motion data including distance, velocity, and acceleration. Students might use a CBR to "match" a graph of distance versus time by walking toward a wall where the motion detector measures their distance from the wall over time; as the student moves toward the wall, the plot of the "walked" graph is superimposed on the "graph to match" so that the student can compare the two graphs.

The student teachers designed a sequence of lessons for one of the classes they planned to teach during student teaching. The objectives of the lessons focused on specific content standards in mathematics, earth science, life science (biology), or physical science (chemistry or physics). After they taught their lessons where their students had hands-on experiences with the technology as a learning tool, they submitted these reflections on teaching science or mathematics with technology.

> Although the most difficult task with regards to this lab was finding the time to include it, as it was a course requirement, overall the lab was successful. Students seemed interested that the CBL system provided results that were similar to what they had experienced by hand, but that the rate of sampling was faster although they had to perform one test at a time.
> *(Middle school earth science student teacher)*

> The next time I do this lab I will schedule another class just for a class discussion about comparing the two labs. I would talk about technology, and why scientists use it instead of taking data manually.
> *(Middle school life science student teacher)*

> I think that the use of technology in my demonstration of household acids and bases was great. . . . The probes used in this manner [are] very similar to the pH meters found in all sorts of research labs and on testing equipment.
> *(High school physical science student teacher)*

> It is clear to me that even if the class did not use the technology to learn the topics . . ., they still would have learned the information. However, by using the technology the students were able to cover some objectives that wouldn't be so easily or quickly met without the use of technology.
> *(Middle school mathematics student teacher)*

> I am convinced that students will retain this knowledge much longer because of the physical/graphical/instant nature of the technology. Students don't have to "take my word for it," rather they can test their own hypotheses in an instant.
> *(High school physical science student teacher)*

> The integration of the technology into the classroom was amazing—I have yet to see students so focused and interested in taking the temperature and pH of water! . . . Overall, I feel that this week really was the highlight of my student teaching experience. . . . Students were interested, engaged, and enjoying science to a higher degree than normal (and way higher for some!).
> *(High school life science student teacher)*

> Science goes wrong all the time and scientists repeat experiments over and over to get results. These are several concepts that I would incorporate into this type of lab. . . . I would incorporate these concepts into all labs especially as I am gaining insight into my students' understanding of science.
> *(Middle school physical science student teacher)*

◈ Developing a TPCK, a Pedagogical Content Knowledge for Teaching with Technology

Knowledge has been framed as "the amount of information necessary to function and achieve goals; the capacity to make information from data and to transform it into useful and meaningful information; the capacity with which one thinks creatively, interprets and acts; and an attitude that makes people want to think, interpret and act" (uit Beijerse, 2000). How does this description apply to the knowledge you need for teaching with the twenty-first-century technologies? Technological pedagogical content knowledge (TPCK) is the body of knowledge you need to teach both *with* and *about* these technologies. TPCK is highlighted as the interconnection and intersection of content, pedagogy (teaching and student learning), and technology (Margerum-Leys & Marx, 2002; Mishra & Koehler, 2006; Niess, 2005a; Pierson, 2001; Zhao, 2003). Certainly developing the "capacity, with which one thinks creatively, interprets and acts" is a critical attribute in teaching. Shavelson, Ruiz-Primo, Li, and Ayala (2003) provide a more detailed view about the thinking which can be applied to that involved in TPCK. They describe four specific types of thinking: *declarative* (knowing that, including definitions, terms, facts, and descriptions), *procedural* (knowing how, which refers to sequences of steps to complete a task or subtask), *schematic* (knowing why, by drawing on both declarative and procedural knowledge, such as principles and mental models), and *strategic* (knowing when and where to use domain-specific knowledge and strategies, such as planning and problem solving together with monitoring progress toward a goal). These ideas point toward a teacher's TPCK as a way of thinking strategically that involves *planning, organizing, critiquing, and abstracting* for specific content, specific student needs, and specific classroom situations. What experiences do you need in developing this way of thinking?

Putnam and Borko (2000) stated, "How a person learns a particular set of knowledge and skills, and the situation in which a person learns, become a fundamental part of what is learned." Your beliefs about how your content knowledge is learned are likely affected by how you learned that content. If you learned with paper and pencil tools, you may believe that is the best way to learn the content when perhaps other more advanced technologies may be as useful in learning in the content. Furthermore, newer and emerging technologies challenge you to consider teaching your content differently than how and even what you were taught. The challenge for you is to overcome and enhance your prior learning experiences, learning that was likely without twenty-first century technology tools. The challenge is for you to develop new ways of learning your subject with technology so you are prepared to teach your students. For as John Dewey was quoted as saying, "If we teach today as we taught yesterday, then we rob our children of tomorrow." You need to learn the strategic thinking of analyzing and critiquing your content and the teaching of your content so that you know when and where to use the pedagogical reasoning strategies, such as planning and problem solving, together with monitoring your instruction toward a goal of guiding the *children of tomorrow* in engaging appropriate technology tools in learning the subject matter content.

The Snapshot of Student Teaching with Technology portrays student teachers' thinking after teaching with electronic technologies. Prior to their one-year, graduate teacher preparation program, these students had completed a bachelor degree with sig-

nificant coursework in science or mathematics. During their student teaching, they were expected to teach their content using technology as a tool to support their students' learning. In most cases, they had learned their content in a different way—through lectures and perhaps some verification lab experiences. The Calculator Based Ranger (CBR) and the Calculator Based Laboratory (CBL) were new to them (see Chapter 10 to learn more about CBLs and CBRs). In their teacher preparation program, the student teachers needed to learn about these technological devices along with other computer-based technologies while they also learned about teaching and learning mathematics and science; they were supported in planning and organizing a sequence of lessons that integrated these technologies as tools for learning the content; and they taught their lessons during student teaching, critiquing and analyzing the results of their teaching experiences.

What was the result? Was it easy for them to do? Are they now ready to teach effectively, to integrate technology in their teaching of their subject? Do they have a TPCK that prepares them for integrating technology as a tool for learning mathematics or science? Have they incorporated the pedagogical reasoning to integrate:

- what they know about their subject, with
- what they know about technology, and
- what they know about teaching and learning

for designing curriculum and instruction to support their students in constructing understandings of the content? Have they learned to think strategically about their teaching with technology?

These questions are important for you to consider as you prepare for teaching. In 2002, new standards were developed as a guide for what teachers need to know and be able to do to prepare future citizens for an Information Age punctuated by electronic technologies. Your understanding of these standards will help you gain a better understanding of the expectations in your teacher preparation program as you prepare for teaching and learning in this new age.

NETS · T: Technology Standards for Teachers

The International Society for Technology in Education (ISTE) through the Preparing Tomorrow's Teachers to Use Technology (PT³) grant program created a set of educational technology standards for shaping what teachers need for teaching with technologies, namely, "the fundamental concepts, knowledge, skills, and attitudes for applying technology in educational settings" (ISTE, 2002). The

National Educational Technology Standards for Teachers (NETS·T) are described in six standard areas with accompanying performance indicators for preparing teachers for teaching in the Information Age. Carefully investigate each of these standards as a guide for thinking about teaching and learning your content with technology.

NETS·T Standard I. Technology Operations and Concepts   The first standard directs teachers toward the importance of developing an in-depth understanding of the operations and concepts of particular technologies (ISTE, 2002). ISTE identifies two indicators that more explicitly describe the knowledge, skills, and understandings you need to develop to meet this standard. You need to

A. *demonstrate introductory knowledge, skills, and understanding of concepts related to technology; and*

B. *demonstrate continual growth in technology knowledge and skills to stay abreast of current and emerging technologies.* (ISTE, 2002, p. 9)

Key questions arise when interpreting this standard and its performance indicators. What is meant by technology? What are the introductory concepts for technology? And, what are the important technologies to be considered?

Chapter 1 challenged your understanding of the word *technology*. Obviously, technology is much broader than many people consider when they first hear the word. Some think of technology as computer-based and electronic—a narrow subset of tools that humans have invented to make work easier and life better. Others recognize the importance of systems and processes in defining technology. Bugliarello (1995) includes technological systems, like medicine, that "encompass many pieces of hardware, software, and know-ware" (p. 228). Research and development are considered as technological processes. Thus, in its broadest interpretation, technology is an amalgamation of products, systems, and processes focused on enhancing the quality of life.

More locally to education, though, classroom technologies have traditionally included tools for writing (pens, pencils) along with tools for measuring, drawing, and designing. The microscope is a technology used in science classes. Films and television are included as technologies that are often used in many subject area classes. With the advent of computers, computer-based technologies are now added to the list of classroom technologies that can be used to support teaching and learning. Thus, a list of classroom technologies must consider the broad range of tools for enhancing teaching and learning, including the newer information and communication technology inventions.

Perhaps the newer technologies offer the biggest challenge for teachers in gaining a basic understanding as described in NETS·T Standard I, Performance Indicator A (NETS·T I-A). Teachers need to understand how to use computer systems with devices such as keyboards, printers, and scanners. As for the introductory concepts with computer systems, the emergence of new operating systems like OSX for the Mac lessens the computer platform (PC or Mac) issue. These two platforms have similar operations for

1. accessing and launching computer software,

2. entering and manipulating data,

3. copying and incorporating data and graphics, and

4. saving, printing and sending documents.

In essence, this standard recommends that you learn to use a computer system, operate its basic peripherals, and troubleshoot its problems including those with its basic peripherals.

Depending on your particular subject or classroom level, you may need skills with other subject-specific technologies. For example, some of you will need an understanding of basic calculators and their peripherals since more and more of the students are using them as tools in learning. Calculator peripherals can be added that allow students to collect and store real-time data, such as temperatures and speed of movement. Both the CBRs and CBLs that the student teachers used in the Snapshot of Student Teaching with Technology are such peripheral devices. In addition to skill in performing basic operations, graphing data, and analyzing data with a calculator, some teachers need a basic understanding of CBRs and CBLs to be prepared to troubleshoot the basic operations for guiding student learning both with and about the technology.

You are encouraged to consider technologies that offer promise for your students' learning. As a new teacher, you cannot possibly have an understanding of operations and concepts of all technologies any more than you can have a mass of activities for teaching your subject. You need to begin with an understanding of some of the basic technologies that you plan to use in your beginning teaching. In the same way that you will add activities to your instructional toolkit, as you teach you will be in a position to build your repertoire of technologies for which you have a basic understanding. Certainly you will expand your understandings as you explore and teach with emerging technologies for the classroom.

Software applications are important potential technologies in this first standard. Word processing, spreadsheets, databases, multimedia authoring tools (such as PowerPoint), and Web authoring

In the Classroom 2.1

ALPHABET, ANIMALS, COMPUTER MICE, AND HYPERLINKS

TECHNOLOGY OBJECTIVE: **NETS · S I, IV**

- **PowerPoint:** Technology as a communications tool.
- Become familiar with hyperlinks and the computer mouse in presentation software.

CONTENT OBJECTIVE: **Reading:** Students identify alphabetic animal words and connect the words with their pictures.

GRADE LEVEL: K–2

PROBLEM: Which is the animal word?

Create a PowerPoint presentation that shows words for students to specifically identify animal words.

Introduce students to the PowerPoint application by demonstrating how they will practice using the computer mouse to identify the alphabetic animal words while they also practice proper posture as they work on the computer.

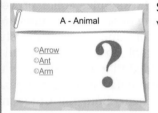

Students are to find the animal word that begins with the letter A. If they click the wrong word they are given another chance to find the animal word and get a picture of the animal!

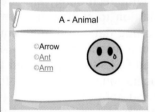 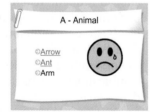 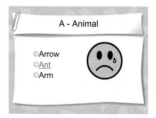

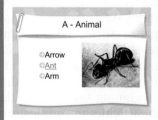 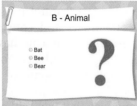

When they select the right animal word, clicking on the word moves them to the next animal (in this case the B animal).

tools provide a basic list of software expertise that Part II of this book is designed to support you in gaining knowledge of the basic concepts and operations with these applications. In the Classroom 2.1 introduces a sample activity that demonstrates how you might create technology activities to guide your students' learning. In this case, the teacher creates a presentation for a lesson where students practice using the computer mouse to click on hyperlinks to identify alphabetically arranged animal words to connect written words with the pictures. Chapter 8 of this book guides you in developing PowerPoint presentations; use Technology Link 2.1 to obtain a start for this PowerPoint alphabet animal presentation. The activity shows that even if you teach in grades K–2, you may use your technology knowledge and skills to create activities to guide students as they learn both *with* and *about* technology.

Technology Link 2.1

*U*se the **Animal** link at this book's website for beginning for an alphabet animal presentation.

www.wiley.com/college/niess

The Internet (sometimes referred to as the Net), including the World Wide Web (Web or WWW) and e-mail, is another broad-based technology application where teachers need familiarity with basic operations and concepts. Some people inaccurately equate the Internet with the Web. In reality the Web is built on the Internet. The Internet is the physical background of computers, networks, and servers that allow the connection of a multitude of computers around the world.

The Web is one of the important services provided by the Internet. The Web provides a set of protocols and tools to allow for sharing information. Users of the Web need browsers to read basic Web pages and Web authoring tools to add pages to the Web. An important concept with respect to the Web is that it was developed around the idea of universal readership. Anyone can put information on the Web with the appropriate tools. In addition, anyone can read pages that are not restricted by some form of password protection.

The Web has already been identified as a tremendous resource for teaching and learning. Moreover, the Web can be used as a resource for you as you prepare to teach. You can use the various search tools to locate lesson plans and ideas at websites throughout the world. The search tools typically have both a *search engine* (that searches a database or index of Internet sites) and a *subject directory* (that provides quick links to sites of interest). A search using the keywords "*lesson plans, writing, technology*" results in many "hits," many identifying lesson plans for more than writing or even technology.

Figure 2.1 provides a resource idea modified from one found on the Web. This idea may be use-

---

Resource Idea

Title:	A Web-Wall
Topic:	Multidisciplinary, Internet
Grade:	K–12, college, teacher preparation programs
Objectives:	Using Web searches, student teachers are able to identify useful lesson plan resources that integrate technology in teaching or learning.
Idea:	A Web-Wall is a directory that can be prepared by students in a teacher preparation program. Preservice teachers search the Web for useful websites that describe lesson ideas and plans for incorporating technology in specific teaching areas. They prepare several cards for the class bulletin board; each card includes a site location, a one-sentence description of ideas available at the site, a one-sentence description of a useful idea found at the site, their name, and the date they found the site. Preservice teachers are expected to (1) design the format and construct the class bulletin board and (2) add a specific number of ideas during the course. At the end of the course, the class reviews the various sites and identifies the most valuable resources by placing stars on those cards. Preservice teachers should review sites they have not visited recently to identify whether the ideas for their planning are still active.
Materials:	Bulletin board materials, 5 × 8 blank cards for information, access to Web
Modifications:	

1. Build a bulletin board where students in grades 5–8 search for more information about a specific topic of interest. Have the students discuss the various websites posted on the bulletin board for their accuracy and reliability.
2. Have student teachers search lesson plan resources on the Internet. Collect information such as technology use, grade level, topic, and other important information to include in a class database of resources. Use database searches and sorts to organize and display the information. Which websites were the most useful in obtaining information in explaining the topic? What technologies are most commonly used?

Source:	Wynn, Elissa, *Web-Wall*. Retrieved March 20, 2004, from http://www.LessonPlansPage.com/CIWebWallBulletinBoardIdea49.htm

FIGURE 2-1   Gathering ideas through Web searches in a preservice teacher's program.

ful in your teacher preparation program but, as one of the modifications suggest, the idea may be adapted to a lesson that you might use with your students.

If you plan to use this activity, however, you need a basic knowledge of how to search the Web and how to limit the searches. Not all browsers use the same database and, as a result, different browser search engines return different information. For most search engines, the results are based on how close the Web page titles and their descriptions are to your keywords. Not all of the hits will necessarily meet all of the search criteria; you are more apt to be more selective if you use the operator AND or the plus sign (+) to connect your keywords. The browser's Help section provides important information for conducting your searches. Probably the most important concept around the Web is that, besides universal readership, the Web is designed around a concept of universal contribution. The ideas you find may not have been tested or may have been tested in situations different from your intent. You must evaluate the products that you find and make important decisions about their usefulness.

In summary, the NETS·T Standard I describes a basic technology expertise needed by all classroom teachers as they seek to integrate technology in teaching and learning. Again, Part II of this book is designed to assist you in gaining basic knowledge, skills, and concepts of various technologies to support you in working on this standard. An important note is that the chapters are focused on more than just technology operations and concepts. The chapters are focused on preparing you to teach about the technology as you teach your subject(s) with technology—a TPCK that integrates the technologies as "integral components or tools for learning and communications within the context of academic subject areas" (ISTE, 2000, p. 17).

NETS·T Standard II. Planning and Designing Learning Environments and Experiences   The second NETS·T standard focuses on teachers planning and designing "effective learning environments and experiences supported by technology" (ISTE, 2002, p. 9). A major task for teachers is to plan and design learning environments that support learning. Each of the performance indicators describes the thinking and planning that teachers need to do in planning lessons and units. Teachers need to

A. *design developmentally appropriate learning opportunities that apply technology-enhanced instructional strategies to support the diverse needs of learners;*

B. *apply current research on teaching and learning with technology when planning learning environments and experiences;*

C. *identify and locate technology resources and evaluate them for accuracy and suitability;*

D. *plan for the management of technology resources within the context of learning activities; and*

E. *plan strategies to manage student learning in a technology-enhanced environment.* (ISTE, 2002, p. 9)

Consider the Learners   Students are central to the decisions a teacher must make in accomplishing this expectation. Who are they? Current views of learning highlight not only the importance of knowing who the learners are, but also taking into account their prior knowledge and understandings, their experiences, their attitudes, and their social interactions. Even at the same grade level, students are diverse when viewing them as individuals. And, with respect to technology experience, students are obviously diverse.

Although many households have computers, many do not. Although many schools have technology access, many are limited in what they are able to provide for the students. Although many teachers incorporate a variety of technologies in their lessons, many do not. As a result, students have not had the same experiences with technologies and, thus, come to the learning environment with diverse needs with respect to the question of integrating technologies in the learning environment. Teachers need to plan for this diversity along with a consideration of the myriad of other diverse needs of the students in their classes (NETS·T II-A).

Suppose you are planning to have your students do a Web search for information about a topic. Some of your students may be curious about the topic of tornadoes and others may not. How do you plan for this diversity? Perhaps you can incorporate the video *Raging Planet: Tornadoes* that shows what happens when warm air and cool air collide while introducing a famous geographic location, Tornado Alley. After this introduction, you can show the students that they actually live in the path described by Tornado Alley. What if only some of your students have had experiences with tornadoes? How do you plan for this diversity? Perhaps you can have those students share their experiences with the others. You also note that some of your students have experience with searching the Web, whereas others do not. How do you plan for this diversity? Perhaps you can pair students (expert, novice) in the Web search process.

Investigate the Research   Recognition of the diverse needs of your students is essential in making a decision about the opportunities you plan to incorporate in your lessons, particularly when you involve technology. But you are not alone in your efforts to design the lessons. Current research on teaching and learning with technology provides some guidance (NETS·T II-B). Project-based learning (PBL) has been found to support student learning. Student gains have increased significantly in technology-enhanced PBL environments helping students learn to effectively use the Web as well as attacking interdisciplinary problems (Sandholtz, Ringstaff, & Dwyer, 1997). Given this research you might plan on having students investigate the history and power of tornadoes and challenge them to develop a tornado preparedness and safety brochure for the students, parents, and community members. In this manner you have applied current research on teaching and learning with technology and provided students with a useful, authentic experience that connects their work in school with the larger community outside the classroom walls.

Consider Various Technology Resources   With a more refined idea about the project, you must consider potential technology resources to help your students (NETS·T II-C). In addition to the video, Web searches are valuable for identifying appropriate sites for your students to visit. Word processors and a presentation tool (such as PowerPoint) can be used to help students as they design their brochure and prepare to present their findings. In considering each of the technology resources, you need to identify their usefulness as well as consider the issues of access.

Manage the Technology and Student Interactions   In planning the tornado unit to include various technologies, you will be faced with important management issues: managing the technology (NETS·T II-D) and managing the student interactions with the technologies (NETS·T II-E). You may need to reserve time in a computer lab; but you must also develop a schedule for how the students work with that equipment. The plans must be integrated with other learning activities. You need to factor into your plans how you will deal with assuring that the students have the necessary skills for working with the equipment. Providing students with specific websites may be more useful than having the students wander around the Web since a simple search on tornadoes results in over 86,000 news articles and perhaps thousands of Web pages devoted to the topic. Alternatively, you might help them identify searches that will limit the number of hits that are returned. You might consider the instructional time and resources available. For example, does the class-room have a projector? Can the lesson be a whole-class inquiry? Or is it better for independent work in a lab?

Another useful management technique is to organize the students in teams and give each team a specific task rather than responsibility for the whole project. Identify one team as the Meteorologist team, charging this team with responsibilities like these:

- Describe the formation of tornadoes.
- Describe the threat of tornadoes to your state and, in particular, your community. How great is the risk for tornadoes, what is the history of tornado damage, and what do meteorologists predict for your weather this year?
- Outline the warning systems available in your community and schools.
- Work with the Presentation team to provide the information for both the PowerPoint presentation and the community safety brochure.

Plan Strategies for Student Learning   Ultimately, these efforts in planning and designing the learning environment and experiences in a unit that is enhanced with technology have the effect of helping you focus on the needs of your students, so that they can be actively engaged in learning. These explicit considerations during the planning stage result in helping you organize your students' time and experiences with the technology and in avoiding lost time due to confusion and misunderstandings about the project. Chapter 11 of this book is designed to help you extend these ideas in designing and developing instructional plans that integrate technology.

NETS·T Standard III. Teaching, Learning, and the Curriculum   The third NETS·T standard highlights teachers implementing "curriculum plans that include methods and strategies for applying technology to maximize student learning" (ISTE, 2002, p. 9). For this standard, ISTE identifies four indicators. Teachers need to

A. *facilitate technology-enhanced experiences that address content standards and student technology standards;*

B. *use technology to support learner-centered strategies that address the diverse needs of students;*

C. *apply technology to develop students' higher order skills and creativity; and*

D. *manage student-learning activities in a technology-enhanced environment.* (ISTE, 2002, p. 9)

Although many countries have a national curriculum, the United States does not. In the United States teachers are expected to design the curriculum based on local, state, and national standards.

Curriculum standards have been developed by professional organizations, such as the National Council of Teachers of English (1996), the National Council for the Social Studies (1994), the Consortium of National Arts Education Association (1994), the National Center for History in the Schools (1996), the National Academy of Sciences (1996), and the National Council of Teachers of Mathematics (2000). Chapter 4 of this text focuses on integrating student technology standards with these national curriculum standards.

In addition to these curriculum standards, each state has carefully considered the national standards in the design of their state-recommended standards and benchmarks. Schools and school districts must consider these state standards and benchmarks as they personalize their curriculum expectations to incorporate local interests. Given the national emphasis on testing what students know and are able to do, some states are more explicit in describing a curriculum that recognizes what the tests are testing. For those states, teachers do have less autonomy for designing and developing the curriculum. But they do have the responsibility for designing the lessons and instructional units to address the identified curriculum standards and benchmarks. Essentially, U.S. teachers have far greater opportunity and responsibility for designing the methods and strategies for integrating technology-enhanced experiences to address the content standards guiding the curriculum.

Figure 2.2 illustrates multiple content curriculum standards supporting the tornado unit. Three specific science standards for grades 5–8 are identified by the social studies middle grades curriculum

---

Unit: Tornadoes

Standards
Science
1. Science as inquiry, specifically abilities necessary to do scientific inquiry: develop descriptions, explanations, predictions, and models using evidence and explanations.
2. Science as inquiry, specifically understanding about scientific inquiry: scientific explanations emphasize evidence, have logically consistent arguments, and use scientific principles, models, and theories.
3. Science in personal and social perspectives, considering populations, resources and environments, natural hazards, and risks and benefits. (National Academy of Sciences, 1996)

Social Studies
1. Time, continuity, and change: use knowledge of facts and concepts drawn from history, along with methods of historical inquiry, to inform decision making about and action taking on public issues.
2. Study of people, places, and environments: describe physical system changes such as seasons, climate and weather, and the water cycle and identify geographic patterns associated with them.
3. Civic ideals and practices: practice forms of civic discussion and participation consistent with the ideals of citizens in a democratic republic. (National Council for the Social Studies, 1994)

Technology
1. Technology productivity tools: students use productivity tools to collaborate in constructing technology-enhanced models, prepare publications, and produce other creative works.
2. Technology research tools: students use technology to locate, evaluate, and collect information from a variety of sources. (ISTE, 2000)

Resources
1. *Raging Planet: Tornadoes* video
2. Internet resources
   • Lesson ideas: http://school.discovery.com/lessonplans/programs/ragingplanet-tornado/
   • The Fujita scale for measuring tornado intensity: http://www.fema.gov/kids/fscale.htm
   • Maps of tornado alley: http://www.tornadochaser.net/tornalley.html
   • Facts about tornadoes: http://www.noaa.gov/tornadofacts.html
   • Safety procedures: http://www.tornadoproject.com/safety/safety.htm
   • Preparation and building safety: http://www.disastercenter.com/tornado.html
3. Bulletin board background, cards, staples, pens
4. Technology
   • Computer Internet, PowerPoint, word processor, graphics package, spreadsheet
   • Video camcorder, digital camera
   • Video projector for computer presentations

(continued on next page)

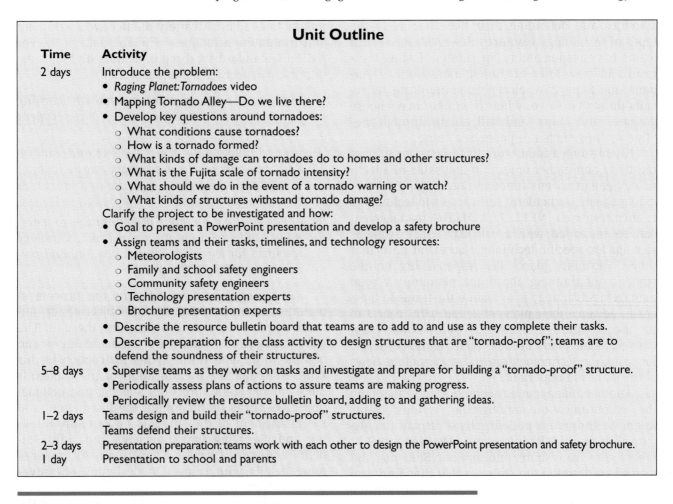

FIGURE 2.2   A teacher's thinking and planning for a tornado unit that integrates technology in a problem-based learning manner.

standards to frame this interdisciplinary unit. The National Education Technology Standards for Students (*NETS · S*) (ISTE, 2000) provide direction for the integration of technology in this unit through two of its standards. These technology standards support teachers as they facilitate the technology-enhanced experiences so that students learn both about the technology and with the technology. Teachers also design technology integration to create and support learning that could not otherwise be accomplished without it. The technology in the unit is for a purpose, not just for "fun days with technology." The purpose is to create and support learning that could not otherwise be accomplished without the use of the technology. From an observation of one of the student teachers described in the Snapshot of Student Teaching with Technology, "by using the technology the students were able to cover some objectives that wouldn't be so easily or quickly met without the use of technology." In other words, teachers must purposely plan that the technology-enhanced experiences

address content standards and student technology standards (NETS · T III-A).

In developing the unit, teachers must address the diverse needs of students, specifically considering learner-centered strategies (NETS · T III-B). The use of teams for doing the research and developing the presentation products is an example strategy. In addition to the Meteorologist team, the teacher might consider developing specific tasks for each of the teams described in the unit outline (Figure 2.2). Each team needs specific content and technology responsibilities as well as a responsibility to communicate and work with the other teams.

Another consideration is important. The teams' work with the technology needs to be directed toward developing students' higher-order thinking skills and creativity (NETS · T III-C). Creating tasks assuring that all teams and all students on a team work toward these goals is particularly important. More generalized tasks that provide some direction are useful, but the tasks need to stress the importance of the teams developing their own plans of activities and defending their decisions as to the types of technology resources they wish to use. All teams have responsibility for communicating their results in two different presentation formats. Perhaps one team may elect to communicate its results through a video, whereas another may choose graphics and maps, and still others through creative writing, such as a poem or a story.

Establishing a framework that allows for student creativity and higher order thinking skills in a technology-enhanced environment does require teacher management, particularly since access to technology is often restricted (NETS·T III-D). This management can be supported with a calendar where students sign up for specific technology access at particular times. Flexibility places the responsibility on the students for thinking ahead and planning. A good management strategy is to require the teams to present in advance their plans of action with respect to the use of various technologies with possible alternatives. Their plans become their "entrance ticket" for using the technology resources. Periodic reviews of the plans are important.

Another management technique for enhancing the communication among the various teams might be through a bulletin board display (as discussed in the *Web-Wall Resource Idea* in Figure 2.1) where they can share information. Students and teams can describe the websites that they find useful as well as other information that will help the other teams.

Probably one of a teacher's most challenging tasks is the development of a comprehensive unit plan. This plan coordinates the thinking about the unit. The content and technology standards lead to specific activities. Careful attention to the learners and their needs shapes the unit and the strategies that involve technology in support of higher order thinking skills and creativity. This plan includes management strategies that are aligned with each of the previous considerations. The organization of the unit plan often begins with broad points and is then expanded by specifics as the teacher thinks through the various activities. Figure 2.2 provides an example of the unit plan ideas discussed to this point. Chapters 11 and 12 of this book guide your thoughts about important decisions that teachers need to make when designing and developing a unit that integrates technology.

NETS·T Standard IV. Assessment and Evaluation
The fourth NETS·T standard emphasizes the importance of assessing and evaluating students' progress toward the standards and outcomes for the unit and in particular assessing how and what they have learned with the technology. This standard directs the teacher's attention toward applying "technology to facilitate a variety of effective assessment and evaluation strategies" (ISTE, 2002, p. 9). For NETS·T Standard IV, three indicators highlight the important aspects. Teachers need to

A. *apply technology in assessing student learning of subject matter using a variety of assessment techniques;*

B. *use technology resources to collect and analyze data, interpret results, and communicate findings to improve instructional practice and maximize student learning; and*

C. *apply multiple methods of evaluation to determine students' appropriate use of technology resources for learning, communication, and productivity.* (ISTE, 2002, p. 9)

An essential activity early in the process of planning a unit is to identify the objectives or outcomes desired as a result of teaching the unit. The question is clear: What are students to know and be able to do as a result of the instruction in this unit? Although the identification of the standards does provide some direction, specific instructional objectives focus the planning, the instruction, and the assessment of the students by carefully thinking and clarifying the knowledge and skills students will gain. Chapter 12 of this book provides more details with respect to designing objectives that involve learning with technology.

Consider a couple of possible objectives for the tornado unit as described in Figure 2.3. Both objectives consider the highest risk areas in Tornado Alley, but the students need to be able to describe their knowledge at different levels. For the first objective, the teacher might assess students' knowledge through a written test, verbal questioning, or perhaps a report that specifically requires the identification of the highest risk states. The second objective requires that the students use computer graphic tools and a computer graphic of the United States; the students are expected to provide a graphical rendition of the highest risk areas. This rendition might be expected in a report or during a testing session where the students have access to the appropriate technology. The depth of knowledge expected is also different in the two objectives. For the first objective, a student might identify Arkansas as a highest risk state and be correct; in the second objective, however, the student must show graphically the portion of Arkansas that is at highest risk. In other words, these two objectives describe different knowledge and understandings as well as different skills in expressing that knowledge.

The graphing calculator research of the early 1990s emphasized the importance of connecting the manner in which students learn their knowledge

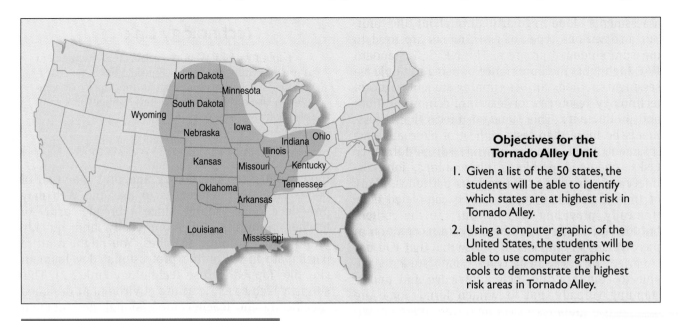

Objectives for the Tornado Alley Unit

1. Given a list of the 50 states, the students will be able to identify which states are at highest risk in Tornado Alley.

2. Using a computer graphic of the United States, the students will be able to use computer graphic tools to demonstrate the highest risk areas in Tornado Alley.

FIGURE 2.3 Objectives for the tornado unit.

and understanding with the manner in which they are to use and express their knowledge (Dunham & Dick, 1994). Many teachers allowed (and even encouraged) students to use calculators in solving mathematics problems. Yet, when assessing the students' knowledge of the mathematics, the students were not allowed to use the calculators to solve similar mathematics problems. Unfortunately, the students had learned to solve those problems using a particular tool, a tool that lessened the need to complete numeric computations. When the students were required to complete numeric computations to solve the problems by hand, they were more likely to take longer to solve the problems and were more prone to making errors in numeric computations. The environment in which the students were to demonstrate their knowledge resulted in assessing numeric computations rather than solving problems in the same manner they had been solving them in class. Dunham and Dick (1994) declared that this assessment of what the students had learned was "much like comparing apples and oranges."

The NETS·T Standard IV addresses the importance of applying technology in assessing student knowledge. NETS·T Standard IV-A advocates that teachers use a variety of assessment measures in the process of identifying what students have learned; furthermore, this performance indicator challenges teachers to consider technology performance in assessing students' progress in meeting the specific instructional objectives.

Objectives such as the second one on Tornado Alley (Figure 2.3) describe both the content knowledge and the technology performance that students are to gain as a result of the instruction. The specifics in the objectives have implications for instruction. During the unit, students need to have instruction and access to graphics packages if there is an expectation for demonstrating a particular level of performance with technology. As a result, each team's task may need to include an expectation of using graphics software in producing the products for either the PowerPoint presentation or the brochure.

The NETS·T Standard IV-B suggests that teachers use technology resources to collect and analyze various assessment data. Spreadsheets offer teachers the opportunity to design personalized grade books, to record and analyze the assessments, making use of the functions available in the spreadsheet. Chapter 6 of this text guides your thinking about different spreadsheet formats that you can create to collect, store, and analyze student results from various assessments for the unit. The data are more apt to be in a form that helps you reflect on the instruction and the students' learning if they are personalized in your grade book; ultimately such a grade book results in helping you improve your future instructional practices. Using an electronic version of a grade book allows you to maintain an up-to-date analysis as the data are entered. Therefore, you are able to more quickly determine students' progress; moreover, you can more easily prepare individual reports for each of your students or their parents.

Of course this up-to-date information is only useful if students' progress has been measured in a variety of ways *throughout* the unit. Providing students or their parents with an ongoing assessment of their progress requires that not only are assessments done regularly throughout the unit, but also various types of assessments are used to measure students' progress. The NETS·T Standard IV-C highlights the importance of using multiple assessment methods for determining students' uses of technology resources for learning, communication, and productivity. This standard directs that assessments be more than tests. A host of alternative assessment types can be considered: performance tasks, open-end problems, observations, journals, interviews, drawings, and perhaps portfolios. Many of these assessment types can be completed electronically, providing data not only on the content but also on the use of technology. In recognition of the diversity of students, it is essential that you use a variety of assessment types. Some students are able to communicate their knowledge and understanding verbally and in written form. Some are able to use graphics to communicate their knowledge and understandings more clearly. Some might be more interested in displaying their knowledge in an electronic portfolio. It is important for teachers to select appropriate task formats from among a myriad of available methods, carefully considering the intended purpose of the assessment. Chapter 13 of this book is dedicated to help you expand your knowledge and skills with more accurately assessing your students' learning with technology and their learning about technology.

NETS·T Standard V. Productivity and Professional Practice   The fifth NETS·T standard describes the importance of teachers using technology "to enhance their productivity and professional practice" (ISTE, 2002, p. 9). For this standard, ISTE describes four indicators teachers need to:

A. *use technology resources to engage in ongoing professional development and lifelong learning;*

B. *continually evaluate and reflect on professional practice to make informed decisions regarding the use of technology in support of student learning;*

C. *apply technology to increase productivity; and*

D. *use technology to communicate and collaborate with peers, parents, and the larger community in order to nurture student learning.* (ISTE, 2002, p. 9)

The NETS·T Standard V-B recognizes the importance of continuous growth in technology knowledge and staying abreast of current and emerging technologies. NETS·T Standard V-A reiterates that ongoing professional development and lifelong learning are important habits for a teacher. With access to the Web, teachers have the capability of accessing a broader range of references for researching and designing new units. Although

Technology Link 2.2

Tapped In is a Web-based learning environment to provide online professional development for teachers. Visit the various buildings in the Tapped In community. Use the **Professional Development** link from this book's website.

www.wiley.com/college/niess

they could go to the library and find a myriad of books and other references to use, the Web may provide a richer source since a broader array of teacher resources are more easily and quickly found through online searches. You might want to participate in an online professional development site, like Tapped In (use Technology Link 2.2). This site is a Web-based learning environment designed specifically for teacher professional development focusing on significant issues in teaching and learning and on ways that innovative uses of technologies can help address those issues.

While you are learning to teach, you will be required to design new units around specific content standards. Web resources have the potential of providing you with access to many teacher-tested ideas. Creating a Web-Wall as described in the resource idea in Figure 2.1 is one way to obtain help from others in your class in identifying resources that are better than others. As each student teacher finds valuable links for teacher resources, posting them on the Web-Wall helps the others. You are not only maximizing your efforts, you are establishing a professional practice of sharing your ideas with other teachers that will support you when you are teaching.

In your practical teaching experiences, such as student teaching, an important activity for your professional growth is to reflect on your instruction, on your students' interactions in the instruction, and on the adequacy of your plans in supporting their learning. The student teacher reflections in the Snapshot of Student Teaching with Technology are samples of the reflections that student teachers wrote after having taught with technology. They were asked to reflect on the ease of teaching with technology. Their comments demonstrate their recognition of the importance of both planning and preparation:

I had thought it would be quite easy to integrate the use of technology into my lesson plans, and soon discovered that if I hadn't actually tried the lab a few times to work the "kinks" out then I would have really been in trouble.

When using technology, I have to spend time on what directions are absolutely necessary. Then think about how to make the directions succinct.

I felt very well prepared for this sequence of lessons. I spent a good deal of time, at least 10 hours after the lesson plans were completed, getting ready.

A follow-up question about whether the time spent was worthwhile resulted in comments such as these:

I wanted students to be able to see what was happening as it happened, and this technology allowed them to do just that. I had a great time teaching these lessons to the students. It just made so much sense to them when they saw the graph forming as they titrated the acids with the bases. I remember having to manually graph changes in pH vs. volume of base added, and I hated it.

The lab work did lead to a good closing discussion. Summarizing what had happened helped the students make the connections, which was the objective of this lesson.

My mentor was skeptical about the use of the CBLs in this lesson, but admitted to being surprised and impressed by what this technology was able to show to the students. I concur with her assessment; I was also pleasantly surprised at what the technology demonstrated.

Reflective exercises support your continued professional growth. Rather than simply reflecting at the end of the class that "everything went well," these student teachers reiterated some important practices that were needed for integrating technology in support of student learning. They were able to use what they learned in this experience as they planned for additional experiences.

The third performance indicator, NETS·T Standard V-C, advises teachers to apply technology to increase their productivity. Keeping an electronic journal is one way to maintain the commitment to reflect on your teaching. Maintaining a weblog (see Chapters 5 and 10 for a more detailed description of weblogs) is another way to increase the community of teachers with whom you communicate and share reflections as you teach with technology. Word processing your lesson plans may assure that you more consciously think through the lesson by providing a file that can be edited after having taught the lesson. Graphics packages are useful in creating your own worksheets, designing them to fit your particular purposes and student interests. If you can create PowerPoint presentations for your classes, the availability of the presentation allows students with an opportunity to work on the presentation as a whole group or even refresh their understandings on their own or in smaller groups.

You may even create a website that contains assignment information that both students and parents can access. One of the outcomes for Part II of this book is to have you think about these different technologies and consider how you might use them to improve your teaching and increase your productivity.

The fourth performance indicator, NETS·T V-D, challenges you to use technology to communicate and collaborate. Many of the ideas that help teachers become more productive also have potential for supporting communication with parents and students. Weblogs are easily accessed online resources to use for exchanging ideas on content, or even for online collaborative development of courses and other resources. Maintaining a Web page can provide parents access to ongoing assignments. E-mail is one way of contacting a student or the student's parent(s). Databases provide a "mail merge" option where you can add specific student assessment information into separate form letters to the parents; in this way, the parents are provided with their children's individual progress. Putting a special comment field in the database allows you the option of requesting a personal meeting with the parents, indicating that the child is making excellent progress, or adding whatever comment is warranted.

Technology offers many tools to consider for improving instruction. Advancement in the technology and improved access to technology will continue to require more teacher investigation. Teachers need to continue to grow in their ability to use the technology but must also continue to examine the curriculum, student learning needs, and the opportunities provided by integrating technology. This professional expectation requires that teachers establish a mechanism for ongoing communication and collaboration around the issues of integrating technology. The National Board for the Professional Teaching Standards (NBPTS) identifies a specific standard to address this expectation: "Teachers are members of learning communities" (NBPTS, 1994, pp.13–14). NETS·T Standard V recommends that teachers use technology to enhance their professional responsibilities, as they become active members of learning communities.

NETS·T Standard VI. Social, Ethical, Legal, and Human Issues The final NETS·T standard describes the importance of teachers understanding "the social, ethical, legal, and human issues surrounding the use of technology in PK–12 schools and apply that understanding in practice" (ISTE, 2002, p. 9). This standard has five indicators for teachers' activities. Teachers need to

A. *model and teach legal and ethical practice related to technology use;*

B. *apply technology resources to enable and empower learners with diverse backgrounds, characteristics, and abilities;*

C. *identify and use technology resources that affirm diversity;*

D. *promote safe and healthy use of technology resources; and*

E. *facilitate equitable access to technology resources for all students.* (ISTE, 2002, p. 9)

Educational access to technology includes the responsibility for appropriate use and this appropriate use involves legal, ethical, and social considerations. Students observe teachers' actions and often model their own behavior after what they have observed, regardless of what they have been told. Teachers model the behavior that students assume is appropriate. Copying pictures from the Web without appropriate citations or appropriate approvals teaches students that this behavior is legal and ethical. It is not. In essence, as in NETS·T Standard VI-A, teachers must model, as well as teach, legal and ethical practices related to technology use. Excusing the action because of "limited school funding and the high cost of computer software" is not an acceptable practice, either legally or ethically. Part II of this book specifically focuses on social, ethical, legal, and human issues as each of the technologies are discussed.

Teachers have the responsibility for establishing classroom policies and practices that promote legal and ethical uses of the technology resources their students use (NETS·T Standard VI-D). If students are involved in making movies to demonstrate their knowledge and understanding, it cannot be acceptable for them to download and use copy-protected music and other videos for inclusion. Teachers need to have clear guidelines and expectations that do not encourage their students to break the rules. Online resources such as those described in *Technology Link 2.3* may provide helpful ideas for explaining and maintaining these rules. Besides a list of rules and expectations, however, teachers need to be careful about the scoring criteria that are used for assessing the end product. Grading on creativity may unintentionally encourage students to include these copy-protected effects.

With respect to social concerns, teachers must consider the needs of diverse learners, their backgrounds, their characteristics, and their abilities. Using a variety of technology resources as described in NETS·T VI-B is more apt to provide the diversity for meeting diverse student needs and abilities. Another consideration that is important in the selection of various technology resources is the representation of diversity. This concern is as important as the concern for assuring that textbooks highlight and celebrate diversity. When you view specific software packages, you should question the graphics, the verbal presentations, as well as the educational logic that is used. Do the graphics support a particular type of individual such as boys and exclude graphics that might appeal to girls? Is the verbal presentation at a level higher than some of the students are able to understand? Does the progression in the ideas make those ideas misunderstood by some children? Teachers have the responsibility for assuring that the technology resources they select affirm diversity (NETS·T VI-C). However, the logistics of scheduling access for all students should not be used as an excuse for abandoning a technology-infused lesson.

Another social concern deals with access. Assignments that require students to use a word processor must be considered carefully. Teachers must recognize the access that *all* students have to word processors. Some may be able to work on their assignments only at the school, whereas others may be able to work on it both at school and at home. This inequitable access results in different opportunities to participate in the assignment, certainly affecting the quality of the end product. Teachers have the responsibility to facilitate equitable access for all students as described in NETS·T Standard VI-E.

In essence, in addition to encouraging you to consider using a variety of technology resources as you prepare to teach, we also encourage you to consider important social, ethical, legal, and human issues. Although some of the problems have been highlighted to explain the concerns, the concerns should not result in discarding the idea of integrating technology. The concerns simply present challenges that you must attend to as you design *all* of your instruction. Your legal and ethical use of the technology provides an important model for student learning. Your attention to the diverse needs of your students and an equitable access to technology resources is as important with technology resources as it is with all other books and materials you use in your classroom. The performance indicators in NETS·T Standard VI encourage your development as a professional who integrates technology in a manner that attends to social, ethical, legal, and human concerns.

Technology Link 2.3

*A*ccess to online resources to support appropriate legal and ethical uses of technology resources is available on the **Legal** link at this book's website.

www.wiley.com/college/niess

Standards for Preparing New Teachers

What impact will the NETS teacher standards (NETS·T) have on your preparation as a teacher? Will you be required to meet these standards in order to be a teacher? Although not all state teacher licensing or certification requirements require that you demonstrate the knowledge, skills, and dispositions addressed in the NETS·T standards, as of 2005 over 70% of the states have either adopted, adapted, or referenced the NETS teacher standards in their licensing requirements.

Irrespective of whether the teacher licensing agencies currently require evidence of the NETS·T standards, most teacher preparation programs are guided by other national standards. The National Council for Accreditation of Teacher Education (NCATE) accredits about half of the 1300 teacher preparation programs throughout many states, including all those states without specific requirements. NCATE has acknowledged the importance of preparing teachers to teach *with* and *about* technology. To be accredited by NCATE, a teacher preparation program must address and meet standards that demonstrate a commitment to technology:

> The unit's conceptual framework(s) reflects the unit's commitment to preparing candidates who are able to use educational technology to help all students learn; it also provides a conceptual understanding of how knowledge, skills, and dispositions related to educational and information technology are integrated throughout the curriculum, instruction, field experiences, clinical practice, assessments, and evaluations. *(NCATE, 2002, p. 13)*

This technology commitment is further reflected in NCATE's rubrics used to evaluate each of the standards. One of the six standards specifically addresses a pedagogical content knowledge (PCK) for teacher candidates. More specifically the target for this standard states,

> Teacher candidates reflect a thorough understanding of pedagogical content knowledge delineated in professional, state, and institution standards. They have in-depth understanding of the subject matter that they plan to teach, allowing them to provide multiple explanations and instructional strategies so that all students learn. They present the content to students in challenging, clear, and compelling ways and integrate technology appropriately. *(NCATE, 2003, p. 4)*

Another important set of national standards has impacted teacher preparation programs by describing outcomes that new teachers must demonstrate. The Interstate New Teacher Assessment and Support Consortium (INTASC), a consortium of more than 30 states, identified 10 basic principles focused on the essential knowledge and abilities new teachers need regardless of grade level or subject taught. These principles highlight that in order for beginning teachers to be effective, they need to be able to integrate content knowledge with their pedagogical understanding in order to assure that all their students learn (INTASC, 1993).

Since technology is not specifically mentioned in the INTASC principles, the question arises as to how the NETS·T standards relate to INTASC. Is technology simply another tool that teachers use for their instruction? Does technology require more attention to a teacher's preparation? Appendix B provides one view of the alignment of INTASC principles with respect to the impact of technology on the preparation of teachers. Connecting the INTASC principles with the NETS·T standards highlights the importance of considering technology when considering what you need to know and be able to do as a new teacher. Given NCATE's technology emphasis on teachers' development of a TPCK, the preparation of teachers for the twenty-first century requires a different preparation than that of previous decades. Ultimately, the three sets of standards (NCATE, INTASC, and NETS·T) provide an important lens for framing the expectations for teachers in the twenty-first century. More specifically, they provide a lens for preparing you to teach *with* and *about* technology while focused on teaching your subject matter at your chosen grade level.

Summing It Up

Preparing teachers to teach in the twenty-first century requires attention to the developing impact of newer information and communication technologies on society. With increased access to a variety of technologies, what your students need to know and how they need to know it have shifted. Students need to learn both about technology and how to use that technology for learning. You must be prepared to meet this challenge. You need to learn about these new technologies. You need to learn how to learn with the technologies. And you need to learn how to guide your students' learning with technology. This learning cannot be confined to your initial teacher preparation program. This learning will be a lifelong professional development.

Several professional organizations have actively supported the redesign of teacher preparation programs toward preparing preservice teachers with a pedagogical content knowledge for teaching with technology (TPCK). The International Society for Technology in Education (ISTE) promoted the development of a set of teacher standards to guide your learning throughout your career as you enhance your knowledge and abilities in scaffolding your students' learning with technology, namely, the National Educational Technology Standards for Teachers. Six standards help to clarify the knowledge, skills, and abilities all teachers need to teach with and about technology. Teachers need to

- demonstrate a sound understanding of technology operations and concepts;
- plan and design effective learning environments and experiences supported by technology;
- implement curriculum plans that include methods and strategies for applying technology to maximize student learning;
- apply technology to facilitate a variety of effective assessment and evaluation strategies;
- use technology to enhance their productivity and professional practice;
- understand the social, ethical, legal, and human issues surrounding the use of technology in education and apply that understanding in practice. (ISTE, 2002, p. 9)

In concert with these NETS·T standards, other national organizations have supported the idea that teachers need to develop a pedagogical content knowledge for teaching with technology (a TPCK). The National Council for Accreditation of Teacher Education (NCATE) requires that preservice teachers need to develop a "conceptual understanding of how knowledge, skills, and dispositions related to educational and information technology are integrated throughout the curriculum, instruction, field experiences, clinical practice, assessments, and evaluations" (NCATE, 2002, p. 13). A second organization, the Interstate New Teacher Assessment and Support Consortium (IN-TASC), described 10 important principles for beginning teachers to be effective in assuring that all their students learn. A careful analysis of how the NETS·T standards align with the NCATE and IN-TASC standards provides an important lens for beginning your preparation to be a teacher in the twenty-first century—a teacher with a TPCK for teaching with and about technology. As you teach, you will gain increased knowledge, skills, and abilities for integrating technology as a tool to enhance your students' learning. As a result of your efforts, your students will learn about technology but, more importantly, will be able to use technology as a tool for learning. This notion is at the heart of the NETS·T standards.

End-of-the-Chapter Activities and References

PRACTICE PROBLEMS

1. Search the Internet to identify a useful teacher website that provides a variety of lesson plans for your subject at the grade level you plan to teach.

2. Search the Internet to identify an idea for teaching your subject with technology at the grade level you plan to teach. Describe your idea in the format provided in Figure 2.1 (resource idea).

3. As a class develop a Web-Wall as described in Figure 2.1 (resource idea).

4. Search the Internet to identify a lesson idea for teaching your grade level that includes technology objectives and activities to support learning both with and about technology.

5. Investigate some lesson idea publications such as those identified in the Annotated Resources section or in another resource available for your content area; identify a lesson idea for teaching at one of the grade levels that includes technology objectives and activities to support learning both with and about technology. Describe the idea in the format provided in Figure 2.1 (resource idea).

6. Outline a unit where you integrate technology in teaching that unit. Use the format of Figure 2.2 (tornado unit) to describe your unit.

IN THE CLASSROOM ACTIVITIES

7. Work with students at the elementary or secondary level who are searching the Internet for assistance in a particular project. Record their attempts, successes, failures. What do these students think about the information they are retrieving? Do they accept all information without question? Do they understand it?

8. Observe a teacher teaching a lesson where students have hands-on access to technology. How does the teacher prepare the students for working with the technology?

9. Observe a class where the teacher incorporates technology in the lesson. What is the purpose for using the technology? How does the technology help students to learn the subject?

ASSESSING STUDENT LEARNING WITH AND ABOUT TECHNOLOGY

10. Interview a teacher about how she or he assesses students' knowledge about technology. What kinds of assessments are used? What is the purpose of the assessment?

11. Interview a teacher about how she or he assesses students' knowledge of content they learned *with* technology? What kinds of assessments are used? What is the purpose of the assessment?

12. How do teachers use technology in education? Construct a survey to collect data to answer this question. If possible, ask at least 10 teachers to respond to your survey. Analyze the results to develop a response to the question.

E-PORTFOLIO ACTIVITIES

13. Prepare a graph that you will use to chart your progress with a variety of technologies that you will learn about in this course. Be prepared to scan this document at the end of the course to be included in your E-portfolio.

14. Write a reflection on how you see the NETS·T standards represented in your own program of study in preparing for a teaching career.

15. Outline a lesson plan that does not include technology at all. Be prepared to reconsider the impact of your developing knowledge about teaching with technology on your plans for the lesson.

REFLECTION AND DISCUSSION

16. Discuss the strategic thinking that the teacher needed in developing the tornado unit lesson plan.

17. Consider your specific discipline.

- Identify technologies that may be useful teaching the discipline.

- Identify examples of how technology has shifted how the knowledge in the discipline is known.

18. Discuss your beliefs about teaching your content area with technology as a learning tool.

    a. Select a particular topic for your content that you think would benefit from the use of technology as a learning tool. Discuss how the topic is enhanced with the use of the technology.

    b. Select another topic in your content for which you believe technology might hamper the development of the important ideas.

    c. Prepare a statement about your general ideas about teaching your subject with technology. Be sure to date this reflection for review after you finish the course.

Annotated Resources

International Society for Technology in Education. (2002). *National educational technology standards for teachers: Preparing teachers to use technology*. Eugene, OR: ISTE. This document presents a set of standards to guide teacher preparation programs as they redesign their programs for preparing future teachers to teach with and about technology.

Wang, L., Ertmer, P. A., & Newby, T. J. (2004). Increasing preservice teachers' self-efficacy beliefs for technology integration. *Journal of Research on Technology in Education, 36*(3), 231–250. This reference contains a self-efficacy beliefs inventory for technology integration.

Lesson Ideas: These references provide classroom lessons for integrating *learning about technology* while *learning* academic subject matter content *with technology*.

Carroll, J. A., Kelly, M. G., & Witherspoon, T. L. (Eds.). (2003). *Multidisciplinary units for prekindergarten through grade 2*. Eugene, OR: ISTE.

Hannah, L., Menchaca, M., & McVicker, B. (Eds.). (2002). *Multidisciplinary units for grades 3–5*. Eugene, OR: ISTE.

O'Hara, S., & McMahon, M. (Eds.). (2003). *Multidisciplinary units for grades 6–8*. Eugene, OR: ISTE.

CHAPTER 3

Learning and Knowledge in the Twenty-first Century

Tim Platt/Iconica/Getty Images

Introduction

With the major impact of information and communications technologies on civilization today, what knowledge is worth knowing for citizens who will live and work in this century? The Snapshot of Examinations of Eighth-Grade Student Learning portrays the knowledge eighth-grade students were asked to demonstrate in the previous two centuries. Could you pass these examinations? What knowledge was examined and for what reason? Compare the items from a test given as an eighth-grade final exam in Salina, Kansas, in 1895 with items from the 1994 National Assessment of Educational Progress (NAEP). (NAEP has monitored students' progress in reading, mathematics, science, writing, U.S. history, civics, geography, and the arts in grades 4, 8, and 12 since 1969.) Has what students need to know in the eighth grade changed over the past century?

The 1895 test was given during a specific time in American history as the Agricultural Age was giving way to the Industrial Age. Careers shifted as settlements moved westward. Human economic activity began to centralize in urban areas, focused around mechanized production of goods. Rather than growing all that was needed, families traded services and materials. Trading was more formalized, however, with an increased emphasis on paying for services and materials using the nation's

currency. The nation's educational goals shifted too. Industrialization exposed expanded knowledge and generated new educational needs. Increasingly, America's citizens needed to be able to read, write, and do simple calculations in order to pay for the services they received. More children attended schools for at least some of the elementary grades.

The general belief about learning shifted along with the progression of knowledge needed for effective participation in society. Prior to the 1900s, the belief was that the mind was a muscle that needed to be exercised; repetition was an important exercise. Children learned arithmetic through daily repetition and practice with many problems. Test questions had single correct answers. Essays were given, but to demonstrate the scoring emphasis on the essay the questions were labeled as questions "2–5." Students were expected to demonstrate their ability to write by writing a composition describing their understanding of the rules of grammar. The rules for grammar and pronunciation were to be memorized and regurgitated on the tests. Expertise with reading and writing was interpreted with a demonstration of knowledge of the rules.

By the end of the twentieth century, though, the society shifted into an Information Age, an age marked by information and communications electronic technology inventions. Although this new period was not identified by large-scale changes in settlement patterns, the educational needs of workers dramatically changed. Fewer people were needed for the repetitive work of factories. With increased access to information, more people were needed to think creatively, make decisions, and solve problems. Now, more of America's children are not only expected to complete secondary schools but to also complete college. What schools need to teach, therefore, has become quite different from the previous centuries. With increased technology access to information, what students now need to know continues to shift; they need to know how to process information, how to analyze and use information, and basically how to use information for lifelong learning. As noted by Eisner (2003), the best way to educate America's children is to focus on teaching judgment, critical thinking, meaningful literacy, and service.

With these transformations of the educational goals for the twenty-first century, learning is also viewed much differently. Today, a consideration of learning is focused on how students construct their individual understandings from personal experiences. When thinking about learning, educators highlight the internal mental processes involved in learning. They think about learning by considering how students organize and connect their personal experiences and understandings, their knowledge schema (or knowledge structures) that connect huge amounts of information for recall, application, and expansion of their understandings.

Today, the shift of attention to learning from the perspective of students' constructions has influenced how and what teachers are taught to teach. Both curriculum and instruction have shifted from teacher-centered to student-centered. Although the school curriculum still includes core academic areas such as English and language arts, mathematics, science, and social studies, these subjects are directed more toward a consideration of the challenges of the twenty-first century, namely, the importance of lifelong learning and the development of learning processes. The mathematics curriculum includes data analysis and statistics along with an emphasis on guiding student learning of five processes for learning and doing mathematics: problem solving; reasoning and proof; communication; connections; and representations. The social studies curriculum is refocused around 10 themes for teaching students the content knowledge, intellectual skills, and civic values necessary to fulfill the duties of citizenship in a participatory democracy: culture; time, continuity, and change; people, places, and environments; individual development and identity; individuals, groups, and institutions; power, authority, and governance; production, distribution, and consumption; science, technology, and society; global connections; and civic ideals and practices. The language arts curriculum is directed by the recognition that

> Being literate in a contemporary society means being active, critical, and creative users not only of print and spoken language but also for the visual language of film and television, commercial and political advertising, photography and more. Teaching students how to interpret and create visual texts such as illustrations, charts, graphs, electronic displays, photographs, film, and video is another essential component of the English language arts curriculum. (National Council of Teachers of English, 1996)

The core academic subjects have collaborated in integrating information and communications technology literacy skills into their curriculum in recognition of the intersection of information and communications technology literacy and the core subjects as developing a more relevant curriculum for meeting the demands of the twenty-first century. With the challenges of the twenty-first century, different forms of assessment now include fewer structured and more open-ended responses where attention is on the reasoning students use in explaining their responses. The NAEP career question is an example of a question that was not likely to be asked a century ago but today is an important type of question used to assess students' reasoning skills.

Teachers today must know much more than what they needed to know to teach a century ago. They can no longer assume their job is to simply transfer information that they learned in the same way that they learned it. Knowledge is expanding daily, and how people understand and gain that knowledge is also changing. Emphasizing the principal parts of verbs has given way to a focus on communicating through a wide range of both print and nonprint texts. Knowing how to take the square root of a number using paper and pencil is no longer essential knowledge; using the appropriate technological tool to find the square root in solving problems is now more essential. Teachers need to be prepared to guide students' in constructing knowledge rather than simply telling them what they need to know. Teachers need to be prepared to guide students in learning how to learn. They need to guide their students as they learn *about* technology. An even more critical teaching skill, however, is the skill to teach students to learn *with* the technology.

The important difference between the tests described in the Snapshot of Examinations of Eighth-Grade Student Learning is not whether you or your students can answer the questions. The tests demonstrate that the kinds of knowledge and how that knowledge must be known have changed substantially. How many students from 1895 could use a spreadsheet to find the average of a set of scores? How many students from 1895 could prepare a digital story that blends audio, voice, and images in a persuasive essay. Certainly the time spent learning to use the spreadsheet and various audiovisual technologies influences the curriculum. But learning to learn with technology is an important skill for the future. Teachers today must know how to scaffold their students' learning so that they are prepared to participate in the society in their future—a future that must grapple with the impact of a knowledge explosion with crucial information and communications technological changes.

CHAPTER LEARNING OBJECTIVES

After reading this chapter, you should be able to:

1. Discuss the Information Age of the twenty-first century and identify what knowledge is worth knowing.

2. Illustrate *learning* and how it happens.

3. Explain a behaviorist's view of learning and how it influences teaching and learning today.

4. Describe a cognitive scientist's view of learning and how it influences teaching and learning today.

5. Explain *constructivism* and how it affects teaching and learning today.

Snapshot of Examinations of Eighth-Grade Student Learning

Russell Schoolhouse, 1896

The eighth-grade teacher at Russell Schoolhouse, Mrs. Baxter, announced that the students needed to prepare for the final examination of the year. She found some items from the 1895 examination[1] to give students practice with the type of questions they would have on the final day of school. Before school, she had written the problems on the board and covered the board until the students were in their assigned seats with their pencils and tablets ready. The students knew that they were expected to neatly copy each question from the board. They were to write their responses neatly following each question so that their work was easily read. As soon as the students were ready, Mrs. Baxter uncovered the board.

Mrs. Baxter: You have two hours to complete these test items. Remember to write neatly and there will be no talking. If you need something, raise your hand and, when I recognize you, you may come to my desk to ask your question. Begin.

---

[1] Test items were taken from the Eighth Grade Final Exam from 1895, Salina, Kansas. The original document is on file at the Smoky Valley Genealogical Society and Library in Salina, Kansas. *The Salina Journal* reprinted the entire test on Sunday, July 9, 2000. Retrieved January 2004 from http://www.saljournal.com/sub/1895/

1. Grammar: What are the principal parts of a verb? Give principal parts of do, lie, lay, and run.
2–5. Grammar: Write a composition of about 150 words and show therein that you understand the practical use of the rules of grammar.
6. Arithmetic: A wagon box is 2 ft. tall, 10 ft. long, and 3 ft. wide. How many bushels of wheat will it hold?
7. Arithmetic: What is the cost of a square farm at $15 per acre, the distance around which is 640 rods?
8. Arithmetic: What is the cost of 40 boards 12 inches wide and 16 ft. long at $0.20 per inch?
9. History: Show the territorial growth of the United States.
10. History: Who were the following: Morse, Whitney, Fulton, Bell, Lincoln, Penn, and Howe?
11. Geography: Name and locate the principal trade centers of the United States.
12. Geography: What is climate? Upon what does climate depend?
13. Geography: Describe the mountains of North America.
14. Orthography: Write 10 words frequently mispronounced and indicate pronunciation by use of diacritical marks and by syllabication.
15. Orthography: What is meant by the following: alphabet, phonetic orthography, etymology, syllabication?

Westlake Middle School, 2003

Justin is in the eighth grade at Westlake Middle School. His teacher, Ms. Harrison, announced that all of the students in the class were to take the National Assessment of Educational Progress (NAEP) next month. She explained that this test is known as the "Nation's Report

Card" to document the progress of what America's students know and can do in various subject areas.

Justin:	What's on the test?
Ms. Harrison:	Reading, mathematics, science, writing, U.S. history, social studies, geography, and the arts!
Justin:	Oh man, I'm in trouble!
Ms. Harrison:	Not really. How about if I give you practice tests so you can see what the test is like and how you might prepare yourself?
Class:	OK.

Ms. Harrison suggested that over the next week she give them a practice test in the different areas, one each day for part of the class period. She indicated that she would give them a mathematics test tomorrow so they definitely would need to have their calculators. The following day they would take a reading test, and the day after that she would give them a history test. Each test would take about an hour. Then, on Friday, they would talk about the tests and determine how they had done on the practice tests.

On Tuesday, the students sat in their assigned seats at the various tables organized around the room; they had sharpened pencils, erasers, and calculators. Ms. Harrison began by distributing the mathematics test, indicating that they had 45 minutes for these five questions.

Mathematics[2] (45 minutes)

Name: _____

1. How many feet are in 15 miles?   1 mile = 5,280 feet
   - A) 352
   - B) 35,200
   - C) 79,200
   - D) 84,480
   - E) 89,760

2. If $3 + w = b$, then $w =$
   - A) $b/3$
   - B) $b \times 3$
   - C) $b + 3$
   - D) $3 - b$
   - E) $b - 3$

3. The perimeter of a square is 36 inches. What is the length of one side of the square?
   - A) 4 inches
   - B) 6 inches
   - C) 9 inches
   - D) 18 inches

4. What is the median of these numbers?
   4, 8, 3, 2, 5, 8, 12
   - A) 4
   - B) 5
   - C) 6
   - D) 7
   - E) 8

5. A high school ordered 11 buses to transport 418 students. If each bus can seat 35 students, will the number of buses ordered be enough to provide a seat for each student.
   Yes_____   No_____

   Explain your answer:

   _____

   [2] *Source:* National Center for Education Statistics, National Assessment of Educational Progress (NAEP), 1994, 8H7.

Wednesday, the students were prepared to take the reading and writing test. Ms. Harrison indicated that they needed to read an article titled "The Sharebots," by Carl Zimmer and then they would have three questions—one where they would need to write an essay. They had an hour for this test.

Reading and Writing[3] (60 minutes)

Name: _____

1. The main purpose of the article is to describe:
   - a. how robots locate metal pucks.
   - b. how robots work with each other.
   - c. how robots recharge their own batteries.
   - d. how robots perform five basic behaviors.

2. The following sentence appears in the next-to-last paragraph of the article:

   With this simple social contract, the robots needed only 15 minutes of practice to become altruistic.

   Based on how the word is used in the article, which of the following best describes what it means to be "altruistic"?
   - a. to engage in an experiment.
   - b. to provide assistance to others.
   - c. to work without taking frequent breaks.
   - d. to compete with others for the highest score.

3. Do you think it is a good idea for Matari to "produce more complex robot societies"? Support your opinion with information from the article.

   _____

   [3] *Source:* National Center for Education Statistics, National Assessment of Educational Progress (NAEP), 1994, 8H7.

On Thursday, Ms. Harrison described the test for the day, the U.S. history test. She had selected some of the eighth-grade test questions but had also identified some of the twelfth-grade test questions as ones they might be able to answer.

Ms. Harrison:	I thought you might like to try some of the twelfth-grade questions since one of the questions discusses future career paths that might be of interest to you. We talked about some of these careers last week and discussed the type of courses you needed to take in high school to prepare yourself. I'd like to see what you have to say about this question. You'll have an hour for this test. Remember, on Friday we'll talk about the questions and how to prepare to take the NAEP test next month.

U.S. History[4] (60 minutes)

Name: _____

1. What is the main reason the Pilgrims and Puritans came to America?

   a. To practice their religion freely

   b. To make more money and live a better life

   c. To build a democratic government

   d. To expand the lands controlled by the king of England

2. Between 1960 and 1990, what invention most changed the way people in the United States worked?

   a. The typewriter

   b. The computer

   c. The superconductor

   d. The radio

3. Imagine you could use a time machine to visit the past. You have landed in Philadelphia in the summer of 1776. Describe an important event that is happening.

4. Refer to the survey information shown below. (These questions were asked in public opinion polls in July 1950.)[5]

July 12, 1950—Professions

"Suppose a young man came to you and asked your advice about taking up a profession. Assuming that he was qualified to enter any of these professions, which one of them would you first recommend to him?"

Doctor of medicine	29%	Professor, teacher	5
Engineer, builder	16	Banker	4
Business executive	8	Dentist	4
Clergyman	8	Veterinarian	3
Lawyer	8	None, don't know	9
Government worker	6		

July 15, 1950—Professions

"Suppose a young girl came to you and asked your advice about taking up a profession. Assuming she was qualified to enter any of these professions, which one of them would you first recommend?"

Nurse	33%	Actress	3
Teacher	15	Journalist	2
Secretary	8	Musician	2
Social service worker	8	Model	2
Dietician	7	Librarian	2
Dressmaker	4	Medical, dental technician	1
Beautician	4	Others	2
Airline stewardess	3	Don't know	4

• Identify one way an imaginary 1990 survey and its results would probably be similar to the 1950 survey

• Suppose that similar surveys were conducted in 1990. Identify one way an imaginary survey and its results would probably be different from the 1950 survey.

[4] Source: National Center for Education Statistics, National Assessment of Educational Progress (NAEP), 1994, 8H7.

[5] Twelfth-grade sample item. Source: National Center for Education Statistics, National Assessment of Educational Progress (NAEP), 1994, 12H7.

Learning and Knowing in the Twenty-first Century

You are preparing to teach and your primary task as a teacher will be to assure that your students learn the knowledge that is important for their future as citizens in the twenty-first century. However, this idea means you must respond to an important question: What knowledge is worth learning and knowing? Along with that question you must also consider how you will teach the knowledge. Will you use electronic technologies? How will teaching with such technologies help?

What Knowledge Is Worth Learning and Knowing?

Can you find the cube root of 14,172.488, *without* using a calculator or computer? Probably not! Figure 3.1 shows how Gertrude Baxter was able to find that 24.2 is the exact cube root of 14,172.488. The key is that Gertrude used paper and pencil and not an electronic technology! This problem was a mathematics problem for eighth-grade students in 1896! Now, in the twenty-first century, this method of finding the cube root might at best be considered a lost art.

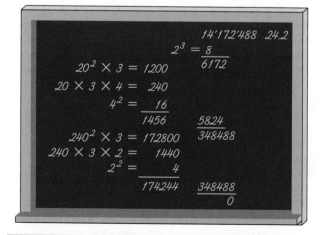

FIGURE 3.1 Gertrude Baxter's method for finding the cube root of 14,172.488.[6]

[6] Source: Found in Gertrude Baxter's school notebook, written on April 27, 1896; found in an old basement in Rhode Island in 1990.

Not only has instruction changed in the twenty-first century but the curriculum encompassing the subjects to be learned has also changed. Assessments of students' progress provide a lens for viewing what students need to know and be able to do to be successful citizens. The *Snapshot of Examinations of Eighth-Grade Student Learning* displays how some items given to eighth graders have changed since the late 1800s.

Social scientists often use broad descriptors to portray human activity, including what citizens need to know over time. One of the most commonly used descriptions places human economic activity in three broadly defined periods: the Agricultural, Industrial, and Information ages. This language actually derives from social scientists' efforts to describe changes since the mid to late 1800s in Europe and the United States. These changes represent a shift from the persistent, almost ancient, agricultural practices marking human activity to that time in history.

In the late 1800s, the Agricultural Age was giving way to the Industrial Age. Beginning in Britain with the development of mechanical devices, such as the steam engine, and rapidly spreading throughout Europe and the United States, the evolution toward an Industrial Age represented a sharp break from America's agrarian past. During the Industrial Age, human economic activity centralized in urban areas, focusing around mechanized production of goods. Industrialization resulted in new forms of knowledge and generated new educational needs. Thus, what productive citizens needed to know shifted in recognition of the difference.

By the late 1800s, most states expected children to attend school through eighth grade but had not yet moved to a requirement or provision for a high school education for all. Although some students were destined to operate and manage the farms, others were urged to prepare for work in factories. Now, more than ever, citizens needed to know how to read and write and how to deal with simple financial transactions. In addition, those who worked in factories needed to be able to do repetitive tasks quickly and accurately. With increasing numbers of citizens working in factories, schooling began assuming additional duties including that of taking care of America's children while their parents worked in the factories. Thus, the goals of a high school education, previously identified as college preparation, needed to shift. What should the curriculum be for a broader range of students? Did all of America's citizens need the Latin and Greek classic curriculum? Did America need a curriculum designed to prepare its students for college, or was there a need for a more terminal education (called the "people's" school)?

In 1892, the National Education Association established the Committee of Ten to make recommendations for a standard high school curriculum. This committee recommended eight years of elementary education and four years of secondary education for *all* American children. The committee described the goal of high school to prepare all students to do well in life. In its recommendations, the committee liberalized the high school by offering alternatives to the traditional Latin and Greek classic curriculum. They called for a curriculum that included more emphasis on modern languages (in particular, English), mathematics, science (including physics, chemistry, zoology, and natural sciences), and history.

The recommendations of the Committee of Ten directed a change from a traditional emphasis on language, number, and geography as highlighted in the test questions in the Snapshot of Examinations of Eighth-Grade Student Learning. The tests not only mimicked what knowledge was worth knowing but also what skills needed to be reinforced. Tests in 1895 focused on memory, speed, and repeatability—skills important for working in the factories. Students needed to demonstrate an ability to read, write, and compute. But how they demonstrated this ability lay in their ability to identify the "principal parts" of a verb, to identify the correct "diacritical marks" for different vocabulary words, and to write paragraphs that described the rules of grammar.

Fast forward from 1895 to today to a remarkably different society. The knowledge explosion, particularly over the past 60 years, has resulted in a society increasingly dependent on newer technologies. In the 1950s, television was a new technology for citizens; now cables and satellites serve multiple televisions throughout the home. Rather than waiting for information about a war, citizens watch the war on television and are provided with 24-hour, updated information. In the 1950s citizens wrote letters to communicate; now they are more likely to use electronic mail, text messaging, or cell phones. The speed of communication has increased in such a manner that responses to questions are expected within the day, and sometimes in hours, rather than in the multiple days needed for sending letters. And, instead of calling from home, many citizens respond by cell phones from wherever they are. Students at colleges and universities are often seen traveling from class to class talking on cell phones rather than waiting to meet at a local coffee shop.

Perhaps the Internet is a more significant example of the shift to the Information Age. Cetron and Davies (2003) claim that 80% of all scientists, engineers, and physicians who have ever lived are alive today and are probably actively trading ideas in real time on the Internet. Libraries, once highlighting their in-house treasured books, have today added access to information throughout the world with the provision of access to the Internet. Internet searches guide citizens to a multitude of responses to their questions. Whether the answer is credible is a more critical concern. More than ever before, citizens need to question the sources of their answers.

How should an American education prepare citizens to be able to make sense of the mass of and access to information? According to the International Society for Technology in Education (ISTE), schools need to prepare students to

- Communicate using a variety of media and formats
- Access and exchange information in a variety of ways
- Compile, organize, analyze, and synthesize information
- Draw conclusions and make generalizations based on information gathered
- Know content and be able to locate additional information as needed
- Become self-directed learners
- Collaborate and cooperate in team efforts
- Interact with others in ethical and appropriate ways. (2000, p. 5)

These expectations for schooling have clearly increased along with the change in the valued content. Social studies is an academic content area included in the early twentieth-century school curriculum, whereas orthography is no longer considered an important content area as in the late 1800s. However, the expectations are not so much of "what" but "how" a student must know the "what." The inclusion of calculators as tools has resulted in questions allowing students to use calculators in the process of demonstrating what they know in mathematics; certainly finding the cube root of a number using the cumbersome algorithm demonstrated in Figure 3.1 is no longer considered as knowledge worth knowing. For students to demonstrate an ability to write in 1895, they needed to demonstrate their skill by responding to structured response grammar questions, where the questions pointed to specific comprehension such as naming the "principal parts of the verbs do, lie, lay, and run." Today, literature in English and language arts has increased its focus toward more real-world communications, such as job applications, resumes, and invoices, in the pursuit of today's goals and expectations. Open response questions include either short or long essays providing students

with the opportunity to develop and sustain a stance or argument. In social studies the changes in the questions for the twenty-first century reflect the addition of content. The questions, such as asking students to form career advice based on the information provided in the tables, reflect a reasoning skill that might not have been common or valued in the Industrial Age. In mathematics, open response questions now promote "more than one way" to approach and solve a problem.

As technology continues to transform the workplace, schools are expected to provide time to allow students to build their skills and knowledge about electronic and communications technologies. More importantly, these future citizens must not only learn *about* the technology but they also must learn how to learn *with* the technology; in other words, they need to learn to use technology as a tool for learning. The knowledge worth knowing in the twenty-first century, a century marked by easy access to information, includes critical thinking, problem solving, and decision making. Citizens need to be able to make sense of masses of information, to analyze, synthesize, and evaluate the information in order to make decisions about what to do as a result of the information. Technology not only supports easier access to information but it provides tools for analysis and decision making. As indicated in the National Educational Technology Standards for Students (NETS · S),

> To live, learn, and work successfully in an increasingly complex and information-rich society, students must be able to use technology effectively. Within an effective educational setting, technology can enable students to become:
> - Capable information technology users
> - Information seekers, analyzers, and evaluators
> - Problem solvers and decision makers
> - Creative and effective users of productivity tools
> - Communicators, collaborators, publishers, and producers
> - Informed, responsible, and contributing citizens. *(ISTE, 2000, p. 2)*

How Is Knowledge Learned?

Educational psychologists indicate that learning happens "when experience causes a relatively permanent change in an individual's knowledge or behavior" (Woolfolk-Hoy, 2004, p. 198). Consider this case where learning does happen:

Three-year-old Kim loves animals! Her favorite animal is a dog, called Reno. Reno has spots on her back and a tail that often wags and brushes against Kim's face. Unfortunately, Reno lives at Kim's grandmother's house in Oregon and Kim now lives in Athens, Georgia. She misses playing with Reno and often asks, "Where's Reno?" Her mother does show her pictures of Kim and Reno explaining that Reno is at Grandma's house over 3000 miles away!

One day Kim's mother needed to drive to Atlanta to shop and Kim rode along. As they traveled, her mother noticed some animals in the farmyards they passed. "Oh look Kim, cows!" Upon seeing the animals, Kim exclaimed, "Doggies!" Her mother chuckled and kindly corrected Kim, "No, those are cows." As they continued on the road, Kim identified the cows as "doggies" and her mother continued to correct her with, "No those are cows." This interchange continued for over an hour as they drove to Atlanta. "Doggies," "No those are cows," "Doggies," "No those are cows," . . . . As they neared the outer edges of Atlanta, Kim saw some more cows and excitedly exclaimed, "Cow-doggies!" Kim's mother smiled, accepting Kim's new classification for cows. On the trip home, Kim called them all "cow-doggies."[7]

Views of Learning In Kim's case her behavior did change and the change seemed to be relatively permanent. Psychologists thus claim that she has learned. However, what prompts different psychologists to make this statement is different depending on how they view learning. Behavioral and cognitive views are the two primary views promoted for explaining the concept of learning. Although both views result from observing the same events, as in Kim's case, they focus on different aspects. Behavioral psychologists focus on the observable behaviors and the role of external stimuli in changing those behaviors. Cognitive psychologists, on the other hand, focus on internal mental activities that cannot be observed directly. Basically, behavioral psychologists are interested in the observable "stimulus–response" and cognitive psychologists are more interested in the "hyphen," or what happens mentally for the learner between the stimulus and response.

Stimulus ———————— Response

Behaviorists' View of Learning Behaviorism spotlights external and observable behaviors. Questions behaviorists typically ask include, What stimulates the learner and what responses does the learner make to those stimuli? Behaviorists see that Kim's mother continued to correct Kim with "No, those are

cows." And, when Kim finally used "cow-doggies," her mother smiled and supported her. Behaviorists see the role of the mother as important for Kim's learning—her mother reinforced the change with her smile and acceptance after 80 miles of not accepting Kim's identification. In essence, for a behaviorist, Kim's learning was externally motivated by her mother and her mother provided the reinforcement Kim needed to learn that the animals were not "doggies." Behaviorists are likely to explain the jump from "doggies" to "cow-doggies" as an accumulation of bits of knowledge (doggies and these new animals that did not seem to be accepted as doggies) transferred to a larger class of animals (cow-doggies) with four legs, a tail, two ears, and a spotted coat.

Behaviorists assert that behavior is shaped and strengthened through reinforcement, or practice promoting the desired behavior. The value and power of meaningful practice are well documented and used in education. Consider all the practice that is used to help children learn:

- Counting numbers and letters of the alphabet
- Spelling and meaning of many words
- Adding, subtracting, multiplying, and dividing
- States and their capitals in the United States

Many educational technology applications have relied on drill and practice applications designed basically from a behaviorist perspective. In fact, drill and practice is a common application of technology in elementary education. A quick Web search reveals many technology applications that can be used to increase skills in mathematics, reading comprehension, parts of speech, phonics, synonyms and antonyms, spelling, basic science, and geography. These applications invite students to "climb aboard the next boat, plane, or train to take off to faraway worlds of learning" while playing fun games that provide drill and practice with educational topics.

Research and a long history of use have demonstrated that using educational technology for drill and practice of basic skills can be highly effective in many content areas (Kulik, 1994). Conversely, research has reported negative effects associated with excessive practice, premature practice, or practice without understanding (Koehler & Grouws, 1992). Think about the times that you have made up acronyms to remember a mathematical process. For example, do you remember the phrase "My Dear Aunt Sally" that reminds you to **M**ultiply and **D**ivide first and then **A**dd and **S**ubtract to find an answer to this problem?

$$20 - 6 \div 2 \cdot 5 + 1 = \textbf{What?}$$

---

[7] Actual event took place in fall 1969 on the road from Athens to Atlanta, Georgia.

The result is 6 and not 36. When you try to remember what letter of the alphabet comes after "h," do you mentally say or sing the alphabet? Such practice often focuses students on the algorithm rather than sense making. Students are often taught to "invert and multiply" when dealing with division of fractions. Yet, after excessive drill with those types of problems, some students when given the problem 2/3 ÷ 1/6 = ? respond by inverting the 2/3 (3/2 × 1/6) and finding a solution of 1/4. They have remembered to "invert and multiply" but not which of the fractions to invert. With the focus on following a procedure without making sense of the problem, the students have no idea that their answer is not even close to the correct answer of 4.

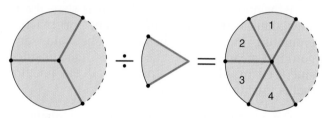

2/3 divided by pieces of 1/6 size   =   4 of those pieces

Ultimately, without students' understanding and making sense of the problems, research has shown that they develop a fear or dislike for the subject along with an attitude that the subject does not need to make sense. Certainly, these results about the effects of drill contradict a major goal of education today, namely, that sense making is important in learning if ideas are to be remembered and expanded.

Behaviorists consider learning as both sequential and hierarchical. Think about the elementary curriculum and how it is organized. How are the textbooks organized? Look at a number of textbooks from different publishers for the same grade. Each text sequences most of the topics in the same order, supporting the behaviorist's view that learning occurs by accumulating bits of knowledge in a particular order. Some might consider learning about technologies from a hierarchical perspective, resulting in a curriculum using a behaviorist approach to guiding student learning.

Many behaviorist educators consider learning to use particular technologies (such as learning to use databases) as being sequenced in a linear fashion, where one idea builds on another. Many technology manuals suggest this sequential hierarchy. Behaviorism promotes learning a fixed set of skills in a fixed order. From this perspective, learning to sort data in a database may be viewed as dependent on knowledge about data types, say, text versus numeric. Figure 3.2 shows a sorting of text data.

Chapters of Book	Title	Chapters of Book	Title
5 th Chapter	All About E	1 st Chapter	All About A
9 th Chapter	All About I	10 th Chapter	All About J
2 nd Chapter	All About B	2 nd Chapter	All About B
7 th Chapter	All About G	3 rd Chapter	All About C
6 th Chapter	All About F	4 th Chapter	All About D
10 th Chapter	All About J	5 th Chapter	All About E
4 th Chapter	All About D	6 th Chapter	All About F
3 rd Chapter	All About C	7 th Chapter	All About G
8 th Chapter	All About H	8 th Chapter	All About H
1 st Chapter	All About A	9 th Chapter	All About I
Before sorting Chapters of Book field		After sorting Chapters of Book field	

FIGURE 3.2   Sort of text data in a database.

The field Chapters of Book lists information that appears to be numeric data with the leading numbers in the string of characters (e.g., 5th Chapter). When the sort is conducted, the titles remain connected with the chapter numbers but the results do not make sense. Why isn't the 10th Chapter at the end of the list? These results suggest to behaviorists that students need to understand the different data types *before learning about* sorting various fields in a database.

Basically, behavioral explanations of learning hold that

- Learning is a change in behavior motivated by external experiences.
- Motivation is external to the learner and is best if positive.
- Learning is an accumulation of bits of knowledge.
- Learning is sequential and hierarchical.
- Learning is reinforced through drill and practice that includes both positive and negative feedback; positive feedback is more pleasurable.
- Transfer of ideas is limited to ideas with high degrees of similarity.

Cognitive Psychologists' View of Learning Cognitive psychologists focus on changes in knowledge and think of learning as an internal mental process. The cognitive view of Kim's learning proposes that her understanding of the class of "doggies" has been transformed. They note that Kim experienced disequilibrium when her mother indicated that the animal was a cow. Previously, Kim had experienced animals called cows but never from close up. She had personal experiences with a dog that, to her, looked like what she was seeing. She had not yet learned the effect of distance on the size of animals. Thus, her observations were guided by the pattern of the animal that she observed: spots, four legs, and tail. These animals looked like Reno and, therefore, must be "doggies."

Chapters of Book	Title	Chapters of Book	Title
Chapter 5	All About E	Chapter 1	All About A
Chapter 9	All About I	Chapter 10	All About J
Chapter 2	All About B	Chapter 2	All About B
Chapter 7	All About G	Chapter 3	All About C
Chapter 6	All About F	Chapter 4	All About D
Chapter 10	All About J	Chapter 5	All About E
Chapter 4	All About D	Chapter 6	All About F
Chapter 3	All About C	Chapter 7	All About G
Chapter 8	All About H	Chapter 8	All About H
Chapter 1	All About A	Chapter 9	All About I
Before sorting Chapters of Book field		After sorting Chapters of Book field	

FIGURE 3.3 Change in the information in the Chapters of Book field.

The fact that her mother continued to challenge the "doggy" proclamation created Kim's disequilibrium. Cognitive field psychologists stress that this disequilibrium is motivation for learning. In Kim's case, her mental construction of "doggies" did not include "cows." She needed to reorganize her personal understandings to accommodate this new information. When she described the animals as "cow-doggies," cognitive field psychologists say she has learned as a result of reordering her mental structures and how those structures are linked.

Cognitive field psychologists view learning as "transforming significant understandings we already have, rather than simple acquisitions written on blank slates" (Greeno, Collins, & Resnick, 1996, p. 18). For them, one of the most important elements in learning is the knowledge that learners bring to situations. What learners know determines to a great extent what they will pay attention to, learn, remember, and forget. Research has documented that a student's level of development provides a window of opportunity for a range of activities. At each stage of development, the lower limit of this window of opportunity rests on previous knowledge, concepts, and skills that have been established. An upper limit is determined by tasks that can be successfully completed only with step-by-step instruction. Lev Vygotzky termed this area where students cannot solve a problem alone but can succeed with adult guidance as the *zone of proximal development* (Vygotzky, 1962; Wertsch, 1991).

©Sovfoto/eastfoto

Cognitive psychologists think about the database activity differently. They consider the problem of sorting in a database as an introduction to the instruction dealing with data types. The teacher's role is to guide the students' thinking by asking, "Why did the database sort this information this way?" If the students are unable to respond, the teacher follows up with a clarifying question, "Why does the tenth chapter follow the first chapter when I use the database to sort on the Chapters of Book field?" Students might suggest that the data should be entered differently (without the "st" after the 1). The change is made and the sort is redone as in Figure 3.3.

The new data and the corresponding sort on the field Chapters of Book is still incorrectly sorted. Again, the teacher asks, "What causes Chapter 10 to be sorted before Chapter 2?" The teacher continues asking questions to guide the students in developing conjectures as to why the sort does not seem to recognize that the number 10 is greater than the numbers 2, 3, . . ., 9. At an appropriate point, the teacher may guide the students to notice that the data are entered into the fields as *text* and that there are other formats for the data to be entered. After exploring this information, the students instruct the database to consider the information in the Chapters of Book field as *numbers* but retain the information in the Title field as *text* (see Figure 3.4). Finally, after changing the data *type* to be number and sorting on Chapters of Book, the sort is completed as students expect (see Figure 3.5).

With this experience, from the cognitive perspective, students are engaged in the process of expanding their personal conceptions about databases, sorting in databases, and data types while establishing new connections among their *schemas*.

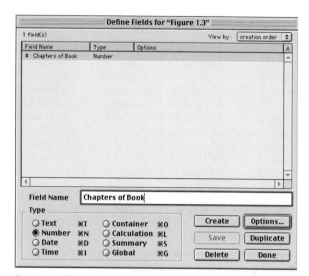

Entering Chapters of Book with the data type of Number

Entering Title with the data type of Text

FIGURE 3.4   Selecting the data type for the fields.

Chapters of Book	Title	Chapters of Book	Title
Chapter 5	All About E	Chapter 1	All About A
Chapter 9	All About I	Chapter 2	All About B
Chapter 2	All About B	Chapter 3	All About C
Chapter 7	All About G	Chapter 4	All About D
Chapter 6	All About F	Chapter 5	All About E
Chapter 10	All About J	Chapter 6	All About F
Chapter 4	All About D	Chapter 7	All About G
Chapter 3	All About C	Chapter 8	All About H
Chapter 8	All About H	Chapter 9	All About I
Chapter 1	All About A	Chapter 10	All About J
Before sorting Chapters of Book field		After sorting Chapters of Book field	

FIGURE 3.5   Sorting data identified as *number* results in a correct ordering.

Woolfolk-Hoy (2004, p. 250) explains, "A schema is a pattern or guide for representing an event, concept, or skill. . . . Schemas are abstract knowledge structures that organize vast amounts of information." Thus, as a result of the experiences, these students are reorganizing their own schemas in the process of adapting to new experiences with this database sorting activity.

Piaget (1954) clarifies how the experiences with the database impact children's schema adaptations.

©Getty Images News and Sport Services

He talks in terms of two cognitive processes as directing how students use and adapt their schemas: *assimilation* and *accommodation*. The students in this example have prior knowledge about the concept of sorting: Sorting puts items in order. The students are assimilating when they accept that the database completes a sort and recognize the results do not match their existing notions of the concept of sorting. With the teacher's questioning, the students engage in the process of altering their schema of database sorting—accommodating the new knowledge by adjusting their schema to consider the importance of data types when sorting data.

Piaget's perception of assimilation and accommodation are expanded with a proposal that the shift from one cognitive state to another is instigated by conflict or, in his terms, *disequilibrium* created by inconsistent ideas. He claims that a natural desire for *equilibrium* is motivation for the activation of the processes of assimilation and accommodation. In the database example, the initial problem of sorting data in the database created disequilibrium for the students. Why does the database sort the information this way? The teacher engages the students in the problem by asking questions, challenging them to search for a solution to the problem; in other words, the students are challenged to search for equilibrium in their understandings about sorting in databases.

Jerome Bruner describes this teacher guidance and assistance as *scaffolding* (Wood,

©AP/Wide World Photos

Bruner, & Ross, 1976). Scaffolding student learning requires that teachers determine what kinds of help to give students as well as when and how to provide the help. Vygotsky adds the importance of *discourse* in the scaffolding as a way to mediate and transform the mental activities students are engaged in and the importance of recognizing each student's zone of proximal development. Thus, teachers need to pay careful attention to students' experiences and understandings as well as plan to engage them in discourse about the ideas as they make decisions of what, when, and how they plan to guide their students' learning (Santrock, 2006; Woolfolk-Hoy, 2004).

Children develop preconceptions that often do not stand the test of extension as in the database example and with Kim and her understanding of "doggies." Children's early conceptions about technology provide another example of their schema developed through guided experiences. Teachers need to explicitly plan activities to engage them in developing a more mature understanding of technology. It is important to begin early, helping them gain a broader understanding that does not support a misconception that technology equals computers and the Internet.

In the Classroom 3.1 presents an idea for guiding elementary students in organizing their schema

In the Classroom 3.1

WHAT IS TECHNOLOGY?

TECHNOLOGY OBJECTIVE: **NETS · S I, IV, V**

- **Internet, digital images, word processor:** Technology as a communications and research tool.
- Gather and incorporate digital images in a word-processed document.

CONTENT OBJECTIVE: **Language arts:** Develop ability to use written and visual language to communicate ideas and understandings with words and pictures with a variety of audiences and for different purposes.

Social studies: Identify and describe examples in which science and technology have changed the lives of people, such as at home and work.

GRADE LEVEL: Partnering K–2 students with grade 3–5 students

DEFINITION: Technologies are tools invented by humankind to make work easier and life better.

PROBLEM: What are your ideas about technology?

Engage: Ask children to think about technology as an invention that makes work easier and life better. Give them some ideas like chairs, bikes, . . ., followed by collecting their ideas. Be sure that each student responds.

Demonstrate: Show the students some digital pictures of different technology inventions and ask them how these inventions make work easier and life better.

Search: Show the students how to gather images using Web searches. An easy way to find the pictures they want is to do a Web search searching by phrases such as "telephone images" or even "stove images." Google has an easy page to search for images: http://images.google.com/

Challenge: Create a book of Technology Inventions, where students gather images to be entered in a word-processed template. See Figure 3.6, which displays the pages of the template that are ready for student use. Use Technology Link 3.1 to obtain this template.

Create: Partner K–2 students with fourth- or fifth-grade students—one fourth- or fifth-grade mentor and one K–2 student—to make a book. Instruct the mentors to record the words, ideas, and pictures that the K–2 student identifies in the word-processed book.

Technology Link 3.1

*U*se the **Book** link at this book's website to access the template for your use in developing the Technology Inventions book.

www.wiley.com/college/niess

about technology. The activity partners early elementary children with upper elementary students. Together they produce a Technology Inventions book. Figure 3.6 provides template pages to outline what the children need to accomplish. The early elementary students generate the ideas about technologies by identifying technologies in the home, at work, and in school. The task for the upper elementary students is to assist in gathering digital images and entering the images in the book as well as the early elementary students' dialogue using features of the word processor. Together the partners gain experiences with Internet searches for digital pictures and entering pictures into a word-processed template.

As their teacher, you need to build from their understandings about technology inventions and experiences. Begin with their ideas about technology, helping them expand the ideas. For example, if they say *cars*, ask them how cars make work easier and life better. You can even ask that the upper elementary mentors ask for extensions as they are working on the book. When you discuss various technologies, you can demonstrate how to find digital images of these technological inventions using Web searches. As they select their images, you might ask if they were to draw the image, what technology they might use if they did not have access to the Web. Engaging students in discussions about what they are thinking and learning about technology inventions is essential if they are to actively rearrange their schema toward a more insightful and useful understanding.

From a cognitive field view, the children (both the early elementary ones and upper elementary ones) are actively engaged in rearranging their internal mental organizations with respect to the concept of technology. In this activity, they are thinking and learning about technology inventions using technology tools for communicating their ideas about the concept of technology.

Basically, cognitive field psychologists' explanations of learning hold that

- Learning is an internal adaptation to experiences, a reordering of mental structures or schemas as a result of experiences.
- Learners are intrinsically curious and curiosity motivates them to learn.
- Disequilibrium is motivation for learning.
- Learning is a result of disequilibrium shifted into equilibrium.
- Vygotsky's zone of proximal development describes the optimal size of the disequilibrium for learning to take place.

- A variety of experiences that differ in outward appearance while retaining the basic conceptual structure support the learner in identifying patterns, generalizing, and making connections.
- Learners ultimately construct their own understanding but adults (teachers) can scaffold the experiences to support students in building or constructing a firm understanding (reordering their mental structures as they adapt to the experiences).
- Big ideas and pictures transfer to other contexts.

Constructivism and Contemporary Views of Learning   Arguably the most popular view of how students learn is connected with a constructivist perspective. Constructivists hold the view of learning that "emphasizes an active role of the learner in building understanding and making sense of information" (Woolfolk-Hoy, 2004, p. 323). Constructivists believe that learners are the primary agents in developing their own knowledge and understandings. Learners bring to each event or situation their personal experiences, and those experiences influence how they operate with each new event. If a learner is instructed to color a wagon blue but has only had experiences with red wagons, the learner is apt to overlook the word blue in the instructions and simply color the wagon red.

Cognitive field psychologists' explanations of learning (including those of Piaget, Bruner, and Vygotsky) incorporate some kind of constructivism because of the emphasis on individuals constructing their individual understandings (cognitive structures or schemas) as they interpret their experiences in specific situations. Constructivist approaches support student-centered over teacher-centered instruction and curriculum. Students' knowledge constructions are the center of learning. In essence, constructivists' approaches recommend that educators

- Embed learning in complex, realistic, and relevant learning environments
- Provide for social negotiation and shared responsibility as a part of learning
- Support multiple perspectives and use multiple representations of content
- Nurture self-awareness and an understanding that knowledge is constructed
- Encourage ownership in learning. (Woolfolk-Hoy, 2004, p. 327)

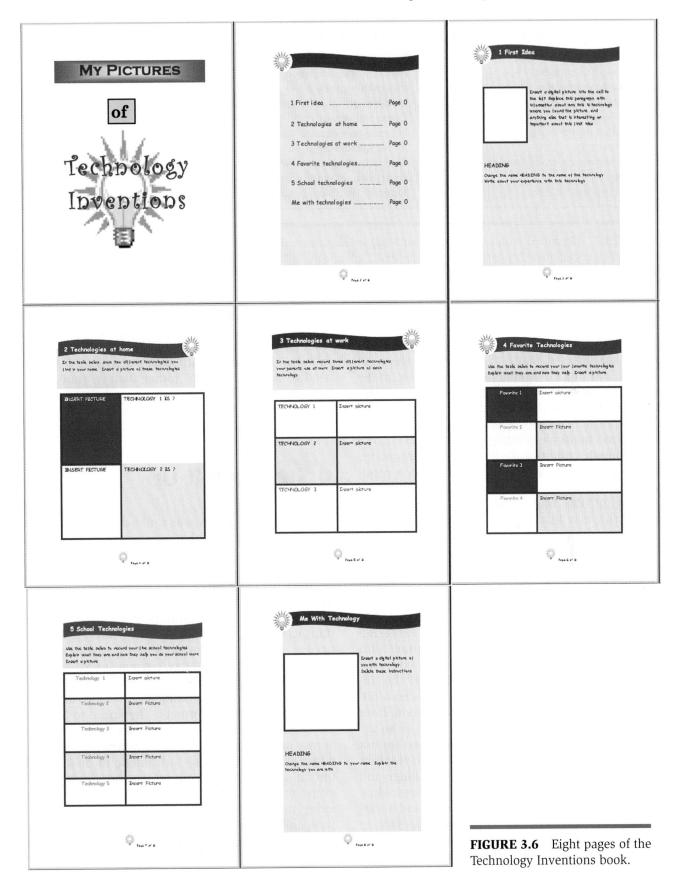

FIGURE 3.6 Eight pages of the Technology Inventions book.

Traditional Learning Environments	⇔	New Learning Environments
Teacher-centered instruction	⇔	Student-centered instruction
Single-sense stimulation	⇔	Multisensory stimulation
Single-path progression	⇔	Multipath progression
Single media	⇔	Multimedia
Isolated work	⇔	Collaborative work
Information delivery	⇔	Information exchange
Passive learning	⇔	Active, exploratory, or inquiry-based learning
Factual, knowledge-based learning	⇔	Critical thinking and informed decision making
Reactive response	⇔	Proactive or planned action
Isolated, artificial context	⇔	Authentic, real-world context

FIGURE 3.7   Reprinted with permission from *National Educational Technology Standards for Students: Connecting Curriculum and Technology*, ©2000, ISTE ® (International Society for Technology in Education), iste@iste.org, www.iste.org. All rights reserved. Permission does not constitute an endorsement by ISTE.

Over the past 15 years, this constructivist emphasis has directed many of the current views on creating learning environments. In particular, as described in the National Education Technology Standards for Students (NETS·S, 2000), the traditional approaches to learning are merging with new learning environments as identified in Figure 3.7.

Although traditional learning environments have not disappeared, the trend, partly as a result of the constructivist influence, has been toward a melding of the traditional educational environments with new learning environments. An important indicator of this shift is that many classrooms, once organized with individual student desks in rows, have succumbed to tables arranged so that students can share and discuss ideas, work on problems in small groups, collaborate, and work with materials and other manipulatives designed to provide multiple representations of key ideas. Accompanying this shift is an equally important shift in the role of the teacher. Embracing constructivists' views, educators have highlighted the notion that students construct their own understanding, rather than simply absorb information from their teachers. Teachers think of learning as an active, sense-making process where learners are not passive recipients of information. Instead, teachers work at considering students' understandings and realize that each student's learning is influenced by prior knowledge, experience, attitudes, and social interactions. Students use cognitive processes to construct understanding of the ideas to be learned rather than simply receiving the information from the teacher. Unlike the behaviorists who focus on the directly observable, external behaviors, constructivists focus on the cognitive processes and strategies that students use as they learn. As a result, in accordance with constructivism, teachers need to act as a "guide" rather than a "translator" as students work on problems that help them develop and construct their own personal understandings.

Summing It Up

America in the 1600s was quite different from today. Then knowledge that was useful was reading, writing, and some arithmetic and that could be completed after at most an elementary education. Citizens read the Bible, they wrote letters to communicate with their families in the European countries, and they used arithmetic in their trading transactions. Only doctors and lawyers really needed more education, and their numbers were few. That was then! Today citizens need reading, writing, and arithmetic and a whole lot more. They need to be able to communicate in many different ways, using multiple formats. They need to be able to access and exchange information in a variety of ways that utilize the current technologies. They need far more than basic arithmetic to understand the massive amounts of information that affect even general household decision making. Citizens today need to be able to compile, organize, analyze, and synthesize this information. Moreover, no longer can formal schooling signal the end of learning. The normal mode is now for lifelong learning. Careers have significantly changed due to the impact of communications and information technologies. Now more than ever before citizens need to be technology literate. As indicated in the National Educational Technology Standards for Students (NETS·S),

> To live, learn, and work successfully in an increasingly complex and information-rich society, students must be able to use technology effectively. Within an effective educational setting, technology can enable students to become:
> - Capable information technology users
> - Information seekers, analyzers, and evaluators
> - Problem solvers and decision makers
> - Creative and effective users of productivity tools
> - Communicators, collaborators, publishers, and producers
> - Informed, responsible, and contributing citizens. *(ISTE, 2000, p. 2)*

An important question for educators has been and continues to be, How do students learn to be this type of citizen? The job of educators is to build an educational system that supports students in learning, and thus educators consistently ask whether students have learned what they need to learn to be productive citizens.

Beliefs about learning have significantly changed in the last 50 years. Early in the 1900s, people believed that students learned as a result of responding to specific stimuli. Behaviorists explained learning as a change in behavior that was motivated by external experiences, namely, the stimuli for learning. They viewed learning as an accumulation of bits of knowledge that together added to knowledge of the whole. As a result, teachers were expected to package the curriculum in pieces providing extensive drill and practice to reinforce the ideas being transmitted to students. From a behaviorist perspective, learning is sequential and hierarchical. Students need to learn specific pieces in a specific order for them to transfer that knowledge to solve specific problems.

Over time and with significant increases in knowledge, educators' views on learning have changed. Cognitive psychologists shifted the focus in learning from the external stimuli to thinking of learning as an internal mental process. Cognitive psychologists view learning as a reordering of mental structures called schemas and see learning as resulting from disequilibrium shifted into equilibrium. Piaget talked specifically about this process toward equilibrium as involving assimilation and accommodation where first the learner recognizes and comprehends a discrepant event from within the existing schema, gradually makes a mental adjustment to comprehend the new information, and thus accommodate the discrepant event. Vygotsky described the zone of proximal development as a window of opportunity for the learner to engage in the learning process with respect to the particular event. He also identified the importance of discourse in the learning process. Bruner added the notion of teachers scaffolding the learning experiences based on the window of opportunity and engaging students in discourse. These theories about learning collectively incorporate an emphasis on individuals constructing their individual understandings.

Today, how students learn is connected with the constructivist perspective. Constructivism encompasses a view of learning that "emphasizes an active role of the learner in building understanding and making sense of information" (Woolfolk-Hoy, 2004, p. 323). The constructivist's belief is that learners are the primary agent in constructing their own knowledge and understandings. The learner brings to each event or situation his or her personal experiences, and those experiences influence how the learner operates within each new event. Piaget, Bruner, and Vygotsky incorporate constructivism in their views with an emphasis on individuals constructing their personal understandings (cognitive structures or schemas) as they interpret their experiences in specific situations.

These current perspectives on how students learn have lead to significant redirections in establishing learning environments. Teachers think of learning as an active, sense-making process where learners are active participants in generating their own understandings. They see their role as scaffolding the learning experiences using student-centered instruction that incorporates collaborative work with multiple paths to exploring ideas. They see their role as a guide rather than a translator for students.

In essence, over the past century, the view of student learning has shifted from passive to active engagement in constructing personal understandings. With the shift of what citizens need to know to be productive members of society in the Information Age, teachers must establish learning environments that guide their students in making sense of masses of information, analyzing, synthesizing, and evaluating the information to make decisions about what to do as a result of the information. Technology not only supports easier access to this information, it provides tools for analysis and decision making. However, the technology focus is an education directed at accommodating future citizens in learning not only *about* technology but also how to learn *with* technology, to learn to use technology as a tool for learning.

End-of-the-Chapter Activities and References

PRACTICE PROBLEMS

1. Investigate some current textbooks for the grade level and subjects that you plan to teach. Which view of learning (behaviorist or cognitive field) do these texts seem to follow? Provide several examples that support your position on this question.

2. Conduct a Web search to identify lesson ideas for the grade level and subject matter that you plan to teach. What view of learning do these lesson ideas support?

3. Create a Technology Inventions book using the template from Technology Link 3.1 as described In the Classroom 3.1.

4. Select a particular lesson you find on the Web that might include student use of some technology as a tool for learning. Prepare an outline of the lesson from a behaviorist perspective. Prepare another outline of the same lesson from a cognitive field perspective. Write a summary of the major differences in how the lesson unfolded.

5. Identify a lesson from either the Annotated References or one you find in a journal reference for your grade level and subject matter focus. Review the lesson to identify the author's perspective on how students learn. Explain your reasoning.

IN THE CLASSROOM ACTIVITIES

6. Ask a teacher if you can observe a specific classroom activity and ask what the teacher's objectives for the activity are. Focus your observations on two or three students during the specific activity. Interview the students individually after the lesson. How did they describe what they learned? Did they learn what the teacher wanted them to learn?

7. Ask a teacher if you can observe a specific classroom activity that includes students' hands-on use of a technology. Ask for the teacher's primary objectives for the activity. Observe the lesson carefully, noting times when the lesson uses a behaviorist approach and when the lesson uses a cognitive field approach. Interview the teacher, asking for the rationale for the approaches used during the lesson.

ASSESSING STUDENT LEARNING WITH AND ABOUT TECHNOLOGY

8. Explain how assessing student learning from a behaviorist perspective might differ from that of a cognitive psychologist.

E-PORTFOLIO ACTIVITIES

9. Use a graphics package to prepare a visual description of how students learn.

10. Create a one-page summary that describes the major contribution of these theorists toward an understanding of how students learn: Piaget, Bruner, and Vygotzky. Insert a graphic that supports your discussion.

11. Begin a reference list for your E-portfolio that is a collection of ideas for teaching your subject area and grade level with a variety of technologies. Continue to enhance this collection as you learn about new technologies.

REFLECTION AND DISCUSSION

12. Describe your understanding of what learning is and how students learn.

13. Think about the primary subject that you hope to teach. How did you learn what you know in that subject area?

14. Identify concepts or ideas that you learned in your precollege education that are probably no longer considered as important. Explain why you think these ideas are no longer important.

15. Reflect on your classroom learning experiences in elementary or secondary school levels. Describe a classroom experience that you believe the teacher relied on as a constructivist perspective in guiding the lesson.

Annotated Resources

Bell, R. L. & Garofalo, J (Eds.). (2005). *Science units for grades 9–12*. Eugene, OR: ISTE.
Units for consideration for incorporation of technologies in teaching science.

Carroll, J. A., Kelly, M. G., & Witherspoon, T. L. (Eds.). (2003). *Multidisciplinary units for prekindergarten through grade 2*. Eugene, OR: ISTE.
Units for consideration for incorporation of technologies in teaching in prekindergarten through grade 2.

Hannah, L., Menchaca, M., & McVicker, B. (Eds.). (2002). *Multidisciplinary units for grades 3–5*, Eugene, OR: ISTE.
Units for consideration for incorporation of technologies in teaching in grades 3–5.

McKenzie, W. (Ed.). (2004). *Social studies units for grades 9–12*. Eugene, OR: ISTE.
Units for consideration for incorporation of technologies in teaching social studies.

O'Hara, S., & McMahon, M. (Eds.). (2003). *Multidisciplinary units for grades 6–8*. Eugene, OR: ISTE.
Units for consideration for incorporation of technologies in teaching in grades 6–8.

CHAPTER 4

Technology Standards for Students

Patrick Olear/PhotoEdit

◆Introduction

You are preparing to teach in the twenty-first century. Does that mean that you will teach what you learned in the same way you learned? Think back on how you learned about π (pi or 3.14. . .). Can you explain π or do you just know the value? Did you ever use a string to measure around the circumference of a circle and realize that it was about three times as long as its diameter? Or did your teacher just tell you what π was and expect you to use it in solving some problems?

Mr. Dixon in the *Snapshot of a Twenty-First-Century Teacher's Unit Outline* was concerned that his students develop a deep understanding of π based on an exploration of circles, their circumfer-ences, and their diameters. He did not want to just tell them that π was the ratio of the circumference of a circle to its diameter. He hoped that they would tell him what it was.

- Why use all this valuable teaching time to have the students develop an understanding of pi?
- Why involve various technologies—Geometer's Sketchpad, National Institutes of Health imaging software, spreadsheets, World Wide Web?
- Why waste time with a digital camera?
- Why can't you just teach the idea the same way you were taught?

Part of the answer to those questions is that the knowledge that is valued in the twenty-first century has changed. Knowledge that 3.14 is an

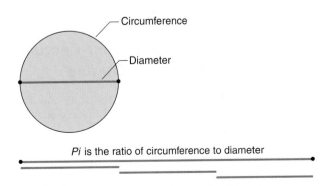

Approximately 3 lengths of the diameter equal the length of the circumference!

approximation for pi is no longer considered as essential as knowing what to do with pi. Now, simply pressing the π button on the calculator returns an acceptable approximation for pi. Understanding pi as the ratio of the circumference to the diameter and being able to use that ratio in thinking about and solving problems is more important knowledge in the twenty-first century. Today, what is more important is that students are able to determine how to use the available technologies appropriately, using them to solve problems and make decisions.

Another part of the answer to all of those questions is the increased access to information and multiple information technologies. When you purchase a computer, even if you have the most advanced system on the market, your system is quickly outdated by a more powerful and more accessible system—likely for much less! For this reason, contemporary, content-area curricula require that students continue to learn basic skills with multiple current technologies, learn to use the technologies in the search for solutions to problems, and basically learn to use technologies as tools for learning and solving problems.

Another part of the answer is that the views of learning and teaching have changed. Students' learning is now focused on multiple experiences to support them in constructing their own understandings rather than simply receiving information. Teachers are expected to guide students as they explore the various experiences and build their knowledge. Teachers need to engage students in learning to use a variety of tools through a variety of activities. Teachers need to scaffold their students' learning activities, guiding the students' progress in learning.

To adequately prepare students for living, learning, and working in the twenty-first century, you, as their teacher, must be prepared to enable your students to learn differently than how you learned. The nation has reached consensus that an American education needs to be transformed to meet the needs of the Information Age. Policy makers and public citizens have called for higher standards for what the children need to know and be able to do. As a result, most content areas have identified new curriculum standards to guide the education of the twenty-first century. With a recognition of these new directions, the National Educational Technology Standards for Students (NETS·S) describe six areas that promote the use of technology as an "integral component or tool for learning and communications within the context of academic subject areas" (ISTE, 2000, p. 17). These standards provide a framework to guide your curriculum and instruction in support of your students in meeting the twenty-first-century goals for education.

CHAPTER LEARNING OBJECTIVES

After reading the chapter, you should be able to:

1. Identify what is meant by technological literacy for the twenty-first century.
2. Describe why it is important to learn to use technology as a tool within the context of the academic subject areas.
3. Discuss the National Educational Technology Standards for Students (NETS·S).
4. Identify ways teachers can redesign their curriculum and instruction to support students in meeting the standards for students (NETS·S).
5. Explain how teachers might use the NETS·S standard performance indicators in developing their curriculum.
6. Discuss how the NETS·S guidelines are connected with subject area curriculum standards.

Snapshot of a Twenty-First-Century Teacher's Unit Outline

Mr. Dixon is teaching sixth grade in a self-contained classroom. As he considered the mathematics lesson he was to teach, he wanted to connect the mathematics they were learning with the real world and at the same time introduce his students to some new technologies to use as learning tools. More importantly, he wanted to use a problem to actively engage his students in an exploration about π (pi) rather than simply telling them its value and the important formulas for circles. This rationale guided him in outlining the unit on pi.

Unit: Pi, Circles, and Their Diameters

Problem for sixth-grade students to investigate:

What is the relationship of the circumference of a circle to its diameter?

Supporting questions for this problem:

- What is a circle?
- What real-world objects have a circular appearance?
- What information defines a circle?
- How can the circumference and diameter be measured for large, distant circular objects like the Moon, Venus, or Earth?

Day 1

1. Student Activity. Students work in pairs on a worksheet (Figure 4.1) to sort two-dimensional objects, given instructions to identify as many different ways as they can to sort the objects and explain their decisions.

2. Student Activity. Students work in groups of four, compare their ideas for sorting the objects.

3. Class discussion. Talk about the various sorts. **Key questions for discussion:**

   a. What are the different sorts? (Possible sorts: polygons, round objects; circles, noncircular objects; objects with angles, oval objects; polygons, circles, ovals.)

   b. How does the group of polygons differ from the group of round objects? (Possible differences: corners versus no corners; sides versus no sides; angles versus no angles.)

   c. How does the group of circles differ from the groups of polygons and ovals? (Expected response: You can fold circles in half at any point in the curved edge.)

   d. If you take a picture of real-world objects, which would have the shape of a circle? (Possible objects: coins, bicycle wheels, clocks, door knobs, Moon, Sun, Earth, lamp shades.)

4. **Homework.** For class on Day 2, bring pictures of objects that show circular forms.

Day 2

1. **Demonstration.** Demonstrate different ways to create circles.

   a. Tack one end of string at the center of the paper on the bulletin board, tie pen to other end, and use the pen to draw the circle on bulletin board paper.

   b. Use a compass to create a circle on paper. How is this method like the method with the string?

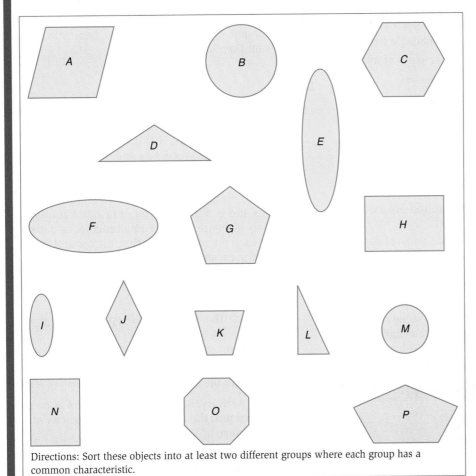

Directions: Sort these objects into at least two different groups where each group has a common characteristic.

FIGURE 4.1 Two-dimensional object worksheet.

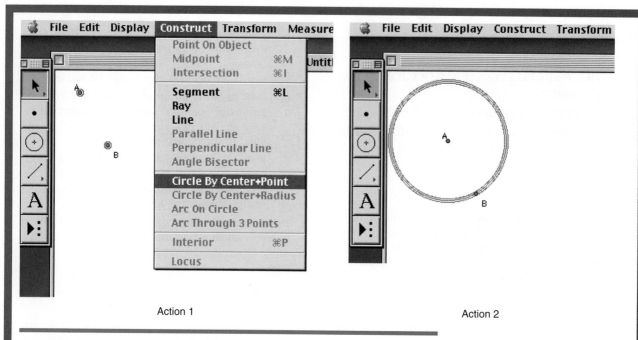

FIGURE 4.2   Progression for creating a circle with Geometer's Sketchpad.

c.   Using Geometer's Sketchpad software, create two points, labeling them A and the B. Select first point A and then point B; choose Construct Circle By Center + Point. See Figure 4.2. Have students explain how this method is similar to the other two methods for creating a circle.

2. **Class discussion.** Identify major parts of a circle.

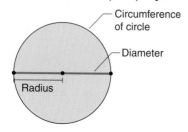

a.   Circumference: distance around object, similar to perimeter of an object.

b.   Radius: distance from center point of circle to circle circumference.

c.   Diameter: distance from one edge of circle to other edge of circle when folded in half. Equal to twice the radius.

3. **Measurement activity.** Students use string and rulers to measure circumference, diameter, and radius of objects in the classroom (clock face, doorknob, wastebasket top, etc.). Record data in a table:

Circumference	Radius	Diameter

4. **Digital camera activity.** Groups of two take digital pictures of several different circular objects, perhaps of the pictures they brought to class.

5. **Homework.** Collect circumference, radius, and diameter data of circular objects from home. Bring to class on Day 3.

Day 3

1. **Demonstration.** Describe a different way to measure circumference and diameter of circular objects using new technology, NIH Image software, a public domain image processing and analysis program that was developed through the National Institutes of Health (NIH). This software can acquire, display, edit, enhance, analyze, and animate digital images and is similar to the ultrasound software used to measure the circumference of a baby's head. Explain to students that ultrasound technology uses sound waves to create images of shapes inside our bodies and that the data are used in determining the health of the unborn baby.

a.   Launch the software and open an image of Venus (Figure 4.3).

b.   Measure the diameter of Venus in pixels. Explain pixels as the unit of measure.

c.   Measure the circumference of Venus in pixels.

2. **Student Activity.** Students work in pairs at computers to repeat the measurements of diameter and circumference of Venus.

3. **Demonstration.** Demonstrate opening additional graphic images.

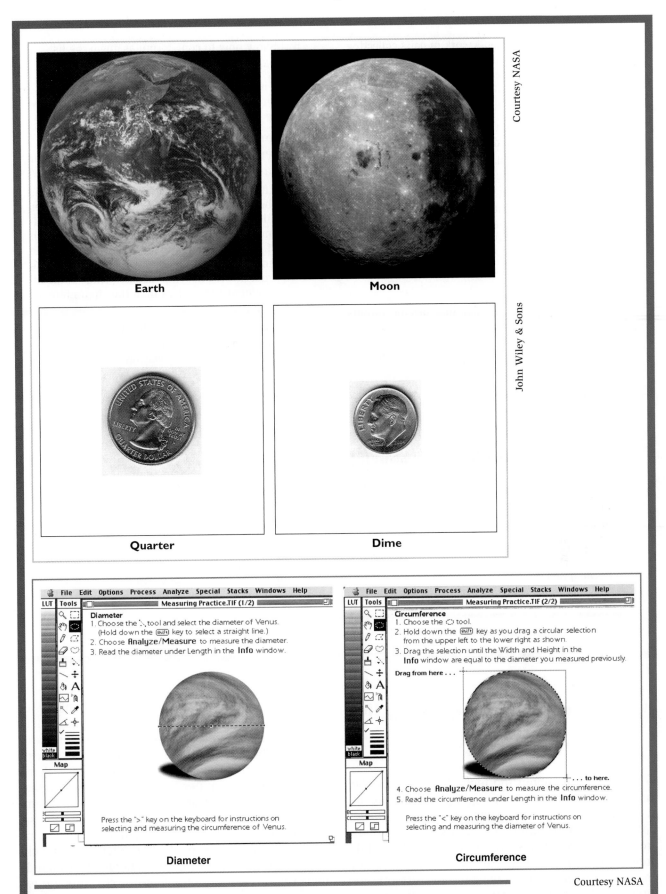

FIGURE 4.3   Measuring the diameter and circumference of Venus using NIH Image.

4. **Student Activity.** Students work in pairs collecting data from at least 20 different images stored in the image file that includes images that they captured with the digital camera.

5. **Closure Questions**

   a.   How accurate is the measurement in pixels? (Depends on the detail of the image.)

   b.   How would you find the radius of the objects? (Divide the diameter by 2.)

   c.   Is there any relationship between the circumference and the diameter like there is between the radius and diameter? (Record all student suggestions on overhead.)

Day 4

1. **Demonstration**

   a.   Set up a spreadsheet that includes the various student ideas of possible relationships: adding, subtracting, multiplying, dividing the circumference and the diameter. See Figure 4.4 for format.

   b.   Show how to copy formulas down the list.

   c.   Record the various image labels.

2. **Student Activity.** Students enter data and use the spreadsheet to compute the relationships. See Figure 4.4 for sample data.

3. **Closure Questions**

   a.   What relationship do you find from your data?

   b.   After recognizing that the circumference is about 3 times the diameter, ask, What does this mean about the circumference and the diameter? If you had a string that was the length of the diameter and a string that was the length of the circumference, can you show me what this relationship means? (Three of the diameter strings is less than the circumference string.)

4. **Homework.** Research pi on the Web. What do you find about the relationship between circumference and diameter and how it was discovered?

⬭ Circle.xls

	A	B	C	D	E	F	G
1	What pattern do you see for the relationship of the circumference to the diameter?						
2							
3	Object	Circumference [C]	Diameter [D]	C+D	C-D	C*D	C/D
4	Venus	629	200	829.00	429.00	125800.00	3.15
5	Earth	1112	354	1466.00	758.00	393648.00	3.14
6	Moon	1216	387	1603.00	829.00	470592.00	3.14
7	Quarter	493	157	650.00	336.00	77401.00	3.14
8	Nickel	440	140	580.00	300.00	61600.00	3.14
9	Fan	697	222	919.00	475.00	154734.00	3.14
10	Fire Hydrant	681	217	898.00	464.00	147777.00	3.14
11	Bicycle Wheel	895	285	1180.00	610.00	255075.00	3.14
12	Bowling Ball	631	201	832.00	430.00	126831.00	3.14
13							
14							

FIGURE 4.4   Spreadsheet of circle data. Is there a pattern?

◀Preparing Technologically Literate Students

When you think about the tools that students use for learning in schools, you might picture a student at a desk with a pencil, some paper, and a book. Certainly at the beginning of a school year, parents are asked to provide a variety of tools for their children as they prepare for the school year. Paper, crayons, scissors, rulers, pencils, and erasers are typical tools for elementary-aged students; secondary students are more apt to be asked to bring spiral-bound pads of paper or 3-ring notebooks with paper, pens, pencils, erasers, and perhaps a calculator. Schools provide students with tools for learning, too. Then during the first week of classes, textbooks are handed out in the various classes. Some schools have computer-based technologies (computers with Internet access, digital cameras, camcorders, etc.) available as tools for students to use, but many others do not. Some students have some of these technologies available in their homes. Others do not. Today, learning in schools must include increased access to technologies if students are expected to learn how to learn and solve problems using appropriate technological tools.

Technological Literacy

For hundreds of years, schools have had the primary responsibility for teaching children to be literate citizens. This literacy included teaching children reading, writing, and mathematics. Concerning writing, education was charged with teaching children to learn to write letters both in print and cursive forms and to arrange those letters into words and sentences. In the process schools have assumed the primary responsibility for guiding students as they learn to write and communicate with the writing tools of the time. Essentially, schools have been expected and continue to be expected to assure that all students can write and communicate using the appropriate technologies of the times.

In the twenty-first century, computer and electronic technologies have significantly affected how people work and communicate. Thus, any discussion of preparing literate citizens must necessarily include a discussion of *technological literacy*. Today students need to know what technology is, how it works, what purposes it can serve, and how it can be used efficiently and effectively to solve problems and make decisions. Furthermore, they need to learn to think *strategically* with respect to technology, developing a knowledge that supports them as they solve problems with appropriate technologies, make decisions based on their use of the technologies, and monitor their progress in obtaining appropriate technological solutions. This technological literacy does not imply just knowing about technology. Technological literacy, developed from within the context of academic subject areas, ultimately directs how they will implement technologies to solve problems as productive members of society.

Schools carry the primary responsibility for literacy, including technological literacy. Schools must make changes in both the tools used to attain literacy and the curriculum that supports this learning. Students need to learn basic skills with technologies, learn to use technologies in the search for solutions to problems, learn to use technologies to learn, and basically learn to think strategically with technology. Although some students come to school having had experiences with some of the technologies, schools are expected to assure that all students have at least a basic knowledge of using technology for learning and communicating.

In the 1990s technology classes at elementary, middle, and high school levels were available to provide a foundation with technology. Today, fewer and fewer of those classes are available. As with writing and communicating with pencils and pens, learning to learn and communicate with technology has become a responsibility of all teachers regardless of their subject matter content so that the learning is in concert with learning in the various academic contexts. Elementary teachers now work with technology teachers to design the context in which students will learn with the technology. Secondary subject specific teachers, too, must consider how students can use the technologies to learn, integrating student learning with the technology in concert with their learning in the subject area. Through this education, what knowledge should *all* students gain to be able to live and work in the twenty-first century?

NETS · S: Technology Standards for Students

Before the school year begins, teachers consider what technologies they want to be sure that their students are able to use throughout the year. Once identified, the goal is to support students in learning to use these technologies as they learn and think within the context of specific content areas. For this goal to be met, teachers, such as Mr. Dixon in the Snapshot of a Twenty-First-Century Teacher's Unit Outline must strategically plan how the technologies are introduced and supported as their students learn within the context of the subject matter throughout the year. A critical task for the teacher is to scaffold learning about each technology within the specific subject matter context. In essence, teachers need to include technology as an integral component of learning within the subject area in order to accommodate students as they learn how to learn and think with the technology.

Another important concern in each teacher's planning is to consider the variety of ways to integrate each technology as a tool for learning and communicating within the context of the specific content. The International Society for Technology in Education (ISTE, 2000) provides teachers with guidelines through the development of student technology standards to be used in concert with subject-specific standards. From this perspective, teachers need to reconfigure their curriculum and instruction in ways that guide students' learning of the subject, the technology, and the technology within the context of the subject. The National Educational Technology Standards for Students (NETS · S) are organized in six standard areas along with clarifying features for each standard. These standards describe a breadth of potential uses for teachers to consider in connecting the curriculum with technology.

NETS · S Standard I. Basic Operations and Concepts

The first standard aims at students' understanding of the basic operations and concepts of technology. Two statements further describe this standard. Students

A. *demonstrate a sound understanding of the nature and operation of technology systems;*

B. *are proficient in the use of technology.* (ISTE, 2000, p. 14)

Teachers cannot expect that students come to their classes with knowledge of the basic operations and concepts of various technology systems or that they are proficient users of technology. This recognition, however, must not be used as an excuse for not incorporating technology in the classroom learning activities. Rather, this recognition challenges teachers to design a curriculum that guides students in learning *about* the specific technology within the context of the curriculum.

In the Snapshot of a Twenty-First-Century Teacher's Unit Outline in this chapter, Mr. Dixon's primary goal was content-specific, requiring students to understand and be able to use the value of pi (the mathematics goal). He arranged the students' work with a variety of technologies throughout the unit to support them in learning both about the mathematics and about the technologies. The demonstration with Geometer's Sketchpad was designed as the students' first experience with that software. Mr. Dixon planned that his students observe how to use this new sketchpad and some of its drawing tools to create a circle. As they watch him use the tools to construct the circle, he plans that they observe the relationship between two points in a new visual form, reinforcing their previous work with the string and the compass. All three of these technologies are valuable in his class in that they provide multiple and unique representations of the same phenomena. Geometer's Sketchpad may prove to be most useful to students as they expand their work with geometric shapes. The focus at this time, however, is to explore how to create a circle, paying careful attention to specific characteristics of a circle. Later, in another unit on polygons, they might have an opportunity to experience more of the tools and have hands-on work using the tools to create polygons.

Mr. Dixon also designed the unit with circular objects so that the students could work with the NIH Image software. The students had previously taken digital pictures and learned how to incorporate their digital pictures in this software. For this unit, he planned to use the activity to guide them in measuring specific parts of digital circular images, such as dimes, quarters, Moon, and Earth.

In other words, for this unit, Mr. Dixon had carefully considered what technologies were useful for content-specific goals and for students' growing technology-specific skills. Mr. Dixon had previously incorporated instruction with the basic operations of NIH Image with the intent that during this unit their skills with this technology would be enhanced. Simultaneously, he planned for this unit to introduce his students to Geometer's Sketchpad in preparation for future lessons where they would learn more about its basic operations and use it for exploring mathematics concepts.

The message in this Snapshot of a Twenty-First-Century Teacher's Unit Outline is that when students need instruction with the basic operations and concepts of a particular technology, teachers need to consider how to use the curriculum context to teach the needed technology skills. But how will you know what your students know about the technology you want to use? Rather than making unsupported assumptions, it is your task to determine your students' readiness to use a particular technology for learning. Chapter 13 of this book will help you think about how to preassess your students' readiness for using technology for learning.

Now suppose that you are a language arts teacher at the ninth-grade level. You are planning to have your students read *The Adventures of Huckleberry Finn* by Mark Twain at the end of the school year. You know that you will want your students to use several different technology tools in that unit to support their learning and communications. You are unsure about their technology skills and abilities with keyboarding and word processing, but you are certain they will need help gaining skills and concepts of some of the other technologies where they will be able to demonstrate proficiency by the concluding unit.

How will you make sure that the students are proficient users of the technology for that unit? You begin the year by preparing them! You recognize that reading *The Adventures of Huckleberry Finn* will present difficulties for the students because of unfamiliar dialects and unique approaches to humor. As Twain explains, "in this book a number of dialects are used, to wit: the Missouri negro dialect; the extremist form of the backwoods South-Western dialect; the ordinary 'Pike-County' dialect; and four modified varieties of this last" (Twain, 2001, p. 2). One instructional goal for teaching this novel might be to not only make the dialects accessible to the student readers, but to help them see how Twain used language as a literary device in the novel. Remember, you want to use technology when it accomplishes something that you could not otherwise do with more conventional tools. Use of technology early in this unit allows access to unique instructional resources while allowing you, as their teacher, to provide your students with an introduction to technologies that you will be developing throughout the unit.

In the Classroom 4.1 requires that students transcribe a conversational speech event that they witness, ranging from a family discussion at dinner to a conversation between friends in the hallway. In this activity, students use a word processing application with either a handheld device or a laptop to write as much of the event as they can capture, including notes about cues, vocal inflection, visuals, and physical movements between speakers. In

In the Classroom 4.1

WHAT DID YOU SAY AND HOW SHOULD I WRITE IT?

TECHNOLOGY OBJECTIVES: **NETS · S I, III, IV**

- **Word processors:** Technology as a communications tool and learning basic operations of technology.
- Keyboarding, spelling and grammar checking, formatting tools.

CONTENT OBJECTIVE: **Language arts:** Understand textual features for expressing language in various dialects.

GRADE LEVEL: 5–9

PROBLEM: How do speakers use dialect? How does dialect impact how meaning is communicated? How does what we know about oral speech influence how we read dialogue and dialect in a novel?

❏ Here are some phrases from Mark Twain's novel, *The Adventures of Huckleberry Finn.* The novel is written in the first person voice of Huck Finn. Enter these phrases in a word processing document as they are written:

You don't know about me, without you have read a book by the name of "The Adventures of Tom Sawyer," but that ain't no matter. (p. 3)

The Widow Douglas, she took me for her son, and allowed she would sivilize me; but it was rough living in the house all the time, considering how dismal regular and decent the widow was in all her ways; and so when I couldn't stand it no longer, I lit out. (p. 3)

Well, three or four months run along, and it was well into the winter, now. I had been to school most all the time, and could spell, and read, and write just a little, and could say the multiplication table up to six times seven is thirty-five, and I don't reckon I could ever get any further than that if I was to live forever. I don't take no stock in mathematics, anyway. (p. 14)

"Don't you give me none o' your lip," says he. "You've put on considerable many frills since I been away. I'll take you down a peg before I get done with you. You're educated, too, they say; can read and write. You think you're better'n your father, now, don't you, because he can't? I'll take it out of you. Who told you you might meddle with such hifalut'n foolishness, hey?—who told you you could?" (p. 18)

❏ Using a different font color, rewrite each phrase using traditional English grammar, punctuation, and spelling. Insert your rewritten phrase after the phrase in the word-processed text and then put a box with some shading around each phrase.

Example:

> You don't know about me, without you have read a book by the name of "The Adventures of Tom Sawyer," but that ain't no matter. (p. 3)
>
> You don't know me unless you have read a book by the name of "The Adventures of Tom Sawyer," but that does not matter. (my revision)

❏ Observe and transcribe a speech event. Listen carefully, perhaps audiotaping different voices so you can transcribe them accurately. Be sure to note vocal inflections, visuals, and physical movements passing between the speakers engaged in the speech event.

❏ Trade your transcription of each phrase with a peer. After reading the transcript, use a different color to rewrite the phrase in traditional English as you did with those phrases of *Huckleberry Finn.* Frame each grouping of phrases as you did previously.

❏ The final section of this document is your response to the problem that began this exercise. Write your response as if you were explaining the answer to your friends orally—only you will be doing this explanation in writing using your word processor.

class they can share their documents by using the beam feature of the handheld or by storing their document in a shared folder. Or, in a computer lab, they can switch seats with a peer (perhaps only exchanging the keyboards), to convert the phrases to more academic or formal English using various tools in the word processor: different colors of fonts, borders, and shades, along with the spelling and grammar tool. The emphasis is on the language arts issue of considering how speakers use diction, dialect, conversational, and academic speech in order to communicate specific, intended meaning. Although this activity guides students in learning some basics of the word processor (or perhaps to see what skills they do have with the basic tools), you are maintaining the focus of the lesson on the context of the curriculum.

As noted in the technology objectives description of In the Classroom 4.1, this activity focuses on multiple NETS student standards. NETS·S I refers to learning some basics of word processors as discussed in this section. However, as with almost any activity you integrate in your classes, the activity also meets other student standards, to be discussed in further detail later in this chapter. For now, this activity also focuses on NETS·S III that refers to using technology as a productivity tool and NETS·S IV that refers to using technology as a communications tool.

NET·S Standard II. Social, Ethical, and Human Issues
The second student standard focuses on the social, ethical, and human issues when using technology. Three statements clarify this standard. Students

A. *understand the ethical, cultural, and societal issues related to technology;*

B. *practice responsible use of technology systems, information, and software;*

C. *develop positive attitudes toward technology uses that support lifelong learning, collaboration, personal pursuits, and productivity.* (ISTE, 2000, p. 14)

Much of how children learn begins with observation. They observe, mimic, and implicitly are taught by others' actions, including their teachers. In this manner, teachers implicitly teach students acceptable behavior with respect to scholarly, legal, and ethical uses of technology. Suppose a teacher copies or uses software without paying for it so that students can use that software as a tool for learning. Is that legal? Is it ethical? What do students learn?

If teachers use copyrighted materials for educational uses without identifying the author, they are implicitly teaching their students that copying materials is acceptable. Fair use guidelines under the U.S. Code, Title 17, Chapter 1, Section 107 of the Copyright Act of 1976 allow teachers to use and copy certain copyrighted work for nonprofit education uses. One key to the fair use guidelines lies in the "effect of the use upon the potential market for or value of the copyrighted work." Certainly copying an entire copyrighted document should not be considered legal because making such a copy may affect the potential market for or value of the work. The question remains, however, as to "how much" can be copied for educational uses. This question is a concern for many schools or districts and their

interpretations vary widely. Typically, they identify specific policies in describing their interpretation. Teachers must be concerned both with the Copyright Act and their school's policies when considering copying. If uncertain, teachers can contact the author for permission. At the very least, the author must be cited in an appropriate manner. Therefore, if teachers copy others' materials from a website, they should (1) assume it is copyrighted material, (2) check with the school or district policy, and (3) identify the author(s) in an appropriate citation.

Schools typically have rules and guidelines for legal and ethical behaviors that are designed to inform teachers and students as they use technology. Furthermore, parts of the overall school curriculum explicitly focus on ethical, cultural, and social issues related to technology as well as other materials used in learning. Perhaps this explicit instruction incorporates the goal of guiding students in understanding the scholarly, ethical, and legal issues related to technology use. Nevertheless, these policies and the instruction do not absolve teachers' responsibility for this technology standard. As technology is incorporated throughout the curriculum, attention must be given to this standard, in particular for having students practice responsible uses of technology systems, information, and software.

Think about this standard in relationship to designing the *Huckleberry Finn* unit. The students need some familiarity with the Mississippi River before reading the novel. So you might plan that they take an imaginary trip on the Mississippi River and write a journal of their travels. In doing so, you require they use existing interpretations of the *Huckleberry Finn* story from online resources relating to some aspect of their journey. This activity can integrate social, ethical, and legal concerns when copying materials from the Web. You need to plan to encourage the students to look for evidence of authorship for any material they plan to incorporate. And you need to require that they provide the appropriate citations either obtained through a website or obtained by personal contact with the creator. In such an activity, students are not only encouraged to practice responsible uses of technology information but perhaps will develop positive attitudes toward technology uses that support their personal pursuits.

NETS·S Standard III. Technology Productivity Tools
The third student technology standard directs their attention to the use of technology as a productivity tool. Two statements clarify this standard. Students

A. *use technology tools to enhance learning, increase productivity, and promote creativity;*

B. *use productivity tools to collaborate in constructing technology-enhanced models, prepare publications, and produce other creative works.* (ISTE, 2000, p. 14)

The idea of technology as a productivity tool engages students in using technology to support them in producing creative works, designing models, and publishing their creative works. Prior to the advent of computer-based technologies, students had few tools to use for producing creative works. Since the late 1980s and early 1990s word processing programs have provided drawing capabilities to allow students tools to illustrate their ideas as they described them. Now, many powerful graphics packages are available to help students produce diagrams and visuals that communicate information far better than in words. OmniGraffle (a software designed specifically to create diagrams and charts as a way to organize thoughts visually, documenting thoughts through graphics) supports students in transferring their ideas sketched out in a group discussion to a more formal description of their plans for a project. With access to numerous digital images, students can use digital imaging editors like Photoshop to enhance or otherwise change the images. Perhaps students may wish to include images of the imaginary people they interview during their trip on the Mississippi River. By selecting and altering images in such digital imaging editors, students can produce a more vivid description of their trip. Also, with access to applications such as Adobe Premiere, iMovie, or even iPhoto, students can turn digital photos, photographs, video, and audio clips into movies as they demonstrate their thoughts in a more creative manner than if they only used a word processor.

The Web provides students with an environment for searching a tremendous volume of information to identify information that can aid in the solution to particular classroom assignments. This information is certainly more diverse than simple print media since the Web provides access to audio and visual clips to use for supporting ideas. Compare this capability with students' opportunities for searching extensive volumes of information in a library.

Such technologies only begin to highlight the wealth of different technologies that are currently available to support students in becoming more productive and creative. What is your role as a teacher in helping students learn to use the various technologies as productivity tools? Certainly, an important task is to continue searching for alternative tools. Technologies are being developed and become available for helping students. Have you had experience with electronic text (e-text) programs like Microsoft Reader that allow readers to annotate and mark up electronic text? Perhaps this tool will help students as they read novels such as *The Adventures of Huckleberry Finn*. The Electronic Text Center at the University of Virginia Library currently has an online archive of tens of thousands of electronic texts and images with a library service that offers "Ebooks" for the Microsoft Reader or the Palm Pilot along with access to technologies for the creation and analysis of text materials. Use the Library link described in Technology Link 4.1 to review this service.

Technology Link 4.1

*A*ccess to the Electronic Text Center at the University of Virginia Library is available by using the **Library** link at this book's website.

www.wiley.com/college/niess

You do need to help your students become proficient with the basic operations and concepts of the particular technology (NET·S Standard I). But as the students learn about the basic operations, they can also be learning to use the technology as a productivity tool. It is likely they will learn more about the basic operations and concepts when they use the specific technology in an activity that helps them to be more productive and creative.

What about encouraging students to be more productive and creative in the *Huckleberry Finn* unit? Preparation might extend to a more interdisciplinary unit while still retaining the language arts focus. Mark Twain lived at a time of American history with which the students need to become familiar if they are to understand the context and function of the novel that they will be reading. Humor was a key tool that Mark Twain used in contrast to the harsh realism of the frontier times. Humor is entertaining and is a colorful way of expressing ideas, whether it is communicated through puns, tall tales, wit, or even satires. The teaching of Twain's novel lends itself well to examination through a variety of perspectives: literary, historical, and social. However, in order to get to the roots of the multiple issues and delights that the text presents, teachers and students need to explore the complex satirical structures that were the framework on which Twain constructed his social commentary. In fact, when the book was first banned in Concord, Massachusetts, it was the satire within the text that incited the attack against a text "whose satire was suitable only for the slums."

In the Classroom 4.2 suggests how a social studies emphasis might be used to extend and support a more interdisciplinary direction by engaging students in developing their own interpretive description of Mark Twain, using images of him with accounts of his personality along with an investigation of the reality of the times of his childhood. In the process of interpreting the Mark Twain of the frontier times, students have the opportunity to use technology as a productivity tool through the

In the Classroom 4.2

WHO WAS MARK TWAIN?

TECHNOLOGY OBJECTIVES: NETS·S I, II, III, IV

- **Internet, word processing, and concept mapping software:** Technology as a communications and productivity tool with consideration of ethical issues.
- Use a Web-based search engine to locate, copy, and cite appropriately illustrations and cartoon images of Mark Twain and the times in which he lived.

CONTENT OBJECTIVE: Social studies: Develop an interpretive description of Mark Twain, the frontier humorist who wrote *The Adventures of Huckleberry Finn*. Fit this description with information from his childhood years.

GRADE LEVEL: 6–12

CHALLENGE 1: Who was Mark Twain?

- ❑ Locate cartoon images that appeared in *Life* magazine using an Internet search. Can these cartoon images be copied, according to the Copyright Act under the fair use guidelines? Identify at least three cartoon images that can be copied and cited. How should they be cited?
- ❑ Locate Steve Railton's collection of illustrations of Mark Twain using a Web search. Determine which illustrations can be copied to your word-processed document and the appropriate method for citing the illustrations.
- ❑ Copy and paste three cartoons and three illustrations and write a short descriptive essay which puts into words the various graphic depictions of Mark Twain.

CHALLENGE 2: What were the times like when Mark Twain lived?

Mark Twain was born Samuel Langhorne Clemens on November 30, 1835. He was born in Florida, Missouri, and lived in Hannibal, Missouri, from ages 4 to 18. His memories of his childhood provided the framework for three stories including *The Adventures of Huckleberry Finn*, which was published in 1885.

- ❑ Where is Hannibal, Missouri? Create a map that shows this town and its surrounding areas using the draw tools in the word processor.
- ❑ What was life like in Hannibal, Missouri, during Twain's childhood? Using concept map software, describe Mark Twain's childhood. What influenced his life during the period of his childhood, 1840–1853?

development of a descriptive essay using a word processor and incorporating graphic images to support their description. In the process they must deal with social, legal, and ethical issues of copying images from the Web.

NETS·S Standard IV. Technology Communications Tools   The fourth student technology standard focuses on communicating with technology. Two statements help to explain this standard. Students

A. *use telecommunications to collaborate, publish, and interact with peers, experts, and other audiences;*

B. *use a variety of media and formats to communicate information and ideas effectively to multiple audiences.* (ISTE, 2000, p. 15)

Enhanced technologies have most certainly altered communications today. E-mail and fax have largely replaced letter writing. Responses are expected sooner. Fifty years ago, students developing a project notebook to describe the frontier times on the Mississippi River might have written to the chambers of commerce of various towns along the Missis-

sippi River, requesting artifacts from that time period. Today, students can search the websites of the chambers of commerce for towns along the Mississippi and even send e-mails with follow-up requests.

E-mail has expanded the community of available experts for help on questions. Students could e-mail nonfiction writers who have studied Hannibal during Twain's time, experts on Twain, experts on southern frontier literature and humor, and even students across the country who are also studying this novel. Another idea might be to connect with students in towns across the nation where Twain wrote to see the kinds of connections between places as well as the ways in which they perceive Mark Twain.

The Web offers additional ways to communicate with others, even those in your own class. A class wiki (Hawaian word for fast, sometimes referred to as "what I know is" uses html for Web communication) can be used to post ideas on the development of a full-class collaborative document about the novel. Wikis offer open editing of pages in a website, a potential extension for In the Classroom 4.2. In this wiki, students could post their ideas and growing understandings to add to the description of Mark Twain as a humorist. The teacher might consider having the students use the class wiki as a collaborative space dedicated to bringing together students from across the nation who are working with the novel where they might work with the ideas of the historical context of the novel. Another extension might use the class wiki for students to collaborate in writing a full-class essay on a variety of ideas that they have learned about Mark Twain or Hannibal.

Another new form for communication on the Web is called a weblog (described more commonly as a blog). Blogs are Web writing spaces that can function as online journals. In the *Huckleberry Finn* unit, English or language arts teachers might use a blog as a personal reflective space for student readers. Specific prompts might help focus student responses as they read. For example, in the *Huckleberry Finn* unit, "parody" is an important literary device and concept. Teachers might ask students to respond to the following questions in a blog post:

- What is a parody? How does Mark Twain use parody in this novel?

- How is what Mark Twain does similar to Whitman's preface in *Leaves of Grass*, Wilson's apologetic preface to *Our Nig*, and Hawthorne's parodic preface to *The Scarlet Letter*?

- What current texts can you identify as a parody? How are they similar to or different from Twain's novel?

A social studies activity might direct students to use blogs for reflecting on how race is portrayed by Twain through his characters, primarily Huck Finn and Jim, and what Twain was saying about race in the mid-nineteenth-century world portrayed in the book. Through the students' personal blog postings, they demonstrate their developing understanding of the use of parody in this novel and other, more contemporary texts. Further, because blogs are collaborative spaces, students can post responses to one another's ideas.

NETS · S Standard V. Technology Research Tools
The fifth Student Technology Standard focuses on using technology for research. Three statements expand on this standard. Students

A. *use technology to locate, evaluate, and collect information from a variety of sources;*

B. *use technology tools to process data and report results;*

C. *evaluate and select new information resources and technological innovations based on the appropriateness for specific tasks.* (ISTE, 2000, p. 15)

Technology has increased students' ability to conduct research. The Web provides access to a tremendous amount of information not traditionally available in school libraries. Now students can search library and electronic text collections from around the world as they research specific topics. More than ever, however, they must learn to carefully cite the works that they do access as well as to evaluate them. Whether these works are valid and reliable is an important question that student researchers must consider in their investigations.

Student research can be an important activity in the *Huckleberry Finn* unit. One research idea is to involve them in the controversy and question of whether the novel is appropriate for teenagers to read. The novel contains references to the practice of slavery, views particular to the reformation, language that is offensive to many, and images that present Black characters as little more than laughable. In 1957, the National Association for the Advancement of and Colored People (NAACP) charged that the novel contained "racial slurs" and "belittling designations," a stance that has been cited in the banning of and controversy over the book for well over the past 40 years. However, a 1999 position paper by the NAACP provides an alternative consideration about the teaching of *The Adventures of Huckleberry Finn*.

> You don't ban Mark Twain, you explain Mark Twain! To study an idea is not necessarily to endorse the idea. Mark Twain's satirical novel, *The Adventures of Huckleberry Finn*, actually portrays a time in history—the nineteenth century—and one of its evils, slavery.

With this suggestion, teachers may consider work with the novel as a means of addressing what it means for a book to be offensive and even banned. The newer technologies might become value added by making accessible resources and information that students might not otherwise be able to access as they consider the question of whether to ban the novel. For this project, students participate in a class-enacted mock trial exploring the banning of the novel in their high school. In the Classroom 4.3 proposes another interdisciplinary activity involving students in conducting extensive online and textual research into the current ethical, social, and cultural expectations of the society as it might exist in their own community. Additionally, the students must gather data about other legal cases and national organizations that have addressed the teaching of this controversial novel.

NETS · S Standard VI. Technology Problem-Solving and Decision-Making Tools The sixth student technology standard directs the students' use of technology toward problem solving and decision making.

In the Classroom 4.3

CASE #123: THE BANNING OF *THE ADVENTURES OF HUCKLEBERRY FINN*

TECHNOLOGY OBJECTIVES: NETS·S I, II, III, IV, V

- **Internet, e-mail in search of supporting evidence using movie editing or presentation software:** Technology as a communications, productivity, and research tool.
- Use technology to search for supporting evidence for presentation at a mock trial that explores the banning of the novel.

CONTENT OBJECTIVE: **Language arts:** Students acquire new information and respond to needs and demands of society; students use a variety of technological and information resources to gather and synthesize information and to communicate an analysis of social issues.

Social studies: Students construct reasoned judgments about specific cultural responses to persistent human issues; students examine persistent issues involving the rights, roles, and status of the individual in relation to the general welfare.

GRADE LEVEL: 9–12

CHALLENGE: Your task is to enact a mock trial that explores the banning of the novel in a fictional high school in your community. The class will be divided into teams to enact the mock trial where there will be a jury composed of your peers from other class periods. Judge (insert teachers' last name) will make the final ruling.

TEAMS AND TASKS: Each team is expected to prepare evidence and other important artifacts for the trial. They need to select a way to communicate their evidence, perhaps using technologies such as digital cameras, digital video cameras, digital editing, movie editing and presentation tools such as iMovie, Windows Movie Maker, PowerPoint, or Photoshop. All teams are expected to work collaboratively, sharing information and expectations to support the preparation for the trial.

- Attorneys, prosecution and defense
  - Collect evidence in support of the position.
  - Select key arguments that need to be made, citing evidence from the text as well as from real-life cases.
  - Determine witnesses needed for the presentation.
  - Organize the presentation of the evidence and arguments.
- Witnesses
  - Identify potential witnesses for both the prosecution and defense.
  - Prepare a witness statement that outlines the personal perspective and observations.
  - Check with the attorneys to determine if other witnesses are needed and, if so, prepare similar descriptive documents to describe the statements and perceptions of that witness. Provide that information to the attorneys who requested the witness.
- Jury members
  - Jury members must come from the local school county. Identify potential jury members. Provide ethnic backgrounds and other background information that may be requested by the attorneys or judge: family, employment, age, experiences in various countries or cultures.
- Enactors
  - Identify the lead attorneys and support personnel to work with the various teams in preparation for the trial.
  - Identify potential jury members who might be chosen for the trial; these potential jury members should work with the jury member's team to clarify background information.
  - Record enactments that will be used in the trial using appropriate technologies.

Two statements illuminate this standard. Students

A. *use technology resources for solving problems and making informed decisions;*

B. *employ technology in the development of strategies for solving problems in the real world.* (ISTE, 2000, p. 15)

The preparation of problem solvers and decision makers is an overarching goal for education. Problem solving requires higher order thinking skills, such as analysis, synthesis, or evaluation of knowledge from multiple disciplines. Problems differ from exercises at the end of a chapter primarily because students know that the solutions to the exercises can be found in the ideas from the chapter. Problems are different from the infamous "word problems" in a mathematics textbook because the primary distinguishing feature from an exercise at the end of the chapter is that the problems are expressed in words; solving these problems can also be done using the information in the chapter. Problems challenge students to think outside a particular chapter or unit, to think more broadly than from within the confines of the information in a chapter or unit.

This sixth standard suggests that technology is one of the tools that can support higher order thinking. Simulation software is one type of technology that is often promoted as engaging students in problem solving and decision making. SimCity 4 is an example of a simulation that engages students in designing their own city, making decisions about the city budget, size of the population, and operation of the city in the face of problems including random disasters such as flooding, fires, or even twisters.

In the Snapshot of a Twenty-First-Century Teacher's Unit Outline, the Geometer's Sketchpad provides a different type of problem solving technology, a drawing pad that students can use to explore mathematical relationships and make conjectures based on these explorations. In this example, they see how to construct an equilateral triangle and then are challenged to construct a regular hexagon (six-sided figure with equal sides).

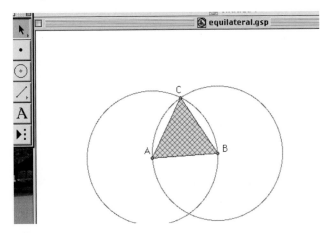

In the Classroom 4.3 can be extended to involve students in problem solving and decision making in the unit on *The Adventures of Huckleberry Finn*. As a follow-up to the mock trial, students are challenged to compose letters to the school board ad-dressing other controversial texts, some that they independently research, read, and believe should be added to the curriculum. In this problem-based, real-world activity, the students must address a controversial text, develop an argument, and then present their findings to the school board. Technology can be used as a research tool and as a presentation device. Perhaps students could use a class wiki to collaborate and correspond with students in other schools where the students are reading the proposed controversial novel. A discussion board can be used as a forum for sharing and responding to ideas as they are developed. Students can use e-mail to discuss ideas with authors and others concerned with the specific controversy. The letter to the school board might be accompanied by a PowerPoint presentation of the evidence or a student-designed and student-created movie (using movie editing software) providing a debate about the controversial aspects of the proposed novel.

By now you have perhaps considered that many of these activities actually respond to more than one of the NETS·S standards, at least in some way. Students constructing a defense to the school board must demonstrate understanding of basic operations and concepts of the technology they use to solve this problem (NETS·S I). They must consider the scholarly, ethical, and legal considerations of copying clips or other items from the Web (NETS·S II). The technology they select for their final presentation to the school board is a productivity tool as it is used to display their argument (NETS·S III). In the development of their product, they may use a variety of technologies, including e-mail, the class wiki, and discussion boards, to identify and share their developing defense for their specific controversial texts (NETS·S IV). They must do some research to develop their argument, and much of the research involves the use of various technologies such as the Web and e-mail (NETS·S V). The idea was posed as a problem requiring that they use appropriate technologies in presenting their solution using tools like presentation or movie editing software (NETS·S Standard VI).

Careful consideration of each of these standards along with subject matter standards providing the context requires attention in advance of teaching a unit such as described for *The Adventures of Huckleberry Finn*. Figure 4.5 displays one way the final unit might be conceived. An important point, however, is that throughout the discussion of the NETS·S standards, the expectation has been that students will be prepared for this unit, prepared both for work with the technology as well as for reading the classic novel. Without the technology preparation, the unit might become a unit about technology, which is definitely not the intention.

Language Arts Unit: *The Adventures of Huckleberry Finn*

Premise

You don't ban Mark Twain, you explain Mark Twain! To study an idea is not necessarily to endorse the idea. Mark Twain's satirical novel, The Adventures of Huckleberry Finn, *accurately portrays a time in history—the nineteenth century—and one of its evils, slavery.*

—NAACP, 1999 Position Paper on the Teaching of The Adventures of Huckleberry Finn

Standards

English/Language Arts

1. Students read a range of print and nonprint texts to build an understanding of texts, of themselves, and of the cultures of the United States and the world; to acquire new information; to respond to the needs and demands of society and the workplace; and for personal fulfillment. Among these texts are fiction and nonfiction, classic and contemporary works.

2. Students read a wide range of literature from many periods in many genres to build an understanding of the many dimensions of human experience.

3. Students apply a wide range of strategies to comprehend, interpret, evaluate, and appreciate texts. They draw on their prior experience, their interactions with other readers and writers, their knowledge of word meaning and of other texts, their word identification strategies, and their understanding of textual features.

4. Students employ a wide range of strategies as they write and use different writing process elements appropriately to communicate with different audiences for a variety of purposes.

5. Students use a variety of technological and information resources to gather and synthesize information and to create and communicate knowledge. (National Council of Teachers of English/IRA Standards, 1996)

Social Studies

1. Students use experiences to study individual development and identity.

2. Students study people, places, and environments. (National Council for the Social Studies, 1994)

Technology

1. **Basic operations and concepts:** Students are proficient in the use of technology.

2. **Social, ethical, and human issues:** Students practice responsible use of technology and develop positive attitudes toward technology uses.

3. **Technology productivity tools:** Students use technology tools to enhance learning, increase productivity, and promote creativity.

4. **Technology communications tools:** Students use a variety of media and formats to communicate information and ideas effectively to multiple audiences.

5. **Technology research tools:** Students evaluate and select new information resources based on the appropriateness for specific tasks.

6. **Technology problem-solving and decision-making tools:** Students use technology resources for solving problems and making informed decisions. (ISTE, 2000)

Resources

1. PBS Video: *Born to Trouble: The Adventures of Huck Finn*

2. Internet resources:
   - http://etext.lib.virginia.edu/railton/huckfinn/huchompg.html
   - http://cte.jhu.edu/techacademy/web/2000/kajder/texts/huckfinn/huckintro.html
   - http://www.pbs.org/wgbh/cultureshock/beyond/huck.html

3. Butcher paper, cards, staples, pens

4. Technology:
   - Computer, Internet, class collaborative wiki, weblog account (for each individual student), Photoshop, PowerPoint, iMovie or Windows Movie Maker
   - Digital cameras and digital video cameras

Unit Outline

Time	Activity
2 days	Introduction to the humor of the nineteenth century: Who influenced Twain?

- Frontier humor and harsh realism
- Puns, tall tales, wit
- Who was Mark Twain?
  - http://etext.lib.virginia.edu/railton/enam482e/mtassoc.html

(continued on next page)

	• Small group problem: Small groups select and read a range of texts, develop a list of "criteria" identifying the elements of frontier humor. Small groups use the class wiki to post their ideas to a full-class collaborative document. Texts include these:

• Small group problem: Small groups select and read a range of texts, develop a list of "criteria" identifying the elements of frontier humor. Small groups use the class wiki to post their ideas to a full-class collaborative document. Texts include these:
  ○ Olmstead's "Old Willy"
  ○ Twain's "The Notorious Jumping Frog of Calaveras County"
  ○ Twain's "How I Edited an Agricultural Paper"
  ○ Additional texts by Washington Irving, James Russel Lowell, Ambrose Bierce, Bret Harte
  ○ http://etext.lib.virginia.edu/railton/huckfinn/suggs.html
Introduce *The Adventures of Huckleberry Finn* and the mock trial project:
• Each student will participate in a class-enacted mock trial exploring the banning of the novel in Hannibal High School, a "fictional" high school classroom.
• Technology (PowerPoint, iMovie or Windows Movie Maker) will be used to present evidence to the jury.
• Teams and their tasks, timelines, and technology resources
  ○ Attorneys (prosecution and defense)
  ○ Witnesses
  ○ Jury members
  ○ Enactors

1 day	Introduction to parody: Twain's distortion of the preface • Examine Whitman's preface to *Leaves of Grass*, Wilson's apologetic preface to *Our Nig*, Hawthorne's parodic preface to *The Scarlet Letter*, and Twain's anti-preface to *Huckleberry Finn*. • Students post responses to reflective weblogs. • Begin reading and discussing the novel (chapters 1–11).
2 days	Small groups design and create a literary map of the Mississippi, based on Huck and Jim's journey. • Construct a map of the Mississippi River to highlight Mark Twain's literary and real-life relationship with the river. Begin with a blank map or obtain one from http://memory.loc.gov/ammem/gmdhtml/gmdhome.html; have butcher paper, cards, staples, and pens available for student use. Assignment: Read chapters 12–18.
1 day	Conduct an online "slanguage" search. Is the language and dialect presented within the novel exaggerated? What is its effect?
1 day	Introduction to satire • Read Suess' *Butter Battle Book* • Examine Horatian and Juvenalian forms of satire and satirical attack. • Identify "satirical elements" in place in *Huckleberry Finn* (i.e., the tacky grandeur of the Grangerford House). • Examine the illustrations in the text as caricature. Assess the satire within the presentation of Jim, Huck, Pap, and the Widow Douglas. Use online sources to find additional representations of each character. Assignment: Read chapters 19–31.
1 day	In-class "read in" of scholarly articles addressing the nature of satire in Twain's *Huckleberry Finn*.
2 days	Mapping the literary plot using Kernan's elements of satire. PBS video *Born to Trouble*: Use selected portions to support discussion about satire. Assignment: Read chapters 32–43.
1 day	In groups of four, design a raft that Huck and Jim could have used to navigate the Mississippi. • Determine the size of the logs needed to build the raft and how many logs would be needed. • Describe the raft, its length, width, and area for Huck and Jim. • Use details in the text to support your design proposal, including a potential cost for building the raft. • Present your proposal for the raft using a PowerPoint presentation that incorporates the language that might be used by Huck and Jim.
1 day	Develop two visual open minds (using Photoshop) of the satirist at two selected key moments in the novel.
2 days	Trial preparations. Develop arguments, script scenes, and record enactments or develop evidence using the digital camera, digital video camera, iMovie or Windows Movie Maker, PowerPoint and Photoshop. Use PBS video *Born to Trouble* to support students in working on the trial.
3 days	Conduct mock trial.

FIGURE 4.5 Unit plan on *The Adventures of Huckleberry Finn* that integrates the NETS student standards with the content area standards.

NETS · S Performance Indicators

The NETS student technology standards provide a structure for guiding students in using technology as an integral tool for learning. However, in order for these standards to be more useful, teachers can benefit from more specific performance indicators that describe specific performances for various grade levels. The NETS project also developed performance indicators of achievement for grades preK–2, 3–5, 6–8, and 9–12 as a means of clarifying important student considerations in working toward their technology literacy.

As shown in the unit described in Figure 4.5, the language arts teacher has made some assumptions about the technology literacy of the students. For the mock trial activity, students are expected to work with technologies such as a digital camera, iMovie or Windows Movie Maker, PowerPoint, and Photoshop. The teacher described a time allotted for the trial preparation—only two days—clearly demonstrating this teacher's expectation that students are able to use the technologies without special instruction on the technologies. This expectation is perhaps better reflected in one of the NETS student performance indicators for grades 9–12:

Prior to the completion of Grade 12 students will select and apply technology tools for research, information analysis, problem solving, and decision-making in content learning. *(ISTE, 2000, p. 24)*

An important note about this particular indicator is that it is identified as supporting technology as a communications tool (NETS · S IV) and technology as a research tool (NETS · S V) but it could have as well been aligned with technology problem-solving and decision-making tools (NETS · S VI). What is important about the performance indicators is that they provide some assistance for teachers in designing their K–12 curriculum in support of working on the six student technology standards categories in the context of learning the subject matter.

Figure 4.6 shows a sample of the performance indicators, specifically the indicators for grades 6–8. A link for accessing all the performance indicators for the various grade levels aligned with the NETS · S guidelines is provided in Technology Link 4.2. As you investigate these performance indicators to design your lessons and units, you need to think about them from within the context of the academic subject areas as well as within the context of your students' technology understanding. In this way, the

NETS · S Standards	Prior to completion of grade 8 students will:
I. Basic operations and concepts	1. Apply strategies for identifying and solving routine hardware and software problems that occur during everyday use. (I)
II. Social, ethical, and human issues	2. Demonstrate knowledge of current changes in information technologies and the effect those changes have on the workplace and society. (II)
III. Technology productivity tools	3. Exhibit legal and ethical behaviors when using information and technology, and discuss consequences of misuse. (II)
IV. Technology communications tools	4. Use content-specific tools, software, and simulations (e.g., environmental probes, graphing calculators, exploratory environments, Web tools) to support learning and research. (III, V)
V. Technology research tools	5. Apply productivity/multimedia tools and peripherals to support personal productivity, group collaboration, and learning throughout the curriculum. (III, IV)
VI. Technology problem-solving and decision-making tools	6. Design, develop, publish, and present products (e.g., Web pages, videotapes) using technology resources that demonstrate and communicate curriculum concepts to audiences inside and outside the classroom. (IV, V, VI)
	7. Collaborate with peers, experts, and others using telecommunications and collaborative tools to investigate curriculum-related problems, issues, and information, and to develop solutions or products for audiences inside and outside the classroom. (IV, V)
	8. Select and use appropriate tools and technology resources to accomplish a variety of tasks and solve problems. (V, VI)
	9. Demonstrate an understanding of concepts underlying hardware, software, and connectivity, and of practical applications to learning and problem solving. (I, VI)
	10. Research and evaluate the accuracy, relevance, appropriateness, comprehensiveness, and bias of electronic information sources concerning real-world problems. (II, V, VI)

FIGURE 4.6 *NETS* student performance indicators for technology-literate students in grades 6–8.

standards support technology use as "an integral component or tool for learning within the context of academic subject areas" (ISTE, 2000, p. 17).

The performance indicators provide a skeleton for organizing activities, planning units and lessons, and assessing units and lessons. They are not intended as a script for the lessons and units. You can use them to identify key features of particular

---

Technology Link 4.2

*A*ccess to a complete electronic copy of the NETS student technology standards and performance indicators is available by using the **NETS** link at this book's website.

www.wiley.com/college/nie*ss*

---

activities along with your subject area performance indicators. Additionally, you might identify specific *NET·S* standards and performance indicators that reflect the goal for the use of the technology as an integral component for learning in the activity. Figure 4.7 shows how you might describe the resource ideas as you collect them for future consideration when you design lessons and units.

In planning your units, you might also use the *NET·S* standards and performance indicators as a guide to help you organize the unit in much the same way as you do with the content standards. Review the *Huckleberry Finn* unit in Figure 4.5 and consider how the *technology standards* section might be rewritten to incorporate appropriate performance indicators from Figure 4.6.

Title: *Huckleberry Finn Today*

Content: English/language arts analysis of a satire

Grades: 11–12

Standards

1. **National Council of Teachers of English/IRA Standards, 1996:** Students apply a wide range of strategies to comprehend, interpret, evaluate, and appreciate texts. They draw on their prior experience, their interactions with other readers and writers, their knowledge of word meaning and of other texts, their word identification strategies, and their understanding of textual features.
2. **National Council of Teachers of English/IRA Standards, 1996:** Students use a variety of technological and information resources to gather and synthesize information and to create and communicate knowledge.
3. **NETS·S Performance Indicator 10 for grades 9–12, Standards IV, V, VI:** Collaborate with peers, experts, and others to contribute to a content-related knowledge base by using technology to compile, synthesize, produce, and disseminate information, models, and other creative works.

Idea

After reading the novel *The Adventures of Huckleberry Finn* students in small groups are to write and produce a movie set in today's times where Jim and Huck meet and become friends. The movie needs to describe how they would act today. What real-world issues would they confront today? Where would they begin their journey? Where would their journey take them? How might they respond to the confrontations?

Students will use the Web to gather information that suggests important issues that might confront Jim and Huck and in which regions of the country those issues might be of particular concern. One group will conduct a survey of the school to identify contemporary issues of importance for teens; a spreadsheet graphical analysis can be used to provide a visual display of the data, highlighting the various ideas. Other groups will contact experts (via e-mail) outside the school to identify potential issues for various regions of the country. A class wiki is used to share information among small groups. A weblog account for each small group supports small groups in synthesizing their ideas for determining current issues that they want to consider in their movie.

When the movies are presented, class discussion is centered on the question of why NOW is an important time to read *The Adventures of Huckleberry Finn*.

Materials

- iMovie or Windows Movie Maker software for making the movie
- Digital camera and camcorder for collecting clips for the movie
- Spreadsheet, word processor
- Class wiki and individual student blogs
- Web and e-mail access

Modifications

1. Students create their movie storyboards sketches with paper. They scan the final sketches and incorporate them in a PowerPoint presentation to finalize their proposed movie.
2. Students individually write a diary of Huck's adventures in the modern day scene.

Source

PBS's Culture Shock, *Huck Finn in Context: The Curriculum, Section 6, Final Projects*, Retrieved June 27, 2004, from http://www.pbs.org/wgbh/cultureshock/teachers/huck/section6.html

---

FIGURE 4.7   Sample for describing teaching resources.

The performance indicators also direct the assessments you might use to determine the students' achievements in the unit. The performance indicators, if revised within the unit context, provide specific outcomes for students to demonstrate. Chapter 13 of this text will provide you with more details in using the performance indicators as you think about student assessment.

You have probably noticed that each performance indicator often attends to more than one standard. But you also may see that an activity reflects more than one performance indicator. The mock trial activity in the *Huckleberry Finn* unit is an activity that reflects work aimed at performance indicator 8 (in Figure 4.6) where students must select and use appropriate tools and technology resources to accomplish the various assigned tasks in preparation for the trial. However, that activity also reflects work on performance indicator 10, where the students need to research and evaluate methods for presenting the evidence to determine which best supports the question of whether to ban the novel or not. Should they use digital photos as evidence or would iMovie or Windows Movie Maker evidence be more persuasive? One technology provides audio along with the video with the capability of displaying the language used in the novel. Using a digital camera, on the other hand, does provide the opportunity for close-up stills that might more graphically express a person's scorn.

Connecting the Standards for a Twenty-first-Century Education

Two important considerations are key in beginning the curriculum and unit or lesson planning process: (1) the students and (2) the subject matter. Curriculum content standards have been developed by national organizations for most of the subject areas to specifically discuss student learning at different grade levels. Appendix D contains a listing of the national organizations and their accompanying websites for the primary curriculum areas in schools today. When considering student literacy, the curriculum standards for four major content areas are typically identified:

- *Standards for the English Language Arts* prepared by the National Council of Teachers of English, 1996

- *Principles and Standards for School Mathematics* prepared by the National Council of Teachers of Mathematics, 2000
- *National Science Education Standards* prepared by the National Academy of Sciences, 1996
- *Curriculum Standards for Social Studies* prepared by the National Council for the Social Studies, 1994

These standards provide a national perspective suggesting curriculum guidelines for grades K–12 (often broken into grade level groupings such as K–2, 3–5, 6–8, and 9–12). Also, the states provide specific guidelines for grades K–12 for each of these content areas. All of these documents have starting points for thinking about the content to be taught at particular grade levels. These guidelines suggest the general content that students need to learn in the specific content areas. The grade level organization provides important direction for designing the overall curriculum considering the needs of the students in developing their knowledge in these content areas.

The NETS student technology standards and their accompanying performance indicators for the various grade levels explicitly provide additional support for (1) designing sequences of instruction for the various content areas, (2) developing appropriate sequences of instruction to support students in learning about technology, and (3) preparing for the use of technology as a tool for learning in the content area.

One technique for considering the content area standard and the NETS student technology standards and Performance indicators collectively is to specifically investigate possible connections with the content area standard. Each of the national organizations (identified in Appendix D) provides national standards for teachers to use in building their individual curricula and these standards are often available through the websites. Begin with your subject area standards. Ask yourself questions such as these:

- What technologies can serve as tools for learning this content?

- How can technology serve as a productivity tool, a communications tool, a research tool, or a problem-solving and decision-making tool for learning in this area?

- What preparation will students need in order for the technologies to be tools that support students in learning?

- What social, ethical, and human issues need consideration if the technology tools are used in this area?

- What activity will assure that the technology is an integral component for learning and communication within this content area?

Responses to those questions from each of the content standards will help you in seeing the connections of specific grade level content standards and their performance indicators with the NETS·S technology standards and performance indicators. For each subject matter standard, consider the corresponding performance indicators. Then consider the NETS·S guidelines in relationship to those performance indicators. Does the technology provide a potential for supporting that indicator? If it does, identify a NETS·S technology performance indicator that seems connected. And finally, if you can, think of an instructional example that might be used. Appendix C provides a matrix for grade 8 Language Arts that demonstrates the connections of the standards and performance indicators of both the language arts recommendations with those supplied by NETS·S that a language arts teacher might consider. You can use Technology Link 4.3 for access to similar electronic matrices to use as you investigate the connections with subject area standards.

Technology Link 4.3

*A*ccess to electronic copies of national standards for language arts, mathematics, science, and social studies to investigate connections with the NETS student technology standards and performance indicators is available by using the **Standards** link at this book's website.

www.wiley.com/college/niess

As you learn about different technologies you can continue to add ideas to the matrices that are of interest for your own teaching. Ultimately, this process helps you become more familiar with the standards and how technology can be used as an integral tool for learning and communication. When you begin to plan units, you will then have had some experience identifying ways that technology can become integral to your students' learning. Again, the important starting point is with the students and what they need to learn in the particular content area. You may even begin to see that how that knowledge is known is shifting with the impact of technology.

With the *Huckleberry Finn* unit, the language arts teacher was concerned that students investigate topics of literary style (humor in parodic and satirical forms) of a particular author (Mark Twain) in a particular time of American lives (1850–1900). *The Adventures of Huckleberry Finn* provided the environment for a consideration of controversial issues and literary criticism. Then the teacher considered potential strategies for engaging the students in the content (the learners and pedagogy) amid possible tools for guiding their learning (including the po-

tential of technology in supporting learning). Although the NETS·S standards and performance indicators for technology helped the teacher to think about how technology might be used, a primary concern for the teacher was the students (their backgrounds, experiences, and learning needs) and the school (access to various technologies). Yet, the intersection of all of these concerns is what assures that the unit incorporates technology tools at the appropriate level as integral components of learning the content. Teachers use this technological pedagogical content knowledge (TPCK) to design lessons and units to enhance students' learning at a time when technology is viewed as a powerful tool with enormous potential for supporting the work, communications, learning, and living in the twenty-first century (ISTE, 2000).

Although you may not think that all units should incorporate technology, you need to think about the possibility of assuring that technology is included. Some important questions can be used to guide your thinking about your units.

- What specifically is the focus of the unit and lessons (the subject matter focus)?
- What available technologies might be supportive of learning this subject matter (technology and the subject matter focus)?
- What are the varied learning needs of students as they learn the subject matter (learners and the subject matter focus)?
- How might the technologies be used to help students learn the key subject matter concepts (technology and subject matter focus)?
- Will the technologies alter how students learn the subject matter (technology and the subject matter focus)?
- How should the identified technologies be integrated in the lessons to maintain the importance of learning the subject matter (technology and subject matter integrated with teaching and learning concerns)?
- How should the technology activities be integrated with other student explorations of the concepts (subject matter and technology integrated with teaching and learning concerns)?
- What skills do students need in advance in order for the technologies to support the learning of the key concepts (technology and subject matter integrated with teaching and learning concerns)?
- How should students' knowledge and understanding of the key ideas of the unit be assessed? Should technology be a component of that assessment (subject matter, technology, and teaching and learning)?

As you consider those questions, the NETS student technology standards provide an important perspective in a consideration of technology as a tool for learning. Part II of this text is designed to expand your knowledge of a variety of technologies and, more importantly, to help you think about using those technologies in a variety of ways for incorporating various technologies as tools for learning. These tools can be integral to learning and communications and ultimately prepare your students for their future where technology is an integral component in their lives, work, and continued learning.

Summing It Up

The twenty-first century requires a preparation of the nation's future citizens in markedly different ways than in the past. Students today are engaged in a visual, oral, and textual world that calls for a different conceptualization of what it means to be a literate citizen. Schools are expected to respond with changes in both the tools used to attain this literacy and the curriculum that supports this learning. Students need to learn basic skills with technologies, learn to use technologies in the search for solutions to problems, and basically learn to use technologies to learn.

The National Educational Technology Standards for Students (NETS·S) were developed to promote the use of technology as "an integral component or tool for learning and communications within the context of academic subject areas" (ISTE, 2000, p. 17). Six standard areas describe a breadth of potential uses for teachers to consider in connecting the curriculum with technology.

Students must become proficient in the use of technology, recognizing important social, ethical, and human issues that are related to technology use. Students need to learn to use technology as a productivity tool, a tool that while increasing their productivity also promotes creativity. Students need to use technology as communications tools, utilizing a variety of media and formats to communicate information. Students need to have experiences in using technology research tools, using the tools to locate, collect, process, and evaluate data and information in ways that extend their knowledge of the subject matter and that helps them answer important questions. Students need to think in terms of technology as problem-solving and decision-making tools. As they learn the subject, they need to be involved in experiences where they can use technology for solving real-world problems.

How can students work toward these standards? You, as their future teacher, need to be prepared to guide them in working toward these technology standards. This experience must be framed within the context of their learning of the various subjects asking important questions. What is to be learned and what are the learner's needs? In identifying and designing the curriculum, consider the connection of the NETS·S guidelines with the subject area standards such as those developed for English and language arts, social studies, science, and mathematics. Connecting those standards with the technology standards as you learn about teaching and learning is an important goal for developing your own pedagogical content knowledge for teaching with technology (TPCK)—the knowledge and skills that go beyond simply teaching subject matter content. You are preparing to integrate how you know your subject matter with your knowledge of the technology and of teaching and learning to prepare literate citizens for the twenty-first century.

End-of-the-Chapter Activities and References

PRACTICE PROBLEMS

1. Review the *Huckleberry Finn* unit and extend the technology standards section to incorporate appropriate performance indicators from Figure 4.6.

2. Conduct an online search for technology ideas that might be used in guiding student learning while studying the controversial novel, *The Adventures of Huckleberry Finn*. Describe at least one idea using the format in Figure 4.7.

3. Search the Web or use one of the resources identified in the Annotated Resources section of this chapter to find a lesson idea that engages students in using technology as a tool for learning the subject and grade level you plan to teach. Describe your idea using the format in Figure 4.7.

4. Select one of the electronic standard matrices from the Standard link identified in Technology Link 4.3. Connect the NETS·S technology standards and performance indicators with one grade level in the content area that you plan to teach.

5. Begin your own blog using the instructions in the article by Bull, Bull, and Kajder (see Annotated Resources). In your blog discuss how the particular technologies you are learning in this course can be used to guide students in meeting the student technology standards.

6. Conduct an online search of wikis and blogs to identify how those technologies might support learning in your particular subject area. Record your ideas in the format shown in Figure 4.7.

Computer Beliefs Inventory

Scoring the inventory:

a. Strongly Agree = 5; Agree = 4; Uncertain = 3; Disagree = 2; and Strongly Disagree = 1.

b. Reverse the order of the scores in a for the following items: 4, 6, 7, 13, 14, 15, 16, 17, 18, 19, 23, 24, 25, 26 (i.e., Strongly Agree = 1; . . .; Strongly Disagree = 5).

c. The instrument is intended to measure two distinct constructs (self-efficacy beliefs and outcome expectancy). The two subscales are defined by the following items: Self-efficacy beliefs in Items 1, 2, 4, 6, 7, 9, 11, 13, 17, 19, 22, 24, and 25; Outcome expectancy in Items 3, 5, 8, 10, 12, 14, 15, 16, 18, 20, 21, 23, and 26. Do not add the two subscales together.

SA = Strongly Agree   UN = Uncertain   D = Disagree   A = Agree   SD = Strongly Disagree

1	I know how to use the computer.	SA	A	UN	D	SD
2	I am always finding better ways to use the computer.	SA	A	UN	D	SD
3	If I got better in using the computer, it would help me do better in school.	SA	A	UN	D	SD
4	I am not very good at using a computer.	SA	A	UN	D	SD
5	When students' attitude toward math improves, it is often due to their having learned how to use the computer.	SA	A	UN	D	SD
6	Even when I try hard, I do not use the computer as well as others do.	SA	A	UN	D	SD
7	I generally use the computer poorly.	SA	A	UN	D	SD
8	Learning how to use the computer well would help me in my classes.	SA	A	UN	D	SD
9	I understand what a computer can do well enough to use it correctly.	SA	A	UN	D	SD
10	My success in school work is related to how well I can use a computer.	SA	A	UN	D	SD
11	I know how to use a computer as well as most students.	SA	A	UN	D	SD
12	Learning how to use a computer can help me.	SA	A	UN	D	SD
13	I find it difficult to use a computer.	SA	A	UN	D	SD
14	Learning how to use a computer will not help my future.	SA	A	UN	D	SD
15	It is not worth my time to use a computer.	SA	A	UN	D	SD
16	I will probably never use a computer once I leave school.	SA	A	UN	D	SD
17	Given a choice, I would not let the teacher grade me on using the computer.	SA	A	UN	D	SD
18	It is really not necessary to use a computer.	SA	A	UN	D	SD
19	When I have an assignment which involves a computer, I am usually at a loss as to how to do it.	SA	A	UN	D	SD
20	Computers can be helpful.	SA	A	UN	D	SD
21	I might someday make more money if I learn to use a computer.	SA	A	UN	D	SD
22	I feel comfortable when I use the computer.	SA	A	UN	D	SD
23	Most good jobs do not require computer skills.	SA	A	UN	D	SD
24	I do not know how to use the computer well.	SA	A	UN	D	SD
25	Whenever I can, I would avoid using computers.	SA	A	UN	D	SD
26	Success in school has nothing to do with being able to use the computer.	SA	A	UN	D	SD

IN THE CLASSROOM ACTIVITIES

7. Observe a teacher teaching a lesson where students have hands-on access to technology. Describe how the NETS student technology standards are evident in the lesson.

8. Observe a class where the students are using technology in the lesson. How does the technology help them learn the subject?

9. Interview three students in a class where they have just used technology in their lesson. Ask them to explain what they learned and how the technology helped them in learning those ideas. Create an online blog (see Bull, Bull, & Kajder, 2003, in Annotated Resources) to record your summary of how students learn with technology.

ASSESSING STUDENT LEARNING WITH AND ABOUT TECHNOLOGY

10. Beliefs are the foundation on which attitudes and behavior are built. A Computer Beliefs Inventory, developed by Riggs and Enochs (1993), provides one way to identify students' beliefs about the use of computer technology in learning. Have several students respond to this survey and compare their responses to your observations of them in a classroom

where they are using computers. Discuss how their results on this instrument match their verbally expressed beliefs about learning with technology.

11. Design and prepare a chart that you can use to describe your students' progress with a variety of technologies as they learn with technologies. Be prepared to scan this document to be included in your E-portfolio.

12. Collect from various school districts any written guidelines for legal and ethical technology use. If the schools have computer labs, interview the technology support person. Does any firewall or filtering software to prevent access to specific websites protect the computer systems? If so, what is filtered?

◆Annotated Resources

Bull, G., Bull, G., & Kajder, S. (2003). Writing with weblogs: Reinventing student journals. *Learning and Leading with Technology, 31*(1), 32–35.
Weblogs provide a personal online diary that can be updated on a regular basis. Construct your own blog using online templates that allow you to focus on the writing.

International Society for Technology in Education. (2000). *National educational technology standards for Students: Connecting curriculum and technology.* Eugene, OR: ISTE.
This document provides technology standards for students along with performance indicators, curriculum examples, and scenarios to guide teachers in reconfiguring the curriculum to promote the use of technology as an integral component or tool for learning and communications within the context of academic subject areas.

International Society for Technology in Education. (2002). *National educational technology standards for students: Curriculum series.* Eugene, OR: ISTE.

• *Multidisciplinary Units for Prekindergarten through Grade 2*
• *Multidisciplinary Units for Grades 3–5*
• *Multidisciplinary Units for Grades 6–8*
• *Social Studies Units for Grades 9–12*
• *Science Units for Grades 9–12*

These publications provide a resource for integrating technology in teaching specific content areas and grade levels with conscious attention and connection to the NETS·S technology standards.

Kajder, S., & Bull, G. (2003). Scaffolding for struggling students: Reading and writing with blogs. *Learning and Leading with Technology, 31*(2), 32–35.
This article discusses weblogs (also called blogs) along with their use in teaching reading and writing. Ten instructional activities describe how blogs can be helpful tools for learning in the classroom. As noted, "Blogs provide a multi-genre, multimedia writing space that can engage visually in-need students and draw them into a different interaction with print text. Students at all levels learn to write by writing" (p. 35).

Lee, J., & Molebash, P. (2004). Using digital history for positive change in social studies education. *Journal of Computing in Teacher Education 20*(4), 153–157.
This article is an example of social studies teachers learning to use digital historical inquiry methods integrated in their teaching.

Twain, M., (2001 reprinting). *The Adventures of Huckleberry Finn.* New York: Modern Library, a division of Random House, Inc.
This American classic novel follows the adventures of a youth, Huck Finn, who flees from Pap, his father and the town drunk. The first person voice of Huck tells the intriguing adventures of Huck and Nigger Jim, who is fleeing from slavery, as they pilot their raft on the Mississippi River among dangerous waters, steamboats, and people.

PART II

Connecting Technology with Learning

The illiterate of the twenty-first century will not be those who cannot read and write, but those who cannot learn, unlearn, and relearn.

—*Alvin Toffler*

You along with most teachers today were educated primarily in the twentieth century. When you graduated from high school, your diploma recognized you as being *literate*. This education was primarily without the integration of technology in both what you learned and how you learned it. You may have learned about multiple information and communications technologies and perhaps you consider yourself *computer literate*. Are you *media literate?* As a *literate* citizen for the twenty-first century, you need to be able to read and write using the multitude of current technologies in your communications. Literacy in the twenty-first century requires that you are a critical thinker and creative producer of an increasingly wide range of messages using image, text, and sound along with the ability to locate, access, analyze, evaluate, manipulate, and communicate information effectively in a variety of formats including printed text, graphics, animation, audio, video, and motion.

What other skills, knowledge, and understandings do you need for teaching in the twenty-first century? Does your twentieth-century education adequately support you for teaching in the twenty-first century, a century where new and emerging technologies are impacting what and how students learn in elementary, middle, and high school? Although you may have knowledge and skills about the current technologies, you probably do not have the knowledge and skills for using the technologies for learning. Does that present a problem? Yes, because when you think about the important tools for learning, you are not likely to think about using even current information and communications technologies. In essence, you need to *learn, unlearn, and relearn* about the current and emerging technologies, including ways that the technologies can become integral tools for learning in the subject area that you are planning to teach. You may need to *unlearn* how and what you have learned and *relearn* your subject with the technologies as tools in order to support you as you *learn* with and about the technologies as learning tools. Your experiences will prepare you to be a *literate* teacher in the twenty-first century and are essential for developing your TPCK focused on teaching with and about technology as an integral component in learning.

The goal for this part of the book is to engage you in learning, unlearning, and relearning with some of the key information and communications technologies for teaching in the twenty-first century. These experiences are framed within multiple content areas and multiple grade levels. Each chapter is focused around a technology capability (such as word processing or multimedia) and integrating that in teaching various subjects and grade levels. The emphasis is on exploring how technologies can be used as learning tools that not only support learning the subject matter content but also support learning about specific technologies in meeting the national student technology foundation standards (NETS·S):

I. Basic operations and concepts;
II. Social, ethical, and human issues;
III. Technology productivity tools;
IV. Technology communications tools;
V. Technology research tools; and
VI. Technology problem-solving and decision-making tools.

Classroom suggestions are embedded in language arts, mathematics, science, or social studies lessons for grades K–12 as guides for you as you *learn, unlearn, and relearn* toward integrating technology as an integral tool in teaching and learning.

CHAPTER 5
Writing and Word Processing

Michael Newman/PhotoEdit

Introduction

Readin', Ritin', and Rithmatic—the basic three R's of an educashun. This phrase conveys a message in writing that suggests that the essential knowledge and skills for an educated person in society are reading, writing, and arithmetic. But the written message portrays much more—the times when those skills are considered as essential (the nineteenth century) and perhaps the education and beliefs of the person writing the message.

Learning to read and write has long been an expectation of schooling along with learning to do arithmetic. Teaching arithmetic is typically considered the task of elementary teachers and secondary mathematics teachers and, more often than not, reading and writing are considered curricular tasks for the elementary teachers and secondary language arts teachers. However, as beliefs about how students learn have shifted, so have the beliefs about how students learn best to communicate through reading and writing. Both are forms of communication that students are more apt to learn to read and write within the context of specific subject areas.

With the importance of communication in the twenty-first century, all teachers are expected to think in terms of broader forms of communication (reading and writing, as well as visual and aesthetic communication) as a responsibility of *all* teachers regardless of their subject matter or grade level expertise. Mathematics teachers expect their

students to communicate their processes, conjectures, and reasoning in writing. Science teachers expect their students to explain their lab procedures and their results in writing. In art, students are asked to explain their interpretations of particular pieces. Students in music often write descriptions of composers' intentions in specific musical scores. National standards and high-stakes testing in most content areas have similar expectations. As you plan to guide your students in learning to communicate, you certainly need to include writing as one form of communication, and probably the best and most efficient way to teach writing is within the context of various subject areas.

Communicating in writing requires much more than putting correctly spelled words together in a grammatically correct form. Multiple forms of writing are important in education (e.g., essays, persuasive essays, research reports, plays, outlines, fiction versus nonfiction writing, narrative writing, and creative writing). Students need to learn to write in these different modes since each mode has specific functions, forms, and expectations. Students need instruction that helps them in the prewriting stages to develop their ideas, in revising and editing to clarify and extend those ideas, and finally in the various ways of publishing their work for the greatest impact with the intended audience.

Along with changes in expectations for teaching writing, changes have certainly arisen with the availability of a broader array of tools for writing. Graphite and ink were found to be useful for recording ideas in early ages. But in the 1800s the pencil with an eraser was the primary tool for writing completely changing how student writers could compose. In the twenty-first century, newer technologies, including word processors and desktop publishing software, expanded the collection of writing tools, each offering unique capabilities to support student writers in composing and revising their ideas. Today, in the classroom, word processing is intertwined with the *writing process*—the development of a piece of writing by prewriting, revising, editing, and publishing to an intended audience. These tools allow students to work as writers in fulfilling each of the steps in the writing process within the context of learning in a variety of content areas.

As early as the elementary grades, teachers design their curriculum and instruction to help their students build skills in the writing process. Word processing can be incorporated in this curriculum and instruction in much the same way that paper, pencils, and pens are, that is, within the context of the subject matter. Middle and secondary teachers, not just the language arts teachers, must incorporate activities directed at improving their students' written communications while they also gain additional skills in writing with word processors. With this approach, students have the opportunity to gain essential experiences in improving their communication through writing. Instruction within the context of the different subjects provides the framework for written communication within a context and ultimately enhances learning in that subject.

CHAPTER LEARNING OBJECTIVES

After reading this chapter, you should be able to:

1. Describe basic capabilities of word processors that students need in order to use word processing as a tool for learning.

2. Explain how and why students need to learn to keyboard.

3. Illustrate how word processing can be used to engage students in the writing process: in prewriting, revision and editing, and publishing stages.

4. Identify activities that support learner-centered explorations of content, engaging students in a consideration of social, ethical, and human issues when using word processing as a tool.

5. Describe activities that support learner-centered explorations of content while concurrently engaging students using word processing as a productivity tool, a communications tool, a research tool, or a problem-solving and decision-making tool.

Snapshot of a Classroom Writing with Word Processors

Students in Mrs. Whitaker's tenth-grade English class were working to revise and edit persuasive essays they developed in class over the past two weeks. Their essay topics addressed student-selected issues presenting multiple platforms for a "Great Debate" held at the close of the unit. Mrs. Whitaker also designed this unit to help her students investigate the capabilities of various writing tools for improving their work.

Mrs. Whitaker's primary goal in the lesson was for her students to develop and rethink their drafts. Secondarily, she also wanted students to understand how the word processor can be used to improve their writing, thinking beyond the use of this tool for simply entering text displayed on a screen. Revision and editing stations were formed around the classroom computer lab, each posing "challenges." Students in groups rotated through a minimum of four of the revision and editing stations, applying the strategies and tasks described in their essays. Lianna's group completed all five stations in the time allotted. Her progress shows how the work at each of the stations helped her to revise her essay.

Station 1. Ratiocination

Station 1, *ratiocination*, offered a cluster of five computers where students work as a group, exchanging ideas and responses to what the process reveals about their individual drafts. An instruction sheet posed the expectations for the students to complete individually at their computers:

Ratiocination Editing

1. Change the text color of the first sentence to blue.
2. Change the text color of the second sentence to orange.
   Continue alternating colors throughout the paper. Once you complete that, check for run-ons or fragments. Is there much more of one color than another? Check for varied sentence structure.
3. Copy the first word of each sentence into a second Word document.
   Check for capitalization. Is any word used too often? If so, revise those sentences.
4. Italicize the state of being verbs (am, is, was, were).
   Eliminate half by using active voice.
5. Bold the "rich, complex" words.
   Count and double the number when revising.

Lianna and four other students selected this station for their first activity. Lianna's essay addressed a poem by Robert Graves, and as Figure 5.1 shows, this activity revealed multiple areas where she might revise for clarity, content, and precision.

Station 2. Nutshelling

Mrs. Whitaker identified precision as one of the areas where her students' writing needed the most improvement, explaining, "students typically

---

Lianna's essay development from Station I

"The Legs" by Robert Graves *is* an **interesting** poem. It has a very strong message. The message *is* about life. The person talking in this poem *is* an observer in life. He does not join in with other people, and *is* happy with this, thinking that everyone else is going nowhere. But when he wants people to listen to what he says or does, they do not pay attention. He has distanced himself from everyone so long as they don't really care. Finally, he realizes that it might not be so bad to join in with other people. He does, and likes it so much that he finds it hard to be so bad to join in with other people. He does, and likes it so much that he finds it hard to stop.

The author conveys this message in many ways to the reader. One way the author shows the meaning of this poem *is* through the use of metaphor. In fact, the whole poem *is* one extended metaphor. People in this poem *are* compared to legs when walking down a road. The legs and their activities *are* made to seem **unappealing**, which *is* shown when the author says, "What drew the legs along Was the never-stopping, And the senseless, frightening Fate of being legs." It *is* made to seem like it *is* the "fate" of the people to keep going, *as* if it *were* punishment. The main character *is* not on that road. It says, "On grass By the road-side entire I stood. . . ." This tells us that he *is* apart from everyone else, as if he were standing on the side of the road. But the legs do not pay attention to what he does or says. The author writes, "Though my smile was broad The legs could not see, Though my laugh was loud, The legs could not hear." Then it says, "My head dizzied, then: I wondered suddenly, Might I too be a walker from the legs down?" meaning that maybe if the main character would associate with other people, he could become a "walker" and people would listen to him. The last stanza reads, "Gently, I touched My shins. The doubt unchained them: They had run in twenty puddles before I regained them." He finally joins in and cannot stop.

This extended metaphor *is* the main way for the poem's message to be expressed, but it *is* not the only way. The author also uses lining and format to make the poem more effective. All of the stanzas are made up of four lines and most of the lines are short. This makes the poem seem like legs in an **orderly**, compact way without stopping. The stanzas also read without pauses, like legs coming and going without stopping.

The author also uses rhythm for effect. The rhythm of this poem *is* quick and hardly ever stops. For example, consider the stanza, "Watching the unstoppable, Legs go by, With never a stumble, Between step and step." There *are* no pauses in this stanza. It reads like legs walking on a road without stopping. This stanza *is* read fast, like the speed of the legs described in the poem. The rhythm definitely adds to the **effectiveness** of the poem.

Lastly, the author uses description to enhance the poem and help **convey** its message. For instance, the author describes the legs walking on the road in detail. An example of this *is* when it says, "Watching the unstoppable legs go by With never a stumble Between step and step." The author also describes the road that the legs *are* walking on. For example, the first stanza reads, "There was this road, And it led up-hill, And round in and out." Further, "And the gutters gurgled With rain's overflow, And the sticks on the pavement Blindly tapped and tapped." The description in this poem helps the readers to visualize what *is* happening. This helps express the meaning of this poem and makes it better.

This poem uses figurative language, lining, rhythm, and description to communicate its message. The message *is* clear, which means that the devices in the poem work together to lead somewhere that the use of just one or two wouldn't allow. Further, as a reader, I *am* swept along, almost as if I *am* in the same **trance** as the legs. This *is* Graves' biggest point.

3. First words list (paragraph one):

The

It

The

The

He

But

He

Finally

He

He

FIGURE 5.1   Lianna's work at the ratiocination station.

Further, as a reader, I am swept along, almost as if I am in the same trance as the legs. It's surprising and quite disconcerting, the emotions that I believe Graves deliberately builds into his poem. He doesn't want us to admire the legs. It's a call to resist, to acknowledge our humanness, and to question the paths that we travel. We rarely step out onto the side of the road to reflect upon the journey. This poem creates a space for the reader to do just that.

FIGURE 5.2 Lianna's work on the first sentence of her last paragraph after the nutshelling activity.

have an uncanny knack for writing for pages and pages that don't say much of anything at all." Station 2 began with a challenging quote by Maya Angelou:

> *Putting down on paper what you have to say is an important part of writing, but the words and ideas have to be shaped and cleaned as severely as a dog cleans a bone, cleaned until there's not a shred of anything superfluous.*

Nutshelling, the activity focused on in Station 2, aided in cutting through the superfluous text and getting to the core of the students' thinking. To nutshell, students examined their writing, looking for the one sentence that captured the core ideas they hoped to express. They then copied and pasted that sentence into a second Word document (or an additional page within the document) and wrote from there. This station was motivated by Strickland's (1997, p. 66) comment, "Real writers can't help but cross out, start over, and move things around, and a computer's

word processing facilitates this activity. Only a few keystrokes are needed to delete, copy, move, and rearrange text."

Students in the nutshelling writing center worked collaboratively, color-coding recommended sentences, and passing keyboards to each other to receive help in the development of ideas. Lianna's work is demonstrated in Figure 5.2. Mrs. Whitaker followed Calkins' (1994) recommendation to have students discuss positive rather than negative aspects of their writings: "Why not ask them to find bits of their writing — words, lines, passages—which seem essential, and then ask them to explore why these sections are so very significant?"

Station 3. Devil's Advocate

At the third station, the students worked with a strategy referred to as *devil's advocate*. The instructions asked them to open two windows in their word processor, splitting the full screen equally between their existing essay and a blank document. Working from the content of the original essay, the students used the blank document to write the opposite case, pushing the reasoning and logic and questioning the content of the original piece. Figure 5.3 displays Lianna's work. Mrs. Whitaker explained, "The fusion of the two allows students to locate the flaws in their argument, add depth to their original writing, and to strengthen their reasoning." Although other stations featured collaborative tasks, the students were now expected to work individually, using the opposite case to strengthen the stance of their original document. To conclude this task, the students revised the paragraph in the next row of the table, where they merged the two columns into one.

Lianna's Original Paragraph:
This extended metaphor is the main way for the poem's message to be expressed, but it is not the only way. The author also uses lining and format to make the poem more effective. All of the stanzas are made up of four lines and most of the lines are short. This makes the poem seem like legs in an orderly, compact way without stopping. The stanzas also read without pauses, like legs coming and going without stopping.

Devil's Advocate Comments:
(First, this seems like a weak point—one that I'd attack quickly if I were arguing against it. The writing is awkward.)
The brevity of the lines makes them read as commands, mirroring the instructions that must be followed. They aren't legs. They are simply straightforward, clear instructions—like you'd get in an army. There is no need for a pause because of the needed precision and necessity for each command.

Revised Paragraph:
Where the extended metaphor is a significant method for expressing intended meaning, Graves also takes advantage of line structure and format. All of the stanzas are made up of four lines and most of the lines are short. This leads the lines to read quickly, precisely, and sharply, just like the steps of the marching legs. The stanzas also read without pauses, emphasizing the mindless following insisted upon and practiced by the legs.

FIGURE 5.3 Lianna's revised paragraph as a result of the devil's advocate work.

Station 4. Swapping Conclusions for Introductions

In the fourth station, Mrs. Whitaker challenged the students to swap their *conclusions for introductions*. Each student cut the conclusion of the essay and pasted it as the introduction. This change effectively moved the real *meat* of the essay to the beginning, allowing the students to revise the essay from the best points of the previous draft. Lianna's work at this station is shown in Figure 5.4.

Station 5. Exploding Sentences

Revision is often the most difficult of the writing tasks for students to understand.

> To students, the process of revision usually means to write the composition neater this time and to use only one side of the paper and . . . oh, yes, check the spelling. But using the computer in class to demonstrate the revision process can change students' perception and understanding suddenly, dramatically, and permanently. (Golub, 1999)

Heard (2003) extended these ideas, explaining that revision "involves changing the meaning, content, structure or style of a piece of writing rather than the more surface changes that editing demands" (p. 1). Word processors supported them in engaging their writing in a more visual, compelling way.

Mrs. Whitaker framed the instructions for the *exploding sentences* station on ideas she gathered from Heard's book. The instructions read as follows:

> Consider one of two possible plans of attack for revision of *position* sentences that make claims without much explanation:

> **1.** Explode the sentence into a slow-motion retelling of the piece. This process helps to develop an argument or explain how evidence actually provides support for your position.

> **Lianna's Conclusions for Introductions Outline:**
>
> Robert Graves' poem, "The Legs," uses figurative language, lining, rhythm, and description to communicate its message. The message is clear, which means that the devices in the poem work together to lead somewhere that the use of just one or two wouldn't allow. Further, as a reader, I am swept along, almost as if I am in the same trance as the legs. This is Graves' biggest point.
>
> I. Extended metaphor
>   a. Unappealing legs (with quote)
>   b. Distance from the road (with quote)
>   c. Lack of control (with quote)
> II. Lining and rhythm
>   a. Short length
>   b. Precision
>   c. (Need to pull from former paragraph) Pace/march
> III. Description
>   a. Road (Note: This is important because we need to see the road, it's length, and the way it winds on and on.)
>   b. Legs (Note: This is important because if we can't understand the bodiless, mindless legs, the whole point of the poem is missed.)
>   c. Gutters (Note: I read this as reflective of the hopelessness of the situation and the following. The legs are drowning in misery that they don't seem to feel anymore.)
> IV. Interpretation/conclusion

FIGURE 5.4 Lianna's effort after swapping the conclusion and introduction of her essay.

> **2.** Explore the sentence and consider it as a magnifying glass for identifying and pinpointing targeted specifics to improve the development of your position.

Lianna's work in the exploding sentence station is shown in Figure 5.5.

Former Sentence:	Exploded Sentence:
1. The author conveys this message in many ways to the reader.	1. Graves exercises his craft through the use of extended metaphor, lining, rhythm, and description, demanding that the reader break from routine and pay mindful attention.
2. The main character is not on that road.	2. The speaker is not on the road, allowing him to witness and closely describe the senseless routine of the followers.
3. He finally joins in and cannot stop.	3. Though he has witnessed and argued against the mindless path taken by the followers, the speaker is unable to resist, joining into the lines and losing the limited control that he exercised earlier in the poem.
4. The description in this poem helps the readers to visualize what is happening.	4. It is only through description that we can see the headless, mindless legs, feel the hopelessness of the road they follow, and experience the seductive rhythm and pace that calls us to join in the march.
5. This is Graves' biggest point.	5. The entire poem drives us to this, that there is something inherently human and easy in the act of following, and that our possibilities lie in our ability to step outside and see.

FIGURE 5.5 Lianna's work at the exploding sentence station.

Basic Operations and Concepts of Word Processing

The word processor is a tool for writing, designed primarily for communication with words and graphics in written form. A word processor is a computer application that has not only replaced the typewriter but has supplanted it with its capabilities and versatility. In fact, you might not have ever used a typewriter as a student writer. Although both the typewriter and the word processor use a keyboard for text entry, their similarities quickly diminish from that point. With word processors, the writer prepares the document on a display screen, deletes and changes information directly within the document, and then electronically stores the document for distribution, perhaps printing on paper and saving for future needs. Basically, a word processor is designed for the writer to create, edit, format, and present documents in written form.

Desktop publishing software contains word processing capabilities that also support writers in the communication of ideas through text and page appearance. With advancements in technology, the distinctions between word processors and desktop publishers have blurred. Both are used to design, produce, and deliver documents containing text, color, and graphics. Capabilities for arranging text and graphics in a document, at one time considered the advantage of desktop publishers, are capabilities now available in word processors. The one advantage that desktop publishers have over word processors is the treatment of pages as separate entities to allow ease in formatting and placing the pages. Text in word processors is developed in a continuous stream of pages requiring the writer to scroll through the text for viewing, editing, and formatting pages. However, rather than focusing on the distinctions between the two types of tools, it is far more useful for teachers to focus students on the process of improving and enhancing their written communications—a writing process that involves creating, editing, formatting, and publishing as a means of communicating ideas.

Basic Operations in Word Processing

Creating documents in a word processor requires some form of data entry, usually with a keyboard. Touch-sensitive screens provide a form of data entry for the early grades where children can touch objects they wish to include in a story they are composing. Some audio input is available, but that technology has been difficult to perfect because of complexities with voice recognition as a result of accents, dialects, and languages.

Today, the most common method for creating written materials is via keyboarding, exposing an issue of teaching keyboarding skills. Should keyboarding be taught? If so, who teaches it, when, and how? Elementary and middle school levels seem to be the places where keyboarding is more commonly integrated with a computer/technology literacy curriculum. More and more, *technology* teachers work with content-area teachers to identify the context and needed skills for working with keyboarding and the computer.

An elementary school technology teacher described the design of her curriculum this way: "The librarian and I each get an outline for the classroom teachers' curriculums and then we spend time planning projects between the two of us and the classroom teachers. This way, we can integrate what the students are learning, reinforcing the curriculum while bringing in technical skills." Using this process, they focused their attention on designing a progression for developing keyboarding skills over grades K–6 within the context of supporting the classroom activities.

Each task described in Figure 5.6 is linked to a valuable, authentic curricular project connected to content standards. The students are not expected to create a class book just to demonstrate their keyboarding skills, nor do they use software teaching them to find the "I" key during instructional time.

Ease of editing continues to be the attraction of word processors over typewriters and pens. In the Snapshot of a Classroom Writing with Word Processors, Mrs. Whitaker's tenth-grade students work to revise their essays, investigating their writing through a variety of techniques. They use different colors for every other sentence, copied text, italicized verbs, and bolded "upper level" words to view their essays differently than with just plain text. Students see *nutshelling* and playing *devil's advocate* as authentic parts of a writer's work, made more accessible and efficient with the editing features of the word processor: deleting, copying, moving, and rearranging text. Even rewriting the essay beginning with the *conclusion as the introduction* does not seem to be a daunting task with the editing features of the word processor. These activities guide students not only in learning to use some of the editing capabilities of the word processor but also in learning to use those capabilities to improve their writing. Maintaining a focus on writ-

Grade	Keyboarding	Subject Context
Kindergarten	• Introduction of the keyboard and its keys	• A class book describing *what I will be*
First Grade	• Introduction to the keyboard, correct hand position, and correct body posture • Introduction to the home row keys • Introduction to word processing	• ABC book project
Second Grade	• Introduction to the right and left division of the keyboard • Introduction to the keyboarding with the top and bottom row keys	• Personalize a poem by changing words and phrases
Third Grade	• Reinforcement of keyboarding with correct hand and body position and correct finger placement (home row, top row, and bottom row keys)	• How am I like and different from my mother, father, sister, or brother (display text in a Venn diagram)
Fourth, Fifth, and Sixth Grades	• Reinforcement of proper keyboarding skills	Fourth Grade: Fiction book report Fifth Grade: Investigation of Native American myths Sixth Grade: Newsletter about ancient Egyptians

FIGURE 5.6   Curriculum outline prepared in collaboration with content area teachers.

ing and thinking skills, when more advanced word processors are developed or even whatever technology replaces the word processor, supports those thinking skills and the writing skills in the proper perspective.

Formatting tools provide student authors with a variety of ways to present their written messages. The font type, color, style, and size are just a few of the changes that students can use to manipulate the text format and its message. Graphics can even be embedded in the text to focus attention, convey information, and add interest in the idea.

Even in a mathematics class, students can use various word processing features in ways that help them make sense of problems. Students often have difficulty when reading mathematics problems, getting confused when translating the words into some method for solving the problem. Figure 5.7 shows how students use the formatting tools to explain the words in the problem as they work toward a solution. The technique is similar to that used by Mrs. Whitaker's students as they revised their essays in the Snapshot of a Classroom Writing with Word Processors. For mathematics, however, students' difficulties are in translating the words to a mathematical form. Part of the difficulty is that, when solving word problems, students typically overlook important words. Coloring the different numbers to represent the hats of the respective colors helps highlight that some of

the numbers are percents and others are the actual numbers. Another part of their difficulty is that they do not focus on what they are being asked to

---

The Hat Problem

Problem:
Today was hat day for our class of 40. In our class, 10% of the hats were red, 20% were blue, 25% were green, 5 students had orange hats, and the rest of the class had black hats. How many black hats were brought to class today?

Reformatting the problem:
Today was hat day for our class of **40**. In our class, **10% (of the hats)** were **red**, **20% (of the hats)** were **blue**, **25% (of the hats)** were **green**, 5 students had orange hats, and the **rest of the class** had **black** hats. <u>How many **black hats** <u>were brought to class today</u>?</u>

Rephrasing the problem:
   40 = number of hats in the class
   B = number of black hats
   B = 40 − [10%(40) + 20%(40) + 25%(40) + 5]
   B = 40 − [0.10(40) + 0.20(40) + 0.25(40) + 5]

Finding the solution:
   B = 40 − [4 + 8 + 10 + 5]
   B = 40 − [27]
   B = 13 or there were 13 black hats brought to class today.

FIGURE 5.7   Formatting the text to aid in interpreting and solving a mathematics problem.

find; underlining and making the font larger for the important question in the problem helps with this difficulty.

Publishing is another capability of word processors. Students typically publish their written communications in one of two ways: on paper or electronically. Some printers support color and others do not, making the consideration of the type of printer an issue when writing the document. If color is important in the communication as it is in Station 1 of Snapshot of a Classroom Writing with Word Processors, then looking at a noncolored printout would not help the students see the ratio of one color to the other. Viewing it electronically does. If students want to save a copy of the document to demonstrate their progress with the activity, then they may want to save it in an electronic portfolio developed over the course of the year as a demonstration of their writing improvement. Or, they may elect to save the document in a Web page format for publication on their website. If they want to send a copy to others electronically, they might choose to save the document in a format that is more easily read as an attachment in e-mail, such as in a rich text format (RTF). In each case, the means of publishing impacts their writing and must be considered as the last stage of the writing process.

Learning with and about Writing with Technology

The Snapshot of a Classroom Writing with Word Processors demonstrates several word processing activities designed to guide students as they revise their written work. As they explore their own writing, they also gain facility with word processors. They change the colors of the text, copy and paste words and phrases and even entire paragraphs, and use multiple documents to challenge the assertions in a paragraph. Further, keyboarding is an important skill in using a word processor. As students learn to use the keyboard, they can compose essays and reports for some of their work in each of the different subject areas they are studying, such as social studies, science, language arts, and even mathematics. As they explore different problems, they begin to recognize word processors as more than just a tool for learning in their language arts classes. They see the word processor as a writing tool where they must consider its social, ethical, and human issues as well as increasing and enhancing their productivity and communications. They also can use this writing tool as a research tool and a problem-solving and decision-making tool as they learn in various subject areas. The important consideration, however, is thinking of the word processor as a writing tool—considering the basic concepts of writing that can be included as they work with a myriad of subject area problems. In other words, learning to write with a word processor needs to be embedded throughout the curricula as students learn to write within the context of the different subject areas.

Basic Concepts of the Writing Process

Although research on word processing in education has been mixed, the results do suggest a positive impact in two areas: improvement in the quality of writing and the development of students' improved attitudes toward writing (Bangert-Drowns, 1993; Snyder, 1993). With the various capabilities of the word processor, students are writing more and are more willing to make revisions. Activities such as those in the Snapshot of a Classroom Writing with Word Processors encourage students to reconsider their writing as they learn more about the features of the word processor for improving their writing. With the advancements in this technology, teachers, regardless of content area, ask students to write more and have higher expectations about the quality of that writing. Increasingly, teachers are incorporating the process of writing in their instruction as a means of guiding students who are learning to work as writers using a writing process that includes prewriting, revision and editing, and publishing.

Word Processing Instructional Ideas: Prewriting
Student writers insist that simply getting started is the hardest part in writing. Why? Student writers often question what they have to say. Lucy Calkins (1994) clarifies, "The powerful thing about working with words is that we are really working with our thoughts. Writing allows us to put our thoughts on the page and in our pockets; writing allows us to pull back and ask questions of our thoughts." Student writers need space to explore their thoughts and to test how they look on paper (or, with word processing, on the screen). Writers use prewriting to rehearse mentally, verbally, and on paper, to discover the voice and form that lead them in communicating ideas. Donald Murray (1994) describes prewriting as "everything that takes place before the first draft" and as the phase

of writing that "takes about 85% of a writer's time." Adding the computer into the mix not only provides additional efficient tools for brainstorming and organizing ideas but it lowers the stakes and raises students' engagement.

Five Minute Monitors-Off Free Writing   Free writing is described in several different ways, from "quick writing" to "invisible writing" to "tactile writing." Perhaps these ways are best described through Gertrude Stein's mantra: "To write is to write is to write is to write is to write is to write is to write." Prewriting allows students to do just that. For this activity, students turn off their monitors and, in a quiet classroom, focus intensely on "screen-less" writing. With practice, they experience fluency and flow while also lessening the need for control over their writing (Ayers, 2002). Students who were completely "blocked" open up with this freedom, no longer confined or overwhelmed by the blank screen. As Shayla, a ninth-grade English as a Second Language (ESL) student, writes, "Monitors-off writing allows me to concentrate on my thoughts and figuring out what I have to say. I don't have to worry about translation or grammar or how my work looks—I simply think about what I want to say."

Collaborative Free Writing   Working collaboratively as a full class prompts students to brainstorm, building ideas from the ideas offered by others in their classroom community. Instead of calling out ideas and listing them on a whiteboard, students think about writing by writing. In a small-group, collaborative activity, student teams pass the keyboard around while clustered about a workstation. Alternatively, with access to a computer lab, teachers can provide students the opportunity to roam from computer to computer at a cue. Students liken this activity to a writer's version of musical chairs—only, now, no one is "out." These activities can be done with word processors or even concept map software such as Inspiration and Kidspiration to generate graphic organizers or mindmaps. Figure 5.8 suggests a concept map prompt for engaging students in a prewriting stage when they are preparing to write a new fairy tale. This tale is to be about Goldilocks and three different animals: a monkey, an elephant, and a lion. Students are to brainstorm what actions might happen with each animal.

Word Processing Instructional Ideas: Revision and Editing   Although Donald Murray (1982) argues that writing is rewriting, students often do not see revision as an opportunity to develop and improve a piece of writing. Rather they see rewriting as an indication that they have failed to write the paper right the first time. For them, revision means correction.

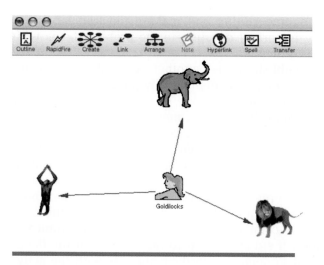

FIGURE 5.8   Goldilocks Inspiration concept map prompt to encourage student brainstorming.

Golub (1999) suggests that students' vision of incorporating the computer at this stage is that they need to "write the composition neater this time and to use only one side of the paper and. . . oh, yes, check the spelling."

On the contrary, revision is not editing. They are separate steps. One is "rethinking" and the other looking at word choice, grammar, semantics, and syntax. Students are able to use features of a word processor, such as cutting and pasting, spell check, and grammar check, as both revision and editing tools. But word processors can be used in several other ways to aid them in revising the writing. Golub recommends computer-based technologies, like word processors, as a way to demonstrate the revision process and change "students' perception and understanding suddenly, dramatically, and permanently." Actually, a word processing tool helps to lead students through the differences between the processes of revision and editing, each with distinctly different sets of tasks for them to consider in the development of all of their writing.

Revision on the computer can sometimes cause student writers to lose sight of the drafting process in that they continually retool and revise using a single copy of the writing. Encourage them to keep track of their drafts so they can later examine how their work evolved by adopting a coding system such as "name of piece (version 1.0)." For example, the initial draft of this chapter is saved as *chapterfive(v1)* and successive drafts are saved as *chapterfive(v2), chapterfive(v3), chapterfive(v4),* . . . . With this strategy students not only see how the written piece develops, they have previous versions that they may want to resurrect. Another strategy might be to set up a wiki for each student's writing space. In this environment, each successive draft is saved, allowing the writer the opportunity to revisit a previous version more easily.

Writer's Journal   While students are writing, encourage them to maintain another document: a writer's journal. In their writer's journal, they record ideas along with reflections on the process of writing a particular piece or even ideas for its development. As they are writing on the computer, suggest that they keep both their writer's journal and the "new" piece open. Reflection allows student writers to gain additional control over the thinking that runs throughout their work. The journal permits them to question their own wording and ideas in a way that helps them discover "what they're doing well—and what they need to improve—their subsequent performance can incorporate these important insights and lead to greater control" (Golub, 1999).

Nutshelling   The most difficult skill for students to learn is to write *precisely*. They have an uncanny knack for writing for pages and pages without saying much of anything at all. Nutshelling is one of the strategies used in the Snapshot of a Classroom Writing with Word Processors. This strategy aids students in cutting through the superfluous text and getting to the core of their thoughts. With this strategy, they examine their writing, looking for the one sentence that captures the core ideas they are trying to express. They then begin with that sentence and write from there. Word processors make color-coding, cutting, and manipulating text as easy as a keystroke, making this strategy quick and effective.

Color-Coding Topic Sentences   Again, when writing with a word processor, revising and editing are made more accessible and efficient. Strickland (1997, p. 66) writes, "Real writers can't help but cross out, start over, and move things around, and a computer's word processing facilitates this activity. Only a few keystrokes are needed to delete, copy, move, and rearrange text." With a word processor, students can be directed to color-code their drafts, for example, highlighting topic sentences in green, supporting details in red, and transitions in blue. This process ensures, first, that these elements all exist in the paper and, second, that students are actively thinking about how they are using and identifying these components. Make the colors a standard in each piece of writing, and use the strategy in peer reviews and conferences as well.

Highlight Your Text with Color	
Green	Topic sentences
Red	Supporting details
Blue	Transitions

Conclusions for Introductions   Many writers often begin writing by writing for a few pages before really figuring out what it is that they have to say. Student writers are the same. When it comes to revising their work, cutting the conclusion of their essay and pasting it for the introduction is a technique that encourages moving the real *meat* and discovery of the writing to the beginning. Then the students are more apt to develop a new draft from the best points of their previous draft. Though this activity is initially met with groans, students later see the fruits of the increased labor. Figure 5.4 in the Snapshot of a Classroom Writing with Word Processors presents Lianna's new outline for her persuasive essay as a result of using this strategy.

Combining Sentences   Text is easily manipulated with a word processor. Students can work to alter the structure of their sentences using both the insert and delete features available in the spaces of existing sentences. Although drill and practice sentence-combining software does exist, this strategy is more effective for students to do within the context of their own writing. Begin by having them open some text and review the techniques in a short lesson. Then challenge them to work with their own essays to examine, manipulate, and enrich the sentences.

Database of Effective Transitions and Great Leads   Mark Twain explained, "The difference between the right word and the wrong word is the difference between lightning and the lightning bug." Help trigger student writers' thinking and repository of effective words and phrases by encouraging them to reference a class-constructed database filled with effective transitions, leads, and strong verbs and descriptors.

Comments in Hidden *Fields*   Regardless of whether students receive feedback from teachers or peer reviewers, it is difficult for them to take negative comments and engage in revising their work. Instead, they get locked into editing while dismissing the negative comments as a product of an *unfair reading*. Atwell (1998) explains, "Writers are vulnerable. Our essential selves are laid bare for the world to see. Writers want response that gives help without threatening." Calkins (1994) recommends that students discuss positive rather than negative aspects of their writings. "Why not ask them to find bits of their writing—words, lines, passages—which seem essential, and then ask them to explore why these sections are so very significant?" Student writers can begin by using the embedded comment features in a word processor to annotate their own writing. Peer readers then insert their comments, sharing their reactions to the ideas. When student writers start the dialogue with their readers, they are more open to other areas of discussion.

Devil's Advocate   A devil's advocate station was one station in Mrs. Whitaker's class in Snapshot of a Classroom Writing with Word Processors. At that station (Figure 5.3), Lianna opened two documents in her word processor, effectively splitting the screen into two columns. She posted a paragraph from her original essay in one column. Then, she used the other to write the opposite case, challenging the reasoning and logic and questioning the content of the original paragraph. Through this process she was able to locate flaws in her argument, and she rewrote the paragraph adding depth and strength to her reasoning in a second row of the table where she merged the cells to have an entire row for the paragraph.

Word Processing Instructional Ideas: Publishing the Writing   After revising and editing their writings, students need to consider communication in published form. This portion of the writing process requires much more than simply printing the piece on the printer. Challenge students to enhance their written communication to assist readers in understanding the ideas. Are the points made with simple text? Should some words be highlighted for emphasis? Would colored text help? Would graphics help the presentation? Should the lines be both left- and right-justified? Could a table or graph help in presenting some ideas more clearly? Are the page breaks appropriate? Many of these changes are made using the editing and formatting features of a word processor.

Enhance Presentations with Graphics or Digital Images   A simple means to enhance student work is to add graphics and images before printing on the classroom printer or posting to the Web. The trick is to make sure that the added *bells and whistles* supplement and enrich the content, not distract the readers' focus or lead them down a side path. Word processors have formal ways for inserting images and graphics. However, the low-tech version also works: Simply cut and paste a digital image. Students can use a scanner or even take a picture with a digital camera to get the electronic image they want. They do need to be sure to credit the source if the image or graphic is not created from scratch.

Consider a Variety of Audiences   Often students think they are writing only for teachers. Without specific directions, students tend to publish their writing in a traditional manner: printing and stapling the pages in the upper left-hand corner or perhaps placing the pages in a folder. Incorporate the audience in the assignments to engage them in thinking beyond this tradition. Lots of ideas can challenge them to think about the community be-

yond the classroom. Brochures, newspapers, and booklets are just a few different publishing forms:

- Create a travel brochure along the Oregon Trail to describe towns, events, and sights, encouraging people to consider reenacting the famous trip. Distribute the brochure to the various chambers of commerce along the Oregon Trail.
- Create the *Salem Sentinel* newspaper as it might have appeared in Salem, Massachusetts, in 1692 (the time of the Salem witchcraft trials) as an anticipatory activity prior to studying Miller's *The Crucible.*
- Create a brochure of animal life in a *protected* area near your town. For each animal include pictures, a description of its habitats, and its protection needs. Share the brochure with community members to help inform them of this protected area.
- Compile student poetry into a class literary magazine. Print in both an electronic and paper form.
- Prepare a business plan for implementing an original business idea. Be prepared to present the plan to a panel of business executives.
- Collect histories of residents of the area, publishing the histories with digital images of the interviewees along with photos and memorabilia to enhance their story. Share these histories with the community historical society as well as with the interviewees.

By encouraging students to publish their work in a variety of ways, you also have the opportunity to teach some of the basics of design and layout when using word processors to achieve these results.

Electronic Portfolios   Portfolios are purposeful collections of a student's work over time. Typically, the collections are of the students' *best* work, perhaps including drafts of various pieces leading to that best work that demonstrates their growth and development in particular classes. These collections are often more manageable in an electronic form. Electronic portfolios have proved invaluable for students in college interviews, providing a succinct means of presenting an information-rich source that describes their progress in previous educational situations.

Encourage students to save their work in the school server space and to periodically copy the collection to a CD (Compact Disc). Have the students create their own table of contents, include reflective writing about each piece, add evaluations made by teachers and peers, and include original art, photos, and illustrations. Encourage students to serve as peer reviewers for each other. Areas in the portfolio can be provided for readers to make direct comments, provide feedback, and even include their own writing. In this manner, the electronic portfolio becomes an organic compilation allowing both the writer and readers to work interactively through each piece.

An electronic portfolio (often referred to as an e-portfolio) also provides an idea for you as you prepare to teach with technology. This book is designed to support you in the development of a publication about your growth in preparing to teach with technology. Thus, throughout the book you will be creating many artifacts that you might compile as electronic artifacts as described in Resource Idea: Electronic Portfolio in Figure 5.9. Besides saving the files electronically from word-processed documents, most word processors have a feature for saving files as a Web page. You can use this feature to develop your own website portfolio or simply publish your electronic portfolio on a CD. The End-of-the-Chapter Activities and References section for each chapter of this book includes specific ideas for E-Portfolio Activities. Consider these ideas as starting points for collecting artifacts to provide evidence of your progress with the National Educational Technology Standards for Teachers (NETS·T; ISTE, 2002). Such an electronic portfolio provides an effective, concise compilation for presenting you as a teacher ready to integrate technology in your teaching. Potential school personnel looking for new teachers appreciate seeing these portfolios as a demonstration of knowledge, skills, and preparation for a possible teaching position.

Social, Ethical, and Human Issues

What social, ethical, and human issues are of concern with computer-based technologies such as word processing? The Web provides a myriad of sites to locate and copy pictures. The Web also provides

---

Resource Idea: Electronic Portfolio

Title: An Electronic Portfolio Describing a Teacher's Preparation to Teach

Topic: Teaching with Technology

Grade: Teacher preparation for all grades

Objectives: Student teachers compile and publish a purposeful collection of artifacts providing evidence of their progress with the six NETS standards for teachers.

Idea: Student teachers gather artifacts for an electronic portfolio that contains artifacts demonstrating the growth and development in preparing to teach with technology. The electronic portfolio is framed by the six teacher technology standards:

1. Technology Operations and Concepts

2. Planning and Designing Learning Environments and Experiences

3. Teaching, Learning, and the Curriculum

4. Assessment and Evaluation

5. Productivity and Professional Practice

6. Social, Ethical, Legal, and Human Issues

Throughout their preparation program, student teachers gather a variety of electronic artifacts within the six standards. Lesson plans, essays, reflections, worksheets, and other specific ideas for teaching at the specific grade level and in specific subject areas are maintained in an electronic composite of the artifacts and, periodically, student teachers review the collection to find the best pieces of evidence and the organization that best represents their progress in each standard area. At the completion they prepare a summary reflection for each standard explaining how the artifacts provide evidence of their progress. A final reflection summarizes and analyzes the evidence and their preparation for teaching with technology. The final portfolio is recorded on a CD that also contains information about the student teacher as an introduction to the portfolio and information for viewing the portfolio.

Materials: Network space for collecting the electronic artifacts, CD, a variety of computer-based technology resources

Modifications:

1. Prepare an electronic portfolio that demonstrates progress in a specific course.

2. Publish the electronic portfolio on a student teacher website that allows the user to click on the subject area and grade level to view the various portfolios.

3. Develop an electronic portfolio using the NETS student technology standards as the organizer.

FIGURE 5.9   Format for describing a resource idea.

In the Classroom 5.1

A PICTURE IS WORTH A THOUSAND WORDS

TECHNOLOGY OBJECTIVE: **NETS·S I, II, III, IV, V**

- **Internet, word processor:** Technology as a communications, productivity, and research tool while also focusing on social, human, and ethical issues.
- Use a word processor to express thinking elicited by a picture gathered electronically, appropriately referencing the picture.

CONTENT OBJECTIVE: **Science:** Students demonstrate an understanding about science and technology, specifically that technological solutions have intended benefits and unintended consequences.

Social studies: Students identify and describe historical examples of the interaction and interdependence of science, technology, and society.

Language arts: Students apply a wide range of strategies to comprehend, interpret, evaluate, and appreciate text in the form of a picture.

GRADE LEVEL: 6–12

PICTURE EVENT: The explosion of atomic bombs in Hiroshima and Nagasaki, Japan, in 1945.

PROBLEM: What was the impact of the explosion of the atomic bomb on society?

- ❏ Find a picture of the event, copy and paste it into your written document, and appropriately reference the picture. Use Technology Link 5.1 to obtain the picture.

- ❏ Prepare an essay of 1000 words that uses the picture event to discuss intended and unintended consequences of the dropping of atomic bombs on Hiroshima and Nagasaki.

- ❏ Revise your essay using at least two of these strategies:

   1. Nutshelling   **2.** Conclusions for introductions   **3.** Devil's advocate

   Save the different versions of your essay in separate files for inclusion in your electronic portfolio [essay_title(v.1), essay_title(v.2), and essay_title(v.3)].

- ❏ Publish your essay in two formats:

   1. Written, using double space, placing your name and date in the header and the word count and page numbers in the footer.

   2. Electronically, in your portfolio, where you include the various versions resulting from the revision stage and the final version that you printed.

---

students with easy access to *well-researched and high quality* essays, written for them by *experienced writers*. With the copy and paste features of computer technology, students can easily copy phrases, pictures, and other ideas created by others and use those items to enhance their own ideas. Are these responsible uses of the technology?

Students need to understand that although the ideas of others, including experienced writers, may seem to be more eloquent, their writing assignments are designed to help them develop and practice the skills to improve their own writing and thinking. In this vein, you need to guide your students in understanding the difference between paraphrasing and plagiarizing. Focusing students on the writing process (prewriting, revision and editing, and publishing) discourages them from using the writings of others as their own. More importantly, a consistent emphasis in all classes throughout the grades results in students appropriately using word processing technologies and provides a greater likelihood of develop-

ing a positive attitude toward using word processing technology as a tool for improving their writing.

With the impact of technology on society, the school curriculum needs to include consideration of social, ethical, and human issues with technology. The curriculum needs to incorporate a consideration of both current and historical examples of the interaction and interdependence of science, technology, and society in a variety of cultural settings. Student writing is an important activity that provides them with opportunities to express their expanding knowledge and understanding about this interdependence. Further, the greater range of publishing options and audiences presents challenges—and opportunities to exercise their independence.

Word Processing Instructional Ideas: Science, Technology, and Society   In the Classroom 5.1 is an example of a multidisciplinary activity concerned with important social, human, and ethical issues of technology, in this case, the dropping of two atomic bombs on Hiroshima and Nagasaki, Japan, in 1945. Students are asked to prepare a 1000-word essay using a picture of one of the atomic bombs dropped on Japan as a prompt; the essay is focused on their interpretation of the intended and unintended consequences of the use of the atomic bombs.

As the students review their essays using at least two of the revision strategies to improve their essays, they are able to refine their thoughts and arguments. Of course they need some instructional support first in framing their understanding and ideas and second in rethinking their ideas. Guide them in investigating the question of the consequences of the technological solution. They can search the Web for various points of view about the use of the atomic bomb; they can interview people from their local areas, gathering their perspectives on the issues identified through their Web searches; they can use primary sources to consider the rationale of President Harry S. Truman and his advisors for using the bomb (sources such as those found in Technology Link 5.1). Similar investigations provide them opportunities to seek and study the perspectives of a variety of others and to report those ideas appropriately. Provide time for them to publicly share their findings and results of their investigations. Engage them in a consideration of the credibility of the sources for their ideas as well as biases in the sources they identify. This emphasis supports responsible uses of technology systems and information. The essays they write serve as the culmination for their consideration of the interaction and interdependence of science, technology, and society—an activity that focuses on developing their understanding of the ethical, cultural, and societal issues related to technology in the broadest terms.

Technology Link 5.1

*T*he Truman Library contains several documents about the atomic bomb. A link to the library is available at this book's website. The **Truman** link connects you to a website where you can conduct a search on the atomic bomb for a special presentation on the decision to drop the bomb.

www.wiley.com/college/niess

Word Processing as a Productivity Tool

Word processing is particularly useful in learning to use technology as a productivity tool. This application provides a broad array of features for students to use to express their thinking and ideas, including but not limited to text, color, and graphics.

From a constructivist's viewpoint, students actively construct their own understandings of ideas and concepts from a variety of experiences, intended or unintended. Teachers need to support students with a variety of experiences differing in outward appearance while still retaining the basic conceptual structure so that they can begin to make essential connections. Encouraging a variety of publication options is one way to have them display and communicate their knowledge and understanding in various ways.

Assignments directing students to produce an expression of their understandings in different formats offer ways for them to consider how they can use technology as a productivity tool. Different display formats can motivate and engage their creative spirit and ultimately provide them with the variety needed to help them make important connections. Moreover, multiple opportunities using word processing help them gain a perspective of the technology as a productivity tool.

Word Processing Instructional Ideas: Estimation in Metric Units   The United States uses two measurement systems: the metric system and the customary system. Students are more familiar with the customary system with its inches, feet, and yards, but they must learn to use the metric system since that system is used worldwide. In the Classroom 5.2 is an activity to guide students in gaining important experiences with measurements in the metric system. As a result, they are better able to make estimates in that system. Because of multiple experiences with measurements in inches, they are better able to imagine lengths in inches. If they are asked to imagine 5 centimeters (cm), however, they often have difficulty because of their lack of experiences with this system. This activity gives them some experiences designed to build their estimation skills in the metric system. In the process they also use the capabilities of the word processor as a productivity tool. For this activity, they use tables in the word processor for recording and organizing their estimates and measurements and they produce a new set of objects for estimation and measurement. For this part of the activity they copy and paste graphics, sizing the graphics appropriately so that they create a one-page printed document of another 10 objects similar to the object worksheet in Figure 5.10. Trading their new

FIGURE 5.10   Objects worksheet for Estimation Activity One of In the Classroom 5.2.

In the Classroom 5.2

ARE YOU GOOD AT ESTIMATION?

TECHNOLOGY OBJECTIVE: **NETS·S I, II, III, IV, V**

- **Word processor:** Technology as a communications, productivity, and research tool.
- Create a table and design worksheets that contain digital graphics.

CONTENT OBJECTIVE: **Mathematics:** Understand attributes, units, and systems of measurement and make reasonable estimates of length.

Science: Work with and estimate measurements in the metric system.

GRADE LEVEL: 5–9

PROBLEM: Investigate your ability to estimate measurements of length in the metric system. How good are you at estimation?

❑ With the printed worksheet (as in Figure 5.10), estimate the lengths of the objects in centimeters. Record your estimates in a table in a word-processed document.

Object	Estimate (cm)	Measurement (cm)	Difference
1. Width of the school crosswalk sign at the base			
2. Longest length measurement of the football			
3. Length of the pen from the tip to the cap			
4. Height of the wastepaper basket (without the paper)			
5. Height of the tack, not including the point			
6. Circumference of Earth			
7. Length of the diagonal of the calculator			
8. Height of the flask			
9. Length of the scissors (the cutting portion to the joint, not including the handle)			
10. The width of the envelope			

❑ **Estimation Activity One**
- ○ Measure the objects with a centimeter ruler and record in the appropriate portion of the table.
- ○ Find the difference: Estimate − Measurement.
- ○ Evaluate the results to answer the question of whether you are a good estimator with centimeters. Do you over- or underestimate? Do you overestimate with larger objects or smaller ones? Explain your results.

❑ Prepare your own collection of 10 different objects by inserting pictures in a landscape version of a Word document. Center your name in the footer:

DESIGNER: YOUR NAME

❑ Prepare an attachment to your collection of 10 objects, accurately referencing the sources of the graphics.

❑ **Estimation Activity Two**
- ○ Trade your document with another student and redo the estimation and measurement activities.
- ○ Prepare a report describing the results of this second estimation activity. Did your estimates improve? What techniques do you use to obtain a better estimate? Why is estimating in centimeters difficult or easy for you? Explain your results.

❑ **Publish Your Work**
1. Prepare a written report that includes your printed copies of the objects you did for the first estimates, the objects your partner created, and your tables for each of the activities. Place your name and date in the header of the first page; number each page in the report in the header at the upper right.
2. Prepare a copy electronically in your portfolio, where you include copies of graphics that were used in both estimation activities.

In the Classroom 5.3

SHARING OUR STORIES

TECHNOLOGY OBJECTIVE: **NETS · S I, III, IV, VI**

- **Word processors and Internet:** Technology as a communications tool.
- Use technology to collaborate, publish, and interact with peers, experts, and multiple audiences.

CONTENT OBJECTIVE: **Social studies:** Students explore and describe similarities and differences in ways that groups, societies, and cultures address similar human needs and concerns.

GRADE LEVEL: K–5

PROBLEM: How are families alike and different around the world?

❏ Begin this worldwide project by joining a service such as iEARN, a network open to all teachers and students in a school to create and facilitate a project around families around the world. See Technology Link 5.2. Establish a project to find out how families are alike and different around the world.

❏ Create a word processing template for children to use in creating a story about their families including a space for a picture. The template might be a one-page Word document with spaces for students to insert information about the siblings, home, daily life, typical weather, short stories about daily activities, pictures of home life, and pictures of family members. Children use the template to create stories and pictures that describe their families.

❏ After revising and editing the stories, the children publish their stories for others around the world to read using the worldwide service.

❏ As children read the stories of others from around the world, they create a brochure of "Families Around the World" to share what they learn about how their families are alike and different from those around the world.

---

object worksheet with peers helps them visualize and gain experience with lengths in terms of centimeters. At the conclusion they prepare a report that describes their improvement in estimation abilities. In essence, through this project, while they are measuring and making estimates, they are also using word processing capabilities to enhance their estimation skills in a different and more creative way than simply measuring objects and comparing them with their estimates.

Word Processing as a Communications Tool

Communicating in writing is an essential skill in the twenty-first century. Lots of ideas are available to help students learn to communicate in writing beginning in the early grades. As you collect ideas to encourage students to communicate using word processing, the writing process emerges as an important consideration when you design activities and lessons to support their progress.

Word Processing Instructional Ideas: Sharing Stories
In the Classroom 5.3 is an idea that encourages students to use technology as a tool for communications by collaborating, publishing, and interacting with various audiences. The intent of the activity is for students to learn how families are alike and different, but

not just families in their neighborhood. For this activity to succeed, students must communicate with other students outside their neighborhood, perhaps in completely different cultures. Technology Link 5.2 provides a link for a Web-based service called iEARN that is designed, specifically for classroom teachers and students, as a highly interactive resource that connects schools and classes throughout the world around specific learning projects. Through such a resource, children have an opportunity to share stories about their families with other children around the world. The aim is to learn how families are alike and different around the world. Children use a word-processed template designed specifically for the development of their stories by the teachers from the various schools in the project. A variety of revision and editing activities can be incorporated to help the children review their stories to make sure they adequately represent their families. Graphics and digital pictures can be incorporated to enhance the communication about their families.

Technology Link 5.2

*T*he **Families** link connects you to the iEARN website to join and begin a classroom project among schools around the world.

www.wiley.com/college/niess

In the Classroom 5.4

WHAT IS MARRIAGE?

TECHNOLOGY OBJECTIVE: NETS·S I, II, III, IV, VI

- **Internet and word processors:** Technology as a research tool.
- Use technology to locate, evaluate, and collect information from a variety of sources. Use word processing to process the collected data and report the results.

CONTENT OBJECTIVE: Social studies: Compare and analyze societal patterns for preserving and transmitting culture while adapting to social change.

Language arts: Conduct research on issues and interests by generating ideas and questions, and by posing problems. Gather, evaluate, and synthesize data from a variety of sources to communicate discoveries in ways that suit purpose and audience.

GRADE LEVEL: 9–12

PROBLEM: The meaning of the term *marriage* is often contentious. What are various cultural experiences and expectations relating to marriage that ultimately define the term?

- ❏ Describe a research project to collect data from a variety of sources concerning the question of various societal and cultural experiences and expectations related to marriage. These resources might include family members, secondary sources such as history books, along with cultural resources such as religious documents. Explain why this collection of data will provide information for considering the question of preservation and transmission of culture while adapting to social change.

- ❏ Conduct the research project using word processing as a research tool.
  - Organize the collected data taking advantage of the available technology tools. Using your writer's journal, record any patterns that appear as you organize and evaluate the data.
  - Synthesize the data in response to the research questions.
  - Prepare a research report responding specifically to the research question(s), referencing the data that were collected. Use your writer's journal to support the patterns that you have identified.
  - Use the devil's advocate strategy to revise your research report from an alternative perspective. Revise your research report based on this new vision.

- ❏ Publish your research report in two formats.
  - Write a double-spaced paper, placing your name and date in the header and the word count and page numbers in the footer.
  - Save in your electronic portfolio, where you include the version before and after the devil's advocate activity and the final version that you printed.

Word Processing as a Research Tool

Asking questions is important in student learning. Collecting, analyzing, and reporting information to answer their questions is a useful part of the learning process. Word processing enables students with a myriad of features as they collect and report the results of their research efforts. As they learn to use word processing capabilities, they enhance their understanding and appreciation for the word processor as a research tool.

Word Processing Instructional Ideas: Writing and Researching a Nationally Debated Topic   In the

Classroom 5.4 provides a challenge for students to study a nationally debated topic. The question for their study is, What is marriage? Students use writers' journals to record the data, where they develop patterns they discover as they organize and evaluate their research data about the concept of marriage. The devil's advocate revision strategy is particularly helpful in challenging the patterns and ideas they have proposed in their research report. By opening two documents on the screen, they have an environment to challenge the ideas and to reframe and substantiate their proposals prior to publishing their papers.

Word Processing as a Problem-Solving and Decision-Making Tool

Making decisions is not a matter of rolling the dice and choosing. Students must practice to learn processes that they can use for making decisions. Problems within the context of the various disciplines are important for guiding students in developing these abilities. Features of word processors provide useful ways to engage in the problem-solving and decision-making processes. Encourage students to use these features in decision-making with respect to context-rich questions that help them gain a respect for word processing as a problem-solving and decision-making tool.

Word Processing Instructional Ideas: Constructing Historical Understandings   Social studies is a text-rich discipline that emphasizes reading and writing skills and as displayed in several of the previous instructional ideas. Students at all levels need opportunities to make use of word processing skills to support the construction of a variety of text-based representations of their knowledge. In the Classroom 5.5 is an example of a social studies project where students are challenged to make interpretations based on the perspectives of historical persons. This project guides students in developing an understanding of how historical understandings are constructed using authentic primary sources. Students work in collaborative groups to develop a word-processed tabular comparison of the various perspectives of two women in the late 1700s, one the wife of a famous man and the other who is neither famous nor married to a famous man. Students must describe the perspectives of each woman from the perspective of the other. Students working in small collaborative groups are supported in their work by various features of the word processor as described in Step 1. For example, in the groups, one student might construct a list of complaints in Abigail Adams' letter as well as the implied threats mentioned by Adams in her letter. A second student in the group might suggest what Abigail Adams hoped to achieve as well as interpreting her tone. Two more students could work on an analysis of the Martha Ballard diary entry. One student might attempt to describe in modern vernacular some of the events that occurred on March 31, 1786, in Ballard's life. The second student might describe some of the hardships confronted by Ballard in the day she describes in her diary.

A word-processed table provides the spatial arrangement that supports a comparative analysis. Different text colors are used to highlight the different perspectives. Huddled around one electronic document, the students are able to make comparisons, discuss their ideas, and challenge the different perspectives. In this way, the word processor supports them in focusing on the overall question of considering how historical understandings are constructed using primary sources such as the original letters.

Summing It Up

Writing is an essential form of communication in the twenty-first century. In fact, national standards across content areas and high-stakes testing emphasize the importance of written communication. The word processor is a tool for writing that provides far more capabilities than the typical writing tools such as pens and pencils. Word processors allow writers to more easily and efficiently brainstorm ideas, to organize ideas by moving, copying, pasting, and even deleting, to revise and edit their ideas, to format the ideas for a more exciting presentation, and even to publish ideas in a variety of ways—electronically or in hard copy.

Guiding students in entering their ideas in a word processor requires teachers to consider the issue of keyboarding. Who teaches it, when, and how? More and more technology teachers work with content-area teachers to identify context and needed skills for working with keyboarding and word processors.

Although students may get an introduction to keyboarding with a technology teacher, reinforcing skills with keyboarding is an instructional responsibility of all teachers, regardless of content and grade level, as they integrate computer technologies such as word processors.

With word processors, the quality of students' writing has improved along with their attitudes toward writing. Teachers are more apt to incorporate the process of writing in their instruction as a means of guiding students' learning in a variety of subject areas. As a result, students are writing more and are more willing to make revisions. Word processors support them in several ways in the writing process: prewriting, revision and editing, and publishing.

The school curriculum must include social, ethical, and human issues of working with technologies such as word processors. As students write more and more with word processors, they need to understand the difference between plagiarizing and paraphrasing. An emphasis on the writing process where students are consistently expected to revise and edit their work supports students in expressing their personal ideas rather than relying on the ideas of others.

In the Classroom 5.5

CONSTRUCTING HISTORICAL UNDERSTANDINGS

TECHNOLOGY OBJECTIVE: **NETS · S I, II, III, IV, V, VI**

- **Word processors:** Technology as a problem-solving and decision-making tool.
- Use technology to organize an analysis of two letters and construct comparative interpretations of the documents using formatting tools of the word processor.

CONTENT OBJECTIVE: **Social studies:** Understand how historical understandings are constructed through the study of two letters from the past.

GRADE LEVEL: 9–12

PROBLEM: How are historical understandings constructed?

Organize the class in groups of four to study two letters (one from a famous person and one from a not so famous person) from the past. Students use a word processor to organize an analysis of the letters and construct comparative interpretations of the documents using the formatting tools of the word processor.

❏ **Step 1:** In small groups, study the letter by Abigail Adams and the diary entry by Martha Ballard. The analysis is organized around these tasks:

1. Adams' complaints and threats
2. Adams' hope and tone
3. Ballard's daily life
4. Ballard's hardships

Report the results of this study of the four tasks in a word-processed document using this spatial arrangement.

Adams' complaints and threats	Ballard's daily life
Adams' hope and tone	Ballard's hardships

❏ **Step 2:** Shift perspectives and read about the other historical person. If the student worked on Martha Ballard's daily life, that student now looks at Abigail Adams' complaints and threats, and vice versa. If the student worked on Ballard's hardships, that student investigates Adams' tone in her letter.

❏ **Step 3:** Write what you think the author of the original document would have thought about the other person's hardships or complaints. If a student worked on interpreting Adams' tone, that person now projects what Adams might have thought about Ballard's hardships. These new entries are highlighted in a new color to emphasize the position taken and listed directly below the original work.

Adams' complaints and threats	Ballard's daily life
Ballard's thoughts about Adams' complaints	Adams' thoughts about Ballard's daily life
Adams' hope and tone	Ballard's hardships
Ballard's thoughts about Adams' hope and tone	Adams' thoughts about Ballard's hardships

❏ **Step 4:** With a round robin analysis use new highlighting techniques (different colors) for developing the interpretations and perhaps introduce a third character that could have been living at the same time.

Adams' complaints and threats	Ballard's daily life
Ballard's thoughts about Adams' complaints	Adams' thoughts about Ballard's daily life
African enslaved person's thoughts about Adams' complaints	Native American's thoughts about Ballard's daily life
Adams' hope and tone	Ballard's hardships
Ballard's thoughts about Adams' hope and tone	Adams' thoughts about Ballard's hardships
African enslaved person's thoughts about Adams' hope and tone	Native American's thoughts about Ballard's hardships

(continued)

❑ **Step 5.** In groups, summarize your analyses developed through the round robin process. Relate your analysis and efforts to respond to this question: How are historical understandings constructed using authentic primary sources?

PRIMARY SOURCES

Writing 1: Abigail Adams wrote this letter, requesting that her husband consider the plight of women as he participates in the Continental Congress to draft and approve the Declaration of Independence. She implores her husband to "remember the ladies" as he, along with the other colonial leaders (all men), considers declaring independence from Great Britain. Part of the letter written by Abigail Adams to John Adams, March 31, 1776:

> *I long to hear that you have declared in independency. And, by the way, in the new code of laws which I suppose it will be necessary for you to make, I desire you would remember the ladies and be more generous and favorable to them than your ancestors.*

> *Do not put such unlimited power into the hands of husbands.*

> *Remember, all men would be tyrants if they could. If particular care and attention is not paid to the ladies, we are determined to foment a rebellion, and will not hold ourselves bound by any laws in which we have no voice or representation.*

> *That your sex are naturally tyrannical is a truth so thoroughly established as to admit of no dispute; but such of you as wish to be happy willingly give up the harsh tide of master for the more tender and endearing one of friend.*

> *Why, then, not put it out of the power of the vicious and the lawless to use us with cruelty and indignity with impunity?*

> *Men of sense in all ages abhor those customs which treat us only as the (servants) of your sex; regard us then as being placed by Providence under your protection, and in imitation of the Supreme Being make use of that power only for our happiness.*

Writing 2: Martha Ballard, who was neither famous nor married to a famous man, described her chores and tasks on the same day, March 31, ten years later.
Martha Ballard diary entry for March 31, 1786:

> *Rained Last night, Snowd ys morn. [ye] dam broke ys morn. mr. Ballard & Brooks [had] Some uneasiness. I am unwell. Isaac Savage to Breakfast here, had some phisick for his Dafter Hannah. ye Northern Light appears this Evinng. Cyrus & Ephm ointing for ye itch.*

> *Birth. Eliab Shaws Son*

> *A frosty morn. I finnisht knitting Cyruss Buskins, the Girls washt. I was Calld to Eliab Shaws at half after 5/O Clock PM, his wife in Travil, & Shee was Safely Delivrd between 6 & 7 of a Son, her 4 th child. I slept at mr Browks.*

> *I Came home from mr shaws at 10h / [morn]. mr Cowen & others Brought Loggs to ye mill. I went to See Polly Hamlin, Shee is unwell. old mrs Hardin Sleeps here.*

> *mrs Hardin wnt from here. mr Ballard went to atetnd town meeting. mr Sual Sent a man to attend me to his hous to hear Mr Pother speak. after meeting I went to See mrs Weston. Shee ebing unwell. I Rode hom, found mrss Becke, Lidia Bisbee, Polly Hamlin & Polly Adams here. Ephrm is 7 years old ys day.*

> *A Stormy day. Mr Ballard Left home for Sebestakuk. mrs Farly here, says her family are in Sufering Circumstances. I cardid Tow for Hannah & Dolly to spin.*

> *A Cloudy, Cold Day, thee ground frose. I have been at home Carding Tow.*

> *it began to Snow at one O Clok ys morn, a tedious Storm till 4 ys. Afternoon. Mr. Ballard not Returnd. Ye Severest Storm we have had this winter.*

The word processor is a productivity tool. The ease of revision and editing encourages students to challenge their first ideas and even rewrite their ideas. Students are equipped with a variety of ways to present their ideas; using different font sizes, styles, and colors, incorporating graphics, creating tables, etc., also can use the capabilities of the word processor. Capabilities of the word processor provide an environment where students can explore various ways of displaying and communicating their knowledge. In the process of exploring the different capabilities they gain a perspective of the word processor as a productivity tool.

Written communication is an essential skill in the twenty-first century. Word processors are powerful communication tools. Word processing intertwined with the writing process offers a myriad of features to support students' inquiry as they collect and report the results of their work in the search for answers to questions. In these experiences, students learn that the word processor is a research tool as well as a problem-solving and decision-making tool. With consistent expectations for the use of the word processor as a writing tool for learning throughout the curriculum, students expand their knowledge and understanding of the tool, using the tool for improving their writing while learning in a variety of subjects.

End-of-the-Chapter Activities and References

PRACTICE PROBLEMS

1. Here is a mathematics problem. Use the word processing capabilities to clarify and solve the problem in a similar manner as was done in Figure 5.7.

   The middle school has a requirement that all students are involved in at least one of the following sports: soccer, basketball, and baseball. Soccer is a popular sport, with 75% of the students in the school involved; 30% of the students in the school are involved in basketball; and 40% are involved in baseball. Forty students are involved in at least soccer and basketball; 90 are involved in at least soccer and baseball; and 30 are involved in at least basketball and baseball. Ten students are in all three sports and 116 students are involved in only one of these sports. How many students are there in the school?

2. Use Figure 5.8 as a graphic organizer to describe a new fairy tale about Goldilocks, the monkey, the elephant, and the lion. Work in groups of three, passing the keyboard around to brainstorm ideas for the fairy tale.

3. What words can describe the picture of the atomic bomb? Use Technology Link 5.1 to access a picture of the atomic bomb from the President Truman website to complete the activities as described for In the Classroom 5.1.

4. How good are you at estimating in centimeters? Complete the activities described for In the Classroom 5.2.

5. Design a template that children can use to gather data about families around the world (see In the Classroom 5.3).

6. Use the format in the Resource Idea: Electronic Portfolio described in Figure 5.9 to describe an idea that incorporates writing and word processing in teaching in your specific content and grade level (some sources are described in the Annotated Resources section).

IN THE CLASSROOM ACTIVITIES

7. Observe classroom activities, noting and describing the writing that the students do in the process of learning the subject. Which of the activities might be enhanced by incorporating word processing as a writing tool? How might the tool be incorporated in these areas: productivity, communications, research, problem solving, and decision making?

8. Observe some classroom activities to consider how learning might be enhanced while incorporating the capabilities of word processing in student writing.

9. Talk with various teachers in the grade level and content area you hope to teach about word processing and the writing process. What are their concerns about incorporating word processing? What are their suggestions for incorporating word processing?

10. For your specific content area, design (or find in the literature) a word processing activity that would support students in learning the content while also learning about the capabilities of a word processor as a writing tool. What content area standard(s) does the activity support? What technology standard(s) does the activity support? Outline how you envision students working on this activity.

ASSESSING STUDENT LEARNING WITH AND ABOUT TECHNOLOGY

11. Complete In the Classroom 5.5: Constructing Historical Understandings. Identify the word processing operations and concepts that are key to this activity that you would use in describing a scoring guide for the activity. Describe how you would assess students' capabilities with those key ideas.

E-PORTFOLIO ACTIVITIES

12. Plan an outline for your own electronic portfolio to match the expectations described in the Resource Idea shown in Figure 5.9.

13. Prepare a reflection about teaching and learning *with* and *about* word processors with respect to your specific content area. How can you incorporate word processors and the writing process so that students use them as tools as described in the student technology standards? How can word processors be used as tools in learning your subject area? Save this reflection as a Web page so you can consider using it as a reflection in your E-portfolio.

REFLECTION AND DISCUSSION

14. Begin a teacher's journal where you describe your ideas and reflections on integrating instruction about the word processor as you teach your subject at the specific grade level.

15. Prepare a discussion of what you have learned with respect to each of the chapter learning objectives. Select one objective on which to expand how the ideas in the objective impact your preparation to teach with word processing.

16. Find a word processing activity (see Annotated Resources for suggestions) to use with students you are preparing to teach (grade level and content). Describe how you would prepare students to be ready to use the word processor as a tool for learning in the activity.

17. Respond to this statement: Word processors are tools for learning in language arts.

Annotated Resources

Brown, N. M. (1993). Writing activities. *Arithmetic Teacher, 41*(1), 20–21.
    Describes a class activity where students create word problems associated with specific arithmetic problems that are then edited using a word processing program.

Dexter, S., & Watts-Taffe, S. (2000). Processing ideas: Move beyond word processing into critical thinking. *Learning and Leading with Technology, 27* (6), 22–27.
    Posters, newsletters, and other ideas use word processing as an idea processor that engages critical thinking in language arts.

Francis, J. W., & Sellers, J. A. (1994). Studying amino acid sequence using word processing programs. *American Biology Teachers, 56*(8), 484–487.
    Describes simple methods to enhance the teaching of protein structures and function by analyzing amino acid sequences using word processing programs.

Hagins, C., Austin, J., Jones, R., & Timmons, T. (2004). Authors "in residence" making writing fun! *Learning and Leading with Technology, 31*(6), 36–30.
    Fourth graders use online mentors to help compose original stories.

International Society for Technology in Education. (2000). Population growth and urban planning. In *National educational technology standards for students.* Eugene, OR: ISTE.
    Students investigate world population growth as a major global issue and then write a one-act play, poem, or short story about the quality of life in a location in the year 2050.

Jankowski, L. (1998). Educational computing: Why use a computer for writing? *Learning and Leading with Technology, 25*(6), 30–33.
    Word processing can be used for beginning writers in elementary grades; the article includes sample student assignments and a sample writing task card.

Kajder, S., & Bull, G. (2003). Scaffolding for struggling students: Reading and writing with blogs. *Learning and Leading with Technology, 31*(2), 32–35.
    Blogs provide teachers and student writers with an engaging, rich writing space while offering access to an instant publishing press on the Web. This article provides a beginning look at a multigenre, multimedia writing space to engage visually minded students to involve them in learning to write by writing.

Lewis, P. (1997). Using productivity software for beginning language learning—Part 1. The word processor. *Learning and Leading with Technology 24*(8), 14–17.
    Activities demonstrate how word processors can be productivity software to motivate beginning elementary or middle level foreign language students in creating language fluency and spelling.

Reissman, R. (1991). Using computers: Movie matters. *Learning, 20*(4), 48.
    Help students improve their critical thinking skills by watching movie segments then write and or draw what they think happened earlier or would happen later in the movie.

Reissman, R. (1996). Computerized fortune cookies—A classroom treat. *Learning and Leading with Technology, 23*(5), 25–26.
    Use fortune cookie fortunes in a middle school class combined with word processing technology to create writing assignments, games, and discussions.

Wiebe, J. H. (1992). Word processing, desktop publishing and graphics in the mathematics classroom. *The Computing Teacher, 19*(5), 39–40.
    Mathematics involves words, numbers, symbols, and pictures, all of which can readily be produced and manipulated in word processors and with graphics tools. These products are powerful tools for organizing and representing mathematical information.

CHAPTER 6

Spreadsheets

Bill Aron/PhotoEdit

Introduction

Spreadsheets! Aren't they just tools for mathematics classes? They certainly appear to be tools for mathematics students because spreadsheets use numbers, formulas, and graphical representations. In this chapter you will see that spreadsheets are not just tools for the mathematics class. Rather, as Drier (2001) challenges, teachers need to think of the spreadsheet as a cognitive tool that can enhance student learning of content material in many different content areas. Burns expands on this idea suggesting that "spreadsheets enable learners to model complex and rich real-world phenomena that can be manipulated, analyzed, evaluated, and displayed both quantitatively and visually" (2002, p. 23). Such phenomena are found in many content areas besides mathematics, such as fine arts, language arts, science, and social studies.

If you want your students to be able to use spreadsheets in powerful ways, they need to learn *about* the tool, including the concepts and basic skills required to use spreadsheets. Simply entering numbers in cells does not ensure that the spreadsheet can *think* with those numbers. Students need to learn how to *explain* to the spreadsheet how to *think*. An important question for you as their teacher is, How do I teach students about the spreadsheet when I have so much else to teach?' The answer is that students can and should learn *about* the spreadsheet while they are learning important concepts and ideas in a variety of content areas *with* the spreadsheet.

Perhaps as early as the elementary grades, students can be engaged in working with a model of a spreadsheet on a bulletin board divided into cells for information that contains their names and ages. As a class they can simulate putting a formula in a cell to find the average age. Then they can practice this same activity with an actual computer spreadsheet as perhaps they learn to make a bar graph of their ages. Throughout the elementary grades more and more capabilities can be considered in a similar way as problems in the curriculum seem reasonable for spreadsheets and, over time, as the students are learning to use the spreadsheet as a tool for learning.

As you prepare to teach, you need to think about ways to guide your students' learning with and about spreadsheets in the following:

- making connections between ideas and concepts from multiple subject areas (e.g., social studies, science, art, and mathematics);

- developing higher level conceptual understandings in various content areas;

- expanding the students' problem-solving skills and abilities by exploring problems that require investigation of real-world data.

The decision to incorporate spreadsheets as a tool for enhancing student learning must be made carefully. Be sure to ask yourself questions like these:

- Is the time spent learning about and solving problems with spreadsheets at the expense of the development of important concepts that would not benefit from a spreadsheet application?

- Do spreadsheet functions divert students' attention to the academic concept being studied (e.g., enhancing graphs with color and graphics)?

- Do students use functions and graphics just because those capabilities are available and become dependent on the spreadsheet to do the thinking about problems?

The spreadsheet is a powerful, yet complex, learning tool. And, like any tool, spreadsheets can be misused. But students can also use spreadsheets to work problems and ideas in ways that may not have been possible previously. Your role as their teacher is to guide their learning with and about spreadsheets. This task requires that you think about your content differently than when you learned it. You need to create new ideas and new lessons to guide their learning in ways that integrate learning *about* the spreadsheet while also learning subject matter concepts and ideas *with* the spreadsheet.

CHAPTER LEARNING OBJECTIVES

After reading this chapter, you should be able to:

1. Identify activities that simultaneously support learner-centered explorations of both subject matter content and spreadsheets.
2. Describe important spreadsheet basic skills for working with user-defined and built-in formulas and creating charts.
3. Explain how a spreadsheet chart may misrepresent data.
4. Explain how a spreadsheet can be used as a communication and a productivity tool.
5. Illustrate techniques students need to learn for locating Internet data for spreadsheet analysis in conducting research.
6. Show how spreadsheets can be used as problem-solving and decision-making tools.
7. Discuss how designing dynamic, dependable spreadsheets supports problem solving and decision making.

Snapshot of a Classroom Investigation of Spreadsheets

Have you heard the rumors about the different colored candies in the M&Ms bags? Did you know that when you first open a bag of M&Ms, you should pick out all the reds and then eat all the other colors? Then, before you eat the reds, you should make a wish and your wish will come true. Some people even suggest that the greens have special powers! However, according to the manufacturer of M&Ms, Mars, Incorporated, "We cannot explain any extraordinary 'powers' attributed to this color, either scientifically or medically."

If you opened a bag of M&Ms to test these special powers and took out only one M&M, what are your chances of getting a green M&M? Ms. Hernandez posed this problem to her sixth-grade class, first asking them to tell her what colors of candies were possible. They quickly called out the right colors: red, yellow, green, orange, blue, and brown.

Ms. Hernandez:	Do all the bags have the same number of each color in them?
Sara:	No, I have even had a bag where there were no greens. But it had lots of browns!
Ms. Hernandez:	Does that mean the bags are packaged so that there will always be more browns?
Shawn:	I don't think so. It just always seems like there are more browns than any of the other colors.

Ms. Hernandez:	If I take one candy from a new bag of M&Ms, do you think the chance of getting a brown is greater than getting a green?

The class enthusiastically agreed. So Ms. Hernandez suggested that they test their conjecture by collecting some data. She told them she would provide them each with a bag of M&Ms if they followed the instructions on the overhead:

1. Make a candy bar chart with the M&M candies.

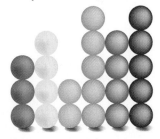

2. Use the data from your chart to count the number of each color.
3. Record the information for each color on individual 3 × 5 Post-it notes. For each color, prepare each note like this example.

Red

12

1. Record each of these labels on individual 3 × 5 notes: NAME, RED, BLUE, YELLOW, GREEN, BROWN, and ORANGE. Example:

NAME

2. Place the cards next to each other across the wide part of your table.

NAME	RED	BLUE	YELLOW	GREEN	BROWN	ORANGE

3. Take turns placing 3 × 5 data notes in a row in the appropriate columns underneath the column headings. Your table data should look like this example.

NAME	RED	BLUE	YELLOW	GREEN	BROWN	ORANGE
Sara	13	9	5	6	15	8
Maria	10	6	3	9	13	13
Shawn	9	12	8	3	12	12

4. After all candies are counted and the number of each color is recorded on the 3 × 5 notes, you may eat your data!

The students were already organized at the four large tables in the room—8 students at one table, 7 at the second table, 6 at the third table, and 8 at the fourth table. Once the students had recorded their data, Ms. Hernandez gave each table 25 more blank 3 × 5 notes and displayed new instructions on the overhead.

When all the students had displayed their data, Ms. Hernandez asked each group to describe where the note with the label "GREEN" was in their table data.

	A	B	C	D	E	F	G
1	NAME	RED	BLUE	YELLOW	GREEN	BROWN	ORANGE
2							
3					Y		
4							
5		X					
6							
7							
8							
9							

Table 1:   It's the fifth note on the top.

Table 2:   It's the fourth note after the note with "NAME."

Table 3:   It's the third note in from the right.

Table 4:   It's the note to the right of the "YEL-LOW" note.

Ms. Hernandez: Let's fix your note display so that we can communicate better. I'm giving each table a new set of notes. These notes look like arrows. We'll use these as row and column markers. Use the numbers 1, 2, 3, etc., to label each of the rows and use the letters A, B, C, etc., to label each of the columns similar to this overhead:

Now, I can say the note with the X is located in cell B5 and the note with the Y is located in cell E3. Where will the note with the word "GREEN" be identified?

Class: Cell E1.

Ms. Hernandez: Right! Now we have a way to talk about our different table data sets. At each of your tables, identify the cell names for the information on this overhead:

Find the cell names for the information that contains the following:

a. most M&Ms for each of the colors;
b. fewest M&Ms for each of the colors;
c. name of the student with the most number of green M&Ms;
d. name of the student with the fewest number of green M&Ms.

As Ms. Hernandez walked around the classroom, she could see that the students were correctly using the cell names to locate information in the data sets. Ms. Hernandez felt it was time to explain the different types of data in the cells.

Ms. Hernandez: In cell A1 you each have a *label*. What is the label in cell A1?

Jeremy: NAME.

Ms. Hernandez: Right and that label is different from the contents of cell B2. Sharon, what does your table's cell B2 contain?

Sharon: We have 11. Actually that's the number of red M&Ms that Karen had in her bag.

Ms. Hernandez: Good. And, Wayne, what value does your table have in cell B2?

Wayne: We have 15 and that is the number of red M&Ms that I had in my bag of M&Ms.

Ms. Hernandez: Yes, so you are using the labels that you put in column A and row 1, or cell A1, to help you describe the data more clearly. That is why you often will need labels in cells. And, in cell B2 you had a *value* not a *label*.

Ms. Hernandez wrote the words *Labels* and *Values* on the board and indicated that there was still another type of cell that they will be using. That type of cell is a *Formula*. She asked the students to add another column heading label, called TOTAL, as she demonstrated the addition of the column H on the overhead.

	A	B	C	D	E	F	G	H
1	NAME	RED	BLUE	YELLOW	GREEN	BROWN	ORANGE	TOTAL
2	Sara	13	9	5	6	15	8	
3	Maria	10	6	3	9	13	13	
4	Shawn	9	12	8	3	12	12	

Ms. Hernandez: Using the cell names, will the person whose name is in cell A4 describe how to find the TOTAL value for row 4? Maria, that's you for your table. Can you describe what needs to be done?

Maria: We would add the values in the cells B4, C4, D4, E4, F4, and G4.

Ms. Hernandez: Right. Here's a shortcut for this formula so that you can get it on the back side of your 3 × 5 Post-it. To indicate that you want to calculate a value, use the equal sign. Then use the SUM formula like this:

= SUM(B4:G4)

Each of you should prepare a note for your row that contains the *formula* on the underside of the note and put the *value* on the other side. Then place that note card down with the *value* showing in the appropriate place in the table data set.

	A	B	C	D	E	F	G	H
1	NAME	RED	BLUE	YELLOW	GREEN	BROWN	ORANGE	TOTAL
2	Sara	13	9	5	6	15	8	56
3	Maria	10	6	3	9	13	13	54
4	Shawn	9	12	8	3	12	12	56

After all the students had completed this task, Ms. Hernandez asked the students to "show formulas." To follow this command, the students lifted up their note cards in column H to display the formulas and Ms. Hernandez confirmed their efforts with the overhead.

	A	B	C	D	E	F	G	H
1	NAME	RED	BLUE	YELLOW	GREEN	BROWN	ORANGE	TOTAL
2	Sara	13	9	5	6	15	8	=SUM(B2:G2)
3	Maria	10	6	3	9	13	13	=SUM(B3:G3)
4	Shawn	9	12	8	3	12	12	=SUM(B4:G4)

Ms. Hernandez then asked the students to "show values" and they turned over their note cards in column H so that they could see the actual values they had calculated.

Ms. Hernandez: Now let's see about answering the question that started this whole experiment. How can we find the chances of getting a green M&M in your experiment?

Maria: I think we could find the average for each color. Then the chance of getting a green would be the average for GREEN divided by the TOTAL of the averages.

Ms. Hernandez: Good idea, Maria. How would you find the average for the REDs? Be sure to use the cell names to describe what you would do.

Shawn: We would add B2 + B3 + B4 + B5 + B6 + B7 + B8 + B9 and then divide that sum by 8.

Ms. Hernandez: Yes and a shortcut for that formula could be =AVERAGE(B2:B9) since you are averaging the values in cells B2, B3, B4, B5, B6, B7, B8, and B9. This formula does the same as adding the values and dividing by the number of cells. Identify someone in each of your groups to prepare the average formula for each color on the underside of a note card and then record the calculated average on the top side. Show the formulas when you put the notes in place so I can check your work.

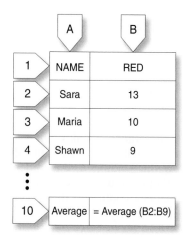

	A	B
1	NAME	RED
2	Sara	13
3	Maria	10
4	Shawn	9
⋮		
10	Average	= Average (B2:B9)

Ms. Hernandez: For each of your data sets, find the chances of picking a green from your specific data. Remember that you need to also find the TOTAL for the averages using the =SUM(B10:G10) formula. Have someone in your group prepare that card, too. Then let's check to see if we all have the same values. Do you think we will?

Sara: We aren't all the same size of groups. I think that might affect the value.

Ms. Hernandez: How?

Sara: Well, I'm not sure but I think the more bags of M&Ms you have, the closer you will be to the actual chance for picking a green.

Ms. Hernandez: Interesting conjecture, Sara. We'll investigate that tomorrow when we work on the computers. Today you have all been building a spreadsheet that describes your data. Tomorrow we will enter these data into a computer spreadsheet. Before you leave though, let's review what you have learned today.

Ms. Hernandez directed questions to students who had not yet participated in class to review the new terms that they had learned today. To support this review, she handed them each the Spreadsheet Summary in Figure 6.1 and asked them to review this sheet as homework. She instructed them to be prepared to identify any new information on the sheet that was not covered in class or that confused them. Finally, Ms. Hernandez reminded the students

Spreadsheet Summary

Spreadsheets are used to display data just like your M&Ms model using the 3 × 5 cards! They extend in two directions: **Rows** and **Columns**.

Rows
Spreadsheet rows are identified by numbers: 1, 2, 3, ...
How many rows are possible?

Columns
Spreadsheet columns are identified by letters of the alphabet: A, B, C, ...
How many columns could there be? What strategy would you use so there can be columns past the Z?

Cell names
Each cell of the spreadsheet is identified by a column and a row:
B3 is in column B and row 3
E10 is in column E and row 10
Z100 is in column Z and row 100

Cells can contain different types of information

Labels
A cell containing a letter of the alphabet or other nonnumeric character is a **label**. In the M&Ms model, cell A1 contained a label with the information NAME.

Values
A cell with a number is a **value**. In the M&Ms model, cell B2 contained the number of red M&Ms for the first person in the group.

Formulas
Values are entered into a cell either directly or as a result of a **formula**. When formulas are recorded in a cell, the spreadsheet immediately follows the instructions and places the value that results in the cell. The spreadsheet recognizes a formula if the entry begins with an equal sign (=).

=SUM(B2:G2)
This formula computes B2+C2+D2+E2+F2+G2 and places the results in the cell that contains the formula.

=AVERAGE(B2:B9)
This formula adds the values in cells B2, B3, B4, B5, B6, B7, B8, and B9, divides that sum by 8, and places the result in the cell that contains the formula.

FIGURE 6.1 Summary of key ideas explored in the introductory lesson on spreadsheets.

that their work for tomorrow will focus on finding the effect of different sample sizes for answering the question, "What are the chances of getting a green M&M?"

Basic Operations and Concepts of Spreadsheets

The spreadsheet is a tool for collecting, displaying, and analyzing information. Its two-dimensional display is similar to the way many classrooms are arranged—in rows and columns, creating multiple "cells." Each cell holds "information" just as each classroom desk is assigned to a specific person. Cell B3 is a location assigned to Karen and cell D1 is assigned to John.

	A	B	C	D	E	F	G
1	Alice	Same	Joel	John	Roberto	Kristi	Lana
2	Hans	Jason	Maria	Kim	Melissa	Hank	Tom
3	Zoey	Karen	Justing	Juan	Aaron	Jana	Mason
4	Dianne	Sharon	Wayne	Sally	Marissa	Harrison	Edwardo
5	Ava	Duane	Carol	Katie	Marty	Joni	Mary
6							

However, spreadsheets are much more complex tools than this simple introduction suggests. The Snapshot of a Classroom Investigation of Spreadsheets describes a simulation activity designed to help students model the actions of a spreadsheet as they begin learning about the spreadsheet. Although this model introduces the students to the basic framework of a spreadsheet, it does not completely answer the mathematics problem the students are investigating nor does it completely explain a spreadsheet. At the end of their first activity, the students identify two important questions to explore; these questions provide the framework for an actual hands-on exploration of a computer spreadsheet.

* What is the chance of getting a green M&M?
* What is the effect of different sample sizes in exploring this probability of getting a green M&M?

Entering and Differentiating Data Types

Ms. Hernandez used the classroom simulation to help the students see that the spreadsheet cells can hold different types of information. The next step is for the students to enter their M&M data in an actual computer spreadsheet. Working in partners at this point is a good idea so that the students can help each other.

The names of the students in each row are *labels* that identify each student's M&M data. The colors (RED, BLUE, etc.) label the columns containing the number of M&Ms for each color. The numbers of the different colors of M&Ms are *values* that the computer spreadsheet can use in numerical calculations.

Look carefully at this sample data as it appears on the computer screen. Do you see any difference in how the labels and numbers are placed in the

cells? The M&Ms data values are *right-justified* while the labels are *left-justified*. Although you can change this formatting, when you first enter the information, if the information is a label, the spreadsheet will automatically place it at the left of the cell; if the information is a value, it will be right-justified.

M&M Data

	A	B	C	D	E	F	G
1	NAME	RED	BLUE	YELLOW	GREEN	BROWN	ORANGE
2	Sara	13	9	5	6	15	8
3	Maria	10	6	3	9	13	13
4	Shawn	9	12	8	3	12	12

Ms. Hernandez asked the students to tell her, using the cell names, what they needed to do to find the total number of M&Ms in their bags; in other words, she asked them to describe the formula for finding the total number in their bags. Then, she translated their identification to a shorthand form of the formula, =SUM(B2:G2), explaining that the equal sign (=) was used to signal the entry as a formula. Without the equal sign, the spreadsheet treats such an entry as a label because the characters entered contain at least one piece of text information.

In the computer hands-on activity, the students need to enter the formula =SUM(B2:G2) into cell H2. Pressing the <return> or <enter> key immediately signals the computer to calculate a value and the value is displayed in the appropriate cell. Note, in this example, the Formula Bar displays the formula in cell H2 and the calculated value in H2 is right-justified.

=SUM(B2:G2)

M&M Data.xls

	A	B	C	D	E	F	G	H
1	NAME	RED	BLUE	YELLOW	GREEN	BROWN	ORANGE	TOTAL
2	Sara	13	9	5	6	15	8	56
3	Maria	10	6	3	9	13	13	54
4	Shawn	9	12	8	3	12	12	56

The copy feature of the spreadsheet makes copying a similar formula to the succeeding rows an easy process. Notice the handlebar in the lower right-hand corner of the outline around the value 56. Click on the corner handlebar and drag it down the rows to copy. The formulas are copied *relative* to the specific rows. This term means that the formula is changed to represent the specific row and column in which the formula is placed. Thus, the formula in cell H3 is recorded as =SUM(B3:G3) and the formula in cell H4 is =SUM(B4:G4). The values for the formulas are determined and displayed in cells H3 and H4. As you move the cursor from cell H2 to H3 and H4, you see how the formulas change relative to the specific row and column by looking at the Formula Bar.

Spreadsheets have many *built-in* functions besides the SUM function. Ms. Hernandez' students know how to find the average: add the values and divide by the number of values. Now at the computers, they can investigate the AVERAGE function that Ms. Hernandez shows them.

NAME	RED	BLUE	YELLOW	GREEN	BROWN	ORANGE	TOTAL
Sara	13	9	5	6	15	8	56
Maria	10	6	3	9	13	13	54
Shawn	9	12	8	3	12	12	56
Average	10.6666667						

In this example, rows 5 through 9 are empty. What does the spreadsheet do with the empty cells? The sum of the values is 32. But, does the computer divide by 3 or by 8? If the computer uses five zeroes for the blank cells to find the sum of 32 and divided this sum by 8, the average is 4. On the other hand, the sum of 32 is divided by 3 if the spreadsheet considers only the cells with values. Through this experience, students are in a position to gain a better understanding of the AVERAGE function when they actually enter the formula and explain the results. This example shows that the AVERAGE formula only uses cells with values, divides 32 by 3, and finds the average to be 10.666667. This example guides students in identifying the advantage of using a *built-in* formula over a *user-defined* formula. If students define formulas with the value of 3 for the divisor (to fit the current data in the spreadsheet), the spreadsheet does not easily support additions or subtractions of additional data. Yet, the AVERAGE formula only considers cells that contain values that can be averaged, identifying the number for the division in the average algorithm.

The result of this average calculation leads to another useful built-in function in spreadsheets, the *ROUND* function. The general format for this function references two parameters, (1) <number to be rounded> and (2) <number of decimals in the value>.

=ROUND(<number to be rounded>, <number of decimals in the value>)

For this problem, the <number to be rounded> is the average found by the formula *AVERAGE(B2:B9)*. To round the average number of red M&Ms to the nearest whole number (because you are interested in whole M&Ms), the formula is

=ROUND(AVERAGE(B2:B9),0)

With this instruction, the spreadsheet returns the value 11 for the average number of red M&Ms. Again, the copy feature helps to copy the appropriate functions across to column H, changing the column indicator relative to the appropriate column.

NAME	RED	BLUE	YELLOW	GREEN	BROWN	ORANGE	TOTAL
Sara	13	9	5	6	15	8	56
Maria	10	6	3	9	13	13	54
Shawn	9	12	8	3	12	12	56
Average	11	9	5	6	13	11	55

Charting Data

Numerical values are one way to display the data. The same data, put into graphical form, typically help students visualize what is happening more clearly. Spreadsheets offer many different types of graphs and allow students to highlight certain features of the graphs using the draw tools. When working with the M&Ms data, students naturally think about a pie chart for graphing the averages, probably because the candies are round. Obviously that is not a particularly good reason for using the pie chart. A better reason for using the pie chart is that the average data provide a single row of data that describe an average bag of M&Ms. The pie chart does a good job representing each color's portion of the 100% total. If you highlight cells B10 through G10 and select the pie chart from the charting menu (Excel calls this menu the Chart

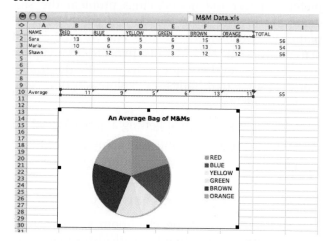

Wizard), you immediately notice that the slices of the pie representing the different colors are not the right colors. And, the legend is labeled 1, 2, 3, 4, 5, and 6, which is not descriptive either.

NAME	RED	BLUE	YELLOW	GREEN	BROWN	ORANGE	TOTAL	
Sara	13	9	5	6	15	8	56	
Maria	10	6	3	9	13	13	54	
Shawn	9	12	8	3	12	12	56	
Average	11	9	5	6	13	11	55	

An Average Bag of M&Ms

RED
BLUE
YELLOW
GREEN
BROWN
ORANGE

A descriptive chart needs to include a title, needs to have a legend that identifies the colors for each of the slices of the pie chart, and needs to have the slices appropriately colored for the colors of the M&Ms data. First, add the labels by highlighting cells B1 through G1 and select Copy from the Edit menu. Click on the pie chart and select Paste from the Edit menu. Immediately, the legend is corrected with the color names, only perhaps you notice that the colors in the pie chart do not match the color names in the legend.

Now, you need to guide the students in changing the colors of the slices so that the colors match the labels that were just created in the legend. Click on the specific portion of the legend (say, the first box which is labeled RED). Then select the appropriate color from the Fill Color menu (found in the Drawing menu). Continue this process until all the slices are the appropriate colors.

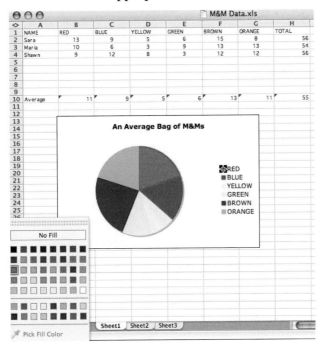

As nice as this chart is, it does not provide the answer to the question the students are to answer. What is the chance of selecting a green M&M from a bag of M&Ms? Introduce the students to the Chart Options (in the Chart menu). In the Data Labels tab, they have a number of options for labeling the slices of the pie. Select the "show label and percent" option as in this example. The percent information helps to answer the question about the chance of getting a green. One final display capability of the spreadsheet might be to explode the GREEN slice, highlighting the importance of this information for answering the question. Select the green slice and drag it to the location desired.

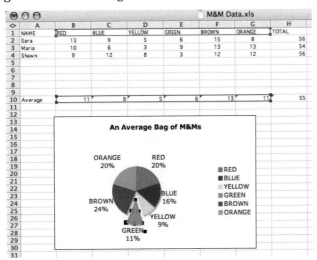

This analysis of a sample of three bags of M&Ms indicates an 11% chance of selecting a green M&M. Also, the chart clearly displays the chances of getting the other colors. But the important considera-

tion is whether this sample represents the percentages the manufacturer uses to fill the bags. In the Classroom 6.1 is an activity where students gain familiarity with charting spreadsheet data while exploring an important mathematical question. How does the actual probability used by the company to fill the bags compare with the experimental probability (as identified in selected sample sizes)? Technology Link 6.1 contains three sample sizes (5, 50, and 100 bags) for students to explore the effect of sample size in determining the actual probability.

Technology Link 6.1

An Excel spreadsheet called M&Mexperiment.xls is available at this book's website. This spreadsheet contains samples of 5 bags, 50 bags, and 100 bags to be used for In the Classroom 6.1. The **Actual** link connects you to the M&Ms websites to find the actual probability. The challenge is to determine whether the bag is from the United States or the United Kingdom. They use different percentages in packaging their candies.

www.wiley.com/college/niess

Learning with and about Spreadsheets

The M&Ms activities demonstrate one way to introduce students to spreadsheets while also guiding them in learning about the basic operations and concepts of a spreadsheet. With this preliminary knowledge, students (as early as fifth grade) are ready to begin using spreadsheets as an important tool for learning in a variety of subject areas. Students can research questions that require them to integrate their knowledge of mathematics, geography, geology, history, and other subjects with that of spreadsheets. As they explore different problems, they begin to recognize that spreadsheets are more than mathematical tools. They learn about the spreadsheet as a tool to explore social, ethical, and human issues. They learn how to use the spreadsheet as a productivity tool, a communication tool, a research tool, and a problem-solving and decision-making tool. As with any tool, attention to basic operations and concepts is essential if students are to learn to use the spreadsheets efficiently and accurately with a myriad of subject area problems.

Basic Spreadsheet Operations and Concepts

How can you scaffold your students' learning experiences about spreadsheets as they learn with spreadsheets? As their teacher, you must identify

---

In the Classroom 6.1

WHICH SAMPLE SIZE BEST ESTIMATES THE ACTUAL PROBABILITY?

TECHNOLOGY OBJECTIVE: NETS · S I, III, VI

- **Spreadsheets:** Technology as a productivity, problem-solving, and decision-making tool while building understanding of basic concepts.
- Use a spreadsheet to prepare graphical representations of data from different sample sizes of bags of M&Ms.

CONTENT OBJECTIVE: Mathematics: Analyze the effect of sample size to identify the best estimate for the actual probability.

GRADE LEVEL: 5–9

BACKGROUND: The M&Ms company fills the bags of candies using a specific weighting for each color. They mix a large amount with the different colors in the specified proportions. The individual bags are filled from the mixture.

ACTUAL PROBABILITY: The probability of each color used to fill the bags of M&Ms at the company.

EXPERIMENTAL PROBABILITY: The probability of each color from an experiment of some number of bags of M&Ms.

PROBLEM: What sample size produces an experimental probability to best estimate the actual probability?

❑ Display the data for different sample sizes of bags of M&Ms in a spreadsheet:

   A. 5 bags of M&Ms

   B. 50 bags of M&Ms

   C. 100 bags of M&Ms

❑ Analyze each experiment:

   A. Find the average number of M&Ms for each color in the experiment.

   B. Create a pie chart that displays the label and percent for each color.

   C. Compare your results from each experiment; propose the actual probability that the company uses for each color of M&Ms.

❑ Visit the M&Ms website to find what the M&Ms company posts as the actual probability. Does the candy come from the United States or the United Kingdom? Be sure to check the websites for both countries.

❑ Explain whether these data seem to be from the United States or the United Kingdom. Write a paragraph explaining the effect of sample size in estimating the actual probability.

---

specific capabilities of the spreadsheet that your students will need for their future explorations of the content. At the same time, you must identify a subject-specific content area within which their exploration can be embedded. Often these explorations of content are easily embedded in mathematical and real-world business applications since many of the capabilities are based in mathematics and various content areas. Notice how the first two Spreadsheet Instructional Ideas encourage students to explore the basics of the spreadsheet and at the same time connect their use with mathematical content.

Spreadsheet Instructional Idea: Working with User-Defined Formulas

Suppose you are working with a spreadsheet and you enter this formula in cell C4:

=B3−B5+D3/D5

How would a computer spreadsheet respond to this formula? Would the subtraction be done first, then the addition, and finally the division? In other words, are the operations computed in the order that they appear from left to right? Or, does the computer spreadsheet follow the mathematical convention that would have multiplication and division done first (from left to right) and then the addition and subtraction (from left to right). This convention is the one that elementary-grade students learn. How can explorations with this formula help them learn both with and about spreadsheets?

In the Classroom 6.2 is a student investigation that is concerned with the order of operations. But this activity does more! Students learn about spreadsheets and they use the spreadsheet as a problem-solving tool. Begin with a whole-class discussion of the problem that introduced this section. Using the numbers 3, 3, 4, and 9, which numbers should be

In the Classroom 6.2

TARGET MATH

TECHNOLOGY OBJECTIVES: NETS · S I, III, VI
- **Spreadsheets:** Technology as a productivity, problem-solving, and decision-making tool while building understanding of basic concepts.
- Create spreadsheet formulas referencing cells using cell names.

CONTENT OBJECTIVE Mathematics: Use the order of operations to calculate solutions in a problem-solving investigation.

GRADE LEVEL: 5–9

PROBLEM: Use mathematical operations $(+, -, *, /, \wedge)$ and perhaps parentheses to construct a formula that uses cell references to the four predetermined numbers to result in the target numbers. Then design your own target problem.

	A	B	C	D	E	F	G	H	I	J
1	Target Math									
2										
3		Directions:			Use math operations to create a formula that uses these 4 numbers					
4					to create the TARGET number. Put the formula in the cell in the center.					
5										
6							Do it a different way:			
7		1. The target is 13					2. The target is 13			
8										
9			1		4			1		4
10										
11			8		6			8		6
12										
13		3. The target is 12					4. The target is 6			
14										
15			1		5			3		4
16										
17			8		6			3		9
18										
19	5. Now creat a target problem and challenge your neighbor to solve it									
20										
21					The target is		?			
22										
23										
24										
25										
26										
27										

target.xls

Possible solutions: Cell D10=C11/E9*E11+C9 and Cell I10=H9^J11+(J9+H11)

placed in the yellow cells (B3, B5, D3, and D5) so that the formula in the blue cell C4 that contains the formula =B3−B5+D3/D5 returns the value 6?

the spreadsheet returns a strange statement #DIV/0! and also shows an exclamation point, indicating that the result is unexpected and may be an error!

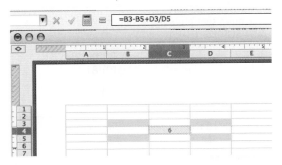

The problem begins by setting up this spreadsheet. When the students enter the formula in C4,

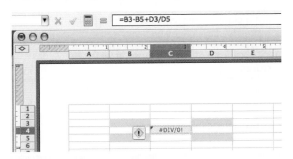

Encourage the students to suggest values to put in the yellow cell locations to see how the formula

changes. The statement #DIV/0! remains until a number is entered in cell D5. This information is the spreadsheet's way of indicating that, without a value in that cell, the value in D5 is assumed to be zero and, of course, division by zero is undefined! As students suggest different arrangements for the values of 3, 3, 4, and 9, they need to explain why the arrangement results in the display in cell C4.

Now the students are ready for In the Classroom 6.2 where they must identify a formula in the center cell (C4) that results in the target number using the surrounding cells (such as B3, B5, D3, and D5). Through this investigation the students are (1) exploring the order of operations using addition, subtraction, multiplication, and division along with parentheses to direct the order and (2) recognizing that the order of operations in the spreadsheet matches the mathematical convention:

1. operations within parentheses;

2. multiplication and division operations in the order they occur (left to right);

3. addition and subtraction operations in the order they occur (left to right).

Spreadsheet Instructional Idea: User-Defined versus Built-in Formulas   During the month of March, the high temperatures in Portland, Oregon, often vary drastically as winter shifts to spring. Last year, the highs reported for one week were as follows:

Sunday	Monday	Tuesday	Wednesday	Thursday	Friday	Saturday
55	60	64	68	60	58	55

What was the average high temperature for that week? Most students in the upper elementary grades are able to determine the average by adding the values $(55+60+64+68+60+58+55 = 420)$ and dividing by seven $(420/7 = 60)$.

In the Classroom 6.3 challenges students to explain why using a *built-in* function for the average is generally better than personally defining a formula. With the *user-defined* formula for the average (where the sum is divided by seven), seven data points are *always* required whereas in the built-in AVERAGE formula, the spreadsheet ignores empty cells and nonnumeric cell data. This result is similar to the previous mathematics problem (discussed in Spreadsheet Instructional Idea: Working with User-Defined Formulas) where the lack of a value in cell D5 is interpreted to be the value zero when responding to a user-defined formula. In other words, when a *built-in formula* references empty cells or nonnumeric cell data, the calculation ignores those cells. On the other hand, *user-defined formulas* require a value for cells that are identified in the formula. If the cells are blank or contain nonnumeric data, the spreadsheet uses the number zero for that cell.

Designing dependable spreadsheets is an important outcome for this activity. What happens to the spreadsheet when different data are entered? How can the spreadsheet be designed to continue returning correct results for different data? Important fundamentals for spreadsheet design need to be emphasized (as in Figure 6.2) to assure the accuracy of the results of a spreadsheet.

Social, Ethical, and Human Issues

As students work with data in computer spreadsheets, they are able to analyze and reconstruct others' analyses, and even question their proposals. However, in using the spreadsheet as a tool, the accuracy of the analysis is critical. Some graphs may tell one story, while others suggest a different story. Teachers need to include instruction for guiding students in understanding ethical, cultural, and societal issues involved in the use of spreadsheets. Thus, students need to learn to be responsible for the results generated through their spreadsheet analyses.

Spreadsheet Fundamentals	
Do not include numeric values with formulas.	Avoid formulas that embed the values like the 8 in this formula: =SUM(B2:B10)/8
Refer to values by the cell names in which the values are stored.	Spreadsheets use the values in cells B2 through B10 and B1 in computing the value =SUM(B2:B10)/B1
Use spreadsheet built-in formulas.	=AVERAGE(B2:B10) is more dependable than =SUM(B2:B10)/8
Focus on dependability by testing.	Use values like 10 to test cells—easier to test!

FIGURE 6.2   Spreadsheet design fundamentals that support the design of dependable spreadsheets.

In the Classroom 6.3

ON AN AVERAGE!

TECHNOLOGY OBJECTIVE: NETS · S I, III, VI

- **Spreadsheets:** Technology as a productivity, problem-solving, and decision-making tool while building understanding of basic concepts.
- Compare built-in formulas with user-defined formulas. Identify strategies for design of reliable and dependable spreadsheets.

CONTENT OBJECTIVE: **Mathematics:** Find the average of a set of data.

GRADE LEVEL: 5–9

PROBLEM: Kelly collected the high temperatures for three weeks. She entered the data but left the value for Saturday of the second week blank. She did enter "not reported" for Wednesday of the third week. She defined two different ways to find the average for the first week:

- **User-defined average in cell B12** as

$$=(B4+B5+B6+B7+B8+B9+B10)/7$$

- **Built-in AVERAGE** in cell B13 as

$$=AVERAGE(B4:B10)$$

Then she used the copy feature of the spreadsheet to copy the formulas across the two rows.
To her surprise while the values were the same for the formulas in the first week, they were not for the following weeks. What happened?

	A	B	C	D
				$=(B4+B5+B6+B7+B8+B9+B10)/7$

average.xls

	A	B	C	D
1	High Temperatures for three weeks in March			
2				
3		Week 1	Week 2	Week 3
4	Sunday	55	52	59
5	Monday	60	55	61
6	Tuesday	64	54	62
7	Wednesday	68	56	not reported
8	Thursday	60	59	62
9	Friday	58	60	59
10	Saturday	55		60
11				
12	User-defined Average	60	48	#VALUE!
13	Built-in AVERAGE	60	56	60.5
14				

1. Create this spreadsheet entering these formulas in the appropriate cells.

Cell	Formula
B12	$=(B4+B5+B6+B7+B8+B9+B10)/7$
B13	$=AVERAGE(B4:B10)$
C12	$=(C4+C5+C6+C7+C8+C9+C10)/7$
C13	$=AVERAGE(C4:C10)$
D12	$=(D4+D5+D6+D7+D8+D9+D10)/7$
D13	$=AVERAGE(D4:D10)$

2. Why are the values in cells C12 and C13 different? Which formula calculates the average correctly? How can the formula in cell C12 be changed to have the average identified correctly?

3. Why are the values in cells D12 and D13 different? What causes the message #VALUE! to be displayed? How should the formula in D12 be changed to get the average of the data?

4. Why might you prefer to use a built-in formula to a user-defined formula in the spreadsheet?

5. What ideas do you have for designing dependable spreadsheets that are important for obtaining correct results for multiple data sets?

The Internet provides students access to a myriad of data sets. And access to these data sets provides opportunities for students to investigate statements, positions, and arguments. The data are easily obtained and fairly easily placed in a spreadsheet. Yet, it is essential to challenge the validity and reliability of the data before challenging widely held positions with data they use in supporting their challenge. As teachers, you need to help your students identify sources that are accurate, relevant, appropriate, and comprehensive. Rather than just providing data sets in a spreadsheet, students should be encouraged to research the sources of the data as an important part of their investigation of data to support their arguments through an analysis of spreadsheets. Spreadsheet Instructional Idea: Analyzing Authentic Data provides one example of how data can be used to challenge a commonly held position. Moreover, the source of the data for this activity is a widely recognized valid and reliable source, which lends credibility to the challenge.

Spreadsheet Instructional Idea: Analyzing Authentic Data   What is your understanding of the American South prior to the Civil War? Do you believe that the Southern economy was agriculturally based while the Northern economy was primarily focused on manufacturing? This belief is widely held and widely taught. Does that make this belief accurate?

The National Council for the Social Studies has called for social studies to be active, authentic, integrative, meaningful, and values-based. Students need to be encouraged to question the "accepted" views about the past. Spreadsheets can be used for analyzing the census data on manufacturing activity in various parts of the South as well as the agrarian activity of the North in the process of investigating the authenticity of the "accepted" view. This approach to studying about the past requires that students view the past as a series of unresolved problems. Some of the problems may be obvious, such as the original exclusion of blacks and women from participation in the American democratic process. Others, such as the problems stemming from common misconceptions about the North and South before the Civil War, are not so obvious. As students consider the period before the American Civil War, they need to understand that accepting the view of the North and South as being vastly different leads to conclusions suggesting that the Civil War was unavoidable. The idea that the North and South were culturally at odds makes it easier to suggest that the Civil War had to be fought in order to unify separate national experiences. The idea that the Civil War was an unavoidable cultural clash discounts the role of slavery; Southern apologists later used this idea to excuse

segregation and racial discrimination. Yet, this question challenges the "accepted" view. Were the North and South really so different?

What type of data makes sense to investigate such a challenge? Where might the data be found? The United States Census has traditionally collected important data concerning the economic, social, and cultural conditions of towns, counties, and states. This type of data may be useful in challenging the ideas. But where can these data be found that are accurate, authentic, and reliable? An Internet search of the U.S. Census quickly identifies the Geostat Center at the University of Virginia (see Technology Link 6.2).

Technology Link 6.2

*T*he best source for data concerning the economic, social, or cultural conditions in the United States is the United States Census. Data from historic U.S. censuses are available on various websites, but one of the best is the University of Virginia's Historical Census Browser. Use the **Census** link to access this Web browser.

www.wiley.com/college/niess

The Geostat Center is widely recognized as providing an authentic and reliable database to access data for various times, including the 1850 period. In accessing these data, you might first identify the data you need to examine if the North and South were vastly different in terms of the agriculture (or farming investments) as well as in their manufacturing investments. Once at the Geostat site, select the census year to examine the data for 1850. Now you need to identify the variables of interest:

- Within the Agriculture window select cash value of farms.
- Within the Economy/Manufacturing/Employment window select capital invested in manufacturing investments.

Submit your query using the appropriate selection at the bottom of the page.

The data are presented in columns like a spreadsheet. While you can use the options at the bottom of the page to resort the data, you can work with these data in a spreadsheet, too. Highlight the states and their data, then copy and paste the material into the spreadsheet. With some formatting and sorting of the data on the column titled Cash Value of Farms (in descending order), your spreadsheet looks like the one in Figure 6.3.

You can now use this spreadsheet to investigate the original question while also exploring a number of spreadsheet features such as sorting and charting. In the Classroom 6.4 discusses some activities you

In the Classroom 6.4

HOW DIFFERENT WERE THE NORTH AND SOUTH BEFORE THE CIVIL WAR?

TECHNOLOGY OBJECTIVE: NETS · S I, II, III, VI

- **Spreadsheets:** Technology as a productivity, problem-solving and decision-making tool while building understanding of basic concepts.
- Investigate Internet data for authenticity and using spreadsheet sort and charting capabilities.

CONTENT OBJECTIVE: **Social studies:** Challenge accepted views of the past.

GRADE LEVEL: 8–12

PROBLEM: Was the North primarily industrial and the South primarily agricultural?

Use U.S. Census Bureau data to describe the economic characteristics of the North and South during 1850. With a spreadsheet of 1850 data for the states for (1) cash value of farms and (2) capital invested in manufacturing establishments, complete the following:

1. Sort the state data by the cash value of farms. What do these data suggest about the Northern states versus the Southern states with respect to agricultural production?

2. Sort the state data by the capital invested in manufacturing investments in descending order. What does this information suggest about the Northern states versus the Southern states with respect to investment in manufacturing?

3. Find the total cash value of farms for all states. Calculate the PERCENT of each state's investment in farms to the total cash value of farms for all states. Sort the state data by this PERCENT. What does this information suggest about the South's dominance for agricultural production in the United States?

4. a. Reorganize your data to compare the data for the five largest states from the North (New York, Pennsylvania, Ohio, Massachusetts, and Indiana) and the South (Virginia, Tennessee, Kentucky, Georgia, and North Carolina).

	Region	State	Cash Value of Farms	Capital Invested in Manufacturing	
1		1850 CENSUS DATA			
2					
3	Region	State	Cash Value of Farms	Capital Invested in Manufacturing	
4	North	NEW YORK	554,546,642	99,904,405	
5		PENNSYLVANIA	407,876,099	94,173,810	
6		OHIO	358,758,603	29,019,538	
7		MASSACHUSETTS	109,076,347	83,357,642	
8		INDIANA	136,385,173	7,842,362	
9					
10	South	VIRGINIA	216,401,543	18,109,993	
11		TENNESSEE	97,851,212	6,975,279	
12		KENTUCKY	155,021,262	12,350,740	
13		GEORGIA	95,753,445	5,460,483	
14		NORTH CAROLINA	67,891,766	7,252,225	

b. Create a stacked column chart to compare the North versus the South displaying both the farming and manufacturing data for each state. From the information in this chart, which states were primarily responsible for the agricultural production in the United States?

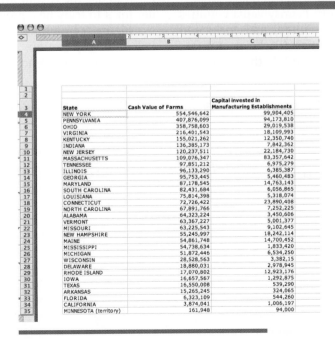

	State	Cash Value of Farms	Capital invested in Manufacturing Establishments
4	NEW YORK	554,546,642	99,904,405
5	PENNSYLVANIA	407,876,099	94,173,810
6	OHIO	358,758,603	29,019,538
7	VIRGINIA	216,401,543	18,109,993
8	KENTUCKY	155,021,262	12,350,740
9	INDIANA	136,385,173	7,842,362
10	NEW JERSEY	120,237,511	22,184,730
11	MASSACHUSETTS	109,076,347	83,357,642
12	TENNESSEE	97,851,212	6,975,279
13	ILLINOIS	96,133,290	6,385,387
14	GEORGIA	95,753,445	5,460,483
15	MARYLAND	87,178,545	14,763,143
16	SOUTH CAROLINA	82,431,684	6,056,865
17	LOUISIANA	75,814,398	5,318,074
18	CONNECTICUT	72,726,422	23,890,408
19	NORTH CAROLINA	67,891,766	7,252,225
20	ALABAMA	64,323,224	3,450,606
21	VERMONT	63,367,227	5,001,377
22	MISSOURI	63,225,543	9,102,645
23	NEW HAMPSHIRE	55,245,997	18,242,114
24	MAINE	54,861,748	14,700,452
25	MISSISSIPPI	54,738,634	1,833,420
26	MICHIGAN	51,872,446	6,534,250
27	WISCONSIN	28,528,563	3,382,15
28	DELAWARE	18,880,031	2,978,945
29	RHODE ISLAND	17,070,802	12,923,176
30	IOWA	16,657,567	1,292,875
31	TEXAS	16,550,008	539,290
32	ARKANSAS	15,265,245	324,065
33	FLORIDA	6,323,109	544,260
34	CALIFORNIA	3,874,041	1,006,197
35	MINNESOTA (territory)	161,948	94,000

FIGURE 6.3   Census Bureau Data for 1850.

can use to guide students' explorations of the question of whether the South dominated agriculturally and the North dominated in manufacturing in 1850.

Exploration of the capital invested in manufacturing per state (sorting the data by that column) suggests that indeed the northern states had a distinct manufacturing character. However, if the cash values of farms are totaled for all states and each state's percent of that total is calculated, a different picture emerges. Additional evidence to challenge the notion of a dominance of the South in agricultural production unfolds with this graphical comparison of the five largest states from the North and the South.

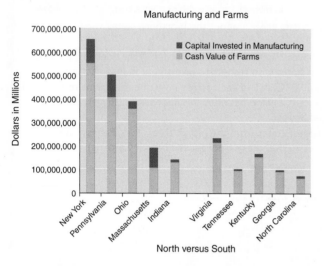

A host of alternative perspectives and interpretations might also emerge as students conduct more analysis with the data in this activity. For example, students might want to look at county data from border states such as Virginia and Pennsylvania. If students isolate five southern Pennsylvania counties (Adams, Bedford, Franklin, Fulton, and York) and five northern Virginia counties (Berkeley, Fairfax, Hampshire, Jefferson, and Loudon), they find that the economic similarities are striking. Graphing the cash value of farms and the capital invested in manufacturing for these 10 selected border counties using a stacked column chart shows that those counties in both states were heavily agrarian.

An alternative approach for representing the data on the economic difference between the North and South might be to calculate the cash value of farms as a percentage of the total economic activity in each state. If the cash value of farms and the investment in manufacturing of the year are summed, students are able to sense the relative extent of each type of economic activity. Again comparing the five largest northern and southern states challenges the conventional notion. With the exception of Massachusetts, all nine states are exceedingly agrarian.

As students explore the various hypotheses about the antebellum South, they must pay careful attention to which data they use, to the functions that they use in the analysis, and to the types of graphs for communicating their position. Through such an activity they have the opportunity to practice a responsible use of the spreadsheet technology in developing accurate and appropriate information that challenges widely held assumptions and beliefs.

Spreadsheets as Productivity Tools

One advantage of spreadsheets is that they help people become more productive by saving time. The speed and accuracy of the calculations allow them to consider different options quickly. Changing one piece of data initiates an automatic recalculation of all embedded formulas. However, students need to learn to use the capabilities of the spreadsheet in order for it to truly be a productivity tool for them.

Figure 6.4 outlines a simple multiplication problem for exploration of copying *relative* versus *absolute* cell references in spreadsheet formulas.

	A	B	C	D	E	F	G	H
1	Formula Challenge							
2								
3	Find a formula that could be entered in cell B4 that could then be							
4	copied down the rows and across the columns							
5	to complete the Multiplication Table.							
6								
7								
8	X	1	2	3	4	5	6	
9	1							
10	2							
11	3							
12	4							
13	5							
14	6							
15								

Multiplication.xls

FIGURE 6.4 Designing a spreadsheet multiplication table.

Typically, copying a formula adjusts the formula for the particular row and column. If, in the multiplication spreadsheet, you put the formula =B8*A9 in cell B9 and copy that formula across the row, the formula changes relative to the particular row and column. Cell C9 becomes =C8*B9 which returns the correct product of 1 and 2, or 2. But cell D9 is =D8*C9 which is 6 and, to make matters worse, cell G9 becomes =G8*F9 which is 720 (clearly not the product of 1 and 6).

To change this *relative* formula, you can use the symbol $. What happens if, instead of =B8*A9 you enter the formula =B8*$A9 in cell B9? With the $, you are creating an *absolute* reference to the object that follows the $. That means that column A is to remain A as the formula is copied. When this formula is copied across row 9, the products are then as they should be.

Can these new formulas in row 9 be copied down the rows? Try it. Unfortunately, cell G14 becomes =G13*$A14 instead of =G8*$A14. The rows were not held constant because of the relative references to the particular row into which they were copied. What formula could you enter in cell B9 so that when you copy it across and then copy the resulting formulas down the rows, the appropriate multiplication is completed? What happens if cell B9 is set as =B$8*$A9. This formula indicates that, when copied, row 8 in the B$8 portion is to remain constant and column A in the $A9 portion is to remain constant. The spreadsheet produces the correct multiplication results when the formula is copied to the other cells. Test it out by entering different values to be multiplied in row 8 and column A. You will find that this one formula in cell B9 (=B$8*$A9) can be copied to all the other cells of the multiplication table to assure that the products are correct. In the process of creating this multiplication table, students directly experience the difference between copying referenced and absolute formulas in a spreadsheet.

Spreadsheet Instructional Idea: Using Relative and Absolute Cell References   Teachers must maintain accurate records of students' grades. Often this activity is completed using a grade book—the bound, paper version. This compilation of grades, however, requires that the teacher manually compute the final grade, a process that is both tedious and, unfortunately, error-prone. Alternatively, if an electronic version of a grade book is maintained, it can be used to continuously update each student's progress in the class as new grades are entered. While there are many prepackaged electronic grade books available for teachers, you and your students can design a grade book program that specifically describes the work expected for the grading period.

When you are student teaching, you are expected to maintain student grades and keep your students updated on their progress. Perhaps you can use In the Classroom 6.5 with your students to challenge them to design a grade book that they can use to maintain a record of their progress in the class. In the process, they will learn more about the spreadsheet and the use of a spreadsheet as a productivity tool.

In the Classroom 6.5 designs a grade book that returns a "Percent to date" for each student. As students complete each assignment, the students' grades are entered. When Homework 1 grades are entered, the teacher also enters "Points to date" for that homework, or 2 in cell B17. The spreadsheet is set up to accumulate the "Points to date" in column M for each student and in cell M17 to identify the total points to date.

Problem 2 guides you in instructing the computer to return the "Percent to date" in column N. The formula =ROUND(M4/$M$17,2) in cell N4 instructs the spreadsheet to compute the division of the value in cell M4 by the value in cell M17 (2/2); the result is 1.00 since the ROUND function indicates the value is to be rounded to the hundredths place. But 1.00 does not look like the percent that is desired. You need to *format* the cell to return a percentage with zero decimal places. With this instruction, the value in cell N4 becomes 100%.

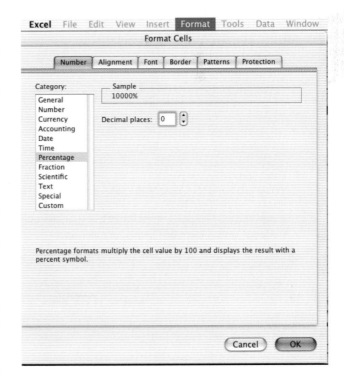

Once the formula and formatting in cell N4 are completed, you can simply copy the formula down the column to find the "Percent to date" for

In the Classroom 6.5

HOW ARE MY GRADES DETERMINED?

TECHNOLOGY OBJECTIVE: NETS · S I, III, VI

- **Spreadsheets:** Technology as a productivity, problem-solving and decision-making tool while building understanding of basic concepts.
- Absolute and relative cell referencing; formatting in percentage; using the IF formula to print appropriate grade.

CONTENT OBJECTIVE: All Subjects Areas: Determine grades.

Mathematics: Explore greater than and less than in conducting logical tests.

GRADE LEVEL: 8–12

PROBLEM: How does the teacher determine our grades?

Mr. Harris announced that grades for the grading period are determined with the following assignments and point values:

Homework	2 points for each, 5 homework assignments
Quizzes	10 points for each, 4 quizzes
Midterm test	50 points for one midterm
Final test	100 points for one final test

Grades for the quarter are based on this grading scale:

89% <	A	<= 100%
79% <	B	<= 89%
69% <	C	<= 79%
59% <	D	<= 69%
	F	<= 59%

1. Create this basic grade book. What formula should you use to determine the "Points to date" for each student (M4, M5, . . ., M14), the "Points possible" for the assignments (M16), and the "Points to date" for the assignments (M17)?

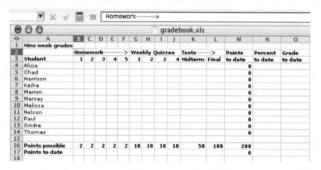

2. Enter some data for Homework #1 and then enter this formula in N4: =ROUND(M4/$M$17,2). The result is 1.00. While still in cell N4, change the value to a percent: Format the Number to a Percentage with zero (0) Decimal places. The result is 100%. Copy the formula and formatting from cell N4 down the column to have the spreadsheet create the correct percentage for all the students. Explain why this formula creates the correct percentage for the students' grades identified in this spreadsheet.

(continued on next page)

3. Instruct the spreadsheet to calculate the grade to date by entering this formula in O4 and copying the formula down the O column.

$$=IF(N4>89\%,"A",IF(N4>79\%,"B",IF(N4>69\%,"C",IF(N4>59\%,"D","F"))))$$

Explain how this formula works to determine these grades.

| | =IF(N4>89,"A",IF(N4>79%,"B",IF(N4>69%,"C",IF(N4>59%,"D","F")))) |

gradebook.xls

	A	B	C	D	E	F	G	H	I	J	K	L	M	N	O
1	Nine week grades														
2		Homework-------->					Weekly Quizzes				Tests------>		Points	Percent	Grade
3	Student	1	2	3	4	5	1	2	3	4	Midterm	Final	to date	to date	to date
4	Alicia	2											2	100%	A
5	Chad	1											1	50%	F
6	Harrison	2											2	100%	A
7	Keiha	2											2	100%	A
8	Marion	1											1	50%	F
9	Marsay	2											2	100%	A
10	Melissa	2											2	100%	A
11	Nelson	1											1	50%	F
12	Paul	2											2	100%	A
13	Sindra	2											2	100%	A
14	Thomas	2											2	100%	A
15															
16	Points possible	2	2	2	2	2	10	10	10	10	50	100	200		
17	Points to date	2											2		

4. Test your grade book with these grades for each of the assignments. Enter the grades for Homework 2 and then enter the "Points to date" for Homework 2. Explain why you must enter the "Points to date" for each assignment in order for the correct grade to be determined.

gradebook.xls

	A	B	C	D	E	F	G	H	I	J	K	L	M	N	O
1	Nine week grades														
2		Homework-------->					Weekly Quizzes				Tests------>		Points	Percent	Grade
3	Student	1	2	3	4	5	1	2	3	4	Midterm	Final	to date	to date	to date
4	Alicia	2	2	2	1	2	9	8	10	9	47	92	184	92%	A
5	Chad	1	2	2	1	0	8	7	9	9	40	75	154	77%	C
6	Harrison	2	2	2	2	2	9	9	8	8	39	70	153	77%	C
7	Keiha	2	0	0	1	2	5	5	7	6	30	60	118	59%	F
8	Marion	1	2	2	2	2	8	7	9	7	48	91	179	90%	A
9	Marsay	2	2	2	0	0	7	9	9	8	47	77	163	82%	B
10	Melissa	2	0	0	2	2	9	7	8	8	45	72	155	78%	C
11	Nelson	1	2	2	2	2	9	6	9	9	38	62	142	71%	C
12	Paul	2	2	0	2	2	7	9	10	7	39	80	160	80%	B
13	Sindra	2	0	0	1	0	7	6	5	4	38	72	135	68%	D
14	Thomas	2	0	2	1	2	8	8	10	9	35	73	150	75%	C
15															
16	Points possible	2	2	2	2	2	10	10	10	10	50	100	200		
17	Points to date	2	2	2	2	2	10	10	10	10	50	100	200		

5. Change this spreadsheet grade book so you can keep track of your grade in one of your classes.

all students. Notice how the formula does not change for the $M$17 portion because the dollar signs indicate an absolute reference. On the other hand, the M4 changes for the appropriate row for each formula. Another advantage is that the formatting is also copied. So the resulting values are all percentages.

With the percentages, you can easily determine the appropriate grade and so can the spreadsheet with the proper instruction. The IF function requires a logical test to be performed in order to determine the action to be completed. A simple example of this formula is

IF(N4>89, "A", "not A")

If this formula is inserted in cell O4, the logical test is whether the value in N4 is greater than 89; 100% is greater than 89% resulting in a "true" statement. Thus, the spreadsheet enters the grade "A" and is finished. Now suppose the value in N5 is 50 and the formula in cell O5 is

IF(N5>89, "A", "not A")

The test leads to a false statement because the value in N5 is 50, a value that is clearly not greater than 89. As a result, the spreadsheet enters "not A" in O5.

However, for the In the Classroom 6.5 activity, the instructions are more complex in order to match the instructions the teacher presents in the problem. The formula for cell O4 is

=IF(N4>89%,"A",IF(N4>79%,"B",IF(N4>69%, "C",IF(N4>59%,"D","F"))))

In this case, the value in cell N4 is a percentage requiring the % sign to be included with the numbers in the formula. For this formula, the spreadsheet first checks whether the value in cell N4 (Alicia's grade) is greater than 89%. The test is true, so "A" is recorded. If the test is false, the spreadsheet refers to the next condition to determine if the value is greater than 79%.

When this formula is copied to cell O5, the formula becomes

=IF(N5>89%,"A",IF(N5>79%,"B",IF(N5>69%, "C",IF(N5>59%,"D","F"))))

Since Chad's grade is 50%, the computer returns a grade of "F." Each of the tests that need to be done returns a "false," so the last action is to record an "F" for Chad's grade.

Spreadsheets as Communication Tools

Spreadsheets communicate data through a variety of forms including tables and charts. The communication requires that the creator manipulate and represent data far beyond what might be done with a simple display of the raw data. Thus, a spreadsheet-produced chart or graph carries with it a specific intent and certain values. These values must be recognized and carefully implemented when creating spreadsheet products.

One of the value-based concepts that teachers need to guide students' understandings when working with spreadsheets relates to bias and distortion in the presentation of graphs. For example, consider the question of the rising cost of stamps by examining the increase in the cost of stamps over the past century.

Year	Cost (in Cents)
1919	2
1932	3
1958	4
1963	5
1968	6
1971	8
1974	10
1975	13
1978	15
1981	18
1981	20
1985	22
1988	25
1991	29
1994	32
1997	33
1999	34
2002	37

Does this cost increase seem unreasonable? Many students do not see the changes by simply looking at the numbers. A graphical look provides a more visual representation of the numbers. One interpretation of this graph suggests that the cost of stamps has gradually increased over the past century and the rate of increase does not appear to be particularly steep.

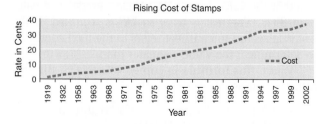

But look more carefully at the horizontal axis (or x-axis) on this chart. The years of the increases

are distributed equally in the chart. Yet, from 1919 to 1932 is a 13-year span while from 1999 to 2002 is a 3-year span! This inconsistency in the intervals is a common mistake in communicating data that leads to a misunderstanding of the information.

Notice how the graph appears when the intervals are consistent. Now the picture is quite different. The rate of increase in the cost of stamps has dramatically increased since 1970. Now, you probably have a different perspective on the question of whether the increase has been unreasonable.

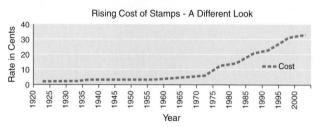

Has this increase in cost really been at an unprecedented rate? Some people might say this graph supports the position that the increase in the costs of stamps has been unreasonable. On the other hand, a better presentation of the data is a comparison with some other costs over the same period. Has the rate of increase in stamps been similar to the rate of inflation as described by the consumer price index? Compare the stamp graph with a graph of the rate of inflation. Perhaps the rate of increase in costs of stamps no longer seems unreasonable as previously suggested. However, as these comparisons show, manipulation and presentations of graphical data from a spreadsheet can be used to communicate the values the creator wishes to advance.

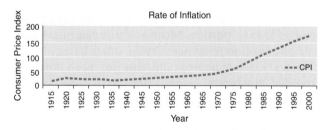

Spreadsheet Instructional Idea: Charting That Misrepresents Data   Do you think crime is a big problem? Has the rate of homicides increased dramatically since 1970? Has the rate of homicides leveled off? What do the data suggest?

You can use examples of charts with misrepresented data from textbooks or original sources to help students understand how values can be transmitted using charts and graphs. A number of common mistakes are made when charts are distorted. In addition to the manipulation of the horizontal axis (*x*-axis), another serious error involves the use of inconsistent intervals on the vertical axis (*y*-axis).

In the Classroom 6.6 engages students in exploring the effects of adjusting the scale on the vertical

In the Classroom 6.6

IS THE HOMICIDE RATE CONTINUING TO INCREASE?

TECHNOLOGY OBJECTIVE: NETS·S I, II, III, VI

- **Spreadsheets:** Technology as a communication, problem-solving and decision-making tool while building understanding of basic concepts and considering ethical issues in presenting data.
- Consider ethical presentations of data when changing the scale on chart axes.

CONTENT OBJECTIVE: Social studies: Determine the value of various graphical representations of data on the homicide rate in the United States.

GRADE LEVEL: 8–12

PROBLEM: Use the homicide data to create various charts to describe the rate of homicide over the past 50 years. Does this change in the homicide rate indicate an increasingly lawless society?

1. Create a spreadsheet data table with the homicide rate data for 1950–2000. Be sure to format the "Year" column as text, rather than as numbers.

Year	Estimated Number of Homicides
1950	7,020
1955	6,850
1960	9,110
1965	9,960
1970	16,000
1975	20,510
1980	23,040
1985	18,980
1990	23,440
1995	21,610
2000	15,517

2. Create a chart of the data where the vertical axis (y-axis) has a scale ranging from 5000 to 50,000. Describe the message that this chart gives about crime in American society.

3. Create a second chart of the data where the vertical axis (y-axis) has a scale ranging from 7500 to 19,500. Describe the message that this chart gives about crime in American society.

4. Create a third chart of the data where the vertical axis (y-axis) has a scale ranging from 0 to 25,000. Describe the message that this chart gives about crime in American society.

5. Which scale provides the most accurate description of crime in American society? Explain how changing the vertical axis affects the message that is communicated.

---

axis of charts. Typically, the spreadsheet creates charts with scales beginning at zero, adjusting the upper limit of the scale to a value similar to the largest value in the data. However, you can alter the look and potential meaning of the chart by reformatting the scale (highlight the axis, choose Format, Selected Axis, and then Scale). This action allows you to change the minimum and maximum values as desired, and that is how easy it is to change the message that is given by the chart. As students in sixth through twelfth grades explore social studies problems such as this one, they also learn more about spreadsheets and how people are able to manipulate the messages that they communicate through a spreadsheet graphical presentation.

In this problem, the charts represent data on the homicide rate in the United States over the last 50 years. Depending on your intent, these very straightforward numbers can be used to make not so obvious political statements, that carry hidden values and ideologies.

The first chart that students create for In the Classroom 6.6 suggests that homicide rates have not fluctuated much over the last 50 years. This effect is produced by extending the range of the y-axis well beyond the highest value for any single entry. In this example the range extends to 50,000 deaths per year, whereas the highest value is 23,440. Someone who wishes to suggest that crime is not a big problem might use this chart.

In the second example the range of the vertical axis is limited. In fact, the value for 1950 is below the beginning value on the vertical axis. Moreover, the values for 1975, 1980, 1990, and 1995 are above the highest possible printed value of 19,500. The impression is then that the homicide rate has risen from virtually zero to something off the charts. Someone who wants to idealize the 1950s as a time of innocence might use this chart to suggest that changing societal values or lax law enforcement resulted in a massive jump in the homicide rate.

The third example is the best representation of the data illustrating a rise in the homicide rate through the 1970s with a slight decrease after 1995. This rise is relatively consistent and less dramatic than in the second chart. Someone who wants to suggest that the recent rise in the homicide rate has leveled off and is now moving down might use this chart to make the point.

Spreadsheets as Research Tools

The Internet provides access to a tremendous amount of data. You can explore the same data that the scientists analyze about Mars as well as the data that social scientists analyze about who does what jobs and who lives where and why. Extensive data sets are available for teachers to use as they guide students in learning to be critical thinkers. Teachers can create spreadsheets in advance and engage the students in analyzing the information, perhaps making conjectures and using the data to support or refute those conjectures. In the process, the students continue to explore the capabilities of the spreadsheet in supporting their analysis.

Spreadsheet Instructional Idea: Investigating Ideas with Charts   In the Classroom 6.7 introduces students to a study of presidential election statistics from surveys conducted by the National Election Studies. All of the numbers are percentages of the total number of votes cast by people in various demographic categories. For example, in the 1952 election 51% of the grade-school-educated voters voted for Eisenhower (Republican) and 49% of grade-school-educated voters voted for Stevenson (Democrat).

This spreadsheet supports the study of voting patterns among a variety of demographic groups. What voting patterns do students see in this spreadsheet? Why did African-American voting patterns change from 1952 to 1976? How does the percentage of votes cast by people living in urban areas for Democratic candidates for president from 1952 to 1976 compare

with those in suburban and rural areas? Johnson and Kennedy split the Catholic vote, despite the fact that Kennedy was one of the few Catholics ever to be nominated for president by a major political party. Since Johnson was not Catholic, how is Johnson's maintenance of the Catholic vote explained?

Many interesting and important lessons can emanate from the questions that arise. Teachers may want students to explore the overall voting patterns among all groups. Students can make pie charts to compare groups on individual elections. Other spreadsheet functions can also be used. For example, students can arrange the percentages per candidate in descending order and compare levels of demographic support from year to year to year. They can also experiment making charts in a search for patterns. They may also be asked to discuss how data presentation is influenced by what a person wants to portray.

Spreadsheets as Problem-Solving and Decision-Making Tools

Solving problems and making informed decisions are important parts of many content areas. Spreadsheets can be useful tools in solving problems that result in students learning more about the subject involved in the problem. In the process of solving the problems, they also are able to learn to design dynamic spreadsheets where changing variables important to the decision can be changed as a way of extending the problems to explore different questions about the initial problem.

Spreadsheet Instructional Idea: Which Chart Best Describes the Data?   An interesting science problem challenges students to identify a town in the United States based solely on wind frequency data. Figure 6.5 presents a set of wind frequency

| | | | | | | | | | | | | | | =SUM(B5:M5) |

Wind.xls

	A	B	C	D	E	F	G	H	I	J	K	L	M	N
1	Mystery Town Wind Frequency Data													
2	Number of days per month for each wind direction													
3														
4	DIR	Jan	Feb	Mar	Apr	May	Jun	Jul	Aug	Sept	Oct	Nov	Dec	Total
5	N	0.25	0.36	0.62	1.11	1.49	1.65	2.08	1.4	0.99	0.47	0.36	0.28	11.06
6	NNE	0.19	0.2	0.28	0.33	0.53	0.42	0.4	0.31	0.36	0.16	0.21	0.12	
7	NE	0.31	0.31	0.31	0.54	0.5	0.45	0.47	0.37	0.42	0.31	0.3	0.22	
8	ENE	0.34	0.2	0.34	0.39	0.31	0.33	0.28	0.25	0.42	0.19	0.3	0.25	
9	E	1.55	0.95	1.33	1.32	0.99	0.72	0.53	0.34	1.05	0.9	1.29	1.3	
10	ESE	8.99	5.82	4.53	2.64	1.49	1.38	0.68	0.78	1.83	4.03	6.15	7.72	
11	SE	4.31	3.47	2.54	1.56	1.02	0.9	0.34	0.81	1.65	3.47	3.75	4.09	
12	SSE	1.95	1.51	1.67	1.14	0.68	0.69	0.5	0.68	0.96	1.58	1.71	1.64	
13	S	2.98	2.18	2.76	2.01	1.43	1.44	0.74	1.18	1.44	2.82	2.61	2.88	
14	SSW	3.29	3.25	3.66	1.92	1.46	1.47	0.65	0.78	1.08	1.89	2.25	4.15	
15	SW	1.27	1.26	1.95	1.44	1.15	1.08	0.56	0.68	0.93	1.52	1.14	1.49	
16	WSW	0.62	0.53	1.15	1.14	0.84	0.6	0.37	0.47	0.81	0.74	0.69	0.71	
17	W	0.65	0.84	1.09	1.35	1.18	0.96	0.68	0.96	1.62	1.43	1.05	0.74	
18	WNW	0.9	1.37	2.05	3.3	4.56	4.17	5.08	5.21	4.41	2.79	1.68	0.96	
19	NW	0.99	1.65	2.42	4.44	6.54	6.42	9.7	9.39	5.76	3.01	1.92	1.3	
20	NNW	0.37	0.62	1.02	2.1	3.6	4.29	5.74	4.46	2.52	0.99	0.54	0.4	
21	Calm	2.11	3.44	3.35	3.24	3.22	3.09	2.23	2.95	3.75	4.74	4.05	2.76	
22	Total	31	28	31	30	31	30	31	31	30	31	30	31	

FIGURE 6.5   Wind frequency data for a mystery town in Oregon.

In the Classroom 6.7

HAVE THE VOTING PATTERNS CHANGED?

TECHNOLOGY OBJECTIVE: **NETS · S I, II, III, IV, V, VI**

- **Spreadsheets:** Technology as a communication, productivity, research and problem-solving and decision-making tool while building understanding of basic concepts.
- Create and manipulate charts to communicate responses to proposed hypotheses.

CONTENT OBJECTIVE: **Social Studies:** Identify voting patterns in presidential elections from 1952 to 1976.

GRADE LEVEL: 8–12

PROBLEM: Have there been any big shifts in voting patterns from 1950 to 2000?
Use these presidential election statistics to create various charts that demonstrate voting patterns from 1950 to 2000.

1. Create this spreadsheet including the appropriate coloring to highlight specific years. The * indicates the candidate who won the election.

2. Review the data in the spreadsheet table for the African-American voters and conjecture as to why their voting patterns changed from 1952 to 1976. Construct this chart and use its information in describing your conjecture. The * indicates the candidate who won the election.

   - Invoke the chart wizard from the menu (Insert→Chart).
   - Select Column charts (the default).
   - Select Cluster column chart subtype (first option available).
   - Select next.
   - Make sure the data range field is blank and then with the chart select A2 through P3.
   - Hold (on the Mac) or Control (on the PC) an drag and select A13 though P13.
   - Continue to format the chart.

3. Repeat the steps to make charts for other demographic comparisons, such as the percentage of votes cast by people living in urban areas for Democratic candidates for president from 1952 to 1976.

4. Prepare a narrative that describes voting patterns for three different demographic groups. How can the data from this spreadsheet be used to generalize the demographic groups you selected?

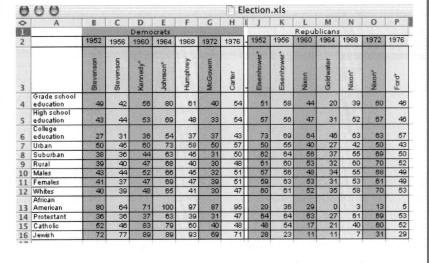

| | Democrats | | | | | | | Republicans | | | | | | |
| | 1952 | 1956 | 1960 | 1964 | 1968 | 1972 | 1976 | 1952 | 1956 | 1960 | 1964 | 1968 | 1972 | 1976 |
	Stevenson	Stevenson	Kennedy*	Johnson*	Humphrey	McGovern	Carter	Eisenhower*	Eisenhower*	Nixon	Goldwater	Nixon*	Nixon*	Ford*
Grade school education	49	42	56	80	61	40	54	51	58	44	20	39	60	46
High school education	43	44	53	69	48	33	54	57	56	47	31	52	67	46
College education	27	31	36	54	37	37	43	73	69	64	46	63	63	57
Urban	50	45	60	73	58	50	57	50	55	40	27	42	50	43
Suburban	38	36	44	63	45	31	50	62	64	56	37	55	69	50
Rural	39	40	47	68	40	30	48	61	60	53	32	60	70	52
Males	43	44	52	66	45	32	51	57	56	48	34	55	68	49
Females	41	37	47	69	47	39	51	59	63	53	31	53	61	49
Whites	40	39	48	65	41	30	47	60	61	52	35	58	70	53
African American	80	64	71	100	97	87	95	20	36	29	0	3	13	5
Protestant	36	36	37	63	39	31	47	64	64	63	27	61	69	53
Catholic	52	46	83	79	60	40	48	48	54	17	21	40	60	52
Jewish	72	77	89	89	93	69	71	28	23	11	11	7	31	29

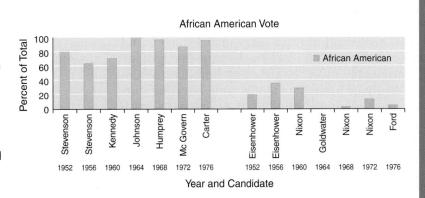

directional data for a town in Oregon. Students are expected to describe the wind pattern, using an appropriate graph of the number of days in the year that the wind has come from that direction. Their first task is to find the number of days in the year for each wind direction in column N of the spreadsheet in Figure 6.5.

Once the total number of days for the different directions is identified, students need to display the information in an appropriate graph. Which one of

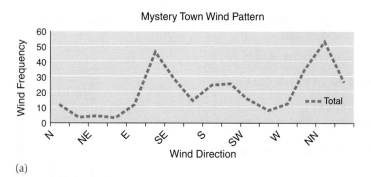

(a)

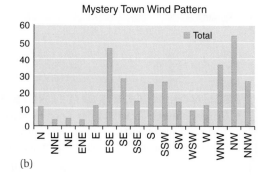

(b)

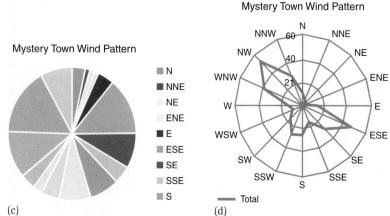

(c)

(d)

FIGURE 6.6 Graphs of wind frequency data for a mystery town in Oregon. (*a*) Line chart. (*b*) Bar chart. (*c*) Pie chart. (*d*) Radar chart.

the graphs in Figure 6.6 provides the best description of the wind pattern in the mystery town?

The radar chart provides the clearest description of the town's wind patterns and provides information about its geography. This town is not likely on the Pacific Ocean coast. If it were, there would be more wind coming from the west. Obviously, the predominant winds come from the northwest (NW) and the east southeast (ESE), but as students look more carefully at when the winds come from those directions, they also note that the winds from the NW are in the summer months and the ESE are in the winter months. What geological formations support such wind patterns? When students investigate the geology of various towns in Oregon, they find that the Columbia River has winds of the same direction during those seasons. Another river connects with the Columbia River in Portland, Oregon. That river moves southward to define the Willamette Valley. This chart shows some winds from that direction suggesting that perhaps this town might be Portland. In fact, the wind frequency data are for Portland, Oregon.

Spreadsheet Instructional Idea: Analyzing Data with Functions and Charts Climate information, including temperature and precipitation, further defines many locales. Summer temperatures like those in Death Valley certainly are not found in Idaho. Nor does lots of precipitation (all the moisture from the

sky including rain, snow, sleet, and hail) appear throughout the midwest during the summer. Latitude, longitude, elevation, and landforms (mountains, rivers, and oceans) are factors in defining the climate for specific locales.

Climatologists use 30-year data sets of climate data to describe the typical climate for locations at different times of year. You can use In the Classroom 6.8 to guide your students in an investigation of temperature and precipitation data for multiple mystery towns. Begin with a search of the Regional Climate Centers for data or use Technology Link 6.3 to access 10 different western town data sets to give to your students. The students' tasks are to identify their towns based on this climate information.

Technology Link 6.3

*T*he best source of data for In the Classroom 6.8 is available on the Web by searching for Regional Climate Centers. In particular, the Western Regional Climate Center provides the most complete climate data sets. Historical data are available in the Historical Climate Information section. You can download the data or use the **Climate** link to download ten different mystery town data sets, both temperature and precipitation data. Change the town names to Mystery1, Mystery2, etc., and provide the data sets to your students as they work collaboratively in groups to identify all ten mystery towns.

www.wiley.com/college/niess

In the Classroom 6.8

WHERE ARE THESE TOWNS IN THE WEST?

TECHNOLOGY OBJECTIVE: NETS·S I, III, IV, V, VI

- **Spreadsheets:** Technology as a research and problem-solving tool while building understanding of basic concepts.
- Analyze data using averages and standard deviations to prepare charts that help in identifying mystery towns.

CONTENT OBJECTIVE: Science, mathematics, and geography: Develop and evaluate inferences about U.S. towns based on predictions based on data analysis.

GRADE LEVEL: 5–9

PROBLEM: Are towns in the western coast states of the United States identifiable by their temperature and precipitation data? Select from: San Diego, California; Los Angeles, California; San Francisco, California; Newport, Oregon; Portland, Oregon; Olympia, Washington; and Seattle, Washington.

Students in teams of four are provided with four mystery towns. Each person in the team is responsible for completing the analysis of the temperature and precipitation data from one of the mystery towns. The students work as a team to make the final analysis of where the towns are in the western coast states.

1. Find the average for each month based on the multiple years of temperature data provided for the mystery town.

2. One standard deviation describes a range about the mean that encompasses about two-thirds of the temperature data. Find the standard deviation for each month. Then find the upper and lower limits for this one standard deviation band by (a) adding the standard deviation to the average and (b) subtracting the standard deviation from the average temperature.

3. Create a chart that shows the one standard deviation band for a 12-month period for the mystery town. The team must determine the vertical axis scale to be used for this chart. Then compare the "average temperature band" with your team members. Make an initial decision about the identity of the four mystery towns.

4. Complete Steps 1–3 for the precipitation data. As a team, reconsider the decisions as to where the mystery towns are.

5. As a team, solidify your decision and be prepared to defend the analysis to the class.

Through this investigation students must use their knowledge of geology, atmospheric science, geography, and mathematics to identify the towns. What kinds of land formations are in the various towns and how do these land formations affect the climate? What is the latitude and longitude of the towns, and how might that affect the climate? What is the geography of western U.S. states? How does the ocean affect their various climates? What is an average temperature and precipitation for the towns? Why do climatologists use a one standard deviation band about the average to describe a typical temperature or precipitation for various locations? How is this band calculated? With these questions, students must explore a new function, the standard deviation (STDEV) function.

Isn't the standard deviation function too advanced? No! Middle-school students grasp that this function identifies a range about the average, encompassing approximately two-thirds of the data in that set. For example, Portland's January precipitation data averages 5.97 inches with a standard deviation of 2.76 inches. Therefore, a "typical" precipitation band for the month of January is 3.21 inches (5.97 − 2.76) to 8.73 inches (5.97 + 2.76). On the other hand, in July the standard deviation is only 0.72 suggesting much less variability in

precipitation, from 0.03 to 1.47 inches. That makes sense since July is not necessarily a rainy month, even for Portland, Oregon!

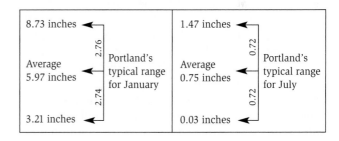

When the data are graphed to show the band about the mean for each month, the graph is like that shown in Figure 6.7. This band shows that while there is more precipitation in the winter months there is also more variability in the amount of precipitation in those months. Therefore, the band width is wider in the winter months than for the summer months.

For In the Classroom 6.8, provide students with a list of possible towns to help them begin their explorations. They can investigate the land formations, the geology, and the climate for the various towns to guide them in their identification of their mystery town represented by the data they are expected to

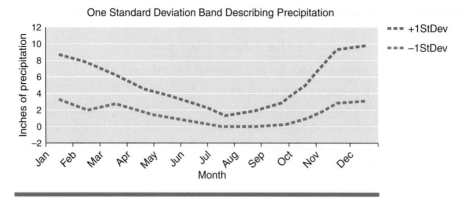

FIGURE 6.7 Portland's typical precipitation throughout the year.

analyze. This activity is best done with students working in collaborative teams where each student is responsible for analyzing the data for one of the towns. The team then shares and compares their graphs and analysis to assist in making a decision as to which towns are represented by the mystery data. A key to maintaining the focus on problem solving and decision making is have the class as a whole decide where *all* towns are located; only indicate that they are correct if they get all towns correctly identified. You can tell them the number of correct towns, just not which ones are correct. Thus the class, as a whole, must work together sharing their data and their analyses.

Spreadsheet Instructional Idea: Which Is the Best Deal? Suppose you were asked to find five numbers with an average of 12. That's easy, five 12s average five! But so do the numbers 1, 2, 3, 4, and 50! In fact this problem has lots of solutions and a spreadsheet can help to find many different ways. Figure 6.8 shows a spreadsheet with four ways that are really quite different. For column E, the average is only 2.4 at this point, suggesting that some of those zeroes need to be changed. For column F, as values are entered the average is being computed for the numbers that are shown. This sample shows the dynamic nature of spreadsheets. The average formulas in cells B9, C9, D9, E9, and F9 are automatically recalculated with each new entry.

Find five numbers who average is 12. How many ways can this be done?

Ways	A	B	C	D	E	F
	12	1	1000	0.5	0	2
	12	20	-200	30	0	13
	12	10	-780	20.5	0	
	12	14	0	3	0	
	12	15	40	6	12	
Average	12	12	12	12	2.4	7.5

FIGURE 6.8 Finding averages of 12 with five numbers.

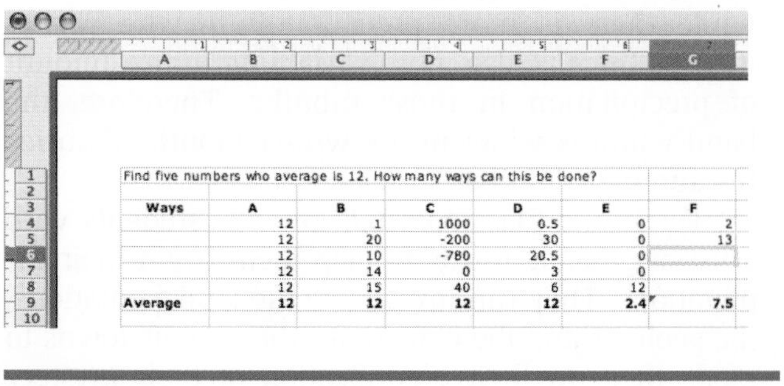

This dynamic capability of spreadsheets results in a wonderful tool for problem solving and decision making if students learn to design spreadsheets to take advantage of the capability. The keys to designing dynamic spreadsheets rely on

- Displaying all important variables in the problem;
- Adequately labeling all the variables in the problem;
- Assuring that the embedded formulas only refer to the cells where the values reside (rather than embedding an actual value in the formulas);
- Using absolute references to cells containing values that are to be always used (if adjustments are made in the spreadsheet, perhaps copying the formula to another location in the spreadsheet, the references remain with the correct value).

In essence the goal is to design spreadsheets that are dependable and maintain the accuracy of their results under changing conditions, as is often the case when students are engaged in problem solving and making decisions.

In the Classroom 6.9 provides one example where students are asked to make a decision about whether to use a satellite option for receiving movies or to purchase a DVD player and use rentals. In working with this problem, students create a table, a graph, and some expressions to model the problem. Then they compare their hand-constructed versions with the design of a spreadsheet that displays all three representations simultaneously. However, once they have used the spreadsheet for determining which option, they are asked to reconsider their decisions under new conditions for each of the options. With the spreadsheets they are able to explore the new conditions dynamically, making the appropriate changes in the key values that influence expressions for each

In the Classroom 6.9

SATELLITE MOVIES OR DVD MOVIES?

TECHNOLOGY OBJECTIVE: **NETS · S I, III, IV, VI**
- **Spreadsheets:** Technology as a problem-solving and decision-making tool while building understanding of basic concepts about dynamic spreadsheets.
- Creating dynamic spreadsheets that allow for user exploration; using absolute referencing.

CONTENT OBJECTIVE: **Mathematics:** Model problems using representations such as graphs, tables, and equations to draw conclusions.

GRADE LEVEL: 7–9

PROBLEM: The Smith family is trying to decide between installing a satellite dish and receiving movies through the satellite or purchasing a DVD player and signing up for DVD rentals per month. The Smiths need to compare the cost of each option over several months in order to make an appropriate decision. Help them make the decision.

- Satellite: One-time installation of $30 and then $49 per month for the service that allows them to access the movies with the stipulation that they must maintain this system for at least one year.
- DVD: Purchase a DVD player for $250 and buy unlimited rentals of DVDs for $30 per month.

1. Create a table of the costs for the number of months for a 12-month period to explore the cost for the DVD option and the Satellite option. Which is the best deal? Explain why you might choose one over the other.

Number of Months												
	1	2	3	4	5	6	7	8	9	10	11	12
Satellite												
DVD												

2. Create a graph to compare the costs over 12 months (keeping in mind that the satellite choice must be for at least one year).

3. Create two equations of the costs for the different options for the number of months.
   - Satellite (month) = what (month) + (initial cost)
   - DVD (month) = what (month) + (initial cost)

4. Now, put these different representations of the problem together by creating the spreadsheet framework for exploring this problem.

   a.

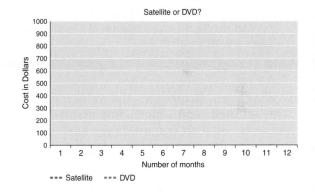

- Format the spreadsheet as in the graphic.
- Insert the value 1 in I3 and the value 1 in L3.
- Insert the cost per month for the Satellite in A7 and the installation fee for the Satellite in D7.
- Insert the cost per month for the DVD in A8 and the purchase price of the DVD in D8.
- Insert a formula in cell G6 that refers **absolutely** to cell I3.
- Insert a formula in cell H6 that references cell G6 plus an **absolute** reference to value in cell L3.
- Insert a formula in cell G7 that uses **absolute** references to cells A7 and C7 and references G6 for the number of months.
- Insert a formula in cell G8 that uses absolute references to cells A8 and D8 and references G6 for the number of months.

(continued on next page)

- Copy the formula in G6 across the row to P6.
- Copy the formula in G7 across the row to P7.
- Copy the formula in G8 across the row to P8.

The values in the spreadsheet table should now match the table you created in Step 1.

   b. Create the graph.
   - Highlight cells F6 to P8.
   - Select Chart Wizard to do a Line Chart.
   - Enter the title for the graph, the descriptions for the *x*-axis (Number of Months) and for the *y*-axis (Cost in Dollars).

   c. The graph shows the rising costs of the two options. But the graph does not go for 12 months nor do the two lines intersect. Use the **dynamic** nature of this spreadsheet you just created to explore the problem. Try these different ideas.

   - Insert the value 3 into cell I3. What happens?
   - Change the value in L3 to 0.5. What happens?
   - Change the value in L3 to 0.1. What happens?
   - Change the value in I3 to 6. What happens?
   - Change the value in I3 to 10. What happens?
   - Change the value in I3 to 11. What happens?
   - What would be your decision about which option to choose? Why do you select that option?

   d. Explore the problem even further using the dynamic nature of the spreadsheet that allows you to change the values in the problem. Try these different options.

   - The satellite company changes its plan to charging $25 per month with free installation of the satellite, still requiring that the user maintain this system for at least one year. Meanwhile, the DVD company changes its plan to charging a $150 fee to purchase the DVD player and $15 per month for rentals. Which company would you choose? Why?
   - Now in a bonus offer, for a limited time only, the satellite company changes its plan to charging $25 per month and will waive the installation fee, still requiring that the user maintain the system for at least one year. Meanwhile, the DVD company changes its plan to charging a $125 fee to purchase the player and $15 per month for rentals. Which company would you choose? Why?

   e. After exploring the problem, respond to these questions:
   - What is the value of creating a dynamic spreadsheet?
   - What are the important features of a dynamic spreadsheet that assure that, as changes are made, the spreadsheet is dependable?

option. With each change, all the values in the table are updated and, more importantly, the graphical representation is immediately updated to aid in reviewing the impact of the change.

Summing It Up

The power of the spreadsheet is in its ability to generate, organize, and display numeric data in a visual format. Because of the reliance on numeric data, the spreadsheet is often viewed as a tool for mathematics. However, spreadsheets have the potential to add rigor to other content areas that are not often considered as quantitative subjects. Elementary children can investigate lunchroom waste to find out whether they are wasting food (Ramondetta, 1992). Social studies teachers can encourage students to challenge existing stereotypical portrayals of economic activity in the North and the South before the Civil War. Biology teachers can use spreadsheets to model population growth, competition, and predation in nature (Carter, 1999). Middle-school science teachers can ask their students to investigate the severity of El Niño by investigating the temperature and precipitation data of various towns in the United States (Bell, Niess, & Bell, 2001–2002). Perhaps, as Hemmer (1998) proposes, the middle-school curriculum can integrate spreadsheet skills in learning history, mathematics, language arts, and science. In essence, the spreadsheet offers a tool for students to use to investigate, explore, and challenge statements, descriptions, and explanations that are more often presented to them to simply accept as they learn in different content areas.

In order for students to use spreadsheets as efficient and effective tools in learning in different content areas, they must *learn about* the tool as they *learn with* the tool. They must learn about basic operations and concepts of the spreadsheet. They need to learn about data in the form of numbers, labels, and formulas. They need to learn how to construct their own formulas, and they need to learn how and when to use the built-in formulas. They need to learn about copying formulas within the spreadsheets and the importance of both absolute and relative referencing. They need to learn how to construct charts—pie charts, line charts, bar charts, etc. As important as these basic operations are, a key concept with spreadsheets is that of designing dependable spreadsheets. Students need to learn to test their spreadsheet designs to assure that the formulas are resulting in accurate results. They must learn not to assume that the results are accurate and learn not to make decisions based on untested spreadsheets.

Just learning spreadsheet basics does not mean your students learn how to *learn with* the spreadsheet. As they are introduced to the basics, they must experience social, ethical, and human concerns related to spreadsheets. They need to question the validity and reliability of data they retrieve from the Internet. With charts used to display the data, students can change the message by making a change in the axes of a line chart. Spreadsheets can immediately recalculate the data on entry of new data; thus, they serve as a productivity tool allowing students to quickly and efficiently investigate different models of data. Students can also use spreadsheets to conduct research. They need to be taught to ask questions, rather than simply accept statements as facts. Spreadsheets can be used in solving problems and making informed decisions. In essence, spreadsheets are tools that students can use to investigate real-world, authentic problems. Spreadsheets are tools that can encourage critical thinking, encourage students to challenge ideas, and at the same time develop their personal knowledge and understanding through their investigations. Burns (2002) suggests that teachers need to understand "the analytical, interdisciplinary, creative, and visual capabilities of spreadsheet software. . . . Spreadsheets enable learners to model complex and rich real-world phenomena that can be manipulated, analyzed, evaluated, and displayed both quantitatively and visually." Teachers, such as you, are key to scaffolding these interdisciplinary possibilities, designing the curriculum and the experiences that focus students on both learning *with* and *about* the spreadsheet.

End-of-the-Chapter Activities and References

PRACTICE PROBLEMS

1. Your district offered you a choice of two pay scales for your first year of teaching. Which scale would give you the greatest total salary for your first year of teaching? Create a spreadsheet to show the monthly salary and the total salary you would receive under each scale given that you work for 9 months.

   Scale A: $4000 per month

   Scale B: $100 for the first month and double the monthly salary for each month that you work

2. Design a dynamic spreadsheet that allows the user to input an initial value and the amount to increase (increment) that value by each time. Have the spreadsheet dynamically produce a multiplication table that identifies the five numbers to be used in the table and correctly multiplies those values.

3. A simple magic square is a 3 × 3 matrix that contains the numbers 1–9 in the cells such that all the rows, the columns, and the diagonals add to the same number. Create a magic square spreadsheet where the formulas dynamically add the rows, columns, and diagonals as various numbers are entered. Finally, place the numbers 1 through 9 in the shaded areas so that the sums are 15 in each row, column, or diagonal.

4. Fill a bag with some colored marbles (or substitute 1-inch paper squares) with these colors: 8 red, 7 black, 5 green, 6 blue, 4 white. Draw a marble from the bag and record the color. Then replace the marble in the bag. Repeat this process until 100 drawings have been made and recorded.

Color	Red	Green	Blue	Yellow	Total
Result					100

   a. Create a spreadsheet to calculate the percentage of times each different color appeared out of the 100 drawings.

   b. Use the data in the spreadsheet to create a pie chart of your results. Explode the section(s) with the largest experimental probabilities. How close were your results to the actual probability for each color? Why might the experimental probability be different from the actual probability?

Percent of Classrooms with Internet Access									
	1994	1995	1996	1997	1998	1999	2000	2001	2002
Elementary	3	8	13	24	51	62	76	86	92
Secondary	4	8	16	32	52	67	79	88	91

5. Create the Target Math spreadsheet as described for the In the Classroom 6.2 activity. Protect the cells where the numbers used in meeting the target are placed so that they cannot accidentally be changed. Use the various color capabilities to highlight the cells where the target formulas are to be entered.

6. Complete In the Classroom 6.3 to compare built-in formulas with user-defined formulas.

7. How long have public schools had Internet access in their classrooms? Note the data above.

   a. Create a spreadsheet and chart the data in a bar chart of year by percent access. What message is communicated with this chart?

   b. Change the percent axis to distort the message of the chart. Explain how this chart describes public schools' access to the Internet.

   c. Make another change in the chart to alter the message the chart provides about public schools' access to the Internet. Explain how this change alters the message.

8. Do all states spend the same amount per school pupil? Below are data for some of the states. Create a spreadsheet of these data.

   a. Select two states of interest and create a line chart of year (x-axis) by dollar (y-axis) for those two states. What message is communicated?

   b. Change the dollar axis of the chart to distort the message. Explain how this chart describes how states fund public school pupils.

9. Create the dynamic spreadsheet as described in the In the Classroom 6.9. Determine which option is best for the original problem as well as for the changes described in part d. Respond to the questions in part e.

10. Obtain one of the articles from the Annotated Resources that you believe is a standards-based activity. Complete the spreadsheet activity. Describe how the activity helps students in working toward the technology standards. Which standard(s) is addressed?

IN THE CLASSROOM ACTIVITIES

11. Try the M&M simulation activity from the Snapshot of a Classroom Investigation of Spreadsheets with some fifth- or sixth-grade children. Follow up on this activity with students doing the same activities with the computer, with students working in pairs. Talk with the children about how they might use a computer spreadsheet. Collect their ideas. Are they all the same? Do they have ideas you had not considered? Did they have any misunderstandings about how the spreadsheet works?

12. Talk with various teachers in the grade level and content area you hope to teach about the type of grade book they use. Create an electronic grade book that you might use when you teach based on the information you gathered. Include a sample data set that demonstrates how the grade book works.

13. For your specific content area, design (or find in the literature) a spreadsheet activity that supports students in learning the content with a spreadsheet tool. What content area standard(s) does this activity support? What technology standard(s) does this activity support? Outline how you envision students working on this activity.

ASSESSING STUDENT LEARNING WITH AND ABOUT TECHNOLOGY

14. Complete In the Classroom 6.6: *Is the Homicide Rate Continuing to Increase?* Identify the spreadsheet operations and concepts that are key to this activity that you would use in describing a scoring guide for the activity. Describe how you would assess students' capabilities with the key ideas.

15. Extend the following list of basic operations and concepts for spreadsheets. Identify all activities in this chapter that provide students with experiences in learning *about* these spreadsheet operations and concepts.

	A	B	C	D	E	F	G	H	I	J	K	L	M	N	O
1	School Expenditures per Pupil														
2	Selected States														
3	States/Years	1959-60	1969-70	1979-80	1980-81	1985-86	1989-90	1990-91	1993-94	1994-95	1995-96	1996-97	1997-98	1998-99	1999-2000
4															
5	Alaska	$546	$1,123	$4,728	$5,688	$8,304	$8,431	$8,330	$8,882	$8,963	$9,012	$9,097	$9,074	$9,209	$9,668
6	Arkansas	$225	$568	$1,574	$1,701	$2,658	$3,485	$3,700	$4,280	$4,459	$4,710	$4,840	$4,999	$5,193	$5,628
7	California	$424	$867	$2,268	$2,475	$3,543	$4,391	$4,491	$4,921	$4,992	$5,108	$5,414	$5,795	$6,045	$6,401
8	Georgia	$253	$588	$1,625	$1,708	$2,966	$4,275	$4,466	$4,915	$5,193	$5,377	$5,708	$6,059	$6,534	$6,903
9	New York	$562	$1,327	$3,462	$3,741	$6,011	$8,062	$8,565	$9,175	$9,623	$9,549	$9,658	$9,970	$10,514	$10,957
10	Texas	$332	$624	$1,916	$2,006	$3,298	$4,150	$4,438	$4,898	$5,222	$5,473	$5,736	$5,910	$6,161	$6,771
11	Washington	$420	$915	$2,568	$2,542	$3,881	$4,702	$5,000	$5,751	$5,906	$6,074	$6,182	$6,535	$6,595	$6,914
12															
13	US States Average	$360	$774	$2,237	$2,489	$3,776	$4,973	$5,252	$5,767	$5,978	$6,135	$6,361	$6,631	$6,991	$7,393

Basic Operation/Concepts of Spreadsheets	Activities
1. Enters numeric data accurately	M&Ms data entry
2. Uses built-in formulas appropriately	In the Classroom 6.3: On an Average
3. Incorporates user-defined formulas appropriately	In the Classroom 6.2: Target Math In the Classroom 6.3: On an Average

E-PORTFOLIO ACTIVITIES

16. Complete one of the In the Classroom spreadsheets in this chapter. Arrange all charts and data so that they can be viewed. In addition to saving the spreadsheet normally, select Save as a Web Page, so you might select it as an exhibit for your E-portfolio.

17. Prepare a reflection about teaching and learning *with* and *about* spreadsheets with respect to your specific content area. How can you incorporate spreadsheets so that students use them as a tool as described in the technology standards? How can spreadsheets be used as a tool in learning your subject area? Save this reflection as a Web page, so you can consider using it as a reflection in your E-portfolio.

REFLECTION AND DISCUSSION

18. Prepare a response to each of the Chapter Learning Objectives. Expand your response on one objective, discussing its importance for you as a teacher.

19. Find a spreadsheet activity (see Annotated Resources for suggestions) that can be used with students you are preparing to teach (grade level and content). Describe how you would prepare students so that they are ready to use the spreadsheet as a tool for learning in this activity.

20. Respond to this statement: Spreadsheets are mathematical tools.

Annotated Resources

ELEMENTARY

Chesebrough, D. (1993). Using computers: Candy calculations. *Learning, 21*(7), 40.
Using data collected from candy and spreadsheets, students work with averages and percentages to make mathematical predictions.

Drier, H. S. (1999). Do vampires exist? *Learning and Leading with Technology, 27*(1), 22–25.
In this activity students use their knowledge of addition and multiplication along with spreadsheets to investigate a common folktale about the existence of vampires. This

activity provides an introduction to mathematical proof by contradiction.

Golden, J. R. (n.d.). *Child mortality in our world.* Available on the Web at http://teacherlink.org/content/social/instructional/mortality/home.htm.
Students create spreadsheets and graphs to determine the influences of clean water, education, and malnutrition on the child mortality rates of several countries around the world.

Holmes, E. D. (1997). The spreadsheet—absolutely elementary! *Learning and Leading with Technology, 24*(8), 6–12.
This article contains six activities for use in an elementary classroom. The first activity has students solve a problem posed by a Mother Goose rhyme using a spreadsheet. The second activity has students use a spreadsheet template to learn shape, color, and numeration concepts. The third activity has students collect data and then use a spreadsheet to analyze the data. In the fourth activity, students use spreadsheets to explore the relationship between "units of liquid measurement and the percentage of a gallon that each unit represents." In the fifth activity students use spreadsheets to collect and analyze data to investigate the problem "How High Will the Ping-Pong Ball Bounce?" In the final activity, students collect measurement data and then use spreadsheets to discover proportions of the human body from the data.

Parker, J., & Widmer, C. (1991). Teaching mathematics with technology: How big is a million? *Arithmetic Teacher, 39*(1), 38–41.
Includes activities that propose ways to make large numbers more meaningful to elementary students along with spreadsheet projects that incorporate National Council of Teachers of Mathematics Standards for number sense.

Ramondetta, J. (1992). Learning from lunchroom trash. *Learning, 20*(8), 59.
Elementary children can help students consider how much trash they create by analyzing lunchroom waste. Their research involves obtaining a list of items thrown away and then collecting data by counting the items that are thrown away in the lunchroom. They enter the information into a spreadsheet and analyze the result by preparing charts that clearly display the lunchroom waste.

LANGUAGE ARTS

——. (2000). But aren't spreadsheets just for math? *TAP into Learning, 2*(2), 7–8. Available on the Web at http://www.sedl.org/tap.
In this activity, students use a spreadsheet to outline and graph qualities and attributes of characters in *The Outsiders* so as to create a personality profile. This profile is then used to justify a character's guilt or innocence in a trial setting.

Lewis, P. (1997). Using productivity software for beginning language learning—Part 2: Spreadsheets, databases & mail merge. *Learning and Leading with Technology, 25*(1), 12–17.
The article contains an activity for using spreadsheets to learn verb conjugation in a foreign language class.

Newman, J. M. (1989). The flexible page (online). *Language Arts, 66*(4), 57–64.
This article deals with spreadsheets as a classroom tool for performing mathematical calculations and creating text matrices. Included are electronic spreadsheet examples for plotting genealogy, comparing types of crocodilians, compiling data for "mystery liquids," and charting the differences and similarities among three versions of *Cinderella*.

SOCIAL STUDIES

Graham, B. (n.d.). *Economic perspectives in colonial America.* Available on the Web at http://teacherlink.org/content/social/instructional/ameconpop/home.html.

Students use spreadsheets to analyze population data to: (1) determine demographic changes in early American colonies, and (2) conjecture about the social, economic, and political influences and consequences relating to the population changes.

Graham, B. (n.d.). *Job distribution after 1945.* Available on the Web at http://teacherlink.org/content/social/instructional/jdistrib/home.html.
Students analyze the changes in the distribution of jobs in America from 1945 to 1995 using spreadsheets.

Lee, J. K. (n.d.). *Social demographics and election statistics.* Available on the Web at http://teacherlink.org/content/social/instructional/election/home.html.
Students manipulate spreadsheets of presidential election returns data from 1952 to 1976 to identify voting patterns of various social demographic groups.

SCIENCE

——. (n.d.). *Periodic table trends: Melting point* and *boiling point.* Available on the Web at http://teacherlink.org/content/science/instructional/activities/melting/
Students create a graph from spreadsheet data to investigate the connection between an element's position in the periodic table and its melting and boiling points.

——. (n.d.). *Where in the world are all the earthquakes?* Available on the Web at http://teacherlink.org/content/science/instructional/activities/earthquakes/.
Using the Internet, students download seismic data from their birth years into a spreadsheet. Next, students manipulate the data in the spreadsheet to create a graph, which is superimposed on a map of the world. Using this visual, students can hypothesize about hot zones and tectonic plates.

Bell, R. L., Niess, M. L., & Bell, L. (2001–2002). El Niño did it: Climate phenomena model integrating technology with teaching science and mathematics. *Learning and Leading with Technology, 29*(4), 18–26.
Students download climate data from the Internet to a spreadsheet in order to calculate average temperatures and precipitation amounts. These results are then graphed and analyzed for climate patterns and effects of El Niño.

Carter, A. J. R. (1999). Using spreadsheets to model population growth, competition and predation in nature. *American Biology Teacher, 61*(4), 294–296.
This article explains how to input mathematical equations in a spreadsheet to model population growth quickly and easily and discusses other experiments that utilize spreadsheets.

Lehman, J. R., & Kandle, T. M. (1995). SSMILes: Popcorn investigations for integrating mathematics, science, and technology. *School Science and Mathematics, 95*(1), 46–49.
Students use spreadsheets to determine relationships about data collected from popcorn while utilizing math, science, and technology skills.

Lucas, K. B. (1994). Charting northern skies with the aid of a spreadsheet. *School Science and Mathematics, 94*(3), 151–157.
Using a spreadsheet, students create their own star charts appropriate for viewing a particular location, date, and time.

MATHEMATICS

——. (n.d.). *Analyzing smoking & lung cancer.* Available on the Web at http://teacherlink.org/content/math/activities/ex-smoking/.
Students use a spreadsheet to investigate the relationship between smoking and deaths from lung cancer.

——. (n.d.). *Collecting and numerically analyzing M&Ms data.* Available on the Web at http://teacherlink.org/content/math/activities/ex-mmnumerical/.
Students use a spreadsheet to collect, organize and analyze data on the colors of M&Ms in an individual bag of M&Ms.

——. (n.d.). *Exploring sunspots.* Available on the Web at http://teacherlink.org/content/math/activities/ex-sunspots/home.html.
Students use a spreadsheet to create a graph of sunspot data and then determine the cyclic pattern of the data from the graph.

——. (n.d.). *Using technology to enhance learning: Charleston housing market.* Available on the Web at http://www.sedl.org/pubs/tec26/nonflash/classtech.html.
Using spreadsheets, students collect and graph real estate data from Charleston, South Carolina. Using linear equations students then examine the house prices.

Allen, R. M. (1999). Ordered-pair relations—a performance assessment. *Mathematics Teaching in the Middle School, 5*(3), 190–194.
Using spreadsheet capabilities, students create a drawing of connected ordered pairs, the inverse, and the negative of the drawing to explore ordered pairs and make connections to other mathematical topics.

Attia, T. L. (2003). Using school lunches to study proportion. *Mathematics Teaching in the Middle School, 9*(1), 17.
Students study proportion in the context of nutritional values of their school lunches using spreadsheets.

Battista, M. T. (1993). Mathematics in baseball. *Mathematics Teacher, 86*(4), 336–342.
This article contains 13 activities that explore the mathematics of baseball. Also discussed is the integration of spreadsheets to explore these concepts.

Friedlander, A. (1998). An EXCELlent bridge to algebra. *Mathematics Teacher, 91*(5), 382.
This articles contains spreadsheet activities for learning algebraic concepts.

Hersberger, J., & Frederick, T. M. (1995). Flower beds and landscape consultants: Making connections in middle school mathematics. *Mathematics Teaching in the Middle School, 1*(5), 364–367.
In this activity, students develop concepts of area and perimeter using spreadsheets to explore, analyze, and hypothesize about real-life problems.

Lesser, L. M. (1999). Exploring the birthday problem with spreadsheets. *Mathematics Teacher, 92*(5), 407–411.
Students use spreadsheets to explore and solve the problem that asks about the probability of having two people in the same room with the same birthday.

Niess, M. L. (1992a). Math: Winds of change. *Computing Teacher, 19*(6), 32–35.
Provides methods for cooperative, student investigation of weather data similar to methods currently used by atmospheric scientists. Utilizes spreadsheets to focus on the analysis and interpretation of wind frequency data for a small town in Oregon.

Niess, M. L. (1992b). Mathematics and M&Ms. *Computing Teacher, 20*(1), 29–31.
An introduction simulation to the computer spreadsheet using M&Ms and a mathematics problem.

Niess, M. L. (1998). Using computer spreadsheets to solve equations. *Learning and Leading with Technology, 26*(3), 22–24, 26–27.
Students use spreadsheets to solve equations and inequalities. Using the graphing features of a spreadsheet, students can visualize these solutions.

CHAPTER 7

The Internet and Databases

©AP/Wide World Photos

▶ Introduction

Our unity as a nation is sustained by free communication of thought and by easy transportation of people and goods. Individual and commercial movement matches the ceaseless flow of information throughout the republic over a vast system of interconnected highways crisscrossing the country and joining at our national borders with friendly neighbors to the north and south.

Together, the united forces of our communication and transportation systems are dynamic elements in the very name we bear—United States. Without them, we would be a mere alliance of many separate parts.

> *President Dwight D. Eisenhower, Speech to Joint Session of Congress, February 22, 1954*

With this speech President Eisenhower requested congressional approval for the development of a system of limited access roads linking major urban areas across the United States. The interstate highway system proposed by President Eisenhower was conceptually quite simple, but in practice was a remarkable technological feat. The plan took an incomplete system of 6,000 miles of interconnected national roads first proposed in the 1930s and begun in 1944, and expanded it to a modern system of 35,000 miles of interstate highways by 1975. The development of the interstate highway system in the 1950s and 1960s enabled the United States to move people and materials in an efficient manner.

The "individual and commercial movement over a vast system of interconnected highway crisscrossing the country" that Eisenhower envisioned in his speech was masterfully executed over the years succeeding his speech, but what he intoned in his speech was more remarkable. Eisenhower recognized the importance of what he called the "ceaseless flow of information." This information flow was significantly and permanently enhanced, beginning in the 1960s, through the development of ARPANET, an interconnected communications network for sharing and distributing electronic information.

ARPANET was created by the U. S. Department of Defense's Advanced Research Projects Agency (ARPA) in an effort to ensure that critical information was able to be protected in the event of a massive offensive attack on the United States. Defense planners in the 1960s were mostly concerned about a Soviet nuclear strike. They wanted to enable critical information to be distributed so that a single attack or even a collection of attacks was not able to eliminate sources of valuable information. If the information were stored in multiple places and were able to be moved from one place to another in a quick and efficient manner, virtually no attack short of complete destruction would result in the loss of that critical information about the U.S. defense system.

ARPANET bore a remarkably conceptual similarity to the interstate system, but ARPANET was constructed to move information instead of people and physical material. Just as the interstate highway system changed the patterns of life in the United States, the ARPANET and its successor, the Internet, has significantly changed the ways people communicate and work. Although the interstate highway system changed the way people lived, enabling the growth of suburbia and fostering the emergence of the modern automobile culture, the Internet is re-making the social fabric, enabling new forms of communications, community building, and resource sharing by decentralizing the distribution of information. The interstate highway system and ARPANET were both reflections of America's Cold War resolve to adequately protect military resources and enable movement. More importantly, though, those two technological advances set the world on a course of social change that continues to affect everyone today.

CHAPTER LEARNING OBJECTIVES

After reading this chapter, you should be able to:

1. Identify basic concepts and constructs students need to learn to make effective use of the broad range of tools offered by the Internet.

2. Explain how e-mail, discussion boards, and list-servs are similar and yet different.

3. Describe real-world, authentic learning experiences that engage students in learning with Internet and database resources as they learn basic concepts, constructs, and operations about the Internet and databases.

4. Show how databases can be used to organize information and data and facilitate access to the analysis of the information.

5. Illustrate ethical and social considerations that are important in using online communications tools in the K–12 classroom.

6. Identify learning opportunities that can be structured to support students in continuing to expand their knowledge and understanding of the resources available on the Internet.

7. Highlight how locating Internet and database information is important for students to learn in conducting research, making decisions, and solving problems.

Snapshot of a Class Investigation with Web Searches

Have you ever been overwhelmed searching for information on the Web? How many times have you tried to find what seemed like the answer to a simple question and found yourself, 30 minutes later, no closer to your answer, but completely confused and frustrated?

In Mr. Nguyen's tenth grade United States history social studies class, students needed strategies to avoid being victims of this all too common phenomenon of what some call being lost in cyberspace. Mr. Nguyen knew when he planned to require his students to use online resources in a research project on human rights that he needed to provide them with some guidance about how to conduct effective Web-based research.

Mr. Nguyen: Today we are going to start a research project that will involve you using the Web to find specific resources to help you answer questions.

Most of the students in the class looked, for the most part, unconcerned. They were used to using the Internet and the Web, but Mr. Nguyen knew their experience using the Web to find content-specific resources was quite limited.

Mr. Nguyen: We're going to search today for information on the Web that will help you answer the questions we developed from our content outline on the Human Rights unit we are studying. Each of you developed a question yesterday. Shana, what is your question?

Shana: Why was Aung San Suu Kyi awarded the Nobel Peace Prize?

Mr. Nguyen: Great topic—remember Aung San Suu Kyi was awarded the Nobel Peace Prize in 1991 and is currently under house arrest in her native Myanmar. Let's use this question as an example to walk through a search. Is that OK Shana?

Shana: YEAH!

Mr. Nguyen:	First, let's talk about the question. I would like to clear up a couple of things with your question. First, we know Aung San Suu Kyi received the Nobel Peace Prize for her work in promoting a peaceful solution to human rights problems plaguing her country of Myanmar. How can we change the question so that we are investigating something more intriguing about her work for peace?
Brad:	How about if Shana asks about the problems Aung San Suu Kyi was attempting to solve when she won the peace prize.
Mr. Nguyen:	Good! That would move Shana past a simple fact finding expedition. Shana, do you know what Aung San Suu Kyi was so concerned about?
Shana:	No, so maybe I could look at her work instead of just asking why she won the peace prize.
Mr. Nguyen:	OK, but that would also be a fairly simple fact finding exercise. You could probably find that information in an online encyclopedia. How about if you try to find out what people around the world think about Aung San Suu Kyi's work? This question would require that you know about her work, but go past it and investigate perceptions.
Shana:	That sounds like a good idea, but how do I find out what people think about Aung San Suu Kyi?
Mr. Nguyen:	Anyone?
Patricia:	How about if she just searches using the whole question. Something like, "What do people think about Aung San Suu Kyi?"
Mr. Nguyen:	Let's try it.

The class conducted the search yielding results that all related to Aung San Suu Kyi, but did not in any way provide information on public opinion or perceptions about her. Instead the results of the search directed students to Web pages that mentioned Aung San Suu Kyi and most often had terms such as "people" or "think" contained somewhere in the text. These results reflected the proximity of words in the searched text, but none of the Web pages had the exact sequence of words. The website that the search engine considered the best result was actually the text of a speech Aung San Suu Kyi delivered accepting membership in the Hague Peace Conference. In the speech, Aung San Suu Kyi said, "It's only by changing the way people think that we progress towards peace." The combination of her name in the title of the Web page and the words "think" and "peace" being close to each other resulted in this page being listed at the top of the list of websites. In fact, nine of the top ten results were

Aung San Suu Kyi speeches or writings. The tenth site was an article summarizing her work.

MR. NGUYEN:	OK, these results are obviously not going to help us. We need to know what other people think of Aung San Suu Kyi. How about if we just search "Aung San Suu Kyi."

The class conducted this search but found mostly biographies and general magazine articles. Another approach was needed, so Mr. Nugyen decided to explain to his students how search engines work.

Mr. Nguyen:	Search engines are primarily either crawler/bot-based or human-based. The crawler-based search engines make use of computer programs that continually search the Web or "crawl" around the Web collecting and storing information about websites. The crawler visits a Web page, reads it, and follows links to other pages in the site. Everything the crawler finds goes into the "index" for the search engine. When we search using these services, we are basically asking the search engine to compare our words to their index or collection of text descriptions of the websites that have been included in the search engine's database.
	Another type of search engine is a human-constructed index of websites. These search sites are much smaller and are prepared by humans after a person or team of people reviews numerous sites. The large mainstream search engines are based on the crawler idea. Smaller indexes of Web resources are more likely human constructions.

Given the uniqueness of the search for the question about Aung San Suu Kyi, Mr. Nguyen decided it would be a good idea for his students to try both types of searches and to use some specific tips for improving the search. First, Mr. Nguyen had his students search using a crawler-based search engine on the words *Aung San Suu Kyi* and *opinion*. He suggested to his students that this search might result in the types of results Shana might find useful.

Second, Mr. Nguyen thought it might also be a good idea to have students search several newspaper resources. He suggested that if Shana looked at one newspaper from five different places, she might find useful types of results. For this search, the students used a school-owned compact disc (CD) database that contained newspaper stories from multiple news sources. This database was compiled by humans and was easy to search due to its hierarchical organizational structure. Through these two search techniques, the students retrieved a more robust collection of resources about Aung San Suu Kyi.

Basic Concepts and Constructs of the Internet and Databases

Although the Internet and databases are different tools, they are inextricably connected. Much of the data and information on the Internet is stored in databases. Much of the way that data and information are retrieved from the Internet is through databases. When you search the Internet you use search tools that provide an index of a database. As Mr. Nguyen described for his students in the Snapshot of a Class Investigation with Web Searches, different database compilations are available: crawler-based or human-based. Crawler-based searches make use of "bots," shorthand for robots. These robots are programmed to "crawl" around the Web collecting and storing information about websites. The crawler or robot visits a Web page, reads it, and follows links to other pages in the site. Everything the crawler finds goes into the "index" for the search engine. When you search the Internet, you are basically asking the search engines to compare your words to their index or collection of text descriptions of the web sites that have been recorded in the their databases. Human-based databases provide smaller indexes that are focused on identifying specific information such as that in newspaper articles. In those cases, humans identify the specific information and store that information in the database fields. This type of a database is more often found on the CDs in libraries.

Today much of the information available through the Internet exists in databases. Once disconnected storehouses of primarily numerical data, today's databases are massive in scope, consisting of electronic representations of every imaginable human expression from music, to text, to still and moving pictures. The databases are storehouses of human knowledge and ingenuity; they might be thought to rival or even replace traditional physical storehouses of knowledge such as libraries. In fact, several major academic institutions no longer purchase or continue to maintain physical copies of text-based resources, instead relying exclusively on database-stored electronic versions.

Students often get the impression, when they are searching the Internet, that the World Wide Web (WWW or Web) and the Internet are interchangeable. In reality the Web is only one of the services available through the Internet. Enabling students to develop a basic understanding of the concepts and constructs of the Internet helps them to challenge this misrepresentation. An understanding of the Internet is not complete without an understanding of databases and how to search and sort them. Ultimately this understanding is useful in helping students identify the best information in support of their investigation of content-related questions and to enhance their learning.

Internet Infrastructure

The Internet is a network of interconnected computers distributed throughout the world. More precisely, the Internet is a collection of connected networks or systems of connected computers. These networks are connected using physical cables collectively known as the *backbone* of the Internet as well as *routers* that essentially direct traffic as information moves along the Internet backbone. The entire system allows a message or piece of information to travel in a matter of seconds to other computers that might in fact be halfway across the world, all in a fraction of a second. Technology Link 7.1 can be used to connect to Opte Project's *visual map* of the Internet traffic, providing you with a visual description of its enormous complexity.

Technology Link 7.1

A visual map of the Internet is available at this book's website. Use the **Internet_Map** link to connect to the Opte Project and download a graphic providing a colorful display of the millions of connections created by the Internet in one day.

www.wiley.com/college/niess

Information is sent across the backbone and routers in *packets*. These packets are electronic bits of information coded to represent some portion of a file, a text message, or an image—whatever is being sent across the Internet. When you create an e-mail message, your computer e-mail system encodes the message into multiple packets. Routers determine what route the packets follow so that they successfully arrive at their destination from one computer to another. Packets are individually routed via the fastest path, meaning that all the packets for your message do not necessarily follow the same path. Computers at the destination for the message then decode the packets, reassembling the information into a readable form. In most cases, all of this activity takes a matter of seconds, giving you the impression that the pieces were sent as one continuous message.

Internet Protocols and Services

A number of protocols make use of the Internet infrastructure. Each protocol is a system for interacting with and arranging information sent across the Internet. The Internet's operational system operates based on a protocol known as the transmission control protocol/Internet protocol (**TCP/IP**). This protocol specifies the rules for dividing a message into the packets, sending those packets along the best route possible, and reassembling the packets. In the earliest days of the Internet, researchers developed e-mail and discussion group protocols, such as simple mail transfer protocol (SMTP), for sending text messages across the Internet. Soon afterward, the file transfer protocol (FTP) was developed for sending complete computer files. Twenty years after the establishment of ARPANET, the hypertext transfer protocol (HTTP) was developed in the creation of the Web. Each of these methods for sending information is unique and important for enabling students as they manage and manipulate information.

Electronic Mail   Electronic mail, more commonly known as *e-mail*, is probably the Internet service you use the most. This service allows you to create, send, and receive messages; for those messages you receive, you can reply, forward, save, delete, or even print. Managing your e-mail is an important task; otherwise, you end up with a mailbox that is full and has no room for more messages. Today, people often rely on e-mail folders instead of printing the messages and storing them in physical filing cabinets. For that reason it is important to identify a storage strategy that you understand. Organizing your e-mails into folders helps you find the messages that you want. You can organize the messages in each folder by date or alphabet.

E-mail is clearly a ubiquitous communication tool. Katie, a ninth grader enrolled in a public high school, explains, "E-mail allows me to share my ideas as they are happening. I can connect with my friends immediately and get their responses just as quick. I can't imagine not having it." Yes, e-mail is a powerful communications tool, but its use raises interesting questions when examining how it works, how it is used, and how to tap into it within classroom study.

Consider what Katie had to say. E-mail is appealing to students (and teachers) due to its speed, its efficiency, and its "commonness" and accessibility. With e-mail, you can attach files to share with colleagues, sharing video, text, photos, and even sounds. This versatility has opened up new worlds when it comes to eliciting feedback on lesson ideas, materials, and even student writing. However, the speed and accessibility continue to pose problems. When rushing to send off an e-mail message, writers do not always take time to consider tone, grammar, and even simple conventions such as capitalization and punctuation. Quick e-mail does not mean e-mail that has been carefully considered and constructed. The *unsend* feature provided by some e-mail software is a useful tool, particularly when a message is sent without necessary time, reflection, and serious consideration. Although e-mail has the potential for opening up rich classroom dialogues, these capabilities are often missed opportunities when *speedily* working through curricular goals.

When teaching students to compose e-mail effectively and efficiently, encourage them to compose messages in a word processor. Students typically take more time to think through the content, while also taking advantage of the editing tools, such as spell check and grammar check. Then, they simply copy and paste the completed message into the e-mail program and send it on its way. Discuss the use of emoticons and the use of words in parentheses to convey emotion and tone. It is also helpful for students to learn effective and appropriate ways of replying to unclear messages that they might receive within the course of their e-mail correspondence. The more tools they have, the more effective they will be as users of e-mail.

E-mail accounts in the classroom can be difficult to manage. Though just about every student with online access has an account through the many *free* options that are available (e.g., hotmail, yahoomail, excitemail), those services are not necessarily the accounts that you want opened in your classroom. In fact, many K–12 schools now have firewalls and other blocking mechanisms in place that prevent student access to those accounts. Student e-mail accounts can either be created through a schoolwide service or through an educational website such as ones identified in Technology Link 7.2.

Technology Link 7.2

*F*ind pen pals all over the world. Use the **Pen_pals** link to access sites where you can collaborate with teachers and students across the globe.

www.wiley.com/college/niess

In a language arts classroom, students can connect with international *pen pals*, or as one class describes it with *think pals*, who are able to provide insight and ideas when studying texts from different cultures and experiences. Reading Amy Tan's novel *The Kitchen God's Wife* is more powerful when the students can exchange ideas with female students in China. When pairing the reading of *The Diary of Anne Frank* and *Zlata's Diary*, students in the United States are able to correspond with students throughout Germany and Eastern Europe, again adding a rich dimension to their study.

With e-mail connections, the classroom community expands to include a variety of voices, beliefs, ideas, and values. Think about an eleventh-grade class where students read Maxine Hong Kingston's *The Woman Warrior* in a thematic unit broadly named Identity. Beginning with *The Woman Warrior*, this unit challenges students to also read Toni Morrison's *Sula* and Denise Chavez's *The Last of the Menu Girls*, bringing African-American, Asian-American, and Hispanic American voices into the classroom. Because the novels mirror students' ethnicities, most students see parts of themselves and their own experiences in the novels. However, as students begin to struggle with Hong Kingston's novel, it is immediately clear that they are not really able to understand the elements of Chinese culture and customs that complicate and enrich the novel.

Though some parents may be willing to participate in class discussions of what it means to immigrate to America as a Chinese daughter, these conversations are largely confined to discussions between the teacher and parents, not the student readers in the classroom. Students are more apt to relate to other students their age thinking, "I just wish that there was a kid like me to talk to about this book. Maybe then it would make sense. . . ." The links in Technology Link 7.2 are useful for registering your class to collaborate with another class in China. A variety of classroom contacts may be available. Teachers in a Chinese international school in Beijing may be looking to develop students' English language skills corresponding with American students; a high school teacher in San Francisco may be looking for a class to correspond with her English as a Second Language (ESL) Chinese-American class filled with recent immigrants; or an advanced-level history teacher in Qufu may want to correspond with American students about the impact of the Civil War on their community's local history and memory of the past. Each opportunity has the potential to enrich the learning experience of students in the language arts study of the various novels. Conversations are likely to explore the present and the past, what it means to be a recent Chinese-American immigrant, what it means to be American, gender roles in both Chinese and American cultures, and how it is that the past gets remembered. The e-mail messages act as a catalyst to involve students, even those who previously have contributed little to class discussions and who have read even less.

It is important to consider the power of student writing when using e-mail as a tool. E-mail allows students to communicate their ideas, no matter how confident or shy they may be. Students appreciate the *lower stakes* environment e-mail provides. Dani, an eighth-grade student, wrote, "E-mail allows me to be secure . . . posing my ideas where they will be pushed and extended without my having to be on the line like in discussion."

Discussion Groups   Discussion groups offer a way to communicate with others about a topic of interest

but, instead of individual discussions via e-mail, discussion boards allow messages to be posted in a central location with a subject heading, date, time, and author's name or e-mail. Students can post to nonlinear discussions, selecting those ideas they find to be the most compelling and offering their ideas for response and development. Students can use the boards both in and outside of class to post questions and access the class *community* as they are working on their homework. Parents also appreciate a discussion area as a tool for monitoring and participating in their children's classes, often responding to questions or posting their own.

The Internet also hosts thousands of discussion groups. Many teacher discussion groups are available that you might consider useful as you prepare to teach and begin your teaching. For example, The Math Forum provides a Public Discussions section with an alphabetic listing of their various discussion groups available. Figure 7.1 shows a sample of a response to a question about percents that might be found in the k12.ed.math section. The original question is placed at the top with each line marked by >; one response is posted after the question. Some of the discussions receive limited responses while others are vigorous for a period of time and then seem to stop. Most discussion boards offer browsing and searching features to help you identify discussions for your area of interest. If you do not find the right

---

Subject:	What's the salary before a percentage increase?
Author:	Dave
Date:	Thu, 01 Aug 2004 17:59:33 GMT

>I can't figure this out . . . Can anyone HELP?
>Kerry's weekly salary was increased 8.5% to 271.25.
  What was her
>weekly salary before the increase?

Not laughing. This is a commonly discussed problem and worth looking at. Let's use simpler figures.

Steve's investment of $100 increases by 10%? What does he have now?
Hint: $110

Now John has $110, it is that amount we are referring to when we say "it" is now reduced by 10%.

So what is 10% of $120? If "it" is reduced by that amount, what remains? [Hint ... spend 10% and you are left with 90%, but use that fact after thoroughly understanding this stepwise process.]

Try to take it from there. After some study and practice, you can "generalize," and see the overall pattern of behavior with these increases and decreases.

Dave.

FIGURE 7.1   A discussion about percent from The Math Forum discussion group dedicated to mathematics education in grades K–12.

area for your discussion, you can post your own discussion topic message or question.

Teacher preparation programs often use discussion boards to connect their student teachers who are placed at a variety of school placement sites for student teaching. With a discussion group, the student teachers can be grouped in teams to discuss a particular question, or perhaps the entire class is expected to "post one response plus one follow-up response" to a question. All or most of the discussion may in fact be electronic. For example, a teacher preparation class might be asked to discuss the National Educational Technology Standards for students (ISTE, 2000). The instructor could divide the class into the six standard areas. Through on-line collaborative discussion groups, the team members must (1) clarify the expectations in the standard, (2) discuss ways that the standard is being implemented (or barriers that make it difficult to be implemented) in their individual school sites, and (3) design at least two activities that might be used in their subject areas at the various grade levels. Their initial discussions probably involve brainstorming about each of the assignment topics. Given time and extended discussion, the teams have the opportunity to compose their approach to each part of the assignment. The advantage of this discussion group assignment is that it provides student teachers with an opportunity to work as a team without having to be at the same location at a common time. The disadvantage is that, after posting an idea, a team member may have to wait some time before receiving a response that may extend the idea.

Multiple online tools support teachers in establishing interactive, threaded discussions for classroom use. Technology Link 7.3 provides links to access current recommendations.

Technology Link 7.3

The **Discussion** link from the text website can be used to find recommendations for use of interactive, threaded discussions in your classes.

www.wiley.com/college/niess

Once you decide to incorporate a discussion board in your class, you must be conscious of the importance of establishing the initial conversations. The teacher must assume the duty of facilitating the initial conversation, building the community, and defining the level of inquiry expected. This facilitator role can and should later be shifted to various students. But, to begin the community, a few rules are important:

1. A discussion community is not just a forum for individual expression. Students need to have space to test their ideas, but the discussion community also must provide a place where the group's voice is gathered and amplified, so that the group can affirm, question, challenge, and correct the voice of the individual.

2. The space should welcome silence and speech. Although this discussion is one that should be full of *talk* and *active idea sharing*, it needs to provide such compelling ideas that students also feel welcome to *lurk*, free to think and explore without the pressure of continuously adding to the conversation.

3. Conflict is okay. It allows students to test ideas in the open in an attempt to stretch each other and make better sense of the world. However, this conflict must be both thoughtful and inclusive. Students need to learn the difference between sharing and pushing thinking versus attacking.

4. The discussion will most likely not facilitate itself. At least one person needs to pay close attention and ask deliberate questions that challenge the participants' ideas, thinking, and meaning. Teachers often think that since students embrace the technology, their participation in this online discussion will automatically lead to high-level thinking. Not true!

5. Take advantage of the technology by providing links to articles and online texts that have potential for enriching and extending the dialogue. These additions often act as immediate catalysts to invigorate the discussion.

Mailing List Servers One of the earliest and most productive means of communicating using Internet protocols is an automatic mailing list service called *Listserv*. The list service is a part of an educational computing network called BitNET (Because it's time NETwork). The BitNET system was developed in 1981 and reached its prime in the late 1980s and early 1990s as the Web was emerging. BitNET users share their interest in subjects by *subscribing* to an electronic discussion topic. Any subscriber wishing to send a message to all those subscribed does so by using the special e-mail delivery protocol (Listserv) to automatically send messages to all subscribers. The result is similar to an online newsgroup or discussion forum, except that the messages are transmitted as e-mail and are therefore available only to individuals on the list. Although Listserv refers to a specific mailing list server (now marketed by a private firm), the term is sometimes used to refer to any mailing list server. Most e-mail providers now make available some form of *listserv* or mailing list for their subscribers.

Listservs provide teachers with an additional method for discussion, with other teachers or perhaps even among the students. You can browse the Web to identify specific listservs where the discussion is of interest to you; or you can add a listserv of interest. Plenty of listservs are available to support teachers. For example, you can join a listserv focused on children's literature or one about integrating technology in education.

One of the most powerful aspects of mailing list services is the community nature. Your students can join an identified private or public list. If they have an idea, they can send it to all of the other students who are subscribed to the list. This action provides them with a captive audience similar to what happens when a student is speaking in front of a class, but the list eliminates the potential intimidation of speaking in front of the class. Although some students are comfortable speaking in front of the class, others are not; on the other hand, they may have items they are willing to share in written form. A list service may provide a more comfortable avenue for them to participate in a class discussion about a particular topic.

Teachers might take advantage of the relative comfort that a listserv can provide by discussing a topic that some students may be reluctant to speak about in class. Religion and evolution are two topics that generate student timidity. Of course, the topics also can bring out passion and emotion in students. Just as the listserv discussion potentially establishes some communicative avenues, such a discussion might eliminate some student participation in a classroom situation. A listserv can temper overly passionate and/or controversial public discussions. Students can say what they would like, within obvious limits, while allowing others to consider the message in a more comfortable manner without immediately reacting to the message. Students can take time for thinking and forming their responses before sending them.

Teachers can initiate a listserv-supported discussion of such topics in a number of ways. Some teachers may want to develop specific questions, such as setting the context of religion in a cultural or historical context. For instance, students might write a response to a query about the justification for Martin Luther's condemnation of the Catholic Church. Teachers might simply tell students that Luther was opposed to the selling of indulgences or pardons for sin. This introduction avoids the more fundamental disagreements Luther had with the Catholic Church due to the higher level of religious intensity of these disagreements and the continued disagreement among Protestants and Catholics over these issues. Teachers may even want to allow students to remain anonymous. Obviously, for these types of listserv discussions, teachers must screen messages, particularly if student anonymity is allowed.

World Wide Web   The World Wide Web, or Web, is often thought of as interchangeable with the Inter-

net. However, the Web is only one of the many services offered by the Internet. The Web is a valuable resource for finding information and is, thus, a valuable resource for education.

The Web is a collection of pages connected by *hyperlinks* that allow the user to navigate quickly among the various pages using the hypertext transfer protocol (HTTP). Each Web page has its own unique address called a *uniform resource locator* (URL), such as the address for this book's website.

http://www.wiley.com/college/niess/ch7links.html

A   B   C   D

A. The Internet protocol used in transferring the data.

B. The Web (www) domain name identifying the computer where the pages are stored.

C. The directory path (or folder) on the particular computer identifying where the Web page is stored. The specific folder that contains the Web pages and links for this book are stored in a folder labeled **niess**.

D. The document name for the Web page that contains links for Chapter 7 of this book.

The links described in Chapter 7 are identified in the document called ch7links.html. On this page you might find the various Technology Links for Chapter 7. These links allow you to move quickly among the pages without having to enter the addresses. Later in this text you will learn how to create Web pages of your own design (Chapter 9), but for now, the emphasis is on navigating Web pages and using the information to enhance learning in various content areas.

Searching the Web is often a described as a *time sink*, or where you are lost in cyberspace. You have probably experienced this loss of time, as you search for some particular information. Web search engines provide some assistance. As Mr. Nguyen explained in the *Snapshot of a Class Investigation with Web Searches*, he needed to provide his students with experiences to guide them in conducting effective Web searches. However, he wanted to make sure that this instruction was within the context of the work that they were doing in the class. Although he explained the different types of search engines, crawler-based versus human-based, he also required that the students conduct searches using the two different types, comparing the quality of the information and the ease of identifying the information. Nevertheless, while learning more about conducting searches on the Web, the students were focused on their research questions in the Human Rights unit.

File Transfer Protocol (FTP)   File transfer protocol (FTP) is a procedure for transferring electronic files from one computer to another. Today, FTP is most often used as a way to transfer Web pages that Web authors have created on their personal computers to the Web server computer hosting a website. Most Web authoring software programs include a way to FTP files from a local personal computer to a Web server computer.

FTP might best be envisioned as an idea instead of an actual procedure. The ability to transfer files from one computer to another is quite powerful. File transferring enables portability and the publication of students' work in ways that increase visibility and promote social interaction. Without FTP, students are not able to post their work on the Web, and without FTP and HTTP, students are not able to download and use other files, including freeware (free computer programs), shareware (computer programs for which producers request a payment), and for pay software computer programs. Chapter 9 guides you in using FTP to transfer Web files.

Databases

The Web has a tremendous volume of information, making locating specific information difficult. The Web in fact is much more than the Web pages you view because it also contains multiple databases of information and nontextual files such as graphical files and documents in formats such as PDF (portable document format). The recognition of the magnitude of databases available on the Web has lead to the phrase *invisible Web* because Web searches do not invade these databases and nontextual files. The term *invisible* is actually not accurate because no information on the Web is really invisible. Perhaps the term more recently coined as the *deep Web* is more accurate since Google has identified a way to include the deep Web content into their search functions.

The important point, however, is that databases are critical to the Web and to searching the Web. The students in the Snapshot of a Class Investigation with Web Searches learned more about conducting Web searches using different types of search engines. In actuality these search tools work with database-type software to store a variety of data. These databases need to be continuously updated in order to provide the most current information available on the Web. Thus, rather than actually searching the entire Web, the students only searched a database, looking for word matches or phrase matches.

As previously indicated, the Web contains many large databases. The U.S. Census Bureau, the U.S. Patent and Trademark Office, and the National Climate Data Center maintain their information in searchable databases for users to access. All the users need to do is identify the data of interest, using search or browse functions available on their Web pages. This process is the same as the process of searching and sorting databases. For students to use these Web features effectively they need a basic understanding of databases and that understanding is enhanced if they create and manipulate their own databases.

Databases look similar to spreadsheets because they are often displayed in columns and rows. However, databases do not use the cell designations like spreadsheets do. The columns are called *fields* and the rows are called *records*. An elementary class might develop a database to describe specific information about the children in the class using fields for their first name, height (in inches), hair color, number of brothers, number of sisters, number of dogs, and number of cats. Each record contains a field for each of these categories. Figure 7.2 shows

My Class						
Name	Height	Hair color	Brothers	Sisters	Dogs	Cats
Melissa	40	Blond	0	2	1	0
Tommy	48	Brown	1	0	2	1
Joe	45	Brown	1	0	2	1
Sharon	46	Blond	1	1	0	0
Maria	40	Black	1	2	0	1
Tawny	47	Red	1	2	1	1
Shana	45	Blond	1	1	1	0
Brad	52	Brown	1	1	0	0
Hunter	48	Blond	0	2	1	0
Madison	53	Red	1	1	1	0
Makenna	49	Blond	1	1	1	0
Ken	50	Black	1	2	1	1
Danny	51	Brown	1	0	1	0
Kevin	52	Black	1	1	1	2
Ava	46	Brown	0	1	0	0
Keith	52	Brown	2	0	2	1

FIGURE 7.2   Database of 16 student records for the class.

Name	Height	Hair color	Brothers	Sisters	Dogs	Cats
Ava	46	Brown	0	1	0	0
Brad	52	Brown	1	1	0	0
Danny	51	Brown	1	0	1	0
Hunter	48	Blond	0	2	1	0
Joe	45	Brown	1	0	2	1
Keith	52	Brown	2	0	2	1
Ken	50	Black	1	2	1	1
Kevin	52	Black	1	1	1	2
Madison	53	Red	1	1	1	0
Makenna	49	Blond	1	1	1	0
Maria	40	Black	1	2	0	1
Melissa	40	Blond	0	2	1	0
Shana	45	Blond	1	1	1	0
Sharon	46	Blond	1	1	0	0
Tawny	47	Red	1	2	1	1
Tommy	48	Brown	1	0	2	1

FIGURE 7.3 Class database after an alphabetic sort on the field Name.

that Melissa's record is the first record that was entered. She is 40 inches tall, blond, and has two sisters and one dog (but no brothers or cats).

An important distinction between a database and a spreadsheet is in its organization. Each record retains all of the fields. In fact, the first step in creating a database requires the identification of the fields or categories of the data that are to be gathered. Besides labeling each field, you must determine the data type. In this class database, the name and hair color are *text* data, and all the other fields are to be entered as *numbers* so that they can be treated numerically instead of alphabetically in any sorts and searches.

The primary functions used in a database involve sorting on any field and searching for specific data. An alphabetic *sort* on the field Name results in changing the order of the records as in Figure 7.3. Notice that for a sort, all the records are presented. The difference is that Ava's record is at the top of the list of records and Ava's record still includes a height of 46 inches, brown hair, and one sister.

Suppose the students want to identify the students who have red hair. A *search* on the field Hair color equal to Red results in just two records identified; Tawny and Madison are the only two students with red hair, as shown in Figure 7.4. Databases have capabilities for conducting searches on multiple fields. The search of all the student records for

those who are taller than 50 inches *and* have brown hair results in three student records. For this search to be successful, it is important that the heights are labeled in the database as "numbers" so that the search can use the mathematical notation > (for greater than). This search results in the identification of three records of data matching these conditions of the search request (see Figure 7.5).

Another classroom suggestion that helps connect students' understanding of databases with the large databases available on the Web involves the U.S. Census Bureau data. The U.S. Census Bureau collects specific data every 10 years in order to count the population in the United States. The census exists as a means to determine representation in the House of Representatives. The 435 seats available in the House are apportioned to the states based on their population as determined through the census every 10 years. One of the extended uses of this tremendous data set is to measure the diversity of the nation.

Although students can access this database directly, a preliminary activity is useful in helping them see ideas they might retrieve from that database. To help students understand how the census database is constructed, have them gather data about their families similar to that gathered by the U.S. Census Bureau. Using a word processor to create a questionnaire, they can outline the

Name	Height	Hair color	Brothers	Sisters	Dogs	Cats
Tawny	47	Red	1	2	1	1
Madison	53	Red	1	1	1	0

FIGURE 7.4 Search results from the class database on the field **Hair color** where the color matches the word **Red**.

Name	Height	Hair color	Brothers	Sisters	Dogs	Cats
Brad	52	Brown	1	1	0	0
Danny	51	Brown	1	0	1	0
Keith	52	Brown	2	0	2	1

FIGURE 7.5 Search results on the class database on the fields of *Height* and *Hair color*.

data they want from each family. Household size, ancestry of parents or guardians, age of each member of the household, occupations of the adults in the family, and language spoken in the household are possible categories of information they might collect. Before collecting the data, the class needs to create the database fields corresponding to the questionnaire data. Once the data are gathered and entered, the students sort and search the database to describe their families as a group. This analysis might be compared with the description of their local community or another community of their choice using the actual census data through Virginia's Historical Web Browser. Use Technology Link 6.2 (as discussed in Chapter 6) to access that website.

Learning with and about the Internet and Databases

The various activities previously described provide some ideas and directions for guiding student learning with and about the Internet and databases. One experience, however, is not all that is needed. Students need to consistently experience expanding instruction that engages them in exploring the basic operations, concepts, and constructs with the various Internet services and database capabilities. You cannot assume that students have learned about the various features and capabilities somewhere else, in some other class. You need to guide their learning with these tools by providing them with opportunities to explore the National Educational Technology Standards for Students (NET·S). As noted in the NET·S guidelines, the best ways to enhance student learning is within the context of the academic subjects. That way, students are more apt to naturally incorporate those tools as they explore more ideas within that content area. This approach supports them in examining various ideas within the context of their academic subjects: basic operations and concepts of the Internet and databases; social, ethical, and human issues related to their use; uses of the Internet and databases as productivity tools; uses of the Internet and databases as communications, research, and problem-solving or decision-making tools.

Basic Web Operations and Concepts

The Web offers tremendous potential for student involvement in searching for answers to important questions. Determining ways to focus student learning within the time available requires careful planning. Without some direction, students may or may not be able to identify quality sites in their quest for answers to questions.

Internet and Database Instructional Idea: Searching the Web In the Classroom 7.1 presents a problem for a class investigation that uses both the Web and library resources. The expectation is that students identify a route from the Atlantic to the Pacific and explore that route to investigate the people, wildlife, and geography along the way. In the process they also become more familiar with navigating the Web.

In the Classroom 7.1 is clearly designed to take more than one day. To maintain the focus of the lesson on the tasks desired in both social studies and science, planning is critical. In addition, to assure that students are able to gain experience using the Web as a tool for learning, the students definitely need support in the identification of appropriate websites.

In 1995 Bernie Dodge with Tom March at San Diego State University developed an instruction model, called *WebQuest*, to guide teachers in designing task-oriented activities that focus students on analyzing and synthesizing the information rather than simply identifying the information on the Web as well as from other resources (ISTE, 2002, pp. 32–33). They identified six building blocks for the WebQuest model to guide the development of lessons that focus students on the learning both with and about Web searches:

- **Introduction**: Interest and orient the students to the inquiry they will be doing.
- **Task**: A concise description of what the students complete in the activity.

In the Classroom 7.1

PEOPLE, PLACES, AND WILDLIFE FROM THE ATLANTIC TO THE PACIFIC

TECHNOLOGY OBJECTIVE: NETS·S I, II, V, VI

- **Navigating the Internet:** Technology as a research and problem-solving tool while building understanding of basic concepts.
- Navigate websites in search of valid information.

CONTENT OBJECTIVE: Social Studies: Study people, places, and environments across the United States. **Science:** Develop an understanding of animal populations and ecosystems and study various landforms across the United States.

GRADE LEVEL: 5–9

PROBLEM: How do people, geography, and animal wildlife vary from the Atlantic Ocean to the Pacific Ocean?

- ❑ Select one location along the Atlantic and another on the Pacific.
- ❑ Small groups identify various routes between those two places that demonstrate the diversity of geography, of people, and of wildlife across the United States.
- ❑ As a class, select the most interesting of the suggested routes.
- ❑ Divide the selected route into sectors to be analyzed by the small groups.
- ❑ Small groups collect historical, geographic, biological, and cultural information about their sector using information from various websites and reference books in the library. Some types of information students might select include the following:
  - Stories about Native Americans
  - Descriptions of animal wildlife
  - Descriptive journals kept by historical figures who have explored the area
- ❑ Map the area to describe various points of interest.
- ❑ Display the information about the sectors investigated by the groups.
- ❑ Reflect on the value of the various websites used for obtaining information for the trip.

- **Process:** Steps students do to complete the task.
- **Resources:** Resources (Web pages, journal articles, videos) the teacher preselects to guide the students in accomplishing the task rather than searching for the resources.
- **Evaluation:** Specific benchmarks along with scoring rubrics used to assess students' progress with the task.
- **Conclusion:** Thoughts for concluding the activity, along with ideas to guide students in reflecting on the learning experiences.

More detail about each of these building blocks can be found at the WebQuest site by using Technology Link 7.4. This site is a valuable resource for WebQuest task-oriented lesson ideas at many grade levels and in a variety of subject areas.

Creating your own WebQuest activity helps in extending your knowledge of teaching with and about the Web through a task-oriented activity. As you might notice from the WebQuest site, the les-

sons are presented for students in a Web format beginning with an introduction and a task much like the presentation in Figure 7.6 parts *a* and *b*. In this activity students investigate the geography, the society, and the wildlife from the Atlantic to the Pacific in the twenty-first century. The introduction is based on a task similar to that given to Lewis and Clark by President Jefferson over 200 years ago. The task, however, is set in today's time. Students

Technology Link 7.4

*W*ebQuest, created by Bernie Dodge with Tom March at San Diego State University, is a task-oriented activity that focuses the students on using information rather than searching for it. **WebQuest** links you to more information about the model and to a large number of predesigned WebQuest activities.

www.wiley.com/college/niess

(a) From the Atlantic to the Pacific

Introduction

On October 14, 1803, Meriwether Lewis and William Clark formed one of the most famous and successful partnerships in history. President Jefferson instructed them to

- Map a new route to the Pacific Ocean.
- Make contact with the Native Americans.
- Obtain specimens for further study.
- Maintain a full record of the activities of the expedition.

They began their journey, leaving from Camp Dubois at the mouth of the Missouri River on May 21, 1804. For 28 months and nearly 8000 miles, they mapped the route of their travels, documented their interactions with the Native American tribes, collected specimens, and maintained a full record of journals of their expedition. Throughout the trip, Lewis and Clark equally shared the leadership of the group. When faced with decisions, they polled all members, regardless of their status in the group (even Sacagawea once she joined the group). On November 16, 1805 at "Station Camp" in full view of the Pacific Ocean they recognized the completion of their journey in one of their journals:

We are now of the opinion that we cannot go any further with our canoes and think we are at the end of our voyage to the Pacific Ocean.

(b) From the Atlantic to the Pacific

Task

Your task is to map a trip from the Atlantic Ocean to the Pacific Ocean. You are instructed to

- Map a route from the Atlantic Ocean to the Pacific Ocean.
- Make contact with Americans along the way.
- Obtain virtual specimens of animal life along the way.
- Maintain a full record of the activities of the expedition.

Prepare a visual recounting of the trip through a video presentation that provides the stories of Americans and animal wildlife found along the way. Provide journals of specific stories along the way. Support your presentation with an annotated map of the trip that describes various points of interest and activities of the expedition.

FIGURE 7.6   (a) The **introduction** building block of a WebQuest model.
(b) The **task** building block of a WebQuest model.

---

are to map a route from the Atlantic to the Pacific and in the process they are to study the geography, the society, and the wildlife. In their account of the trip, they are to be prepared to use a variety of documents: a video presentation describing locations, people, and wildlife; journals that provide a written account of the journey; an annotated map describing the landmarks along the expedition; and a trip log that clarifies the daily progression of the journey.

The process building block is the next part of the model. Here you must describe what processes the students need to do in the task. You have lots to think about at this stage. How much time do you plan to allot for the task? How should the students be organized? What group size is best? Who should do what and when? Assume that you divide the task into three days of work and that you plan to divide the class into groups of size four where each group must plan a portion of the route between the Atlantic and the Pacific. Determining which route is the task for the first day.

What exactly do the students need to do? A Web page description outlines the process for the students. Figure 7.7a shows the top level of the process Web page, explaining in general terms the goals for each day of the project. Students

find the details for each day by selecting the appropriate hyperlinks labeled <u>Instructions Day 1</u>, <u>Instructions Day 2</u>, and <u>Instructions Day 3</u>. The extended detail in these pages presents the subtasks along with specific roles for each member of the group. Parts *b*, *c*, and *d* of Figure 7.7 detail the instructions for each day. As students investigate the instructions, they actually learn more about the Web. They use the hyperlinks to navigate the instructions. When they finish reading the instructions for the first day, they simply click on the hyperlink titled <u>Return top level</u> to return to the general outline of the processes for the task. In actuality they never leave the specific Web address where the processes Web page is stored; all the instructions are contained in one document, using hyperlinks to navigate within that document.

The next building block for the activity, the resources block, guides students in using specific resources. Websites are among the potential resources for students to use in this type of task. The teacher needs to preselect valuable sites to guide the students' investigations, focusing them on the topic rather than becoming lost in cyberspace. Again, a Web page is useful for guiding the students in their explorations of the different websites. Figure 7.8 displays a Web page

(a) From the Atlantic to the Pacific

Process

Day 1

The primary task for today is for each group to propose a route for the class to research for the overall task.

Instructions Day 1

Day 2

The primary task for today is to research the assigned sectors in preparation for the trip.

Instructions Day 2

Day 3

The primary task for today is to travel your sector in the coast-to-coast route, developing the visual production to describe your sector of the journey along with the appropriate maps and trip logs.

Instructions Day 3

(b) Instructions Day 1

Day 1:

The primary task for today is for each group to propose a route for the class to research for the overall task. As a group, select a route. Each team has four members and while the group must work as a whole, each person has a specific focus.

- Geographer: Focus on identifying a beginning and ending location; consider potential routes connecting them.
- Social scientist: Identify the people and societies across the United States.
- Ecologist: Identify a variety of wildlife across the United States.
- Recorder: Lead the group's efforts in identifying a route.

As a group, describe your selection:

- Identify the benefits and interesting features of the route. What can you learn about the geography, the people, and the wildlife across the United States by taking the route?
- Divide your route into six sectors, explaining the greatest values for traversing these sectors in the overall task.
- Prepare a map showing the routes, the sectors, and important features for consideration.

Recorders will present the routes for consideration. As a class agree on the route to be used and assign sectors.

Return top level

(c) Instructions Day 2

Day 2:

The primary task for today is to research the assigned sectors in preparation for the trip.

1. Assigned roles from the first day continue; expectations for each include:

- Geographer: Identifies specific places to investigate.
- Social scientist: Identifies specific events and people to visit along the sector journey.

- Ecologist: Identifies specific wildlife to document along the route.
- Recorder: Maintains a database of potential events along with the appropriate Web links for review.

2. Use Web links in a search for information relevant to your specific route. Keep a database file of Web links that identify important information: geography, people, events, or wildlife.

3. Select specific daily activities for the sector of your route.

Return top level

(d) Instructions Day 3

Day 3:

The primary task for today is to travel your sector in the coast-to-coast route, developing the visual production that recounts your sector journey and the appropriate maps and trip logs.

1. The duties of each member of the groups are extended to assume responsibilities associated with the preparation of the end product, the video presentation.

- Geographer: Organizes the video description of the geography of your sector; has primary responsibility for the development of the annotated map.
- Social scientist: Organizes the video description of the people and events and prepares annotations for the map; prepares trip log entries to tell the story of interactions along the way.
- Ecologist: Organizes the video description of the wildlife and prepares annotations for the map; prepares trip log entries to tell the story of the variation in the wildlife along the way.
- Recorder: Directs the video presentation, assuring that the video accurately tells the story. The recorder also maintains the trip log, calculates the distance traveled, and figures the cost.

2. Prepare a video presentation of the journey to answer these questions:

- How does the geography and landscape change along your sector? What obstacles does the land present in completing your journey? What is the weather like and why?
- What animals do you see that you have never encountered before? How would you describe them? Why are these animals only found in certain parts of the country?
- What are the people like in this sector of the route? How would you describe them? How are they different from people in the other sectors of the route? What jobs do they hold? What is important to them in their lives?
- What were the highlights of this sector of the journey from the Atlantic to the Pacific? How does the journey in this sector differ from the others across the United States? Why are there differences? What was similar and why?

3. Prepare an annotated map of the journey that is coordinated with the trip as described in the video presentation.

4. Prepare a trip log that specifically describes the daily adventures, the length, and the cost of the trip.

5. Present your work as the class as a whole makes the planned journey across the United States.

Return top level

FIGURE 7.7   (*a*) Outline of the **processes** for the task. (*b*) Instructions for the first day of the task. (*c*) Instructions for the second day of the task. (*d*) Instructions for the third day.

highlighting some resources that students might use for this task. In this example, pictures and descriptions identify the resources; in fact, the pictures are hyperlinks. All the students need to do is click on the pictures to visit the specific links. An important distinction between these hyperlinks and those in Figure 7.7 is that clicking on these hyperlinks moves the students to different Web addresses. No links are

Resources	
Day 1: Searching for a route	
What are possible routes?	
	Search the Atlas in our library for locations along each of the coasts you think are reasonable for the route.
	**Investigate different possible maps on the Web using MapQuest.**
What about the people?	
	Investigate different American Indian tribes across the United States.
What about the geography?	
	Color landform atlas of the United States. **Topographical maps.**
What about wildlife?	
	**Search for fish and wildlife on the U.S. fish and Wildlife website.** **Search for wildlife, farm, and marine mammals in different regions of the United States.**

FIGURE 7.8   Day 1 of the resources building block for the WebQuest model.

Evaluation

At the conclusion of this task, you will be evaluated on your work on the various outcomes for your sector of the trip.

Video	25%	See <u>Video Evaluation</u> for scoring guide on this major part of the project.
Journals	15%	<u>Journal Scoring Guide</u> describes the expectations for the journal.
Annotated map	25%	See <u>Map Evaluation</u> for scoring guide on this major part of the project.
Trip log	25%	See <u>Trip Log Evaluation</u> for scoring guide on this major part of the project.
Group evaluation	10%	As a team effort everyone in your group should contribute equally on the final products. Each team member will rate the other members of the team using the <u>Group Scoring Guide</u>. This feedback and teacher's feedback will be summarized to determine each team member's score for this portion of the project.

FIGURE 7.9   Evaluation building block for the Atlantic to the Pacific task.

available on those sites to return to the *resources* Web page. To navigate in this mode students must use the browser tools: the back arrow or the Go menu. Once they reach the sites the teacher has identified, they often use links from those sites to gain more information. To return to the teacher's menu of resources, they can either select the back arrow a number of times until they reach the correct location or they can use the Go menu of sites visited to immediately return to the desired Web address. These tools help them navigate the Web without having to enter the website addresses, an action often fraught with typographical errors. Chapter 9 of this text guides you in creating hyperlinks for navigating within a Web page as well as to other addresses as described in both the process and resource sections of this WebQuest activity.

The evaluation building block emphasizes important pieces of the task and how those pieces will be assessed. In the case of the Atlantic to the Pacific task, each group must produce four primary outcomes: video presentation highlighting the geography, people, and wildlife along the trip; annotated map; journals; and trip log. Figure 7.9 presents an example of how you might begin this section of the task showing the percentages to be allotted for each of the outcomes. As you can see by the figure, however, the work in identifying this building block includes the preparation of specific scoring guides for determining the value and progress of each student's work with each outcome. In this case, the evaluation menu directs students to specific scoring guides for each outcome; links are provided to the scoring guides rather than complicating the message about the percentages for each outcome. Teachers need to clearly describe the expectations and varying levels of accomplishments in the expectations for each scoring guide, presenting these expectations in a separate Web page format. Chapter 13 of this text provides directions for developing such scoring guides and Chapter 9 shows you how to make this evaluation block a Web page with links to the scoring guides.

The final part of the WebQuest model is the conclusions building block. This block is critical for sup-

porting the students in summarizing and reflecting on the information they have collected as well as the processes they used to collect the data. Questioning is a useful strategy for guiding their thinking at this time. Since this task uses Web-based research, one key is to engage the students in a discussion about the sites they visited as they gathered the evidence and artifacts for the different outcomes. Questions such as those in Figure 7.10 are useful in extending students' thinking beyond just a collection of data to specifically considering the Web resources they used for investigating the people, the wildlife, and the different geographies across the United States. Explicitly questioning them about their work with websites is important if the goal is for them to learn more about using Web resources in content-specific inquiry projects such as the Atlantic to the Pacific task. Ultimately, the students gain experience needed in learning to use the Web as they learn within the context of their subject matter.

Conclusion

Brand X Pictures

Congratulations! You have completed a fantastic journey across the United States—from the Atlantic to the Pacific. In the process you have investigated the diversity and complexity of land formations, people and social groups, and wildlife. Be prepared to discuss these questions when the class evaluates the various websites used to gather data and information:

• What websites provided you the most information? What was there about the website that made it so informative?
• What websites provided you the most valuable information? What made it valuable?
• What websites provided you with the least accurate information? How do you know it was not accurate?
• Did any of the websites provide you with biased information? Why do you think it was biased?

FIGURE 7.10   Conclusion building block for the Atlantic to Pacific journey.

Social, Ethical, and Human Issues

Mr. Nguyen's efforts to help his students untangle the mass of information available on the Web in the *Snapshot of a Class Investigation with Web Searches* was one way to help students understand how they can use the Internet to be more productive as they conduct research. Teachers can easily extend students' work with the Internet and databases to problem solve and make decisions. The Internet also offers critical new communications techniques. As students work with these new capabilities, however, they must also wrestle with social, ethical, and human issues.

The social, ethical, and human problems children encounter when using Internet resources might be the most significant limitation of the Internet in school-based settings. Considerable effort has been expended toward the goal of protecting children from inappropriate Web-based resources and predators who might attempt to interact and/or entice children through various Internet applications, such as e-mail discussion groups. One common danger for children is in chat rooms. As soon as children can type simple words, they can participate in an online chat. Many of these chat rooms are unmoderated. Children must be taught to take care when chatting just as they are taught to take care when in public places such as a playground. In this activity, teachers help young students understand the potential dangers of chat rooms.

Internet and Database Instructional Idea: Chatting Safely Many chat rooms look like playgrounds or lunchrooms. Kids in these rooms talk in groups or one-to-one about their friends or their schoolwork or maybe their favorite games. Of course, there is one important difference. In a physical place you can see the person you are talking with and make a reasonable decision about who they are and why they are in that place. In the chat room children have no reliable way to know why the people they are talking to have *entered* the room or who they are. Herein lies the problem with chat rooms. Children have no way of knowing what their new *friends* are up to and, as young and potentially vulnerable human beings, they may be susceptible to a wide array of harmful interactions.

Chat rooms are places where people are linked together via a host computer or server and conduct live text-based conversations. In most chat rooms the only limitation is the ability to access the Internet and type in your thoughts. Whatever you type in a chat room appears instantly on the screen for everyone else in the room to see as if it were just spoken in a real-time conversation. Only the log-in names (nicknames or screen names) on the screen identify the individuals in the chat room. Often more than one *conversation* is happening. In fact, the "chatter" may seem very chaotic and not at all like a real-life conversation.

To help children understand the dangers of chat rooms, explain how chat rooms work and provide them with some simple and easy to remember rules for participating in chats. One way to help children remember to be safe is to teach them some heuristics for being safe in chat rooms. Create and post an acronym for the word CHAT to consistently remind students about safety concerns. Figures 7.11*a* and 7.11*b* provide two examples.

Chat rooms can provide children with an opportunity to express their ideas in writing. But you must guide them by reminding them to be careful

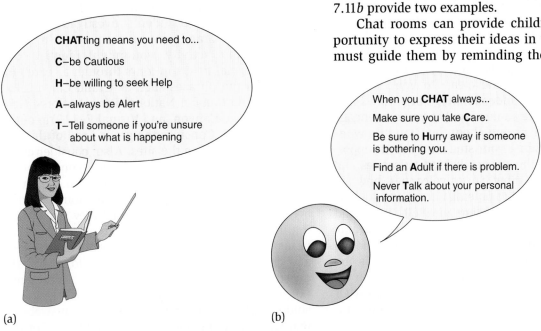

(a)   (b)

FIGURE 7.11   (*a*) A bulletin board to remind students of the important rules for chat rooms. (*b*) A poster designed to help children remember the chat room rules.

about what they tell other people in these environments. It is also important to check out chat rooms before allowing students to enter the room. Use these criteria to evaluate chat rooms:

1. **Does the chat room have a moderator?**

   Chat rooms for children should have a human moderator (as opposed to a software program) who checks what users are saying and monitors the rules of behavior for the chat room.

2. **Are users' rights to privacy protected?**

   Chat rooms should have very clear terms and conditions and privacy statements posted on the site.

3. **Are the topics open for discussion clearly posted and enforced?**

   Educational chat rooms should limit the topics and questions being discussed, and a moderator should be present to ensure the chat stays focused.

4. **Does the chat room promote commercial interests?**

   Some popular chat rooms have advertising and links to other sites and services. These links should be limited and must be checked out by the teacher.

Internet and Databases as Productivity Tools

Field trips provide marvelous opportunities to take the classroom activities to the real world. Imagine providing your students with an opportunity to explore the Grand Canyon, to investigate the geology of this marvelous geological sight. How was it formed, where did the rock come from, why does the Grand Canyon look the way it does, and how did it happen? These questions can be used in a guided tour of the actual site. However, a field trip to the Grand Canyon is unlikely, particularly if your school is not in the area. Do your students have to miss out on understanding about the Grand Canyon? Or is there some way that you can engage your students in learning about the Grand Canyon?

Imagine providing your students with an opportunity to explore the science behind volcanoes and volcanic processes. What causes volcanoes, how are scientists able to predict potential eruptions such as occurred on Mount St. Helens in 1980, 1986, and again in 2004? What is the composition of volcanic ash? These questions can guide a tour of an actual volcano. But perhaps this type of field trip is too dangerous and is not available locally. Do you ignore units on volcanoes and volcanic processes? Or is there some way that you can engage your students in an investigation of volcanoes?

Imagine an astronomy unit where students are learning about Mars and other planets. What is Mars made of? Is there a likelihood of life on Mars? Is there water on Mars? These questions can be used in guiding an investigation of the planet Mars, but certainly an actual field trip to Mars is not possible! What can you do to help students investigate a planet such as Mars?

Although the idea of field trips is an appealing solution for each of these situations, there are important reasons that field trips are not the best solutions. The Grand Canyon may not be near your school; a trip to an active volcano is probably not a safe trip; and certainly a trip to Mars is out of the question! Yet, science teachers are encouraged to incorporate fieldwork in their instruction. Field trips offer authentic learning experiences for students, giving them greater understandings of the natural and technological world in which they live. Also, field trips are often the most memorable and meaningful experiences for students in their study of science. It is true that field trips cost time and money and are not always productive in meeting the goals. The question then is, How can you incorporate the educational and motivational elements achieved with field trips in a more productive way?

Internet and Database Instructional Idea: Virtual Field Trips   Science is not the only subject area that is benefited by field trips. Literally all subject area instruction at all grade levels can benefit. As a teacher, however, you need to expand your understanding of field trips to include the idea of virtual field trips. The Web provides a myriad of resources to engage students in a virtual field trip during class time. All you need to do is spend some time searching using key phrases like *virtual field trips*. In the Classroom 7.2 describes plans for a virtual field trip of the Grand Canyon where students investigate the question of how the Grand Canyon was formed. In preparation for this activity, you might identify four different virtual field trip tours through a search on the Web using phrases such as Grand Canyon Explorer, Grand Canyon National Park, National Geographic: Grand Canyon, and Virtual Field Trip of the Grand Canyon. Consider the grade level of the students when selecting the sites. Also, consider creating your own virtual tour where you create a website that has the links for students to explore.

As the students explore the virtual tours, encourage them to keep a journal of what they find. Working in small groups, one of the group members can be assigned to assure that they record their efforts and findings in an electronic journal. To answer the questions, each small group must prepare a presentation of their findings. It is important to engage the students in a consideration of the different websites that were useful in answering the questions. For this lesson, the closure uses that information to direct them to a new exploration — an exploration of the fossils that might be found in each of the layers of the Grand Canyon. Through their virtual tour, the

In the Classroom 7.2

FORMING THE GRAND CANYON

TECHNOLOGY OBJECTIVE: NETS · S I, II, III, V, VI

- **Internet:** Technology as a productivity, research, and problem-solving tool while building understanding of basic concepts.
- Navigate websites to gather information.

CONTENT OBJECTIVE: Science: Students investigate the physical processes that shape the patterns of Earth's surface and expand their abilities in scientific inquiry by developing descriptions, explanations, predictions, and models based on evidence and explanations.

GRADE LEVEL: 5–9

PROBLEM: How was the Grand Canyon formed?

❏ Introduction:

- Locate the Grand Canyon on a map of Arizona that is available on the Web. Search other Web pictures of the Grand Canyon and ask the students to brainstorm ideas on how the canyon was formed. Introduce the idea of conducting a field trip directed at investigating these questions:
  - ○ How was the Grand Canyon formed?
  - ○ Where did the rock come from?
  - ○ Why does the Grand Canyon look the way it does?
  - ○ When did all this happen?

❏ Virtual field trip:

- **Teacher preparation**: Identify four different websites that provide virtual field trips of the Grand Canyon.
- **Organization**: Divide the class into groups of four students each.
- **Instructions:** Each student in the group leads one of the four virtual tours of the Grand Canyon investigating the four questions, gathering data along the field trip. Record your work in an electronic journal describing the four different virtual field trips. Be sure to maintain a list of the websites that were used in answering the questions.
- **Board the bus** (the computers): Begin the tours with your electronic journal ready for the data collection.

❏ After completing the virtual tours:

- Small groups use their electronic journals in creating PowerPoint presentations explaining their responses to each of the questions.
- Groups share their presentations.

❏ Closure:

- Engage the students in summarizing the answers to the four questions, discussing how the virtual Web tours helped them learn to use the Web as a productivity tool.
- Ask the students to brainstorm the types of animals that might have existed at each of the layers they found in the Grand Canyon. Explain that their next journey will be to identify the fossils that might be found in each of the layers. Ask them to indicate websites they visited in their previous virtual tour that might help to explore this idea, sharing why these are useful sites.

students navigate the Web, exploring different sites and recording their visits. In the process they find some sites more useful than others, and a specific closure discussion helps them to think about how the Web can be used as a productivity tool in answering important content questions, in this case about the formation of the Grand Canyon.

Internet and Database Instructional Idea: A Website Resource Database   In the Classroom 7.2 asks that

students maintain an electronic journal describing the websites and the information that they gathered about the Grand Canyon. A specific closure activity might be for the class to create a database with fields that are useful in searching for resources for the next class investigation about the types of fossils at each layer. The class decides which fields would be useful. In this manner, they learn more about creating a database within the context of the subject and in the end have a tool that enhances their productivity on the next project.

The Resource Idea: Database Productivity Tool described in Figure 7.12 can be used to extend this idea to your teacher preparation program where you create and maintain a database describing the websites that you find useful in teaching your subject. Note that the database includes a field to align each idea with the NETS·S guidelines. You might also have a field for the teacher standards (NETS·T). If this database is maintained, you will find that you are more productive in designing lessons, including those in the WebQuest format. The database is a *library* of resources that you can quickly consult, conducting a search for specific topics, content areas, and grade levels to identify ideas. You save lots of Web searching time if you consistently add to and maintain your database. A good idea for supporting this database is to create electronic files describing each resource in more detail. Label each file with the corresponding title in the database; store the files in a folder that also contains the database so that all the information is in the same location on your computer.

Internet and Databases as Communications Tools

The rapidly emerging access to the capabilities and services of the Internet are impacting education's literacy goals. Internet literacy is intertwined with reading, writing, and communications goals. In fact, literacy researchers have turned their attention to the Internet. Blanchard (1996) claims that, across all disciplines, telecommunication via the Internet changes how teachers and students exchange information and ideas.

The Internet offers plenty of opportunities for students to learn to use it as a communications tool within the context of learning the various subject areas. For example, students can use some of the many services available to ask questions of experts: Ask Dr. Math, Ask Dr. Science, Ask Miss Grammar, and even Ask Dr. Universe. Web services such as these provide students with another avenue for finding answers to their curriculum-related questions. But students must be able to express their questions clearly and succinctly in written form. Thus, teachers must guide students in learning to communicate and use written language for corresponding with distant readers. Garner and Gillingham (1998) proposed that teachers incorporate instruction to guide students in monitoring their own written communications. Does the writing communicate? Is the writing grammatically sound? Is the communication clear and unambiguous?

Internet and Database Instructional Idea: Written Debates When you hear about a debate, you probably think in terms of a verbal encounter. With the

---

Resource Idea: Database Productivity Tool

Title: A Database of Resources

Topic: Multidisciplinary, database

Grades: K–12, college, teacher preparation programs

Objectives: Using databases, student teachers maintain a database of resources that integrate technology in teaching or learning.

Idea: A resource database is a collection prepared by students in a teacher preparation program. Preservice teachers search the Web for useful websites that describe lesson ideas and plans for incorporating technology in specific teaching areas. They prepare records in the database with these fields: Title, Topic, Content area, Grade level, NETS Student Standards (NETS·S), Website. Student teachers add a specific number of website ideas over the term of the course. When preservice teachers are designing future lessons, they are able to search the database for useful websites that might be used in lessons described in the WebQuest format. Preservice teachers should review the database websites periodically to consider lesson ideas and the currency of the website resources.

Materials: Database program, Internet access

Modifications:

1. Use database searches and sorts to organize and display the information. Which websites were the most useful in obtaining information in explaining the topic? What technologies are most common?

2. At the beginning of the school year, help the students develop a database to provide them with a productivity tool to be used throughout the year as they conduct Web research. This database is to be extended throughout the year as they continue to use the Web as a research tool.

FIGURE 7.12   One idea for creating a database to assist in gathering resources in the teacher preparation program.

In the Classroom 7.3

FOR OR AGAINST?

TECHNOLOGY OBJECTIVE: NETS · S I, II, IV, V, VI

- **Internet:** Technology as a communications, research, and problem-solving tool while building understanding of basic concepts.
- Use an e-mail listserv to communicate ideas in support of or against a particular proposal.

CONTENT OBJECTIVE: **All subject areas:** Students organize and consolidate their thinking through written communications. They analyze and evaluate their written expressions. They must express ideas precisely in writing.

GRADE LEVEL: 6–12

DEBATE STATEMENT: Use of the Web is more valuable and important for learning today than use of the school library.

❏ Prepare students for the debate: Before proposing the debate statement, students need multiple experiences using both Web and library resources within the context of learning the subject matter content. While they work on these activities, have them maintain a journal describing the benefits and disadvantages of using the different resources.

❏ Organize for the debate:

- Announce the statement and provide a sign-up debate list with the number of potential debate forums (Forum A pro, Forum A con, Forum B pro, Forum B con, etc.).
- Form debate groups of two or three students and have them sign up for a position on the debate list.
- Announce the debate to be completed in three rounds:
  - Round 1: Present initial position.
  - Round 2: Rebut arguments communicated in Round 1.
  - Round 3: Recap position and make concluding arguments.
- Create the listservs that contain only the students signed up for a particular forum.
- Announce that the teacher is the judge who will moderate the lists.

❏ Group preparation for the debate:

- Allow groups preparation time to set up arguments, preparing an outline for the logic to be used in presenting the arguments.
- Group members must share the debate position equally. Determine who will prepare the written response for each argument.

❏ The debate:

- Debate occurs on the listserv only, with each position group assigned to a specific computer and a specific forum.
- Round 1: Groups send their positions to the listserv simultaneously, with individual group members sending their portions of the argument to the listserv.
- Round 2: Groups rebut the arguments presented in Round 1 with each student in the group sending an e-mail in response to the previous arguments.
- Round 3: Groups send their recap and concluding arguments to the listserv. Each group member must send a response.

❏ Summarize and reflect:

- Judge presents the decisions and rationale for the decisions.
- In a whole-class discussion discuss the writing techniques that were successful in communicating positions.

shift toward the importance of written communication, a debate in writing offers an instructional opportunity for students to learn to use the Internet as a communications tool. One idea for this type of activity is the Great Debate Project, a Web and problem-based activity that provides a service of ongoing debates by e-mail and Internet. Debate topics are posted for class participation. The class chooses a position (for or against) on one of the topics and sends their intent to participate. The debate takes place and is judged by a panel of teachers.

In the Classroom 7.3 is an extension of one of the debate topics posted in the Great Debate Project Web page. This idea, however, uses a class discussion in a classroom listserv established and moderated by the teacher. The students engage in the debate via e-mail. The debate about whether the Web is a better learning resource than the library is an important question as more and more students rely almost solely on the Web for their research. The debate requires the students to discuss the pros and cons of both avenues of research. For an effective debate, students need experiences using both for research in specific subject areas. Those experiences along with information that they may gather about the proposal are important for developing their positions. Since the debate is conducted through a written communications mode, they must develop their arguments and present those arguments in writing on the listserv. The conclusion of the activity needs to consider writing techniques that are useful in communicating the arguments most clearly.

Internet and Database Instructional Idea: A Blogging Experience   Another classroom communications tool is a *weblog*, or *blog*, an online personal journaling tool. Blogs developed from the work of heavy Web surfers who created Web logs to capture their journeys and discoveries. At last count, several hundred thousand diarists were actively posting as they created blogs about almost every conceivable topic. Blogs provide teachers and student writers with a writing space that requires no technical knowledge of the Web authoring language HTML, while offering access to an instant publishing press. Technology Link 7.5 provides a link to a free weblog website that allows you to quickly construct your own weblog, working from online templates that take care of the design and allow you to focus on the writing.

Technology Link 7.5

*F*or access to the free website to quickly construct your own weblog, working with online templates to support your writing, use the **Weblog** link.

www.wiley.com/college/niess

A weblog is a communications tool that is more structured than an e-mail list and more intimate than a discussion board; it offers a conversation space for student readers, writers, and thinkers transcending other similar applications known to this point. Perhaps even more key for connecting weblogs to classroom work is the multitextual capacity of the weblog space. Writers are able to import audio files, images, and movie files, tapping into the wealth of compelling materials available online.

A weblog writing space contains two parts: online journal and class discussion tool. With weblogs,

students are provided with a forum for engaging in written discussion that features the following:

1. Economy: Weblogs demand precision. The well-developed weblog post requires no scrolling—it is a brief, targeted set of words that communicates the intended idea.

2. Archiving: Each posting is dated and archived by week or day. This structure allows readers (and student writers) to explore how ideas unfold, connect, link, and synthesize.

3. Feedback: The "comments" feature in a weblog expects peer review and sharing from the start. Instead of opening selected passages for periodic feedback (often teacher-driven), a weblog begins the communication with the initial posting.

4. Multiple representations: Weblogs allow writers to post images or even record postings as sound files. By tapping into a variety of student writers' literacies, weblogs offer student writers multiple means of communication, again within a confined space.

5. Immediate publishing: As soon as students post and publish to their weblog, their entry appears online. Not only does this feature allow for an immediate accomplishment, it enables the feedback and response loop to begin.

6. Participation: Classroom discussion rarely allows each student an opportunity to share a substantive idea at the moment that it is conceived. Weblogs provide a communications tool where each student *can* participate. The learning community, posting, connecting, seeing, reading, thinking, and responding, leads to greater participation.

Through the precision and economy of each posting, student readers and writers have smaller chunks of text to consider. Emphasis is on exploration of the language used during the writing process. On the simplest level, this emphasis directly supports student textual and cognitive confidence. It works to build stamina needed to continue reading difficult texts. It provides a space for readers to talk about the reading process while they are immersed in the text, as opposed to having to reconstruct meaning away from the text.

Perhaps the most significant instructional power of the weblog is its ability to support, reflect, and convey student comprehension. One of a teacher's greatest challenges is to lead students to connect, synthesize, and apply understanding in a variety of contexts and situations. The weblog space demands that students consolidate their writing and demonstrate how to think when working as a reader or as a writer. The scaffolding provided through the immediate archiving allows teachers an opportunity to

In the Classroom 7.4

WHAT WILL BE REMEMBERED FROM 9-11?

TECHNOLOGY OBJECTIVE: NETS · S I, II, III, IV, V, VI

- **Internet:** Technology as a communications, productivity, research, and decision-making tool while building understanding of basic concepts.
- Incorporate a weblog for communicating ideas triggered by digital images.

CONTENT OBJECTIVE: All Subject Areas: Students organize and consolidate their thinking through written communications. Students analyze and evaluate their written expressions. Students express ideas precisely in writing.

GRADE LEVEL: 6–12

QUESTION: What really happened on September 11, 2001?

- ❏ Prepare students for viewing the images: Engage students in a classroom development of important questions to be asked about the September 11, 2001 attacks. Sample questions might include the following:
  - What happened? Who did what? Where?
  - Who was responsible?
  - Were the actions legitimate reactions to the beliefs of those who were responsible?
  - What was the reaction of people around the world?
- ❏ Introduce the Smithsonian Institution's September 11 Digital Archive as a collection of the history of the September 11, 2001 attacks. The archive is designed to collect first-hand accounts of the attacks and the aftermath, archiving e-mails and digital images both of the events and people's reaction.
  - Access the website (use Technology Link 7.6).
  - Explore the site to become familiar with the various artifacts and collection techniques for developing the collection.
- ❏ Challenge students to discuss their ideas about media and literacy as a means of triggering ideas and reactions, using their weblogs as a response journaling tool where they share comments and feedback. Encourage them to make postings whenever the texts trigger ideas or reactions. Allow them to have their journal blogs as either public or private.

support and examine students' work with a text that progressively increases in difficulty.

In the Classroom 7.4 describes one idea for engaging students in expressing their reactions and thoughts triggered by digital images available in the Smithsonian Institution's September 11 Digital Archive (see Technology Link 7.6). The overriding question is framed around how the events of September 11, 2001, will be recorded in history and the effect of the media in framing that record.

Technology Link 7.6

*I*nvestigate the **Digital** link to access the digital archives that the Smithsonian Institution is collecting to preserve and present the history of the September 11, 2001, attacks in New York, Virginia, and Pennsylvania and the public responses to them.

www.wiley.com/college/niess

Using a weblog as a journaling tool, students select, read, explore, probe, and connect online texts housed within the Smithsonian Institution's September 11 Digital Archive. Students maintain their weblogs as response journals, posting their ideas and reactions triggered by the images and text. The journals challenge student writers to enter into and meaningfully engage in the questions posed by the images. The journal space provides the students with a space to consider new ideas, structuring and synthesizing what is known as opposed to retelling. Here they are asked to choose when to write, take risks, think differently, and voice honestly within a space where they select the audience they wish to share their ideas—using either a public or private selection of their written ideas. The capability of inserting images and sound files into their response entries provides a rich environment for expressing those thoughts and reactions.

Through this activity, students are drawn into the media offered through the digital archive by both their memories of the past and their needs for the present and future. In class, they might speak of this investigation as an experience that disquieted what they had previously thought while providing them the space to make meaning out of where they are at this particular moment. Each student weblog grows with multiple entries, all of which use the texts as a springboard into making meaning out of current events and their own beliefs.

It is important to use class time for face-to-face classroom discourse to build a community of growth and verify that the weblogs are writing spaces to be viewed by the student writer, the teacher (who would comment in an area away from the student's weblog), and only those students who the student writer selects.

Internet and Databases as Research Tools

The Internet is a useful research tool with an extensive collection of data and access to experts. Experiences that guide students in learning about this resource as a research tool have become an increasingly important activity at both elementary and secondary levels. Although teachers may establish activities that require students to use the Internet as a research tool, they must scaffold their students' experiences to assure that they are growing in their knowledge and understanding of finding valid and reliable data and information. From the beginning of the school year, you need to begin helping your students expand their knowledge. The ideas developed through the WebQuest model are useful in that teachers are more apt to identify good resources for students and, in the conclusion of the lessons, guide the reflection on the value of those resources. Students need to learn to continually challenge the validity and reliability of the sites. At some point, however, you must allow and encourage them to identify resources on their own. An extension of the WebQuest model called the Web Inquiry Project enables students to look for sites on their own and, more importantly, to use information from the sites to conduct authentic inquiries in various academic disciplines.

The Web Inquiry Project (WIP) model was developed by Philip Molebash at San Diego State University. The model shares a conceptual likeness to the WebQuest model, but with at least two important distinctions. First, the WIP model encourages students to locate their own Web-based resources. Second, WIPs allow for authentic inquiry, including the development of a focused and inquiry-based question, whereas WebQuests are focused on tasks, which might or might not be inquiry-orientated. Use Technology Link 7.7 to access the website that contains examples and templates for creating your own WIPs. The WIP model is framed in six stages as described by Molebash (2004).

1. Hook students by focusing them on some relevant and intriguing content.

2. Guide students toward the development of inquiry-based questions.

Technology Link 7.7

Investigate the **WIP** link to access examples and templates for creating your own Web Inquiry Project (WIP) as designed by Philip Molebash.

www.wiley.com/college/niess

3. Expect students to develop a procedure for addressing the question, including the identification of appropriate Web-based materials.

4. Provide students time and support for accessing the identified materials to gather information aimed at responding to the question.

5. Encourage students to manipulate or analyze the information toward responding to the question.

6. Expect students to report their findings and draw conclusions using the data and/or evidence uncovered in step 5.

Internet and Database Instructional Idea: Who Are the Inventors?   Who invented the cotton gin? You probably think it was Eli Whitney. Or did Catherine Green, Whitney's employee, actually invent the cotton gin for which Eli Whitney obtained the patent? How many inventions have been identified with a male name, ignoring the fact that a woman was the actual inventor? You can probably name many inventions that have been created by men. How many inventions can you find that were created by women? Does the lack of women inventors give the impression that women did not invent anything? Using the web inquiry model, students can research women inventors and move toward dispelling the myth that women are not contributors in mathematics, science, and technology inventions and advancement domains.

The middle school years are the grades when girls begin making decisions about whether to pursue high school mathematics and science courses. Part of their decision-making process involves their understanding of the disciplines and who works in mathematical or scientific careers. Role models affect their personal views. If they do not see women models, either historically or in the present times, they envision the domains as male-dominated and not for them.

In the Classroom 7.5 describes a WIP research project that can be incorporated in a mathematics or science class particularly during the middle school years. For this project, the students work in groups of two to research women contributors to the fields of mathematics, science, or technology. This research project focuses them on a consideration of the reliability of the Web-based resources and the extent to which women have contributed to the traditional understanding of mathematics, science, and technology. Students identify resources

In the Classroom 7.5

WOMEN IN MATHEMATICS, SCIENCE, AND TECHNOLOGY

TECHNOLOGY OBJECTIVE: **NETS·S I, II, III, IV, V, VI**

- **Internet:** Technology as a communications, productivity, research, and decision-making tool while engaged in understanding basic technology concepts.
- Identify valid and reliable Internet resources for use in conducting a research project.

CONTENT OBJECTIVE: **Science and mathematics:** Students inquire about the role of women in science and mathematics disciplines.

GRADE LEVEL: 6–12

PROBLEM: Do the fields of science, mathematics, and technology welcome women's participation?

❏ "Hook" students by telling them the story of Catherine Green.

Eli Whitney invented the cotton gin, right? Well, not so fast. Some historians are now suggesting that Eli Whitney might have had some help. In fact, they say he might have had a lot of help. Eli Whitney invented the cotton gin after he moved in 1782 to Georgia from his home in New England and observed the desperate need for a device that would remove cotton fibers from their seeds—or so the story goes. Some historians now argue that Whitney "borrowed" the idea from slaves who were using a comblike device to separate fibers from the seed. Others suggest that Whitney's gin (machine) was simply an adaptation of existing devices that just did not work very well. The story can certainly be authenticated with historical and archeological evidence. Planters did use drum-like devices or rollers to remove fibers from cottonseeds. The problem with those devices (used in North America as early as the sixteenth century) was that they did not work well with short fiber cotton typically grown in the southern United States. Whitney was essentially trying to improve on the roller gin and apparently decided to make use of sharpened teeth extended from the roller or drum – maybe based on the combs he saw slaves use. Now, Catherine Green comes into the story. A third group of historians claim Eli Whitney's employee, Catherine Green, provided Whitney with the final inspiration that enabled his invention to work. The story goes that Whitney was unable to solve a problem with his simple device. The teeth were pulling the fibers away from the seed, but the fibers would stick to the teeth, clogging the machine. According to some historians, Catherine Green showed Whitney how a brush could be used to remove cotton fibers sticking to the teeth on the cylinder of Whitney's device.

The rest, as they say, is history. Whitney perfected his device, applied for and received a patent, and to this day receives sole credit, in most sources, for the invention.

❏ Guide students toward the development of authentic questions about the role of women in science, mathematics, and technology. This work will most likely require that you find additional women, like Catherine Green, who may have contributed in the fields of science, mathematics, and technology, but their contributions are not so well publicized.

❏ Groups begin to conduct research by developing a procedure for addressing their question. This effort includes the identification of Web-based resources to help students address their questions.

❏ Students gather data from their identified Web-based resources.

❏ Students analyze the data as evidence to address their questions.

❏ Students develop a report or some conclusions that include some clarification of their proposed answer and their research methods.
- Answer the questions you identified.
- What methods did you use to conduct your research?
  - Describe the methods.
  - Identify all resources used for gathering information. Provide evidence for the accuracy of the resources.
  - Identify resources that you identified as less reliable. How did you know?

within the context of inquiries about the contributions of women, and as they collect data, they are asked to evaluate both the validity and reliability of the resources. In the process they expand their understanding of using such Web-based resources as research tools.

Internet and Databases as Problem-Solving and Decision-Making Tools

The availability of databases on the Internet affords teachers and students numerous opportunities to engage in problem-solving and decision-making

In the Classroom 7.6

WORLD HUNGER

TECHNOLOGY OBJECTIVE: NETS·S I, II, III, IV, V, VI

- **Internet:** Technology as a research and decision-making tool while building understanding of basic concepts.
- Access Internet databases about the availability of food in various places in the world.

CONTENT OBJECTIVE: Social studies: Students analyze the problem of world hunger and propose solutions to the problem of hunger on a local level.

GRADE LEVEL: 6–12

PROBLEM: Where and why are people hungry in the world and what can be done locally to alleviate hunger?

PREPARATION: Promote understanding of the relative production capacities and food needs of various countries.

- ❏ Research online databases to find the types of crops grown in various countries.
  - What countries produce agricultural crops such as rice, wheat, corn, and potatoes?
    - ○ The Central Intelligence Agency (CIA) World Factbook (http://www.cia.gov/library/publications/the-world-factbook/) provides reliable information about national agricultural crop production.
  - Compare the production of staple crops such as corn, rice, and wheat to the population of the identified countries.
    - ○ Students use the online resource, called Nationmaster (http://www.nationmaster.com/index.php) to find the top 20 corn, rice, and wheat (grain) producers. Older students might want to create ratios of the population and a given food production.
- ❏ Are there imbalances between the needs of people and the country's ability to domestically produce enough to meet the demand?
  - Brainstorm ideas about whether the crops grown in a given country provide enough to feed the population.
  - If the production does not seem to be enough, where do the people in the country get their food?

PROBLEM SOLVING: Think globally but act locally! What happens when countries cannot meet the demand for food in their country?

1. *Students develop and expand the problem.*
   - Questions for students:
     - ○ What do you know about hunger given your analysis of the country data on food production?
     - ○ Have you ever seen pictures on television or in magazines of children who are hungry?
     - ○ Do you know of places where people might be hungry?
   - Distinguish between chronic hunger and the more short-term quenchable hunger that they may feel.
   - Consider the scope of hunger in a given place.

2. *Students should identify alternative opinions about the problem.*
   - Consider how people think about hunger and to some extent why it exists.
   - Prompt students to think about the food system that sustains the production and distribution of food throughout the world using a version of this story about a food system.

   The Story of Akeyo's Corn. Akeyo lives in eastern Kenya. He and others in the town grow corn for a living. They are, of course, dependent on rain for the corn to grow. Sometimes the rains fall and Akeyo's corn grows. Other years the rain does not fall and Akeyo's corn does not grow. What else will Akeyo need besides rain for his to corn grow? (Hints: He will need to keep the weeds and animals out of his cornfield, he will need enough sun, and he may need fertilizer.) Once Akeyo's corn is grown, he will need to do a lot to get the corn ready to sell. What types of things will Akeyo need to do? (Hints: He will need to pick the corn, shuck it, and store it.)
   Some years Akeyo has too much corn for his family. He sells the corn to make money to pay for others things his family needs. What might prevent Akeyo from being able to sell his corn? (Hints: He needs a way to get the corn to the market and he needs people who are willing to buy the corn.)

3. *How might the problem of hunger be solved?*
   - ❏ Extend the story of Akeyo to consider the larger question of hunger.
     - Use Internet research to look at corn production and consider why corn production might have been down in some years. (Hints: Limited rainfall, disease, problems with distribution.) Guide students in understanding that if corn production is down then the amount of corn available for purchase will also go down, thereby causing some with limited access to corn markets to go hungry.

(continued on next page)

- Have students think of ways that Akeyo and other corn producers can be helped so that they can produce and sell enough corn each year to provide for their families. Prompt the students for multiple solutions.

4. *Students determine which solution best solves the problem.*

❏ Create a two-column list where students list each of the ideas they thought would result in the failure of the corn crop; in the second column they should list the solutions they suggest.

❏ Identify what you consider as the best solution to solve the problem.

5. *Implement the solution.*

❏ Since this step would be impractical given students' work thus far, have them shift gears and think about hunger in their own community.

- Questions:

  ○ Are there people in our community who are hungry?

  ○ Why might those people be hungry? Their ideas may be very similar to the items discussed about Akeyo.

  ○ How can you help alleviate hunger in our community?

❏ Repeat steps 3 and 4 until one solution has been developed. Ask students to think about how they might implement the solution and proceed to do just that.

6. *Adapt the implemented solution as needed.*

❏ After students implement their solution, ask them whether they think their solution is working. If they have reasons to believe it is not working, then adapt the solution and reimplement.

---

activities. One problem-solving technique popular in education is the problem based learning (PBL) model introduced in Chapter 2. The PBL strategy essentially involves students identifying and confronting ill-structured problems while attempting to find some meaningful real-life solution to the problem. The most important aspect of the PBL strategy is that the problem is set in the context of the real world.

The PBL procedure can involve numerous steps, but is best imagined as a means of enabling students as they consider meaningful problems and propose solutions that ideally would be implemented. Jonassen's (1997) model for solving ill-structured problems recommends steps for facilitating a PBL activity.

1. Develop or identify a problem for students. Ideally, the problem emerges from students' interest. The problem does not, and in fact should not, have an obvious solution. Importantly, the problem should be grounded in the real world and be ill-structured, meaning the problem should not have a simple or best solution.

2. Identify and clarify alternative opinions, positions, and perspectives. These ideas should not be thought of as solutions or hypotheses. Instead, students should think about what is known and unknown about the problem.

3. Generate possible solutions to the problem. Prior to developing the solutions, students can prepare a list of questions that might help in solving the problem. Questions may be in the form of requests for more information. The questions can guide research that may include questioning an expert, accessing data online, or visiting a library to find answers to the questions.

4. Assess the likelihood of each of the various solutions to actually improve the problem situation.

5. Select what seems to be the best solution to the problem and if possible implement the solution selected.

6. Adapt the solution, given problems that emerge after the solution's implementation.

Internet and Database Instructional Idea: Addressing Hunger   Why are some people hungry? Where do those people live? Students in grades 6–12 can investigate the problem of world hunger using the PBL strategy and resources available in databases on the Internet. (In the Classroom 7.6 presents a detailed description of this activity.) Through this activity, students must think about what they can do to solve the problem of hunger. The problem is ill-structured, with no simple or obvious solution, and the problem is most certainly fixed in the real world. The problem, particularly as it relates to the reasons some people are hungry and where the hunger is worst, can be addressed using online resources, particularly online researchable databases. The primary goal is to allow students to understand how the food system works from farming and production to distribution and consumption. The problem is best addressed on a global scale using a modified version of Jonassen's steps and online resources.

Hunger is a problem all over the world. In exploring the problem of world hunger, students need to consider the problem in ways that might potentially solve the problem; however, the most practical solutions require actions close to home. For this reason, students need to be guided in thinking on a global sense about the problem of hunger but to act locally in addressing the problem. This *think globally and act locally* process begins by identifying production capacities of various countries, researching the online databases provided in the Central Intelligence Agency's (CIA) online searchable World Factbook and the Nationmaster online data. First, with the CIA online fact book, select the option to **search** the fact book and use **Agriculture** to identify the category for the search. Next select the **Agricultural-products** hyperlink to find the listing of countries and their agricultural products, listed in order of importance (see Figure 7.13). This listing allows students to distinguish between countries with major agricultural products of rice, wheat, corn, and potatoes and those without.

Then they can find additional information on the production of various staple crops such as corn, rice, and wheat related to the population of the identified countries. Here they investigate the Nationmaster Web page as shown in Figure 7.14.

Country	Agriculture - products
Afghanistan	opium, wheat, fruits, nuts; wool, mutton, sheepskins, lambskins
Albania	wheat, corn, potatoes, vegetables, fruits, sugar beets, grapes; meat, dairy products
Algeria	wheat, barley, oats, grapes, olives, citrus, fruits; sheep, cattle
American Samoa	bananas, coconuts, vegetables, taro, breadfruit, yams, copra, pineapples, papayas; dairy products, livestock
Andorra	small quantities of rye, wheat, barley, oats, vegetables; sheep
Angola	bananas, sugarcane, coffee, sisal, corn, cotton, manioc (tapioca), tobacco, vegetables, plantains; livestock; forest products; fish
Anguilla	small quantities of tobacco, vegetables; cattle raising
Antigua and Barbuda	cotton, fruits, vegetables, bananas, coconuts, cucumbers, mangoes, sugarcane; livestock
Argentina	sunflower seeds, lemons, soybeans, grapes, corn, tobacco, peanuts, tea, wheat; livestock
Armenia	fruit (especially grapes), vegetables; livestock
Aruba	aloes; livestock; fish
Australia	wheat, barley, sugarcane, fruits, cattle, sheep, poultry
Austria	grains, potatoes, sugar beets, wine, fruit; dairy products, cattle, pigs, poultry; lumber
Azerbaijan	cotton, grain, rice, grapes, fruit, vegetables, tea, tobacco; cattle, pigs, sheep, goats
Bahamas, The	citrus, vegetables; poultry
Bahrain	fruit, vegetables; poultry, dairy products; shrimp, fish
Bangladesh	rice, jute, tea, wheat, sugarcane, potatoes, tobacco, pulses, oilseeds, spices, fruit; beef, milk, poultry
Barbados	sugarcane, vegetables, cotton
Belarus	grain, potatoes, vegetables, sugar beets, flax; beef, milk
Belgium	sugar beets, fresh vegetables, fruits, grain, tobacco; beef, veal, pork, milk
Belize	bananas, cacao, citrus, sugar; fish, cultured shrimp; lumber; garments
Benin	cotton, corn, cassava (tapioca), yams, beans, palm oil, peanuts, cashews;

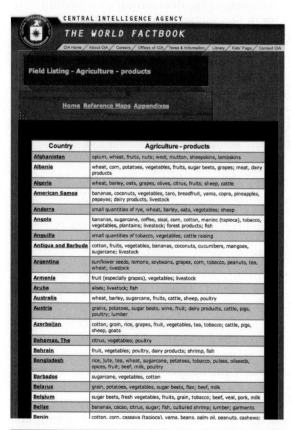

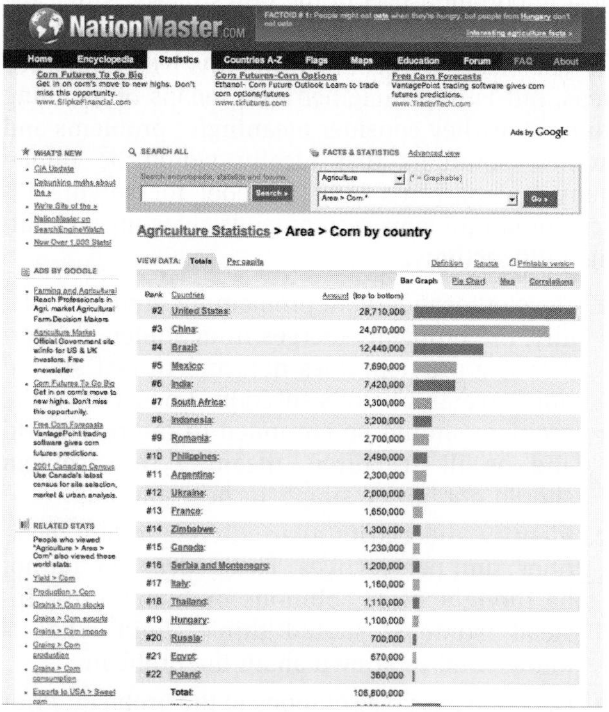

FIGURE 7.13 CIA online fact book search results for the agricultural products of the countries around the world. (https://www.cia.gov/library/publications/the-world-factbook/fields/2052.html)

Using the information from both sites, students identify whether there are imbalances between production and country needs. An important distinction between the two representations is that the fact book is a *static* presentation, data collected at one time and presented in the description. However, the data in Nationmaster page provides a *dynamic* presentation, periodically adjusted with the most current data. Helping students understand the differences is an important consideration as they make comparisons of the data available on the Web.

Summing It Up

The Internet is an extensive and complex structure with potential as a valuable resource in guiding student learning. The various services such as e-mail, discussion groups, and listservs offer a means for connecting students with others throughout the world and provide the avenue for extending ideas and perspectives beyond those described in textbooks or other single presentations. The Web provides a valuable resource for finding information, investigating ideas and conjectures, and researching questions.

To take advantage of this tremendous resource, teachers must reconfigure both what they teach and how they teach to include learning about these

Rank	Countries	Amount (top to bottom)
#2	United States:	28,710,000
#3	China:	24,070,000
#4	Brazil:	12,440,000
#5	Mexico:	7,690,000
#6	India:	7,420,000
#7	South Africa:	3,300,000
#8	Indonesia:	3,200,000
#9	Romania:	2,700,000
#10	Philippines:	2,490,000
#11	Argentina:	2,300,000
#12	Ukraine:	2,000,000
#13	France:	1,650,000
#14	Zimbabwe:	1,300,000
#15	Canada:	1,230,000
#16	Serbia and Montenegro:	1,200,000
#17	Italy:	1,160,000
#18	Thailand:	1,110,000
#19	Hungary:	1,100,000
#20	Russia:	700,000
#21	Egypt:	670,000
#22	Poland:	360,000
	Total:	106,800,000

FIGURE 7.14 Corn production analysis from the Nationmaster website. (http://www.nationmaster.com/graph/agr_are_cor-agriculture-area-corn)

technology resources. Students need a basic understanding of databases to efficiently use and evaluate the results of Web searches. They need instruction that guides them in conducting searches more efficiently and effectively. And they need experiences that engage students in learning with these resources while they are learning about them.

The WebQuest and Web Inquiry Project models provide helpful ideas for scaffolding student learning about the Web as they explore content-related tasks or inquiry problems. The WebQuest model guides students in exploring and using teacher-identified resources. This model provides the structure and guidance for the students so that they are less likely to become lost in cyberspace. At some point, however, students must learn how to search the Web, identifying keywords that help in streamlining Web search results. The Web Inquiry Project model focuses on encouraging students to locate their own Web-based resources, while engaged in the investigation of authentic inquiry-based questions.

Important social, ethical, and human issues must be considered as students begin working with the extended Internet and database resources. Although students have extended access for exploring ideas and questions, they must also be protected from and yet learn about inappropriate Internet resources. Chat rooms, while providing students with the opportunity to share their ideas and to talk in groups or one-on-one about their classroom, are susceptible to a wide array of harmful interactions. In the same way that children are taught to safely cross streets, they must be taught about the dangers of chat rooms and how to be safe in them. Similarly, students need to be taught cautions as they learn to search the Internet. These cautions expand to include a consideration of the validity and reliability of the various sites they identify. Is the information accurate? Who authors the information? Students need to be taught to challenge the information rather than merely accepting it as fact.

Both the Internet and databases are productivity tools. Access to information through the Internet helps students become more productive in their research than allowed by school libraries that may or may not have the references needed. The Internet provides access to extensive databases that students can access for investigating problems. Virtual field trips offset some of the difficulties presented by actual field trips, such as cost, access, and time.

The Internet and databases are also communications tools. Clearly e-mail, discussion groups, and listservs offer multiple opportunities for students to communicate with others, including, perhaps, students in other countries, extending their knowledge and perspectives. A weblog, an online personal journaling tool, supports students in communicating as writers. In a weblog, students communicate developing ideas and positions that they are pursuing. However, the weblog allows for, and in fact demands, peer review of the ideas, aiding the student in the development of the ideas. Weblogs offer more than simple text communication; students are able to incorporate images and sound files to better communicate their ideas.

Problem-based learning is a popular strategy in education to engage students in conducting research and in problem-solving and decision-making activities. Students can identify and confront authentic and real-world problems that previously they have not been able to investigate because of a lack of access to actual resources. Now with access to extensive searchable databases such as the Central Intelligence Agency's World Factbook and the U.S. Census Bureau, they can investigate problems of world hunger and its relationship to their own local areas.

The "ceaseless flow of information" that President Eisenhower envisioned in 1954 as an essential element for uniting the nation set the world on a course of a significant shift in education. With the Internet and its myriad of databases, students and teachers are no longer confined to textbooks and limited library resources. With access to these extended resources, classroom activities can be redirected to more student-centered investigation, where students are actively engaged in inquiry-based learning within authentic, real-world contexts. And, through these activities where they are extending their knowledge of the content, they are learning more about the technologies they are using. Teachers who pay attention to scaffolding students' learning experiences with the technologies support their students in learning how to learn with the technologies.

End-of-the-Chapter Activities and References

PRACTICE PROBLEMS

1. Conduct an online Web search for one of the following:

   - Teacher discussion groups focused on discussions about teaching and learning for your particular subject area or grade level.

   - Education listservs focused on communication about teaching your particular subject area or grade level.

   Review the communications up to the time you entered the discussions. What are the primary topics that are discussed? How can you use this communication mechanism as you prepare to teach?

2. Create a database of content and grade level websites that you can use and maintain as a teacher resource.

3. Conduct an online Web search for educational chat rooms. Evaluate the chat room websites using the criteria described in this chapter. Identify at least one chat room that meets the criteria. How and why might you use this form of communication in your classroom?

4. Use Technology Link 7.4 or Technology Link 7.7 to investigate the WebQuest site or the Web Inquiry Project site for subject and grade level specific activities that engage students in using the Web as a resource for completing specific tasks. Complete the task. Search for additional websites that might be used in the task. Record the tasks in your teacher resource database.

5. Use Technology Link 7.6 to investigate the digital images provided by the Smithsonian Institution. Then use Technology Link 7.5 to access the free weblog space as your journal space for posting your thoughts about the images and how 9-11 needs to be remembered.

IN THE CLASSROOM ACTIVITIES

6. Observe students in a classroom as they navigate the Internet. How successful are they at answering their questions that lead them to conduct the search?

7. Talk with various teachers in the grade level and content area you hope to teach about the use of the Internet services and supporting student investigation. What are their concerns about incorporating the Internet? What are their suggestions for incorporating the Internet?

8. For your specific content area, design (or find in the literature) an activity that incorporates student work with the Internet in learning the content. What content area standard(s) does the activity support? What technology standard(s) does the activity support? Outline how you envision students working with the Internet in the activity.

ASSESSING STUDENT LEARNING WITH AND ABOUT TECHNOLOGY

9. Conduct an Internet search for scoring guides that might be used in assessing student learning with the Internet. Based on your search results, propose a scoring guide for one of the activities identified in this chapter.

10. In groups of two or three students, complete In the Classroom 7.3. Identify the Internet operations and concepts that are key to successful work in the activity. Describe how you would assess students' capabilities with those key ideas.

E-PORTFOLIO ACTIVITIES

11. Prepare a reflection about teaching and learning *with* and *about* the Internet and databases. How can you incorporate the Internet in your classes so that students use its services as tools as described in the student technology standards? How can the Internet be used a tool in learning your subject area? Save this reflection as a Web page, so you can consider using it as a reflection in your E-portfolio.

REFLECTION AND DISCUSS

12. Explore the virtual field trip offered by In the Classroom 7.2. What are the advantages of such field trips? What are some disadvantages and how can they be lessened?

13. Find an Internet or database activity (see Annotated Resources for suggestions) that can be used with students you are preparing to teach (grade level and content). Describe how you would prepare students so they are ready to use the technologies as tools in learning.

14. Describe the similarities and differences in WebQuests and the Web Inquiry Project. Discuss how you might use each in your own classroom.

15. Respond to this statement: The Internet is not a valid resource for student research.

◆ Annotated Resources

Barrett, J. R. (2001). Indispensable inventions. *Learning and Leading with Technology, 29*(1), 22–26.
Students research historic events and inventions that lead to creation of databases for use in future assignments.

Bull, G., & Bull, G. (2001). Virtual art. *Learning and Leading with Technology, 29*(3), 54–58.
Use electronic picture frames and Web collections of art and art-based lessons to enrich your classroom activities. A number of websites are featured to support language arts instructional ideas.

Bull, G., Bull, G., & Walker, L. (2000). Writing with abandon. *Learning and Leading with Technology, 28*(1), 54–57.
The Internet offers a research tool for acquiring background information needed for development of an effective parody. Use writing resources on the Web to engage students in becoming less intimidated by the writing process.

Dodge, B. (2001). Five rules for writing a great WebQuest. *Learning and Leading with Technology, 28*(8), 6–9, 58.
A description of the key rules for developing a WebQuest model. Includes links to various subject specific WebQuest pages.

Elfrank-Dana, J. (2001–2002). Building and using a Web database with FrontPage. *Learning and Leading with Technology, 29*(4), 14–17, 62–63.

A Web-query project of a U.S. history class focuses students in developing a research project that requires they collect data and build a database to investigate the problem.

Goldberg, K. P. (1992). Database programs and the study of seashells. *The Computing Teacher, 19*(7), 32–34.
Students discover different types of questions that can be answered by a database providing characteristics of seashells.

Harris, J. (2000–2001). Virtual vantage points: Using webcams for teleresearch. *Learning and Leading with Technology, 28*(6), 14–17, 54–55.
A plethora of ideas suggest incorporating webcam data to demonstrate teaching process as students learn content.

Harris, J. (2003). Generative connections: An Internet-supported response to standards schizophrenia. *Learning and Leading with Technology, 30*(7), 46–49, 59.
James Burke's books and public television programs connect seemingly unconnected ideas, for example, how the origins of margarine connect it to plankton shells. This Web project identifies the topic of "time" where students must gather data from the Web to contrast, analyze, and draw comparative conclusions about seasonal changes among different geographic locations.

Hollis, R. (1990). Database yearbooks in the second grade. *The Computing Teacher, 17*(6), 14–15.
Second-grade students create a database about their class and then use the data to describe their class using graphs.

Holmes, B. (1998). The database: America's presidents. *Learning and Leading with Technology, 25*(7), 6–11.
Students organize information using a database on U.S. presidents and in the process learn more about both databases and U.S. presidents.

Insinnia, E. Skaecki, E., & Tucker, J. (2000). Teach a novel without the Internet? Never again! *Learning and Leading with Technology, 27*(8), 28–35.
Authentic Internet research adds a new dimension to students' experiences of reading a novel.

Lee, J., & Molebash, P. (2004). Using digital history for positive change in social studies education. *Journal of Computing in Teacher Education 20*(4), 153–157.
Create digital primary historical source materials using Web Inquiry Projects as described in this article about exploring the potential of the Internet to support historical inquiry.

Mittlefehldt, B. (1991). Social studies problem solving with databases. *The Computing Teacher, 18*(5), 54–55.
Students collaborate in an investigation of a database, using the data to define an underlying problem in one of the poor states or poor nations of the world.

Morrison, C., Moor, D., & Numaly, D. (1999). Traversing the Web up the Mississippi to Lake Itasca: An Internet experience. *Learning and Leading with Technology, 26*(7), 14–17.
A project-based learning approach expands the students' horizons through a virtual field trip where they plan the trip themselves, identify the itinerary, and then visit various websites along the Mississippi.

Norton, P., & Harvey, D. (1995). Information knowledge: Using databases to explore the tragedy at Donner Pass. *Learning and Leading with Technology 23*(1), 23–25.
Students create a database that is then used to investigate questions about he tragic journey over the Donner Pass.

Strickland, A. W., & Hoffer, T. (1990–1991). Integrating computer database with laboratory problems. *The Computing Teacher, 18*(4), 30–32.
This problem-solving activity integrates a laboratory investigation in high school chemistry with a database activity.

Truett, C. (2001). Sherlock Holmes on the Internet: Language arts teams up with the computing librarian. *Learning and Leading with Technology, 29*(2), 36–41.
Mystery stories and the WebQuest format team for the Sherlock Holmes WebQuest where students must determine the key elements of the mystery story and how the universal literary elements of plot, characterization, theme, etc. support the development of the mystery story.

CHAPTER 8

Multimedia and Media Literacy

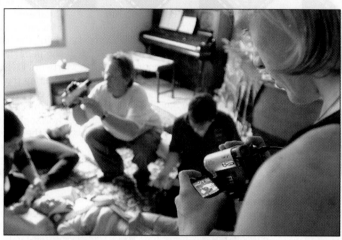

©AP/Wide World Photos

Introduction

Education is expected to prepare literate citizens, but what does it mean to be literate in the twenty-first century? The dictionary connects *literacy* with reading and writing. Yet, you probably immediately think in terms of reading and writing as you know them: reading books, newspapers, and other printed materials; writing with pens, pencils, and perhaps word processors in an effort to communicate ideas and information. The idea of reading and writing is much broader. When you think about what you read and write, you are focusing on the content of the reading and writing. You might think about the scribbles that are either written or read and, in this case, you are thinking about the language (and perhaps grammar) for the communication. You might think about the presentation of the written and verbal communication and, in this instance, you are thinking about the constructions of reading and writing. In essence, the preparation of literate citizens requires learning to both read and write, learning to use the symbols or languages, and learning to use the constructions of reading and writing in addition to learning the content that is being communicated.

Reading and writing have been skills used by humankind for many centuries—probably longer ago than you think because there is evidence of these skills dating even before 15,000 B.C. In those early times, the content was more focused on business transactions rather than recording conversations and history. The language was more pictorial or graphical than today's more abstract combination of alphabetic images. People used marks to communicate ideas, perhaps using clay tokens, sand, or walls as the display space. Those tools for reading and writing were dependent on the ingenuity and technological advancements of the time. And, because writing did not begin in any one place and develop in a single path, a multitude of writing methods and styles evolved.

Today, students in America are primarily taught to read and write with alphanumeric symbols, a, b, c, …, 1, 2, 3, …. They are taught to form the symbols with a writing utensil, to express sounds the symbols represent, to combine symbols to form words, and to combine words to form sentences that convey meaning. Whereas the early grades emphasize basic tools and symbols for reading and writing, the content of reading and writing expands with each year of education. Thus, the concept of literacy for an educated citizen has expanded over the centuries to focus on putting words together using the most powerful cultural tools at your disposal to understand and communicate ever more complex ideas. This expectation is one that depends on and builds toward higher order critical thinking skills in order to develop citizens who know how to identify key ideas, make connections among a myriad of ideas, ask pertinent questions and identify inaccuracies, and formulate a response that clearly communicates and expresses the ideas. Perhaps the best way to think about the goals of education is to think of education as being designed to prepare literate citizens, citizens who have the ability to locate, access, analyze, evaluate, and communicate information effectively.

Advances in reading and writing technologies have also evolved along with the notion of literacy. Clay token, stylus, pen, pencil, typewriter, printing press, telephone, telegraph, motion pictures, radio, television. All of these media have been used at times and in various ways to exchange ideas among humankind. Although some are no longer or rarely used, the media available have significantly advanced with the invention of computer technologies. And with the advancements the phrase *media literacy* has been framed to expand the notion of literacy to more than words on a piece of paper, to include a variety of message forms including image, language, and sound—for sharing ideas. Some people suggest further that media literacy is a phrase that will be needed until the common understanding of literacy basically incorporates the idea of *fluency* in both print and nonprint forms. For the time being, though, media literacy as described in Figure 8.1 is useful in highlighting a broader understanding of what it means to be literate.

A literate citizen is media literate: a critical thinker and a creative producer of an increasingly wide range of messages using image, language, and sound along with the ability to locate, access, analyze, evaluate, manipulate, and communicate information effectively in a variety of formats including printed text, graphics, animation, audio, video, and motion.

FIGURE 8.1   A description of a media literate citizen.

With education's goal of preparing literate citizens, teachers must think in terms of a curriculum that also guides students in learning with and about multimedia. *Multimedia* encompasses those applications that support a combination of media to communicate information, media including text, still pictures, graphics, animation, sounds, motion, and video. Given this understanding, many word processors today offer multimedia ca-

pabilities. Other types of multimedia include presentation software and video or movie production packages as newer ways for students to display what and how they understand what they are learning.

Hypermedia is another term often entangled with multimedia. In fact, hypermedia can be considered a subset of multimedia. Hypermedia is an expression for the media that provide the ability to link media and with this capability offers users control of the sequence of the ideas. The most familiar hypermedia is probably the Web.

This chapter is devoted to creating multimedia presentations as another means to communicate ideas and information. The focus is on learning to *write* or *author* with those tools and use the tools to address or target unique instructional challenges inherent in specific content areas. Chapter 9 continues your exploration on multimedia authoring, specifically on authoring in Web environments. Together, the two chapters guide your preparation for supporting your future students in becoming multimedia literate: students who are literate in the uses and creation of multiple forms and multiple genres of texts.

CHAPTER LEARNING OBJECTIVES

After reading this chapter, you should be able to:

1. Identify authoring tools that offer a multimedia environment for students to express and communicate their ideas.

2. Describe guidelines that deserve careful attention when authoring multimedia.

3. Clarify actions that are important in each of the multimedia design process phases: the preproduction phase, the production phase, and the postproduction phase.

4. Explain how experiences that develop basic concepts of communicating with multimedia can be incorporated in various content area learning experiences.

5. Identify social, ethical, and human issues that are important with respect to multimedia.

6. Recommend activities that support learner-centered explorations of subject matter content to engage students in using multimedia as a productivity tool, communications tool, research tool, and problem-solving and decision-making tool.

Snapshot of a Class Designing a Movie

Class: [In a circle, singing, and performing the actions described in this song.]

Pon el **pie** aquí.

Pon el **pie** allá.

Pon el **pie** aquí y sa cudela.

Baila el joqui poqui,

Da la vuelta ya.

¡Todo mejor será!

Mr. Lopez: And now in English?

Class: You put your **foot** in.

You put your **foot** out.

You put your **foot** in

And shake it all about.

You do the Hokey Pokey and shake it all about.

That's what it's all about!

Mr. Lopez: Terrific! You have just visually shown me the words you were singing. Now let's all sit in the circle.

The fourth–fifth combination class students quickly organized their circle around their teacher, Mr. Lopez. He then showed them a picture of a young child wearing her father's tennis shoes.

Courtesy M. Niess

Mr. Lopez: What is this child doing?

Marie: Wearing tennis shoes that are too big!

Mr. Lopez: Actually, she was singing the song you just sang with her parents. And, whenever her parents say, "Zoey, do you have happy feet?" she quickly shuffles and stamps her feet in her dad's tennis shoes.

Then she begs to sing the song again! My question for you is, "What makes your feet happy?"

Carlos: Jumping around in the puddles in my red boots!

Cynthia: Dancing in my tap shoes!

John: Running barefoot through the sprinklers in the summer!

Mr. Lopez: These are all great ideas! What if we make a movie that describes "happy feet" that also shows our progress in learning both Spanish and English?

Mr. Lopez is fluent in both Spanish and English, an important skill for this class of half native English speakers and half native Spanish speakers. He works to help his students communicate with each other in each language and has been teaching them words and phrases in both languages. The suggestion that they demonstrate the words they have been learning sounded fun to the class. Making a movie was even more exciting since previously they learned to use the digital camera. They had taken special pictures and used them as writing prompts in their writing class.

Mr. Lopez: Now we will learn to use the camcorder as a way to communicate our ideas about "happy feet" while we also demonstrate our knowledge of the two languages, Spanish and English. But, we don't just begin filming with the camcorder. There are lots of activities to be done before any filming begins. What do you think might be important?

Sarah: What do we want to say in our movie?

Mr. Lopez: Yes, we need to write a script that explains what we want to say! What else?

Cynthia: Who is the audience?

Mr. Lopez: Right! If we are making the movie for our parents we might do it differently than if we were making it as a movie for the first and second graders in school. What else?

Carlos: Mr. Lopez, are we making one movie or can we make one in Spanish and one in English?

Mr. Lopez: That's an interesting point. We need to decide whether the movie will be a comparison of the words from English to Spanish. Or, do we want an English version and a Spanish version to demonstrate how we are able to communicate in each other's language? We have lots of decisions and activities to do in preparation!

To begin, we need to focus on the concept for the movie—making happy feet! Each of you needs to share what makes your feet happy. Go to your desks, take out your writing journals, and describe your ideas to these two questions: What footwear makes your feet happy? And, what are you doing when you are wearing that footwear?

We'll gather all your ideas as we begin the next activity in preparation for making this movie!

After the children had completed their journals, Mr. Lopez felt it was important to give them an idea of the overall process needed for creating a movie. He could tell by their responses that they had the notion that the major part of the project would be using the camcorder. He had prepared a presentation using PowerPoint to guide them in completing and learning about the process.

Mr. Lopez called the class to attention and began the presentation of the process with the first two slides, in Figure 8.2.

Mr. Lopez: [Displaying Slide 1.] To guide you in the making of our movie, I have prepared this presentation describing the process we will use in making our movie called *Happy Feet*.

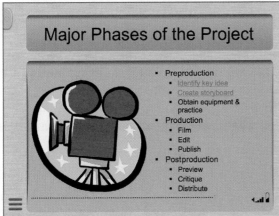

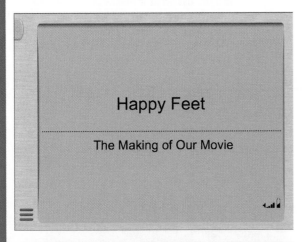

FIGURE 8.2   Slides 1 and 2 of the movie presentation.

[Moving to Slide 2.] Basically, there are three major phases to the project: the preproduction phase, the production phase, and the postproduction phase. We have already started with the preproduction phase because you have just finished writing your ideas in your journal. Our goal is to come up with the key idea for our movie.

[Clicking on the *Identify key ideas* link in Slide 2, the slide in Figure 8.3 appeared.] To do that, I will arrange you in small groups to share your ideas and create a summary of all of your ideas. When the groups have finished their tasks, I will ask that you enter your ideas in a slide in this presentation as a way of sharing your ideas.

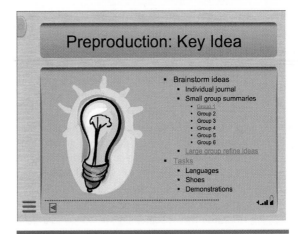

FIGURE 8.3   The general tasks to be completed in identifying the key idea for the movie.

[Selects the *Group 1* link to display the slide in Figure 8.4.] I will have a slide in this presentation for each group, as in this display. Notice the group number? There will be a slide for each group to complete. Each group will enter their five favorite *Shoes* and *Action* ideas.

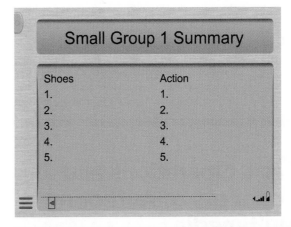

FIGURE 8.4   The small group summary task slide to be used to summarize ideas for the movie.

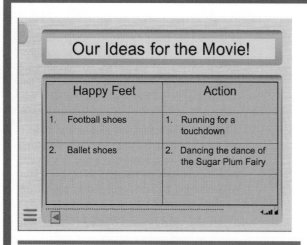

FIGURE 8.5   Slide to capture the movie decisions suggested in the whole-class discussion.

| | Notice the small arrow at the bottom of this slide. What do you think happens if I click on that arrow? |

       Notice the small arrow at the bottom of this slide. What do you think happens if I click on that arrow?

Juan: I know! It will take you back to the slide that has the links to the other small group summaries. But . . . but they aren't highlighted the same way as the one for Group I was. Right?

Mr. Lopez: [Clicking on the return arrow and returning to the slide shown in Figure 8.3.] No, they aren't because that is something we will do as a class so that everyone learns how to make active links to your particular summaries.

       When all the summaries are completed we will move to the next step of finalizing our key ideas for the movie. What should I do to display that task? Marie, why don't you come up and show us?

Marie: [Goes to the computer and clicks on the *Large group refine ideas* that displays the slide in Figure 8.5.] See, when I click on it, here it is [pointing to the screen that all the students are watching]. But I'm sort of confused. Why do we have this slide?

Mr. Lopez: [Pointing to the slide.] Because as a class we will use this slide to display our final key ideas for the movie. I just put a couple of ideas that I saw you had written in your journals. But, as a class we will enter our decisions for the key ideas of

shoes and their actions that make our feet happy.

    [Selecting the return arrow that returns to the slide in Figure 8.3.] Once we have decided on the key ideas, then it will be time to clarify what we mean by those ideas. We'll work in three groups to do this — languages, shoes, and demonstrations.

    [Selects the *Tasks* link to display the clarification of the tasks duties shown in Figure 8.6.] This slide gives you a general introduction to the tasks to help clarify and more fully describe the key ideas for the movie. But that's getting way ahead of ourselves! Hopefully, you can see that we have lots of work to do in creating the movie.

    [Selecting the return arrow to display Figure 8.3 slide.] All that we have been discussing is just so we can identify the key idea for the movie.

    [Selecting the return arrow to show slide 2 in Figure 8.2.] Once we have that, it will be time to write the storyboard. As we get to that point, we'll discuss what it means to create a storyboard. I'll add more to this PowerPoint presentation when we are ready for that stage. But for now, I'd like to assign the six small groups to discuss the ideas in your journals.

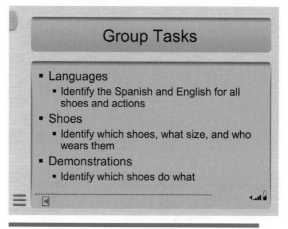

FIGURE 8.6   Group tasks for clarifying and enhancing the description of the key ideas for the movie.

Basic Operations and Concepts of Authoring Multimedia

Multimedia authoring typically engages the user in designing presentations that potentially incorporate

text, graphs, video, audio, and animation. The children in the *Snapshot of a Class Designing a Movie* initially focused on designing a movie to communicate their understanding and facility with two languages, Spanish and English. In the process, however, they also extended their knowledge about presentation software such as PowerPoint with an introduction to using hyperlinks in their presentation in a way that put the user in control of the display of the slides. In other words, they were learning to utilize a variety of multimedia authoring software tools for communicating their ideas.

Multimedia Authoring Tools

Early in the introduction of computers in education, authoring tools were programming languages like Logo. In Logo, students created instructions to move a turtle about the screen while drawing with a pen to create shapes and designs. The authoring effort required them to think about the mathematics embedded in the creation of the designs. And through this creative experience, the creator of Logo, Seymour Papert, felt that students engaged in a thinking process that is required in problem solving and doing mathematics. As Papert (1980) described it, "You can't think seriously about thinking without thinking about thinking about something." While Papert talked in terms of *microworlds*, those microworlds did offer children opportunities to create with multimedia—creating graphics, describing motions, and manipulating text.

With advancements in technology, multimedia authoring might be viewed as having morphed from the original microworld authoring idea to the use of very different tools. Today, students can access a variety of media capabilities including text, still pictures, animated graphics, sound, and motion video. Each multimedia tool offers more than one of these capabilities and each tool offers different means for describing and presenting ideas and understandings. In essence students have access to many different multimedia tools to think with, to create, and to communicate what they know and how they know it.

Concept Map Communications Tool   You have probably heard the phrase, "A picture is worth a thousand words." Graphics tools provide students with opportunities to describe their thinking in ways other than simply through words. Pictures describe ideas that often words only intimate. Draw and paint tools provide students with a sketchpad for describing their thoughts. And, for students who are less artistically inclined, clip art, screen captures, scanners, and digital cameras are tools with the potential to enhance students' expression capabilities.

Concept maps have been proposed as a means to help students organize their thinking as well as communicate their thoughts. Concept maps can be used to display the attributes and relationships of concepts as well as to brainstorm and plan. In much the same way that an outline provides an overall perspective, a concept map typically incorporates visual graphics as a means for enhancing the communication of a student's thinking. However, a concept map provides more than an outline in a graphic; it provides a visual communication and display of the ideas. Perhaps part of the power of a concept map is in the incorporation of a description of how the ideas in the outline are linked.

Concept mapping software is typically a graphics-based tool that allows students to organize their thinking and communicate their thoughts in a concept map format. Most often concept maps are single page presentations, but they can have elements like sounds and active links to the Web or other documents. Figures 8.7*a* and 8.7*b* present a comparison of two students' descriptions of three- and four-sided polygons. Kyle's attention is focused on the angles of the polygons because he classifies rectangles as different from parallelograms. Shannon's description, on the other hand, depicts the set of rectangles as a subset of the set of parallelograms. Through these concept maps, their teacher can see how they see the ideas differently. More importantly, Kyle's teacher can guide him to consider the sides, rather than the angles, of the rectangles and parallelograms, to help him recognize that rectangles are actually parallelograms.

Slide-Based Communications Tools   Students are often expected to make presentations to describe their work on various projects. Slides and overheads have traditionally been used. These tools have more recently been replaced by presentation software, such as Microsoft's PowerPoint. Presentation graphics software uses slides to display the message. Unlike capturing the slides with a camera, presentation software provides an environment where students create the slide using the vast array of embedded capabilities, such as backgrounds, designs, text formatting, and drawing tools. Students are able to incorporate audio and video on the slides. Furthermore, the software allows them to arrange and rearrange the slides, including transitions as well as a variety of animations on each slide.

At the end of the Snapshot of a Class Designing a Movie, the children were organized into small groups to identify their five best ideas for the *Happy Feet* movie. Mr. Lopez indicated that he wanted them to share their ideas in the presentation that evolved as they learned the movie-making process.

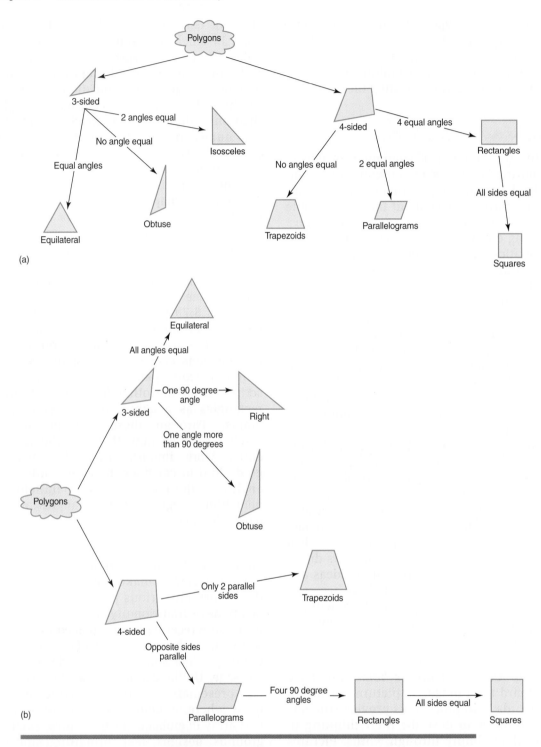

FIGURE 8.7 (*a*) Kyle's description of three- and four-sided polygons focused on angles. (*b*) Shannon's presentation of three- and four-sided polygons.

Figure 8.8 displays Group 1's slide presentation of their ideas where they have added pictures they had taken when they were getting used to taking pictures with digital cameras. Alternatively, they might have used some clip art images to display the actions that they envisioned for the different feet and shoes.

Clip-Based Communications Tools Video and audio editing offer many opportunities to extend students' multimedia literacy. Although presentation tools can, and often do, include both video and audio elements, those elements are formally presented in separate slides. Motion pictures are different tools, using clips rather than slides. However, the essential

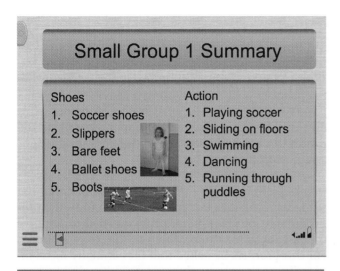

FIGURE 8.8   Group 1's summary ideas for the *Happy Feet* movie.

feature of motion picture clips is the timeline that describes how the clips are presented. Although the presentation software slides can be animated, motion pictures offer a continuous stream of clips over a time period in which audio and video elements are integrated to change the nature of the communication.

In the Snapshot of a Class Designing a Movie the students prepared to display their knowledge about Spanish and English using the idea of activities that indicate happy feet. When their movie is complete, they will have incorporated video action displaying feet in various types of shoes doing the actions that they think will be joyous. They plan to use audio to sing, play background music, or perhaps to verbally say the words in both English and Spanish. In addition, they probably plan on using text and graphics to display the words that are spoken in the two languages. These audio and video elements have the potential to add to the entertainment value of the communication. Ultimately, the process of developing the movie, the use of the presentation software to explain the process of developing a movie, and the final movie display not only their English and Spanish literacy but also their literacy with respect to using multimedia in developing their critical thinking and creative production capabilities.

Multimedia Authoring

Authoring a multimedia production is both an art and a science. Specific techniques and guidelines clearly support the development of the production to better communicate the intended message; attention to the guidelines recognizes the science of multimedia production. Yet, the guidelines do not provide an algorithm for a successful communica-

tion. They do provide hints and concepts from which the art of multimedia authoring proceeds. Students can be taught the hints and guidelines. However, they must also be guided in developing the art of multimedia authoring.

Basic Building Blocks   Authors of papers or books record their creations with sheets (perhaps on paper or even in word processors). Authors of concept maps develop their creations with a blank screen that looks like a blank sketchpad. Presentation software authors work on their creations in slides. And authors creating movies think and work in terms of clips framed by a timeline. Actually, multimedia authors must think in terms of the basic building blocks for their creations. They need to make important decisions as to which format has the most potential for communicating their ideas. If audience interaction and discussion are desired for expanding or clarifying the ideas, a continuous video stream may not be the best option. If the intent is to demonstrate actions both in real time and again in slow motion, then a continuous video stream may be the best option.

In the Snapshot of a Class Designing a Movie, Mr. Lopez had already identified that the production was going to be a movie because he wanted to help his students learn the process of creating such a production. He was careful to present the students with a beginning challenge that was more likely to lead to a movie production. He captured the students' attention with the song and actions that they were doing as they spoke in both English and Spanish. He challenged them to think in terms of actions that they saw as making their feet happy. The idea that he proposed involved action; it involved sound that matched the action and it involved displaying visually the actions. Furthermore, a movie production was envisioned as the final outcome of the learning process, the product that demonstrated what they had learned.

On the other hand, Mr. Lopez also selected a PowerPoint presentation to be developed as they learned to make the movie. His intent was that they would expand the presentation as they learned. This decision called for a slide-based approach where both he and his students could add to the presentation to describe the process. Thus, Mr. Lopez envisioned the presentation as much as a teaching tool as a communications tool, a tool focused on the process of learning about creating a movie.

- **The intent and content of the message dictate the decision on the basic framework and format for the multimedia presentation.**

Multimedia authors need to formulate the basic arrangement for the framework of the presentation. What background video or audio will enhance the presentation? An extensive library of backgrounds is available for slide-based presentation options. However, availability does not endorse the use of multiple backgrounds. The backgrounds framing the presentation are not the focus of the presentation. Multiple backgrounds can distract the audience from the message that is intended. Similarly, audio streams provide an option for a background to a video stream. Authors have a tremendous variety of sounds available, but that does not mean authors should incorporate multiple sound tracks in a presentation. As with visual backgrounds, multiple audio backgrounds often have the effect of distracting the audience from the message.

- **Multiple audio or video background elements can distract from the message and communication.**

Multimedia Objects   Once the decision for the basic building block is made, authors need to direct their attention to the addition of the desired multimedia objects. Here again, they have many choices among text, graphics, audio, and video objects to be interspersed throughout the presentation. Text in words can be selected, formatted, and organized on a slide or to appear, fade, and even disappear in clip-based blocks. Graphics can be drawn, painted, captured, scanned, or clipped from a variety of sources. Students can even take their own digital pictures (as in Figure 8.8), enhance, and format them to obtain the desired visual. Video clips can be obtained from disks, Compact Disc (CD), videotapes, digital disks, and the Web. Authors can choose to reorder the clips or repeatedly replay particular parts in various motions for effect. Audio can be collected or recorded. As with video, the objects can be altered for effect. Slow motion sounds have the effect of drawing out the words, perhaps helping the audience hear specific sounds that in regular motion they overlook.

- **Enhance the message with supporting text, graphics, audio, and video interspersed throughout the presentation.**

Another decision that authors need to make in the design of the presentation concerns the proposed transitions from one object to another, from one slide to another, or from one clip to another. As with the variety of object sources, authors have multiple options from which to choose. Availability does *not* endorse the use of multiple transitions throughout that presentation because that variety might in fact distract the audience from the message. Ultimately, the important message about objects and transition selection is to be mindful of the intent of the presentation. Direct the audience to the message or intent, not the objects and transitions.

- **Multiple transitions among various objects can distract from the message or communication of the presentation.**

Multimedia Design Process

Multimedia productions require much more than making selections from among the tremendous variety of multimedia options. As the children in the Snapshot of a Class Designing a Movie quickly discovered, they had a lot of work to do before actually making the movie. Mr. Lopez described the process in three phases: preproduction, production, and postproduction.

Preproduction Phase   Mr. Lopez explained that the students needed to begin at the beginning—the preproduction phrase—where they needed to identify the key ideas for the production that they planned. For this process, he asked that they initially focus on identifying their individual ideas. This individual activity encouraged all students to become part of the process of suggesting ideas and verbalizing those ideas in writing. Then, in small groups, they brainstormed and clarified their cumulative ideas. In the process, Mr. Lopez planned for them to present their small group ideas to the whole class. After sharing their ideas and identifying some tasks, Mr. Lopez assigned groups to work on providing more clarification on the various ideas that were suggested. For reporting the results of the work from the different tasks, Mr. Lopez provided time for the whole class to share their ideas, discuss the various ideas, and come to consensus on the key ideas for their production. This work encouraged the class to solidify and articulate their key ideas for the production.

Still in the preproduction stage, the class moved to the storyboarding stage. Figure 8.9 shows the description Mr. Lopez added to their presentation for explaining this stage in the process of producing a movie. Part of the preproduction process was to prepare a script for the production. The

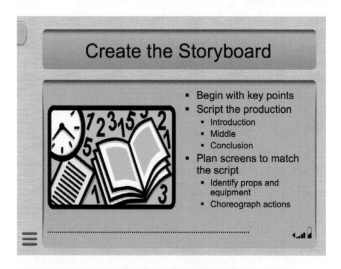

FIGURE 8.9   The storyboarding activities in the preproduction phase for designing a movie.

script for this production is similar to a script for a play or, perhaps, a lesson plan for teaching a class. The introduction needs to get the attention of the viewer as well as motivate the viewer to watch the rest of the movie. The script needs to expand the key ideas in clear and engaging ways. Finally, the script must have a conclusion, bringing the movie to a climax while also assuring that the key ideas have been communicated.

In developing the script, the students must choreograph actions, assuring that those actions support the message and do not detract from the message. One useful tool for this process is a storyboard. A *storyboard* supports the collection of the multimedia descriptions for each clip of the script and includes the order and timing for the clips. The storyboard also supports student work in the computer lab because they have a plan for their work, as opposed to the more time-consuming approach of creating as they go.

In the storyboard, the basic information must be identified for each clip in the movie; a form such as the one shown in Figure 8.10 is a useful tool. This example describes the title of the clip and the media objects (video and audio) that are to be included along with proposed formats and times. You can create your own storyboard format for the students or perhaps consider an electronic version to encourage this level of planning (see Technology Link 8.1).

Along with storyboarding and scripting, students must consider the equipment, costumes, and actions that they want to incorporate in the project. Perhaps

they plan to show happy feet in a dance similar to the dance they used in singing their song. If so, they need to have the appropriate shoes and know the specific steps for the dance. They also need cameras to take close-ups, focusing on the feet rather than faces. Scheduling, testing, and becoming comfortable with the equipment and actions are among the important activities in this preproduction phase.

Schools or districts have at most one camcorder or video system, requiring scheduling of needed equipment. Students need to learn to use the equipment, making sure they are able to obtain the desired effects. Nevertheless, the equipment probably has to be reserved for a specific time period, a limited time. If the students have to continually gather retakes, valuable time and energy are lost as they become familiar with the desired actions. Besides the equipment, they need to practice any actions they plan, obtain the props, and make sure that everyone knows what is to happen. They may even see that their plans are not exactly as they envisioned, forcing them to make appropriate changes in the storyboard and script. Although this portion takes time, it ultimately saves time!

- **Create a storyboard with script details to save time in authoring multimedia.**

An important task in the preplanning stage is to obtain permissions as needed to assure that the video is available for public display. It is important to have permissions *before* collecting video and audio. If you plan to use copyrighted effects, you need permission. In the Snapshot of a Class Designing a Movie, Mr. Lopez focused the movie on the children's feet specifically to avoid having to video student faces. It is still important to have the parents' permissions and to, at the very least, notify the parents of the actions planned in the movie. Technology Link 2.3 offers a link to access some information about legal and ethical uses of technology resources.

- **Obtain permission releases for elements (people, sound, video) in a product that will be displayed publicly.**

As with preplanning the design of the movie, preplanning is key to the quality of slide presentations; they also benefit from the storyboarding process. This preplanning phase requires authors to think through the key ideas to be presented and to

☐ Still	☐ Audio	☐ Video	☐ Music	■ Title
Length	30 sec	Order		I

- **Title and subtitle**

Happy Feet
An English and Spanish Presentation

- **Action**

Children, in different types of shoes, dance to the tune (sung by the children) of "Hokey Pokey." Clips of the song sung in English and then in Spanish, are in background.

Description

Pan on the various feet with different shoes as described by the song.

Film tip

Title fades in and holds for 20 second then fades in the subtitle.

Editing key

FIGURE 8.10 Basic information for a clip in a storyboard.

identify in advance the particular objects that are planned to enhance the presentation. The Outline section of PowerPoint's presentation may seem like an environment for prethinking, but it actually does not replace the need for advanced thinking. Unfortunately, authors often design their presentations in an ad hoc manner, letting their creativity flow. That strategy often leads to unclear messages that are complicated and even lost among the varied objects that have been inserted to create a flashy presentation. Then, the presentation becomes a presentation of the variety of objects available in the software and the desired message is lost.

Production Phase   Once the planning is completed, the production phase can begin. This phase is often the one that students are anxious to begin; yet they quickly realize the value of the preplanning phase. If students are preparing a slide presentation, they simply follow the directions as designed in the storyboard and script. Similarly, if they are preparing a movie, they follow the directions in its storyboard and script. They film the clips they need, collecting all the clips as described in the storyboard. For each clip, they need to make sure to collect more than the time indicated in their storyboard for that clip. When using the video camcorder, they need to begin taping at least 30 seconds prior to the action that is desired; similarly, they need to tape past the action so they are assured that they do not cut off the end of the action during the editing phase.

- **Collect footage with extra seconds of footage before and after the desired action.**

An important filming technique prior to the editing stage is to keep in mind that you are able to edit the film. Students might collect film of some of the students saying the words in Spanish with the intent that they would overlay the audio with the video of the variety of footwear that students use to make their feet happy. Be sure to consider a variety of video angles. One continuous video from the same angle can become boring. Close-ups of the shoes next to the feet and the feet in the shoes might add interest to the action that is planned. Think of ways to display the action from a variety of perspectives in order to add interest.

- **Shoot footage with a recognition of the editing capabilities that can be incorporated.**

When all the audio, video, and stills are collected, students are ready to begin the editing phase using some movie production software, such as iMovie or Movie Maker. At this point, they follow the instructions that were carefully preplanned in the storyboard, merging and editing the objects and transitions. The software is designed in such a way that they are able to continuously review their

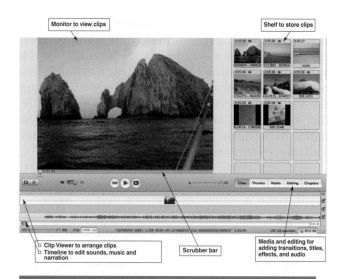

FIGURE 8.11   Interface for iMovie in support of the production of the movie.

work, editing, cutting, and extending as needed to obtain the effects desired.

Figure 8.11 shows an iMovie interface for the editing phase. Clips can be stored in the *shelf* and viewed in the *monitor viewer*. The movie is designed in the Clip Viewer and Timeline by dragging clips from the shelf to the clip viewer. The clips can be arranged, rearranged, and even deleted to build the movie. In the editing process, transitions and titles can be added to the clips; then, audio and other effects can be added at the timeline. As objects are added, the author is able to review the movie by selecting the right arrow below the Scrubber Bar to see if the effects are as intended.

After completing the editing phase, students need to publish the production in the desired format. Students typically transfer movies into a Quicktime version and put that version on a CD. The Quicktime version of the movie can also be imported into other applications, such as a word processing document, a slide in a presentation slide show, a link in a Web application, or even a multimedia field in a database. The Happy Feet movie the children were developing in the Snapshot of a Class Designing a Movie might even be imported into the PowerPoint presentation for describing the making of a movie as the closure demonstrating the end product of their creative efforts.

It is important to understand that Quicktime is based on the idea of flip-card animations, where the images are shown in succession to simulate the motion. This technology is designed to create moving pictures and synchronize the desired sounds without creating excessively large files that require large amounts of storage space. Unfortunately, the compression techniques for video do not work as well for titles because of the number of frames per second involved. If you export to Quicktime's CD-ROM Movie,

Medium format, the movie is one-quarter the size of a TV quality movie, meaning the text should be reasonably easy to read. A technique to improve the quality of the Quicktime version makes use of its capabilities to add the opening title and closing credit frames from a second movie. First, export a version of your movie without the opening title and closing credits. Then create a second movie with only the title and credit sequences, including a few black frames between the title and the credits so that it will be easier to edit. Export this movie to the same-size Quicktime movie, using a compressor such as Animation that is better suited for computer-generated graphics. Finally, paste the credits back into the first movie.

- **Consider the quality needed for the final product.**

Postproduction Phase   Once the production is completed, concerns must turn to previewing, critiquing, and distributing. Previewing is more than just watching the movie or clicking through the presentation slides. Here, the students must think through and plan the proposed presentation. Four questions can be used to guide this process:

- How should the prepared presentation be introduced?
- What happens after the prepared presentation is completed?
- What kinds of lighting and sound facilities are needed?
- What if the technology does not work as planned?

Practicing for the viewing of the presentation is an important postproduction process. A couple of considerations are important when presenting to the audience.

- **Bright lights can interfere with the visual presentation; the frames fade into the light.**
- **Explain slides, do not read them. Use the slides as main points for the discussion.**

A practice session might also be a good time to complete a peer review of the project. Figure 8.12 provides a simplified example of a scoring guide review for a movie presentation. For this particular scoring guide, the student peers are asked to rate the amount of *persuasive evidence* for each of the categories used to describe the final product. As

Peer Review Movie Presentation		
Movie Title:	**Movie Author:**	**Movie Reviewer:**
Criteria	**Persuasive Evidence** 0- None 1- Little 2- Adequate 3- Extensive	**Explanation**
Content		
1. The entire presentation is excellent, with the movie integrated in a thoughtful manner to clearly express the content.		
2. The introduction to the movie is solid and interesting.		
3. The content of the movie is clear throughout.		
4. The movie expresses the content in a creative, thoughtful, and imaginative manner.		
Media		
1. The audio is consistent, audible, and supports the presentation of the message.		
2. The video is consistent, clear, visible, and supports the presentation of the message.		
3. Effects support the presentation of the message, including timing, pacing, and presentation.		
Additional comments:		

FIGURE 8.12   Sample scoring guide for peer review of the preview of the movie and its presentation.

the students use the scale, they must provide a written explanation for each of their ratings. Teachers might also add other categories to focus on how the group worked in the development phase. Chapter 13 of this text helps you in the development of scoring guides that you can design for assessing student work with multimedia.

When the presentation has been completed, authors must consider additional distribution possibilities. For example, students may want to use the movie in an electronic portfolio to provide evidence of their media literacy. In the case of the Snapshot of a Class Designing a Movie, students might want to have the PowerPoint presentation of the process followed by the Quicktime version of the movie. If the electronic portfolio is focused on the development of their facility in both English and Spanish, they may only include the Quicktime version as evidence of their growing ability to communicate in multiple languages. In other words, how the products are distributed depends on the purpose of the distribution. If the movie and slide presentations are sent via e-mail, consideration must be made for the recipient. Does that recipient have the capability to view the presentation? Is the file too big? Should a movie be exported using the Email Movie, Small option? Should the presentation be saved as a Quicktime movie to be displayed? Is the appropriate software available? Those and other questions are important considerations in the postproduction stage of the project. Too often, however, that stage is not even seen as part of the activities of the production process and is overlooked.

◀Learning with and about Multimedia

Mr. Lopez, in the Snapshot of a Class Designing a Movie, incorporated important experiences with multimedia to guide the development of his students' media literacy along with their educational experiences with learning multiple languages, English and Spanish. Mr. Lopez wanted to help his students understand the importance of the translation from one language to another—that translation is not simply a word-for-word translation. Languages are embedded in cultural contexts. For example, the actual "Hokey-Pokey" song translation is difficult to obtain because the original song is U.S. folk music requiring a certain rhythm to be maintained to fit the music. Since the song is so familiar to certain populations, multiple competing translations exist, each with their own following for one reason or another. As Mr. Lopez helped the students in the development of their storyboard and script, he was able to help them begin to recognize the difficulties of translations of more than one word. In other words, their work with multimedia was embedded within the context of the academics of languages. Moreover, although the experiences of the production were rich experiences with multimedia, they simply must not be the only experiences students have. They need multiple learning experiences if they are to understand general media operations and concepts, methods for selecting among the various multimedia tools, and facility with the incorporation of various multimedia tools to communicate information—experiences that support the development of media literacy.

Basic Concepts of Communicating with Multimedia

Multiple experiences with a multimedia application are essential for the learning process. Students need to experiment with the capabilities, reflecting on and evaluating the effects in the communication of the ideas. They need lots of practice in gathering pictures with a camera; they need lots of practice in electronic editing. They need lots of practice collecting video clips and editing those clips. They need lots of practice merging audio with video. In essence, becoming media literate does not happen as a result of participation in a single multimedia project; rather, experiences must be incorporated throughout their educational programs in all subject areas.

Multimedia and Media Literacy Instructional Idea: Observing Change When you were born you weighed less than 15 pounds and were less than 2 feet tall. Certainly, that has changed! If you visited the school where you went to first grade, you would surely find there have been changes: the teachers have changed, the books have changed, and perhaps the desks have changed. If you placed a camera at a particular location to follow the growth of the landscape throughout the years, you can see that it undergoes changes. Perhaps the land is cleared, houses are built, and trees planted; perhaps it only changes subtly but certainly it changes. In fact, it has been said that the only true constant today is change itself.

Change is a guiding theme in the language arts curriculum where students study reading, writing, listening, and speaking as change processes. They must develop an understanding of the concept of change to enhance their study of other disciplines and provide insights into their own lives. By reading the literature and engaging in shared inquiry, students develop an awareness of the nature and importance of change as it relates to people in various circumstances, times, and cultures.

Change is an important concept identified in the social studies curriculum. In particular, the middle grades standards indicate the importance of students gaining the ability to "identify and use key concepts

In the Classroom 8.1

EVIDENCE OF CHANGE

TECHNOLOGY OBJECTIVE: **NETS · S I, IV**

- **Multimedia:** Technology as a communications tool while building understanding of basic concepts
- Morphing pictures in slide-presentation applications.

CONTENT OBJECTIVE: **Social studies:** Analyze patterns of change.
Science: Provide evidence of change.
Language arts: Study the change process.

GRADE LEVEL: 6–12

INTRODUCTION: Two pictures of Mount St. Helens were taken, one on May 17, 1980, and the other on September 10, 1980. What evidence for change is displayed in these pictures?

PROBLEM: What pictorial evidence can display the change process?

- Capture pictures of the change in process, taking succeeding pictures of the change. Note that the following three pictures provide clear evidence of the eruption that changed Mount St. Helen's landscape.

- Create a PowerPoint presentation, animating the process by morphing one image into the other.
- Complete your presentation by describing the process of change that is occurring. For example, for this eruption, you might describe the process of a volcanic eruption and what happens to stimulate the eruption.

such as chronology, causality, change, conflict, and complexity to explain, analyze, and show connections among patterns of historical change and continuity."

Change is a theme that runs throughout both the science and mathematics curricula as they emphasize the importance of understanding how change occurs in nature and in social and technology systems. The concept of rate of change is difficult. Whether the rate of change is constant, increasing, or decreasing has important implications for interpreting situations. Beginning early in their education, children must be guided to recognize and describe change. "Only after they have a storehouse of experience with change of different kinds are they ready to start thinking about patterns of change in the abstract" (Project 2061, 1993, p. 272).

Change is obviously a theme across the grade levels in many major academic areas as it also is with technology. Computer technologies have changed, evolving in hardware and software, en-

hancing the capabilities. As a result, changes have occurred in the way people communicate their thoughts and ideas; changes have occurred in the way people do business. Thus, important aspects of media literacy involve recognizing, understanding, and coping with change.

As more and more students incorporate multimedia applications to communicate their recognitions, their understanding and ability to obtain desired effects change. One of those effects might be to demonstrate the process of change visually and identify the various indicators of a particular change.

Morphing is an animation effect that can be used to demonstrate the change process by gradually blending one image into another. Although morphing software is available, students can create a similar effect using the presentation software transitions and animations. In the Classroom 8.1 describes an activity where students are asked to identify and demonstrate evidence of a change process. The activity is introduced and displayed by the evidence of the change created by a volcanic eruption of Mount St. Helens in 1980 from one day to the next. Clear evidence of the change is that there are trees in the foreground on one day and the next day there are none. Similarly, the snow and the mountaintop disappear from one picture to the next. Students might also note the appearance of steam rising from the center of the mountain and speculate the cause for this change as a volcanic eruption.

To model change using presentation software, students need to obtain numerous pictures over the change period as demonstrated by the three pictures of the eruption on Mount St. Helens. Pictures need to be taken from roughly the same distance and perspective. Another key is to identify central points about which the transformation is to be displayed. The base of the mountain might be one of the consistent features of the images with another point a specific land characteristic on the mountain. The more central points you can identify on the images, the better for displaying the morphing process. Simulating a person aging over years can be accomplished more smoothly using the nose, eyes, ears, and head shape as central features of the image. Simulating the growth of a plant might incorporate a measurement stick and the pot holding the plant.

PowerPoint offers many transition capabilities such as fade smoothly displayed in Figure 8.13. In this example, the slides are also set for automatic movement from one slide to the next showing each for only one second. This action gives a more consistent simulation of the change over time than requiring the presenter to click the mouse for the next slide.

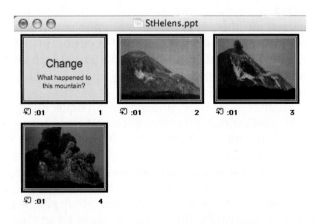

FIGURE 8.13 Morphing using a fade smoothly transitions from one slide to the next with the timing set automatically to move from one slide to the next after one second.

Social, Ethical, and Human Issues

What social, ethical, and human issues are of concern in the consideration of a multimedia perspective in the development of a literate citizen? Certainly, ease in copying electronic graphics, animation, audio, video, and motion presents a need for teachers to help students understand the legal concerns of copying and develop an ethical perspective toward the use of media elements created by others. The notion of a literate citizen as a person who is able to communicate information effectively using a variety of formats must also include the practice of legal and social uses of media elements.

Social issues are important, too. Teachers must consider the needs of diverse learners, their backgrounds, their characteristics, and their abilities with respect to multimedia. In the Snapshot of a Classroom Designing a Movie, Mr. Lopez had to make sure that the ideas of what makes feet happy represent his diverse student population. While the students were focused on displaying their knowledge of the two different languages, the activity needed to accurately represent their diversity. For example, "Hokey Pokey" is American folk music that is difficult to translate and still maintain the rhythm and actions. Thus, it is important for the Hispanic children to offer ideas for songs and actions that represent their culture.

Multimedia and Media Literacy Instructional Idea: Representing and Valuing Diversity   The settlers of colonial America brought their personal experiences from their previous countries, and primarily from Europe. Yet, with the American Revolution of 1776-1783, America officially declared independence from England. By this time, the original settlers had been replaced by a new generation whose roots were American. And, with the official Declaration of Independence, the mood of the country focused on the importance of American freedom and what it meant to participate as members in this new democracy. The overriding feeling was for citizens to clearly define what it meant to be American. The importance of one American culture was viewed as essential for America to retain its freedom, a freedom that had cost many lives. Education was essential to the preservation of this freedom since education shaped the future citizens into what was valued for good American citizens. As a result, America's emphasis was on the development of a monoculture as the American culture. Perhaps in these early days, this view included the idea of all children learning the same way with the same curriculum.

Fast forward to the twenty-first century to see a difference in emphasis. Rather than the promotion

In the Classroom 8.2

MULTIMEDIA COMMUNICATION—VALUING AND RESPECTING DIVERSITY?

TECHNOLOGY OBJECTIVE: **NETS · S I, II, IV**

- **Multimedia:** Technology as a communication tool while building understanding of social, ethical and legal issues involved with basic concepts of technology.
- Evaluating and appreciating the capabilities of multimedia in promoting respect for diversity.

CONTENT OBJECTIVE: **Social studies:** Study of America's cultural diversity, explaining how information describes diverse cultural groups.

GRADE LEVEL: 6–12

PROBLEM: **A variety of media have projected perceptions of the various people of America visually:** Indians as Redskins, Latinos as banditos, African-Americans eating watermelons, Asians with chopsticks and black, horned-rim glasses. Multimedia has tremendous capabilities to communicate ideas and impressions about people, places and environments. Are these types of communication accurate?

- ❑ Select a particular subgroup within the diversity of American society.
- ❑ Collect a variety of resources (library, Internet, textbooks, video collections, magazines) for visual, audio, and text presentations about this subgroup.
- ❑ Analyze the various presentations to answer these questions about your particular group:
  - Do the various presentations accurately describe your group?
  - Do the various presentations promote a respectful view of your group?
  - What has the role of the various presentations had in perpetuating a stereotypical view of your group?
  - What is the role of multimedia in perpetuating inaccurate understandings of diversity in the American society?
- ❑ Develop a multimedia presentation to describe your analysis through printed text, graphics, animation, audio, video, and motion.

---

of a *melting pot* working to erase diversity, American education has been guided toward a more inclusive perspective, a multicultural education, an education that provides opportunities for all students to learn while also recognizing and valuing differences. An important question for students to consider with respect to multimedia is: What is the role of multimedia in building a respect for diversity? In the increasingly global media environment, does media blur cultural identities? Do media artifacts promote stereotypes rather than accurately representing the cultures? What is the role of multimedia in presenting and valuing the diversity of American culture?

In the Classroom 8.2 describes one idea for guiding students in analyzing and evaluating the use of multimedia in recognizing and valuing different cultures. While the students are challenged to investigate a particular segment of the diversity of American culture (Asian-Americans, African-Americans, Native Hawaiians, Hispanic Americans, Latinos, Native American Indians, . . .), they are expected to evaluate the variety of media presentations that communicate views of that segment. The overall question is to consider the part that multimedia plays in supporting and valuing the diversity

in American culture. While studying America's diversity, these students are also investigating social issues with respect to multimedia.

Multimedia as a Productivity Tool

Multimedia does offer students a variety of tools for enhancing their educational experiences. Many of these tools have the capability to enhance student learning, increase productivity, and promote creativity. When students are assigned to prepare reports, they are no longer restricted to text writing for describing their thoughts about specific content. They can incorporate pictures, videos, and even audio elements in their documents to capture and display the depth of their thinking. They are not restricted to static visuals of posters; now they can incorporate resources of pictures, sounds, and even movies to creatively present their positions, responses, and solutions to assignments. As a result, they may, in fact, engage in more and deeper thinking about the ideas as they develop their presentations using multimedia tools. And, as they learn about the subject, they are also engaged in experiences that support the development of their media literacy.

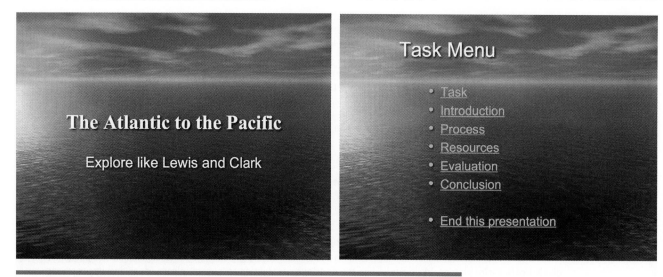

FIGURE 8.14   WebQuest task using presentation software to guide students in the exploration.

Multimedia and Media Literacy Instructional Idea: Instructions, Hyperlinks, and Presentation Software
Imagine for a moment your own classroom. Perhaps you see it as a place where students are actively involved in hands-on activities that you have designed to help them build their own personal understanding of the ideas. Now, think about how the students were introduced to those ideas. Did they just know what to do in the activities? Obviously not!

Providing students with instructions is an essential part of preparing them for the activities. Often teachers assume the responsibility for delivering the initial instructions to assure that all students understand the expectations by providing an outline of the processes students need to follow. One problem with this teacher-centered, verbal presentation is that students are usually not as engaged in understanding the instructions as they are in thinking about getting to do the activity. They may listen politely but do not necessarily follow all that is being said; they may be confused by one part of a task or perhaps quit listening because of some distraction. When the activity begins, you as their teacher find that you must answer lots of questions about what to do next.

Consider a different approach for providing the instructions, one that requires the students to be responsible for identifying what needs to be done and one that allows the students choices in how the instructions are presented. This more student-centered approach places the teacher in the role of guiding the students as they seek to make sense of the instructions. Presentation software has capabilities to present the instructions while at the same time allowing students to select the manner in which they explore the instructions.

In the previous chapter you explored the design of Web-based lessons that involve students in the exploration of Web-based resources to complete tasks (WebQuest). Presentation software hyperlink capabilities can be incorporated to allow the students control of the presentation in much the same way the instructions might be available in a Web presentation. Figure 8.14 shows the first two slides of the WebQuest model that was designed in Chapter 7. Students, working in small groups at a computer where the presentation is loaded, are able to select the links in any order they want depending on their discussions. And they are able to easily revisit instructions as needed.

Teachers create the set of instructions with the presentation software by using hyperlinks as shown in Figure 8.15. The Task Menu contains bullets that are linked to the appropriate slide using the Action Settings available in the Slide Show menu bar option. Similarly, links from each of the slides can be created to go to the other parts of the presentation as in Figure 8.16.

In essence, determining the instructions now becomes the students' responsibility and they are

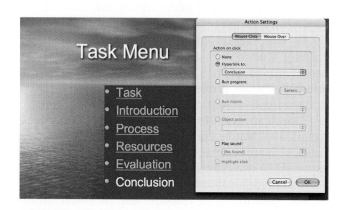

FIGURE 8.15   Creating a hyperlink in PowerPoint.

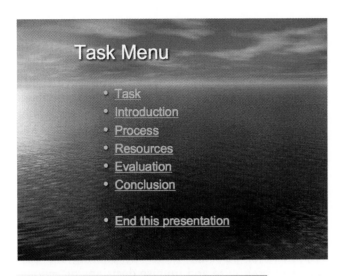

FIGURE 8.16 Demonstration of completed hyperlinks to key slides of the presentation.

free to choose the direction of the presentation. The instructions become a part of the work of the project and, as their teacher, you are able to go from group to group directing specific questions to the smaller groups of students and clarifying their specific questions. Ultimately, you, as their teacher, are more productive and able to concentrate on the important task of guiding student learning.

Multimedia and Media Literacy Instructional Idea: Lectures and Multimedia Presentations   One of the most important tasks for teachers is to design and describe the students' educational experiences. Multimedia offers capabilities that teachers can incorporate to become more productive in engaging their students in learning. As teachers use the capabilities, they are modeling for their students how they, too, might incorporate various media elements to explain and present their thinking. As a future teacher, you must also consider how you can utilize media elements to become more productive in engaging your students in learning in ways that help your students expand their media literacy.

One of the most difficult and overused teaching methods for presenting content is through lecture. Lectures are depicted as teacher-centered and teacher-delivered, where the basic purpose is to disseminate information. Students often describe them as dull and boring, where the teacher likes hearing the sounds of his or her voice. Yet, lectures do have strengths making them useful for instruction. An obvious value of lectures is that a large amount of material can be presented in a short time. Lectures can be used to arouse interest in a topic, introduce an idea, give directions for a task, provide an organization for ideas, and explain material that is not easily available. Ausubel (1961) proposes, however,

that the weaknesses often attributed to lectures are not due to the method itself but to the abuse of the method by those who use it. Lectures can be effective when delivered in an active manner while being supplemented through the use of multimedia presentations shifting the learning experience to more than just verbal learning.

One of the attractions of the lecture method is that the teacher (the lecturer) is able to control the flow of the content, assuring that the students are at least exposed to the topics. Whether the students learn from this exposure is a major question. If students are allowed to remain passively engaged in the ideas, they are less likely to construct personal understanding, now viewed as essential to learning. By teachers' expanding both the visual and auditory elements of the lecture and encouraging a dynamic structure to the lecture, students are more apt to become involved in thinking about the ideas being presented.

Examine two presentation slides for a lecture on Hammurabi's code, a topic for a seventh-grade social studies class. Figures 8.17a and 8.17b show the outline view and the slide view for each lecture. The

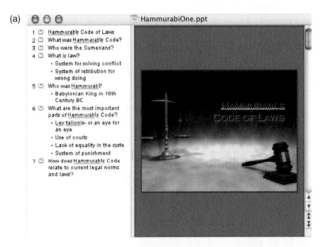

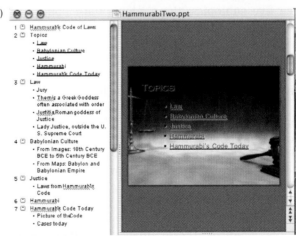

FIGURE 8.17   (*a*) Lecture One for Hammurabi's code. (*b*) Lecture Two for Hammurabi's code.

first slide is the same for both since the teacher's introduction for both begins with a general description of Hammurabi, a Babylonian king who was the first ruler to record laws of the land. Hammurabi, relying on his royal charge as given by divine commission from the gods to secure the general welfare of the people, published a Code of Laws for every man and his servant, for every man and his wife, as well as for every ruler and the ruled. The laws had been in practice for hundreds of years under various Sumerian kings, but no one had previously recorded and codified them as Hammurabi did.

Besides a similar introduction and the same slide background, the similarities in the two presentations diminish after the teacher's introduction to the lecture. In the first lecture (Figure 8.17a), the teacher, as the lecturer, uses the succeeding slides to guide the presentation. Major questions are posed sequentially, with discussion points as needed. In the second lecture (Figure 8.17b), the second slide is a list of topics that are also hyperlinked to future slides. Here the teacher provides these topics as links for selection by the students as possible explorations:

- Laws: Explore the reasons that civilizations and nations have laws.
- Babylonian culture: Explore the culture of the Babylonians where Hammurabi's code was in practice.
- Justice: Explore ideas about justice proposed in Hammurabi's code.
- Hammurabi: Explore Hammurabi himself.
- Hammurabi's Code Today: Explore how Hammurabi's code has influenced the U.S. system of laws and justice today.

The key difference in these lectures is that in the second lecture the teacher asks the students where to begin since the lecture is not driven by a linear presentation of slides. Hyperlinks allow student interest to guide the discussion. Even within each of the five subtopics, the students have opportunities to direct the discussion using additional hyperlinks. The teacher must develop the possibilities, the students listen to a general description about how these topics might be discussed, and the class determines the direction they feel is of most interest.

This nonlinear technique allows the teacher to organize the lecture around topics and possibilities for discussion. The structure requires active student involvement in the lecture, thus attending to a common problem with lectures, namely, student passivity. Furthermore, in the case of this presentation of the ideas, the teacher is able to include a number of visual images, requiring that the students analyze these images as they progress through the lesson. In essence, then, the students are cognitively and actively engaged in the lecture.

Multimedia as a Communications Tool

What do you remember about your childhood? Have you looked at pictures of you as a baby, as a toddler, or even as a first-grader? At best, you have spotty memory of those years! How can you find out about your childhood? One way is to ask your parents or grandparents to describe those years for you. They likely will tell you different stories because the events they remember had special significance to them. One may remember your first steps while another may remember you on your first birthday, playing in your birthday cake rather than eating it.

The ancient art of storytelling has been used to nurture children and young people, guiding their development of personal values by sharing the outcomes of both wise and unwise decisions or actions. Recall the story of the tortoise and the hare where slow and steady wins the race. Perhaps you remember this tale from a story read to you by your parents, grandparents, or a teacher. Historically, village elders transmitted stories and personal histories verbally. As civilization advanced, writings in journals, letters, photograph albums, and even books were more commonly used as ways to share stories. Now in the fast-paced, media-driven world, however, other ways compete as better ways to communicate and share stories with broader audiences. Parents might even communicate via video letters rather than letters written with paper and pen.

Multimedia and Media Literacy Instructional Idea: Digital Storytelling   A digital story is a melding of human voice and personal narrative, using technologies as tools for merging verbal and visual elements into one. Digital storytelling has emerged from the work of Dana Atchley, Joe Lambert, and the Center for Digital Storytelling at the University of California Berkeley in 1993. Technology Link 8.2 provides a link to the Center and other digital storytelling projects.

Effective digital stories use only a few images, a few words, and even fewer special effects to clearly and powerfully communicate intent and meanings. As students learn to communicate through digital stories, they need to work to include only what is necessary as opposed to what is possible. In the Classroom 8.3 describes an idea for guiding students in learning to communicate through digital storytelling using movie technology. Images, narration or

Technology Link 8.2

*I*nvestigate different online digital storytelling resources by selecting the **Storytelling** link.

www.wiley.com/college/nies*s*

In the Classroom 8.3
LETTER OR VIDEO STORYTELLING

TECHNOLOGY OBJECTIVE: NETS · S I, IV

- **Multimedia:** Technology as a communications tool while building understanding of basic concepts of technology.
- Investigate the making of a movie for communicating a story digitally.

CONTENT OBJECTIVE: Language arts: Students extend their literacy skills with respect to spoken, written, and visual language to communicate effectively with different audiences and for a variety of purposes.

GRADE LEVEL: 5–9

SCENE: [Father and daughter in a phone conversation.]

Audrey: Dad, can you send me a story about what you think was a turning point in your life that really changed your future?

Dad: Would you like it in a letter or a video letter?

TASK: Create a digital story that conveys a 3–5 minute personal narrative in response to a significant question and experience from your personal life.

MULTIMEDIA TOOL: Prepare a response in a movie video presentation.

Preproduction Activities

- **Prewriting:** What do you have to say? Identify a specific story worth telling. Use one of these exercises to help you:
  - Draw a detailed map of your neighborhood in which you grew up; include the layout of the streets, homes of friends and strange neighbors, location of school, location of local hangouts, and other personal details.
  - Write a detail journal in response to this question: Think of your favorite childhood coat. What do you have in your pockets?
  - Write a journal response describing a decisive moment (one that you remember as changing your direction in life).

- **Artifact Search:** Search for photos or other printed media that describe your life at this point.

- **Storyboarding:** Map out each image, technique, and element of your story in a storyboard.

- **Story Circle:** Share your drafts and help your partners work through their expressions in telling their stories. Questions to ask:
  - Why tell this story now?
  - Considering the images in the story, are there places where they can do the heavier narrative work and you can reduce the number of words?
  - Who is the intended audience?
  - What do you see happening on the screen at this point in the story? How do the images and the words work together?
  - What is the most important moment (or even sentence) in the script? What happens if we just start from there?

- **Revising the Script:** Consider one of these options for revising your script; then transfer your script to a readable form using one side of a 4 × 6 card.
  - Highlight all the action in green and all the reflection in pink. Too much pink is too much preaching. Too much green means that you are telling anecdotes with no implications.
  - Create a timeline and consider rearranging the order of events, either more or less chronological.
  - Consider exploring sentences, either to a slow-motion retelling or perhaps to more of an extension that focuses on pinpointing and targeting specifics.

Production Activities: Lights, camera, action! Emphasize 80% content and 20% effect.

  - Collect video motion clips.
  - Import or digitize photos.
  - Add transitions and special effects.
  - Record narration.
  - Add a soundtrack.
  - Burn the finished work on a CD.

Postproduction Activities

  - Screen the finished product.
  - Peer review how the stories communicated, exploring techniques and suggestions for both the presentation and the content.

voice, and motion are critical features of this idea for guiding students in digital storytelling. Six key elements are important for students to consider in digital storytelling:

- **Point of View:** What is the purpose of telling the story? Whose perspective is being told in the story?

- **Dramatic Question:** Most stories follow a structure based on somebody desiring something, then they act on that desire, and the audience sees the results. It is important to identify a question that will grab the audience.

- **Emotional Content:** What is powerful and engaging about this story that is often difficult to write, requiring a different form of communication?

- **The Soundtrack:** The soundtrack sets the mood for the story with music and other sound effects that make the story seem more real.

- **Economy:** The storyteller needs to choose key points and then choose still images or video clips that demonstrate these key points. It is important for you to show your audience just enough information to understand what you are trying to say and then change to another image.

- **Pacing:** Pacing is the secret to successful storytelling. A good story moves at a comfortable pace, perhaps pausing so that the audience has a chance to think about the idea. Pacing the breaks is key to the rhythm of the story.

While students are focused on for developing the art of digital storytelling in the activity for In the Classroom 8.3, they are also engaged in processes designed to guide them in learning more about creating a movie where the story is clearly communicated without being overshadowed by the media effects. Before they begin assembling the story, they are engaged in brainstorming ideas, writing, planning, and discussing their ideas that leads to the development of the script and storyboard. These products become their *entrance tickets* to the computer lab where they produce the digital story. Some tips you should consider as you guide students in assembling their story in this laboratory setting are as follows:

- Encourage students to save early and often along with maintaining backup copies of their work.

- Have students narrate in small pieces, maybe even one sentence at a time. This technique gives them maximum control over the pacing of their work. If the movie becomes too wordy, removing or redoing one or some of the pieces is more easily accomplished.

- Focus students on the writing and reading elements of the story. Guard against the technology overshadowing the story.

- Work within the copyright laws. Images and music bits are easily downloaded from the Web. Students need to understand and follow the laws. Require that all images be original and soundtracks be royalty-free. Technology Link 8.3 contains a link to an Internet site that provides legal sounds that can be considered.

Technology Link 8.3

*T*he link **Sounds** accesses free, legal sound effects to be considered when searching for audio media effects.

www.wiley.com/college/niess

Multimedia as a Research Tool

Multimedia tools provide students with multiple ways to collect data and information and to present results of questions they have researched. In the past, students have been required to write research reports to describe the research question, the research methodology, the data collected, analysis of the data, their conclusions, and a reference section. In preparation of such reports, the students followed the same format, basically filling in the blanks.

Today, students are often required to present their research results to the class. Unfortunately, the previous research format has more commonly been transferred to their slide-based presentations. One student follows another, using a presentation they created to describe the research question, the research methodology, the data collected, analysis of the data, their conclusions, and even the references. Such presentations only serve to support Edward Tufte's (2003) portrayal of presentation software as presenter-oriented where both the audience and content suffer. The audience is not involved and the content is reduced to a presentation at the lowest level, certainly not at the analysis and synthesis level that is hoped for in a research assignment.

Challenge students to be creative in their presentations of the results of their research. Encourage them to think about and incorporate a variety of multimedia tools as they conduct their research as well as when they display the results of their research. Part of the challenge, though, is for you to present the assignment using multimedia as you describe different types of research tasks.

Multimedia and Media Literacy Instructional Idea: Presenting the Research Task Frog deformities have been identified throughout the world. The question as to the cause of such deformities is often a challenge for science classes to consider. Part of the science that students need to learn is how to

Resource Idea: Presenting an Assignment

Title:	Motivating Study through Motion Pictures
Topic:	Introduce a new unit to motivate student interest
Grades:	Any grade level
Objectives:	Create a motivational introduction to a new unit that also encourages incorporation of a multimedia approach to communicate their learning.
Idea:	Create a motion picture introduction to a new unit of study to engage student interest in the unit. The movie can take the place of a field trip where students are able to see animals, events, places, or actions that are a part of the study in the new unit.
Materials:	Storyboard of the movie, camcorder, movie application along with additional audio and visual elements.

Modification:
1. Create a movie conclusion to the unit.
2. Incorporate a movie development assignment in the unit.
3. Assign students to develop a new introduction for the unit as a culminating activity for the unit.

FIGURE 8.18   Resource idea for presenting alternative ways to motivate student engagement in assignments.

conduct research. What causes the deformities? Students need to identify and investigate probable hypotheses as to the cause. But their laboratory is in the classroom, not out in the field where the deformities have been identified in specific geographical locations. Students can be shown pictures of the types of deformities. Nevertheless, the location is critical to identifying potential hypotheses. A field trip to search for animals with such deformities is one idea. Of course a field trip is time-consuming and what if the students are unable to find any? Figure 8.18 provides a resource idea for an alternative for the introduction of this problem that may in fact be more successful in helping students conduct observations of the deformities and the environment in which the frogs lived. On the other hand, teachers might develop a movie to show close-ups of specific frog deformities as well as the various geographic and environmental locations where the frogs were found. Some of the slides that might be included are depicted in Figure 8.19. However, a movie provides an advantage over the single slides by displaying the action of finding the frogs, seeing them in action as they move in their environment despite their specific deformities. The movie serves as an introduction to the problem and then as a catalyst for generating student discussion of possible causes.

FIGURE 8.19   Four slides in the frog deformity movie showing two of the possible deformities and two of the environments in which the frogs were found.

In the Classroom 8.4

WHY DO I NEED TO LEARN THIS STUFF?

TECHNOLOGY OBJECTIVE: NETS·S I, IV, V

- **Multimedia:** Technology as a communications and research tool while building understanding of basic concepts of creating movies with available technology.
- Investigate the making of a movie.

CONTENT OBJECTIVE: All subject areas: Investigate and explain why an educated citizen needs to know the subject.

GRADE LEVEL: 5–9

QUESTION: I really don't understand why I will ever need to know this stuff! Why do I have to learn this stuff?

- Prepare a concept map that describes your individual response to the question, Why do I need to learn this stuff?
- In groups of three develop a 5 minute movie response to the question.
  - ❑ **Preproduction**
    - Devise a research procedure for answering the question. Consider these questions:
      - ○ Who might be able to help you?
      - ○ How do people in different businesses use this subject?
      - ○ How is this knowledge helpful in everyday lives?
      - ○ Do only adults use this knowledge?
      - ○ Is there any evidence of knowledge of this subject involved in your activities?
      - ○ What kind of information about this subject is involved in the recreation industry?
      - ○ Is there any evidence of knowledge of this subject in the entertainment industry?
    - Create a storyboard to describe your multimedia approach to data collection in considering the questions.
    - Collect the various multimedia elements needed for your movie.
  - ❑ **Production.** Produce the movie, presenting the results of your investigation on the importance of this knowledge in your life.
  - ❑ **Postproduction.** Present your movie to the class, explaining to them the results of your investigation.
- Conclusion
  - ❑ Students revise concept maps based on the various movie responses to the research question.
  - ❑ Class discussion: What was the impact of developing the movie and seeing other students' movies on expanding your response to the research question?

Multimedia and Media Literacy Instructional Idea: Video Research   The frog deformity movie is used to introduce students to their research project, helping them to identify possible hypotheses to research. However, students can also incorporate movies as a means of communicating the results of their research.

Students typically challenge their teachers with this question: Why do we have to learn this? Although it sometimes feels like they are just trying to divert the class discussion, consider the question as a challenge for them to investigate and answer. In the Classroom 8.4 summarizes a multimedia approach for their research of the question that also challenges them to communicate the results of their investigation in a movie. Their personal research is more apt to provide answers they might accept. With a limitation of 5 minutes for the movies, different groups can be directed to investi-gate different age levels, different uses, different occupations, and even different cultures. You can also include a pre- and postassessment of their responses by having them create a concept map to show how they would respond to the question at each of these points. Finally, a class discussion focuses on the use of movies as a means of communicating the results of their research along with helping them consider presenting different perspectives on the question.

Multimedia as a Problem-Solving and Decision-Making Tool

Multimedia tools support students in investigating problems and using different media elements to clarify and provide information for finding solutions and making informed decisions.

In the Classroom 8.5

DOES CLIMATE IDENTIFY A TOWN?

TECHNOLOGY OBJECTIVE: NETS · S I, IV, V, VI

* **Multimedia:** Technology as a communications, research, and decision-making tool while building understanding of basic concepts of technology.
* Incorporate multimedia elements in a software presentation.

CONTENT OBJECTIVE: Social studies: Identify and describe people, places, and environments.

Language arts: Develop an understanding of and respect for diversity in geographic regions and social roles.

Science: Develop descriptions analyzing data and using evidence to support explanations.

GRADE LEVEL: 5–9

PROBLEM: What climate data distinguishes one town from another?

❏ Distribute mystery town locations to students organized in groups of two. Inform the class of the possible towns. Distribute all but one of the towns without informing the students which town is not being investigated.

- ○ San Francisco, California
- ○ San Diego, California
- ○ Phoenix, Arizona
- ○ Las Vegas, Nevada
- ○ Salt Lake City, Utah
- ○ Denver, Colorado
- ○ Boise, Idaho
- ○ Cheyenne, Wyoming
- ○ Missoula, Montana
- ○ Santa Fe, New Mexico
- ○ Portland, Oregon
- ○ Seattle, Washington
- ○ Anchorage, Alaska

❏ Download the temperature and precipitation data for each town from the Western Regional Climate Center website. Copy the data, pasting it into spreadsheets for analysis to identify the average temperature and precipitation for each month over the year. Relabel the towns as Town1, Town2, ... Distribute the data analyses for each town. (See In the Classroom 6.8 for more details of the analyses.)

❏ Develop a presentation that provides clues for solving a mystery as to the identity of the town. Groups must include geographical clues along with temperature and precipitation information clues to describe the climate of the town. The presentation is to include a variety of multimedia elements to enhance the mystery of the identity of the town.

❏ Present town clues to the class for their investigation of your mystery town.

❏ As a class, determine the names for each of the mystery towns.

Multimedia and Media Literacy Instructional Idea: Where Is My Town?   In Chapter 6, one of the spreadsheet ideas challenges students to investigate the climate data for various towns in the western United States by creating spreadsheets to analyze the 30-year data sets of temperature and precipitation data. After the students have completed their analyses, a problem-solving activity can be used to challenge them to design a mystery presentation that provides geographical, temperature, precipitation, and perhaps wind information about their town. In the Classroom 8.5 is a challenge for students to investigate their specific towns and use multimedia to develop a mystery presentation with clues about the town. A presentation tool provides an appropriate multimedia application for this project. Students in groups of two develop the presentations and present them to the class in a manner that challenges the audience to solve the mystery of where this town is in the western United States. If the students utilize the nonlinear features as shown in a slide in Figure 8.20, the class can be encouraged to select and revisit clues in

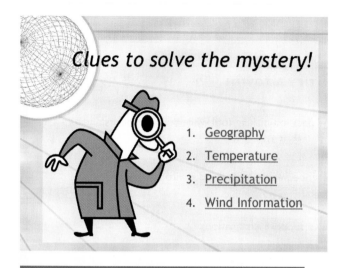

FIGURE 8.20   Nonlinear strategy to provide clues about the mystery town.

their quest to identify the town using the links to the clues of interest.

After all the presentations, the class must make a decision as to which town is which, without presenters divulging the identity of their towns. One way to organize this decision-making process is to have them record either *hit* or *miss* on a piece of paper, fold it, and place the slips into a bag. The teacher counts the number of hits and the number of misses at this point. If there are misses (and typically there are), the class must revisit the question of which town is which. Each group of students might be assigned to review other's presentations, reconsidering the clues and revising their decisions. Again, the groups record hit or miss for their town, placing the slips of paper in the bag. The process continues until all are hits. This process allows for more discussion and investigation about the towns and the differences in the climate data with respect to the geography of the towns.

Summing It Up

Advancements in technology have impacted the meaning of literacy. In the twenty-first century, being a literate citizen is one who is also media literate—a critical thinker and a creative producer of an increasingly wide range of messages using image, language, and sound along with the ability to locate, access, analyze, evaluate, manipulate, and communicate information effectively in a variety of formats including printed text, graphics, animation, audio, video, and motion. Society challenges education to prepare future citizens, citizens who are able to think with

and create with multimedia. Multimedia encompasses those applications that support an integration of media elements to communicate information. Text, still pictures, graphics, animation, sounds, motion, and video are potential selections.

The challenge for teachers is to design their instruction to accommodate learning about multimedia in a manner that helps their students learn various subjects as they also learn about the media elements. Students are used to a visual culture that bombards them with visual stimuli while not requiring a critical analysis. Although some suggest that the benefit of multimedia tools is in engaging visual learners (the students who are *gamers* or into films, television, etc.), multimedia tools provide an avenue for all students to learn to incorporate a wide range of media capabilities while exploring a variety of content-specific ideas.

Students have access to slide-based tools as well as clip-based tools. Messages can be delivered in slides using presentation software; messages can be delivered in movies; messages can be delivered in concept mapping software. Students need to learn both the science and the art of authoring messages in these various applications. Several guidelines are important when authoring multimedia, but these guidelines do not necessarily mean that the presentation communicates the message. Attention to each of the production phases (preproduction, production, and postproduction) is important in becoming a multimedia author. However, these activities do not guarantee the success of the communication. Students engage in strategic thinking to discriminate among the applications to determine which combination is best for each message. Students must learn to put various media elements together in ways that communicate. In addition, multiple experiences in authoring presentations while they are learning within the context of the various subjects are essential for the development of media literacy.

End-of-the-Chapter Activities and References

PRACTICE PROBLEMS

1. Use a concept map application to describe the concept of *media literacy*.

2. Create a concept map that describes knowledge you believe is essential to teach in your subject area for the education of literate citizens.

3. Design an introduction to an assignment to motivate and guide students in developing a multimedia report to describe the results of their work.

4. Collect digital images of an object that is undergoing change. Show the change in the object using the capabilities available in a slide presentation or in a movie.

5. Using In the Classroom 8.3 to guide your work, create a *digital teaching narrative* where you share your story about what led you to teaching, and more specifically to teaching your particular discipline and grade level.

6. Create a movie that responds to the question that students often ask, Why do I have to learn this stuff?

7. Problem-based learning typically begins with a problem that engages students in a question that they will investigate. Often their work requires that they use technology to solve the problem, too. Create a movie presentation that introduces them to the problem in an engaging way and that introduces them to the particular technology that might be used in solving the problem.

8. In Chapter 7 you explored a variety of WebQuest problems for your grade level and subject. Present this WebQuest using presentation software, where hyperlinks allow the user control in accessing the different parts of the problem assignment.

9. Use presentation software to create a document that describes the key stages in developing a multimedia production (such as presentation or movie applications).

IN THE CLASSROOM ACTIVITIES

10. Interview teachers about ways that they might incorporate multimedia tools in their classrooms. What is their preparation for teaching students to use multimedia tools for learning?

11. Interview students about their access to multimedia in their homes that they might use to demonstrate their work on particular class projects.

ASSESSING STUDENT LEARNING WITH AND ABOUT TECHNOLOGY

12. Create a scoring guide for a slide-based presentation that students use to give feedback to each other on the quality and communication of their presentations.

13. Create a scoring guide for a movie presentation that students use to give feedback to each other on the quality and communication of the movie.

E-PORTFOLIO ACTIVITIES

14. Create a commercial that encourages teachers to incorporate media literacy in their instruction.

15. Prepare a reflection about teaching and learning *with* and *about* multimedia. How can you incorporate multimedia in your classes so that students use its elements and capabilities as tools as described in the student teaching standards? How can multimedia be used as a tool for learning in your subject area?

REFLECTION AND DISCUSSION

16. Reflect on the idea of media literacy and what that means for what and how you will teach in the twenty-first century.

17. Discuss the pros and cons of presentation software, taking into account some of the challenges levied by Edward Tufte (2003).

18. Create a digital reflection about multimedia and media literacy in education.

19. Authoring multimedia has been described as both a science and an art. Explain this perception, helping the reader to understand the science of multimedia authoring and how that differs from the art of multimedia authoring. Examples are important in the discussion.

20. Learning to author multimedia is often described as instruction belonging in art classes. Discuss how multimedia authoring can be taught as students learn subject matter content. Use specifics from your subject matter and grade level in your explanation.

Annotated Resources

Bowen, A., & Bell, R. (2004). Winging it: Using digital imaging to investigate butterfly metamorphosis. *Learning and Leading with Technology, 31*(6), 24–27.
A science lesson that incorporates digital photography to show emerging and time-lapse photography to display the metamorphosis of a caterpillar to a butterfly.

McCombs, J. (2001). Coloring outside the lines. *Learning and Leading with Technology, 29*(1), 28–30, 57.
Connect important art concepts with technology skills in a multimedia exploration.

Reissman, R. (2001). Someone's in the kitchen: Multimedia activities for multidisciplinary exploration. *Learning and Leading with Technology, 28*(7), 46–49.
A kitchen/house unit leads to a pool of potential classroom-initiated investigations that can incorporate scanning, audiotaping, and digital photography along with families talking, contributing, and doing multimedia projects.

Sims, K. C. (2001). Great U.S. women: Student research projects with a multimedia twist. *Learning and Leading with Technology, 29*(1), 42–47.
Students learn essential research skills in the middle grades while focused on researching great U.S. women. Multimedia presentations provide the platform for expressing students' ideas and understandings.

Tufte, E. R. (2003). *The cognitive style of PowerPoint*. Cheshire, CT: Graphics Press LLC.
Author challenges the impact of PowerPoint for communicating ideas, describing how the presentations "weaken verbal and spatial reasoning and almost always corrupt statistical analysis."

Hypermedia and Web Authoring

Bob Daemmrich/PhotoEdit

◆ Introduction

Have you ever found yourself thinking about something and suddenly noticed that you shifted your thinking to a seemingly unrelated idea? Perhaps you even began thinking about the original idea later. What about the times when you were in the middle of a sentence and you suddenly thought of something you had been trying to remember earlier? Do you remember sleeping, only to awake scratching your head about your weird dream—a strangely jumbled version of things that you had experienced along with others you had only read about? The human memory is a marvelous yet complex system that supports unlimited connections of ideas, pictures, happenings, sounds, colors, and many other elements.

This powerful system—the human mind—was acknowledged by Vannever Bush in the 1940s in his description of the power of computers:

> There should be a tool that would enhance human memory and thinking and that allows people to retrieve information from a computer in many of the same ways in which retrieval is accomplished within human memory. *("As We May Think," The Atlantic Monthly, 1945, p. 101)*

Bush proposed that the ability to navigate enormous amounts of data was more important than

the futuristic hardware as he described a device he called *memex*, a device where an "individual stores all his books, records, and communications, and which is mechanized so that it may be consulted with exceeding speed and flexibility" (1945, p. 102). Even in those early days of computing systems, Bush visualized *memex* as a device for connecting information:

> When the user is building a trail, he names it, inserts the name in his code book, and taps it out on his keyboard. Before him are the two items to be joined, projected onto adjacent viewing positions. At the bottom of each there are a number of blank code spaces, and a pointer is set to indicate one of these on each item. The user taps a single key, and the items are permanently joined. . . . Thereafter at any time, when one of these items is in view, the other can be instantly recalled merely by tapping a button below the corresponding space. Moreover, when numerous items have been thus joined together to form a trail, they can be reviewed in turn, rapidly or slowly, by deflecting a lever like that used for turning the pages of a book. It is exactly as though the physical items had been gathered together from widely separated sources and bound together to form a new book. *(1945, p. 103)*

In the 1940s, Bush proposed the notion of hypertext without ever using the word! Yet, it was not until 1965 that T. H. Nelson coined the word *hypertext*, as he envisioned all of the world's literature in one publicly accessible global online system:

> "everything" written about the subject, or vaguely relevant to it, tied together by editors (and NOT by "programmers," dammit), in which you may read in all the directions you wish to pursue. There can be alternate pathways for people who think different ways. *(Dream Machines, 1974, p. 45)*

These early visions eventually gave way to reality, to hypertext and the hypermedia systems that today in some sense mimic how the human mind makes connections. Now, hypertext is considered as information "linked and cross-referenced in many different ways and is widely available to end users" (Hooper, 1990) and as a "database in which information (texts) has been organized nonlinearly. The database consists of nodes and links between nodes" (Multisilta, 1996). The notion of hypertext eventually extended to hypermedia: nonsequential documents containing not only text, but also elements such as audio, video, graphics, drawings, photographs, and animation, along with computer systems on which these components are stored and displayed. Probably the most familiar hypermedia system to you is the World Wide Web.

Along with the development of hypertext and hypermedia systems, the notion of literacy has shifted, too. Whereas literacy typically referred to reading and writing in traditional forms (letters, papers, and other sequential forms), today, literacy is extended to include the ability to read and write (or author) new types of documents that, in addition to normal text and graphics, offer the freedom to pursue the information in a nonsequential manner. In essence, this description of literacy is expanded to endorse a communication more like that of the actions involved when the brain is engaged in accessing, processing, managing, integrating, and communicating information—the ability to communicate through interwoven ideas connected by links and to pursue ideas in a nonsequential manner of personal choice.

With this shift in the idea of literacy, educating a literate citizen has also shifted. Learning to read this new type of information is important but so is learning to write this type of information. As Web-readers, literate citizens need to learn to access and process the information. As Web-writers, they need to learn to create electronic paths through related material, to cross-reference other documents, to annotate text, and to create notes. In *Dream Machines* (1974), Nelson characterized this new form of writing this way:

By "hypertext" I mean nonsequential writing. Ordinary writing is sequential for two reasons. First it grew out of speech . . . which [has] to be sequential, and second, because books are not convenient to read except in a sequence. But the structures of ideas are not sequential. They tie together every which way. And when we write we are always trying to tie things together in nonsequential ways.

As a teacher, your task is to prepare literate citizens. You need to teach your students to read and write in a manner that takes advantage of tools supporting nonsequential communication if they are to develop this expanded form of literacy. The challenge is to engage your students in the forms of reading and writing that are currently available in books and on the Web. Authoring, distributing, and viewing hypermedia documents provide important activities to guide them in learning to communicate in the nonsequential format. The key for you, however, is to guide your students in learning to read and write within the context of the academic subject areas important in the twenty-first century.

In recognition of this notion of integration of learning to use the twenty-first-century tools within the context of various subject areas, the Partnership for 21st Century Skills (2004) developed Information and Communication Technology Literacy Maps in geography, mathematics, and English to assist teachers like you in developing lesson plans for students to integrate their learning with twenty-first-century tools, such as hypertext and hypermedia, with core academic subject areas. These maps provide a vision of an education different from the one you experienced. For example, by twelfth grade, students

- In English, will be able to navigate a nonlinear text to access relevant information or follow the sequence of nonlinear narratives;

- In mathematics, will be able to create a presentation that uses dynamic images to illustrate a mathematical concept, connection, or problem and its applicability to a real-world context;

- In geography, will be able to work on a team to prepare a multimedia presentation on toxic and hazardous waste management at local and global levels (Partnership for 21st Century Skills, 2004).

These sample outcomes describe the use of twenty-first-century tools in communicating student learning. Your job is to redesign and create the curriculum and instruction to prepare your students with the twenty-first-century skills of a literate citizen.

CHAPTER LEARNING OBJECTIVES

After reading this chapter, you should be able to:

1. Identify authoring tools that provide an environment for students to communicate their hypermedia ideas on the Web.

2. Describe the elements that are useful in authoring Web hypermedia.

3. Illustrate activities and guidelines that deserve careful attention in the hypermedia and Web authoring design process phrases: the preproduction phase, the production phase, and the publication phase.

4. Explain how nonsequential reading and writing differ from the more traditional, sequential forms of reading and writing. Describe experiences that support the development of basic concepts of this nonsequential form of communication with hypermedia when learning in a variety of content areas.

5. Identify Web authoring experiences that support students in gaining an understanding of the importance of challenging the credibility of Web resources.

6. Explain how authoring of electronic portfolios can be used to guide students in learning to use technology productivity tools while also enhancing their creativity.

7. Describe hypermedia and Web authoring experiences that have potential to enhance students' visual narrative communication abilities.

8. Describe how Web authoring is useful in guiding students in learning about hypermedia as a research tool and a problem-solving and decision-making tool.

Snapshot of a Class Investigation of Web Hypermedia

Mrs. Harrison's sixth-grade class was accustomed to searching for information on the Web. One day they asked Mrs. Harrison how the information had been placed there. They thought of Web information much like the information they found in books in their library. Someone wrote the books and someone wrote the information they found on the Web. They were familiar with the production of books, published on paper and bound. But they were not familiar with how the Web materials were published.

Shannon: It seems easier to access information on the Web than it does in the library. You just click on the links and you get the information immediately. So all the information must be in the same place like in a book, only different chapters.

Mrs. Harrison: Not exactly. I think we should explore more about the Web to get a better understanding of what is happening when you use hyperlinks on the Web. I have a model that may help. I'll bring it in tomorrow. Tomorrow will be our first day in preparation for creating your own Web pages.

Aaron: Wow, that's great. I can hardly wait!

Mrs. Harrison: I know but it will be important to understand what you are working with when you begin. So tomorrow, we'll begin by discussing three types of hyperlinks you can create.

Mrs. Harrison had developed a model of Web pages using cardboard rectangles. Each rectangle contained information along with specific links for additional information. Mrs. Harrison found some $1\frac{1}{4}$ inch Velcro poster squares with adhesive backings and placed one side of a Velcro square for each link. She connected the other part to a piece of string to demonstrate the action when the link was selected. Figure 9.1 describes the separate boards and the simulated links she made for this demonstration. She began with the first two boards in a stack on her desk. The third board she placed in a closet near her desk.

Mrs. Harrison: Today I want to demonstrate the three types of hyperlinks: first, within a page; second, from one page to another within the same computer location; and third, from one computer page to an address at a computer not even in our state! Does that sort of confuse you?

Class: YES!

Mrs. Harrison: Remember when you are searching the Web, there are addresses connected with all the different Web pages? We have a computer in our school district that provides space for us to create and provide Web pages for distribution throughout the world. Our server has this address [pointing to the information she had placed on an overhead transparency].

Hypertext transfer protocol is the system for interacting with and arranging informa-

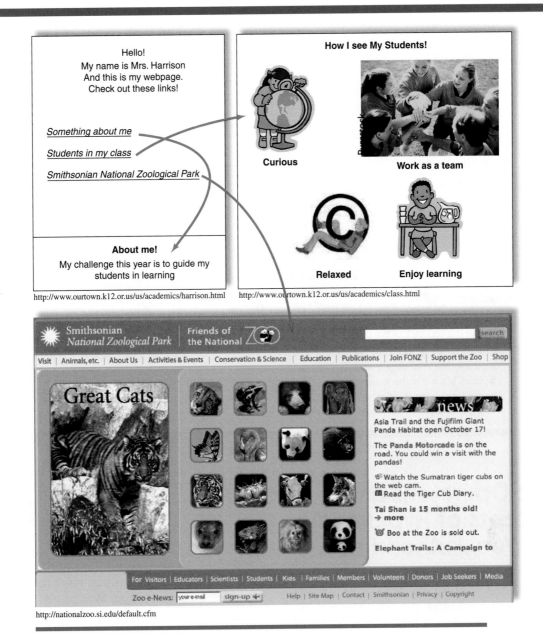

FIGURE 9.1 Boards, Velcro poster markers, and strings that Mrs. Harrison used to describe the three types of hyperlinks.

HyperText Transfer Protocol

HTTP

School's Web address

http://www.ourtown.k12.or.us

Mrs. Harrison's Web address

http://www.ourtown.k12.or.us/academics/harrison.html

tion on the Web. So this address begins by identifying the system with the HTTP. My Web pages are in a subdirectory called academics. So the address to my front page

directs the user to that location. If you entered this address in a Web browser, you would see a frame like this [displaying an overhead of her front page].

Hello!
My name is Mrs. Harrison
And this is my webpage.
Check out these links!

Something about me

Students in my class

Smithsonian National Zoological Park

The important lesson for today, though, is that these links are three different types of hyperlinks. The first link is something about me and is linked to another location in this same page [pointing at the bottom of the first page in Figure 9.1]. You just can't see it when you first enter my website. But, when I click on this link, the computer responds by connecting to the information about me in the same page below.

[Mrs. Harrison unfolded the cardboard demonstration of her home page to display the additional part and then demonstrated this type of link by connecting the two squares using the string with squares at each end.]

This is a target hyperlink—a link within the page so that it has the same Web address. For this link, I don't leave the Web page! I just displayed a part that you didn't see that was below the top part of the page.

The next link is about my class. I have created another Web page that uses a different address, but it is at the same storage location as my front page. If I click on this link, I will be sent to another Web page [showing the

board that was behind the other on her desk, as described in Figure 9.1]. This kind of link is called a relative hyperlink because it is being linked to another document in a similar location [demonstrating the connection with the string].

This last hyperlink, to the National Zoo, is different. This link directs the computer to a different computer, one that is not even in Oregon where we are. The National Zoo is in Washington, D.C., and that is where the computer is that contains this page. A hyperlink that links to a different computer is called an absolute hyperlink.

[Mrs. Harrison demonstrates this type of link by connecting the page the students were viewing to the board that she was placed in her closet.]

Shawn: So, ... do we get to start creating our Web pages now?

Mrs. Harrison: Not just yet. We still have more to learn about creating Web pages! But, knowing that you can make these different types of hyperlinks is an important beginning for when you create your Web pages.

Basic Operatons and Concepts of Hypermedia and Web Authoring

You have probably roamed the Web quite successfully using browser software (Internet Explorer, Safari, Firefox, and Mozilla are just a few). The *back* and *forward* hyperlinks are typical tracking tools to visit and revisit particular sites. Also, since many pages often show information that is updated every few seconds, the *refresh* hyperlink helps you see the latest information displayed on the page. Certainly, you have entered addresses in the address space to move directly to a page of interest. If you were interested in returning to that site you probably saved the address using the *bookmark* feature of the browser. Then all you need to do is to select the appropriate bookmark to move directly to the location without having to enter the more complex Web address.

What about the contents that you have seen on the Internet? You might consider those as a library of multimedia elements including a variety of graphic, audio, visual, and textual elements. Creating (or authoring) such multimedia Web pages offers a new

challenge since you must overcome the traditional approach of presenting information in a sequential fashion; you need to figure out how to communicate in a nonsequential fashion. How are all these elements created? How are they formatted? And how are these pages made available for others around the world to access and read? These questions are only the beginning of questions you must consider as you begin developing your own Web pages.

Web Page Development

With the development of the Web, a new language, hypertext markup language (HTML), was created as a mechanism for linking graphics and text in a new, nonsequential way. Initially, Web developers were required to program in this language in order to create Web pages with hyperlinks that provide the Web reader control of the direction for traversing the Web document.

Figure 9.2*a* depicts a sequence of instructions in HTML that results in the Web presentation in Figure 9.2b. Multiple *tags* indicate the beginning and ending of important sections. The heading (<head>) of the instructions initiates the beginning information: the language is HTML and the title of the document is Introduction. The heading is ended using another tag (</head>). In the body of

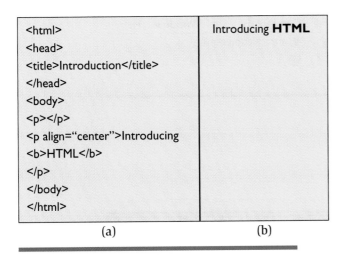

`<html>`
`<head>`
`<title>Introduction</title>`
`</head>`
`<body>`
`<p></p>`
`<p align="center">Introducing`
`<b>HTML</b>`
`</p>`
`</body>`
`</html>`
	Introducing **HTML**

(a)	(b)

FIGURE 9.2 (*a*) HTML coding. (*b*) Presentation created by the code.

the design (`<body>`), other tags describe how to format the information. On a new line, the information is to be centered (`<p align="center">`) but only the word HTML is bolded `<b>`. Then the bolding is turned off (`</b>`) and the line is ended (`</p>`). Finally, the body is terminated (`</body>`) and the html coding is ended (`</html>`).

If you have never designed a Web page using HTML coding, you probably find this language quite complicated with the use of the less than (`<`) and greater than (`>`) signs to begin and end all instructions or tags. Perhaps you noticed the slash (/) sign, a signal used to turn off a previously invoked instruction: `<b>` turns on the bold formatting feature and `</b>` turns off the bold.

Web Authoring Tools Although a basic understanding of coding in HTML is sometimes useful, today many software tools are available to guide you and your students in authoring Web pages. Typically, these tools allow you to format the page as you want without having to program in the HTML language; the tool simply makes the conversion of your design to HTML code. Word processors such as Microsoft's Word, spreadsheets such as Excel, and presentation packages such as PowerPoint, all offer options to save the documents as Web pages. You create the page the way you want it to work and when you save it, the application converts all the features to HTML. When writing this chapter in a word processor, the option to save it as a Web page creates two filenames:

Chapter9.htm

Chapter9_files

The first file is the HTML code and the second file is a folder containing the header and the im-

ages identified in the code. Both the htm file and the files folder (with the files called in the code) must be on the Web server in order to display Chapter 9 as a Web page. Perhaps you noted the shortened extension .htm and wondered why that extension and not .html. Although .html is the typical extension, the .htm is a result of previous limitations by Unix and Linux Web servers. Most Web servers allow either.

In addition to these tools for creating the HTML code for your Web pages, you might use an application whose primary function is to create Web pages. Such packages typically incorporate more Web-specific features than word processors. Both Macromedia's Dreamweaver and Microsoft's FrontPage are two possible options. Each of these packages allows Web authors to view the design and the HTML code that creates the design. Figure 9.3 shows both the code and design views in Dreamweaver. As the page is designed, you can access multiple links displayed on the toolbar just like those in word processors. Although the packages display the design view, an important step in the design process is to view the Web page in an Internet browser as it is being created. This action assures that the features work and the presentations are as intended. Web-authoring packages also offer you the option to view the document in a browser of your choice. Therefore, as you are working, you simply switch between the design in the package and the display in your browser.

Web Elements Web pages can incorporate many different elements invoked through the various toolbar options in the Web-authoring package. Figure 9.4 shows some possible elements. In this discussion of each of these elements, the HTML code is often included. You do not have to know how to create the code because the Web-authoring package offers the tools to create them. However, inspecting the code often helps to troubleshoot problems with Web page displays because of the detailed information in the code.

- **Headings.** As in most word processors, some preformatted headings are available for assuring proportional and easily viewable sizes. For example, in Figure 9.4, Heading 1 is used for the top line, signified by `<h1>`, and is turned off at the end of the line with `</h1>`. The complete HTML code for this line shows that the heading is turned on, the line is to be centered, the phrase Web Authoring is bolded, and, finally, both the bold and heading are turned off:

`<h1 align="center">`Introduction to `<b>`**Web Authoring**`</b></h1>`

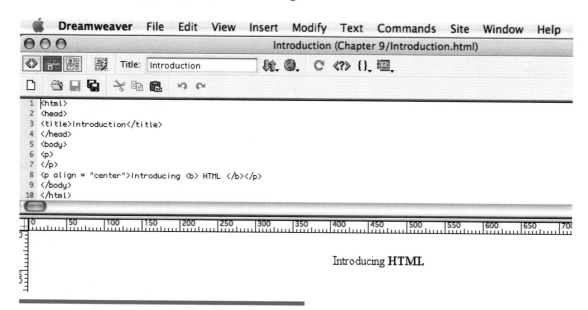

FIGURE 9.3   Dreamweaver code and design view.

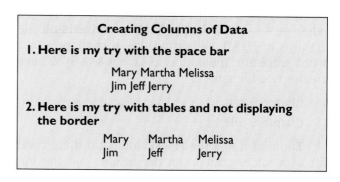

FIGURE 9.4   Elements in a Web page.

- **Backgrounds.** The background of each page can be colored to enhance its visual clarity. Although you can change the background color on every page, the best websites are those where the background does not become the focus of attention. You can even use a graphic (such as a .gif or .jpg) as the background but you must be careful in your selection because the graphic is automatically repeated both horizontally and vertically. This repetition may distract from the message on the page.

- **Text color.** You can change the color of the text but be sure to check that the color is visible against the background and is not confused with hyperlink colors. Make certain that the focus of the text is on its meaning, and not on a rainbow of colored letters.

- **Tables.** Tables can be created in Web-authoring packages as easily as in word processing packages. When you identify the number of columns and rows, you are given the option to either display the borders (<border = "1">)or not (<border = "0">). Another feature with tables is that you can merge some of the cells so that some cells hold more information than others. In Figure 9.4, the cells for Graphics and Hyperlinks are mergers of the cells in columns 2 and 3, providing more space for the information.

HTML is a language that uses a single space to separate instructions but ignores multiple spaces regardless of your intent. If you try to use the space bar or the tab key to line up columns of information, newer Web-authoring packages do not support the use of either for visually aligning the information. Of course, if you create your document in a word processor where you can visually line up data, those multiple spaces may be ignored when converted to HTML. One technique to ensure that information is presented in columns is to use tables and hide the borders of the cells in the tables.

Creating Columns of Data

1. **Here is my try with the space bar**

   Mary Martha Melissa
   Jim Jeff Jerry

2. **Here is my try with tables and not displaying the border**

Mary	Martha	Melissa
Jim	Jeff	Jerry

Each cell of a table can be used to display information. You can format the information in each cell much as you can in a word processor. This technique is used in the Hyperlinks cell in Figure 9.4. Here another table is inserted within a cell. The table shows its border with dashes, indicating that when displayed on the Web, the border will not be visible.

- **Graphics.** You can also insert graphics (in a variety of formats such as .gif and .jpg) into cells and adjust them to the size you want. Remember though, by adding the graphic, you must also include its graphics file in the same computer location as the html-coded document that calls for the graphic.

- **Hyperlinks.** Mrs. Harrison described three different types of hyperlinks in the Snapshot of a Class Investigation of Web Hypermedia. *Target* links are links within a single Web page. In Figure 9.4, the target hyperlink is set to link back to the top of the page. An *anchor* is identified at the top left corner of the page where the target link is to connect (<a href="#top">Top of page</a>). The *relative* hyperlink is defined to link to a page called MyClass.html (<a href="MyClass.html">My Class</a>). For this link to work, both Web pages (Introduction.html and MyClass.html) must be stored in the same location on the computer. Finally, the *absolute* hyperlink uses a complete Web address to this book's Website to find a Web page at a different Web server address (<a href = http://www.wiley.com/college/niess> Book Website </a>).

- **Interactive links.** Web pages can also be created to encourage interactions with the users. Web authors often provide a link for readers to send information, perhaps on problems that might happen in using the page or for more information about the page (< a href="mailto:GuidingAuthor@wiley.com" > Authors </a>).

Sometimes Web authors want to make files available to the users, providing links that download the files to the user. For example, when the authors of this book make the M&M spreadsheet data (from Chapter 6) available, the links are identified in a way similar to other links except that the file has the .xls designator for the type of file (<a href="M&M.xls">M&M Data</a>). The displayed <u>M&M Data</u> link means the file is stored along with the Web page and is available for downloading to the user's computer system. Of course, if users want to access the file, they must have the application that created it, in this case Excel.

Surely you have observed Web pages that support additional elements, including frames, sound, and animation. As you begin learning about Web authoring, though, you need to become comfortable with the nature of a Web page, incorporating just a few elements at a time. Mrs. Harrison began preparing her students to develop Web pages in the Snapshot of a Class Investigation of Web Hypermedia, warning them that there were some basics that they needed before beginning. She planned to scaffold her students' learning about Web pages as they developed them in response to specific subject matter lessons. As they gained expertise, she planned to help them investigate additional elements, much the same way that artists do in adding to their repertoire of design features.

Web Page Design Process   The process for designing and authoring Web pages is similar to that described for movies and presentations. Three phases (preproduction, production, and publication) are framed by the recognition of the potential for a worldwide audience and need for on-going maintenance.

Preproduction Phase In the preproduction phase you must consider both (1) content and (2) design of the Web presentation. Begin with a brainstorming session to consider key ideas for both areas. What information is to be presented? How should the information be communicated? Develop a preliminary outline of the content and ideas.

With this clarity, the storyboarding process is similar to that in the development of presentations and movies. Concept map software, such as Inspiration, provides a nice environment for designing hypermedia applications because of its nonlinear, weblike potential for presenting the ideas. In fact, Inspiration offers a Web page template specifically created for this activity (see Figure 9.5). The storyboard begins with the Home Page symbol, the top level of the website. The numbered boxes show the levels created. Each numbered page (signified by different colors in Figure 9.5) can be relabeled, additional links created as needed at each level, and unneeded links deleted. The Note Tool provides you a way to include notes describing the text on the page along with other Web elements to be included (graphics and sound, for example). Arrows connecting the boxes describe navigation intentions for the website. Double arrows suggest that each page links to the other. Single arrows indicate a link to the page with no return link.

While thinking about the presentation in this storyboard process, you should investigate other ideas for presentation on the Web page. Review a variety of Web pages, noting ideas that might be useful. Prepare for the general look of the website by making some initial decisions about your basic

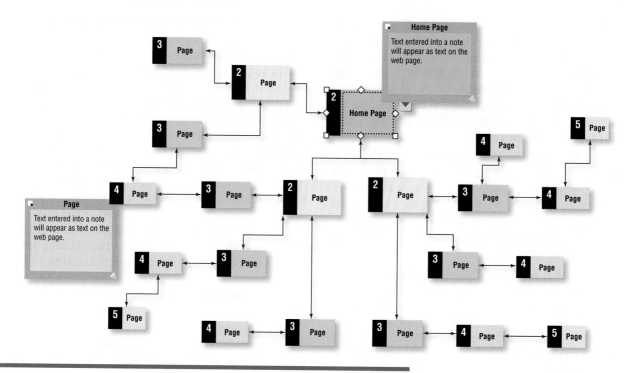

FIGURE 9.5 *Inspiration's;* Web page development template.

Source: Reprinted with permission form *Inspiration Templates (v. 7.5) (Planning Templates: Web Site Plan)* copyright© 2007 by Inspiration. All rights reserved.

plans for the site at this time: background, text font and color, design and placement of navigational buttons, visuals, graphics, and placement of text. The more research and decisions you make at this point, the easier the next phase becomes.

Production Phase The production phase is much easier with a detailed storyboard along with basic design decisions. This phase basically follows the plans. An important first step is to identify a folder on your computer to store the elements you want to incorporate. Working with a dedicated Web-authoring system allows you to create specific pages, place them in the same folder, and test them in a Web browser. If you begin by labeling the folder on your computer with a recognizable name for your Web creation and you store all of the files that are used to create the Web creation, when the site is ready to be transferred to the Web server, you simply move all of the folder contents to the appropriate Web address.

The next useful step in the production phase is to create a general template to be used for all the pages of the website. You might save this template as a file called template.html, establishing the background, fonts, and other basic elements. Another piece of information that is good to include on this template is text indicating the dates you worked on the file, such as Date last updated: <insert date>. This addition helps keep track of changes and updates in the files.

As you begin the home page, you use the template, but save it as index.html. Web browsers iden-

tify this filename as the starting point at a specific Web address. As you begin each page in your storyboard, you again begin with the template.html file, renaming it to identify the specific page you are currently creating. When you need to incorporate an element you have previously planned, such as a graphic, you have that element in your Web folder—since you planned ahead! All you need to do then is to create the link and then the element can be tested.

In some senses, developing Web pages is similar to developing presentation software as was described for PowerPoint presentations in Chapter 8. However, several important points are worth reiterating as you think about producing your Web pages.

- Maintain consistency throughout the pages with respect to the background, headings, colors, navigational buttons, and general format. Using the template.html idea helps you in this case.
- Too many media elements can distract from the message.
- Many times graphics and movies take a long time to load on the Web, so it is wise to keep the number of such elements to a minimum.
- Too much text on a page interferes with the communication of the message.
- Be sure to preview each page in various Web browsers as pages sometimes look differently depending on the particular browser.

Publication Phase Sometimes students are so anxious to see their work on the Web, they move the files to the Web server just to see them. This strategy is not recommended until the pages are completed and operating as expected in the local browser available through your Web-authoring package.

Once the pages and links work the way you want them to, it is time for publication for others to view. There are a number of free and for-pay services that host websites that you can access for publishing your work. You might also be able to use your school's computer resources.

Prior to making the actual transfer, think about how Web pages get on the Web. Some students understand what a Web server is, others need an explanation. The focus should be on how files on the Web-author's computer make it to the Web server. You will transfer or move files from your computer to a computer that could be in a nearby building or possibly hundreds or thousands of miles away. If you have maintained all the files in the same folder on your computer, this process is easy to complete.

The transfer involves the use of an Internet protocol called *file transfer protocol* (FTP). Typically the actual steps to transfer a file are simple, but may include proprietary steps that are dependent on specific software programs. Regardless of the software, the following general steps are almost always involved.

1. Create the file or files you wish to transfer, storing them in the same folder. In some cases you may have subfolders that contain elements and other files that are needed for your Web page.

2. Initiate a software program that uses FTP. The program might actually operate in a Web-based environment.

3. When prompted, select the file or files on your local computer. In the case of the Web production, the files should all be available in that one folder you have used up to this point.

4. Select the folder on the remote computer where you want to transfer the entire contents of the folder.

5. Perform the file transfer.

Note that in steps 3 and 4 students need to work within a hierarchical file structure using folders and subfolders, making sure that the file structure in your primary folder is the same on the Web.

Although the title of maintenance might seem strange, it is an important activity in the publication phase of Web pages. Certainly, as soon as the files are transferred, you need to test the results. If the files have been created using the process described, they are likely to work as they were intended. At this point, however, you need to have someone unfamiliar with the site review it. Others are not familiar with the thinking that you used in the design.

They may be confused by the design or have ideas for easier navigation. If you decide a change needs to be made, you need to make the changes on your local computer and then upload the new Web files using the same FTP process you originally used.

There is much more, however, to maintaining a quality website. This point is important. Quality websites need to undergo regular updates. Review your website, considering the last date the files were updated. Make changes to keep them current. Be sure to make the appropriate changes in the displayed date on your website. Remember that unless you specifically remove the files (using the FTP process), they will remain for everyone to access and use, regardless of the number of years that have lapsed since you last updated them. Thus, the Last date updated: <insert date> information on the page helps to ensure viewers of the currency of the information.

Learning with and about Hypermedia and Web Authoring

The twenty-first century is a new century, one where information and communications technologies direct the activities of productive citizens. Students must become literate in this new environment. In recognition of the importance of such technologies, the Partnership for 21st Century Skills, a collaborative effort of leading content area education organizations and the National Education Association, highlights the critical intersection between learning the technology skills and learning in core academic subject areas through the development of Literacy Maps for geography, mathematics, and English. These maps describe skills, tools, and sample student outcomes to assist educators in developing lesson plans that incorporate learning skills critical for success with twenty-first-century tools. Three broad categories provide the framework for a reevaluation of education in these various academic subject areas:

- Information, communication, and media literacy;
- Thinking and problem solving;
- Interpersonal and self-directional skills.

Technology Link 9.1 provides links to sample literacy maps to assist you in incorporating these skills in your curriculum and instruction, in particular with respect to the tools and student outcomes envisioned in this partnership. Although the tools described include books, newspapers, spreadsheets, and databases, multimedia resources are thoughtfully integrated. Hypermedia tools are considered

Technology Link 9.1

*T*he **ICT** link connects you with the Information and Communication Technology (ICT) Literacy Maps (use the Publications link) for geography, mathematics, English, and science, with additional reports and publications created by the Partnership for 21st Century Skills.

www.wiley.com/college/niess

essential in the development of information and communications technology literacy, indicating that students need experiences in a variety of subject areas for learning. Students need to be able to access, process, manage, create, evaluate, and analyze information with hypermedia tools. In essence, these information and communications technology literacy recommendations challenge teachers to include experiences that guide students in learning Web authoring along with learning in the variety of subject areas.

Basic Concepts of Communicating with Hypermedia and Web Authoring

A literate person is considered to be one who can read and write. Within the framework of the twenty-first century, reading and writing can be thought of as the ability to locate, access, analyze, evaluate, manipulate, and communicate information effectively in a variety of media formats. Hypermedia and Web authoring are integral to the development of media literacy because they direct attention toward a consideration of nonsequential reading and writing.

You have probably heard or even experienced being *lost in cyberspace*. With reader choice in the direction of displaying and reading the ideas, the pathways for traversing a hyperlinked message can look like a child's scribble. Students must be taught to both read and write in this nonsequential manner in order to participate in a society that relies heavily on this form of communication.

Hypermedia and Web-Authoring Instructional Idea: Reading Nonsequential Communications Reading multimedia communications requires skill in understanding and managing information different from the skills in reading a novel. Novels are written in a way that develops a story gradually, building the characters and ideas to a climax. The author's intent is that the reader follows the material sequentially, gathering key points in the process. The development process is a key to the theme or message of the novel.

With hypermedia, direction for the reading is placed in the hands of the reader. Hyperlinks offer readers opportunities to adjust the delivery of the information, to wander and gather additional information in the reading process. Thus, besides reading sequential documents, readers in the twenty-first century need to learn skills for exploring ideas and navigating nonsequential text or for following a set of cues in nonlinear ways.

In the Classroom 9.1 is an activity to guide your students in exploring the differences in thinking in linear versus nonlinear narratives. The activity engages students in reading a poem created by Shel Silverstein (1974) where someone keeps asking, "What's in the sack?" To prepare for this activity, you might create a Web page similar to that shown in Figure 9.6. Link the words in the poem to websites that might have interest for your students. You

---

What's in the Sack?

By: Shel Silverstein

What's in the sack? What's in the sack?
Is it some <u>mushrooms</u> or is it the <u>moon</u>?
Is it <u>love letters</u> or <u>downy goosefeathers</u>?
Or maybe the world's most enormous <u>balloon</u>?

What's in the sack? That's all they ask me.
Could it be <u>popcorn</u> or <u>marbles</u> or <u>books</u>?
Is it two years' worth of your dirty <u>laundry</u>,
Or the biggest ol' <u>meatball</u> that's ever been-cooked?

Does anyone ask me, "Hey, when is your <u>birthday</u>?"

"Can you play <u>Monopoly</u>?" "Do you like beans?"
"What is the capital of <u>Yugoslavia</u>?"
Or "Who <u>embroidered</u> that <u>rose</u> on your <u>jeans</u>?"
No, what's in the sack? That's all they care about.
Is it a <u>rock</u> or a rolled up <u>giraffe</u>?
Is it <u>pickles</u> or <u>nickels</u> or <u>busted bicycles</u>?
And if we guess it, will you give us half?
Do they ask where I've been, or how long I'll be stayin',
Where I'll be going, or when I'll be back,
Or "How do?" or "What's new?" or "Hey why are you blue?"
No, all they keep asking is, "What's in the sack?"
"What's in the sack?" I'm blowin my stack
At the next one who asks me, "What's in the sack?"
What?
Oh no. Not you too!

FIGURE 9.6   Web presentation of Shel Silverstein's poem "What's in the Sack?"

In the Classroom 9.1

WHAT'S IN THE SACK?

TECHNOLOGY OBJECTIVE: **NETS · S I, IV**

- **Hypermedia and Web authoring:** Technology as a communications tool while building understanding of basic concepts of Web technology.
- Comparing communication via Web-based reading with traditional, sequential reading.

CONTENT OBJECTIVE: **Language arts:** Compare students' reading skills used in reading a sequential, linear document with their skills used in reading a hyperlinked document, navigating a nonlinear text to access relevant information or to follow the sequence cues in nonlinear documents.

GRADE LEVEL: 3–5

THE POEM: What can possibly be in Shel Silverstein's sack?

What's in the sack?
by Shel Siverstein
What's in the sack? What's in the sack?
Is it some mushrooms or is it the moon?
Is it love letters or downy goosefeathers?
Or maybe the world's most enormous balloon?

What's in the sack? That's all they ask me.
Could it be popcorn or marbles or books?
Is it two years' worth of your dirty laundry,
Or the biggest ol' meatball that's ever been cooked?

Does anyone ask me, "Hey when is your birthday?"
"Can you play Monopoly?" "Do you like beans?"
"What is the capital of Yugoslavia?"
Or "Who embroidered that rose on your jeans?"

No, what's in the sack? That's all they care about.
Is it a rock or a rolled-up giraffe?
Is it pickles or nickels or busted bicycles?
And if we guess it, will you give us half?

Do they ask where I've been, or how long I'll be stayin',
Where I'll be going, or when I'll be back,
Or "How do?" or "What's new?" or "Hey why are you blue?"
No, all they keep asking is, "What's in the sack?"
What's in the sack? I'm blowin' my stack
At the next one who asks me, "What's in the sack?"
What?
On no. Not you too!

PROBLEM: How does the message change if a poem is read in a printed version versus a hyperlinked version?

- ❏ Divide the class into two groups. One group reads the version of the poem as printed on paper and the other reads the hyperlinked version (see Figure 9.6).
- ❏ Goal: Students are to describe the contents of the sack. Set a time limit for reading the poem. After reading the poem, each student must describe in writing the contents of the sack.
- ❏ Comparison: Ask students to share the contents of the sack items and why they decided on those items. How does reading in the nonsequential Web form differ from reading in the sequential paper format?
- ❏ Discussion: Writing in sequential versus nonsequential formats.
  - What are the advantages of writing in each format?
  - For what type of writing is sequential writing preferred?
  - For what type of writing is nonsequential writing preferred?

might even have the words linked to ideas they have previously studied.

Divide the class into two groups. One group reads the poem as Shel Silverstein wrote it—sequentially; the other reads it on the Web page like Figure 9.6. The goal is for the students to identify what they think might be in the sack, given what they read. Set a time limit for the reading. On the Web, the students choose which of the links they will visit given the time available. This time limit for the exploration is set in order to focus the students on the goal, namely, to describe the contents of the sack.

After reading and recording their descriptions of the contents, ask them to describe the items they identified as being in the sack and why they decided on those items. The discussion reveals how students are guided by the presentation of the poem. Those who read the poem sequentially probably rely on their individual personal experiences, while those who read the poem on the Web are likely to be guided by their explorations of the links. Some students might actually select a link, view the contents, and return to the poem to determine the next item. Others might visit some links and be attracted by the new set of links. This activity provides an opportunity to discuss the format of the presentation for communicating an idea. You can also discuss the navigation skills needed with materials presented in the nonsequential form provided by the Web.

Although In the Classroom 9.1 is focused on reading poetry, students struggle with reading a variety of written, sequential documents and these struggles likely interfere with reading hyperlinked, nonsequential documents. Teaching reading is a responsibility for every teacher. Harris, White, and Fisher (2003) discuss readers from the standpoint of dependence versus independence. Independent readers are able to make causal connections and inferences as they work through a text. Dependent readers are halted by the text and must ask for help in reading. Yet, Harris et al. identify specific strategies for guiding dependent readers in developing their reading skills, such as "grouping dependent and independent readers together to work on learning activities" (p. 41).

Consideration of the type of reading when grouping students for In the Classroom 9.1 is important. As noted in the Partnership for 21st Century Skills (2004), some changes in teaching reading require that teachers need to scaffold learning activities that guide students in:

- learning to skim online materials;
- comparing reading skills used in reading a variety of both sequential and nonsequential literature forms;
- describing their processes for reading a website containing a variety of embedded links;
- navigating nonlinear texts to access information or follow sequence cues in nonlinear narratives;
- reading and understanding the organizational effects of various forms of writing;
- analyzing messages presented by various media elements considering their truthfulness and ability to persuade or mislead a reader.

Hypermedia and Web-Authoring Instructional Ideas: Written Communication in Nonsequential Forms   Although students need to learn to write sequential forms of information, they also need to learn to write nonsequential forms of communication. Reading nonsequential information does provide some assistance in learning to write in this form. But students need specific activities where they develop expertise in communicating through hyperlinks.

You can integrate activities designed to help students understand basic concepts of writing nonsequential, hyperlinked communication and learning within the subject area. Ideas such as these can be used to guide students as they learn to create hyperlinks and communicate in writing on the Web:

- Create a story that uses links to pictures or additional information to enhance the description in the story.
- Beginning with a famous quote, such as, "Ask not what your country can do for you, but what you can do for your country," students create a Web-based hyperlinked response to the challenge—What can you do for your country? Text, images, video, and even audio links should be used to enhance the communication in their responses.
- Describe the water cycle, highlighting physical changes throughout the cycle with hyperlinks at each point in the cycle. Use a variety of media elements to enhance the description.
- Develop a graph to describe the length of a person's hair over time. Use links at various points to describe the activity that explains why the length of the hair changed at those points in time.
- Create a mystery with clues to engage the reader in solving the mystery. Allow the reader to determine the presentation order of the clues by using hyperlinks for obtaining the information.
- Pick a topic that was recently studied in a particular content area. Develop a Web page with responses to "Frequently Asked Questions" about the topic, using hyperlinks from each question to responses to the question. For example, the topic might be fractions (adding, subtracting, multiplying, and dividing). Questions might include "Why do you find a common denominator to add and subtract and not when you multiply and divide fractions?" and "Why do you invert and multiply when you divide fractions?"

Social, Ethical, and Human Issues

Anyone can put anything on the Web! Monitoring of Web information is left to the reader. This notion is frightening considering that children use the Web to gather information.

Hypermedia and Web-Authoring Instructional Idea: Freedom of Speech on the Web   The First Amendment to the Constitution of the United States specifically states,

> Congress shall make no law respecting an establishment of religion, or prohibiting the free exercise thereof; or abridging the freedom of speech, or of the press. . .

The Web is all about reading and writing for the purpose of informing and displaying ideas. People are able to place information on the Web based on their personal perspectives, whether or not those perspectives are supported by truth. Some say that the Web is an avenue where the truth will naturally surface, just as intended by the freedom of speech amendment. Others argue that the presentation of false statements can be harmful. The ability to place information anonymously, while allowing speech without fear, also protects the authors from any defamation lawsuit. In essence the ability to be anonymous may in fact discourage truth by removing accountability.

In the Classroom 9.2 is designed specifically for students to consider the issue of freedom of speech with respect to the Web. In this interdisciplinary activity, the students are both authors of website information and responsible for gathering information from the website readers with respect to the perspectives presented on the issue of whether to regulate the content on the Web. The challenge for the students is to separate the opinions they expressed in their presentations from the data they collect and analyze. They have freedom to develop the arguments for and against the control of the content on the Web. Yet, they are required to analyze data through the online survey that may or may not generate accurate information. Also, they are challenged to investigate the question of the use of Web technology for enhancing the collection of data and how the results of the inquiry vary as a result of different types of investigations for gathering public opinion. Ultimately, they are challenged to consider whether Web content should be controlled.

Hypermedia and Web-Authoring Instructional Idea: Challenge the Source   In general, people seem to rely on the information on the Web as a credible source. Does this reliance make sense? Students need to be taught to ask important questions about the sources they use from the Internet, including the Web. Experiences that require students to question the credibility of their resources are essential with respect to the use of Web resources as supporting evidence. Be proactive by specifically guiding your students to question the credibility of resources they identify on the Web.

- Pick a current topic about which you can find information in a variety of resources, including television reports, newspapers, journals, magazines, and websites. Instruct your students to compare and contrast the information they find in the various sources for details, authenticity, and voice. Which resource provides the most credible information? What is there about the resource that encourages trust in the information?
- Pick a debatable topic and have your students conduct Web searches on the topic. Compare and contrast the information for details, authenticity, and voice. Share the information from different sources and identify features of websites that support the credibility of the information.

Hypermedia and Web Authoring as a Productivity Tool

Hypermedia and Web authoring provide students with a variety of tools to enhance their educational experiences, offering them opportunities to share information as well as collaborate with students outside their own classroom. Students can design Web pages describing their environment, providing information not typically available in other venues. Web authors can even provide links to challenge readers to send data for inclusion in future analyses. In essence, students can use Web authoring as a tool to gather data and develop an analysis based on the most current information. Thus, both hypermedia and Web-authoring tools have the capability to enhance learning, increase productivity, and promote creativity.

Hypermedia and Web-Authoring Instructional Idea: Gathering Data and Updating the Analysis   Weather data are usually obtained from the radio, television, or newspapers for the nearest weather station. Often the data are not precise for locations more than 20 miles away. Students can gather their own data and display the information as a service to others in their local area. In the process they can be involved in cumulating average highs and lows along with providing other descriptive weather information, such as cloud conditions, precipitation, and wind information, along with a visual description of the day. Ultimately, they can compare their data with

In the Classroom 9.2

FREEDOM OF SPEECH AND THE WEB?

TECHNOLOGY OBJECTIVE: **NETS · S I, II, III**

- **Hypermedia and Web authoring:** Consider the ethical, cultural, and societal perspectives displayed by Web presentations in presenting evidence while building understanding of communicating through Web presentations.
- Engage in processes that help in the design and development of Web presentations.

CONTENT OBJECTIVE: **Language arts:** Evaluate the accuracy, relevance, appropriateness, comprehensiveness, and bias of electronic information sources.

Social studies: Analyze the influence of diverse forms of public opinion on the development of public policy and decision making.

Science: Scientific inquiry and using technology to enhance the gathering of data for an investigation. Challenge investigation procedures with respect to guidelines for scientific investigations.

GRADE LEVEL: 5–9

ISSUE: Should content be approved before it is made public on the Web?

- ❑ **Present the Issue:** Challenge students with the issue in question, engaging them in a discussion of various perspectives in response to the question. Divide the class into groups according to the different perspectives on this issue.
- ❑ **Task 1:** Design a Web presentation with the intent of convincing readers about your specific perspective on the issue.
- ❑ **Interactive Website Development:**
  - Develop a homepage for the class website that considers the issue of control of content for the Web and includes hyperlinks to each group's presentation.
  - Develop a form for an online survey to be used for gathering the readers' perspectives on the issue based on their reading of the various presentations provided by the links. The class must consider whether they will accept anonymous responses, whether they want some background information about the respondents in analyzing the information gathered, and, if so, what information they want.
  - Provide a link on the homepage that invites readers to respond to the online survey, sending the information to the class e-mail.
- ❑ **Task 2:** As a group, summarize the results of the online survey and provide a group response to these questions.
  - Based on the results, what are the most persuasive arguments?
  - Can the results of the online survey be trusted? Why or why not? If not, how can more trustworthy information be gathered?
  - How did each group's website presentation affect how you looked at the data?
  - Was the online survey a scientific investigation?
- ❑ **Discussion:** Have the class discuss the issue and the opinions from readers of the Web.
  - Which perspective is the most persuasive and why, based on the results gathered from the online survey?
  - Does the Web promote communication of truth?
  - What are the responsibilities of and challenges for users of Web information if the content is not approved?
  - What are the responsibilities of and challenges for the users of Web information if the content is approved?
  - Will regulation solve the issue?

that provided in the other resources as they investigate specific geographic impacts on weather.

In the Classroom 9.3 describes a classroom project where the entire class is involved in developing a weather description for the month of October for their town. This weather activity requires that they create and produce a Web page (see Figure 9.7a) where specific students are assigned to collect data for individual days, collecting a variety of weather information and including a photo to capture the nature of the day. They are also required to daily recalculate a new average for the month. Finally, at the end of the month, the students must enter the data for the high and low for the entire month, depict the change of the temperature in a spreadsheet graph, and finally insert the updated graph in their monthly calendar Web page (see Figure 9.7a).

In the Classroom 9.3

HOW DOES THE WEATHER VARY IN OUR TOWN?

TECHNOLOGY OBJECTIVE: NETS·S I, III, IV

- **Hypermedia and Web authoring:** Technology as a communications and productivity tool while building understanding of basic concepts of Web technology.
- **Web authoring and spreadsheets:** Integrating, creating, and managing Web information; creating a spreadsheet graphical presentation.

CONTENT OBJECTIVE Science: Investigate weather patterns for specific geographic locations.

Mathematics: Calculate averages for data sets and present data in graphical form in a spreadsheet.

GRADE LEVEL: 5–9

CHALLENGE: Describe the weather in our town for the month of October by creating and maintaining a monthly Web calendar.

- ❏ **Data Collection Tasks**
  - **Daily weather information:** Collect high and low temperatures for each day; provide descriptive information about cloudiness, precipitation, and windiness; obtain a digital picture and write a description of the weather to provide both a visual and textual description of the weather for the day.
  - **Cumulative weather information:** Update the cumulative high and low temperature for the month; at the end of the month, create a graph using the spreadsheet to visually display the changes in high and low temperatures over the month.
- ❏ **Web Tasks**
  - Create and maintain the front page for the weather site including inserting the data in the spreadsheet to update the spreadsheet graph at the end of the month (see Figure 9.7a).
  - Create a daily Web page template (see general idea in Figure 9.7b).
  - Create daily Web pages using the template and creating the appropriate link from the homepage calendar (see link 1 in Figure 9.7a).

The project is a class project with daily expectations and specifically assigned tasks. Over the month, every student needs to be involved with each of the different tasks so that all students have opportunities to collect data and obtain digital pictures, write text information, and work with Web authoring. Assigning tasks and maintaining a calendar of assignments supports project management and communication. Students might be grouped in pairs where the roles alternate between leader and support responsibilities. Requiring partners to maintain a daily journal record of their activities and what they are learning is useful for overseeing the progress of the students and the project.

Hypermedia and Web-Authoring Instructional Idea: Electronic Portfolio Communication The weather Web project can be thought of as an introduction to a yearlong project that students might pursue as a means of continuing to develop their skills with communications and information technologies. Electronic portfolios also provide an on-going activity that can be used to help students learn Web-authoring skills while they are also focused on learning in the content areas.

In the Classroom 9.4 describes a general outline for guiding students in the development of an electronic portfolio, where the students in collaboration with the teacher determine the format and the potential exhibits. Obviously, students working on this project gain additional experiences in developing Web pages, gaining more proficiency with the Web page design process.

Electronic portfolios are selective and purposeful collections of student work available on the Web describing the history of the author's learning. In this example, the electronic portfolio is framed by the National Educational Technology Standards for Students (NETS·S) (ISTE, 2000) described in Chapter 4. Students must think about their work in the various content areas within the framework of their development of expertise with the technology standards: basic operations and concepts; social, ethical, and human issues; technology as a productivity tool; technology as a communications tool; technology as a research tool; and technology as a problem-solving and decision-making tool.

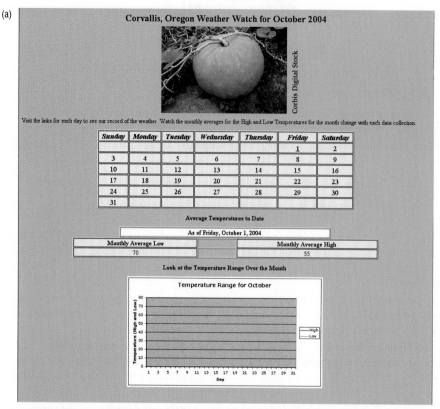

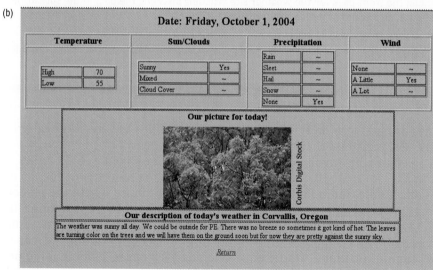

FIGURE 9.7   (*a*) Homepage for weather Web research presentation. (*b*) Weather description for October 1.

In the preparation of the portfolios, the authors need to consider the primary audience. In this case, the students are preparing the electronic portfolio as their primary exhibit in student–parent–teacher conferences to demonstrate their growth with the technology student standards. Electronic portfolios can and should include a variety of links that incorporate text, graphics, video, and sound, extending beyond traditional paper portfolios. With this specific electronic portfolio, this type of presentation provides additional evidence of their work in meeting the student standards. Thus, on completion, the students will be able to describe their work from a variety of perspectives provided by various element capabilities—the subject matter content they learned in the exhibits and their growth in using a variety of media elements to communicate.

An important feature of a portfolio is the set of exhibits that display or showcase the student's work. Reflective pieces encourage them to carefully consider

In the Classroom 9.4

WHAT HAVE I LEARNED?

TECHNOLOGY OBJECTIVE: **NETS · S I, II, III, IV, V, VI**

- **Hypermedia and Web authoring:** Technology as a learning tool while building understanding of basic concepts of Web technology and social, ethical, and legal considerations for Web presentations.
- Integrating, creating, and managing Web information.
- Meeting the NETS · S guidelines.

CONTENT OBJECTIVE: **All subject areas:** Displaying learning outcomes across the content areas.

GRADE LEVEL: 3–12

PROJECT: Create an electronic portfolio displaying up-to-date exhibits across the content areas that display your growth with NETS · S guidelines (ISTE, 2000).

❏ **Preproduction Phase:** Clarify (1) the content and (2) the design of the Web presentation.
  - Brainstorm in small groups ways to present the exhibits around the NETS · S guidelines.
  - Create a storyboard that outlines the basic format for the portfolio.
  - Make basic design decisions.
  - Identify potential exhibits from a variety of content areas.

❏ **Production Phase:** Follow the plan!
  - Set up a template for basic pages in the website, considering background, colors, identification and orientation of graphics, borders, links, and buttons. Be sure to include a date stamp.
  - Save the template and accompanying files in a folder for designing the portfolio.
  - Gather the exhibits in the folder for the portfolio.
  - Create the individual pages of the portfolio, following the directions in the storyboard.
  - Test all files and links.

❏ **Publication Phase:** Test, assess, and manage the website.
  - Before transferring the files to the Web:
    - Have a friend or peer review the website, providing you feedback about the quality of the communication.
    - Have an adult review the website to assure that the presentation meets the social, ethical, and legal standards for Web communications.
    - Have a class discussion about the challenges in presenting such information on the Web for worldwide viewing.
  - Transfer the files to the Web, testing, reviewing, and refining the contents.
  - Maintain the website, updating the elements at least with each grading quarter as the year progresses.
  - Lead the student–parent–teacher conference by presenting the portfolio as a demonstration of your growth over the previous period. Set goals for future work and presentation in the electronic portfolio.

the work that they have created, to evaluate their own work, to consider what they learned as they were creating it, and to establish goals for their future efforts. For this reason, reflective pieces of each of the exhibits should be encouraged in the electronic portfolio. Culminating reflections are also important for engaging students in thinking about what they have learned by the creation of the collection of the exhibits as well as what they learned while designing, developing, and maintaining the electronic portfolio.

Electronic portfolios provide advantages over other forms for describing student's development over a period of time:

- Efficient storage and display of multiple media exhibits, for example, audio of a student reading, video of a student solving a problem, animation of the design of a model along with writings in various formats.
- Ease in periodic upgrading showing progress over the school year or even throughout their school years.
- Dynamic nature of Web pages allowing for cross-referencing student work, linking activities in one content area with those in another content area.
- Ease of access for students, parents, teachers, and others.

Of course, in addition to those advantages, students need time to work on developing the portfolio.

Teachers need to encourage the students to continually evaluate the quality of their work in various content areas, to save various artifacts for consideration, and to review the previously saved work. This process can lead to the development of the reflective pieces. Ultimately, teachers need to provide an expectation and classroom organization for this process.

Finally, before publishing the portfolio on the Web, review of the presentation is essential. Certainly students can review for each other. However, adults should also review the work to assure that the social, ethical, and legal issues are considered. A class discussion of changes that are made to meet appropriate concerns helps students in developing their understanding of the challenges in presenting portfolios on the Web for the whole world to view.

Although this activity is one where the teacher guides students in developing electronic portfolios, as a preservice teacher you should also consider developing an electronic portfolio to describe your professional development in becoming a teacher who is able to guide students' learning with technology. You might even use the teacher standards (NETS·T) to frame your portfolio (ISTE, 2002). With the availability of the portfolio on the Web, as you search for a teaching position, you can direct principals to review your online portfolio that demonstrates your abilities for teaching both with and about technology.

Hypermedia and Web Authoring as a Communications Tool

The advent of the Web has introduced new forms of communication of ideas and information. Moreover, these new forms are shifting what and how students develop skills in both reading and writing while they also learn to communicate and create information in a variety of forms and media. Although the discipline of language arts is probably considered to bear the primary impact of these new forms of communication, learning and communicating in other disciplines is also affected.

History has traditionally been passed from generation to generation through stories, originally verbal and then followed by written narratives describing the past. In the last 35 years, new ways of representing historical knowledge have emerged as alternatives. For historians the impulse to write in narrative form is understandable. As a way for simplifying the complex and connecting cause with effect, narratives have immense value. A narrative's linearity, with its beginning, middle, and end, provides the meaningful chronology essential in the depiction of history and its impact.

Narrative representations, such as that described in most textbooks, rely on the written word. One notable exception is the Bayeux Tapestry, a narration communicated through embroidered, pictorial descriptions of events leading up to and including the Battle of Hastings in 1066. Recent technological advancements in hypermedia relating to visual presentation and representation have enabled a new consideration of how to visually represent a narrative past. Today, increasing numbers of scholars are developing visual representations of historical knowledge that communicate their historical analysis and interpretation.

Hypermedia and Web-Authoring Instructional Idea: Storytelling and Visual Historical Representation Computer technology is well suited for enhancing visual representations of the past. In fact, some scholars, such as David Staley (2002), have suggested that students might better understand history through the visualization process. Imagine that you are the teacher who wants to design a new way of helping students understand history through this process. Consider these efforts of a high school social studies teacher named Tom as he develops a visual narrative on race relations and social interactions in the American South. He wants to challenge his students in a different way, a way that challenges their personal perspectives about race relations in the American South and the advancements made during the period from 1930 to 1970. Rather than having them read various written narratives, he wants to expose them to actual digital images taken during the period, allowing those images to communicate activity to help students begin to describe the growth during that time. Tom's plan is to select a small number of digital images available from a large collection of 35,000 images taken in Atlanta during this crucial period in race relations in the South. The selection of the images is crucial because they need to challenge as well as guide students in their investigations of the history of this period.

Tom's first step is to select the images he might consider for this display. The cataloging methods that are used for archiving the collection are not particularly suitable for helping Tom identify those images he considers most useful. So, Tom must manually sort through various Web pages of archival citations. The process is extraordinarily tedious. Moreover, with so many images he needs a focus and a context for the images. Without that focus, he is unable to make purposeful selections of images.

The key for the design of the visual narrative is that Tom has a good understanding of the subject matter reflected in the collection and is able to use that knowledge for making decisions about which images are significant. After numerous passes through the collection catalogue, Tom settles on a focus inspired by his subject matter knowledge.

Tom recently learned about a promotional campaign launched by leaders in Atlanta's civic, business, and government communities in the first half of the twentieth century. Forward Atlanta was a campaign financed by the city of Atlanta for the purpose of courting northern business and investment to Atlanta. The campaign had multiple iterations beginning in 1928, continuing through the 1960s and to some extent even today. The most lasting legacy of the campaign, though, was a slogan for Atlanta emerging in the 1960s and defining Atlanta for at least a generation: "The City Too Busy to Hate."

The campaign, called Forward Atlanta, provides the context for Tom to tell a story using images. With a context, Tom is able to purposefully immerse himself into the task of deepening his understanding of the Forward Atlanta campaign so that he is better positioned to select images. He wants to use the images to create a context for exploring what it meant for a city to say that it was *too busy to hate*. With what Tom believes to be a clear understanding of the purpose of the Forward Atlanta campaign in mind, he proceeds to select images from the collections for inclusion in his presentation of the story.

Another important skill guiding Tom in developing this visual narrative is his understanding of a pedagogical structure and focus that requires students to design research projects that address the truth or fiction in the claims of the Forward Atlanta campaign. Tom views the students' work with the images as a starting place for inquiry. He wants to use the narrative to disorient students. And he feels that if the visual storyline causes some disruption or does something unexpected, his students would be compelled to work toward some resolution. Tom believes this student work might serve as a starting point for a generalized study of topics in local or U.S. history. He thinks of the pictures as speaking for themselves. With this pedagogical rationale, he works to find particularly powerful images.

With this subject matter understanding and pedagogical intent, Tom produces a visual narrative focusing on the issue of race or social progress in Atlanta. The final visual narrative consists of 10 photos that Tom hopes will generate an empathetic experience for his students. Walter Werner (2002) describes these empathetic experiences potentially generated by visual narrative as times when a "reader imaginatively enters into another's experience" (p. 411). Tom's goal is to, at minimum, generate some empathy for African-Americans in Atlanta during the period between 1930 and 1970.

The completed visual narrative Tom produces has no chronological structure. It centers on a dramatic twist unveiled with the last two images. This twist causes a disruption in the narrative flow and is directed at engaging students' empathic sense.

The first eight images in the visual narrative tell a positive and progressive story of how Atlanta's commercial community was able to benefit from an eager and productive workforce that was highly educated and supported by progressive politics. Tom also includes images that suggest Atlanta had some emerging regional or national cultural status. These eight images collectively suggest that the goals of the Forward Atlanta campaign as expressed with regard to social progress were achieved. The last two images shift the story and inject a sense of drama into the consideration of the success of Forward Atlanta. The first of these last two images shows a group of African-Americans attempting to register to vote. The second is a disquieting picture of a man in a Klu Klux Klan outfit handing a flyer to a passerby on an Atlanta street. Obviously, Tom is inferring that the city may not be *too busy to hate*.

Tom's disruptive visual narrative is reflective of just one way to construct visual narratives. There are at least three additional ways to represent narrative in visual form, including chronological, topical, and spatial. Tom's visual work as a disruptive narrative holds the most promise with regard to encouraging empathetic responses from students. The other three forms of visual narrative are less likely to produce meaningful student inquiry. In essence, though, the keys to the development of an educational experience that effectively communicates with and engages his students are his knowledge of the subject matter intertwined with his knowledge of teaching and learning and his work with digital images as technology communications tools.

As students are engaged in learning through storytelling with visual images, they too learn to identify, design, and develop similar visual narratives in creative ways that communicate their developing knowledge. As a beginning, though, teachers might guide them by providing educational experiences in which they are able to learn with visual narratives. These experiences must not be limited to history.

Storytelling experiences can be used in many subject areas with just a little imagination and by accessing images from the many online digital libraries. Students can be engaged in collecting images from sources such as those available in Technology Link 9.2. They must focus on and identify a context for the communication that they are planning with

Technology Link 9.2

The **Digital Libraries** link connects you with a variety of online digital libraries for exploration of topics in various subject areas.

www.wiley.com/college/niess

the digital images. After working through much the same process as Tom did, they can present their thesis through Web pages where the images are hyperlinked to more detail for telling the story.

Some possible subject area opportunities for designing online visual narratives might challenge students in the exploration of topics such as the following:

- Biology: Examine the causes, consequences, and potential solutions to the loss of biological diversity in rain forests, coral reefs, and wetlands.
- Astronomy: Describe the story of the development of astronomical observations, comparing the nineteenth-century depictions of outer space with the images now created by NASA.
- Geography: Describe the story of the evolution of mapping the American West from an imagined to a defined territory.
- Mathematics: Explore both symmetry and symmetry-breaking with repetitive patterns used in impressionist works of art.
- Mathematics: Explore ancient African mathematics that steered Africans' discovery of the concept of zero.

Hypermedia and Web Authoring as a Research Tool

Research skills typically include problem identification, observation, inference, hypothesis testing, and analysis. Perhaps the most important part of a research project is communicating the entire experience—the procedures, results, reflections on the results, and the conclusions drawn from the experience. Web authoring provides a unique environment for describing and reporting research results while jointly providing the opportunity for students to build their skills with technology research tools.

Hypermedia and Web-Authoring Instructional Idea: Reporting Research Results The major purpose for including laboratory work in science classrooms is to guide students in developing the ability to use one or more scientific process skills. Central to the development of these skills is the communication of the activity, carefully describing the procedures, results, and conclusions. In the Classroom 9.5 describes one way to challenge students to describe their research using a Web presentation. Figure 9.8*a* suggests a main menu for the entire research process that begins with a proposal, maintains reports of the progress in the research, and finally ends with a research report. Figure 9.8*b* shows a menu containing the links for the key parts in communicating the final report: introduction, problem, materials, procedures, results, conclusions, and applications. In this example, students maintain a laboratory notebook using the Research Progress link. As students are working on the research project, others, including the teacher, are able to review the progress and perhaps offer feedback about the communications as well as the activities conducted during the research.

Although this research project is framed for a science class, the process is a general form of inquiry that can be applied to multiple subject areas as students research specific problems. This format is also useful for research that you, as a beginning

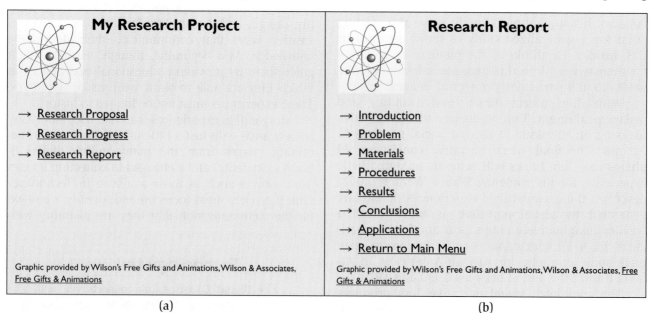

My Research Project	**Research Report**
→ Research Proposal	→ Introduction
→ Research Progress	→ Problem
→ Research Report	→ Materials
	→ Procedures
	→ Results
	→ Conclusions
	→ Applications
	→ Return to Main Menu
Graphic provided by Wilson's Free Gifts and Animations, Wilson & Associates, Free Gifts & Animations	Graphic provided by Wilson's Free Gifts and Animations, Wilson & Associates, Free Gifts & Animations
(a)	(b)

FIGURE 9.8 (*a*) Main menu for research Web page. (*b*) Menu for the final research report, linked from the main menu.

In the Classroom 9.5

A RESEARCH INVESTIGATION

TECHNOLOGY OBJECTIVE: **NETS · S I, II, III, IV, V**

- **Hypermedia and Web authoring:** Technology as a communications and research tool while building understanding of basic concepts of Web technology.
- Integrating, creating, and managing Web information.
- Investigating the use of technology tools to report results of research projects.

CONTENT OBJECTIVE: **Science:** Understanding scientific inquiry, particularly with respect to making results of investigations public, describing the investigation in ways that enable others to repeat the investigation.

GRADE LEVEL: 6–12

PROJECT: Using the Web as a science laboratory notebook.

- ❏ **Design.** Design the Web research communication for the entire research activity: proposal, progress, and report. Figures 9.8*a* and 9.8**b** provide a sample for this organization.
- ❏ **Research Proposal.** An important part of the research is deciding what to study and choosing which data to collect along with how and when it should be collected. Prepare a proposal that provides convincing detail that the study is worthwhile and can be conducted in the prescribed amount of time.
  - Present the proposal in a Web page linked to the main page (as in Figure 9.8*a*) for the Web presentation.
  - Offer Web readers opportunities to comment on the proposal via e-mail to the Web author.
- ❏ **Research Progress.** An essential part of research is the maintenance of accurate records of the procedures. Scientists typically keep a laboratory notebook. In this experience, students maintain this notebook on the Web for all to view the daily progress of the research as well as the researchers developing ideas about the data collected to date.
  - Maintain a daily description of the activities in the research along with materials used in the activities.
  - Prepare a daily reflection on the progress of the research and the developing conjectures about the potential results.
  - Allow the Web reader an e-mail link to provide feedback on the progress.
  - Link the research progress to the main page (Figure 9.8*a*) for the Web presentation.
- ❏ **Research Report.** At the completion of the investigation, the researcher must frame and organize the data for analysis, analyze the data, and present all of this information in a form such that other researchers can replicate the study. The research must also describe the conclusions and suggest applications of the conclusions to work beyond the specific investigation. Basically these activities can be framed in the following categories to become links from the Research Report menu (Figure 9.8*b*).
  - Introduction
  - Problem
  - Materials
  - Procedures
  - Results
  - Conclusions
  - Applications

---

teacher, might do about your own teaching—typically referred to as *action research.*

Action research is a systematic investigation of questions and problems related to the day-to-day activities of teachers and their students (Sowell & Casey, 1982). Some ideas for questions that you might consider include the following:

- Which students do you call on to answer questions? Do you only ask questions of the bright students?

- Do you support males more than females through your attention to their questions, statements, and actions?

- How do you manage the time of a lesson? Do you spend more time with classroom management than with instruction?

This research is important as you grow as a professional. Use the Web as a research communication tool in a manner similar to that suggested In the Classroom 9.5. Engage other teachers in helping you develop as a professional, by providing feedback on your ideas and questions about teaching and learning.

An important consideration when doing research in your classroom is that you must protect the anonymity of your subjects—your students. Pay careful attention to the requirements for the protection of human subjects. Use pseudonyms when you refer to students as well as to your school and class. Do not let this requirement impede you from doing the action research since the work is particularly helpful for your professional development.

Hypermedia and Web Authoring as a Problem-Solving and Decision-Making Tool

Learning to communicate via hypermedia engages students in decision making. The very nature of the activities involved in Web authoring involves problem solving and decision making. Engaging students in designing Web pages along with solving problems in a particular content area provides them with powerful experiences with problem solving and decision making.

Hypermedia and Web-Authoring Instructional Idea: Which Town Is Which?   An important expectation in the social studies curriculum is to provide experiences for students to study people, places, and environments. Typically, teachers begin with the environment in which the students live because of their basic familiarity with that environment. How would you approach a unit that is focused on towns in the United States? Too often teachers begin this instruction in a linear fashion, guiding students in studying one town at a time, learning about the town's history, society, economy, climate, and other special characteristics about the town. Consider a different approach, an approach that puts students in charge of learning about the towns and challenging them to develop mysteries to guide other students in the class in investigating the various towns. In the Classroom 9.6 characterizes this student-centered approach where they investigate, design, and create a mystery for the other students to solve. The problem is to design a mystery about the location of a particular town. The clues provide information pointing toward the identity of the town without specifically naming the town.

In this project, student pairs investigate an assigned town with the expectation that they become experts about the particular town's history, society, economy, climate, and other special characteristics. Rather than giving an oral presentation of the findings, the student pairs are challenged to design a mystery web presentation that is in a mystery format, providing the reader with clues about the town (similar to the idea of In the Classroom 8.5).

Once all the town presentations are created, the challenge for the entire class is to solve the mystery. Again, students work in pairs, using the clues about the town to place the town somewhere in the United States. In the process they learn about each of the towns in order to exclude some of them as potential towns that do not meet the clues provided. Throughout the entire project, students are engaged in problem solving and decision making. They are also expected to use technology as a problem-solving and decision-making tool, authoring Web pages

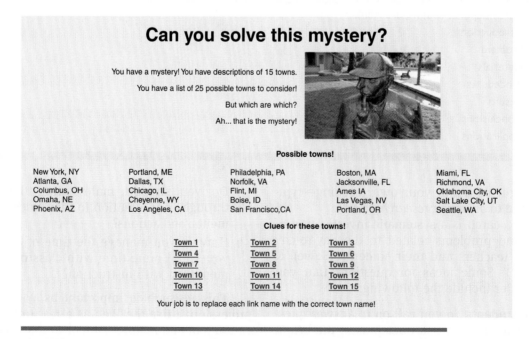

FIGURE 9.9   Mystery Towns Web page presenting the entire town mystery.

In the Classroom 9.6

WHERE ARE THESE MYSTERY TOWNS IN THE UNITED STATES?

TECHNOLOGY OBJECTIVE: **NETS·S I, II, III, IV, V, VI**

- **Hypermedia and Web authoring:** Technology as a communications research, problem-solving, and decision-making tool while building understanding of basic concepts of Web technology.
- Design a Web presentation that includes a variety of media elements and incorporates hyperlinks.

CONTENT OBJECTIVE: **Social studies:** Identify towns based on data about the history, society, economy, climate, and other identifying characteristics.

Language arts: Develop a set of clues to guide readers in solving a mystery.

GRADE LEVEL: 5–9

PROBLEM: Describe a town in a Web-based mystery to guide readers in an investigation of defining characteristics of a town, its people, its culture, its economy, and its history.

- ❏ **Present the mystery.** Identify 25 major towns in the United States for consideration for the project. Assign each pair of students to investigate one town's history, society, economy, and any other descriptive characteristics. Student groups need to keep the names of their towns hidden from the rest of the class during this phase of the activity. Some towns in a list of all possible towns are not assigned, adding to the mystery.

- ❏ **Study one town and develop a mystery website with clues.** Student pairs design their mysteries with clues that involve history, society, economy, and other descriptive characteristics that are presented via a mystery Web presentation.

  - **Preproduction phase to identify the clues and the design of the Web presentation:** What clues provide information about the town? How should the clues be presented? Develop a storyboard for the Web presentation and make basic design decisions.

  - **Production:** Follow the plan established in the storyboard.
    - ○ Set up a template for basic pages in the website, considering background, colors, identification and orientation of graphics, borders, links, and buttons. Be sure to include a date stamp.
    - ○ Save the template and accompanying files in a folder for designing the mystery.
    - ○ Gather the exhibits in the folder for the mystery.
    - ○ Create the individual pages of the mystery, following the directions in the storyboard.
    - ○ Test all files and links.

  - **Publication phase:** Test and present the mystery.
    - ○ Before transferring the files to the Web, have a friend review the website, providing you feedback about the clarity of the clues for engaging the reader.
    - ○ Transfer the files to the Web, testing, reviewing, and refining the contents.

- ❏ **Solve the mystery.**
  - Link the top page of the website that lists the mystery towns (as in Figure 9.9).
  - Student pairs must now identify each mystery town by name. They know one town and must use the clues provided by the other links to identify other mystery towns.
  - After the investigation, change the names of the links in their copy of the Mystery Towns Web page so that each town (Town 1, Town 2, etc.) is now named.
  - Explain the decision in writing, indicating how the clues helped to identify the town.

that demonstrate their understanding of the history, society, economy, climate, and other descriptive characteristics of each of the towns. Although this process may seem to take longer than directly telling students about the towns, the process engages students in a learning experience that leads to a more memorable and thorough understanding

about the towns, where they are asked to describe, differentiate, and explain the people, places, and environments. Also, in the process as they use Web authoring as a tool for their investigation, they learn more about using this technology for communicating their understanding in a different way that incorporates twenty-first-century technology.

Summing It Up

Literacy focuses on skills with reading and writing as mechanisms for communicating. Advancements in technology ultimately mean that the tools for reading and writing change along with the skills for reading and writing. Probably the most significant shift for the twenty-first century is the development of hypertext. Today, hypertext is considered as information that is "linked and cross-referenced in many different ways" (Hooper, 1990). With hypertext the idea of hypermedia is seen as nonsequential documents containing not only text, but also elements such as audio, video, graphics, drawings, photographs, and animations, along with the computer system on which the components are stored and displayed. Thus, educating a literate citizen for the twenty-first century has evolved to include teaching students to read and write in a manner that takes advantage of tools that support nonsequential communication.

Although hypermedia is not unique to the Web, it is a key feature of the Web. And the Web has become an important tool for learning, gathering information, searching for answers to questions, and communicating ideas to a worldwide audience. Web readers must traverse the pages in a nonsequential manner, gathering the ideas and communications using the hyperlinks that are provided. Web writers must learn to communicate in a nonsequential manner that provides hyperlinks allowing the reader to make choices as to the method of gaining the ideas. Today teachers are expected to integrate teaching students to use this new, hypermedia tool along with teaching them important subject matter.

Web pages are displayed using the hypertext markup language (HTML). Although a basic understanding of this language is sometimes useful, today many software tools are available so that students can design the look and communication and the software translates the design to the HTML code. Web elements are similar to basic word processing elements: variety of fonts, colors, sizes, and placements; insertion of tables, graphics, and hyperlinks. The design of the Web page is the part that requires extensive thought and artistic input, similar to that needed in movie and presentation packages; further, this process is described through three phrases: preproduction, production, and publication. Storyboarding is an essential part of the preproduction phase that results in the completion of the content and the design of the Web presentation. The production phase basically follows the plans that have been made, namely, creating pages that are displayed on your computer and not on the Web. The publication phase is when the files are moved to the Web server using the file transfer protocol (FTP) to support the movement of all files and folders needed for the Web production. And, because Web pages are displayed for the world-wide audience, an important part of the publication phase is maintenance of the pages, assuring that the information for worldwide consumption is current.

Guiding students in learning to communicate with hypermedia requires attention to both their reading and writing of nonsequential information. Learning to read and write is integral to all subject areas. Teachers need to provide instructions that guide students in extending their skills with hypermedia as they extend their skills in the subject areas.

Students need to learn to read nonsequential information requiring that they learn to skim online materials, activities that can be within the context of gathering information to answer specific subject matter questions. Students need to learn basic concepts of writing nonsequential, hyperlinked information perhaps by creating a story that uses links to pictures or additional information to enhance the description in the story. Students need to learn to challenge the work that they read on the Web. They need to learn to question the credibility of their Web resources. Students need to practice respectful writing on the Web, modeling legal and ethical practices as they design their Web pages.

Electronic portfolios provide students with an on-going opportunity for help in gaining Web-authoring skills while also learning to present their ideas and work in an online format that incorporates hyperlinks. As students learn new topics in their courses, they can be challenged to describe and communicate their new knowledge using the nonsequential features available in Web authoring. In essence, while the portfolio displays their progress in the content areas, it also displays their development in using the Web as a productivity tool, a communications tool, a research tool, and a problem-solving and decision-making tool.

End-of-the-Chapter Activities and References

PRACTICE PROBLEMS

1. Design a storyboard, using a software application such as Inspiration, to guide the design of your E-portfolio that will be used to demonstrate your progress with the NETS·T guidelines (ISTE, 2002).

2. Design a basic template for an electronic portfolio to demonstrate your progress with the NETS·T guidelines (ISTE, 2002). The template should include the background, any graphics, and location of links that will be consistent from page to page of your electronic portfolio.

3. Create a Web page story that uses links to pictures or additional information to enhance the description in the story.

4. Design a WebQuest or Web Inquiry investigation (as described in Chapter 7) that is designed to have students conduct an investigation via the Web.

5. Create a Web page that is intent on convincing readers to adopt your position on the question, Should content be approved before it is made public on the Web?

6. Use Technology Link 9.2 to collect digital images that you can use to tell a story. Use the Web and hyperlinks in creating a visual historical narrative.

7. Select a question about your teaching that you would like to investigate. Create a Web page to display the research process (as described in the activity In the Classroom 9.5) you used in conducting this action research project about your teaching.

IN THE CLASSROOM ACTIVITIES

8. Read the article by Harris, White, and Fischer (2003) about dependent and independent readers. Observe student readers at your level of interest as they read Web-based information. What do you notice about their comprehension and speed of reading? Describe their processes in using the links for understanding the ideas they are reading. Are students able to read faster with the nonsequential information?

9. Select a poem by Shel Silverstein (or another author of your choice) that would interest students in the classroom. Create a Web version of the poem using hyperlinks that the student would navigate as they read the poem. Ask students to describe the poem after having read the Web version. Do the hyperlinks help or hinder their reading?

10. Observe and perhaps work with students as they gather information from various Web pages. Find out about their use or nonuse of specific links. Do the links help them gather the information? Are there specific links that are more useful than others? Do they become distracted from the message as they traverse the links?

11. Create a "Frequently Asked Questions" Web page about a topic that students are studying in the classes you observe. Ask the students to help you by providing questions that could be used in the Web page. Ask them to help you create the answers. Then encourage them to review your Web page for its usefulness.

ASSESSING STUDENT LEARNING WITH AND ABOUT TECHNOLOGY

12. Conduct an Internet search for a scoring guide that might be used in assessing student work with an electronic portfolio. Review the scoring guide to meet specifics dealing with your particular content area and grade level.

13. Create a scoring guide that could be used in assessing student work in the research activity of In the Classroom 9.5.

E-PORTFOLIO ACTIVITIES

14. Create an electronic resume that could be incorporated in your E-portfolio.

15. Create a Web page that contains a list of your favorite websites for finding resources for teaching your subject at the level of your choice. Each listing should include a description of the value of the resource as well as a link to that website.

REFLECTION AND DISCUSSION

16. Respond to this statement: Having students create Web pages wastes valuable learning time.

17. Respond to this question: How have reading and writing skills shifted in the twenty-first century from those of the nineteenth century?

Annotated Resources

Hanfland, P. (1999). Electronic portfolios: Students documenting their best work. *Learning and Leading with Technology, 26*(6), 54–57.
Electronic portfolios provide an authentic opportunity for students to display their work while also integrating technology in learning. Students are motivated to produce quality work to showcase their best work. Although this article focuses on electronic portfolios created in HyperStudio, the ideas are useful for thinking about Web-based electronic portfolios.

Harris, J., White, P., & Fisher, B. (2003). Helping dependent readers use the Web. *Learning and Leading with Technology, 31*(3), 40–45.
Web-based strategies are proposed to assist struggling readers in improving their comprehension and to ultimately read in a variety of formats, sequential and nonsequential.

Partnership for 21st Century Skills. (2004). Information and Communication Technology (ICT) Literacy Maps. http://www.21stcenturyskills.org/
ICT literacy recommendations and suggestions are provided for action in scaffolding students learning of critical skills for success in the increasingly competitive global economy of the twenty-first century.

Silverstein, S. (1974). *Where the Sidewalk Ends*. New York: Harper and Row.
Come on in to where the sidewalk ends and the poems of Shel Silverstein begin as he shares his perspective of the world. Use the poems as idea starters for Web stories.

CHAPTER 10

Responding to Emerging Technologies

Michael Newman/PhotoEdit

Introduction

Technologies are continually changing and emerging. Just as the methods for teaching with technologies change how and what is taught, new technologies continually transform the potential for these tools to meet new instructional goals. Information and communications technologies keep evolving and improving—increasing in speed, decreasing in size, and becoming more powerful. As the world becomes increasingly digital, the technologies used outside of schools increasingly shape the work inside school classrooms. Some emergent technological developments with educational potential include the following:

- Computer input recognition capabilities that move beyond the keyboard and mouse to include voice, handwriting, and drawing as well as real-time data input from multiple sources, such as temperature, motion, and force.

- Visual displays moving from two- to three-dimensional virtual environments capable of providing students with more advanced ways to explore and visualize abstract ideas.

- Handheld computing devices, with many educational applications, that provide opportunities for simultaneous multiple user participatory input into whole-class investigations.

- Wireless networking that allows educators and students to remain connected as they move from home to school and as they move among the various school classroom activities.

And what about those new wearable computing devices—worn like a belt or glasses—allowing the wearer to communicate and compute, freeing hands for other uses? Do those devices have educational potential? The answer remains within the vision of educators who must carefully investigate what students need to learn as well as how they are most likely to learn this information.

Have you ever participated in one of the many *blogs* (short for weblogs) where someone began with a personal perspective and you and others responded with your perspectives? Perhaps you joined a discussion in a campaign, as many do around election campaigns. Does this new online journaling technology have potential for helping students learn ways to get engaged in important national campaigns?

Today's teachers recognize the importance of student engagement and active experiences in learning and look for authentic opportunities that actively engage students in learning. Maybe blogs provide a mechanism for engaging them in these learning environments. Reflective activities do provide students with important opportunities for learning and building their personal understandings. As you prepare to teach in the twenty-first century, you need to develop an open attitude toward an active pursuit of the advances in emerging technologies, looking for ways that you might use them to support your students' learning. You must

- Consider the capabilities of new tools as well as advancements in older tools.
- Examine the potential of the tools for both a curriculum and instruction designed to prepare future citizens who will live and work in a technology-transformed twenty-first century.

The ideas in this chapter are designed to guide you in developing this attitude toward emerging technologies. The technologies that are discussed serve only as examples to engage your thinking about potential changes in the curriculum you teach and tools that you might use to engage your students in an active learning environment. Ultimately, your considerations toward emerging technology tools must be directed toward providing students with tools for thinking and learning in the twenty-first century.

After reading the chapter, you should be able to:

1. Explain how the emergence of calculators in the twentieth century provides a model for teachers' thinking about emerging technologies.
2. Describe teachers' thinking processes as they consider emerging technologies for educational use.
3. Talk about the value of real-time data collection technologies as tools for learning subject matter content.
4. Differentiate blogs from diaries and traditional journals and ways they can be used to guide student learning.
5. Identify capabilities of RSS (Rich Site Summary or Really Simple Syndication) news readers and podcasting that establishes those technologies as potential tools for learning.
6. Discuss ways that wireless technologies, such as tablet PCs (Personal Computers), might be useful as learning tools in various subject areas.

Snapshot of a Class Developing a Web Blog on a Presidential Campaign

Mrs. Adams teaches eighth-grade U.S. history. Like many social studies teachers, she has a passion for politics. This year Mrs. Adams is particularly excited because it is a presidential election year. By the time she was preplanning for the new school year, both major political parties had completed their state primary presidential elections and held their nominating conventions. When school started, the two candidates were campaigning in earnest and the general election campaign was in full force.

During preplanning, Mrs. Adams consciously thought about ways to encourage her students to get involved in the presidential campaign. She considered many of the standard approaches to teaching during political campaigns, including students making campaign posters or buttons, having debates, comparing the candidates on the issues, and conducting mock elections. Although she appreciated all of these approaches, she wanted to do something different.

Given her deep interest in politics, Mrs. Adams was familiar with an emerging technology called *blogging* that seemed to be influencing the campaign process. She began her own blog as a way to encourage students to get interested in politics and to blog themselves. Mrs. Adams decided to use this new idea

of blogging to facilitate her students' political understanding.

She began class by displaying her website on the overhead screen. Figure 10.1 is her website frontpage and Figure 10.2 expands the text information that Mrs. Adams displayed on the website as she introduced her students to its contents.

Mrs. Adams: As you can see on this screen of the website I created for this class, it's not your typical website. This is a blog. It's a kind of online journal. I am going to be talking to you through this website and using a bunch of other websites to help you think about the upcoming presidential campaign. Do any of you keep a journal or a diary?

Several Students: Yes.

Mrs. Adams: Someone tell me why you do this.

Abigail: Well, I like to write down important things that have happened so I won't forget.

Mrs. Adams: That's good and that is part of what a blog allows you to do, but there is more. With a blog you can write about things that are

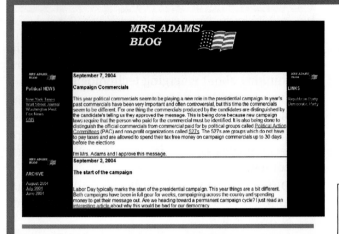

FIGURE 10.1   Mrs. Adam's website for introducing blogging.

	important to you; but unlike a diary or a journal, it is available for anyone to read.
Abigail:	Oh, I don't think I would want anyone reading my diary.
Mrs. Adams:	Good point. Like I said, there is a big difference between a blog and a diary. You are writing in a blog for other people to read. You want them to read it. You can also use the blog to organize links to your favorite websites and you can link to other websites as you write your entries. These hyperlinks allow "bloggers," that's what they call people who write blogs, to back up what they are saying or provide readers with more on a topic. Do any of you read the news or other stories online?
Quincy:	I read the newspaper online. I really look at the music section, to see what new music is coming out.
Amelia:	I read the sports online—stuff like ESPN.
Mrs. Adams:	I'm sure you have both noticed how the sites you are visiting have links to other sites. Well, my blog will be the same. I will have some very short entries and links in

the text of my writing to support and to extend my ideas.

I suppose I should tell you a little more about what a blog is. As I said earlier, blogs are Web-based journals. They are journals in several ways. First, blogs are public and, unlike a diary, others are invited to look at the blogger's thoughts and opinions on a regular basis. I will use my blog to write about what we are learning in class.

September 7, 2004
Campaign Commercials
This year political commercials seem to be playing a new role in the presidential campaign. In years past commercials have been very important and often controversial, but this year the commercials seem to be different. For one thing the commercials produced by the candidates are distinguished by the candidate's telling us they approved the message. This is being done because new campaign laws require that the person or group who paid for the commercial must be identified. It is also being done to distinguish the official commercials from commercials paid for by political groups called Political Action Committees (PACs) and non-profit organizations called 527s. The 527s are groups that do not have to pay taxes and are allowed to spend their tax-free money on campaign commercials up to 30 days before the elections.

I'm Mrs. Adams and I approve this message.

September 2, 2004
The start of the campaign

Labor Day typically marks the start of the presidential campaign. This year things are a bit different. Both campaigns have been in full gear for weeks, campaigning across the country and spending money to get their message out. Are we heading toward a permanent campaign cycle? I just read an interesting article about why this would be bad for our democracy.

FIGURE 10.2   Messages displayed in Mrs. Adams' website.

◀ Educational Acceptance of Calculators

As new technologies become available for general use, teachers are faced with considering their usefulness for supporting students as they learn. This task is not simple nor without problems, as evidenced by the emergence of calculators in the 1970s. Since their emergence, calculators have stimulated an ongoing debate among educators.

Calculators appear to be a tool for adults to use as they wish but not for children to use in their learning! The concern was then and continues to be: How can children learn what they need to learn if they use a calculator? The fear is that the calculator does the thinking for students including calculating sums, differences, products, and quotients needed to solve the problems. Although some educators argue that calculators aid in student learning of mathematics concepts and skills, others argue that it is the calculator that does the mathematics. The challenge for educators as calculators emerged and became accessible for educational uses has been to

1. reconsider the curriculum, searching for artifacts of the previous centuries that are no longer viewed as essential knowledge and skills in the twenty-first century;

2. reconsider instruction, searching how calculator activities might support students in accessing concepts;

3. reconsider what it means to learn when students have access to capabilities that are offered by the technology tool—the calculator.

The challenge was and continues to be to investigate how calculators can be *tools to think with* rather than as *tools to replace thinking*.

Perhaps acceptance of the calculator as an educational tool has been easier for teachers in subject areas other than mathematics. But, such a shift has not been easy for teachers or parents who learned mathematics with an emphasis on computation. They learned how to add, subtract, multiply, and divide carefully following the algorithms that led to the correct solutions. When they were asked to compute $345 \div 23$, they followed the procedures they had learned.

$$\begin{array}{r} 15 \\ 23\overline{)345} \\ \underline{23} \\ 115 \\ \underline{115} \\ 0 \end{array}$$

However, if you ask them to explain why the 1 is placed over the 4 in the procedure, they fumble, stating, "Because 23 doesn't go into 3" or "Because that is what I am supposed to do." Neither response displays an understanding of why the process works in solving a division problem! Their responses suggest that they are following the rules. Neither responses provide evidence that they are thinking about the problem; they are following the rules for finding the solution.

Basic calculator use is actually not much different from the process of solving the division problem. In both cases, the students know the problem requires division. With the calculator the students must accurately follow the correct process for *doing* the division by entering the information in the correct order.

Press these keys in this order: 345, ÷, 23, =

Once the equal sign is depressed, the display returns the result of 15. Rarely is the student required to explain why this process works. Given this de-

scription of the student activity, you might argue that students are not using the calculator as a tool for thinking. Some argue that since they are not having to think about the procedures in division—of how many times 23 goes into 345, what the product of 10 times 23 is, what the difference of 345 and 230 is, how many times 23 goes into 115, and what the product of 23 and 5 is—that they are thinking even less about mathematics and certainly they are not gaining the needed practice with these operations. And so, the argument about the use of calculators in the mathematics classes continues.

Thinking and Learning with Calculators

Keep in mind that the challenge for this chapter is to think about emerging technologies and how they can be used as tools for learning and thinking in a twenty-first-century education. As in the case with educators debating whether to allow calculators, all teachers need to be engaged in the process of challenging the ways that education has always happened and investigating new curriculum and instruction that takes advantage of the capabilities of new technology tools as they emerge.

For the mathematics curriculum, you might begin to think about topics that have not been emphasized without the use of technology. Two important topics, estimation and mental arithmetic, have traditionally been included in the mathematics curriculum but have not been emphasized to the extent that they perhaps should be. Students typically do not see a reason to practice either skill since they learn how to find the *exact* solution, either by long hand or by using the calculator!

With the calculator there is a far more important reason to practice estimation and mental arithmetic. These skills are essential in determining if the solution returned by the calculator makes sense. Is there a chance that a number was incorrectly entered, or an operation mistakenly entered?

Consider this problem:

Mexicans use pesos and Americans use dollars for their currency. Ava is in Mexico and has both dollars and pesos. When she entered Mexico, she had exchanged some of her dollars for pesos at a bank where the exchange rate was 11 pesos for 1 dollar. As she traveled through the country, she noticed that some places allowed paying in pesos or in dollars. Using her estimation skills, she also noticed that sometimes it was better to pay in dollars and at other places it was better to pay in pesos since the stores differed on the exchange rates they allowed. She found a shirt that she wanted to buy that was labeled as costing either 200 pesos or $18. Should she pay in pesos or dollars?

Using her mental arithmetic skills, Ava determined that 200 pesos would be 20 dollars if the exchange rate were 10 pesos to 1 dollar. She also understands that 11 pesos to 1 dollar means the cost of the shirt should be less than $20. But just how much less? She knows that she needs to figure out what 18 times 11 is but she thinks about this multiplication problem differently. She recognizes that 11 times 9 is 99 and twice 99 is 198 (or 11 × 9 × 2 is 11 × 18) or 198 pesos. So she figures that paying $18 is the better deal. If she pays $18 she pays the equivalent of 198 pesos rather than the 200 pesos. Through this thought process, Ava uses both estimation and mental arithmetic skills to determine the better deal and does not need to resort to the long hand calculation or a calculator.

Of course a calculator is much more than a four-function operator. Students can use the calculator as a tool to help verify solutions to equations, visualize functions, and explore the correspondence of a symbolic relationship to its graphical relationship. They can enter functions ($Y_1=2X+5$, $Y_2=3X+5$, $Y_3=4X+5$, and $Y_4=5X+5$) in a graphing calculator as in Figure 10.3 and display the graphs to see how changing the coefficient of X affects the graphical representation. Similarly, with calculators, students can change the value of a variable in an equation to see the change in the outcome.

Without the use of the calculators, students spend time graphing the equations, plotting a minimum of three points per equation to generate a visual representation of the function. Does the calculator capability keep students from learning the skill of graphing, or does the calculator provide a way to help students to more quickly visualize the effect of changes in the coefficients of X that ultimately affects the slope of the line? Teachers must carefully weigh the pros and cons of emerging technologies with respect to what students need to know and what tools they can use in learning.

Using More than Four Functions of the Calculator
With today's calculators, lists of data can be gathered and easily analyzed using the list capabilities. Thus, calculators become a research, problem-solving, and decision-making tool as students learn to apply mathematical models to real-world ideas. In the Classroom 10.1 provides a sample lesson to engage students in using the calculator as a learning tool. In this activity, students use the list of capabilities to explore the relationship of a person's arm reach to height and extend this knowledge to other measurements. For this experiment they collect data from everyone in the classroom, enter the data in a list format in the calculator, and then explore a line of best fit for the data. After they find the best linear fit for the data, one class finds that the line had approximately a slope of 1 while another class finds a linear expression of 1.1X − 18, indicating that the line of best fit has a slope of 1.1. It is important to question students as to what they think would happen if they were able to collect much more data. What would they propose the linear expression might become?

In the second investigation the students investigate the ratio of the distance from their feet to their navel to the distance from the navel to the top of their head. To accomplish this activity, they make measurements of their feet to navel and navel to head, enter the class data, and consider what function best represents the data. Their results might return a linear expression of 1.6X − 15 that suggests that this famous ratio—the golden ratio—is approximately 1.6. Now is the time to discuss the golden ratio that Leonardo da Vinci used in his drawings of human figures. Challenge them to use the Internet to find more about this ratio and to explain its significance in art and architecture.

 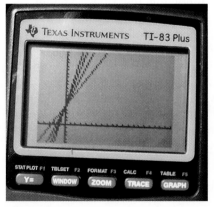

FIGURE 10.3 TI−83+ comparison of changes in the function with the resulting graphical representations.

In the Classroom 10.1

WHAT MATHEMATICS DID LEONARDO DA VINCI USE FOR DRAWING HUMAN FIGURES?

TECHNOLOGY OBJECTIVE: **NETS · S V and VI**

- **Graphing calculators:** Technology as a research, problem-solving, and decision-making tool.
- Enter data in lists in a calculator; use calculator functions to analyze data.

CONTENT OBJECTIVE: **Art:** Consider ratios of human parts in drawings.

Mathematics: Solve problems involving scale factors, using ratio and proportion.

Science: Collecting data to develop a hypothesis about the ratio for a perfect human figure.

GRADE LEVEL: 5–9

PROBLEM: Leonardo da Vinci spent much time drawing human figures. He must have known something because the figures were all pleasing to the eye. What was his secret?

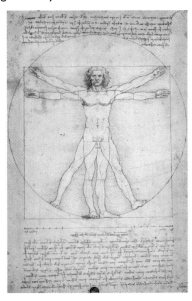

© Galleria dell'Accademia, Venice, Italy / The Bridgeman Art Library

Investigation 1

- ❏ Organize two stations:
    1. Place two measuring tapes (end to end) on a bulletin board flat space so that students can identify their arm reach measurement.
    2. Place two meter sticks (end to end) at the doorway to the classroom so that students can find their heights.
- ❏ Group students in fours to collect the data at each station for each person in their group.
    1. Measure the arm reach, fingertip to fingertip, in centimeters.
    2. Measure the height, head to toe, in centimeters.
- ❏ Record the data on an overhead with a table similar to the following:

Name	Arm Reach (cm)	Height (cm)

- ❏ As the data are collected, students also enter the data (values only) for *arm reach* and *height* into L_1 and L_2 of the calculator list.
- ❏ Graph the data, fitting the window to accurately represent the data.

(continued on next page)

❏ Explore the relationship of the lists by fitting a linear function to the data.

❏ Propose a hypothesis based on your data about the relationship of arm reach to height.

Investigation 2

❏ Provide each group with measuring tapes for student use.

❏ Have each student make these personal measurements:

   1. Measure the distance from foot to navel.

   2. Measure the distance from navel to top of head.

❏ Record the data on an overhead similar to the following:

Name	Foot to Navel (cm)	Navel to Head (cm)

❏ As the data are collected, students also enter the data (values only) for each column into L_1 and L_2 of the calculator list.

❏ Graph the data, fitting the window to accurately represent the data.

❏ Explore the relationship of the lists by fitting a linear function to the data.

❏ Propose a hypothesis based on your data about the relationship of the distance from feet to navel to the distance from navel to head.

Investigation 3

❏ Have each group investigate a specific painting by Leonardo da Vinci, making similar measurements as in Investigations 1 and 2.

❏ What is the ratio of arm reach to height of the figures in the paintings?

❏ What is the ratio of foot to navel to navel to head of the figures in the paintings?

❏ Conduct an Internet search on the golden ratio, discussing your findings on the impact of this ratio in both art and architecture.

Teachers' Thinking and Visioning with New Technologies

Although calculators are no longer considered an emerging technology, their capabilities as a tool for student learning are still debated in educational circles. Will the use of calculators as tools result in a reduction of computational skill development? How important is computational skill development in the twenty-first century? How can education take advantage of the unique capabilities of the calculator for supporting student learning without losing a skill valued by society? These questions are samples of the type of questions teachers must ask as they think about and vision with emerging technologies.

What is the *tipping point* that will push toward whole-hearted acceptance or rejection of an innovation such as calculators in education? Obviously,

this point has not been universally reached. Everett Rogers (2003) explains that each member of the system (in this case the educational system) must progress through a five-step process in facing the ultimate decision as to whether to accept or reject a particular innovation for use:

1. **Knowledge:** person becomes aware of an innovation and has some idea of how it functions.

2. **Persuasion:** person forms a favorable or unfavorable attitude toward the innovation.

3. **Decision:** person engages in activities that lead to a choice to adopt or reject the innovation.

4. **Implementation:** person puts an innovation into use.

5. **Confirmation:** person evaluates the results of an innovation–decision already made. (p. 169)

As new technologies emerge, all members of the educational system must be engaged in the process that leads toward the acceptance or rejection of the technology for an educational application. Teachers are key to this process of diffusion of an innovation. If calculators are to be accepted, teachers must implement and confirm the results.

Teachers' thinking does need to be from a professional position that involves investigation of the emerging technologies, an attitude that involves ongoing evaluation and reflection about the tool for educational purposes. In preparing to teach in the twenty-first century, where advancements and improvements in electronic and information technologies are a constant, you must develop this professional position. This thoughtful visionary attitude places you in the position of questioning these advancements and improvements in technologies from at least six important areas:

1. **Curricular needs in your subject area in the twenty-first century.** Can the technology be used as a productivity, communications, research, and/or problem-solving and decision-making tool for learning in the subject area? Does the technology offer the capabilities to facilitate technology-enhanced experiences that address subject matter content standards and student technology standards? Does the technology offer capabilities that challenge the accepted standards, opening the possibility for a shift in what students need to know to be productive citizens in the twenty-first century?

2. **Instructional needs in your subject area in the twenty-first century.** Can the technology support learner-centered strategies for learning the subject? Can use of the technology as a learning tool help students develop a more robust understanding of the content? Can the technology address the diverse needs of students in learning the subject? How must the instruction be scaffolded to guide student learning with and about the technology?

3. **Student learning in the twenty-first century.** Can the technology engage students in important experiences that support their learning? Can the technology provide multiple perspectives for the students to view the subject? Can the technology be applied to developing students' higher order thinking and reasoning skills? Can the technology maximize student learning?

4. **Unique capabilities of the new tool.** What are the capabilities of the tool? How are those capabilities useful in accomplishing twenty-first-century skills? Do the capabilities challenge accepted ways of knowing and doing? What must be learned before incorporation of the tool as a learning tool?

5. **Student knowledge, access, and management concerns.** Will inclusion of the new tool create student access issues? What preparation must be provided for students working with the technol-

ogy as a tool for learning? What management issues need consideration if the tool is incorporated in the classroom situation?

6. **Assessment and evaluation with the new tool.** How will assessment of students' learning of the subject matter be affected by the incorporation of the new tool? Will performance assessments be important to demonstrate students' knowledge of the content with use of the new tool?

Investigation of Potential Technology Tools for Educational Application

Emerging developments with technologies include at the very least these areas: handheld computing devices and increased input recognition capabilities; Web-based and networked technologies; and wireless technologies. Yet, discussion of specific tools is quickly outdated by newer and more fantastic capabilities. As a teacher, the thinking and visioning processes are essential skills for you to develop. The technology tools discussed in this chapter are presented to engage you in the systematic visionary thinking outlined earlier. You do not necessarily need to make the final decision of whether to implement the technology in the classrooms. As you investigate and evaluate these new applications, you must challenge their use to determine if student thinking and learning within the subject domain are enhanced. Keep in mind the years of investigation that have gone into the question of whether to implement calculators as tools for learning.

Handheld Computing Devices and Increased Input Recognition Capabilities   Today, more and more applications and peripherals have become available for calculators, increasing the calculator's capabilities far beyond the computational capabilities usually associated with calculators. For education, a reconsideration of calculators as a viable educational technology is particularly important because of its reduced cost that provides access for all students beyond the limits of the classroom. With the additional capabilities, calculators are simply becoming more like portable, handheld computers. Thinking about the calculator as a handheld computer helps as you address the six areas in a teacher's visionary thinking process toward acceptance or rejection.

Calculators with Keyboards   One drawback in using a calculator both in mathematics classes and in other subject area classes has been the complexity of entering text information. Strategies for inputting letters have been cumbersome, time-consuming, and error prone. Now keyboards are available to be connected to the calculator for ease in entering text information. Remember the impact that word processors have had on student writing. Does this additional input feature

In the Classroom 10.2

EFFECTIVE LEADS

TECHNOLOGY OBJECTIVE: **NETS·S III, IV**

- **Graphing calculators:** Technology as a productivity and communications tool.
- Use a notetaking application of the calculator with a keyboard attachment for ease in entering text information.

CONTENT OBJECTIVE: **Language arts:** Determine the qualities of an effective lead in a piece of narrative.

GRADE LEVEL: 5–9

PROBLEM: Writers need to seize a reader's attention from the start of a piece of fiction. What are the qualities of leads that are effective in doing just that—getting readers to take notice and compelling them to read further?

- **Collecting data in the library.** Using sample texts in the library, students record and cite those leads they find to be particularly effective and those that are particularly ineffective using the notetaking feature with the calculator.
- **Compile the data.** The teacher uploads the student notes into a database that lists the effective leads as well as those that are found to be ineffective.
- **Analyze the data.** Using a projector to share the contents of the database with the full class, the teacher leads a full-class analytical discussion of the contents of the database.
  - ○ What was it that directed you to describe a lead as effective or ineffective?
  - ○ As *readers*, what do you respond to in the leads that resulted in labeling them effective or ineffective?
  - ○ As *writers*, what do you respond to in the leads that resulted in labeling them effective or ineffective?
- **Synthesize the results.** As a class generate a list of the qualities of an effective lead. Compare and contrast the class list with one found in the textbook.

Certainly, this type of calculator use is not widespread. However, as you consider using the application, think about some critical questions such as these:

- What are the benefits of this technology use over pen and pencil in a language arts setting?
- What are the benefits of handheld technologies with keyboard attachments for supporting student writing?
- Does the technology support the students and their classroom teacher in working with the data and gaining a richer understanding of the content?
- Does the ease of student access provide any benefits?

Whether the technology is integrated in such language arts experiences depends on your responses.

enhance the uses for the calculator technology for educational purposes?

Courtesy Texas Instruments, Inc.

In the Classroom 10.2 is a simple language arts lesson where students are investigating how leads function in selections of narrative text. Their task is to identify stories that have both effective and ineffective leads, using the keyboard attachment to a calculator to enter the text of the leads into a note file. From this in-formation, the classroom teacher aggregates the responses into a shared class database. Students analyze the database of leads to generate a list of qualities of an effective lead. Finally, they compare and contrast the class-developed list to one provided in their textbook.

Advanced Networked Systems Another advancement with calculators is the development of an entire system that allows teachers to gather data about each student's progress during an activity as they work on their individual calculators. Texas Instrument's Navigator is one example of such a system. Consider the difference between the traditional classroom discussion and a classroom discussion where the teacher and students are interconnected.

You can probably easily visualize the typical classroom discussions. The teacher asks questions of the class, calling on students one at a time to share their ideas with the rest of the class. A few students in the class dominate the discussion, and the teacher has little evidence of the thinking of all other students.

With a networked system, the teacher creates the questions on the system and transfers the questions to each student's handheld device simultaneously. The students respond to the questions and when the teacher is ready, they transfer their responses to the teacher's system. With the capabilities in the system, the teacher is able to assess each student's work as well as compile class results to be shared with the class. The teacher can challenge particular responses, asking the students to explain why those responses might be valid or invalid. The teacher can display a bar chart of anonymous student responses for engaging the students in a discussion of what they are seeing, at the same time considering whether the class as a whole mastered the idea. With this information the teacher can immediately discuss questions that did not seem to be mastered and students who made errors in their responses can challenge their own understandings.

A variety of subject area ideas are currently being developed for educational uses of this system. Technology Link 10.1 provides a link to access and investigate some of the activities that use these capabilities. Examples of the activities include the following:

- **Social Studies: Understanding the concepts and flow of legislation.** Through this activity students investigate the process of legislation while working in small groups to investigate words or phrases that are commonly used in the process of a bill becoming a law. As they conduct the research, they keep notes in a notetaking application that is available with the calculator. The goal is to identify the procedure currently used in the U.S. process of legislation, considering what works well in this legislative system and how it can be improved.

- **Mathematics: Increase in volume on the impact of frozen water.** Snow is frozen, crystallized water. In this activity, students investigate the impact of the depth of snow on its weight. The problem is connected with issues homeowners have when snow falls on their roofs repeatedly. Will the weight of the snow cause the roof to collapse? Students collect data about the depth and weight of snow to make estimates of various weights that roofs in their area can support. Then they enter their snow depth in feet in L_1, area of the base in square feet in L_2, and weight of snow in pounds in L_3. Next, they enter a formula for L_4 [$L_4 = L_3/(L_1*L_2)$] to calculate the pounds per cubic foot. Finally, they are able to calculate the mean and median values before discussing the impact of the weight of the snow at different depth levels.

Technology Link 10.1

The **Networked** link connects you with an activities exchange portal for sharing various content area activities to use with networked technologies.

www.wiley.com/college/niess

Real-Time Data Collection

Scientists commonly use real-time data collection devices to measure, store, and analyze data. These devices are often called *probeware* since they incorporate various probes or sensors (such as temperature, pH, sound, and motion detectors) to collect data and software designed to manage and analyze the data. One advantage of this technology is its connectivity with calculators, allowing data gathering to extend beyond the constraints of the classroom. Another advantage of this technology is that as the data are gathered, graphical representations of the data are presented as the probe sends a continuous stream of data from the measuring device. With the collected data, students are able to investigate the connection of the graphical representations of the data and the phenomenon of the data collected. Only recently, through the reduction in the cost to reproduce these technologies, probeware has become more accessible for educational purposes.

Probeware devices provide students with access to investigate science and mathematics concepts through hands-on, student-centered experiences that their teachers have previously described verbally. However, teachers need to carefully design student experiences with the probes. Students need to learn how the probes work, how to gather accurate data, how to use the graphical representations, and basically how to troubleshoot problems that occur. While they are learning about the sensors and understanding how and why the sensors work as they do, they can investigate subject matter problems that have been arranged in an order that provides them with important experiences before progressing to the study of more difficult concepts. Here are a couple of examples of activities that can be used to guide students in learning about the probes along with some important science concepts or ideas.

- **Which cup holds the heat the longest?**

Certainly you have noticed that certain types of cups keep the coffee warmer for a longer period of time. In this activity, students investigate the heat retention of two different types of cups to see which holds the heat the longest. For this experiment, the students connect two temperature probes to a system designed to gather data such as the simultaneous change in the temperature of hot water in two different types of cups. In this activity, students become familiar with the program that manages the recording of temperature measurements every 10 seconds for a period of 5 minutes. As the time progresses, students are able to observe the graphs of the temperatures versus time and immediately see which type of cup retains the heat the longest.

Consider how you might manage this experiment by taking the temperature with regular thermometers. You would have to have multiple thermometers (at least 4, probably 8), each reset to the lowest temperature possible, and a timepiece to check the temperature every 10 seconds. After recording the data, students would need to plot the graph. How valid and reliable will the results be using these materials? Will the graphs that students create be accurate? How many times can this experiment be repeated? How many students need to be in the group in order to manage this experiment with these materials? Where is the focus of student thinking: on the analysis of the data, on gathering the data and creating the chart?

Through this experiment, students are able to learn to use the probeware with the temperature sensors while they investigate graphical representations of temperature change. They are not constrained by the constant need to reset the thermometers and to create the graph. They can even redo the experiment more easily to verify their results. More importantly, this experience prepares them for a more detailed study of the characteristics of the different cups in supporting the retention of the heat. These students have had hands-on experiences with the concept of temperature retention in the process of developing their understanding about collecting data with sensors. And they are learning to use the probes and the technology system for analysis of the data.

- **Can you match my motion?**

If you were given a graph of time versus distance, could you create the motion that created the graph? How would you know if you did recreate the graph?

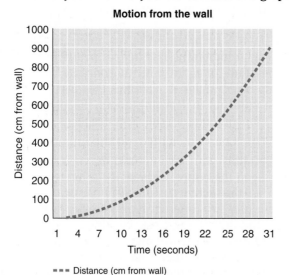

Motion from the wall

- - - Distance (cm from wall)

This activity introduces students to the motion detector with another software program that manages the data collection and analysis. Students fasten a motion detector to a tabletop, at about 15 cm above their waist level, facing an area free of furniture and other objects. As they walk away from the detector, the data are graphically displayed to describe the walking motion.

Understanding how the motion detector works is essential for collecting accurate motion data. With the motion detector, an ultrasound pulse is emitted in

a cone that is about 30° wide. Any object within that ultrasound cone causes a reflection. If a person is wearing a bulky sweater, the target may not supply a strong reflection. Thus, it is important for students to explore gathering data with this probe, to see the graph that results when the object is not within the appropriate cone. It is a good idea for students to hold a large book in front of them as they walk in front of the motion detector in order to smooth out the motion and produce a more accurate graph. Students need to see the difference of their movements both with and without the book.

Once students have had enough experience producing distance versus time graphs, their task is to match the motions of randomly generated graphs by the software program. In the process, students explore velocity versus time graphically, progressing to challenges for matching randomly generated graphs. Ultimately, they learn to work with the motion detector, discovering how it works, determining the quality of the data gathered, and gaining important visual and physical experiences with the concepts of distance and velocity in preparation for a more in-depth study of motion.

Previously, science teachers have tended to teach difficult concepts such as velocity and acceleration through lectures. They provide definitions and verbal explanations of the concepts but students never get an opportunity to gain experience with them. Unfortunately, without the opportunity to experience the concepts, they hear the words without much experiential meaning. The motion detector probes, on the other hand, allow them to gather the data and analyze graphical representations of the data. As a result, they gain valuable personal experiences that provide the instructional variations with the ideas. They are challenged to explain the ideas in their own words based on their personal experiences. However, it is crucial that in the beginning students become familiar with the probes, gaining proficiency with data collection and investigating various graphical representations. As their experiences increase, they are better prepared for more advanced science concepts.

Once students are familiar with the probeware systems, they are ready to tackle bigger problems. Consider the indicators of thermal pollution in rivers and streams. Many human activities affect water's temperature. Industries use river water in their production processes where the water is treated and returned to the river, warming the river. Water runoff from lawns, streets, and parking areas warms river water. Removing trees and vegetation from along a riverbank exposes the river to more direct sunlight that results in warming the water.

A temperature change of only a few degrees over a one-mile stretch of a stream might indicate a source of thermal pollution that can affect the general health of the river, its organisms, and its ecosystem. In the Classroom 10.3 describes a yearlong activity for a class to

In the Classroom 10.3[1]

HOW HEALTHY IS THIS RIVER?

TECHNOLOGY OBJECTIVE: **NETS · S V, VI**

- **Probeware:** Technology as a research and problem-solving and decision-making tool.
- Collect temperatures of water with the temperature probe; analyze the collected data.

CONTENT OBJECTIVE: **Science:** Make observations gathering data over an extended period of time.

GRADE LEVEL: 5–9

PROBLEM: What is the range of temperatures over the seasons throughout the year? Are there any signs of thermal pollution to this river?

Image courtesy of Vernier Software & Technology

- ❏ Identify a river near the school and select two sites approximately one mile apart.
- ❏ Weekly activity throughout the school year (assign tasks to groups of two):
    - Using a stainless-steel temperature probe, mark a distance 4 inches from the tip of the probe. Measure the temperature of the water at each site using the probe. At each site:
        - ○ Place the tip of the temperature probe directly into the stream at a depth of about 4 inches, to the mark.
        - ○ Begin sampling using a clockwise rotation of the probe; after 25 seconds, record the temperature that appears on the screen (to the nearest 0.1 °C).
        - ○ Repeat the measurement, recording the second temperature.
    - Complete the temperature observation record.

Temperature Observation Record

Stream or river:	Date:
Site 1 name:	Time of Day Site 1:
Site 2 name:	Time of Day Site 2:

Distance between sites:

Student 1:

Student 2:

Student 3:

Site	Temperature 1 (°C)	Temperature 2 (°C)	Average Temperature (°C)	Temperature Change (°C)
1				
2				

Field Observations (weather, geography, vegetation, etc.):

_____

If temperature has changed more than one degree, suggest possible reasons for the change (weather, pollution, etc.):

_____

- ❏ At the end of the school year; each pair of students must create a graph of temperature versus time (in weeks) to illustrate the magnitude of the temperature change that occurs in the river or stream throughout the year. Analyze the graph, discussing causes for changes in the temperature of the water and discussing any concerns about the health of the river or stream.

[1]Activity based on "Temperature" created by Johnson, R. L., Holman, S., & Holmquist, D. D. (1999). *Water quality with CBL*. Portland, OR: Vernier Software.

collect important thermal data about a river or stream in their area. Along with the temperature data, they record their observations of the two sites, noting the health of the water, the vegetation, the day's weather, and any other factors affecting the health of the water. At the end of the school year, they review the yearlong data set, charting the change in the river or stream. In the process of conducting their analysis, they use the observations throughout the year to describe the health of the particular river or stream. As they share their analyses, the teacher must encourage them to discuss how the use of the probe for making the measurements is supporting them in completing their research. How is this measurement different from a similar measurement using a simple thermometer?

How does this activity support learning in the classroom? Is the time used worth the effort? After all, the students must leave the classroom to gather the data. What are the issues and concerns when some go out to the stream and others remain in the classroom? Why not just give them the data and have a discussion? What do students gain from the action of collecting the data themselves? These questions are only a few of the important questions teachers must ask when considering the challenge of incorporating the use of the temperature probes.

Consider another use of this technology. Have you ever blown across the opening of the top of a bottle and produced a sound? What created the sound? The bottle seems to pull the air that is above the edge into the bottle, disturbing the air molecules inside the bottle, and producing excess air that attempts to escape out of the bottle. As the air pushes above the edge, the process repeats, producing an air stream that oscillates rapidly above and below the edge of the bottle. This process, called the Bernoulli effect, produces regions of higher than normal pressure in the bottle that ultimately forms a sound in a sinusoidal-shaped graph of pressure versus time. Each musical note is associated with a specific frequency of changes in pressure. The frequency of such a sound wave is measured in hertz (Hz), or cycles per second. For example, 262 hertz is 262 cycles per second and results in approximately a middle C sound.

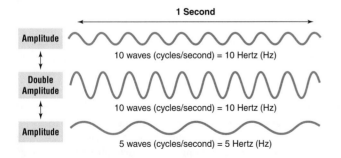

This is a good explanation that probably has little meaning to students. However, coupling this explana-

tion with some guided experiences may more actively engage them in gaining important personal experiences to support their understanding of the various ideas. In the Classroom 10.4 is an activity where students use a microphone sensor to investigate the mathematics of the musical notes by collecting the constants associated with the pressure-versus-time sound wave to produce a particular note when provided with the frequencies of the musical notes. In this scale an octave is divided into two equal intervals, and the higher the note, the greater the frequency. The C notes reveal the doubling of the frequency of corresponding notes in successive octaves. Figure 10.4 displays the frequencies of musical notes.

In this activity, students investigate a sound function created by the changes in air pressure, recorded using a microphone sensor. They are faced with connecting the science of the Bernoulli effect that results in the sound with the mathematics of the sinusoidal-shaped graph of pressure versus time of the sound that is created. In the end they are able to create as many songs as those of the notes they can identify allow. The activity provides a rich opportunity for collaborative group work and for expanding students' problem-solving strategies to include graphical and numerical as well as symbolic representations and ultimately allows students to make important connections among mathematics and science.

Advancing Web-Based Technologies

Web-based advancements in Internet technology over the past 15 years have had a significant impact on education. Today, students search the Web

Note	Frequency (Hz)
C	261.626
C♯ or D♭	277.183
D	293.665
D♯ or E♭	311.127
E	329.628
F	349.228
F♯ or G♭	369.994
G	391.995
G♯ or A♭	415.305
A	440
A♯ or B♭	466.164
B	493.883
Next octave doubles each frequency	
C	523.251

FIGURE 10.4 Frequencies of musical notes.

In the Classroom 10.4[2]

CAN YOU NAME THAT TUNE?

TECHNOLOGY OBJECTIVE: **NETS · S V, VI**

- **Probeware:** Technology as a research, problem-solving, and decision-making tool.
- Use the probeware microphone to collect the sound waves of various notes.

CONTENT OBJECTIVE: **Mathematics:** Identify the amplitude, period, phase shift, and vertical shift in the sine function to produce a specific sound.

Science: Investigate the Bernoulli effect and its connection with the creation of sound.

GRADE LEVEL: 9–12

PROBLEM: Can you play a song using a plastic bottle and a probeware microphone? Below are the notes! Find the notes and play this song.

- ❏ Divide the notes for the song among the class.
- ❏ The students fill their water bottles with water to the level that allows them to produce their notes, using the microphone sensor to identify the cycles per second and measure the frequency of the sound wave produced by blowing across the opening at the top of the bottle.
  - Identify how you found and determined the sound wave corresponding to your note.
  - Identify the amplitude (A), period (B), phase shift (C), and vertical shift (D) for the sinusoidal-shaped graph of pressure versus time that resulted in the note:

    $$y = A \sin(Bx + C) + D$$

- ❏ As a class, play the song. Find other songs and the notes needed to play those songs. Then play those songs.

Image courtesy of Vernier Software & Technology

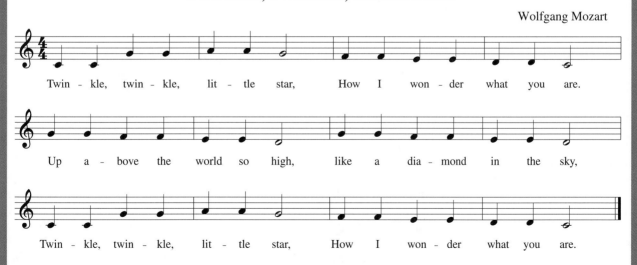

TWINKLE, TWINKLE, LITTLE STAR

Wolfgang Mozart

Twin - kle, twin - kle, lit - tle star, How I won - der what you are.

Up a - bove the world so high, like a dia - mond in the sky,

Twin - kle, twin - kle, lit - tle star, How I won - der what you are.

[2]Activity based on one described by Frenandez, M. L. (1999). Making music with mathematics. *Mathematics Teachers*, 92(2), 90–95.

to find information and they use Web pages as one way to communicate their understandings. More and more publications are readily available on the Web rather than in libraries, allowing students more access to publications that their libraries are unable to obtain. However, as the technology continues to emerge, many have identified limitations that they would like to see overcome with technology advancements. As a result, Web-based technologies are often in flux, generating more change than stability. Examples are plenty and are of course time-bound, but here are a few that are currently having a significant influence on teaching and learning in schools today.

In 2004 a group of leaders in the technology field began to talk about new ways of visualizing the Web. Their discussion was in the shadow of the so-called dot-com bust of 2001. After the fall of the NASDAQ stock market in 2000 and the subsequent collapse of numerous Web-based commercial ventures, many predicted that the Web was overhyped and overvalued. This group of technology leaders thought differently. They saw emerging Web-based technologies that were empowering users at a grassroots level. The new technologies were enabling people to interact, share, discuss, invent, and organize. The group, lead by Tim O'Reilly, dubbed the new technologies Web 2.0. They proclaimed that the Web was far from overhyped; instead it was coming into its own. New technologies were enabling everyday users to organize pictures (i.e., Fliker and Picasa), create spatial representations of personal interest (i.e., Google Mashups), share music and files (i.e., Napster and Kazaa), meet people and create communities (i.e., MySpace), as well as a whole host of other interactive activities. Some of these technologies are reviewed in broad strokes. Remember, technology is emerging, enhancing, and changing even as this chapter is written. The movement is so fast that what is emerging today might not be around tomorrow. With this understanding, look at three emerging technologies that are important in education: weblogs, RSS news readers, and podcasting. The important point is to look for ways their capabilities can support student learning and thinking.

Weblogs and Blogging   One of the earliest limitations identified on the Web was its general lack of interactivity. Although some users have been able to explore, read extensively, and put their own ideas on the Web for others to read, interactive communication open to a broad audience has not readily occurred. Yes, communication has been available on the Web through e-mail lists and discussion boards as described in Chapter 7, but both of those communication methods rely solely on print text presented in a linear fashion. E-mail and discussion board users have not been able

to easily create links expanding on their ideas or easily incorporate multiple elements such as graphics, motion, and visuals. Although some early Web users created personal websites expressing their individual ideas or views, most were limited in their ability to enter (and immediately publish) their ideas. To compound matters, much of what was published on the Web was static. In other words, in the early stages of the Web, website writers did not have the ability to engage their readers in an interactive dialogue other than by e-mail or bulletin boards, and those communication avenues lacked the capability of including visual and moving images.

Weblogs, or blogs, emerged in 2000 as tools for Web users to engage in reflective discourse. They were quickly accepted as a means of communication with the news media, politicians, and ordinary citizens about their private thoughts. Blogs offer much more than a journaling space. Blogs do not require HTML (hypertext markup lnguage) coding, but they can be embedded within a website (like Bernie Dodge is doing with the WebQuest portal with tools like moving type) or published as Web pages (using tools like blogger or modblog). They can display pictures, video, and audio, and even store PowerPoint presentations and Excel spreadsheets to expand on the ideas being discussed. An important point about blogs is that they are not intended to be places to produce technical or formal writing projects; rather, they are spaces designed for meaningful writing that concisely communicates an idea or position.

Blogs have been so quickly accepted as a communications tool that Webster's dictionary added the word to its list of words in advance of its typical requirement for 20 years of use before inclusion. Will Richardson (2004) described the immediate impact of this new communication medium for journalists:

> Howard Dean's weblog vaulted him into the thick of the Democratic presidential race. Companies are using blogs to communicate directly with customers and to provide collaborative space for developers. Journalists at the *New York Times*, ABC News, and other media outlets are using blogs to connect more closely to readers, providing insights and information that might otherwise not make it into print. In fact, in journalistic circles, a debate is raging over whether or not weblogs might change the profession, as we know it.

Although blogs have been quickly accepted in daily lives, educators have been more cautious in considering how they can be used in guiding students in learning. As you saw in Chapter 7, teachers can engage their students in discussing their thoughts in a blog after viewing digital images of the September 11 tragedy (see In the Classroom 7.4 in Chapter 7). And, of course, the work that Mrs.

Adams did with her class in the Snapshot of a Class Developing a Web Blog on a Presidential Campaign represents an idea for the social studies curriculum. Mrs. Adams' interest in the upcoming presidential election provided her with an opportunity to frame the introduction to weblogs. She began by showing the blog that she created to engage them in a discussion about politics. She introduced blogs as Web-based journals that were meant to be public, for others to read and to engage in a discussion about the ideas. She planned that this new form of writing serve as a dynamic means for dialogue, engaging her students in succinctly reflecting on the politics surrounding the upcoming election.

Bull, Bull, and Kajder (2003) promoted the potential for the use of blogs in education: "The sharing of messages, the openness of the thinking, the accessibility of the media . . . it all adds up to a form of communication that warrants our exploration." However, blogs do challenge educators to consider important questions if this technology is to be incorporated in education:

> What does it mean to communicate through a blog? What are the rules? How does that apply to how we communicate and share meaning in open speech? How do we lead students to share and respond to comments shared by other readers? What do the multitextual resources made available online bring into the conversation housed within a blog? How do struggling readers and writers work within this writing space in ways that are different from their engagement with print text? *(Bull, Bull, & Kajder, 2003, p. 32)*

These challenges are directed at more than just language arts and social studies teachers. Blogs provide conversation spaces for students to communicate their ideas in every aspect of their education. The challenge is for each teacher to think of ways that this emerging form of communication guides and aids students in explaining their own thinking. For example, students might

- use blogs for character journals, class travel journals for field trips or study abroad, and for collaborative reading journals;

- use blogs to discuss their developing ideas about the effect of the changes in temperature on the river or stream that they investigate for In the Classroom 10.3;

- discuss their thoughts using wireless notebooks as they progress through a store, identifying items to purchase and considering how their estimate of the costs affects their intent to purchase;

- describe and reflect on their development in a physical education class, when considering their own expanding strength and agility.

Mrs. Adams in the Snapshot of a Class Developing a Web Blog on a Presidential Campaign was experimenting with integrating blogs as a way of engaging students in the political processes in the presidential campaign. She understood the value of journaling as a way of having students think about their own thinking. She planned the lesson to have the students use public journaling as a process of engaging in a discussion with other students. Teachers, such as Mrs. Adams, need to share their ideas and talk about ideas that work for engaging students in writing and communicating; they need to consider how this reflective process, as a form of expression, changes as weblog technology evolves in the preparation of students to become active citizens in the twenty-first century. Perhaps a weblog devoted to engaging teachers in discussing the use of weblog technology in the classroom is a good first step for evaluating the potential of the technology as an educational tool. Better yet, what advantages are there for preservice teachers to enter into a weblog dialog as they interact with the materials and ideas in this book? Could the weblog help them develop a deeper understanding of the potential of weblogs?

RSS News   The explosion of blogs on the Internet led to the rise of another technology tool that makes it easier to filter and track the massively increasing number of online resources. The proliferation of content on the Web is staggering. Just consider blogs. The Perseus Development Group has identified over 4 million weblogs that were created in a 2-year period, with thousands more being created weekly (Richardson, 2004). Add to that the thousands of traditional media outlets that have moved to the Web and the multitude of websites and other dynamic text sources being produced by professionals and enthusiasts around the world. How can one keep up with all this content? First you must realize that it is not possible to keep up with the rapidly expanding set of Web resources. Instead, new technologies offer Web users opportunities to manage the relevant information. Rich site summary or really simple syndication, known as RSS, is one such emerging technology. RSS technology enables simple programs called newsreaders to organize Web-based content. This technology is important for teachers and students in some of the same ways as HTML. Although you do not have to know how to write HTML or RSS code, knowing what the technology tool provides is essential.

RSS is an *aggregator* or *news-feed collector* that allows people to access content using their computer. Think about a particular event, such as the impact of Hurricane Katrina on New Orleans. You might use the aggregator to collect all the new content, or *news feeds*, about this event in order to better understand its impact.

The RSS protocol originated in the mid 1990s as part of an effort to develop Web portals. The portal idea did not go far at the time, but RSS as a background means for gathering portal-based information continues to be an important mechanism for aggregating information. RSS is essentially a simplified XML (extensible markup language) format that calls on remote Web servers to deliver news headlines, summaries, and links to full stories. These RSS feeds must be viewed through a software program called a *news aggregator* or *newsreader*. The full stories provided through RSS are often Web-based, whereas the headlines and summaries are viewable only using the newsreaders. Numerous newsreader programs exist, some running inside Web browsers and others operating as separate programs. For example, the Math Forum through Drexel's School of Education provides access to news feeds that deal with articles of importance to mathematics teachers such as whether or not to allow students unrestricted use of calculators in their mathematics classes. Teachers can access the latest news referring to the concerns and recommendations.

A common use of RSS news aggregators has been in the blog community, where bloggers use RSS to feed readers with updates to their sites. RSS newsreaders allow users to subscribe to specific news or blog feeds, known as channels. After subscribing using a newsreader, users can browse or search for stories, updating the feed whenever they want. In essence, the aggregator checks blogger sites subscribed to and collects all the new content into a folder. As they have time, users can review the headlines, perhaps reading some of the articles in total, deleting some as not of interest, or storing some for future use. Bloglines.com is one Web-based, free aggregator, which can be accessed from any Internet connection, that allows you to start small and experiment, thus getting an idea of the capabilities of aggregators. Technology Link 10.2 provides you with direct access to begin this exploration.

Technology Link 10.2

*T*he **RSS** link connects you to a free Web-based news aggregator that you can use to begin your explorations of RSS as an emerging technology.

www.wiley.com/college/niess

A key activity for historians is to clarify the source of documents that are used in building an understanding of important concepts. And a central concept considered in the social studies curriculum is that of democracy. After exploring newsreaders and recognizing that they are most appropriately focused on current events, Mr. Solomon, a social studies teacher, wanted to design an activity to engage his students in valuable experiences with an emerging technology with potential as a productivity and research tool in social studies. More importantly, he wanted to embed these experiences within a social studies content exploration, namely, the concept of democracy in today's world.

As he thought about the subject matter content of democracy being gathered through a variety of current news sources, Mr. Solomon recalled an important history activity that Samuel Wineburg (1991) called a "sourcing heuristic." Wineburg suggested that as historians work with primary historical sources, they have to identify the source authors along with the motivations for producing the source, as well as how the authors participated in events at the time the source was created. This sourcing technique also carefully describes the intended audience for the document.

In the Classroom 10.5 summarizes an activity that resulted from Mr. Solomon's thinking toward challenging his students to focus on the sources of current news stories related to the concept of democracy. In the activity, the class is expected to collect RSS news feeds using a newsreader for their research project on the understanding of democracy, and complete a sourcing activity. The key to this activity is the manner in which the class treats the newspaper articles as primary historical sources that could be used to investigate global views on democracy.

Prior to the sourcing activity, Mr. Solomon planned to demonstrate how the RSS newsreader might be used to conduct a research project on describing diverse views about democracy. He showed them how to create a channel or news feed for the topic they planned to investigate.

Mr. Solomon identified 17 articles from the newsreader that fit the topic of democracy and assigned each article to one or two students. The students were expected to explore the distributive qualities of newsreaders as well as sourcing each of the news stories using Wineburg's sourcing heuristic. They also evaluated each other's work, focusing specifically on the various perspectives embedded within the news sources that were retrieved. The news stories emerged from a variety of sources, both trusted and suspect, for challenging the students to *source* the information, thereby enhancing their critical reading skills.

Each student read the assigned article on the topic of democracy from the feed. Mr. Solomon asked them to answer a series of questions about the source of the document, the information contained in the article, and the perspective of the article. When the students completed the assignment, the 17 stories were filed in the channel, ranging from a variety of sources including Cairo-based *Al-Ahram Weekly Online*, London-

In the Classroom 10.5

IS DEMOCRACY VIEWED THE SAME BY ALL?

TECHNOLOGY OBJECTIVE: NETS · S III, IV, V

- **RSS and weblogs:** Technology as a productivity, communications, and research tool.
- Use RSS and weblog sources to identify articles about a particular topic.

CONTENT OBJECTIVE: **Social studies:** Explore the concept of democracy portrayed by news articles. Use critical thinking skills in investigating sources of articles.

GRADE LEVEL: 9–12

PROBLEM: Is democracy viewed the same by all? How do current sources portray democracy?

- ❏ **Identify current articles.** Demonstrate using an RSS newsreader with broad access to Internet sites and weblog sources.
  - Create a special channel to automatically gather all stories featuring the word democracy in the article title or brief article summary.
  - Of the articles identified by the RSS reader, assign each article to one or two students in the class.
- ❏ **Identify motivations for articles.** As students consider the article, ask them to respond to the following questions about the source of the current events related to the document assigned:
  - Who wrote the article?
  - What else do you know about the author?
  - Who published the article?
  - What is the business of the publisher of the article?
  - When was the story written?
  - Why do you think the story was written?
  - Who is the audience for the story?
- ❏ **Expectations.** Students write a short summary of the article and prepare to compare the perspectives of the article with those reviewed by the other class members.

based *Guardian News*, the World Socialist Web Site, a Savannah, Georgia, newspaper (*Savannah Morning News*) publication called *Savannah Now, The New York Times International Edition*, and Nigeria-based *Vanguard Niger Delta News*. The stories dealt with a range of democracy-related topics. Twelve of the stories focused on a small number of news-oriented events, whereas the others dealt with less news focused opinion-related items or press releases.

The stories reflected a range of ideological perspectives, resulting in students having conflicting sources of information about three or four stories on the topic of democracy. The students also read stories that reflected perspectives not readily available though mass media outlets in the mainstream press. Through the activity, they learned how newsreaders provided simplified access to news-related stories. But they also learned that they must apply critical thinking skills when using these resources, including the sourcing skills learned in the activity.

Does this application to teaching about democracy create an educational experience that has previously been difficult to obtain? Does the application add value to the classroom discussion? Do students gain an appreciation for differences of opinion about democracy? Do the experiences provide students with valuable experiences in exploring a technology that is useful as a productivity, communications, and research tool in learning social studies? These questions are samples of the kinds of questions you as a teacher must consider when thinking about the value of using RSS newsreaders for your students in your content area. Your task, as a teacher, is to develop and adopt a planning process similar to that which Mr. Solomon invoked for merging his experiences with an emerging technology and with methods for supporting his students in learning in the content area.

Podcasting   Ever think about using a radio program to engage your students in some learning experiences? Of course you do not have a radio broadcasting system, but you do have access to a system that can create audio programs—the Web! *Podcasting* broadcasts audio and/or video (sometimes known as *vodcasting*) via the Web with easy-to-use interfaces. Listeners can subscribe to feeds using podcasting software (another type of aggregator) that periodically checks for and downloads new content automatically; also, listeners can readily create, mix, and post their own recorded content in the podcasting broadcasts. Any digital audio player or computer with audio-playing software can play the podcasts.

Podcasting is an emerging technology that enables users to distribute their own radio shows. American astronaut Steve Robinson made the first podcast from space during Space Shuttle *Discovery* mission STS-114. *Battlestar Galactica* writer Ron Moore created commentary podcasts for viewers to use as they watch the show on television and listen to his comments on each scene. Even President Bush is a podcaster with weekly radio addresses at the White House. Does this emerging technology have potential for education? Yes, podcasting does! Podcasting takes advantage of oral and presentation skills that are not exercised as much given the content pressures of testing. Between providing students access to audio content and giving them the tools for creating their own artifacts, podcasting is an invaluable research, reading, and composition tool. This technology can provide students with new sources of information in formats that encourage their learning in unique and powerful ways. These benefits do indicate that podcasting provides unique capabilities for K–12 education.

The new sources of information made available through podcasting are comparable to the development of Web-authoring tools that enabled people to make text resources available on the Web. In both cases, the technology requires little or no cost and minimal technological sophistication. As with text resources for Web authoring, within a few years tens of thousands of audio resources have been made available on the Web. Students and their teachers can mine these resources for curricular relevant content. For example, podcasts on topics as relevant and diverse as medieval history, a Mark Twain reader, and English as a second language are all available through the link in Technology Link 10.3

Technology Link 10.3

The **Podcast** link connects you to a free space for exploring podcasting as an emerging technology.

www.wiley.com/college/niess

Podcasting technology can also be used as a tool to enable teachers and students to construct their own knowledge. Teachers can create a podcast of supplemental information for student use. Students might prepare podcasts as demonstrations

of their knowledge. For example, students in a language arts class might conduct book talks and use a digital recorder to record the live discussions to be posted online. One of the most important features of this technology as it relates to education might be the ability to control when and where the podcast is used, thereby potentially freeing teachers and students to use fixed classroom time more efficiently. Only by exploring the capabilities of podcasting and using them with students in learning the content can you adequately evaluate their usefulness for education.

In the Classroom 10.6 is one idea that might be useful for even young children to encourage them to improve their reading while also experiencing an emerging technology tool. A key feature in the education of young children is to help them realize that they are improving in their reading abilities. This activity collects evidence of their reading abilities and interests at the beginning of a school year to compare with their reading abilities and interests at the end of a school year. A podcast of before and after evidence of students' reading skills might be used for the children themselves to listen to their own ideas and describe the growth they have made in reading as well as to demonstrate to their parents the progress that they have made over the school year.

Electronic Books   The notion of digitizing a printed book dates back to at least to 1971 when Michael Hart founded Project Gutenberg. Hart visualized an electronic repository of all known literature, freely and easily available to all interested users at the same time. Between 1971 and 1993, Hart and a small group of collaborators digitized about 100 books. Since then they have added thousands of books to the collection. Hart and his collaborators at Project Gutenberg are not alone. Hundreds of initiatives, public and private, have begun the work of digitizing books, and much of the work dates to the early 1990s. Examples include the work by non-profit organizations such as the University of Virginia's eText Center and the Online Computer Library Center (OCLC), as well as for-profit organizations such as Adobe, Amazon.com, and Google's Print project. Together, all these groups have and are continuing to digitize thousands of texts and books. Clearly, the vision of student access to digital versions of an expansive library of writings is a reality, providing students opportunities far beyond that available in current library holdings.

Given the history of the electronic book (or eBook) and the progress made in digitizing books, why consider eBook an emerging technology? Quite simply, the availability of books in electronic format is still enormously insignificant in scope

In the Classroom 10.6

HAS MY READING IMPROVED?

TECHNOLOGY OBJECTIVE: **NETS · S II, III, IV**

- **Podcast:** Technology as a productivity and research tool and considering important human issues.
- Use podcasting technologies to develop an audio program to communicate.

CONTENT OBJECTIVE: **Language arts:** Describe the growth in reading skills developed over time.

GRADE LEVEL: K–2

PROBLEM: Am I a better reader? Have my reading interests changed?

❏ **Beginning of school year**
- Have children select a book they want to read for an audio recording.
- At the beginning of the recording, ask the child to state his/her name.
- The child reads a favorite portion of the book for the audio recording and explains what is being communicated.
- To end the recording the child explains the reason for the choice of the book.

❏ **End of school year**
- Have children select a book they want to read for an audio recording.
- At the beginning of the recording, ask the child to state his/her name.
- The children then read favorite portions of the book for the audio recording. As they read the text, they can be prompted to explain what they are reading.
- To end the recording the child explains the reason for the choice of the book.

❏ **Compile a before and after podcast of each student's growth in reading.** The podcast is available through the class website by clicking on each student's name.

❏ **Share the podcasts.**
- Share with the children, asking them to identify the changes that they hear in their reading ability, their understandings of what they are reading, and their reading interests.
- Share with parents to describe their children's reading improvement. Identify goals for the summer to continue the improvement.

and scale when compared to the number of printed books not available in digital form. Estimates put the number of books now published each year at over one million. The U.S. Library of Congress has over 20 million books in its collection. The total number of books in print could be in the hundreds of millions. Electronic book versions of these publications likely represent less than one-tenth of a percent of all books in print. Still the question must be asked: Why should eBooks be considered a potential technology for education? Perhaps eBooks are similar to calculators. They are available and accessed regularly by many people who have begun reading eBook versions of different texts. Educators need to investigate this technology and ask some basic questions. What do eBooks have to offer education that is better than having students read a bound, paper text version?

When responding to this question, you must consider the multimodal literacy provided by eBooks. More and more electronic books are being created for children and stored on CDs (Compact disc) and the Web, to allow them to engage in stories reconstructed with diverse visual presentations including animation, sound, and other visuals to bring the story to life for the reader. Is this reading as you know it? The format allows the potential for reading to be nonlinear with heavy concentration of multiple inputs. Is this the way reading is to be done in the future? What are students learning when they read using this new format? Educational researchers and teachers need to engage in research to identify what if anything children are learning as they read in this manner. Are they thinking about the text? Is the entertainment value so overwhelming they are simply not thinking?

Much work still must be done if the electronic book is to change book writing, publishing, and reading, but new innovations and efforts are beginning to change the outlook. Two specific innovations may be intriguing for teachers. One involves the systematic digitization of library collections by search engine companies. The plan is to make portions of collections from leading universities and public libraries available to subscribers as well as making portions of these eBooks available to the general public.

Another innovation relates to the means by which eBooks are assembled and distributed. An emerging convention that capitalizes on the ability of computer-based interfaces to deliver nonlinearly structured information is enabling readers to borrow and read eBooks in dynamic ways. Various eBook readers have been developed and are marginally used, but to date no single convention for reading eBooks has emerged. As the number of books made available online continues to grow and as developers continue to tweak delivery mechanisms, eBook readers are likely to increase in popularity.

The area that may be most significantly affected by this emerging technology could be academic books, particularly those aimed at middle school, high school, and college students. Imagine having links to additional information if you need to read more about a particular idea or to see a visual description of the concept. Imagine having the ability to skim a section to see if that section may be of use for answering a question. Imagine linking to a passage that up to this time in the presentation of books has only been referenced. Imagine using digital tools to mark up and annotate electronic texts (such as through Microsoft Reader).

These innovative ideas offer new ways for engaging students in learning, but they also challenge teachers to confront important issues. Electronic books require electronic readers, suggesting that each student needs access, one student to one electronic reading device. With this understanding, successful large-scale integration of eBook activities in education minimally demands classroom sets of the electronic devices. While companies are in the research and development phase for $100 computers, the pocket computer handheld devices provide promise for this access concern.

Think about this example of how a current sixth-grade teacher, Jane Odom, might deal with the access issue along with important pedagogical issues. Jane wonders how she can help her students develop reading skills and habits that will enable them to read in fast-paced technological environments. She knows that students must develop sound reading habits tied to the use of print-based resources, but she also wants to make use of her students' experiences with handheld devices to develop new *electronic reading habits*. To pursue her goal, Jane applies for and receives a small grant to buy a classroom set of handheld computer devices. For less than $10,000, she is able to purchase 25 handheld devices and rights to a small library of 30 books.

During the school year, Jane plans to work with the class, teaching them how to use the device and assigning books or portions of books. She carefully scaffolds the reading activities so that students learn to use the various components of the handhelds, such as word processing, to enhance their reading. Throughout her experience, she holds to one principle. She wants her students to use eBooks to allow them to do things that would not be possible with print versions of the same books. First, eBooks and handheld devices are highly portable, which means that her students are able to carry all 30 books with them virtually at all times. Second, the handheld devices enable the students to directly interact with the text, composing notes, copying text to word processing programs, and transferring work from one handheld device to other ones. Third, the eBooks enable students to connect to related resources; for example, the eBooks and handheld devices provide links to pictures, dictionaries, writing tools, and additional information, including notes on the text in the book.

With the availability of eBooks, teachers, like Jane, must reconsider how to guide students in learning to read in this multimodal fashion as well as how to utilize the capabilities of digital technologies in conjunction with reading the electronic books. Teachers need to develop and provide techniques and sources to aid students in learning within the context of the availability of electronic books.

Emerging Wireless Technologies' Increasing Access

"School swaps books for laptops!" That's the news in July of 2005. An Arizona high school plans to follow an increasingly predominant trend, using electronic materials, readings, and even available electronic books online. Rather than paying for textbooks, the school is issuing students with laptops for use in all instructional areas. Students can link to original information, which was previously at most summarized in often out-of-date textbooks. They access required and ancillary materials over the school's wireless Internet network. And they submit their assignments online from school or home because of the capabilities of the wireless technologies.

With the increasingly available wireless technologies, you can access the Internet from the coffee shop, take notes in classes, beam information to others, send text messages, and accomplish many other activities making use of the emerging wireless network access with various handhelds and laptops. With increased access, how these technology tools will support learning is another emerging question that teachers and students must investigate.

Handheld Computers   Handheld computers are small and portable. Often handhelds are seen as organizers or gameboys that use key taps instead of keyboards. Curtis, Kopera, Norris, and Soloway (2004) challenge teachers to consider ways that these handheld devices can be used as a learning device in the elementary classroom. One application gives students a concept-mapping tool for framing a project, a website, or even a process that they are learning. Brainstorming the ideas using this application clarifies what they want to accomplish; then they can use Kidspiration to formalize their ideas. A simple example of how elementary school children might use this application is to have them identify as many ways as possible to express a chosen number, say 10. They can express the number in letters (ten), expressions (5+5, 8+2, etc.), or even with pictures of 10 items (like 10 apples). They put the number 10 in the center of their screen in a cell and link cells to different ways of expressing it. They can even put some cells that are not 10 that they do not connect with arrows such as 3+3+3 in this display.

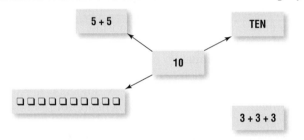

Teachers need to examine handheld devices such as the Palm to determine if they have capabilities that can be used to support learning in their classrooms. Because these devices are more accessible, the children may have more opportunities for learning with technologies. Whether students write more, collaborate more, and read more needs to be researched from within the various subject areas when children have the increased technology access.

Tablet PCs and Other Wireless Devices   Consider the last time you had an eye examination. The nurse gathered data about your eyesight and recorded the information in your chart. The doctor entered the room carrying your chart with all of your past records in a linear array, conducted more tests, and recorded more information about any correction you might need in your lenses. That was yesterday!

Today, the nurse enters the room carrying a wireless, electronic device called a tablet PC, completes the first examination, electronically recording the data that is actually recorded in your online chart for the doctor to review. The doctor enters the room carrying a similar device, accesses your record from online, conducts the necessary tests, and records the prescribed lens correction. All of these actions are actually recorded in your permanent electronic file. If prior information is needed, the doctor is able to directly access that information through a menu selection rather than wading through your past records.

Can this technology be used in education? Similar to the eBook revolution, as technologies such as the tablet PC evolve, educators need to participate, identifying their needs and considering potential uses of the technology. How might you as a teacher be able to use a tablet PC? As you travel throughout the room observing your students in an activity, you can make notes about their progress, assess their skills with particular equipment, and make notes for consideration in future classes. How might your students use a tablet PC? They could take notes using an electronic version of a tablet; they might even have access to an electronic version of the visuals and text so they can make notes or write their questions by the part that is puzzling. Or perhaps students can record the audio of the lecture to accompany their notes of the lecture. Students can work with online tutorials as the teacher guides the activity. Of course students could do other things unrelated to the classroom activities, like send e-mail messages or engage in nonrelated activities.

The most important activity for you as a teacher is to consider how to take advantage of the new wireless technologies. These technologies allow freedom to work from sites other than their classrooms. Imagine students using the devices to take notes while they are on a field trip. Will they be more apt to take notes than if they used paper and pen? Maybe they will if the wireless device is able to connect to a website that has copies of images along with supporting text. They might be more apt to more critically view the images, putting down their emerging thoughts as they are seeing them for real.

Classroom laboratories have restricted science experiments by limiting students to exploring stored samples rather than naturally collected samples. Now, with wireless devices including probeware, students can gather data for lab activities conducted outside the classroom. They can enter the data into spreadsheets, analyze the results to see if they have extraneous data, and consider whether they need to redo the data collection before returning to the classroom.

With handhelds, student writing is no longer restricted to the home or classroom. With handhelds, they can write wherever they are—on the baseball field and the soccer field, at church, or even when they are visiting museum collections. Imagine taking a group of students on a field trip to an art museum; students can take notes on their handheld, wireless devices rather than in their notebooks. Handhelds provide a writing space that may encourage even struggling writers to capture and express their ideas about the artwork they are seeing personally.

What about this idea for a middle school class challenged to develop research questions within a theme, such as "What is an American?" The students have handhelds and work in teams to explore print and online materials in the media center. As they find research questions, they beam their findings to captains in charge of developing the class spreadsheet that lists the questions and resources. Throughout this activity, students' use of the technology is both transparent and essential. The important point is for teachers to consider how the unique capabilities can support what students have not previously been able to accomplish.

"Emerging devices, tools, media and virtual environments offer opportunities for creating new types of learning communities for students and teachers" (Dede, 2004a). Dede proposes a more advanced educational use of wireless devices and a shift toward the learning communities model of education. He describes education where the emphasis is on building learning communities rather than gathering all students into a single classroom space to learn. Furthermore, he suggests that emerging information technologies support this significant shift to communities of learning among schools, businesses, homes, and community settings. The key, however, is for teachers and students to consider each tool's capacities and think about what they can now accomplish that was previously not possible. Does the new technology provide a different way that results in a stronger capacity for learning? Yes, they can learn in the same way with the newer technologies. The challenge is to envision ways that result in a strong capacity for learning.

Summing It Up

Computer-based, communications, and information-based technologies are increasingly evolving, providing more and improved capabilities to support human interactions in the twenty-first century. As these and newer technologies emerge, education is faced with the task of examining them as tools for learning and teaching.

Educators must continually examine the potentials of the new technologies. But they must also continually examine the curriculum and instruction with the new tools. Will the current curriculum stay the same or shift with the impact of the newer technologies? Do students need to learn these concepts or are other concepts more important? Are there better ways to instruct and communicate with students? The technologies considered in this chapter serve only as examples for you to engage in thinking about how emerging technologies might impact the curriculum and instruction as well as ultimately provide tools for students to think and learn with in the twenty-first century.

Teachers need to develop a thoughtful visioning attitude that questions the advancement and improvement in at least six important areas:

1. Curricular needs in your subject area in the twenty-first century.
2. Instructional needs in your subject area in the twenty-first century.
3. Student learning in the twenty-first century.
4. Unique capabilities of the new tool.
5. Student knowledge, access, and management concerns.
6. Assessment and evaluation with the new tool.

Each of the areas requires that teachers challenge the past and consider the future needs of citizens who will live, work, and relax in the twenty-first century.

The calculator has been available for over 30 years and, at first glance, does not appear to represent an emerging technology, except for the addition of peripherals and software to improve their usability and capabilities. If you carefully consider the impact of calculators on education, you find an evolving technology that continues to present questions for educators. Does the calculator disadvantage students in learning mathematics? What do students need to learn without the help of the calculator and what do they need to learn using the calculator as a tool? Meanwhile, calculators evolve to include more and more capabilities that challenge teachers to face the issue of students using calculators as a tool for learning.

Although the mathematics capabilities of the calculator increasingly challenge teachers with the question of how students need to know mathematical concepts and procedures, the addition of a large variety of applications for multiple subject areas has placed calculators as tools to learn in all subject areas. The addition of features that allow teachers to transmit questions to students during the class, to receive responses from each student, and to summarize each student's progress with the ideas have shifted how calculators might be used as *tools to think with* rather than as *tools to replace thinking*.

Calculators with real-time data collection probes provide students with opportunities to experience phenomena they have previously only read or heard about from their teachers and textbooks. They can use a motion detector to investigate distance versus time and velocity versus time as they walk away or toward the detector. They can use temperature probes to investigate thermal pollution. They can collect various sound waveforms and compare the harmonics of different notes.

In addition to the evolution of calculator technologies, Web-based technologies are experiencing significant changes. Weblogs (or blogs) have emerged as a new form of communication that has been quickly accepted by news media, politicians, and ordinary citizens. Blogs have the feel of a journaling space, where the writer expresses his or her personal ideas and impressions, but they offer much more than journaling space. Whereas with journals and diaries you write for yourself, with a blog you write for other people to read. You want them to read it. You can also use the blog to organize links to your favorite website and you can link to other websites as you write your entries. Hyperlinks allow bloggers to support what they are saying or provide readers with more information on a topic. With blogs, you can display pictures, video, and audio, and even store PowerPoint presentations and Excel spreadsheets to expand the ideas being discussed.

With this new form of communication, teachers are faced with important questions about how to incorporate blogging into the curriculum. What do students need to learn and where do they need to learn it with respect to blogs? How will this form of communication change how students learn? What activities in various subject areas can take advantage of this new form of communication to support student learning? Educators have lots of questions for this new form of communication.

The explosion of blogs on the Internet supported the rise of additional technology tools, tools that provide easier ways to filter, track, and make use of the increasing number of online resources. Rich site summary or really simple syndication, known as RSS, calls on remote Web servers to deliver news headlines, summaries, and links to full stories. Students can use the RSS news feeds to complete specific research projects. Nevertheless, while they are gaining access, they must learn to evaluate the perspectives embedded within the news sources, enhancing essential critical reading skills for the twenty-first century.

Podcasting is another emerging technology that enables users to distribute their own radio shows. One of the most important features of this technology as it relates to education might be the ability to control when and where the podcast is used, potentially freeing teachers and students to use fixed classroom time more efficiently. Only by exploring the capabilities of podcasting and using podcasts with students in learning the content can you adequately evaluate the usefulness for education.

Additional emerging technologies that offer challenges for education include electronic books (or eBooks) and increasingly wireless technology access. How will the emerging wireless technologies affect education? Perhaps education will challenge the traditional formation of schools—students learning in a central location. With wireless access you can envision students working in collaborative groups, where some members may be in their homes, other students may be at a computer lab at the school, and others may be at the city library where they have access to important resources for the activity. What are some other ways that students can learn what they need to learn to be successful citizens in a twenty-first century impacted by the capabilities of emerging information and communications technologies? Teachers who maintain a proactive stance toward learning about new and emerging technologies and investigating how they might support learning will be the leaders in responding to the challenges and questions. As a future teacher, you must be willing to challenge both what the students should learn and how they might learn it. You must be prepared to change how you were taught and how you plan to teach, how you might guide student learning, and what you teach given the impact of technology.

End-of-the-Chapter Activities and References

PRACTICE PROBLEMS

1. Conduct the activity described for In the Classroom 10.1 where you enter data into the calculator list.

2. Investigate real-time data collection data probes that are available for use with either a calculator or a computer. Describe a problem that students can investigate using the probe; outline the process that students would follow to investigate the problem.

3. Experiment with weblogs and RSS feeds. Using a free online service (see Technology Link 10.2), start your own blog discussing the use of blogs in education.

4. Aggregate RSS feeds on the topic you chose for Problem 3 to gather various perspectives. Describe the features that are available through the RSS feed. Which features are the most useful?

5. Conduct an Internet search on *emerging technologies*. Identify at least one or two technologies that have potential for education. Explain how these technologies might help students learn.

6. Search the Web for weblogs that are focused on integrating technology into education. Summarize the questions, challenges, or other perspectives on the topic.

7. Explore podcasting using Technology Link 10.3. Create an educational application of the use of podcasting for your subject area and grade level.

IN THE CLASSROOM ACTIVITIES

8. Identify a chapter in a text that students are reading in a classroom that you are observing. Create a list of various ways that the chapter might be rewritten in an eBook format to extend and enhance the students' understanding of the ideas.

9. Interview the teachers in classrooms with respect to emerging technologies. Identify some of the capabilities of the emerging technologies that you have investigated. Ask them how they might use those technologies to enhance student learning.

ASSESSING STUDENT LEARNING WITH AND ABOUT TECHNOLOGY

10. Create a mathematics problem where students are allowed to use the calculator as a tool in the solution. Create a mathematics problem where students should not use the calculator as a tool in the solution. What is the difference in the problems? How would you assess the students' work on the different problems?

11. Identify an educational use of an emerging technology (perhaps using one of the references identified in Annotated Resources). Describe the objectives for student learning and how you might assess their learning both with and about the technology.

E-PORTFOLIO ACTIVITIES

12. Begin a weblog where the discussion is focused on the impact of emerging technologies on the curriculum. Gather other perspectives on this issue and respond to those perspectives in your weblog, creating hyperlinks that allow others to access the additional perspectives.

13. Extend your reference list in your E-portfolio to include ideas for guiding student learning with and about emerging technologies such as those identified in this chapter.

REFLECTION AND DISCUSSION

14. Reflect on your progress toward acceptance of an emerging technology for educational use. Use Everett Rogers' (2003) five steps as you think about your perception of incorporating the specific technology for educational use.

15. Children should not use calculators as they learn mathematics. Respond to that statement in a class weblog.

16. Back to the future: You are teacher in the twenty-second century. Write a journal that describes your typical teaching day. As a class, discuss how your visions of the twenty-second-century education changes from today and how it remains the same.

◄ Annotated Resources

Bull, G., Bull, G., & Kajder, S. (2003). Writing with weblogs: Reinventing student journals. *Learning and Leading with Technology, 31*(1), 32–35.

Investigate weblogs and consider ways that students can engage in blogging in their classes.

Curtis, M., Kopera, J., Norris, C., & Soloway, E. (2004). *Palm OS® handhelds in the elementary classroom: Curriculum and strategies.* Eugene, OR: ISTE.

Consider the variety of ways that handhelds can support education in the elementary classroom. This text contains many thematic units for elementary grades that integrate the capabilities of Palm handhelds in support of learning.

Frenandez, M. L. (1999). Making music with mathematics. *Mathematics Teacher, 92* (2), 90–95.

Explore the mathematics of sound using probeware to create songs.

Gastineau, J., Appel, K., Bakken, C., Sorenen, R., & Vernier, D. (2000) *Physics with calculators.* Portland, OR: Vernier Software.

Review 34 student experiments using the Vernier LabPro interface with Texas Instruments graphing calculators for collecting, displaying, printing, graphing, and analyzing physical science data.

Godsall, L., Crescimano, L., & Blair, R. (2005). Exploring tablet PCs. *Learning and Leading with Technology, 23*(8), 16–21.

Pine Crest School is not a technology school. However, they make extensive use of tablet PCs. Review how they are able to guide student learning with this emerging technology.

Johnson, R. L., DeMoss, G. S., & Sorensen, R. (2002) *Earth science with calculators.* Portland, OR: Vernier Software.

Explore Earth science experiments for middle school level where students use sensors with the Vernier LabPro for collecting, displaying, printing, graphing, and analyzing data.

Johnson, R. L., Holman, S., & Holmquist, D. D. (1999). *Water quality with CBL.* Portland, OR: Vernier Software.

Consult a resource filled with activities for water quality tests using the Vernier sensors with calculators or computers.

Richardson, W. (2004). Blogging and RSS—The "what's it?" and "how to" of powerful new Web tools for educators. *MultiMedia, 11*(1), 10.

Review Richardson's discussion of blogs and RSS. He describes how they can be useful in education and how to get started in using them.

Rogers, E. M. (2003). *Diffusion of innovations* (5th ed). New York: Free Press.

Consider the diffusion model that originally appeared in 1962. Think about this model with respect to the technology innovations that are emerging. Through what process must teachers progress in making decisions about incorporating new and emerging technologies as tools for learning?

U.S. Department of Commerce. (2003). *2020 visions: Transforming education and training through advanced technologies.* Washington, DC: Author.

This volume presents the evolution of learning technologies and discusses how the emerging capabilities for computers and telecommunications might impact the education of future citizens.

Volz, D., & Sapatka, S. (2000). *Middle school science with calculators.* Portland, OR: Vernier Software.

Examine 38 science experiments using probeware with calculators for collecting, displaying, graphing, and analyzing data.

Wineburg, S. S. (1991). Historical problem solving: A study of cognitive processes used in the evaluation of documentary and pictorial evidence. *Journal of Educational Psychology 83*, 73–87.

Presents the cognitive processes used in the evaluation of documentary and pictorial historical evidence that includes background of the historians, presentation of the texts, picture evaluation, ranking tasks, identification of terms, and heuristics.

PART III

Connecting Technology with Teaching

Hope is not a strategy.

—*Thomas McInerney*

Teachers in the twenty-first century cannot teach as they were taught because so much has changed with the integration of information technologies into the fabric of everyday life. Yes, teachers may know how to use the technologies but that does not mean they can simply walk into the classroom and guide students' learning with these newer technologies. Teachers today must learn new strategies for teaching with technologies. And, *hope is not a strategy.*

As a teacher in the twenty-first century, you will need to plan how the technology will be integrated in the classroom instruction to assure that student engagement with the technology supports their learning with the technology. As described in the National Educational Technology Standards for Teachers (ISTE, 2002), teachers implementing technology in teaching and learning need to be prepared to:

1. plan and design effective learning environments and experiences supported by technology; and

2. implement their plans that include methods and strategies for applying technology to maximize student learning.

Hope is not an effective teaching *strategy*. This part of the book is directed toward engaging you in thinking about and investigating various strategies for effective implementation of technology in instruction. This part of the book links technology considerations with the important ideas you encounter in a current methods course in a teacher preparation program. This part of the book focuses on teaching with technologies, integrating the various strategies with the design, implementation, and assessment of instruction with technology as an integral component of the curriculum and instruction. In essence this part of the book is directed toward guiding you in your preparation for guiding students in learning with technology. You need to learn to think strategically as you plan for your students' learning. You must plan carefully, thinking through the lessons and considering not only potential student actions as they work with the technology, but also techniques for scaffolding the students' learning with the technology and methods for assessing student progress with the content ideas and with the technology. You cannot walk into the classroom with *hope* as your only *strategy* for guiding students in effective learning experiences.

CHAPTER 11

©AP/Wide World Photos

Models and Strategies for Technology-Infused Lessons

Introduction

Teaching is a challenging career where teachers represent perhaps the single most important influence, outside the home, on student learning. Each teacher's primary goal is to actively engage students in learning, thinking, and making sense of the experiences as they construct their personal understandings of the ideas. Should teachers simply recreate the experiences and environment in which they learned the content? Does that make sense? Is the content the same? Does everyone learn in the same way? What about the new information and communications technologies? Can they be integrated as tools for learning the ideas?

To make important instructional decisions, teachers must rely on a well-developed and in-depth knowledge of student learning, of the content they are to teach, and of the variety of pedagogical activities that support students in learning. As Shulman (1986) contends, effective teachers need to rely on an integrated knowledge base—one that is an integration of multiple domains of knowledge (knowledge about subject matter, learners, pedagogy, curriculum, and schools)—if they are to be prepared to translate the content in ways that students are able to grasp. Shulman referred to the knowledge that teachers need as pedagogical content knowledge, or PCK.

More recently, with the emerging impact of new information and communications technolo-gies, many have recognized that teachers also need knowledge of multiple technologies that can be used as tools for learning. More critically, teachers must have a well-developed technological pedagogical content knowledge (TPCK), the knowledge that teachers need for teaching *with* and *about* technology in their assigned subject areas and grade levels. Figure 11.1 provides a reminder for you of a picture that helps to describe what is intended by TPCK. From this perspective, teachers need knowledge that is the interconnection and intersection of their knowledge of content, pedagogy (teaching and student learning), and technology (Margerum-Leys & Marx, 2002; Mishra & Koehler, 2006; Niess, 2005a; Pierson, 2001; Zhao, 2003).

What does all this discussion mean for how teachers approach their primary task of actively engaging students in learning, thinking, and making sense of the experiences as they build their personal

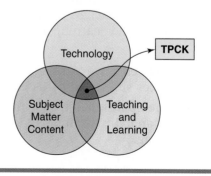

FIGURE 11.1 Pedagogical content knowledge for teaching with technology.

understandings of the ideas? Perhaps adapting Grossman's (1989, 1990) four components of PCK with a consideration of technology provides clarity. This consideration clarifies TPCK as the knowledge, skills, and dispositions that teachers have for teaching with technology, knowledge that includes the following:

- an overarching conception of what it means to teach the content with technology;
- knowledge of instructional strategies and representation for teaching the content with technology;
- knowledge of students' understanding, thinking, and learning of the content with technology; and
- knowledge of curriculum and curriculum materials that integrate technology in their subject. (Niess, 2005a)

Thus as you develop your knowledge base for teaching, an important part of the TPCK knowledge base is a repertoire of instructional techniques, techniques considered when identifying optimal strategies. You will need to ask yourself lots of questions, such as these:

- Is a lecture the best way for guiding students in learning the ideas I am trying to teach?
- How can I challenge the students so that they want to learn these ideas?
- How can I assure they are actively involved in thinking and learning about the ideas that I teach?
- What other strategies might I use that might be more effective for *my* students?

Responding to these questions requires that you use a pedagogical reasoning that integrates what you know about the subject with what you know about potential technologies and what you know about teaching and learning as you select the best strategy for your instruction in a manner that supports students in constructing how they view and are able to use what they are learning. Designing these instructional experiences is an important organizational task that you must consider. Your job requires that you make key decisions in the design, construction, and implementation of the experiences in ways that actively engage students in learning. Also, you must keep in mind that you must consider both teaching *with* and *about* the technology tools you want to integrate in the lessons. You cannot assume that students know how to use the technology as a learning tool. Your instructional strategies must integrate their learning about the technology while they learn about the subject. You need to craft the instruction carefully. Structuring the curriculum and instruction requires that you use a pedagogical reasoning that integrates your knowledge of the students, of the content, and of the instructional strategies, managing the classroom and assessing student learning along with a careful consideration of how the students will interact with the technology and the subject matter concurrently.

CHAPTER LEARNING OBJECTIVES

After reading the chapter, you should be able to:

1. Discuss the impact of current theories of student learning on the instructional choices teachers make in preparing their students to use technology as a learning tool.

2. Identify the affordances and constraints of a direct instruction model when working with students as they learn with and about technology in various subject matter areas.

3. Describe the affordances and constraints of inquiry as an indirect instruction model when guiding student learning with and about technology in various subject matter areas.

4. Clarify key stages in an effective demonstration that guides student learning with and about technology in various subject areas.

5. Illustrate important considerations of effective labs and hands-on activities when guiding student learning with and about technology in the various subject matter areas.

6. Identify teacher behaviors for successful use of questioning and grouping strategies to support student learning with and about technology.

Snapshot of a Technology-Infused Demonstration Lesson

Mr. Porter wanted his seventh grade, self-contained class to use the spreadsheet as a tool for investigating problems in the various subjects in his class through-out the school year. Up to this year, his students had no experience with spreadsheets. Thus, as he outlined his yearly curriculum for each of the subject areas in the curriculum, he constructed a plan to scaffold his students' learning about spreadsheets within different subject matter topics.

He introduced his students to the general framework of a spreadsheet in their mathematics class. The topic he selected was experimental versus theoretical probability where he had the students collect data about the number of each of the different colors of M&Ms in bags of candies (as in Chapter 6 Snapshot). The students in various group sizes (some groups with 4 students, some with 6, some with 8, and some with 10) built a mock spreadsheet, where they were introduced to the rows, columns, cell names, and variety of information that can be entered into the cells. As a result of this lesson, students were excited about actually entering the data they collected into a computer spreadsheet and creating pie charts of their data. Throughout the activities, the class discussed the difference between the theoretical probability of selecting a particular color of M&M from a bag (found from information on the M&M website) and the experimental results they had identified in their varying-sized groups.

In the science class he decided to focus the students' attention on entering formulas and values in spreadsheet cells. They had talked about formulas in the mathematics class activity but had only entered the formulas that they had learned when they were working with the simulated spreadsheet. Now, they were studying atoms and molecules, such as hydrogen and oxygen, along with the periodic chart of elements. The focus of this lesson was on the number of atoms in one mole of a specific element. Mr. Porter began by reminding students that the English language uses grouping words, like dozen for 12, gross for 144, and score for 20.

Mr. Porter: We've been studying atomic structures and have recently discussed that this number on the periodic chart shows the atomic weight of one mole of a particular atom. See, here is the weight of one mole of oxygen atoms [pointing to the oxygen cell in the periodic table]. Kurt, can you read it for us?

Kurt: It says 15.9994 units. That's pretty light I think. A mole of oxygen can't be very big I guess.

Mr. Porter: Right, the units are grams. Now, does anyone know how many atoms are in one mole of oxygen?

Adam: How can we count something that small?

Mr. Porter: Good point, but scientists have identified that the number of atoms in a mole is the same number for each of the elements. They have described that number much like we describe groups of objects—a gross of oranges is 144 oranges and a gross of peanuts would be 144 peanuts. In this case, one mole consists of an *Avogadro's number* of atoms.

Kurt: Hmmm... that number must not be a lot because a mole of oxygen is only 15.9994 grams.

Mr. Porter: I suspect you have no idea about the size of Avogadro's number. So, today we are going to investigate this number.

The Periodic Table of the Elements

1 H Hydrogen 1.00794																	2 He Helium 4.003
3 Li Lithium 6.941	4 Be Beryllium 9.012182											5 B Boron 10.811	6 C Carbon 12.0107	7 N Nitrogen 14.00674	8 O Oxygen 15.9994	9 F Fluorine 18.9984032	10 Ne Neon 20.1797
11 Na Sodium 22.989770	12 Mg Magnesium 24.3050											13 Al Aluminum 26.981538	14 Si Silicon 28.0855	15 P Phosphorus 30.973761	16 S Sulfur 32.066	17 Cl Chlorine 35.4527	18 Ar Argon 39.948
19 K Potassium 39.0983	20 Ca Calcium 40.078	21 Sc Scandium 44.955910	22 Ti Titanium 47.867	23 V Vanadium 50.9415	24 Cr Chromium 51.9961	25 Mn Manganese 54.938049	26 Fe Iron 55.845	27 Co Cobalt 58.933200	28 Ni Nickel 58.6934	29 Cu Copper 63.546	30 Zn Zinc 65.39	31 Ga Gallium 69.723	32 Ge Germanium 72.61	33 As Arsenic 74.92160	34 Se Selenium 78.96	35 Br Bromine 79.904	36 Kr Krypton 83.80
37 Rb Rubidium 85.4678	38 Sr Strontium 87.62	39 Y Yttrium 88.90585	40 Zr Zirconium 91.224	41 Nb Niobium 92.90638	42 Mo Molybdenum 95.94	43 Tc Technetium (98)	44 Ru Ruthenium 101.07	45 Rh Rhodium 102.90550	46 Pd Palladium 106.42	47 Ag Silver 107.8682	48 Cd Cadmium 112.411	49 In Indium 114.818	50 Sn Tin 118.710	51 Sb Antimony 121.760	52 Te Tellurium 127.60	53 I Iodine 126.90447	54 Xe Xenon 131.29
55 Cs Cesium 132.90545	56 Ba Barium 137.327	57 La Lanthanum 138.9055	72 Hf Hafnium 178.49	73 Ta Tantalum 180.9479	74 W Tungsten 183.84	75 Re Rhenium 186.207	76 Os Osmium 190.23	77 Ir Iridium 192.217	78 Pt Platinum 195.078	79 Au Gold 196.96655	80 Hg Mercury 200.59	81 Tl Thallium 204.3833	82 Pb Lead 207.2	83 Bi Bismuth 208.98038	84 Po Polonium (209)	85 At Astatine (210)	86 Rn Radon (222)
87 Fr Francium (223)	88 Ra Radium (226)	89 Ac Actinium (227)	104 Rf Rutherfordium (261)	105 Db Dubnium (262)	106 Sg Seaborgium (263)	107 Bh Bohrium (262)	108 Hs Hassium (265)	109 Mt Meitnerium (266)	110 (269)	111 (272)	112 (277)	113	114				

58 Ce Cerium 140.116	59 Pr Praseodymium 140.90765	60 Nd Neodymium 144.24	61 Pm Promethium (145)	62 Sm Samarium 150.36	63 Eu Europium 151.964	64 Gd Gadolinium 157.25	65 Tb Terbium 158.92534	66 Dy Dysprosium 162.50	67 Ho Holmium 164.93032	68 Er Erbium 167.26	69 Tm Thulium 168.93421	70 Yb Ytterbium 173.04	71 Lu Lutetium 174.967
90 Th Thorium 232.0381	91 Pa Protactinium 231.03588	92 U Uranium 238.0289	93 Np Neptunium (237)	94 Pu Plutonium (244)	95 Am Americium (243)	96 Cm Curium (247)	97 Bk Berkelium (247)	98 Cf Californium (251)	99 Es Einsteinium (252)	100 Fm Fermium (257)	101 Md Mendelevium (258)	102 No Nobelium (259)	103 Lr Lawrencium (262)

1995 IUPAC masses and Approved Names from http://www.chem.qmw.ac.uk/iupac/AtWt/
masses for 107-111 from C&EN, March 13, 1995, p. 35
112 from http://www.gsi.de/z112e.html

To focus the students' attention, Mr. Porter displays the first slide of his PowerPoint presentation. The phrase **Avogadro's number** first appears on the screen, at which point Mr. Porter asks the students what this number might be. The students suggest numbers like 100 or 1000 because they considered that it does not take much to make a mole of only 15.999 grams.

 Avogadro's Number

60,200,000,000,000,000,000,000

or

6.02×10^{23}

Mr. Porter clicks the mouse, displaying an approximate value of Avogadro's number, first in long form followed by the exponential form. He asks if they can read the numbers they are seeing. They make jokes like "6 gazillion" but admit they have no idea because there are just too many zeroes in the number. Although the students are familiar with exponential notation from their math class, even that form does not help them much because they just can not imagine that something with that small mass (15.9994 grams) can possibly contain that many atoms. Mr. Porter expected this lack of understanding because he knows that the students really do not have a good concept of an atom, a mole, or a number this large.

To guide them in developing an understanding of Avogadro's number, Mr. Porter presents them with a problem where they investigate the size of the number in terms of measurements with which they were familiar. He holds up a stack of 10 small, thin chips, which he found among the classroom materials, telling the students that the stack is 15 millimeters (mm) high.

Mr. Porter: If this stack of 10 chips is 15 millimeters high, how high would you expect one of the chips to be?

Ted: 1.5 mm because you just divide by the number in the stack, or 10.

Mr. Porter: Good. Now here is the big question I have for you. Are you ready?

Class: [Unenthusiastically.] Yes.

Mr. Porter: Suppose that I created an Avogadro's number of these chips in one stack, one on top of the other, and assume there is no compression in the stack. How high will the stack be?

Karen: Oh sure, like we would have any idea!

Mr. Porter: Well, guess! I won't take off for guesses! Here let's make a list of all your ideas on the board. Just go ahead and shout them out and I'll put them on the board. As high as what? [He writes as students give suggestions.]

Mr. Porter: This is a good start. Let's use what we know about different measurements to see if we can see which might be the closest to the height of an Avogadro's number of chips. At the same time we can focus on how to enter numbers and formulas in the spreadsheet. Let me show you how we might work on this problem using a spreadsheet. First I'll show you my model of a spreadsheet. [He displays the next slide of his PowerPoint presentation.]

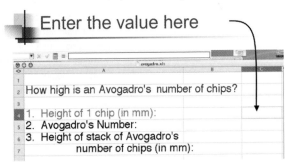

We learned about cell names in the M&M activity. So I want you to focus on the cell names for the spreadsheet. This arrow is pointing at cell C4. What value should we enter here? [He points to the row and column markers and the intersection of row 4 and column C.]

Aaron: 1.5—that's what we said one chip would be from the stack of 10.

Mr. Porter: So the spreadsheet [advancing to the next slide] would look this way. Now look at the next request. What do we enter for Avogadro's number?

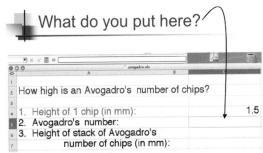

Jamie: I suppose we could enter the long number you showed us.

Mr. Porter: Right, we could do that. But suppose that we decided to enter the exponential form. How would we do that?

Carly: Well, it kind of looks like a formula to me. Could we do it like a formula?

Mr. Porter: Nice idea. Then the computer would show us the value in its own way. Let me suggest a way to enter this formula. The formula we want to enter is like this =6.02 × 10^23 [writing on the board and reminding the students that the equal sign means a formula will be following and the ^ means *to the power of*]. What cell should we enter this formula in? Jamie?

Jamie: C5!

Mr. Porter: Yes, and look at what the computer does when we enter the formula [advancing to the next slide]. The value that it calculated is expressed as 6.02E+23. This notation is important! The *E* means that the base is *10* and the exponent is 23. So the value for Avogadro's number is 6.02×10^{23}, just like we saw in the first slide.

Now we need to find the height of the stack of an Avogadro's number of chips. The cell C7 is where we want that height calculated in millimeters. That means we need to figure out how to find that height. Where are the values we need in order to figure out the height? Michael, can you suggest a formula for the computer to calculate the height, using the cell references for the values?

Reference cells for this formula

Michael: Well, the values are 1.5 for a single chip and Avogadro's number of chips is the number of chips in the stack. Those values are in C4 and C5.

Mr. Porter: Yes, but what calculation do we request that the computer do?

Michael: Multiply C4 times C5?

Mr. Porter: So I use the X for times?

Michael: Hmm? I guess so but I don't remember.

Jason: I know with calculators we use the * to indicate multiplication so I bet we do that with computers too.

Mr. Porter: Good thinking Jason. Now, you are almost there. How do you instruct the computer to do the calculation rather than just print the text that you enter?

Shannon: Oh, oh… [excitedly waving her hand] the equal sign at the front tells the computer to make a calculation!

Mr. Porter: Great! [He brings up the next slide.] Now, as you can see the height of an Avogadro's number of chips is 9.03×10^{23} mm. Can someone come up and write that number on the board? Sherry?

Sherry: [Writing on the board with help from the rest of the class as she struggles counting the zeroes.] 903,000,000,000,000,000,000,000

Ted: But Mr. Porter, that is in millimeters and I really don't know how many millimeters represent any of those places we thought of before we did this calculation. Like the number of millimeters to the moon and back—I have no idea about that.

Mr. Porter: I understand! So let's move to an actual spreadsheet (and not my PowerPoint simulation). First we will review the first three entries in the actual spreadsheet. Then we will investigate converting the millimeters to some measurements with which we are familiar! Here's the spreadsheet we will use [displaying the spreadsheet on the screen].

Mr. Porter: [After students reviewed the entries for cells C4, C5, and C7.] Now, your job is to determine the formulas using cell references like we just did for the height of the number of chips. Again, I'll be your recorder and enter what you say in the cells you tell me to enter. Let's look at the first question where you are to convert the millimeters to centimeters. What would you do? Casey?

Casey: To convert from millimeters to centimeters, you would divide by 10. So enter =C7/10 into cell C8.

Mr. Porter: Ok, will do!

The class continues responding to each of the questions, guided by Mr. Porter's questioning about the formulas for making the conversions. When they find the number of miles for the height of the stack of chips, Mr. Porter adds some other questions to the spreadsheet to get them to think about the number of miles for an Avogadro's number of chips. By answering these questions, the students discover that a stack of an Avogadro's number of chips is not only farther than the distance to the Moon and back but it is more than 6 billion times the distance from the Earth to the Sun!

Through this discussion and the activity with the spreadsheet, the students begin to construct their understanding of the size of Avogadro's number—not only large but *extremely large* from their perspective. Mr.

Porter reminds them that this whole activity began with the idea of the number of atoms in a mole of oxygen atoms, with an atomic weight or mass of 15.9994 grams. Mr. Porter challenges the students to return the next day prepared to discuss these questions, showing they have a better concept of the size of Avogadro's number:

1. Is the national debt larger or smaller than Avogadro's number?

2. How deep would a layer of sand be that covers the state of Texas with an Avogadro's number of grains of sand?

3. Where on Earth can you expect to identify an Avogadro's number of things?

Knowledge about Learning and Implications for Learning with Technology

The National Educational Technology Standards (NETS) for Teachers (ISTE, 2002) highlight the importance of the role of teachers in planning strategies to manage student learning in a technology-mediated environment. Teachers' instructional plans rely on an in-depth knowledge of how students learn and on an ability to apply that knowledge to learning with technology.

Contemporary theories of student learning suggest that students are not simply passive receivers and memorizers of teachers' words (Good & Brophy, 2002). As described in Chapter 3 of this text, current learning thinking is guided by cognitive field psychologists' explanations of learning:

- Learning is an internal adaptation to experiences, a reordering of mental structures or schemas as a result of experiences.
- Learners are intrinsically curious and curiosity motivates them to learn.
- Disequilibrium is motivation for learning.
- Learning is a result of disequilibrium shifted into equilibrium.
- Vygotsky's zone of proximal development describes the size of the disequilibrium for learning to take place.

- A variety of experiences that differ in outward appearance while retaining the basic conceptual structure support the learner in identifying patterns, generalizing, and making connections.
- Learners ultimately construct their own understanding, but adults (teachers) can scaffold the experiences to support students in building or constructing a firm understanding (reordering their mental structures as they adapt to the experiences).
- Big ideas and pictures transfer to other contexts.

Engaging students in constructing their own understanding (i.e., learning), including motivation to challenge preconceived ideas, carefully considering the timing of the challenges, and incorporating a variety of experiences are instrumental in this cognitive science perspective. These ideas direct how teachers construct the learning environment. Their plans for learning encourage the following:

- embedding learning in complex, realistic, and relevant learning environments;
- providing for social negotiation and shared responsibility as a part of learning;
- supporting multiple perspectives and using multiple representations of content;
- nurturing self-awareness and an understanding that knowledge is constructed; and
- promoting ownership in learning. (Woolfolk-Hoy, 2004, p. 327)

The important question for you to consider as you are preparing to teach is: What do these ideas imply about how students learn with technology? Consideration of the ideas of cognitive science and constructivists' perspectives highlights three implications for teaching with technology:

1. **Scaffold student learning with technology within the context of the subject matter so that they also learn about technology.** You need to carefully plan how you guide your students in learning about the technology if you hope they learn to use the technology as a tool for learning. Should students be challenged to learn about the technology by trial and error? The disequilibrium created by such a strategy may be too great, causing students to resist the use of the technology as a tool for learning in the subject. If you carefully scaffold their learning about technology, providing smaller subsets of tasks within the context of the subject to challenge them to learn about the technology, students are more apt to consider the technology as a tool for learning. More importantly, if you embed these tasks within the subject matter content (language arts, social studies, mathematics, science), your students will be more likely to connect the use of the technology as a tool for learning in that content.

2. **Vary the experiences with technology as a tool for learning.** Another implication suggests incorporating a variety of experiences with the technology as a tool for learning in the subject area. Variety is proposed from two perspectives:

   • Students need to learn their subject with the involvement of a variety of technology tools. For example, students can use a variety of technology tools to develop a mystery that describes a town as in Chapter 9 (see In the Classroom 9.6). They could design the mystery using PowerPoint, a movie, or even a Web page. Each of the technologies offers features to develop a creative presentation; yet, the differences in the technologies offer the learner an opportunity to experience the basic notions of developing creative presentations that describe a town in a mystery format. In essence, through the variety of technologies students gather the basic conceptual structure of the ideas they are describing that ultimately helps them to identify patterns and to make generalizations as well as important connections.

   • Students need to use each technology tool in a variety of ways. Your explorations of the various technologies in this text have been guided by using the tool for different purposes: using the technology as a productivity tool, a communications tool, a research tool, or a problem-solving and decision-making tool. For example, using the spreadsheet in these various ways supported a broader, more comprehensive knowledge about using spreadsheets. The charting feature provided you with a tool for preparing graphical representations as a means of communicating your understanding of the data. On the other hand, using some of the built-in functions to explore the data required that you explore techniques to analyze tabular data sets in order to solve a problem or make decisions based on the data.

3. **Select problems that motivate and challenge students to use the technology as a tool for exploration.** If the goal is to use technology as a tool, the problems in which they are engaged need to be realistic and relevant for the use of the technology. The problem for the Snapshot of a Technology-Infused Demonstration Lesson is one that quickly engages students, challenging their perceptions about the size of Avogadro's number. The problem lends itself to an exploration with the spreadsheet with its ease of entering various functions. In essence, the use of the technology does not conflict with the challenge in the problem, namely, to determine the size of an Avogadro's number of chips in a stack in order to comprehend the size of Avogadro's number.

Models and Strategies for Teaching with Technology

What is the best way to teach with technology? The answer to that question is that there are multiple ways to teach with technology, and your task is to identify optimal strategies that support students in meeting the goal of learning the content and gaining skills both with and about technology. Your decisions are most certainly based on (1) your own personal knowledge, experiences, and beliefs about how to learn the content, (2) your students' knowledge, experiences, beliefs, and attitudes, and (3) the goals of the understandings, skills, and attitudes that your students are to gain.

Clearly no one strategy is appropriate for all situations. You might say that the best strategy is the one that results in your students gaining the knowledge, skills, and attitudes for the specific situation. Because your class of students will have great diversity (cultural, educational, social), however, as you prepare to teach you need to focus on developing a repertoire of strategies from which to select for the various educational situations you will plan.

Obviously, the strategies that helped you learn are strategies that you will gravitate toward. If they worked for you, they were surely effective! But your students will not all be just like you. You need to consciously work to build your repertoire of strategies to be prepared for the broadest diversity of students and the shifting educational goals for the twenty-first century. As you consider teaching with technology, specific teaching models and specific teaching strategies can help you expand your own personal repertoire from which you can mix and match ideas as you design lessons and activities for your students.

Teaching Models

Eggen and Kauchak (1996) describe teaching models as "prescriptive teaching strategies designed to accomplish particular instructional goals" (p. 11). Each teaching model is basically a description of student learning since the purpose is to accomplish some instructional goal. Each model incorporates attention to the present-day views about student learning with students actively involved in making sense of their experiences. Each model provides an organizer for you to use as you integrate technology in the classroom instruction.

What are some basic models that you might incorporate as you are faced with teaching with technology? Consider the role of the teacher in each of these models. What is the role of the student? How are students actively engaged in the activities? Are they physically and mentally engaged? How is their thinking involved in the activity? Do these models provide students with experiences within which they are actively engaged in constructing their own understandings of the content and using the technology as a tool? How might these models meet your instructional goals so that students are learning both with and about technology?

Ultimately you need to consider what the particular models afford you to do and how they constrain your plans for students in learning in a technology-mediated lesson. *Affordances* and *constraints* are key terms that can help guide your thinking in making your instructional decisions. Gibson (1979) describes affordances as opportunities for action provided in a specific environment; he proposes that observers need to attend to the affordances of the specific environment rather than abstract physical properties of the objects and environments. He further suggests that constraints "limit possible actions" (p. 78). As in the Snapshot of a Technology-Infused Demonstration Lesson, use of a demonstration with a PowerPoint afforded Mr. Porter the opportunity to focus the students' attention to specific lines in a spreadsheet, yet the PowerPoint presentation constrained the class from seeing the real-time spreadsheet responses. They observed the results that Mr. Porter wants them

to observe. In recognition of this constraint, Mr. Porter moved from the presentation demonstration to a demonstration with the actual spreadsheet after he was comfortable with the students' understandings. He also used this shift to review the actions they had observed and discussed. Once he worked with the actual spreadsheets, he was able to demonstrate possible errors that students might make when they worked with the spreadsheet. At this point, they can explore other questions: What happens when you forget the equal sign with the formula? What happens if you use the X for multiplication instead of the *? However, even that shift in the instruction constrained students from gaining their own personal hands-on work with the spreadsheets, where they would be able to actually enter the formulas and gain personal experiences with spreadsheets. In that class Mr. Porter had the hands-on experience. That particular day Mr. Porter wanted to carefully direct the students' attention; he planned for other spreadsheet experiences at a later date where the students' ideas directed the experiences. In essence, Mr. Porter was aware of both the affordances and constraints of the instructional model he selected and consciously planned in a way that recognized the constraints and what he needed to do to alleviate them.

Consider two basic instructional models and think about the affordances and constraints of the models. Mr. Porter used a direct instruction model where his thinking and ideas directed the flow of the instruction. At other times he might want a different model, one where the students' ideas direct the flow of instruction. Explore these two models, examining their affordances and constraints to determine how you might employ each as you build your instructional plans when teaching with and about technology. Keep in mind that you are designing lessons where you must also guide students' learning about the technology while they are learning within your content area. This recognition means that you have to help them learn how to use the technology and how to use the capabilities of the technology. Also, you must consider this instruction from within your subject area.

Direct Instruction Model   If you want students to know how to work with a particular technology, many times the best model is the teacher-centered, direct instruction model since this model allows you to direct the attention of the entire class toward basics for working with the technology. Joyce, Weil, and Calhoun (2004) characterize this model in five primary phases as shown in Figure 11.2.

Did you notice that the teacher has a primary role and why this model of direct instruction is described as teacher-centered? The teacher is responsible for identifying the lesson goals and, as Eggen

Direct Instruction Model

Introduction	The teacher presents an overview of the concept or skill.
Presentation	The teacher explains, possibly modeling or demonstrating the new concept or skill.
Structured Practice	The teacher leads the students through practice of the concept or skill.
Guided Practice	The students practice the concept or skill under the guidance and monitoring of the teacher; the teacher provides feedback in the form of prompts and praise.
Independent Practice	The students practice the concept or skill independently (in the class or as homework) with delayed feedback after an extended period of time.

FIGURE 11.2 Five phases of the direct instruction model.

and Kauchak (1996) describe, guiding the "transfer of responsibility" to the students. The students are expected to be actively involved in the lesson through their responses to the teacher's questions, and through examples, practice, and feedback. Initially, the teacher does most of the talking through the explanations, but as the lesson progresses the teacher does more questioning as a means of actively engaging the students in developing their own explanations and understandings of the concepts or skills.

Assume that your students have never worked with or even seen any of the real-time data collection probes. They have never used the sensor interface or probes to gather data (as described in Chapter 10). You recognize that you need to introduce them to the basic interface with the temperature probe in preparation for the future activities with the probeware, such as the one described for In the Classroom 10.3 where students must use the temperature probes to gauge the health of a stream near their school. The direct instruction model is particularly effective in introducing the students to using the probes because this approach provides an opportunity to introduce the key instructions for working with the probes. The model provides you with the opportunity to guide the work and practice with the technology for the whole class, rather than having to explain to them individually. Thus, with this model, you can be more efficient and confident that all the students have had basic instruction with the probes in obtaining accurate data.

For the introduction you decide to show the students some film clips of scientists gathering stream data in the field. You describe that the goal of the lesson is for the students to become familiar with a similar technology so that they, too, are able to collect data in the field. You show the students a recent news article that questions the health of the stream near the school site and suggest that when they are familiar with both the temperature and pH probes they will be able to conduct their own research about the stream to determine its health.

The presentation phase of the lesson focuses on demonstrating the probeware interface connected to the calculator while also working with the temperature and pH probes. You use a PowerPoint presentation to describe how to connect the interface to the calculator and to discuss how the interface works. With each step of this presentation, you also model the ideas using an actual interface device with the calculator and the probes so the students are able to see the actions as they are described. As the demonstration progresses, you plan to describe how the temperature probe works with the DataMate application available in the calculator. As a transition to the next stage of the lesson, you demonstrate an activity where the students will be asked to identify how they would measure the temperature of the palms of their hands and of their teammates in assigned groups of four.

The structured practice phase of the lesson focuses on guiding the students in their groups of four. During this phase, you use the demonstration device to model the procedures the students in their groups will follow for setting up the probeware interface, calculator, and temperature probe. You expect that the students will record the instructions in their lab notebooks. Also, during this time, you travel from group to group, answering questions and providing feedback about the process they will be following in the next stage. As a conclusion to this phase, you summarize the work of the student groups by modeling the processes the whole class identifies with another probeware setup, resulting in gathering the temperature of four other members of the class, each from different groups.

For the guided practice phase of the lesson, the student groups have actual hands-on work with the devices with the expectation that they will complete the activity to find the highest palm temperature of their group members. While the students are working on the activity, you monitor their work, provide feedback, and ask questions to assure that all the members are actively engaged in the practice.

For the final phase, independent practice, you provide each group with a set of four beakers, each containing a different colored liquid. You remind them of the safety precautions they must maintain with respect to the various liquids and beakers. Their task is to identify the range of temperatures of the liquids and put the liquids in order of coldest to warmest. They are to record their data along with the processes they used to collect the temperatures. They are to prepare a group description for the next day where they are to work with the pH probes.

The next day continues the introductions to the probeware, again using a direct instruction model where students explore the use of the pH probes and end with an ordering of the different colored liquids by pH (acidic to basic). The conclusion of the two days is planned as a discussion of data collection using the two different probes and the variations in the different liquids by temperature and by pH.

Teacher-directed questions for the students are used for the closure to this work with the probes to assure that all the students have a basic understanding of the probes before moving to the next set of activities. Additional activities are planned where the students have more practice with data collection with the probes prior to conducting the research on the stream. The expectation is that the students will have mastered the concept of how the device makes the measurement, the skills of collecting the data with the probeware, and troubleshooting problems with the probeware (e.g., how the devices react when batteries need replacement). The direct instruction model provided the guided instruction the teacher determined was needed in order that *all* the students were prepared for more independent work as they gained familiarity and comfort with the technology.

Affordances and Constraints of the Direct Instruction Model Under what considerations is it best to use the direct instruction model when integrating technology in instruction? The direct instruction model is particularly useful and efficient not only for introducing students to new technologies and using the technologies for learning content, but also for providing the class with general instructions for working with the technologies. Figure 11.3 summarizes some of the affordances and constraints for the direct instruction model. Think about these ideas with respect to a particular lesson where you might introduce using a new technology in your subject area.

In the example with the direct instructional model for the introduction to probeware, the intent is that the teacher is able to focus the attention of the entire class on setting up the equipment and using the equipment for gathering data. In other words, this model affords the teacher the students' attention. Perhaps the most significant constraint in using this model is that the teacher's ideas guide the flow of the lesson, not the students'. In fact, the students might be lulled into letting the teacher do all the thinking. Thus the teacher's questioning is critical in assuring that the students are engaged and understand the directions. The direct instruction model is an efficient model for assuring that students understand and are able to follow the series of instructions for completing an activity. However, the model is constrained in its ability to encourage student exploration, creativity, and inquiry.

Inquiry-Based Indirect Instruction Model Inquiry, problem solving, and discovery learning are more apt to be supported through a different model, namely, the indirect model of instruction. This model is best suited for teaching concepts, patterns, and abstractions. The critical feature of this model is that the students are at the center and are actively engaged in constructing understandings that make sense to them. The role of the teacher is to guide the student construction, helping them to draw from their own experiences, ideas, and understandings. The teacher provides examples and nonexamples and continually asks questions to challenge the students' thinking in

---

Direct Instruction Model

Affordances
- Teacher guides the classroom discussion and activities.
- Teacher-guided practice provides students with opportunities to gradually develop skills.
- The model is effective for giving directions to the whole class at the same time.

Constraints
- Students' individual ideas or experiences are withheld.
- Teacher's thinking directs the activity.
- Student exploration, creativity, and inquiry are not the focus in the model.

FIGURE 11.3   Affordances and constraints for the direct instruction model.

Inquiry-Based Indirect Instruction Model	
Confrontation with the Problem	Students are confronted by a puzzling situation or a discrepant event.
Data Gathering—Verification	Students gather information to better describe the event.
Data Gathering—Experimentation	Students isolate relevant variables, develop hypotheses, and test them to further clarify the event.
Organizing, Formulating an Explanation	Students formulate their explanations of the event.
Analysis of the Inquiry Process	Students analyze their pattern of inquiry, identifying the lines of thinking that were the most productive in explaining the event.

FIGURE 11.4   Five phases describing the inquiry model of instruction.

ways that guides them in identifying a generalization, analyzing a situation, or synthesizing the ideas. The teacher promotes, supports, and encourages the students in evaluating their own responses directed toward an analysis that leads to a generalization.

Joyce, Weil, and Calhoun (2004) describe one form of this indirect model of instruction in five phases for an inquiry-training model (see Figure 11.4). Their model is designed not only to engage students in inquiry but also to help them improve their skills in working through the inquiry strategies. The five phases are framed by the students' actions because the goal of the model is to encourage a student-centered instruction. The role of the teacher is that of framing the experiences and guiding students through the phases.

How might this model be used to engage students in learning subject matter ideas while also learning about a particular technology? Consider the problem of world hunger and how various Internet databases are useful for gathering information in the various phases of an investigation of the issue (In the Classroom 7.6 in Chapter 7).

Confrontation is the first phase where the students are confronted with the existence of hunger and challenged to think about chronic hunger versus the more short-term quenchable hunger they might feel. Current pictures and news articles depicting people starving are displayed next to current pictures and newspaper articles about people wasting food. The puzzle is why some people are starving while others, often in the students' own area, are wasting food.

The next phase, data gathering—verification, engages students in researching the online databases provided by the Central Intelligence Agency (CIA) along with the online searchable World Fact-book and the Nationmaster online database to identify the production capacities of various countries. This listing allows students to distinguish between countries with major agricultural products

such as rice, wheat, corn, and potatoes and those without. Using the information, students identify imbalances between production and country needs.

Data gathering—experimentation is the phase in which students begin to isolate variables that help them in thinking about the causes of hunger. The story of Akeyo's corn (see In the Classroom 7.6) provides some potential variables for their consideration. The challenge in this phase is for the students to think of ways that Akeyo and other corn producers can be helped so that they can produce and sell enough corn each year to provide for their families. The students create a two-column list, the first column containing the ideas they think would result in the failure of the corn crop and the second column listing the potential solutions. Finally, the students must identify their best solution.

The fourth phase (organizing, formulating an explanation) is the time for them to formulate an explanation. The formulation shifts students' thinking from globally to locally where they are asked to frame their explanation in terms of addressing the problem in their own locations. Ultimately, their explanations are ones that require them to consider solving the local problem.

After students have implemented their solutions, in the final phase, analysis of the inquiry process, the teacher needs to ask them whether they think their solution is working. If they have reasons to believe it is not working, they need to reconsider their solution and reimplement their new ideas. More importantly, at this stage, they need to reconsider how they determined the solution and how they were lead to a strategy that was not productive in solving the problem. Students may question how they used the various online databases and how the databases might have provided better information. Thus, in this stage, while students consider the problem of hunger, they explore more about databases.

Inquiry-Based Indirect Instruction Model

Affordances

- The model focuses on instructional goals of inquiry, problem solving, and discovery.

- Student thinking directs the activity and thus students' individual ideas or experiences direct the progress in problem solving.

- Teacher role is that of guide, not the deliverer of knowledge and information.

- The model is effective for guiding students in gaining a problem-solving stance when working with technology.

- The model is effective for guiding students in gaining a problem-solving stance when working with technology.

Constraints

- The model takes time! Teachers need to organize the classroom in ways that establish an environment that encourages interaction and engagement in the creative process.

- Student diversity results in students completing tasks at different rates.

- The amount of teacher guidance needed varies for individual students. Teachers have to determine when and where to intercede and provide support.

FIGURE 11.5   Affordances and constraints for the inquiry-based indirect instruction model.

Affordances and Constraints with the Inquiry-Based Indirect Instruction Model   The inquiry-based model is a student-centered model where the teacher's role is that of a guide in the inquiry process rather than the director of the process. Such a model has specific affordances and constraints, some of which are displayed in Figure 11.5. This model focuses on establishing a climate of student interaction and exploration that challenges students to search for patterns, frame generalizations, and communicate their ideas. This model certainly begins with the students' personal ideas, knowledge, and understandings. The process allows teachers opportunities to view how their students are constructing their ideas. This process takes time and often results in students completing their work at different rates. In recognizing such a constraint of this model, teachers must carefully manage the varying levels of student progress in ways that do not result in penalizing those who finish early by giving them more work to keep them busy! Similarly teachers must assure that those who need more time, get more time rather than just giving them the answer!

The indirect model is particularly useful for guiding students in developing a problem-solving stance toward working with technology. Teachers need to challenge students to explore the capabilities of the various technologies as well as to work toward solving their problems with the various technologies. Perhaps you have noticed that students do need some basic instruction with the technologies, using a direct instruction model. However, they also need opportunities for exploring the technologies and solving problems with the technologies, opportunities that are more often supported through the inquiry-based indirect instruction model where the teacher is a guide who encourages students to look for solutions rather than giving the right way. Many ideas in the research and in the problem-solving and decision-making sections of Chapters 5–9 are designed with this instructional goal in mind.

Teaching Strategies

In either of the instructional models, teachers can employ various strategies for building on the affordances of the models and working to offset the constraints of the models. Demonstrations, labs and hands-on activities, questioning, and various grouping strategies are some of the typical considerations. As you think about each of these strategies, you should consider how they impact the affordances and constraints discussed with the direct instruction model or with the inquiry-based indirect instruction model. How can you maximize the benefits of the models in your lessons that integrate technology?

Demonstrations   Demonstration is a useful strategy when guiding student learning with and about technology. Demonstrations are typically teacher-centered much as in the direct instruction model. But, do not assume this means the teacher does all the thinking. The teacher typically orchestrates the actions and shows the demonstration while the students assume the role as observers of the demonstration. However, teachers can ask that students follow their verbal instructions, thus giving some of the students hands-on work in presenting the demonstration. As observers, though, students are engaged in thinking about the demonstration and about the questions that

Effective Demonstrations	
Prepare	The teacher identifies and prepares the demonstration to fit the content, to engage the students in the content, and to be visible by all students.
Motivate	The teacher challenges students to become mentally engaged in the demonstration.
Demonstrate	The teacher presents the demonstration while engaging students in the ideas as they unfold. Students observe the demonstration but must respond to questions that challenge their thinking about the ideas.
Closure: Explain, Extend, and Evaluate	The teacher challenges the students to explain the demonstration, extend the ideas to the content, and evaluate the effectiveness of the demonstration in explaining.

FIGURE 11.6   Key components of effective demonstrations.

are posed through the demonstration. Teachers may incorporate either an inductive approach (as with the inquiry-based indirect model of instruction) or a more deductive approach (as often used in the direct instruction model) in guiding the students' thinking. Four key components describe effective demonstrations (see Figure 11.6).

Preparing students to integrate technology in their educational experiences often prompts the use of demonstrations as in the Snapshot of a Technology-Infused Demonstration Lesson. In that lesson, Mr. Porter used a PowerPoint presentation to demonstrate the process for entering formulas in a spreadsheet. At the same time, he challenged the students to investigate the size of the number of atoms in one mole—Avogadro's number. He followed that experience with another demonstration of entering the formulas in an actual spreadsheet in the process of solving the problem of determining the height of an Avogadro's number of chips.

The first stage of a demonstration is to prepare. This stage is critical and requires considerable effort in advance of the actual demonstration. Mr. Porter had to decide how he might present Avogadro's number to his students for their first consideration of its size. He decided to design a PowerPoint presentation that was engaging and visible to the whole class. He decided that the problem of the height of an Avogadro's number of chips would challenge their understanding of that number and be of interest to them. He needed to make sure that students would be able to see the row and column markers and the formulas that he displayed in the simulated version of the spreadsheet in the presentation. He also needed to create the actual spreadsheet that was simulated in the PowerPoint and make sure that he was able to effectively move from one package to the next smoothly.

Before the demonstration day, Mr. Porter made certain that he had access to a computer and a computer projection unit to display both the presentation and the spreadsheet by requesting the equipment in advance and arranging his plans to match the availability. Testing the equipment was essential for assuring the presentation was visible from various locations in the classroom. He was able to complete this test after school a week in advance.

Mr. Porter realized that problems might occur and he wanted to be prepared in the event they did occur. What would he do if the equipment did not work properly? Was he prepared to troubleshoot problems with the equipment or the software? What would he do if the electricity failed that day? In preparation for this problem, Mr. Porter prepared overheads of each of the screens and, while he certainly hoped he would not have to use them, he knew that time in his class was valuable and that he could still do the demonstration with the backup materials.

Mr. Porter did not want to just tell the students how to enter the formulas in the spreadsheet. His plan to actively engage the students in the demonstration inspired him to create the Avogadro's number of chips problem. He knew that his students were more apt to pay attention if they were physically as well as mentally involved with the progress of the demonstration, so he even identified times that he could have students assist him by entering the information into the computer as they worked with the spreadsheet. For this stage, he decided to have his students actually enter the information into the spreadsheet under his guidance. If they did it incorrectly, he could use that event as a teachable moment. If they did it correctly, he could use that to reinforce their new skill.

With his advanced preparation, Mr. Porter felt ready for the demonstration. He planned for his introduction to prepare the students for the lesson, linking their previous work with the periodic table to the idea that a mole represented an Avogadro's number of atoms. Here he wanted to use the PowerPoint presentation to guide the discussion leading to the height of the chips problem.

The next stage was to demonstrate. Mr. Porter had arranged for a smooth transition from the introduction to the demonstration by first having the simulation of the spreadsheet embedded in the presentation so that he could talk about how to enter formulas in a spreadsheet. With the completion of this activity, he planned to switch to the actual spreadsheet where he could review the first three entries in the spreadsheet and then ask the students how to change from one unit of measure (say, centimeters) to another (say, inches). He planned to select another student to come to the computer to enter the formula. If the student made an error in the entry, he asked the class to help that student fix the formula that had been entered. In this process he provided his students with guided practice with the spreadsheet.

Finally, the closure stage was the time Mr. Porter planned for the students to explain, extend, and evaluate the ideas they had explored during the demonstration. In this part of the lesson, Mr. Porter determined that the students needed to summarize the ideas about Avogadro's number and about entering formulas in the spreadsheet. After the discussion, he questioned the students, stimulating their thinking and engaging them in preparing for a discussion the next day.

Demonstrations are most often teacher-centered, but the teacher's role can be that of a guide by having students follow the verbal instructions for conducting the demonstration. Probably the biggest constraint in this strategy is that students may disengage with the classroom interaction and not pay attention. The teacher's questioning is critical in reengaging them in the activity. Questions often need to be directed toward particular students who will support the progression of the demonstration rather than to students who have not been paying attention. Demonstrations do provide a good strategy for introducing technologies and working with the technologies prior to student hands-on use of the technologies.

Labs and Hands-on Activities   Labs and hands-on teaching strategies are essential for teaching with and about technologies. From a constructivist viewpoint on student learning, student-centered, hands-on activities are essential if students are to learn to use the technology as a tool. Labs and hands-on strategies do not provide teachers with free and easy days. If anything, the opposite is true. During such activities, materials and equipment malfunctions, management problems, and instructional shortcomings often occur. Yet, student-centered activities are considered an extremely potent instructional approach for actively engaging students both mentally and physically with the ideas. Organization and planning are critical to the success of these activities. Labs and hands-on strategies are framed by a set of stages as described in Figure 11.7.

Closure The teacher challenges the students to describe the results of the activity, providing them with an opportunity to summarize and explain what they learned from the activity. Students need to reflect on the lab activity and how the particular technology served as a tool for learning the subject. Closure assures that students answer important questions and links to future class instruction.

Preparing students to use technology as a tool for learning often involves students working on lab and other hands-on activities similar to that described in Chapter 5's Snapshot of a Classroom Writing with Word Processors. In that lesson, Mrs. Whitaker used a lab format to engage students in revising and editing their persuasive essays using the capabilities of a word processor as a tool for improving their work. Revision and editing stations were established in the classroom computer lab, each posing specific challenges. Students in groups rotated through a minimum of four of the revision and editing stations, applying the strategies and tasks to their essays.

To ensure that the lab experiences engaged her students in revising and editing their persuasive essays, Mrs. Whitaker needed to carefully prepare the activities and organize the computer lab, the first

Effective Labs and Hands-on Activities

Prepare	Teacher identifies and prepares the lab or hands-on activity to fit the content, engage the students in the content, and assure that all the students are able to work with the materials.
Introduce and Motivate	Students are engaged in the purpose or question of the lab or hands-on activity. They are given explicit instructions about the appropriate procedures with directions for safety, materials organization, clean up, and other expectations.
The Activity	Students participate in the activity, following the instructions. The teacher monitors the progress of groups and individual students, asking questions and notifying students of time constraints. Time for clean up is part of the activity.
Closure	The teacher challenges the students to describe the results of the activity, providing them with an opportunity to summarize and explain what they learned from the activity. Students need to reflect on the lab activity and how the particular technology served as a tool for learning the subject. Closure assures that students answer important questions and links to future class instruction.

FIGURE 11.7 Key features of effective labs and hands-on activities.

stage in planning for an effective lab activity. For this lab, she created five stations, each with a challenge that required students to work on their essays either individually or in groups. The challenges needed to be independent of each other so that the students could select the stations in any order. Also, Mrs. Whitaker needed to arrange for sufficient computer technology and organize the computers into appropriate station groupings. She needed to prepare the students for working with word processors in advance, assuring that they are ready to use the word processing capabilities efficiently. Finally, she needed to have contingency plans in case of problems with the technology or if the students needed additional time with the various challenges.

For the lab activity to be successful, Mrs. Whitaker figured that, for the introduce and motivate stage, she needed to introduce her students to the computer stations on the previous day, explaining what they would be doing on the following day. She decided to use an example essay to demonstrate the specific challenges. The time spent at this stage was essential in preparing the students to use the lab time efficiently.

During the lab activity the students were actively engaged in the work. Mrs. Whitaker, however, needed to observe the actions at each station, assuring that the students understood the challenges, asking questions of various students to ensure their engagement, and answering student questions. Mrs. Whitaker clearly recognized that at this stage she could not sit at her desk and wait for problems to arise. She needed to spend her time rotating throughout the class, observing the students' progress. As the time for the lab ended, she reminded her students of the clean up procedures. The stations needed to be returned to their original state for the next class. If she ignored this step, she would be left with the responsibility of rearranging the lab in time for that next class!

Closure (a stage too often ignored) was essential for the lab. Time was taken to engage the students in summarizing what they learned from each of the stations. This reflective stage was an important time for students to reflect on how the experiences with the technology helped them improve their persuasive essays. This stage was important in guiding their understandings about how the word processor served as a tool for improving all of their writing.

Questioning   Regardless of the general instructional model you might choose, questioning is an important strategy for guiding the instruction while integrating technology. Questions engage students in assessing their own understanding of the technology as a tool for learning the content. Questions are useful for managing students, assuring that they know and understand the expectations for each activity. Questions can be used to assess students' prior knowledge of the technology as well as of the content. In particular, questions can be used to stimulate student thinking in the activity. By focusing questions on students' thinking, you can gain a better understanding of how they construct their ideas integrating their interpretations of the classroom experiences in which they are participating.

The types of questions asked are important if you intend to learn about your students' thinking. Questions need to be clear, brief, thought-provoking, and purposeful, focused on students' thinking rather than on encouraging students to participate in the game of "What Is the Teacher Thinking?" The positive side effect of good questions is that students begin to ask deeper, more thoughtful, and more frequent questions of themselves, their classmates, and the teacher.

Sequencing the questions deserves important consideration. If you begin with a higher order question, the students are likely to be easily confused because they have not been prepared for the intensity of the question. If you want to ask a higher order question, it is better to begin with some lower order questions that set the stage by helping students recall some basic ideas and principles that might be helpful as they ponder the higher order question.

With the importance of a good questioning strategy, you need to plan key questions, carefully considering how you will engage the students in each discussion. Mr. Porter in the Snapshot of a Technology-Infused Demonstration Lesson identified his key question: How high is a stack of Avogadro's number of chips? When he asked about the magnitude of Avogadro's number, the students chided him with the recognition that there was no way they would know. He was prepared (even planned) for them in this case because he quickly asked them to guess, indicating that there would be no penalty in this case for a wild guess. As he guided their thinking about entering formulas in the spreadsheet, he first asked several lower level questions, used a variety of students in collecting answers to the questions, and finally showed them the result of the formula in the PowerPoint presentation.

After this work, Mr. Porter planned to move to the actual spreadsheet demonstration, asking various students to identify the formulas to change from millimeters to centimeters, centimeters to inches, inches to feet, and finally feet to miles. Mr. Porter planned to enter exactly what the students suggested. If the suggestion was incorrect, he planned to use the spreadsheet response as a teachable moment, asking the students to explain why the result was not correct, to suggest a correction, and to explain why their correction should result in the correct conversion. In other words, Mr. Porter did not plan to simply tell students how to enter formulas in the spreadsheet. He preferred to guide the development of their ideas through his questioning strategies along with the spreadsheet demonstration of their ideas.

For a questioning strategy to be successful, however, Mr. Porter knew that he needed to distribute the questions throughout the class, not allowing a few students to dominate the classroom discussion. He planned to call on both volunteers and nonvolunteers, keeping the entire class alert to the discussion. He also knew that he should ask the question first and allow all the students time to think about the response before selecting the student by name who was to respond. He knew to avoid chorus responses from the class so that he could manage the classroom discourse. He planned to ask students if they considered the spreadsheet response correct. He knew that he would need to be prepared to challenge them with questions about the reasonableness of the spreadsheet responses.

Questioning is a powerful strategy for engaging students in thinking about the actions returned by a technology such as the spreadsheet. For this strategy to be successful, however, you need to include techniques such as some of those that Mr. Porter planned. Incorporating a demonstration of the technology as a tool along with questioning requires careful planning. The important point, though, is that the results reveal that students can be engaged in learning about the technology, thinking with the technology, and learning the content with the technology with only one demonstration station where the teacher manages the discourse through carefully planned questions.

Grouping   Small-group investigation is an instructional strategy that uses inquiry to stimulate students' work in solving a problem. Typically, students are confronted with a puzzling situation; groups pursue a solution by exploring their various reactions to the situation, organize their study of the situation, follow their identified plans, reflect and analyze their progress toward a solution, and revise their plans if needed.

You can organize groups in a variety of ways to work on a puzzling situation. The group compositions might be determined randomly or purposefully; purposeful compositions might be students of similar abilities (homogeneous grouping) or varying abilities (heterogeneous grouping). The groups might be asked to work toward a common solution; alternatively, they might work together with the challenge that each group member provides an individual solution.

You can challenge each of these group organizations in many different ways.

- The students in the group can be expected to provide a single solution for the group. In Chapter 8, In the Classroom 8.3, students might be organized in groups, where each group is asked to create a digital story in a 3- to 5-minute narrative response to a significant question. Here the group might identify a common question and then work together in the production process, resulting in one movie response to the question. The composition of each group might be a homogeneous grouping by student interest in a specific digital picture; alternatively, the group might be a heterogeneous grouping with respect to movie-development skills and homogeneous with respect to student interest.

- Each person in the group might be expected to provide an individual solution based on the work of the group. Students for In the Classroom 8.3 in Chapter 8 (where they were challenged to create a digital story that conveys a 3 to 5 minute personal response to a significant question and experience) might begin with groups organized to identify the significant question for the movie solution and to study the production process; however, each student might be expected to develop an individual movie solution. The composition of the groups in this situation might be determined by various skills in working in the production process so that when students work on their individual productions, they have resources for their questions.

- The class, as a whole, divides the problem into subproblems and then each subproblem is assigned to an individual group. The solution to the original problem is thus the result of the sum of the various group solutions where each group shares their knowledge and solution with the class as a whole. This organization might be similar to the strategy used for the study of frog deformities in Chapter 8 (see section on Multimedia as a Research Tool). In this situation, after various hypotheses for the frog deformities are identified, each group is assigned one of the hypotheses to research, and each group is required to develop a PowerPoint presentation to describe and provide evidence for the hypothesis. The class as a whole can then prepare a global presentation with links to each of the hypothesis presentations. Group members might be determined by student experience and understanding with the possible hypotheses since the solution to the problem is the sum of the various presentations.

In each of these situations, students must work collaboratively in learning about the particular technology and learning to use that technology as a tool in the exploration of the subject matter. To assure the success of the group work, when organizing the groups, you need to consider a variety of criteria, such as common experiences or interest and expertise with the technology. Some of the best results occur when students are expected to share their expertise with each other. When considering the use of groups, you need to vary the sizes and expectations for the groups. Smaller groups provide a better opportunity for all members to participate in the solution. Varying expectations for the group work, one solution versus individual solutions, is important. Group work allows students with face-to-face interactions and work with social skills that are important for student learning. Group work also allows for more student involvement than what is typical of whole-class strategies.

Students learn by interacting in multiple environments. Although your primary task is to scaffold your students' learning about technology within the context of the subject matter, you need to develop a repertoire of potential strategies and select those that most efficiently and effectively meet the goals for the instruction. No one strategy is best for all goals. Although various grouping strategies provide positive learning effects, they are best interspersed among and along with other teaching strategies and models. As recommended in the NETS·T guidelines (ISTE, 2002), having a set of generic models and strategies that are multi-purpose in application assists teachers in developing technology-infused lessons. Your set will be continuously modified and expanded as you gain experience in organizing groups for learning various concepts integrating various technologies in the learning experience.

Summing It Up

Your job is to teach. You are guided by goals in the description of what is to be taught. But your task is to design instructional experiences that guide your students in meeting the goals. You must make key decisions in the selection of the design and construction of the experiences in ways to actively engage students in learning. No one single instructional strategy will meet all your instructional needs. You must rely on a well-developed and in-depth knowledge of student learning, of the content you are to teach, and of the variety of pedagogical activities that support student learning.

The ideas of cognitive science and constructivists' perspectives provide you with an important framework for thinking about student learning.

From this perspective, you need to consciously scaffold your students' learning with the technology within the context of the subject matter so that they learn *about* the technology as they learn *with* it, particularly if you hope that your students learn to use the technology as a tool for learning the subject matter. You need to include a number of experiences with the technology, but those experiences need to be varied with how your students might use the technology as a tool for learning. One type of experience, even if students have many opportunities with that same type of experience, results in the students' thinking about the technology only within that type of experience. Varying the experiences provides a breadth of understanding in how the particular technology can be used as a tool in many ways. Finally, you need to select problems that motivate and challenge your students to use the technology as a tool for exploration of the content, rather than just using the technology because it is technology.

As a teacher, you need to have a broad repertoire of potential instructional models and strategies. That way, as you identify an instructional goal, you are able to select from your repertoire, identifying optimal models and strategies that support your intended goal. Several models and strategies can provide a base for your repertoire as you reflect about students and educational environments.

The direct instruction model is best for teaching facts, rules, and action sequences in an efficient manner. This model is useful for guiding students in learning to use the technology while also thinking about the subject matter context. The model is teacher-centered and usually includes a presentation or demonstration accompanied by teacher explanations, examples, and opportunities for practice and feedback.

Inquiry, problem solving, and discovery learning are each forms of the indirect model of instruction, another model that is useful for integrating technology in instruction. This model is best suited for teaching concepts, patterns, and abstractions, and the critical feature is that the students are at the center of this model. Teachers actively engage their students in constructing understandings that make sense to them. They provide examples and nonexamples and continually ask questions to challenge the students' thinking in the process of guiding them in identifying a generalization. The teacher engages students in evaluating their own responses and promotes and moderates the analysis of the process leading them to the generalization.

Demonstrations are useful instructional strategies when introducing technology in the content areas and in helping students understand expectations for future activities. Demonstrations are typically teacher-centered with the teacher invoking either direct or indirect inquiry models to involve students in thinking about the demonstration.

Another important strategy for teaching with and about technology is the labs and hands-on teaching strategy. From a constructivist view of student learning, student-centered activities are a focal point for teaching and learning with and about technology. If students are to learn to use technology as a tool, they will certainly need to have actual hands-on experiences with the technology.

Questioning and grouping strategies are ones that can be effectively integrated with each of the previous models and strategies. Questions are helpful for involving students and assessing their understanding of the technology as a tool for learning the content. Questions are useful for managing students to assure that they know the expectations for each activity. Questions can be used to assess students' prior knowledge of the technology as well as the content. Specifically, questions can be used to stimulate student thinking in the activity. By focusing questions on students' thinking you can gain a better understanding of how they are constructing the ideas as they fit their interpretations of the classroom experiences in which they are participating.

Grouping strategies are important considerations for organizing students in labs or hands-on activities. Teachers can organize groups in a variety of ways to work on an instructional activity. The group compositions might be determined randomly or purposefully; purposeful compositions might be students of similar abilities (homogeneous grouping) or varying abilities (heterogeneous grouping). The groups might be asked to work toward a common solution; on the other hand, they might work together with each group member being responsible for providing an individual solution.

The goal structure of the small group is another important consideration in grouping strategies. Groups can be challenged to work together so that one solution results from the work of all the groups. Individual groups can be challenged to present alternative solutions. Individual members in the groups can be challenged to complete parts of the group's solution. And individual members can be challenged to complete their own solutions in the group structure.

Students learn by interacting in various environments. Although your primary task is to scaffold your students' learning about technology in the context of the subject matter, you need to develop a repertoire of potential strategies and select those that most efficiently and effectively meet the goals for your planned instruction. No one strategy is best in every instructional case. As recommended in the NETS·T guidelines (ISTE, 2002),

having a set of generic models and strategies that are multipurpose in application will assist you in developing technology-infused lessons. Your set will be continuously modified as you gain experience in teaching and in organizing groups for learning various concepts while infusing technology in the learning experience.

End-of-the-Chapter Activities and References

PRACTICE PROBLEMS

1. Select a content goal where you plan to integrate learning with the technology as students also learn about the technology. Selecting from among the models and strategies in this chapter, describe how you might use one or more of the strategies for instruction toward this content goal.

2. Identify a WebQuest from the Web that you find useful for a particular instructional goal. Clarify instructional strategies that you might use to incorporate this activity in instruction.

3. Chapter 7 provides a discussion of a Web Inquiry investigation. Describe instructional models or strategies that might be used with a Web Inquiry.

4. Create a PowerPoint presentation that uses an inquiry-based indirect model of instruction.

5. Select a particular technology that you plan to work with in your teaching.

   a. Outline an activity that might be used to introduce your students to the technology.

   b. Identify some key questions that you might use in the activity to engage students in thinking with and about the technology.

   c. Describe how you might organize the students in groups for a follow-up activity to the one you outlined. How will the students be grouped? What will the goal be for the groups?

IN THE CLASSROOM ACTIVITIES

6. Observe a teacher in a classroom of your level of interest during a lesson in which students are working with technology as a tool or learning about the technology. Identify the strategy and instructional model that the teacher is using during your observations. Identify the key attributes in the success of the strategy or model. How do those relate to the affordances and constraints for the instructional models?

7. Interview three students about the instructional strategies in which they like to learn. Summarize the results, explaining their attraction to learning in the strategy. Relate your results to current learning theory.

8. Videotape your teaching of a particular instructional strategy. Reflect on your teaching with respect to the strength of your use of the strategy to guide students in learning.

ASSESSING STUDENT LEARNING WITH AND ABOUT TECHNOLOGY

9. Select a particular instructional strategy and discuss how you propose to assess student learning with and about technology in that strategy.

E-PORTFOLIO ACTIVITIES

10. Create a Web page that contains hyperlinks matching the strategies that compose your repertoire of instructional strategies for teaching with and about technology. Connect the hyperlinks to plans you have developed for teaching specific content.

REFLECTION AND DISCUSSION

11. Develop a summary comparison of the various instructional models and strategies described in this chapter. Compare the affordances and constraints for each of the models and strategies. Prepare a discussion on how several of the strategies might be used concurrently with a particular instructional model. Use a methods text for you specific subject area or use one identified in the Annotated Resources section.

12. Reflect on this statement: Lectures are not a good strategy for integrating technology because students need hands-on work for learning with and about technology to really learn.

◀ Annotated Resources

International Society for Technology in Education. (2002). *National educational technology standards for teachers.* Eugene, OR: ISTE.

This document provides a variety of instructional ideas for language arts, mathematics, science, and social studies in early childhood, elementary, middle, and secondary programs for integrating technology in the classroom.

LANGUAGE ARTS METHODS

Maxwell, R. J., & Meiser, M. J. (2004). *Teaching English in middle and secondary schools* (4th ed.). Upper Saddle River, NJ: Merrill/Prentice Hall.
This book uses constructivist theory and reflective practice for an integrated approach to teaching English language arts to middle and secondary school learners, containing ideas for effective strategies and planning.

Milner, J. O., & Milner, L. F. (2003). *Bridging English* (3rd ed.). Upper Saddle River, NJ: Merrill/Prentice Hall.
This text presents the organization and planning for instruction with a firm stand on teaching grammar in language arts education. This book explores censorship, national standards, high-stakes testing, multilingual students, and multicultural literature.

Tchudi, S. J., & Tchudi, S. N. (1999). *The English language arts handbook: Classroom strategies for teachers* (2nd ed.). Portsmouth, NH: Heinemann Press.
This book contains classroom strategies in a student-centered approach for teaching language arts.

MATHEMATICS METHODS

Van de Walle, J. (2006). *Elementary and middle school mathematics: Teaching developmentally* (6th ed.). Boston, MA: Allyn & Bacon.
This text provides a student-centered, problem-based emphasis for teaching mathematics.

SCIENCE METHODS

Trowbridge, L. W., Bybee, R. W., & Carlson-Powell, J. (2004). *Teaching secondary school science: Strategies for developing scientific literacy* (8th ed.). Upper Saddle River, NJ: Prentice Hall.
This science methods text reviews planning instruction toward student understanding.

SOCIAL STUDIES METHODS

Lee, J. K. (2007). *Elementary social studies.* Hoboken, NJ: John Wiley & Sons.
This social studies methods textbook is directed at identifying methods and strategies for teaching social studies in the elementary grades.

Martorell, P. H., Beal, C. M., & Bolick, C. M. (2006). *Teaching social studies in the middle and secondary schools.* Upper Saddle River, NJ: Pearson Merrill Prentice Hall.
This social studies methods textbook is directed at identifying methods and strategies for teaching social studies in the secondary grades.

CHAPTER 12

Designing, Implementing, and Reflecting on Instruction with Technology

Introduction

Integrating technology in subject matter activities demands increased attention by and expectations for teachers. The National Educational Technology Standards for Teachers (ISTE, 2002) recommends that teachers implementing technology in teaching and learning need to be prepared to

1. plan and design effective learning environments and experiences supported by technology; and
2. implement their plans that include methods and strategies for applying technology to maximize student learning.

Attention to these requirements demands that teachers draw on multiple domains of knowledge as they plan, design, and implement lessons: their knowledge about the subject matter, their knowledge about teaching and learning, and their knowledge about technology. However, they must not use their knowledge of one domain separately from the other. The key is for teachers to integrate these multiple domains of knowledge when they consider teaching with technology. This integrated knowledge domain is described as technological pedagogical content knowledge (TPCK).

TPCK for teaching with technology means that as teachers think about specific subject matter concepts, they concurrently consider how they might teach the important ideas embodied in the concepts in such a

way that the technology supports the translation of the concepts into a form understandable by their students. For teachers to merge their knowledge, skills, and understandings from these three knowledge domains to transform the subject matter to a form understandable by their students, they must engage in a pedagogical reasoning process, a process that requires preparation, representation, selection, adaptation, and tailoring (Wilson, Shulman, & Richert, 1987). A pedagogical reasoning that integrates the consideration of technologies requires that teachers engage in

- *Preparation*: Teachers need to dissect their own understandings of the content they are to teach, winnowing the topic to its essential ideas. They must critically review the content to examine the essential aspects with respect to the impact of new and emerging technologies. Has the impact of the technology shifted what is important to know and understand and how the ideas are used?

- *Representation:* Teachers need to repackage the subject matter in a manner suitable for instruction with the technologies. Does the technology provide access to new representations of the important ideas?

- *Selection:* Based on the analysis of how and what should be known, teachers then need to select appropriate strategies for facilitating learning those ideas. What technologies help students access the ideas? What must they learn about the technologies if they are to use them for learning?

- *Adaptation:* Teachers must consider the specific students that they will be teaching as they design plans for engaging them in learning. With respect to the technology, what is students' prior knowledge and experience with the technology? How does this prior knowledge influence the pedagogical objectives for the lesson?

- *Tailoring:* Teachers need to configure the instruction in response to the students' individual needs and scaffold their learning experiences about the technology as they learn with the technology. How do student skills and needs with the technology influence the instruction?

Throughout this pedagogical reasoning process and given the impact of technology on the content and the pedagogy, teachers focus on ways to integrate technological visions in ways that add meaning to the topic for the students. However, the teachers' work is not finished, having made those decisions. As with every lesson teachers teach, they must continue to work on planning for the lesson. As the lessons progress, teachers make decisions that perhaps shift their carefully structured plans as they monitor the activities. And, in reflection after the lesson, teachers need to assess the results of the lesson and consider revising the lesson for future implementation.

Those thinking processes in the design and implementation of their lessons are consistent with what research suggests about teacher thought processes. With respect to instructional practices, research has described three important stages around which to focus teacher thinking (Clark & Elmore, 1981; Clark & Peterson, 1981; Clark & Yinger, 1979; Fogarty, Wang, & Creek, 1983; Ross, 1989; Simmons et al., 1989):

1. *Planning* prior to teaching;
2. *Monitoring* and *regulating* while teaching;
3. *Assessing* and *revising* after teaching.

How is a teacher's thinking and decision making affected in each of these important stages of teaching with a focus on promoting technology as an integral component or tool for learning within the subject matter content? What are important considerations when teachers plan to integrate technology as a tool for learning? How are teachers' thinking and decision making affected when they implement the lessons and guide students' learning with technology as a tool? And, finally, what considerations and implications must teachers think about as they reflect and revise their teaching with technology?

Chapter 11 focused your attention on the development of a repertoire of models and strategies for teaching with technology. Yet, the decision of the strategy to be used is only a first step in guiding student learning with technology. This chapter is devoted to an examination of the questions and challenges for expanding and enhancing teachers' thinking and decision-making skills throughout the three stages when teaching with technology. These challenges focus on the development of your ability to integrate your knowledge of the content you plan to teach, your knowledge of teaching and student learning, and your knowledge of the technology. In short, these challenges focus on expanding your pedagogical reasoning that relies on your pedagogical content knowledge for teaching students with technology (TPCK).

CHAPTER LEARNING OBJECTIVES

After reading this chapter, you should be able to:

1. Identify knowledge inputs that are useful in designing lessons that integrate technology.
2. Design important cognitive, affective, and psychomotor objectives teachers might consider for guiding lessons that integrate technology.
3. Clarify important elements of a lesson plan for integrating technology.
4. Describe some guidelines for teachers when engaged in teaching a lesson with technology.
5. Identify some ideas for guiding a teacher's reflections on instruction with technology.

Snapshot of a Teacher Guiding Students' Learning with Technology

Brian Wyngard teaches eleventh-grade U.S. history. One of his goals for the year is for his students to work with primary sources (letters, communications, and other writings) to develop a better understanding of the historical roots of contemporary debates. In particular, he wants to engage his students in considering the current church-versus-state debate from its historical precedence.

Mr. Wyngard: [Pointing to a poster on the bulletin board.] Do any of you recognize this monument?

Jason: Isn't that the one that was removed from one, the court buildings in Montgomery, Alabama?

Mr. Wyngard: Right. This monument was installed in the rotunda of the State Judicial Building in 2001. But Chief Justice Moore was ordered by the Eleventh U.S. Circuit Court of Appeals to remove it because it violated the First Amendment of the U.S. Constitution and the principle of separation of church and state.

Kelsey: Why would a judge do something that violates an accepted principle?

Mr. Wyngard: Because he felt that the order was unlawful, that it placed the federal government in the position of telling us what to think. Others argued on his behalf of the need to recognize God as a part of the moral foundation of the U.S. Tomorrow we'll be looking at some historical precedents of this issue of the separation of church and state by investigating some petitions written during the eighteenth century. That was a time when petitioning the government was more common than it is today.

Catherine: What do you mean by *petitioning the government?*

Mr. Wyngard: U.S. citizens have the right to petition the government for "redress of grievances."

Bill: Huh?

Mr. Wyngard: "Redress of grievances" means citizens can ask the government to address a problem they might be having. This right is guaranteed in the First Amendment to the U.S. Constitution. As I said, petitioning the government was more common in the eighteenth century, but we still see examples of this type of activity particularly with the advent of e-mail and the World Wide Web.

In preparation for the lesson for the following day, Mr. Wyngard discovered the Library of Congress online digital collection called American Memory. He found that this website provided an original collection of religious petitions presented to the state of Virginia government during and just after the American Revolution in the late eighteenth century. With this collection on the Web, he arranged this lesson to guide his students in locating and reading the petitions to gain a perspective of the ongoing national debates about the role of religion in American life and government. He planned for the students to analyze documents, determining the author's intent, the tone of the language, the historical context, and their general content. He felt that after this investigation his students would be prepared to produce written summaries of their analyses and inferences about the level of religious tolerance in colonial America.

From his own work with this website, though, Mr. Wyngard recognized that working with the website might interfere with the content of the lesson. He realized the need to prepare his students for working with the website to assure that their focus remained on the content of what they were reading, not the format in which they were reading the content. After some thought about this problem, he decided to demonstrate the process of accessing the website along with an introduction to the petitions available on the website before sending the students to the computer lab for their individual work with the website.

Mr. Wyngard: Let me demonstrate the website that we are going to use [projecting a display of the website] to access historical documents. This is the American Memory website at http://memory.loc.gov/. Copy down this location accurately so that you will be able to access it when we go to the lab. When you first arrive at the website, you need to click on the Browse button [demonstrating the process on the website projection].

Next you select the period *1700–1799* under the heading Browse Collections by Time Period because that is the period of interest for the work we are doing.

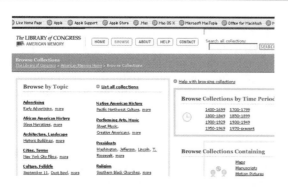

Finally, you need to scroll down the listing of possible petitions during this time period to find the one on religious petitions [pointing to the selection titled Religious Petitions, Virginia, 1764– 1802].

As you can see this collection includes 423 petitions to the Virginia state legislature on topics related to religion from 1764 to 1802. The collection includes petitions from well-known and not so well-known people on topics including separation of church and state, the rights of religious dissenters such as Quakers and Baptists, the sale and division of church property, and the breakup of un-popular religious institutions.

With this preparation for the first activity, Mr. Wyngard decided to engage the students in a whole-class discussion to brainstorm topics that might have been addressed in these petitions. After recording a list of potential topics on the board, Mr. Wyngard assigned each student one of the topics. He explained that in the computer lab, their first task was to take about 5 minutes to search the collection using their assigned ideas.

The next day, the students immediately began working at their computers and within the first 5 minutes had completed the activity; now they were ready to report what they had found. With these reports, Mr. Wyngard started a new list on the board, this time with the titles of actual petitions. With the help of the students, Mr. Wyngard selected 10 petitions and assigned one petition to each group of three students. In each group, the students were instructed to read the petition and then complete three discrete tasks:

1. record the author's name and as much information about that person as possible,

2. write a summary of the petition, and

3. describe the context of the particular request.

Each student was asked to do one of the three tasks and share their results with the others in the group so that each person had information about all three.

While the groups were working on their assigned tasks, Mr. Wyngard visited each group to make sure they were able to locate the document and load it on the screen. He recognized in advance of this lesson at least two limitations that might potentially affect each group's ability to complete the work, so he planned to work directly with students to make sure these limitations did not impede their progress. First, the petitions were not transcribed. Instead, students had to read images of the original handwritten documents. Mr. Wyngard suggested that they transcribe the documents so that the contents could be more easily read.

The document resolution was not a problem, but its quality created the second limitation. The most readable images of the petitions were high quality JPEG images and were as large as 1 megabyte each. He warned the students in advance that the image size would slow down the process and they just needed to be patient. He could have prepared these transcriptions in advance, but since he wanted his students to have the opportunity to work with him in making the selections, he did not know which to transcribe. Hence he simply warned his students and made sure they used their time wisely while the images loaded. To avoid problems during this waiting time, he had the students read a background piece on the collection that was available on the American Memory website. He had printed this piece in advance, made copies, and distributed it just as students were loading images.

With the images loaded, the remainder of the students' work related to transcription and historical analysis. On reflection after the lesson, Mr. Wyngard was pleased with the progress the students were able to make during their time in the lab. He had guided his students with the technological aspects of this lesson, prepared them in advance, and provided them with a 5-minute task to begin their work on the computers. While the students worked in the computer lab, Mr. Wyngard's primary focus was to manage the available time appropriately, guiding the student groups as they progressed through the tasks. He was pleased to note that his students remained on task throughout the class period and completed their tasks within the available class time. In the end, he felt that with his planning and attention to potential limitations, the work with the technology focused students' attention on making sense of the subject-matter-based tasks, rather than shifting to dealing with the operation of the technology.

Designing Instruction with Technology

Teachers face a tremendous challenge when planning to teach with technology because their instruction must establish the benefits of technology as a tool for maximizing student learning of important subject matter content and also support students in meeting the technology standards (NETS·S, ISTE, 2000). Comprehensive thinking and conscientious decision making prior to teaching with technology is obviously a critical part of what they must do in preparation. This planning stage incorporates a systematic process of decision making about what and how the students should learn the content with technology. Although you might wish for a set of specific steps to guide this pedagogical reasoning process toward decision making and planning, in reality, the best approach is a professional consideration of key inputs in the planning process and of important considerations in designing units and lesson plans.

Instructional Planning Inputs

You have been assigned to teach a sequence of lessons that integrates technology. Stop to think about the questions that immediately come to mind when given this challenge. These questions expose some key knowledge inputs to a teacher's planning process that directly utilize and depend on their technological pedagogical content knowledge (TPCK).

Knowledge of the Content   Most likely, when presented with the challenge to teach a sequence of lessons, your first question is, "What content am I supposed to teach?" For Mr. Wyngard in the *Snapshot of a Teacher Guiding Students' Learning with Technology*, the content involved the historical roots of contemporary debates. In his planning, he was forced to carefully dissect his own understanding of the content, extract a specific debate, and investigate the historical roots of that debate. His knowledge of this content reflected many years of learning history. Although he probably was able to discuss the content in fairly general terms, he was certainly not prepared to teach it without further study. He needed to extend his own understanding of the content by reviewing textbooks, curriculum resources, the Internet, and other types of resources. He even discussed the content with other history teachers and other professionals (such as lawyers and legislators). With each of the resources, his own personal knowledge of the content was reconstructed, helping him make new connections. For example, as he read the petitions on the American Memory website, he connected the level of religious tolerance in colonial America with the current debates about the separation of church and state. This connection strengthened his understanding of the historical development leading to the contemporary debates. In essence, then, his own understanding of the content was an important input to what he planned to teach and he needed to have a good grasp of that content.

Knowledge of Technology   As you consider the content you are to teach, another important input is the possibility that the technology might serve as a tool for learning that content. Can you incorporate technology with this content and if so, which particular technologies afford the greatest gain? Technology is not applicable for every topic in your content area, but your knowledge of a variety of technologies and how they might be used in learning content is an important consideration in planning lessons.

Mr. Wyngard clarifies his knowledge of the content he wants to teach by reading historical resources on the American Memory website. In the process, he is alerted to the possibility of using the website as a research tool in the instruction. The NETS·S guidelines (ISTE, 2000) provide a framework for judging potential technologies. Is there a specific technology that might support students in learning to use technology as a productivity tool, a communications tool, a research tool, or a problem-solving and decision making tool? Can you integrate the content to support student learning about the basic operations and concepts of the technology or support students in learning about the social, ethical, and human issues with technology use?

An important consideration with respect to technology is the broad array of potential technological applications. Your knowledge about various technologies positions you for considering them as supporting learning in the content areas. You need to explore your content with potential technologies in mind to see if those technologies might be useful in guiding students in learning the content. If your content is the difference between experimental and theoretical probability (as In the Classroom 6.1 in Chapter 6), a spreadsheet might be a useful tool for problem solving and decision making. On the other hand, calculators might be acceptable. If your content is the role of women in science and mathematics disciplines (as for In the Classroom 7.5 in Chapter 7), you might consider the Internet as a research tool with its worldwide access to a myriad of resources. If your content is the concept of change (as for In the Classroom 8.1 in Chapter 8), you might consider PowerPoint presentations or movies as an appropriate venue for displaying the concept of change. In essence, the depth and breadth of your knowledge of technology is an important input to the planning process.

Knowledge of Teaching and Learning Another key input to your decision-making processes for planning lessons involves your own knowledge and experiences with teaching and learning. So often, beginning teachers teach as they were taught simply because their knowledge and experiences about successful strategies have been limited to their own successes in learning. Teacher preparation programs aim to extend this knowledge and experiential base through academic and practical experiences, including student teaching experiences where cooperating teachers and supervisors mentor student teachers. Through these experiences, the student teachers' repertoire of models and strategies, such as those described in Chapter 11, is expanded. By the time they are ready for their first teaching position, they have expanded their knowledge base of teaching and learning.

As you consider the challenges of teaching, attention to some key characteristics of effective lessons highlights important teaching and learning inputs. Effective lessons are *motivational*, engaging students in the lesson content. Students are challenged to make sense of the developing ideas through the tasks in which they are engaged. In the *Snapshot of a Technology-Infused Demonstration Lesson* (in Chapter 11) the students were challenged to think about the height of an Avogadro's number of chips. The speculations that the students suggested included distances most of them had difficulty imagining (distance to the moon and back), and after their analysis with the spreadsheet they found that the distance was even much more! Mr. Porter did not conclude the lesson with this

recognition; he extended the concept challenging the students to think about this enormous number as they considered where they might find an Avogadro's number of items within their own world.

Effective lessons are *organized*. Students understand what they are to do and are supported in accomplishing the tasks. Mr. Porter had carefully organized his lessons on Avogadro's number using multiple technological applications given a consideration that he needed to guide the students before they had hands-on activities. First he used a PowerPoint demonstration; then he shifted to a spreadsheet demonstration where the students were to describe the formulas using the cell references; finally, he planned that his students would follow up that day with actual hands-on work entering information in a spreadsheet.

Effective lessons are *prepared*. As students work on the tasks with the technology, the technology must be ready for use where the teacher has considered and prepared for problems that might occur. Mr. Porter was prepared for the lesson, testing the equipment in advance. He also prepared for problems by having overheads of the screens that he wanted to display actively. If a problem arose (e.g., the electricity failed, the computer projection light burned out, the computer froze) he was able to immediately switch to the overheads and continue the lesson. With Mr. Porter's extra preparation and planning, the activities were well managed, retaining the focus on the objectives for the lesson.

Effective lessons incorporate a *variety of strategies*. Obviously Mr. Porter had planned for a variety of strategies, beginning with a teacher-directed activity with the PowerPoint, shifting to the spreadsheet where students were asked to guide the work, and finally planning for a follow-up day where the students had hands-on work with the spreadsheet.

A teacher's *enthusiasm* is essential for an effective lesson. If the teacher is not excited by the topic and the activities, why should the students be motivated and engaged? Research shows that teachers who demonstrate their enthusiasm tend to have students who are more attentive and involved (Gillett & Gall, 1982). The students in Mr. Porter's class were more attentive and involved, perhaps partly because of his enthusiasm for the work that they were doing. The variety of activities and his use of students in the development of the spreadsheet are examples of some of the ways that he demonstrated his enthusiasm.

Effective lessons are characterized by the *involvement of students*. Involving students in the classroom actions helped Mr. Porter maintain their attention to the ideas. Spreading his questions throughout the class held the whole class responsible for being involved in the discussion.

Throughout each of these characteristics of effective teaching is an underlying knowledge of the learners. Extensive research supports that teachers on average spend more than 40% of their time planning instruction around considerations about the learners (Clark & Peterson, 1986). Which students are you going to be teaching? What are their preferred learning styles? What is their current level of understanding about the content? What is their current background with and access to the technology that is being considered? A careful consideration of the learners' unique abilities and experiences helps you frame how you will consider teaching them the content with technology. More specifically, this consideration helps you organize, select, sequence, and allocate time to various topics of instruction. For example, in the unit on tornadoes (in Chapter 2), students who actually live in Tornado Alley are better prepared with personal experiences with tornadoes; whereas if students live in Alaska, they may need more preparation for the unit. For In the Classroom 7.2 (in Chapter 7), students are expected to engage in a virtual field trip on the Web. Students with prior experiences with the Web technology are better prepared than those who have not had previous Web experiences. And, in the Snapshot of a Class Designing a Movie (in Chapter 8), students who are native Spanish speakers have different abilities than those who are learning Spanish as a second language.

Extensive research on effective teaching and on student learning in conjunction with the wisdom gained by teaching practice, supports teachers in planning lessons that integrate technology. Such teaching and learning inputs as well as those based on knowledge of content and technology help guide teachers in designing their lessons that integrate technology for guiding student learning.

Designing Instruction

The development of curriculum and instruction for the subject areas is guided by content area standards. (Appendix D contains website links to multiple content area curriculum standards.) The Technology Foundation Standards for Students (ISTE, 2000) also provide important guidelines for integrating technology goals and objectives within the content area standards when planning both the curriculum and instruction. Finally, states and school districts provide additional direction for making decisions about integrating the standards and guidelines in the development of local curriculum and instruction.

Ultimately, teachers make the decisions about their instruction, typically framing these decisions into unit and lesson plans. In Chapter 2, Figure 2.2 presents an outline for a unit on tornadoes as one way of describing decisions a teacher might make about a unit that integrates multiple technologies. Figure 4.5

in Chapter 4 presents another unit around *The Adventures of Huckleberry Finn*. Each outline begins with the standards guiding the unit decisions, and, in both cases, multiple content area standards are identified along with technology standards. These standards are often translated through three to five broad goals for a specific unit in statements such as these:

- **Tornado unit goals**
  - Students will appreciate the impact of use of various scientific methods in the world.
  - Students will develop and apply a variety of technological tools for examining and explaining the science of tornadoes.

- *Huckleberry Finn* unit goals
  - Students will acquire confidence in using technology to study people, places, and environments.
  - Students will value the role of technological resources to create and communicate knowledge.

After committing to general goals and an outline for the unit, the next step in the decision-making process requires planning the details and flow of the daily instruction. Designing the instruction requires some of the most important decisions teachers must make. As you prepare to teach, you must learn to engage in this decision-making process. With the increasingly complex and information-rich technological society, your instructional decisions must reflect an integration of technology inputs into your thinking about instruction along with the inputs of your knowledge of content and teaching and learning.

With the unit goals and an outline that plans for the integration of technologies, you need to decide on the daily instructional activities, carefully structuring the student activities with the technologies. A key concern is the knowledge and experience that students need prior to the use of the technology as envisioned in the unit. Both units expect that students will design a PowerPoint presentation. What if the students have no previous experience with PowerPoint? If not, you need to integrate instruction about PowerPoint somewhere. The result may be that the unit is longer than originally envisioned. If students begin learning about PowerPoint in one unit, their involvement in the next unit can be used to advance their knowledge of working with *PowerPoint* as a tool for learning.

Instructional Objectives   By incorporating multiple inputs to the decision-making process, including technology, as the teacher you are positioned to finalize the design of your instructional plan. In the beginning, you probably sketch out some ideas in your thinking but you have not formally considered them as a cohesive set of activities.

An important first step is to clarify just what you want the students to learn and demonstrate as a result of the instruction. An old saying clarifies this point: "If you don't know where you are going, how will you know when you get there?" Instructional objectives (sometimes referred to as learning outcomes) frame the lessons that extend from the goals you identified for the unit. These objectives focus the instruction by describing the specific student behaviors, actions, and abilities you expect to be able to observe and measure at the end of the instruction.

Instructional objectives are frequently organized in three important categories: *cognitive, affective*, and *psychomotor*. Teachers are most often concerned about the intellectual skills that students gain from instruction; these thoughts are concerned with the cognitive objectives. They must also think about supporting students in becoming committed to the importance of the subject; these more emotional ob-

jectives are in the affective domain. Physical abilities identified in the psychomotor domain point toward students performing skills with strength and endurance. Psychomotor objectives are more often considered the domain of physical educators but in reality become a concern of a wide range of teachers, especially when considering the incorporation of technology where students must physically enter data and manipulate various technologies. Keyboarding may require the consideration of a psychomotor objective if students are in the early stages of working with computer keyboards.

Cognitive objectives are framed in increasing levels of knowledge (in a revision of Bloom's taxonomy described in Anderson & Krathwohl, 2001): remembering, understanding, applying, analyzing, evaluating, and creating. Figure 12.1 provides some

Cognitive Objectives

Objective Level	Objective Statement	Explanation
Remember	The student identifies how to exit a PowerPoint about tornadoes prior to the last slide.	The student is only expected to remember the knowledge that the esc key is used to exit a slide presentation.
Understand	The student clarifies the procedures for viewing a PowerPoint application that describes the Fujita scale of tornado intensity.	Students simply explain the process for viewing the multiple slides in the slide show view using the arrow keys and mouse.
Apply	The student develops one slide about tornadoes for a PowerPoint presentation that includes a picture of a tornado.	Students are expected to create one slide of a presentation with a picture of a tornado inserted from a file and use the various features of the application to communicate a message about tornadoes. They are expected to apply various features of PowerPoint that they have learned, including inserting a picture.
Analyze	The student organizes the presentation on each slide of a PowerPoint presentation that proposes a tornado-proof structure.	Students are provided with a presentation about tornados that is incoherent because all elements on the slides appear at once rather than being animated for a more coherent communication. The students are expected to use the animation features to structure the presentation of the various elements on each of the slides to better communicate the information.
Evaluate	The student reconstructs a presentation of slides for a PowerPoint presentation to allow the user to select the order of the slides about the safety procedures to use in the event of a tornado.	Students must change a linear presentation of slides to one that allows the presenter the opportunity to select the order of the description. They must judge the appropriateness of all the slides and then reconfigure the presentation by inserting a slide to allow the presenter to access the slides that are important for the communication.
Create	The student constructs a PowerPoint presentation that explains how a tornado is formed.	Students must create an original PowerPoint presentation, designing the content and its presentation to communicate their understandings of how a tornado is formed.

FIGURE 12.1   Cognitive domain objectives by increasing level of knowledge.

Affective Objectives

Level	Objective Statement	Explanation
Receiving	The student maintains attention throughout a PowerPoint presentation that describes how tornadoes are formed.	Students are willing to watch a presentation but they make no commitment to liking it and accepting it as a communications tool.
Responding	The student participates in a PowerPoint presentation that requires viewer selection in describing how tornadoes are formed.	Students have begun to consider PowerPoint as a tool for communicating information about tornadoes through their participation in the presentation.
Valuing	The student asks for information describing the process required to create a PowerPoint that requires viewer input into how tornadoes are formed.	Students show some definite involvement with and commitment to PowerPoint as a tool for communicating information about tornadoes.
Organization	The student describes the value of PowerPoint presentations as a means of communicating an understanding about tornadoes.	Students incorporate PowerPoint as a possible communications tool among those that they might consider in the tornado unit. They organize their preferences into a value system.
Characterization	The student selects PowerPoint as a preferred means for communicating an understanding about tornadoes at the end of the unit on tornadoes.	Students identify PowerPoint as a preferred communications tool for explaining ideas about tornadoes.

FIGURE 12.2   Affective domain objectives by increasing level of commitment.

sample objectives that illustrate students' increasing levels of knowledge using PowerPoint as a communications tool in learning about tornadoes. A key distinction among the objective levels is that through the first three levels, students are repeating ideas that were presented to them in instruction, whereas in the upper three levels, they are building **new** ideas and understandings beyond the instruction they have received.

Affective objectives are associated with attitudes, interests, beliefs, and values that describe a student's level of commitment to the idea, topic, or activity (Krathwohl, Bloom, & Masia, 1964). At the highest affective level, students might be expected to value the use of technology as a tool for learning, whereas at the lowest affective level they may simply pay attention to the use of the technology as a tool. Affective domain objectives are described through five basic levels. Figure 12.2 distinguishes the increasing levels of affective objectives describing a student's potential involvement and commitment to PowerPoint as a communications tool when learning about tornadoes. Students are not expected to display all of these levels immediately. If students have never seen a PowerPoint presentation prior to the unit, the teacher might consider an affective objective at the receiving level. On the other hand, if students have been working with PowerPoint throughout the past year, the teacher

might identify an affective objective at the organization (or even the characterization by value) level.

Psychomotor objectives reflect motor skills and eye–hand coordination, such as the ability to use a computer mouse to identify a selection of text in a word processor. These objectives are typically considered as students move from basic perceptions and reflex actions to skilled, creative movements— imitation, manipulation, precision, articulation, and naturalization. Whether or not the teacher explicitly states psychomotor objectives, this type of objective might be considered as students learn about computer technologies such as PowerPoint since they are developing physical skills with the computer keyboard and mouse as they design the elements of each slide. Harrow (1972) outlines five levels of psychomotor objectives that can be used to carefully think through the needed skills with the mouse to draw in PowerPoint slides. For the tornado unit, the teacher might identify that students are able to quickly use a computer mouse to draw a picture of a tornado using the draw tools in PowerPoint; this objective is likely at the articulation level if the teacher does not want to demonstrate the required skills. Figure 12.3 suggests possible objectives for the varying psychomotor objectives to guide you in considering instruction that integrates learning about the technology as well as learning with it.

Psychomotor Objectives		
Objective Level	**Objective Statement**	**Explanation**
Imitation	The student copies the drawing of a tornado that was demonstrated on a PowerPoint slide, using the mouse to select the drawing tool.	Students mimic the drawing action with the mouse after being shown.
Manipulation	The student follows a set of instructions to draw a tornado on a PowerPoint slide using the appropriate drawing tools.	Students use written directions without the aid of a visual model or direct observation to draw the tornado.
Precision	The student independently draws a figure of a tornado using the draw tools in PowerPoint.	Students are more proficient at this level in that they are able to produce a picture without a demonstration or written directions.
Articulation	The student quickly sketches a tornado using the drawing tools in PowerPoint.	Students' control of the drawing tools is increased and demonstrated by increased speed in creating the drawing.
Naturalization	The student spontaneously draws a tornado using the draw tools available in the PowerPoint.	At this level, students are able to repeatedly create the drawing naturally and effortlessly.

FIGURE 12.3   Psychomotor domain objectives by increasing level of abilities.

The important point of this discussion is that as you design your instructional plans where technology is an integral component, you must consider the potential of all three types of objectives—cognitive, affective, and psychomotor—as you describe the technology outcomes you desire from your units. Integrating the subject matter content in the description of these objectives shapes the condition under which the objectives are to be assessed. Basically, these instructional objectives provide directions for the instruction that students need if they are to be able to demonstrate the desired outcomes following the instruction.

Teaching Actions   Each lesson in a unit is organized around the instructional objectives. Further, thinking through every lesson is a process where teachers consider important teaching actions in addition to the potential teaching models and strategies discussed in Chapter 11. The effectiveness of lesson planning, preparation, and organization depends on an explicit consideration of these teaching actions.

Introduction The introduction needs to motivate students to become involved in the lesson. A good introduction captures students' attention and focuses them on what they will learn.

Questioning Asking students questions is important for involving them in the ideas developed in the lessons. Questions require students to actively participate in the instruction. They can be used to gain student interest and attention or to check for student understanding. They can be used to encourage students to engage in higher level thinking, helping them construct and explore their personal conceptions.

Giving Directions Students need to be given directions for each task so that they know what they are to do and how to perform in the lesson. Directions need to communicate these expectations. However, teachers must check, perhaps through questioning, to see if all students understand the directions.

Student–Teacher and Student–Student Interactions A positive and productive learning environment depends on the interactions among the individuals engaged in the lesson. Teachers need to engage all students in the activities, helping them gain a positive feeling about participating and sharing their ideas. They need to establish an environment where student ideas are accepted. Teachers need to monitor student–student interactions to assure that the interactions are positive and productive. In essence, teachers need to manage the classroom in a manner that encourages positive interactions.

Closure Every lesson needs closure. Closure is important for helping students review and confirm the ideas included in the various activities in the lesson. Closure is a time to guide students in making important connections by linking the ideas from the multiple activities throughout the lesson. Ultimately, closure is a time to direct their attention toward the instructional outcomes that guided the design of the lesson.

The Lesson Plan   The planning process for lessons requires more than just thinking about the knowledge inputs (content, technology, and teaching and learning), the instructional objectives, and the important teaching actions. Although that thinking is essential, it does not mean you are prepared to teach the lesson. At some point you need to formally outline and describe the lesson you are considering. Experienced teachers might be able to mentally prepare the lesson, making some organizational notes. Even for experienced teachers, however, a more detailed, written lesson plan offers many advantages. Written plans allow teachers to more easily remember those organizational notes, to review the ideas and consider transitions from one activity to another, and to reflect on and adjust the lesson for future use. More importantly, the integration of technology in the instruction represents a departure from traditional teaching, requiring more in-depth planning and preparation. A written plan is an organizational tool that encourages and supports this explicit and more in-depth planning process.

The sequence, number of elements, and amount of detail in a lesson plan can vary considerably. The plan is a guide for teaching and not a script for a play. Some teachers fear that writing plans will restrict the creative flow and energy of the class. However, when teachers are designing lessons that integrate technologies in the learning activities, the lack of a plan often results in not only the lesson focus being shifted from the primary objectives (perhaps to the technology rather than using the technology as a learning tool), but also loss of valuable instructional time, confusion about the directions, and even lack of preparation of the technology. The process of preparing the plan encourages teachers to think through and imagine how the lessons might proceed in order to maximize students' active engagement in the activities that lead toward the intended outcomes.

Figure 12.4 presents Mr. Porter's plan for the Avogadro's number lesson in the Snapshot of a Technology-Infused Demonstration Lesson in Chapter 11. The information prior to the Instructional Plans might be considered as prelesson information. This information highlights the knowledge students need for the lesson to be successful. If students had not had previous instruction with exponential notation or with general concepts with the spreadsheet, the lesson might have been sidetracked to deal with student confusion. The Purpose of the Lesson is a short description placing this lesson within the context of the unit of instruction. The Instructional Objectives provide the major objectives for the lesson. To clarify the objectives, the type and level have been added as a way of more thoroughly explaining the desired outcome. In particular, the fourth objective is intended to have a cognitive, affective, and psychomotor outcome. Since these objectives describe the outcomes, Mr. Porter numbers them for identification in preparation for designing the As-

sessment Plan that appears at the end of the plan; this way he can use the numbers both in the Closure and in the Assessment Plan to identify what and how the students will demonstrate the objectives by the end of the lesson and by the end of the unit. The Materials section not only describes the major materials needed but also provides notes to remind Mr. Porter of the preparation needed before the lesson. In particular, Mr. Porter recognizes the importance of checking out the technology he needs in advance. The bullets used to highlight each item are purposefully selected in the box (❏) format as a check-off feature. The Classroom information reminds Mr. Porter of the classroom organization for the lesson as well as important information in preparation for the following lesson: Sign up for the computer lab for next lesson!

The core of the lesson is described in the Instructional Plans section of the lesson plan. An important observation about the plan is that it is only an outline and does not prescribe a script for the lesson. Compare the plan with the lesson description in the Snapshot of a Technology-Infused Demonstration Lesson in Chapter 11. Mr. Porter does not follow the plan exactly. The plan was his way of organizing his thoughts before teaching the lesson.

Mr. Porter divides the instructional plans section into three key parts: Introduction, Investigation, Closure—based on his thinking about the importance of introduction and closure. He designs the Introduction to motivate the students, and he reviews the objectives for the lesson to design the Closure. He uses a Key Questions column as a way of describing the flow of the content in the Investigation portion and to indicate his awareness of the importance of questioning to engage his students in the lesson. He also finds that by preparing the questions with potential responses, he is better prepared to respond to students' ideas. The Time column is Mr. Porter's way of thinking through the timing of the lesson, making sure adequate time is available for all parts of the lesson. For beginning teachers, these times are generally guesses; with experience, however, teachers are more accurate in their predictions. In Mr. Porter's plan, the times add to 47 minutes and the class is identified as a 50-minute lesson, allowing time for typical class routines as well as miscalculations on the amount of time the lesson might take.

Recall the importance of clear directions as a key to effective lessons. Mr. Porter's lesson is a demonstration for students where he operates the technology. He uses questions to keep the students actively involved, and they operate the technology only under his guidance, one at a time. But he plans for the students to go to the computer lab the next day to work individually on the spreadsheets. This type of lesson requires that his directions are

Topic: Avogadro's Number: How Large Is It?   **Class:** Seventh grade   **Length:** 50 minutes

Prerequisite Knowledge:
- Students understand general concepts of spreadsheets, entering values, numbers, and formulas.
- Students have been introduced to atoms, molecules, and atomic weight using the periodic table of elements.
- Students understand exponential notation.

Purpose of the Lesson:
The lesson challenges students' knowledge and understanding about the size of a number often used in science, in particular with reference to a mole. The lesson is also designed to provide instruction about entering formulas in spreadsheets using cell references. Collectively the work extends students' understanding of atomic concepts presented in the periodic table.

Instructional Objectives:
1. Students relate an Avogadro's number of objectives to groups of objects on Earth. (Cognitive, Apply)
2. Students willingly express their understanding of the magnitude of Avogadro's number. (Affective, Valuing)
3. Students accurately enter formulas in a spreadsheet using cell references. (Psychomotor, Precision)
4. Students convert among different units of measure using the spreadsheet as a tool. (Cognitive, Understand; Affective, Organization; Psychomotor, Precision)
5. Students describe a mole in terms of an Avogadro's number of atoms. (Cognitive, Remember)

Materials:
- ❏ Periodic table of elements displayed on bulletin board
- ❏ Display chips for demonstrating stacking; ruler for measuring the stack
- ❏ PowerPoint presentation to introduce Avogadro's number + overheads of each slide
- ❏ Spreadsheet for displaying entering formulas + overheads of each result of each formula entered
- ❏ Computer with PowerPoint; whole-class projection device of computer display
- ❏ Overhead projector + overhead with homework challenges

Classroom:
- ❏ Regular classroom with display computer for whole-class demonstration
- ❏ Sign up for the computer lab for next lesson

Instructional Plans:

Time		Activity		Key Questions

Introduction

Time		Activity		Key Questions
1. 2 min	1.	Introduce English grouping words.	1a. 1b. 1c. 1d.	What is meant by dozen? **12** What about gross? **144** What is a score? **20** Why do we need grouping words? **They are means of communicating information efficiently.**
2. 5 min	2.	Recall the periodic table of elements using chart on the bulletin board.	2a. 2b.	What is the atomic weight of one mole of oxygen atoms? **15.9994 grams** How many atoms are in a mole of oxygen atoms? **Avogadro's number**
3. 5 min	3.	Introduce Avogadro's number with PowerPoint presentation. Show first slide; click to add the presentation of the numbers.	3a. 3b.	If Avogadro's number represents the number of atoms in one mole of oxygen, what number do you think it might be? **602,000,000,000,000,000,000,000** How big is this number? **(guesses)**
4. 3 min	4.	Pose a problem: height of an Avogadro's number of chips. Measure the chip and challenge students to suggest comparable distances. Encourage guessing and record on board.	4a.	How high would an Avogadro's number of chips reach? **(guesses)**

Investigation

Time		Activity		Key Questions
5. 5 min	5.	Demonstrate the process for entering values and formulas in a spreadsheet. Begin the investigation of the problem through PowerPoint presentation. • Height of 1 chip is 1.5 mm. • Avogadro's number: Enter as a formula, not ^ for exponential notation. • Height of stack: Use cell references for the formula to have spreadsheet calculate.	5a. 5b. 5c. 5d. 5e.	What value is entered in cell C4 for height of one chip? **1.5** If Avogadro's number is a number, what is put in cell C5? Can we put in a formula? How are formulas entered? Why the ^? $=6.02 \times 10\char94 23$ What does the result of 6.02E+23 mean? $\mathbf{6.02 \times 10^{23}}$ What can be put in cell C7 to have the spreadsheet calculate the height of an Avogadro's number of chips in mm? **=C4*C5** How high is 9.03E+23 mm? **(challenge)**

Time	Activity	Key Questions
6. 5 min	6. Demonstrate the use of spreadsheet to shift height in mm to other units of measure. Use cell references. • mm to cm • cm to inches • inches to feet • feet to miles	6a. How can mm be changed to cm? **=C7/10 in C8** 6b. cm to inches? **=C8/2.54 in C9** 6c. inches to feet? **=C9/12 in C10** 6d. feet to miles? **=C10/5280 in C11**
7. 5 min	7. Compare the distance in miles to distance from Earth to the Sun. Extend spreadsheet for this calculation.	7a. How far is the distance to the Sun? **93,000,000 miles** 7b. How can we find the number of times the distance to the Sun is the height of the chips? **Enter formula =C11/93000000; result is more than 6 billion times the distance from Earth to the Sun**.
8. 7 min	8. Relate the result of an Avogadro's number of atoms in a mole of an element to other amounts around the classroom using these elements: • Oxygen that has a mass of 15.9994 grams • Hydrogen that has a mass of 1.00794 gram Explore the number versus the mass.	8a What is the mass of a mole of oxygen atoms? **15.9994 grams** 8b. What else might weigh 15.9994 grams? **Multiple suggestions from students based on items they have familiarity with—a few particles of sand, handful of pencil shavings from the pencil sharpener.** 8c Do those things have an Avogadro's number of things? **No they are just a few, a very few**. 8d. Pose similar questions for hydrogen. 8e. Which atoms have the greatest mass, hydrogen or oxygen and why? **Oxygen because there are an Avogadro's number of atoms in each mole and O weighs more than H on a per-mole basis.**

Closure

Time	Activity	Key Questions
9. 5 min	9. Summarize with a discussion of student understanding of the size of Avogadro's number.	9a. **Objective 1:** Are there more than or less than an Avogadro's number of people on Earth, ants on Earth, grains of sand on Earth? **Less, less, more** 9b. **Objective 2:** The chip is 1.5 mm. How high would an Avogadro's number of chips that are much thinner be, say, 0.5 mm? **Students need to express how they might figure it out**. 9c. **Objectives 3, 5:** How might you explain an Avogadro's number of items to a friend who was not here today? **(share ideas)**
10. 3 min	10. Summarize entering formulas into a spreadsheet using cell references.	10. **Objective 4:** Explain why it might be better to use cell references in formulas than to enter the values. **Fewer errors in data entry, can make changes in the data to explore different problems.**
11. 2 min	11a. Homework challenge: Ask others, research the Web (show overhead). • Is the national debt larger or smaller than Avogadro's number? • How deep would a layer of sand be that covers the state of Texas with an Avogadro's number of grains of sand? • Where on Earth can you expect to identify an Avogadro's number of things? 11b. Announce: Tomorrow go to lab to explore using spreadsheets to calculate the height of chips that are 0.5 mm thick to compare with homework items.	

Assessment Plan

Objective 1: Questioning, Quiz, Unit Test, e-Portfolio
Objective 2: Questioning, Observation, Journal, e-Portfolio
Objective 3: Observation, Questioning, Lab Quiz
Objective 4: Observation, Questioning, Journal, Quiz, Unit Test, e-Portfolio
Objective 5: Questioning, Quiz, Unit Test, e-Portfolio

FIGURE 12.4 Sample lesson plan used for the Snapshot of a Technology-Infused Demonstration Lesson in Chapter 11.

clear and that the students understand and follow them. Actually, Mr. Porter selects the demonstration model purposefully to show his students how to work with the spreadsheets the following day. His plan for the following day is to provide a 5-minute review of what they are to do and provide them with a handout to guide their work in the computer lab. He still needs to question his students to make sure they understand the procedures and what they are to do in the event of problems.

Possible questions that might be useful for checking your own thinking about the kinds of directions include the following:

- Do the students receive directions for using the technology in advance of the expectation for their hands-on work?
- How do students work on the technology? Individually? In groups? If in groups, how are the groups assigned?
- What should the students do if problems occur with the technology that they are not able to solve?
- Are there worksheets or handouts available to provide students with information and instruction for working with the technology within the context of the subject matter?

Planning for technology as an integral component of a lesson requires even more than just the thinking and decision making. As one student teacher who was planning to integrate technology in a lesson recognized,

> I had thought it would be quite easy to integrate the use of technology into my lesson plans, and soon discovered that if I hadn't actually tried the lab a few times to work the "kinks" out, then I would have really been in trouble.

Planning requires that teachers investigate the ways in which the technology is to be used. During this investigation stage it is important to challenge the expectations of the technology. "What happens if I accidentally press this key instead of this one?" "What happens if I don't do this step?" "What happens if … " challenges provide teachers with important experiences in preparing for the class.

◢Implementing Instruction with Technology

The process of planning a lesson that integrates technology involves extensive consideration of the content and how the technology is involved. Teachers must plan carefully, scaffolding students' learning to work with the technology as a tool as well as to use the technology as an integral component for learning within the context of the content. The lesson plan represents an integration of the teacher's thoughts and decisions about the content, the technology, the students, and teaching and learning prior to actually teaching the lesson. On the day of the lesson, the teacher must implement the plans, monitoring and regulating the activities as the lesson progresses. Teachers make decisions about whom to question, when to move to the next idea, when to repeat an idea, and when to invite students to share ideas with the rest of the class.

Mr. Porter in Chapter 11's Snapshot of a Technology-Infused Demonstration Lesson carefully planned how he envisioned conducting the demonstration. He knew that his students had not had previous hands-on experiences with the technology and that this demonstration is designed to prepare them for hands-on work with entering formulas in a spreadsheet. As the demonstration process continues, he is careful to observe the students, looking for signs of confusion or inattention. He directs his questions throughout the class to make sure that the whole class is attentive and has an opportunity to become involved. Then, as he moves to the demonstration of the actual spreadsheet, he selects students he feels would benefit from actual guided hands-on experience to assist him.

Mr. Wyngard, in this chapter's Snapshot of a Teacher Guiding Students' Learning with Technology, needed to guide his class in hands-on work with the computers. He knows what he hopes will happen in the lesson but he also knows there is potential for problems. He knows that his students are not prepared to work with the American Memory website without some support. He recognizes that he needs to work closely with the students to aid and motivate them as they transcribed the eighteenth-century documents. He knows that he needs to make sure they use their time wisely while the images are loaded. He also knows that he cannot be with every group at the same time.

The experiences of teaching the lessons are different for both teachers. In Mr. Porter's case, the class is directed toward the front of the room with the projection of the PowerPoint and the spreadsheet. Mr. Porter's class incorporates a teacher-centered strategy where he guides the classroom discourse. Mr. Wyngard's organization is different. He needs to manage the students as they work in a student-centered activity, where multiple activities happen depending on each individual student's background, preparation, and understanding. Figure 12.5 summarizes questions that these teachers might be asking themselves while teaching a demonstration or a hands-on laboratory lesson that involves technology.

The important point is that in any technology-infused lesson, teachers must be concerned with

Demonstration	Hands-On Lab
• Are students motivated and engaged with the demonstration? • Do students understand the purpose of the demonstration? • Is the technology working the way it should? • Can all students see the demonstration? • Can all students hear the questions? • Is the demonstration going the way that is intended? • Do the students understand the questions? • Are my questions clear? • Which student should I select for this question? • Are all students paying attention? • Should I involve the students with the demonstration at this point? • Did the students get the main points of the demonstration? • Should students summarize their understandings? Or am I convinced they understand? • What should I do if a small group of students is confused about the ideas in the demonstration? • Should the demonstration be repeated?	• Do the students understand the purpose of the lab? • Do the students understand what they are to do in the lab? • Were my instructions clear? • Is each student actively involved in the lab? • Do students understand what to do if the technology does not work properly? • Do some students need assistance? • Are students following the procedures correctly? • Are students only following procedures rather than thinking about the ideas? • Are all the students trying? • Are the girls letting the boys handle the technology? • Do the students understand the content in the activity? • Are the students using the available handouts that provide assistance? • Should I stop the class and provide an explanation? • Do students know how much time they have left to complete their work? • What should students do if they finish early? • What if some students do not finish in time? How will they have an opportunity to gain the experiences intended?

FIGURE 12.5   Teacher questions considered during instruction.

managing the activity, monitoring the classroom discourse, and monitoring students' progress. They may need to quickly make adjustments in the activity. They may need to troubleshoot the technology. They may have to work more closely with some students with the technology. They may need to reorganize the students to engage them in the activity. They may have to explain ideas that they had not planned on explaining. Regardless of the situation, teachers must be constantly thinking and making decisions about the class activities throughout their lessons. And when the complexity of technology is incorporated, they need to be prepared to troubleshoot problems while maintaining the focus of the lesson on the intended content outcomes of the lessons.

Figure 12.6a describes three scenarios of actual classroom events where technology was integrated in the lesson. How would you handle the situations? Figure 12.6b describes how specific teachers handled the disruptions. In particular, note that the teachers maintained the focus on the lesson and in some cases used the problem as a learning event.

The central lesson in these scenarios is your preparation to deal with problems that might occur with the technology. Practice using the technology in multiple ways; see what happens if you do not follow all the directions; see what happens if you press keys in the wrong order; become familiar with how the technology works. For example, in Chapter 10, since the motion detector uses ultrasound emitted in

a cone about 30° wide, explore what happens when you try to collect data outside that range; then, if you see similar results on the students' display, you can suggest that they are probably not collecting the data within the appropriate range.

Remember, though, you simply cannot predict all that might happen but you need to adjust the lesson when problems do occur. Will you solve the problem or will you let the students try first? The decision will be yours and you must make it on the spot. As one student teacher recognized, "I need to remember to be in more of a troubleshooting mode than a Mr. Fix-It mode. I don't necessarily take over the computer to help them, but I don't always give enough wait time to let students figure things out on their own." Another student teacher's experience shows that teachers confront many challenges that require considerable attention throughout the lesson as they monitor and manage a technology-infused lesson:

The lab activity required that I give a very accurate description of the steps that students were to follow before they began. . . . It was important to constantly be checking their understanding during the activity. I felt that this was difficult to do adequately. . . . Nothing really went wrong, but it was a big headache. I think that by going over all the concepts covered in the activity again in class salvaged the lesson, but it was an additional chunk of time going over the same things.

(a)

Scenario 1

Every student in the class was assigned to create an electronic portfolio that provided links to their favorite science websites. Alice liked the Ask Dr. Science website and created a link along with an annotation that described what she found valuable at the site. On the peer review day, Juan was assigned to review Alice's portfolio. He launched Netscape for his Web browser and entered the link to Alice's e-portfolio. When he clicked on the Ask Dr. Science link, he was transported to a pornographic site.

Scenario 2

Shawn and Kerry were partners in the lab working with a real-time data collection device with a temperature probe and attached to a calculator. They were able to select the Datamate program but were not able to enter instructions for the temperatures to be taken every 10 seconds over a 5-minute period. They figured the batteries might be the problem so they removed the calculator to change the batteries. When they inserted the new batteries, the screen of the calculator display blanked to random square pixels and they were unable to get it to work with the probeware.

Scenario 3

Ms. Lindstrom planned to demonstrate a process for searching the Web using a computer projection unit that displayed the computer actions at the front of the room. She was launching the Internet connection when the projection unit lamp exploded.

(b)

Scenario 1

Alice immediately indicated that the link had worked only minutes ago and demonstrated that the link did work at her computer station. Ms. Watson asked Alice what Internet browser she was using. Alice indicated that she used Internet Explorer, so Ms. Watson launched that browser and entered the address to Alice's website. Sure enough, the link to Ask Dr. Science did connect with the correct website, not the pornographic site that Juan found. Ms. Watson indicated that she would need to research this problem but that this result was a good example of why the students needed to check their work using multiple browsers. She recommended that, for the time being, Alice put a note on her website that the link works only with Internet Explorer in order to warn the viewers. To follow up on this problem, Ms. Watson sent a message to the Ask Dr. Science website indicating the problem. The problem was fixed immediately.

Scenario 2

Mr. Temple asked the students to put a note on the calculator and to get another one from the instrument table for their work this period.

Scenario 3

Ms. Lindstrom had overheads of the demonstration and proceeded with the class simulating the demonstration with the overheads. The next day, after the lamp had been replaced, she did a quick overview of the demonstration to review the key points of the demonstration in preparation for the students' work in the lab.

FIGURE 12.6 (*a*) Actual scenarios of unplanned events in classroom lessons with technology. (*b*) Teachers' responses to the unplanned events in classroom lessons with technology.

Reflecting on Teaching With Technology

Whew, that lesson is over! The lesson is finished but the teacher's thinking is not, if the goal is to assure the effectiveness of teaching that integrates technology with the content. After Mr. Wyngard finishes his lesson in the Snapshot of a Teacher Guid-

ing Students' Learning with Technology that began this chapter, he needs to take time to review what happened in the lesson, to reconsider his thinking prior to the lesson and how that thinking played out in the lesson. He had made several decisions based on what he thought would work for helping his students understand the topic. He needed to assess the results of those decisions. Did the students learn what he hoped they would learn? Had the students met the objectives that he had used in designing the lesson? Did the technology support the students in gaining a better understanding of the historical roots of contemporary debates?

Mr. Porter replays the lesson in his mind using his written plan to guide his reflections on the lesson in the Snapshot of a Technology-Infused Demonstration Lesson in Chapter 11. He makes notes in the plan at points where the lesson was good and where it needed improvement. In particular he notes that his transition from the PowerPoint to the spreadsheet was awkward and took too much time. Shutting down the PowerPoint and searching to find the spreadsheet left his students with unassigned time. They did what most students do. They used the time to engage in off-task behaviors. When it was time to resume the discussion, Mr. Porter had to regain the students' attention as well as reengage them in the activity of finding the height of an Avo-gadro's number of chips. During his postlesson reflection, he realizes that, if he had activated both applications at the beginning of the period, the transition would be a simple click of the mouse, without the loss of student attention.

Reflection on the lesson is an essential activity for teachers to do. Reflection is more than just intensive thinking about what happened in the lesson. Reflection is about change. Teachers need to consider the decisions they made and the success of those decisions. They need to consider the lesson within the context of the lessons designed for the unit. They need to consider how the results of this lesson affect the following lessons. They need to make changes in the future lessons. And, they need to reconsider the unit as a whole. Figure 12.7 highlights some questions that might guide a reflective analysis of the technology-infused lesson.

Reflecting on Teaching with Technology

Questions about the planned activities
1. Did the lesson guide students toward the objectives?
2. Were the activities appropriate?
3. What worked well and what needs improvement?
4. What would you do differently?
5. Was there enough detail in the plan to support the teaching in the lesson?
6. Were the planned times adequate for the different parts of the lesson?
7. Were the key questions adequate in outlining the major content of the lesson?

Questions about the students
1. How did the students respond to the lesson: as you thought they would or differently?
2. Were the students motivated and engaged in the lesson? If some students were not, why not?
3. Did the students work collaboratively in the activities and with the technology?
4. Can you describe each student's progress with the content? Can you describe each student's progress with the technology?
5. Were the students prepared for working with the technology?
6. Are the students prepared for future work with the technology as a tool?
7. Did all the students meet the objectives for the lesson? If not, which students did?

Questions about the technology
1. Was the integration of the technology appropriate for guiding students in learning the content?
2. Did the technology overshadow the content of the lesson?
3. What problems did you note that students had with the technology?
4. What problems did you have in assisting the students with the technology?
5. How might you better prepare the students for working with the technology?
6. Did the students meet the technology objectives in the lesson?
7. What might have aided them in better meeting those objectives?

Questions about the teacher
1. Were you well prepared for the lesson? Classroom arranged? For the activities? Solid understanding of the content of the lesson?
2. Were you well prepared for the technology integration? Materials and technology available and in working order? Organization for access to the technology? Did you have to improvise with the technology?
3. Did anything happen that you were unprepared to handle? If so, how would you handle it in the future?
4. Did you demonstrate enthusiasm and interest in learning the content and learning with the technology?
5. Were your directions clear and supportive of students becoming engaged in the activities?
6. Did your questioning engage the entire class? Did you vary the levels of the questions? Did you engage a variety of levels of students with your questions? Did you use probes to elicit clarification from the students?
7. Were your transitions among the various activities adequate to maintain student engagement in the lesson? Was your closure adequate and useful in helping students to express their knowledge and understandings from the lesson?

FIGURE 12.7   Sample questions for reflection on teaching with technology.

Of course formal and informal assessments of students provides some information for this reflective phase after the lesson. Assessment is explored more fully in Chapter 13. The key at this time is that, as a teacher, you need to be sure to take time to reflect about the impact of the lesson. This reflective phase is an important part of assuring that the lesson accomplished what you hoped it would accomplish as well as determining your next instructional steps.

Teaching requires much more than delivering the lesson. One student teacher identified the importance of planning and preparation for the lesson.

It took some extra planning and some extra time to set up, but I think the payoff of enhanced student interest and learning made it worthwhile. … I think teaching with technology is definitely a little different than standard teaching. It forced me to do more planning and more setup than I had previously.

Of course, planning is of key importance to any lesson. However, careful and deliberate thinking and attention during each of the stages of the instruction with the addition of technology—prior to teaching while designing the instruction, during teaching while implementing the design, and after teaching while reflecting on the instruction—are equally important for the quality of the lesson, for assuring that students learn what is intended, and for teachers to expand in their ability to teach with technology (their TPCK).

Summing It Up

Integrating technology in instructional activities demands increased attention by and expectations of teachers. Teachers must merge their knowledge, skills, and understandings from three knowledge domains to transform the subject matter to a form understandable by their students. Their technological pedagogical content knowledge (TPCK) is the intersection and interdependence of their knowledge of content, technology, and teaching and learning and is key to teaching lessons that integrate technology. This knowledge is used and displayed as they think and make decisions (1) in their planning for teaching, (2) as they monitor and regulate the instruction while teaching, and (3) in their assessments and revisions after teaching. Each of those three stages provides questions and challenges for teachers' thinking and decision making.

As teachers plan lessons, they rely on important inputs: their in-depth understanding of the (1) content, (2) various technologies, and (3) teaching and learning. Typically teachers develop their curriculum and instruction for the year. Given the impact of technology, not only must they rely on important content area standards, they must consider guidelines such as those provided by the technology student standards (ISTE, 2000). Ultimately, teachers frame their decisions into unit and lesson plans. Instructional objectives in three categories aid teachers in focusing the instruction by describing specific student behaviors, actions, and abilities expected at the end of the instruction: cognitive, affective, and psychomotor. Integrating the subject matter content in the description of the objectives shapes the conditions under which the objectives are to be assessed. Basically, the instructional objectives provide directions for the instruction that students need if they are to be able to demonstrate the desired outcomes following the instruction.

The effectiveness of lesson planning, preparation, and organization depends on an explicit consideration of teaching actions that include introductions, questioning, giving directions, student–teacher and student–student interactions, and closure. Because the integration of technology in the instruction represents a departure from traditional teaching, however, these lessons require more in-depth planning and preparation. A written lesson plan provides an organizational tool to encourage and support the explicit and more in-depth planning and thinking prior to implementing a lesson that engages students in work with technology. The sequence, number of elements, and amount of detail in a lesson plan may vary considerably. The important point is that teachers need to think carefully through the entire lesson they are planning. In particular they need to plan for the integration of the technology, to think about what students need to know and be able to do with the technology if they are to use it as a tool for learning. The written lesson plan provides a tool for guiding the thinking and planning process.

On the day of the lesson, the teacher must implement the plans, monitoring and regulating the activities as the lesson progresses. Teacher thinking and decision making shifts to a more active, on-demand mode. Teachers make decisions about whom to question, when to move to the next idea, when to repeat an idea, and when to invite students to share ideas with the rest of the class. When technology is added to the lesson, teachers must constantly monitor the classroom activities and students' progress in those activities. They need to quickly adjust as difficulties arise. They need to be prepared to troubleshoot problems while maintaining the focus of the lesson on the intended content.

In preparation for this action-oriented decision making, teachers need to practice using the technology in various ways, examining "what if" situations. With experience in troubleshooting those types of problems, teachers are better prepared to take immediate action and maintain the focus of the lesson.

At the end of the lesson, the teacher's thinking and decision making must continue if the goal is to assure the effectiveness of teaching that integrates technology within the content. Comparing the lesson as it actually happened with the lesson plan that was designed beforehand helps to guide the thinking teachers need to do at this stage. The reflective stage is more than just intensive thinking about what happened in the lesson. Reflection is about change—change that guides future lessons both with and without the addition of technology. This phase automatically returns to the planning phase, extending the cycle of growth toward effective teaching and learning with and about technology that ultimately enhances a teacher's TPCK.

End-of-the-Chapter Activities and References

PRACTICE PROBLEMS

1. Determine a lesson that you might teach where students use technology as a tool for learning. Identify at least one objective for each of the different types of objectives integrating both the technology and the content in its description: cognitive, affective, and psychomotor.

2. Create a lesson plan for a lesson where students use technology as a tool for learning using the format described in Figure 12.4.

3. Create a set of questions that you could use to review your lesson plan to determine if you have attended to important considerations when thinking through a lesson with technology.

4. Find a set of instructions that guides students in working with a particular technology. Follow the directions to see the activities that students are to do. Next consider how the directions might be misinterpreted to see what happens. Describe at least five errors that might occur with the directions as a result of student misinterpretations.

5. Outline a unit that integrates technology where the technology is new to students. Describe how you would scaffold their learning about the technology while also learning with the technology.

IN THE CLASSROOM ACTIVITIES

6. Interview several teachers who are integrating technology in their lessons about their processes for planning for the lessons. Identify key planning concerns that you can use to review your own plans.

7. Observe students working with technology. Describe actions they do that interfere with their progress with the activity. Describe how they resolve their difficulties.

8. Prepare to teach a lesson with technology demonstrating your thinking about the lesson through a lesson plan. After you teach the lesson, reflect on the effectiveness of the lesson in meeting the stated objectives.

ASSESSING STUDENT LEARNING WITH AND ABOUT TECHNOLOGY

9. Identify cognitive objectives at each of the levels of Bloom's taxonomy (Remember, Understand, Apply, Analyze, Evaluate, Create) that involve the integration of technology in the subject matter content. Describe how you would assess whether students meet each objective.

10. Identify affective objectives (Receiving, Responding, Valuing, Organization, Characterization) involving a particular technology at each of the levels described in the chapter. Describe how you would assess whether students meet each objective.

11. Identify psychomotor objectives (Imitation, Manipulation, Precision, Articulation, Naturalization) involving a particular technology at each of the levels described in the chapter. Describe how you would assess whether students meet each objective.

E-PORTFOLIO ACTIVITIES

12. Create a Web page that contains hyperlinks to lesson plans you develop that integrate technology.

13. Prepare a Web page that contains three hyperlinks:
    - Planning to teach with technology
    - Implementing instruction with technology
    - Reflecting on teaching with technology

    For each of those areas, select and display important artifacts that describe your own progress.

REFLECTION AND DISCUSSION

14. Observe a teacher teach a lesson with technology. Interview the teacher using questions you generated as you watched the lesson and the questions in Figures 12.5 and 12.7 as a guide to determining the teacher's view of the results of

teaching the lesson. Write a reflection on the lesson based on the teacher's responses to your questions.

15. Reflect on this statement: Lesson plans are not needed for teaching with technology.

◆Annotated Resources

Anderson, L. W., & Krathwohl, D. R. (Eds.). (2001). *A taxonomy for learning, teaching, and assessing: A revision of Bloom's taxonomy of educational objectives*. New York: Longman.

This book describes a revised taxonomy that incorporates both the kind of knowledge to be learned (knowledge dimension) and the process used to learn (cognitive process), allowing for the teacher to efficiently align objectives with assessment.

Marzan, R. J., Pickering, D. J., & Pollock, J. E. (2001). *Classroom instruction that works: Research-based strategies for increasing student achievement*. Alexandria, VA: Association for Supervision and Curriculum Development.

This text identifies research-based generalizations that guide instructional strategies for consideration in planning, implementing, and reflecting on the results. Three elements of effective pedagogy (instructional strategies, management techniques, and curriculum design) frame the synthesis of the research-based recommendations.

Woolfolk-Hoy, A. E. (2004). *Educational psychology* (9th ed.). Boston: Pearson Allyn & Bacon.

Discussion of objectives for learning in the cognitive, affective, and psychomotor domains is connected with teaching methods and strategies for designing lessons in various content areas.

CHAPTER 13

Assessing Learning with Technology

David Young-Wolff/PhotoEdit

Introduction

One of the most complex tasks teachers do is measuring each student's understanding and learning. Learning is considered to have occurred when the experiences result in a relatively permanent change in a student's knowledge or behavior. Does this change mean that the student is able to use what is learned in a special way? Is the learning factual and knowledge-based or does it involve critical thinking and decision making? What level of learning is desired? What do the students understand as a result of instruction? Have they had an opportunity to learn? At what level do they understand? Is their knowledge dependent on the way they learned? What evidence is available to describe each student's understanding? How much evidence is needed? What constitutes evidence? What should be the format of the assessments? Does the format of the assessment affect students' abilities to demonstrate their knowledge and understandings?

Now add technology as a tool to the instructional experience where students are engaged in learning. What is the impact of the technology on what students learn? When students are expected to use technology as a tool for learning within the context of the subject, teachers' questions about and challenges for assessment of the learning increase. How should students' understandings be measured when students have learned with technology? What

is important? Is the student's new knowledge dependent on the technology? Should the students demonstrate their knowledge as they use the technology or is their knowledge deeper if they must demonstrate it without the use of the technology?

What must a teacher know about assessing learning? Just as a doctor needs to be knowledgeable of a patient's health history, of multiple tests for providing evidence of the current health of a patient, of potential drug interactions that might mask symptoms, and of how each drug might affect a potential diagnosis, teachers need "to be knowledgeable of the purposes, uses, and values of different assessment techniques and understand how they affect the learner" (Woolfolk-Hoy, 2004, p. 563).

With changes in the ways people communicate and interact as a result of contemporary and emerging technologies, teachers must carefully reconsider how students need to understand and know. Content standards have shifted from fact-based knowledge as essential knowledge toward an importance of conceptual knowledge and higher order and more strategic thinking as essential knowledge and skills. Educational environments have responded by shifting learning experiences to incorporate multimedia, collaborative work, active exploration and inquiry-based learning, critical thinking, and decision-making expectations within more authentic and real-world contexts.

Essentially, twenty-first-century teachers must consider how these changes affect how students must display their knowledge and understandings. Although teachers still must assess student learning, what and how they must assess that learning are evolving. Teachers must be knowledgeable of multiple ways for gathering evidence of student learning. With the addition of learning both *with* and *about* technology, teachers need to assess students' knowledge of the subject matter content in an environment that expects students to incorporate technology as a tool to think and learn with—as a productivity tool, a communications tool, a research tool, and a problem-solving and decision-making tool.

In reality learning, technology and assessment are intertwined. Emerging technologies affect what is to be learned as well as how it is learned. As technologies are incorporated with teaching and learning in K–12 schools, they alter the pedagogy as well as the types of skills and knowledge that students have opportunities to develop. Technology's impact on both teaching and learning also alters how learning needs to be assessed. Traditional testing is no longer the best and only method for assessing student learning with technology. Writing with a word processor is different from writing with a paper and pen. Doing arithmetic with a calculator is different from doing those same problems with paper and pencil.

When technology is added to the educational environment, teachers must consider (1) how technology can be applied to enhance learning, (2) how use of technology changes what is learned, and (3) how technology can be used to enrich the evidence of student learning. New methods, new tools, and new approaches that apply technology to learning must be accounted for when applying technology to the assessment of what is learned and how that learning is known and displayed. This knowledge and understanding are important parts of what a teacher needs to know in the twenty-first century— they are a part of a teacher's technological pedagogical content knowledge (TPCK).

CHAPTER LEARNING OBJECTIVES

After reading the chapter, you should be able to:

1. Describe the relationship of technology-enhanced instruction to assessment.
2. Clarify the purposes for different types of assessments and how those assessments support learning in technology-rich environments.
3. Identify achievement targets related to unit goals and objectives for instruction in technology-enhanced instruction.
4. Illuminate how teachers prepare for gathering accurate assessments and integrating assessment with technology-enhanced instruction.
5. Outline how performance-based assessments provide accurate evidence of student technology-mediated learning.
6. Describe the evidence of student technology-enhanced learning provided through portfolio-based assessments.
7. Identify the usefulness of scoring rubrics when assessing student learning in technology-rich ways.

Snapshot of Integrating Assessment and Learning with Technology

Mrs. Blake's tenth-grade world history class has been studying concepts of time, chronology, and change. The unit revolves around a central question: How has human civilization changed over the past 2000 years? As they explore the question, the students consult multiple resources to explore inventions over various times and reflect on the changes of civilization as a result of these inventions.

To focus the students' explorations, Mrs. Blake engages them in a project requiring that they develop a timeline of technological innovations over the past 2000 years.

Mrs. Blake: Today we are going to talk about technological innovations over the past 2000 years. We want to look at how civilization has changed as a re-

sult of technological innovations. Can anyone tell me what you think of when you think of the word technology?

Jason: Sure, that's easy. Computers and the Internet! But, technology hasn't been around for 2000 years, so why would we want to talk about technological innovations over this 2000-year timeline?

Karen: Right! Technology is an invention of the last 100 years, not 2000 years.

Mrs. Blake: Actually technology is much more than what you are thinking. Technology is actually as old as humanity itself. The word technology is rooted in the ancient past, from the Greek work techne meaning "craft" [writing the word on the board]. Technological inventions have accompanied and sometimes driven human progress and changes in civilizations for thousands of years. Major technological developments over the course of human history have changed the way humans lived in such dramatic ways that understanding those technological developments is itself akin to understanding human progress. That's what we are focusing on in this unit.

Given this information, think back over the past 2000 years. What do you think are some of the most important technological inventions impacting civilization?

Kevin: I think the printing press has to be one of them.

Mrs. Blake: Why? How has society changed because of that invention?

Kevin: Well, for one, people no longer have to share information by verbally telling each other. I read that the elders were responsible for sharing events and their own history with the younger generations so that that information was not lost. With the printing press, people were able to put this information in print to be handed down through the generations.

Mrs. Blake: Good, Kevin. You and many scholars agree. Any other ideas?

Maria: I think the computer has to be the most important invention. Look at how it has shifted the way we communicate and do research. With e-mail we don't write letters like people used to. With the Internet we are able to access lots more information than we could in the library.

Mrs. Blake: Good idea, Maria. Let me tell you about a 1998 author, John Brockman. He proposed a question to an organization of over 100 scholars through a website project called Edge. His question was simply, "What is the most important invention in

the past two thousand years?" Responses to the question varied from the somewhat obscure Public Key Cryptosystems to more expected candidates such as the steam engine or the computer, like Maria said. The inventions nominated by the scholars along with his or her justification are available on the website that we are seeing now [displaying the website]. Brockman has since published a book called *The Greatest Inventions of the Past 2,000 Years,* but we can more easily see the nominations in this website.

Mrs. Blake: As we read through these proposed ideas, you will perhaps find that some of the ideas are strange. For example, Freeman Dyson submitted the invention of hay as the most important invention of the last 2000 years.

Daniel: Whoa, that's weird. Why did he think hay was the most important?

Mrs. Blake: Let's look at his statement on the website.

Mrs. Blake: His choice of hay was to allow civilization to spread north, over the Alps, toward more colder climates. Dyson recognized the need to have a way to feed the animals throughout the year, such as the horses that provided the primary means for transportation.

Basically, you can see that the words technology and technological innovations need to be given a much broader interpretation than you originally thought. So, given that information, I have a task for you to construct an annotated timeline that traces selected technological innovations from the last 2000 years of human history. This handout provides important details about the task [handing the students the handout as shown in Figure 13.1].

THE THIRD CULTURE

WHAT IS THE MOST IMPORTANT INVENTION IN THE PAST TWO THOUSAND YEARS?

Introduction by

John Brockman

A year ago I emailed the participants of The Third Culture Mail List for help with a project which was published on EDGE as "The World Question Center." I asked them: "What questions are you asking yourself?" The World Question Center was published on December 30th. On the same day *The New York Times* ran an article "In an Online Salon, Scientists Sit Back and Ponder" which featured a selection of the questions. Other press coverage can be found in EDGE In The News. The project was interesting, worthwhile,...and fun.

This year, beginning on Thanksgiving Day, I polled the list on (a) "What Is the Most Important Invention in the Past Two Thousand Years?" ... and (b) "Why?"

Freeman Dyson:

This is a good question. My suggestion is not original. I don't remember who gave me the idea, but it was probably Lynn White, with Murray Gell-Mann as intermediary.

The most important invention of the last two thousand years was hay. In the classical world of Greece and Rome and in all earlier times, there was no hay. Civilization could exist only in warm climates where horses could stay alive through the winter by grazing. Without grass in winter you could not have horses, and without horses you could not have urban civilization. Some time during the so-called dark ages, some unknown genius invented hay, forests were turned into meadows, hay was reaped and stored, and civilization moved north over the Alps. So hay gave birth to Vienna and Paris and London and Berlin, and later to Moscow and New York.

FREEMAN DYSON is Professor of Physics at the Institute for Advanced Study in Princeton. His professional interests are in mathematics and astronomy. Among his many books are *Disturbing the Universe, From Eros to Gaia,* and *Imagined Words.*

Historical Development of a Technological Innovation

General Description

Construct a Web-based, annotated timeline that traces selected technological innovations from the last 2000 years of civilization. The timeline is to be a **graphic illustration** of the occurrence of these events. The notations that accompany the timeline should be detailed enough to stand alone as narrative descriptions. The mininarratives should focus on the impact the innovation had on human history and culture; they should include both the positive and negative consequences of the particular innovation. Each note should be at least one paragraph. The items on the timeline are to be taken from the technology developments described in John Brockman's collection of responses.

Task Specifics

1. Rank the technological innovations proposed in John Brockman's responses found at this website: http://www.edge.org/documents/archive/edge48.html#Blakemore

   You need to develop specific criteria for ranking the innovations. Provide an explanation for your criteria in a short paragraph.

2. Select the 10 most important technological innovations over the past 2000 years, using the ideas provided in John Brockman's Web collection. Conduct research to determine the date of each development you select. Suggested resources include your world history textbook and both Web and book resources such as these:

Books
   * *A History of Invention: From Stone Ages to Silicon Chips* by Trevor Williams
   * *The Greatest Inventions of the Past 2000 Years* by John Brockman
   * *Visual Timeline of Inventions* by Richard Platt

Websites
   * Macro History: Prehistory to the 21st Century by Frank E. Smitha at http://www.fsmitha.com/index.html
   * Famous Inventions: A to Z by Mary Bellis at http://inventors.about.com/library/bl/bl12.htm

3. Determine the format of your timeline. You can begin your research of Web timelines at these locations:
   * Technology Timeline from PBS at http://www.pbs.org/wgbh/amex/telephone/timeline/index.html
   * Tommy's History of "Western Technology" at http://www.hbci.com/~wenonah/history/
   * Thousand-Year Timeline at http://www.sunshine.co.nz/nz/31/1000.html

4. Create your Web timeline that shares your nominations for the 10 most important technological innovations over the past 2000 years. Use graphics for illustrating the occurrence of your events on the timeline. Link each graphic to a one-paragraph mininarrative about the impact of the innovation on human history and culture, describing both the positive and negative consequences of the innovation.

5. Share and assess the timelines in class on March 15. Groups of four will be organized to share their timelines with each other, explaining the selections and rationale for the selections. Each student in a group will provide an assessment of the timelines prepared by the others in the group using a scoring rubric.

   Williams, T. I., Schaaf, W. E., & Burnette, A. E. (2000). A History of Invention: From Stone Ages to Silicon Chips, New York: Checkmark Books.

   Brockman, J. (ed). (2000) *The Greatest Inventions of the Past 2000 Years,* New York: Simon & Schuster.

   Platt, R. (2001). *Visual Timeline of Inventions.* London, England: Dorling Kindersley Children.

FIGURE 13.1   Timeline task for displaying the historical development of technological innovations.

After discussing the expectations for the timeline task, Mrs. Blake shared the scoring guide she planned for the groups to use as they assessed the timelines (see Figure 13.2). Mrs. Blake explained that the students would score each of the five expectations separately: the student's criteria for the ranking of the Brockman responses, the ranking and justification with student criteria of the Brockman ideas, the student's own timeline, the graphics used in the timeline, and the mininarratives in the timeline. The scoring guide described the expectations for each proficiency level—advanced, proficient, partially proficient, and not proficient/not enough evidence—for each expectation.

◆Reflection on Learning and Instruction

The twenty-first-century goals for an educated citizen display a perspective different from those envisioned for an educated citizen in the nineteenth century or even the twentieth century. As described in the National Educational Technology Standards for Students (NETS·S), educated citizens need to be able to

* Communicate using a variety of media and formats;

Proficiency Level	Evidence
Advanced	1. The criteria for the rankings include a detailed explanation for how the innovations are to be ranked. 2. Innovations are ranked and the rankings are fully justified using the student's own criteria. 3. The timeline is accurate, complete, and well organized. 4. Graphics are clear, effective, and accurately present the innovations. 5. The mininarratives are accurate and contain positive and negative consequences of each innovation.
Proficient	1. The criteria for the rankings include a detailed explanation for how the innovations are to be ranked. 2. Innovations are ranked and most of the rankings are justified using the student's own criteria. 3. The timeline is accurate, complete, and well organized. 4. Graphics are effective. 5. The descriptions are accurate and contain at least one positive and one negative impact.
Partially Proficient	1. Innovations are ranked but the rankings are not justified. 2. The criteria for the rankings include a partial explanation for how the innovations are to be ranked. 3. The timeline is accurate. 4. Graphics are sometimes effective. 5. The descriptions are limited.
Not Proficient/ Not Enough Evidence	1. Each expectation incomplete, inaccurate, or missing.

FIGURE 13.2   Scoring rubric for the technological timeline task.

- Access and exchange information in a variety of ways;
- Compile, organize, analyze, and synthesize information;
- Draw conclusions and make generalizations based on information gathered;
- Know content and be able to locate additional information as needed;
- Become self-directed learners;
- Collaborate and cooperate in team efforts;
- Interact with others in ethical and appropriate ways. (ISTE, 2000, p. 5)

This description highlights some essential twenty-first-century skills: the ability to make sense of masses of information, to analyze, synthesize, and evaluate the information in order to make decisions about what to do with the information. These skills call for distinctly different knowledge, skills, and abilities than what was defined for educated citizens in previous centuries. Although learning is viewed as occurring when the educational experiences result in a relatively permanent change in students' knowledge, the vision of *how* and *what* students need to learn has evolved. No longer are students viewed as vessels into which knowledge is poured. Students are considered to be active constructors of their personal knowledge and understanding developed from a variety of social and educational experiences.

Given these important shifts in education, teachers are charged with designing instruction to scaffold experiences that guide students in building and constructing a firm and personal understanding. Clearly stated goals and objectives provide the direction for identifying experiences that support students in constructing the important knowledge, skills, and understandings. Chapter 12 describes cognitive, affective, and psychomotor types of objectives and the levels of those objectives that teachers must consider as they arrange the experiences.

Still, teachers are required to determine if and what students learn as a result of the instructional experiences. Are the students constructing their knowledge in concert with the identified goals and objectives? Are the students learning what is to be learned? Are the students developing conceptions that will lead to a continued building of ideas? Or are they constructing misconceptions that will impede their progress? Such questions highlight the importance of the task of assessment for teachers—to assess what their students are learning as well as the effectiveness of the instruction in guiding that learning.

In the Snapshot of Integrating Assessment and Learning with Technology Mrs. Blake designed a task where the students were to explore various resources to construct an understanding of the impact of changes in civilization instigated by technological innovations over the past 2000 years. Her primary goal for her world history class for the year was for the students to become information seekers, analyzers, and evaluators. She believed that those skills would help them consider a variety of historical events and incorporate their understanding of the events as they made sense of world history. She firmly believed in a student-centered approach to instruction, with her students actively engaged in the construction of their knowledge. She also recognized the importance of students using appropriate technologies in the development of their knowledge. Based on her beliefs and knowledge about what the students should gain in the class, she formulated five major objectives for the unit on technological inventions, interweaving what she wanted her students to learn about world history and technology as a tool for learning.

1. Students will identify, describe, and rank significant technological innovations that ignited changes in civilization over the past 2000 years. (Cognitive, Analyze; Affective, Characterization)

2. Students will use technology to locate, evaluate, and collect information about technological innovations over the past 2000 years. (Cognitive, Evaluate; Psychomotor, Precision)

3. Students will use technology resources for making informed decisions about the impact of technological innovations on civilization over the past 2000 years. (Cognitive, Apply; Affective, Organization; Psychomotor, Precision)

4. Students will use a variety of technology media elements to communicate information and ideas about the impact of technological innovations over the past 2000 years. (Cognitive, Apply; Affective, Valuing; Psychomotor, Precision)

5. Students will make judgments about the quality of Web timelines in communicating information and the impact of technological innovations over the past 2000 years. (Cognitive, Evaluate; Affective, Characterization)

As she formulated the objectives, Mrs. Blake realized that she intended more than just cognitive objectives. So she incorporated the multiple dimensions with her descriptions along with the levels she expected in each dimension.

Mrs. Blake found that this direction and her beliefs about how students learn helped in organizing her unit on the impact of technological inventions over the past 2000 years. She knew what she wanted the students to learn and be able to do in the unit! She decided to engage her students in a research effort, encouraging them to construct their understanding; moreover, she designed a technological way for them to communicate their knowledge. The scoring guide for the Web timeline task provided a means of guiding her students' efforts and of notifying them of how their efforts would be assessed in order to provide her with evidence of their learning.

Basic Assessment Concepts

Assessment is an important educational process, a process that involves monitoring students' progress toward important learning goals and objectives. Evidence gathered in the assessment process is designed not only to inform students and their parents but to also inform their teachers about the effectiveness of their instructional decisions. Key to the relationship between assessment and instruction is that assessments are driven by the instructions that students experience. Their responses to the assessments depend on the instruction they receive. Figure 13.3 suggests one model of the interaction of assessment and instruction, in which assessment is depicted as sampling the domain of knowledge and skills taught during instruction. This portrayal of assessment is designed to highlight important ideas about assessment while instruction is taking place.

1. Assessment needs to be interwoven throughout instruction, gathering evidence that reflects and supports the goals of instruction.

2. Multiple assessments need to be completed over time throughout the instruction.

3. Assessments need to sample what students know and are able to do within the framework of the instruction.

4. Each assessment provides some evidence about what and how students learn during the instruction.

The picture in Figure 13.3 actually portrays a specific type or purpose of assessment, namely, *formative* assessment. Formative assessments are those assessments gathered during instruction to check each student's progress and learning. Teachers use that information as feedback to inform students of their progress and to indicate where they can make improvement. Teachers also use that information to

■ Instruction
■ Assessment

FIGURE 13.3   A pictorial description of the relationship between assessment and instruction during instruction.

get a sense of whether the instruction is meeting the objectives and whether the instruction needs adjustment. The evidence may suggest that students are developing misunderstandings from the instruction. In that case, the teacher may need to reframe the instructional experiences to better guide students in meeting the intended outcomes.

Suppose you have students work with spreadsheets as described for In the Classroom 6.4. In that unit the students are engaged in exploring the differences between the North and South before the Civil War by graphing data about the cash value of farms in states in the North versus those in the South. Suppose that when they submit their graphs, you notice that they have inaccurately portrayed the differences because they failed to consider the effect of the scale on the graphs. This evidence suggests that you need to rearrange the instruction to focus their attention on that part of the graph. The formative assessment evidence suggests that the instruction needs adjustment to better guide the students toward attainment of the objectives.

Sometimes during instruction teachers need to anticipate whether students will have difficulty with the subject matter. That purpose for the assessment is not considered formative, rather it is *diagnostic* because its purpose is to anticipate rather than react to instruction. For example, suppose that you developed a sequence of lessons framed by In the Classroom 4.3, where students are expected to use iMovie or PowerPoint to present their evidence for a mock trial considering a ban on the novel *The Adventures of Huckleberry Finn*. You might consider an assessment to identify if students have the necessary skills with these applications, rather than assuming they are prepared to use them as presentation tools. On the basis of that information, you might need to provide some instruction to support use of the applications as presentation tools. Perhaps you plan to use the information to form groups so that there is an expert with the tool in each group. In that way, the diagnosis informs your instructional design. Diagnostic assessment can also be useful prior to a unit of instruction. Again, the information helps to frame the instruction that will be needed for students to have successful learning opportunities.

Preassessments offer another type of assessment used prior to instruction. Preassessments help teachers make decisions about what content needs to be included during the instruction. Suppose that you planned to incorporate the idea from In the Classroom 8.5 where students are asked to describe the climate for a town. Since in this unit students are to develop a presentation that presents a mystery about the town as a challenge for other students to identify the location of the town, they need some background knowledge about the towns if the emphasis is to remain on the climate of the towns. You may elect to identify the background students have with specific towns before selecting the towns. Preassessment information can also support the amount of instruction provided to students prior to their work with the towns by assuring that they have the necessary skills and background for developing the mysteries and for solving the mysteries created by the other students. An additional benefit of preassessment is that it provides a baseline to judge each student's growth in the unit. Comparison of their knowledge and understanding at the end of the unit with that collected prior to the unit provides one measure of their learning.

Assessments at the end of instruction provide another useful tool for developing a comprehensive analysis of students' knowledge and understanding on the completion of the instruction. These *summative assessments* generally are concerned with a comprehensive view of the knowledge, skills, behaviors, and dispositions students have gained through the instruction. They provide information that can be compared with any preassessment as a means of describing each student's learning improvement and are particularly useful for informing students (and their parents). Another purpose for this type of assessment is for reflection on the instructional decisions that were made and for informing future instruction. If student gains do not match the goals and objectives, teachers need to reconsider the instruction. Was the content at the appropriate level? Did the strategies support students in gaining the information? Did the organization of the unit support the development of the ideas? Questions such as those are useful for guiding teachers in redesigning their curriculum and instruction.

Achievement Targets

Assessments must be designed to gather *accurate* information about student learning. This requirement depends on teachers' abilities to define and articulate the student characteristics they want assessed. The goals and objectives for the instruction are essential starting points for assuring accuracy. Mrs. Blake identified five major objectives to help her make decisions about the instruction, and those objectives helped her frame the assessments she needed for gathering accurate information about her students' learning. Mrs. Blake was supported by the identification of specific achievement target questions that helped her in designing the specific classroom instruction and interweaving the instruction with the assessments. Stiggins (2005) identified five specific achievement targets for consideration:

- **Knowledge:** What do students know and understand about the subject matter content (cognitive)?

- **Reasoning:** Can students solve problems using their knowledge and understanding (cognitive)?
- **Performance Skills:** Are students proficient in performing processes based on what they know and understand (cognitive and psychomotor)?
- **Products:** Are students able to create products that provide evidence of their proficiency (cognitive and psychomotor)?
- **Dispositions:** Do students display appropriate attitudes, confidence, and interest toward the content knowledge and understandings (affective)?

The question with each achievement target helps to clarify and articulate the achievement that is desired based on the instruction. The questions assist in the design of more accurate assessments of what students know and are able to do. The questions also guide the identification and selection of assessment tasks for gathering information about the instruction and evidence of student learning.

Formats for Assessments

Stop and make a list of all the kinds of assessments you have encountered. The traditional forms of assessment include various types of test items: true–false, multiple choice, completion, short answer, and essay. But many other forms of assessment are now viewed as more effective in gathering accurate evidence of student learning. A useful way of looking at the various formats is to consider their usefulness in meeting the achievement targets. Figure 13.4 provides one way to analyze how various assessment methods can help to assess the achievement targets. Each assessment method has strengths and limitations for assessing student's achievement.

The accuracy of evidence provided by a particular assessment requires a careful consideration of the format. If students are to provide evidence of analytical thinking, a true–false test is probably not a good choice; students are not required to engage in that level of thinking with a 50–50 chance of simply guessing the correct answer. For many of the assessment methods, teachers can make inferences about the targets and might consider other methods to gather more direct evidence, such as incorporating observations and interviews of students working on the tasks. As students work on projects, teachers can interview them to gather evidence of their knowledge. Portfolios have the potential for gathering evidence for various achievement targets because they are typically developed over time. Teachers can incorporate interviews directed at observing students' reasoning to more directly measure the reasoning achievement target. They can incorporate observations of students using technology as a tool for learning. They can engage students in using journals as a reflective assessment of their own learning. In essence, accurate assessment of the achievement targets depends on the collection of evidence through a variety of assessment formats.

Preparation for Gathering Accurate Assessments

Teachers must prepare for assessment as seriously and consciously as they do for instruction. Just as with instruction, preparation for assessment begins with the goals and objectives. Analyzing the goals and objectives with respect to the five achievement targets is the next step because that process helps to clarify what is to be measured. Then teachers need to consider the variety of formats and uses of assessments with respect to the goals and objectives. Figure 13.5 describes how Mrs. Blake framed her analysis with respect to her first objective. First, she described the evidence that she wanted to observe in terms of the achievement targets. Then, she selected various assessment formats that she wanted to use prior to instruction, during instruction, and after instruction. The analysis helped her organize her instruction since several of the assessments were designed to gather information during the instruction. She planned to have her students working on the project over a period of days, and she knew that she could incorporate several assessments to gather evidence of the students' thinking and reasoning. She planned a warm-up where she could question the students about the technological inventions they identified so that she could obtain some sense of their developing knowledge of technology inventions. She planned for a classroom debate where the students would debate the criteria that were useful for ranking the inventions. This activity would give her information about their reasoning in the development of their criteria. She also planned for a journal writing to gather evidence on their developing dispositions, where they identified how they valued the various inventions.

◢ Assessments with and about Technology

When students learn with technology, what they learn is framed by their learning experiences. If

• **Observation**	Technology impacts what and how students learn.
• **Observation**	Evidence of student learning requires assessments that reflect what and how the students learned.
• **Implication**	Teachers need to reevaluate and redesign their methods of assessing student learning when students learn with technology.

Assessment Method	Knowledge	Reasoning	Performance Skills	Products	Dispositions
Traditional tests: true–false, multiple choice, completion	Lower cognitive levels: knowledge, understanding, apply	—	—	—	—
Essays	Upper cognitive levels: analyze, evaluate, create	Infer reasoning	—	Writing skills in end product	Infer from written expression
Open-ended problems on questionnaires	Upper cognitive levels	Window of reasoning	Infer skills from end product	Assess end product	Reaction to probes depends on format
Papers	Infer knowledge level	Infer reasoning	—	Writing skills	—
Lab performances	Infer knowledge	May observe or infer reasoning	Actual observation of process	—	Infer dispositions
Projects	Infer knowledge; may observe during development	Infer reasoning from end product; may observe during development	Infer skills from end product	Assess end product	Infer dispositions
Portfolios	Infer knowledge from end product; may observe during development	Infer reasoning from end product; may observe during development	Infer skills from end product; may observe during development	Assess product over time and at end	Obtain evidence from reflections
Observations or checklists	Infer knowledge	Infer reasoning	Observe interactions, conversations	—	Infer dispositions
Interviews	Extension probes for knowledge	Potential of probing for reasoning	Potential of probing for process	—	Verbal expression, can probe
Journals or blogs	Infer knowledge	Infer reasoning	Infer skills with technology	Infer from written product	Infer from written expression
Presentations: Web, PowerPoint, movie	Infer knowledge; may observe during development	Infer reasoning; may observe during development	Infer process; may observe during development	Assess specific attributes from the end product	Infer if asked to reflect

FIGURE 13.4   Assessment methods for gathering evidence for the achievement targets.

Objective	Achievement Target Describe the evidence you want to observe.	Format of Task Describe the opportunities for observing the evidence.	Use of Information Describe how the evidence will be used.
1. Students will identify, describe, and rank significant technological innovations that ignited changes in civilization over the past 2000 years. (Cognitive, Analyze; Affective, Characterization)	**Knowledge** • Describe significant technology innovations	• Questioning in warm-up • Journal response where students describe and defend a significant innovation • Web timeline notes • Web timeline ranking explanation	• Formative to determine student progress with ideas • Formative to determine student progress and if additional instruction needed • Summative • Summative
	Reasoning • Identify important technological inventions that ignite changes • Justify rankings with own criteria	• Identify in writing some important technological inventions • Classroom debate on important criteria • Web timeline presentations	• Preassessment • Formative to determine if students are able to identify important criteria • Summative
	Dispositions • Rank significant technology innovations	• Journal justifying one of the criteria to be used • Ranking justifications with the timeline	• Formative • Summative

FIGURE 13.5 Preparation for gathering accurate assessment evidence.

students learn about mathematics *with* calculators, what and how they understand are experienced within an environment that allows calculator use. When they are asked to find the length of a side of a cube given its volume, they need to find the cube root of its volume as in Figure 13.6. Experiences with cubes guide their recognition that the length of the sides of a cube leads to the need to find the cube root of the volume. Their process for finding the cube root involves using the appropriate keys on the calculator. Thus, any assessment that involves the process of finding the exact value of a cube root needs to allow students to use their calculators.

* **Teachers need to reevaluate their methods of assessing student learning in a technology-rich environment with the goal of considering and learning new ways for gathering evidence of learning.**

When teachers engage students in learning subject matter with technology, they need to provide instruction *about* the technology. Besides assessing the subject matter objectives, teachers must identify and assess objectives for developing students' knowledge of the technology. Suppose that students are involved in exploring 100 years of temperature data for a town and they use spreadsheets to calculate the average temperature. Those students are learning more than just about the temperature for the town. They are learning that the formula = AVERAGE(B1:B100) is preferred over the formula = SUM(B1:B100)/100; the AVERAGE function ignores missing data, whereas the SUM function treats missing data as zeros. Therefore, an accurate assessment of the knowledge students gain needs to consider problems such as the one in Figure 13.7 to assess their knowledge about the spreadsheet as a tool for analyzing data.

* **Teachers need to reevaluate their methods of assessing student learning in a technology-rich environment with the goal of considering and learning new ways for gathering evidence of learning.**

Historically, paper and pencil tests have been the preferred method for gathering evidence about what

> **Problem:** What is the length of the side of this cube if its volume is 56 cubic inches? Explain how you find the length of the side.

FIGURE 13.6 Assessment of process for finding cube root.

> **Problem:** Kerry found 100 years of temperature data on the Internet for her town for the month of January. Explain why the function =SUM(B1:B100)/100 may not always return an accurate value for the average.

FIGURE 13.7 Assessment of knowledge of spreadsheet functions.

students know and are able to do. The strength of ease of scoring multiple-choice, true–false, and fill-in-the-blank items makes them attractive to teachers. The limitations include the fact that students' scores may be more influenced by guessing and the assessed knowledge levels are typically low (knowledge, understanding, and apply). In response to the limitations, teachers extend the questions by requiring students to explain why they selected the answers they did; they also include short answer and essay questions to assess the students' thinking about the content. Those test items are more likely to assess student knowledge at the higher levels (analyze, evaluate, create) and allow students to express their understanding in words that are familiar to them. As demonstrated in Figure 13.8, however, students may not be able to provide even a view of their knowledge about the particular question. What does that response tell the teacher? Perhaps the student does not understand the question. Perhaps the student has some ideas but does not know whether to agree or disagree and is, therefore, reluctant to explain her thinking. Perhaps the student has no clue because she used animal faces in her digitized pictures and she was not confronted with the issue. With the potential of multiple interpretations, the evidence of student learning is deficient. Tests sometimes appear to assess more of what students do not know than what and how they know it.

* **Teachers need to reevaluate their methods of assessing student learning in a technology-rich environment with the goal of considering and learning new ways for gathering evidence of learning.**

Alternatives to Testing

Current assessment trends recognize that students have different ways of explaining how they make sense of their learning experiences. The trends support the importance of allowing students to demonstrate their knowledge in a variety of ways: projects, portfolios, reports, videos, or other performances of what and how they know and understand ideas. Two categories of alternatives to testing offer potential for assessing students as they learn with and about technology: performance-based assessments and portfolio assessments. Both categories offer more choices for students to display what they know and are able to do as they learn with and about technology within the context of the subject matter.

In her position as a teacher educator, Professor Summers works with and observes many in-service and preservice teachers. She has noted that both need help in learning new ways for assessing learning given the integration of technology in education. In recognition of the need, she developed a project that required her student teachers to design alternative assessments for integrating learning *with* and *about* technology within the context of their subject matter content. As the students learned more about assessment, they were assigned to work on a project that served both the instruction and assessment components of the methods class. Professor Summers described the project by displaying the class project Web page (see Figure 13.9), outlining the subject matter groups she identified for the project.

Exploring Alternative Assessments

Teaching Content WITH and ABOUT Technology Using *The Wizard of Oz*

- Elementary
- Health
- Lanuage Arts
- Mathematics
- Music
- Physical Education
- Science
- Social Studies

FIGURE 13.9 Professor Summers' class project Web page.

Problem: Is it acceptable to adjust digitized pictures of the characters in *The Wizard of Oz* to have faces of your classmates? Explain your thinking.

Student response:

FIGURE 13.8 A student's response to an ethical issue in the use of technology.

Professor Summers indicated that all groups were to use a common theme, *The Wizard of Oz*, for engaging students in learning specific content in their assigned subject area; they were also expected to design their subject-specific unit integrating learning both with and about technology. As the class explored various alternative assessments, the groups were expected to identify at least one alternative assessment for gathering evidence of students' knowledge and skills about the subject matter content and the technology.

Professor Summers outlined the format the student teachers were to use for summarizing their thinking about their unit and the assessment alternatives (see Figure 13.10). The format was intended to focus their attention on the integrated relationship of instruction and assessment and on three key criteria for the design of alternative assessments: (1) clear purpose; (2) observable criteria; and (3) appropriate setting (Santrock, 2006).

When they finished their documents, the student teachers were to save them as Web pages and create the appropriate links from the class homepage as in the Elementary link. Each group was expected to present their ideas using the Web demonstration at the end of the instruction on assessment. In other words, Professor Summers planned the demonstration presentations as a means of summarizing alternative assessments as well as assessing her students' understanding of alternative assessments for gathering evidence of learning in technology-enhanced units.

Performance-Based Assessment

Stiggins (2005) describes performance-based assessments as activities where students demonstrate performance of certain skills or create products that meet specified quality standards. Performance-based assessments allow direct observation of what students know and are able to do. They encourage open-ended responses. Rather than asking students questions about creating a movie, teachers observe students during the process of creating the movie. Sometimes groups of students work together to produce the product—the movie. Therefore, the assessment is of both the process to create the movie and the movie product.

The word processing subgroup of student teachers in Professor Summers' class designed a performance-based assessment for guiding students as they read the chapters of *The Wizard of Oz*. For individually assigned chapters, the students were expected to create a set of questions for guiding others in identifying key points in the chapter. The product, the set of questions, provided the teacher with an opportunity to assess students' understanding of key points in the chapters. But this student teacher group envisioned more. Figure 13.11 provides their description of this assessment, identifying opportunities for the teacher to observe students as they use word processors in creating their documents with the key questions. Thus, the product is presented in a variety of technological ways—a printout of the document and a Web page—to provide evidence of the identification of key points in a chapter, their writing skills with a word processor, their Web page, and their use of the Web page in their presentations. With this performance-based assessment, the teacher is able to assess the students' presentation and communications skills as they incorporate the Web page in their presentation of the key chapter points.

The social studies group in Professor Summers' class developed a multipurpose assessment for their unit focused on investigating whether *The Wizard of Oz* was really a children's fable or a description of struggles of people against the elite. This group of student teachers designed the unit as a way of engaging students in the study of Populism, a political power at the turn of the twentieth century. Their assessment culminated the study by

Subject Matter Group	
Description of unit (subject matter content, technology content):	
Objectives to be assessed	
Evidence to be observed	
Format of task	
Use of information	
Type of assessment	
Description of assessment:	

FIGURE 13.10   Format for describing alternative assessments.

Subject Matter Group: Language Arts

Description of unit:	This language arts unit focuses fifth-grade students on locating, evaluating, gathering, and presenting key points of chapters in a classic novel.
Objectives to be assessed	• Students locate, evaluate, and gather key points of a classic children's story. • Students use a word processor to create a chapter guide of key points. • Students save a word-processed document as a Web page.
Evidence to be observed	• **Knowledge**: Identification of key points of a chapter. • **Product**: Printout of the document with key chapter ideas, correct spelling and grammar; Web page of the document. • **Performance skills**: Students use word processing, printing and saving as a Web page; students use the Web page as a guide for their presentation.
Format of task	Students are assigned a chapter to read prior to the day where they work in the computer lab using the word processor to prepare a document.
Use of information	Formative to gather evidence about students' skills with a word processor, their ability to gather key points in a text chapter, and their presentation skills.
Type of assessment	Performance-based
Description of assessment:	As students read the book *The Wizard of Oz*, they must focus on an assigned chapter prior to the computer day. On the computer day, they create a set of questions to guide others in identifying key points in their assigned chapter; their questions are prepared in a word-processed document and the document is saved as a Web page. Students use their Web page as a guide when presenting the key points to their chapter.

FIGURE 13.11   Language arts, word processors, Web presentations, and *The Wizard of Oz* performance-based assessment.

challenging the groups of students to analyze the thesis presented by Henry M. Littlefield in a publication in *American Quarterly* in 1964. Littlefield suggested that Baum used the characters, setting, and plot of his book as a lament on capitalist excess and the exploitation of factory workers. He accounted for every character, condition, and theme in the book. For example, he suggested that the Tin Man represented eastern factory workers who, the harder they worked, the worse off they were. The Tin Man was cursed by the Wicked Witch of the East who chopped off body parts with each swing of his ax. Luckily, he had the handy tinsmiths of Oz to replace those missing body parts. Unfortunately, the poor Tin Man just worked that much harder to ease his pain, until his body was nothing but tin. Littlefield suggested that this situation was an allegory for factory workers who, under the oppression of eastern factory owners, worked only to see their conditions worsen, until, like the Tin Man, they were virtually paralyzed.

This group's assessment as described in Figure 13.12 is intended to be summative with respect to the social studies component and formative with respect to developing skills with presentation software, working in groups, and communicating effectively. The teacher has multiple opportunities to observe students as they work on each of the skills in their presentation groups. The final product is the PowerPoint presentation with key points for the arguments for the position taken. The teacher can assess the social studies objectives as the groups present and defend their positions. Thus, both process and product components are provided in the summative evidence. Additionally, the teacher is able to gather data about students' abilities for working in groups during the process, data that are practically impossible to gather with traditional assessments.

Portfolio Assessments   A portfolio provides a systematic and organized collection of evidence of a student's efforts, progress, and achievement in a particular area. The purpose for gathering the evidence can be to show *growth* or *best work*. The purpose affects the compilation. Regardless, compiling and managing the portfolio are integrated with instruction, resulting in a more seamless integration of assessment and instruction. For growth over time, the portfolio contains works from drafts to finished products, stages of concept development, or even stages of performance development. Reflections about the development and improvements in understanding typically provide a student self-assessment component. For portfolios that demonstrate best work, reflections provide students with opportunities

Subject Matter Group: Social Studies	
Description of unit:	This social studies unit engages ninth-grade students in investigating *The Wizard of Oz* as a parable of the turn of the twentieth-century American political Populism. Littlefield (1964) suggests that Baum used the characters, setting, and plot of his book to lament capitalist excess and exploitation of factory workers. Students evaluate Littlefield's criticisms and make a judgment as to the reasonableness of his claims.
Objectives to be assessed	• Students think critically, comparing and contrasting capitalist excess and the exploitation of factory workers with the characters, setting, and plot in *The Wizard of Oz*. • Students work in groups efficiently and effectively. • Students communicate effectively. • Students use technology to critically evaluate Littlefield's thesis.
Evidence to be observed	• **Knowledge**: Recognition and understanding of the Populist party and times around 1890–1910. • **Product**: PowerPoint presentation highlighting key points of the position. • **Performance skills**: Students work in groups on a PowerPoint presentation; students use their prepared PowerPoint in support of the presentation of their position.
Format of task	Students are assigned in groups to compare Littlefield's thesis with Baum's text. In preparation for their presentation, their groups create a PowerPoint for their presentation.
Use of information	• Summative analysis to gather evidence about students' knowledge and analysis of the Populist party, the times, the people, and the conditions. • Formative analysis of students' skills in working in groups, communicating, and using presentation software in support presentations.
Type of assessment	Performance-based
Description of assessment:	Was *The Wizard of Oz* really fiction, a fairy tale for children? Or was it really a lament on capitalist excess and exploitation of factory workers as proposed by Henry M. Littlefield in 1964?
Students analyze the characters, setting, and plot of Baum's *The Wizard of Oz* given Littlefield's analysis in *American Quarterly*. In assigned groups, students study interactions among individuals, groups, and institutions with respect to treatments of factory workers as represented by Littlefield. The group must present a critique responding to the leading questions of fact versus fiction. The groups must prepare and incorporate in the presentation a PowerPoint document that supports the main arguments for their position.	

FIGURE 13.12   Social studies, presentation software, and *The Wizard of Oz* performance-based assessment.

to describe their own progress toward their best work. For portfolios that demonstrate growth, student self-assessments offer a view of their dispositions toward the content in the portfolio.

Portfolio evidence can be compiled in a variety of ways: paper, folders or notebook, computer disk, PowerPoint presentation, Compact disc (CD), or even the Web. With the impact of technology on education, portfolios are increasingly compiled, saved, and displayed in electronic formats. Such portfolios are referred to as electronic portfolios or e-portfolios. Figure 13.13 presents the elementary student teachers' (from Professor Summers' class) description of the electronic portfolio assessment they envision for supporting *The Wizard of Oz* theme over various content areas taught in a sixth-grade, self-contained classroom. In this assessment, each student collects artifacts for the portfolio in the form of digital pictures (using cameras or scanners), videos of work on different projects, and word-processed documents for the Table of Contents and the Reflections.

Weekly, each student makes a CD of the developing portfolio. At the end of the period, their teacher has a summative CD accompanied by the progression of CDs that demonstrate progress over time.

Assessment Scoring Guides

These descriptions of performance-based and portfolio-based assessments are incomplete at this point. Certainly, collecting the artifacts provides evidence of the learning that is taking place. But what does this evidence indicate? How is the evidence scored? Should existence of artifacts indicate the quality of the artifacts? Both types of assessments require an analysis and evaluation of the quality of the work. Both types of assessments require an explanation of how the work will be evaluated—they require a scoring guide or scoring rubric.

Scoring guides establish the criteria that are planned for judging the performance and its product, or the portfolio. They are used to describe the

---

Group: Elementary

Description of theme-based units: Students are reading *The Wizard of Oz* as background for the theme to be used in the sixth-grade class. Each subject area uses some idea from the book to explore a specific subject matter concept or process. These topics or questions were explored:

- **Science:** Water melted the Wicked Witch of the West. What else does water cause to disappear? What solids dissolve in water?
- **Geography:** If there were a yellow brick road from the Pacific Ocean to the Atlantic Ocean, what would be the best route for this road?
- **Mathematics:** If you built a yellow brick road from your house to the school, how many bricks would you need?
- **Language arts:** The newspaper of Oz was called *The Ozmapolitan*. Write and illustrate the news of what is happening in Oz during the time that Dorothy was there using events from the book.
- **Art:** Create a poster about the story by digitizing pictures and replacing the faces of the characters with faces of students in class.

Objectives to be assessed	• Students demonstrate knowledge and understanding of concepts for the specific subject areas. • Students use technology to display their knowledge and skills. • Students reflect on their growth of knowledge, skills, and attitudes toward technology.
Evidence to be observed	• **Knowledge:** Understanding and application of knowledge to solutions to problems in different content areas. • **Reasoning:** Processes used to solve the problems in different content areas. • **Product:** Electronic portfolio display of results of work on different content areas problems. • **Performance skills:** Work with appropriate technologies in solution of problems in different content areas and in preparation of electronic portfolio. • **Dispositions:** Reflections on growth of their knowledge, skills, and attitudes toward technology.
Format of task	Electronic portfolio displaying products from each subject area with reflections about each and about the collection.
Use of information	**Formative** gathering developmental evidence over the time of growth in the various content areas in the different target areas. **Summative** evidence of work in all classes.
Type of assessment	**Portfolio assessment**

Description of assessment: Maintain an electronic portfolio that contains developing samples of work in *The Wizard of Oz* theme. The Table of Contents for the portfolio is

- **Content Work.** Display up-to-date progress on problems, using pictures, video, or other evidence of the work in each area.
  - Science
  - Geography
  - Mathematics
  - Language arts
  - Art
- **Best of All.** Select the work where the most learning progress was made, explaining what was learned.
- **Reflection.** Add journal reflections to identified prompts at various times over the theme project. A final reflection is a self-assessment of learning over the project.

FIGURE 13.13   Elementary, multidisciplinary best work electronic portfolio for *The Wizard of Oz* theme.

range of quality that might occur in the assessments; they describe a score that should be given, what that score means, and how the different levels of quality are differentiated from one another (Arter & McTighe, 2001).

In the Snapshot of Integrating Assessment and Learning with Technology that opened this chapter, Mrs. Blake provided her students with a scoring guide that described her expectations for each part in the assignment. She designed the scoring guide in alignment with the criteria she identified when she assigned the Web timeline project. Her intent

was twofold: (1) the scoring guide would establish the standards for the project and (2) each group would assess the quality of the timelines created by the other groups using the scoring guide.

To begin designing a scoring guide, the criteria of the project or performance must be explicitly identified. What are the expectations or the qualities that are expected in the project? In the Snapshot of Integrating Assessment and Learning with Technology, Mrs. Blake identified five expectations: (1) timeline, (2) graphics, (3) mininarratives, (4) criteria for rankings, and (5) ranking of innovations. These criteria

Expectation	Top Level	Second Level	Third Level	Fourth Level
Timeline				
Graphics				
Mininarratives				
Criteria for Rankings				
Ranking of Innovations				

FIGURE 13.14   The beginning for Mrs. Blake in designing her scoring guide.

were described in neutral terms. Rather than saying *clear mininarratives*, the identification was simply stated as a *mininarrative*.

The criteria might simply be a checklist where the evaluators check yes or no indicating the existence of each. Existence, however, does not differentiate the quality of the work for each one. The purpose of a scoring guide is to allow teachers and their students a way of differentiating the quality. Basically the scoring guide provides a description of different levels of performance on a project as shown in Figure 13.14 using the criteria that Mrs. Blake established. The table provides spaces for presenting the descriptions to differentiate the quality of work on the specified criterion. Danielson (1997) identifies two concerns at this point in the development:

1. When determining the number of levels, an even number of levels is preferable to an odd number because of people's tendency to assign credits in the middle of the range of possible levels. With an even number of levels, there is no middle and the evaluators must make a decision whether the evidence is above or below the middle level quality.

2. Although additional levels allow for a finer distinction of the quality of the work, many points are more time-consuming since the differences are likely to be small.

A good approach to guide your thinking about creating the various levels is to incorporate better descriptors for the levels. Rather than Top Level to Fourth Level, you might describe them as Mrs. Blake did: Advanced, Proficient, Partially Proficient, and Not Proficient/Not Enough Evidence. Those descriptors more clearly delineate between acceptable work (Advanced, Proficient) and unacceptable work (Partially Proficient, Not Proficient/Not Enough Evidence).

A good strategy for preparing the specific descriptions is to begin with the top level, the advanced level. What type of response represents an *outstanding, exemplary,* or *advanced* product or performance? Use several examples to avoid the

implication that one response is right. Descriptors, such as clear, coherent, unambiguous, effective, elegant, accurate, complete, and well organized, are useful at the top level. Once that level is described, the lowest level is described followed by the description of the intermediate levels.

Examples are helpful in determining phrases that might be useful for describing quality at the different levels. Figure 13.15 provides one of the scoring guides that the social studies group in Professor Summers' class developed to be used during the unit to guide students' work in developing their PowerPoint. This group indicated that their intent with this assessment was to provide students and their teacher with evidence of their work in stages as they developed their presentations for describing their position about the Littlefield thesis of *The Wizard of Oz*. They indicated that the information was to be used to alert the groups about their efforts in working as a team, their work on the storyboard for the PowerPoint, and their knowledge of the subject matter content planned for the presentation.

When you develop scoring guides that reflect technology in the learning experience, you need to focus on representing that *integration* of the subject matter content knowledge and the technology content. Often, with the use of technology, there is a tendency to focus on the technology evidence aside from the knowledge of the subject matter content evidence. You need to resist that tendency because it supports technology for technology's sake rather than using technology as an integral component of learning and communication. Mrs. Blake's scoring guide criteria describe an integration of the knowledge of world history with Web-based knowledge. Her scoring guide refers to the importance of the timeline being accurate, complete, and well organized, referring to the display of the content using the Web timeline. The scoring guide also refers to the importance of the graphics on the timeline, with the expectation that students at the advanced level use graphics that portray the technological innovations

Criterion	Advanced	Proficient	Partially Proficient	Not Proficient/ Not Enough Evidence
Storyboard for Power-Point	Complete and well organized, with all assigned media elements and planned formats and identification of needed resources	Somewhat complete with clear organization and many of the assigned media elements, most of the planned formats, and some resources	Not complete but contains a few of the assigned media elements, planned formats, and resources	Incomplete and lacks indication of media elements, formats, and resources needed to complete the project
Content knowledge of Populism	Evidence is accurate, complete, and well organized	Evidence in much of the work that is clear, appropriate, and correct	Some evidence with some confusing, incorrect, or flawed evidence	No evidence; evidence is incorrect, confusing, or flawed
Content knowledge of *The Wizard of Oz*	Evidence is accurate, complete, and well organized	Evidence in much of the work that is clear, appropriate, and correct	Some evidence with some confusing, incorrect, or flawed evidence	No evidence; evidence is incorrect, confusing, or flawed
Organization of content	Logically and intuitively sequenced with clear and direct paths for presenting the information	Logically sequenced with clear and direct paths for presenting the information	Some logical sequence of the information but some of the paths for presenting the information are confusing or flawed	No logical sequence of the information; paths to the information are not evident
Teamwork	Workload is clearly divided and equally shared among the team members	Workload is divided and shared with most team members contributing	Workload is somewhat divided with most of the members participating in the efforts	One or two of the team members are doing all or most of the work

FIGURE 13.15   Scoring guide for a formative performance-based assessment of students' work on the PowerPoint presentation for the social studies unit.

and are clear, effective, and accurate displays of the innovations. Her concern is that the evidence the students provide through their Web timelines identifies, describes, and ranks significant technology innovations that ignited changes in civilization over the past 2000 years, an objective drawn from the subject matter standards as appearing in the 1994 National Council for the Social Studies standards. Equally important to her, though, is that the students provide evidence of using Web technology as a tool for communicating (NETS·S Standard IV) their knowledge of world history as well as displaying their knowledge of basic operation and concepts of Web presentations (NETS·S Standard I).

Keep in mind that scoring guides identify what is valued in the completion of the assessments—the entire work or specific aspects of the work. Scoring guides can be *holistic* (providing an overall judgment about the student's work) or *analytic* (judging the specific parts or criteria separately). From a holistic standpoint, a glitzy PowerPoint or movie that does not accurately display the subject matter content should not be considered proficient. On the other hand, a poorly organized PowerPoint or movie that contains accurate subject matter content should not be considered proficient either. Analytic scoring guides provide the opportunity to recognize strengths for specific criteria. This type

of scoring guide is certainly helpful in guiding student learning with respect to individual criteria. The social studies scoring guide in Figure 13.15 was designed for this purpose. Holistic scoring guides are useful in focusing on an assessment of the entire work. As you prepare to develop your scoring guides, be sure to think about this concern, make a decision as to what you are planning, and carefully describe the objectives and achievement targets for the assessment. Once points are assigned to the specific cells and the points are summed, you are saying that the whole product is valued by the sum of these points whether you are using a holistic or analytic scoring guide.

The elementary group in Professor Summers' class created an electronic portfolio scoring guide in which they identified points for each of the primary criteria for their vision of the portfolios (see Figure 13.16). They indicated that any portfolio with fewer than 32 points needed to be resubmitted. In essence they viewed the scoring guide holistically, providing an overall judgment about the student's work. They were careful to maintain a balance of the score on both the subject matter and technology demonstration through the distribution of the points.

Many examples of scoring guides are available on the Web that identify potential criteria for consideration in assessing learning with and about technology. Technology Link 13.1 links you with one of the possible resources. Remember that with any scoring guide you find, you will probably need to carefully integrate learning the content with the technology. You need to gather not only evidence of how the students know their content with technology but also evidence of what they know about the content.

Technology Link 13.1

The **Scoring Guides** link connects you to Kathy Schrock's Assessment and Rubric Information with multiple links to access rubrics for Web pages, PowerPoints, iMovie video projects, and other types of technologies.

www.wiley.com/college/niess

Electronic Portfolio Scoring Guide

A—Advanced: 37–42 points
B—Proficient: 32–36 points
Partially Proficient or Not Proficient: Needs to be resubmitted; less than 32 points

Criterion	Advanced	Proficient	Partially Proficient	Not Proficient/Not Enough Evidence
Content work	10 points Complete, accurate, and well organized evidence of work in each content area. Selection of artifacts and work samples are effective demonstrations of work in each of the content areas.	7 points Somewhat complete with clear organization and evidence of work in each content area. Selection of artifacts and work samples are appropriate demonstrations in each of the content areas.	4 points Not complete but contains some of the work in some of the content areas. Selection of artifacts and work samples is incomplete with some in most of the content areas.	0 points Incomplete and lacks work in the content areas. Artifacts and work samples are needed to complete the project.
Best of all	10 points Evidence is accurate, complete, and well organized with convincing rationale for inclusion as best work.	7 points Evidence in much of the work that is clear, appropriate, and correct with a reasonable rationale for inclusion as best work.	4 points Some evidence with a confusing rationale for inclusion as best work.	0 points Little if any evidence of best work. Rationale is incorrect, confusing, or missing.
Reflections	10 points All reflections illustrate thoughtful and accurate evaluations of the work in response to the prompts. The final reflection describes why the artifacts in the portfolio demonstrate growth in knowledge, skills, and attitudes toward learning subject matter with technology.	7 points All reflections are clear evaluations of the work in response to the prompts. The final reflection provides some indication of growth in knowledge, skills, and attitudes toward learning subject matter with technology.	4 points Some reflections of the work in response to the prompts. The final reflection is confusing with respect to growth in knowledge, skills, and attitudes toward learning subject matter with technology.	0 points Few if any reflections of the work in response to the prompts. The final reflection is incomplete or missing.
Electronic presentation of portfolio	6 points Logically and intuitively sequenced with clear and direct paths for presenting the information.	4 points Logically sequenced with clear and direct paths for presenting the information.	2 points Some logical sequence of the information but some of the paths for presenting the information are confusing or flawed	0 points No logical sequence of the information; paths to the information are not evident.
Use of multimedia for communication	6 points All media elements enhance the communication of the evidence, support ease of navigation.	4 points Most of the media elements enhance the communication of the evidence and support ease of navigation.	2 points Some of the media elements support communication and ease of navigation.	0 points Few if any of the media elements support the communication and ease of navigation.

FIGURE 13.16 Holistic scoring guide for a summative portfolio assessment for the elementary multidisciplinary best work electronic portfolio.

Summing It Up

Teachers are charged with the responsibility of identifying what students learn as a result of instruction. Today, to meet this charge, teachers need to assess students' knowledge of subject matter content in an environment that expects students to incorporate technology as a tool with which to think and learn—as a productivity tool, a communications tool, a research tool, and a problem-solving and decision-making tool. Ultimately, teachers need to assess subject matter content knowledge, technology content knowledge, and the knowledge of how students process their understandings of the subject matter content with the technology.

Assessment is the process of monitoring students' progresses toward important learning goals and objectives. The evidence gathered in the assessment process is designed to inform parents, students, and their teachers. The evidence provides teachers with information for designing and perhaps redesigning their instruction. Inherently, assessment and instruction are intertwined. Assessment needs to be interwoven prior to instruction, throughout instruction, and after instruction. Assessments need to sample what students know and are able to do within the framework of the instruction. And, multiple assessments need to be completed over time.

Assessments need to provide accurate information about student learning with respect to the identified goals and objectives of instruction. What should students know and how should they know the ideas incorporated in the goals and objectives? Identification of clearly stated achievement targets provides a framework for determining the format of the assessments for gathering evidence: knowledge, reasoning, performance skills, products, and dispositions.

Historically, tests have been considered the preferred assessment method. However, with changes in the goals for educated citizens in the twenty-first century, teachers have been confronted with obtaining assessment evidence of not only what students learn but also how they perform. Current assessment trends recognize that students have different ways of explaining how they make sense of their learning experiences. The trends support the importance of allowing students to demonstrate their knowledge in a variety of ways, including projects, portfolios, reports, videos, or the performance of what and how they know and understand.

With the emphasis on technology as an integral component and tool for learning, two categories of alternatives for assessing students have been increasingly incorporated: performance-based assessment and portfolio assessment. Performance-based assessments focus on students actually demonstrating their knowledge and skills. Rather than answering questions about what they would do, they show what they would do. Identification and preparation of this type of assessment require the identification of a clear purpose, observable criteria, and an appropriate setting. Multiple formats can be used to observe the process and the product produced in the process. Students can be observed working on a PowerPoint presentation as well as when they use that presentation to describe their knowledge and understanding. Thus, teachers can gather evidence of knowledge and skills with the technology as well as their knowledge and skills in the subject matter area.

A portfolio provides a systematic and organized collection of evidence of a student's efforts, progress, and achievement in a specific area. The purpose for gathering the evidence can be to show growth or best work. For growth over time, the portfolio contains works from drafts to finished products, stages of concept development, or even stages of performance development. Reflections about the development and improvements in understanding provide a student self-assessment component. With the access to technology in education, portfolio evidence is increasingly compiled in electronic formats—CDs, PowerPoint presentations, Web presentations—and are often referred to as electronic portfolios or e-portfolios. As a result the electronic portfolios provide a method for assessing what students know and how they know it within the framework of learning with technology.

Determining the quality of the evidence from performance-based and portfolio assessments requires careful consideration by the evaluators, namely, the teachers and even the students and their parents. Scoring guides provide the criteria for judging the performance or the portfolio. The scoring guide must describe the range in the quality possible for each of the criteria. Typically the levels of quality range among advanced, proficient, partially proficient, and not proficient. An important key to developing scoring guides within a technology-enriched learning environment is to include multiple criteria considering the following: knowledge of the subject matter, knowledge of the technology, and knowledge of learning the subject matter with the technology. Holistic scoring guides provide a statement about a student's entire work or effort; students should not be considered proficient without evidence of proficiency in all the criteria, subject matter, technology, and learning with technology. Analytic scoring guides can be used to judge specific criteria separately to provide detailed information about proficiencies and deficiencies.

When technology is added to the educational environment, teachers must consider (1) how technology can be applied to enhance learning, (2) how use of technology changes what is learned, and (3) how technology can be used to enrich the evidence of student learning. New methods, new tools, and new approaches that apply technology to learning must be accounted for when applying technology to the assessment of what is learned and how that learning is known and displayed. This knowledge and understanding are important parts of what a teacher needs to know in the twenty-first century—a part of a teacher's technological pedagogical content knowledge (TPCK).

End-of-the-Chapter Activities and References

PRACTICE PROBLEMS

1. Make a list of 20 different assessment formats. Identify the strengths and limitations for each assessment for use in your subject area and grade level.

2. Outline a unit that you might teach where students use technology as a tool for learning. Identify the key content and technology objectives for the unit. Describe various assessment formats that might be used to assess student learning of the key objectives.

3. Create a performance-based assessment for a unit you might teach. Use the format in Figure 13.10 to describe your assessment and unit.

4. Create a portfolio assessment for a unit you might teach. Use the format in Figure 13.10 to describe your assessment and unit.

5. Create an analytic scoring guide for an assessment you plan for a unit you might teach.

6. Create a holistic scoring guide for an assessment you plan for a unit you might teach.

IN THE CLASSROOM ACTIVITIES

7. Observe a classroom activity that incorporates technology as a portion of the lesson. Identify how assessment is integrated with the instruction and how the teacher uses that evidence.

8. Interview a teacher in the classroom to identify how the teacher uses assessments to inform instruction. What objectives were assessed?

9. Observe a performance-based assessment in a classroom. How is the evidence judged?

10. Collect scoring guides teachers have developed for assessing performance or portfolios. Summarize the key features of the different scoring guides.

ASSESSING STUDENT LEARNING WITH AND ABOUT TECHNOLOGY

11. With a set of objectives for a unit that includes learning with and about technology that you have created, tabulate the achievement targets, formats for assessing achievement of the targets, and the use of the evidence as in Figure 13.5.

12. Collect a variety of scoring guides from the Web or other resources for assessing learning with a technology of your choice. Create your own scoring guide that assesses student learning with and about technology.

E-PORTFOLIO ACTIVITIES

13. Create a Web page introduction to your electronic portfolio that includes hyperlinks to work in the various parts of your teacher preparation program, best work, and reflections on your growth and preparation for teaching with technology.

14. Compile your electronic portfolio on a CD that contains examples of your learning to teach with and about technology.

REFLECTION AND DISCUSSION

15. Observe students as they work with a specific technology. Use your observations to guide you in the development of a scoring guide that would accurately assess student learning in that situation. Write a reflection on the value of the use of your scoring guide for such a performance-based assessment.

16. Reflect on this statement: Tests are the only objective assessments of student learning.

Annotated Resources

Kelly, M. G., & Haber, J. (2006). *Resources for student assessment*. Eugene, OR: ISTE.
Assessment considerations for assessing student learning in technology-enhanced learning are presented in this book that is directed to creating a well-defined assessment program focused on assessing student development of technology knowledge, skills, and application. Linked with the NETS·S guidelines.

Wiggins, G., & McTighe, J. (2005). *Understanding by design*. Upper Saddle River, NJ: Pearson Merrill Prentice Hall.
This book is about design of curriculum, assessment, and instruction focused on planning for student understanding. The text examines an array of methods for appropriately assessing the degree of student understanding, knowledge, and skill through a focus on a *backward design* approach to planning where teachers begin with the desired outputs of instruction.

PART IV

STANDARDS, LINKS, AND MATRICES

Niess, Lee, & Kajder

National Educational Technology Standards for Teachers (NETS · T) and Students (NETS · S)

FOR TEACHERS[1]

All classroom teachers should be prepared to meet the following standards.

I. **Technology Operations and Concepts**

Teachers demonstrate a sound understanding of technology operations and concepts. Teachers:
  A. demonstrate introductory knowledge, skills, and understanding of concepts related to technology (as described in the ISTE National Educational Technology Standards for Students).
  B. demonstrate continual growth in technology knowledge and skills to stay abreast of current and emerging technologies.

II. **Planning and Designing Learning Environments and Experiences**

Teachers plan and design effective learning environments and experiences supported by technology. Teachers:
  A. design developmentally appropriate learning opportunities that apply technology-enhanced instructional strategies to support the diverse needs of learners.
  B. apply current research on teaching and learning with technology when planning learning environments and experiences.
  C. identify and locate technology resources and evaluate them for accuracy and suitability.
  D. plan for the management of technology resources within the context of learning activities.
  E. plan strategies to manage student learning in a technology-enhanced environment.

III. **Teaching, Learning, and the Curriculum**

Teachers implement curriculum plans that include methods and strategies for applying technology to maximize student learning. Teachers:
  A. facilitate technology-enhanced experiences that address content standards and student technology standards.

---

[1] Source: Reprinted with permission from the National Educational Technology Standards for Teachers, copyright © 2002 ISTE.

B. use technology to support learner-centered strategies that address the diverse needs of students.

C. apply technology to develop students' higher-order skills and creativity.

D. manage student learning activities in a technology-enhanced environment.

IV. Assessment and Evaluation

Teachers apply technology to facilitate a variety of effective assessment and evaluation strategies. Teachers:

A. apply technology in assessing student learning of subject matter using a variety of assessment techniques.

B. use technology resources to collect and analyze data, interpret results, and communicate findings to improve instructional practice and maximize student learning.

C. apply multiple methods of evaluation to determine students' appropriate use of technology resources for learning, communication, and productivity.

V. Productivity and Professional Practice

Teachers use technology to enhance their productivity and professional practice. Teachers:

A. use technology resources to engage in ongoing professional development and lifelong learning.

B. continually evaluate and reflect on professional practice to make informed decisions regarding the use of technology in support of student learning.

C. apply technology to increase productivity.

D. use technology to communicate and collaborate with peers, parents, and the larger community in order to nurture student learning.

VI. Social, Ethical, Legal, and Human Issues

Teachers understand the social, ethical, legal, and human issues surrounding the use of technology in PreK–12 schools and apply that understanding in practice. Teachers:

A. model and teach legal and ethical practice related to technology use.

B. apply technology resources to enable and empower learners with diverse backgrounds, characteristics, and abilities.

C. identify and use technology resources that affirm diversity.

D. promote safe and healthy use of technology resources.

E. facilitate equitable access to technology resources for all students.

FOR STUDENTS[2]

All students should be prepared to meet the following standards to achieve success in learning, communication, and life skills.

I. Basic Operations and Concepts
A. Students demonstrate a sound understanding of the nature and operation of technology systems.
B. Students are proficient in the use of technology.

II. Social, Ethical, and Human Issues
A. Students understand the ethical, cultural, and societal issues related to technology.
B. Students practice responsible use of technology systems, information, and software.
C. Students develop positive attitudes toward technology uses that support lifelong learning, collaboration, personal pursuits, and productivity.

III. Technology Productivity Tools
A. Students use technology tools to enhance learning, increase productivity, and promote creativity.
B. Students use productivity tools to collaborate in constructing technology-enhanced models, prepare publications, and produce other creative works.

IV. Technology Communications Tools
A. Students use telecommunications to collaborate, publish, and interact with peers, experts, and other audiences.
B. Students use a variety of media and formats to communicate information and ideas effectively to multiple audiences.

V. Technology Research Tools
A. Students use technology to locate, evaluate, and collect information from a variety of sources.
B. Students use technology tools to process data and report results.
C. Students evaluate and select new information resources and technological innovations based on the appropriateness for specific tasks.

VI. Technology Problem-Solving and Decision-Making Tools
A. Students use technology resources for solving problems and making informed decisions.
B. Students employ technology in the development of strategies for solving problems in the real world.

---

[2] Source: Reprinted with permission from the National Educational Technology Standards for Students— Connecting Curriculum and Technology, copyright © 2000 ISTE.

B

Connecting the INTASC Principles and the NETS Teacher Technology Standards

INTASC Principle	NETS · T Standards	Clarifying the Connection
Principle 1. Subject Matter		
Principle 1. Subject Matter Teachers need to understand central concepts, tools of inquiry, and the structures of the discipline(s). Teachers need to create learning experiences that make these aspects of subject matter meaningful for students.	**Standard I. Technology Operations and Concepts** Teachers demonstrate a sound understanding of technology operations and concepts. (NETS · T I)	• How the subject matter is known and advanced is influenced by technology. With the impact of technology on the advancement of knowledge, technology typically provides tools of inquiry in the subjects. Part of knowing a particular subject matter is knowing the basic operations and concepts of the technology that influences that subject matter. • Technology is one of the disciplines of a teacher.
	Standard II. Planning and Designing Learning Environments Teachers plan and design effective learning environments and experiences supported by technology. (NETS · T II)	• For students to learn the subject matter, teachers need to design and plan learning experiences that integrate technology.
	Standard III. Teaching, Learning, and the Curriculum Teachers facilitate technology-enhanced experiences that address content standards and student technology standards. (NETS · T III-A)	• For students to learn the subject matter the way that subject is known and understood in the modern world requires a curriculum that integrates technology in the students' learning experiences.
	Standard IV. Assessment and Evaluation Teachers apply technology in assessing student learning of subject matter using a variety of assessment techniques. (NETS · T IV-A)	• How students know and understand the subject matter after learning experiences with technology must include some assessment that integrates their knowledge of the subject matter with their knowledge of the technology.
Principle 2. Knowledge of Student Development and **Principle 3. Knowledge of Diverse Learners**		
Principle 2. Knowledge of Student Development Teachers understand how students learn and develop and can provide learning opportunities to support their intellectual, social, and personal development.	**Standard. II Planning and Designing Learning Environments** Teachers design developmentally appropriate learning opportunities that apply technology-enhanced instructional strategies to support the diverse needs of learners. (NETS · T II-A)	• Students have diverse experiences with technologies and need learning experiences of subject matter and the technology that recognizes their diverse needs.
	Standard III. Teaching, Learning, and the Curriculum	
Principle 3. Knowledge of Diverse Learners Teachers understand how students differ in their approaches to learning and create instructional opportunities that are adapted to diverse learners.	Teachers use technology to support learner-centered strategies that address the diverse needs of learners. (NETS · T III-B) **Standard IV. Assessment and Evaluation** Teachers apply technology to facilitate a variety of effective assessment and evaluation strategies. (NETS · T IV)	• How students construct their understanding of the subject relies heavily on their past experiences. Those experiences accentuate the great diversity of students in a classroom. • Identifying the knowledge and understanding of the subject of diverse learners necessitates a variety of assessment strategies. Strategies need to appeal to student diversities and provide multiple opportunities to demonstrate their knowledge both with and without the tools used to explore the ideas.

INTASC Principle	NETS · T Standards	Clarifying the Connection
Principle 4. Knowledge of Multiple Instructional Strategies		
Principle 4. Knowledge of Multiple Instructional Strategies Teachers understand and use a variety of instructional strategies to encourage student development of critical thinking, problem solving, and performance skills.	**Standard II. Planning and Designing Learning Environments** Teachers plan and design effective learning environments and experiences supported by technology. (NETS · T II) **Standard III. Teaching, Learning, and the Curriculum** Teachers apply technology to develop students' higher order skills and creativity. (NETS · T III-C)	• Technologies allow students to explore ideas in a variety of ways, to solve problems, and to describe their understanding. Often the technologies encourage students to engage in critical thinking or higher order thinking skills.
Principle 5. Classroom Motivation and Management		
Principle 5. Classroom Motivation and Management Teachers use an understanding of individual and group motivation and behavior to create a learning environment that encourages positive social interaction, active engagement in learning, and self-motivation.	**Standard II. Planning and Designing Learning Environments** Teachers plan for the management of technology resources within the context of learning activities. (NETS · T II-D) **Standard III. Teaching, Learning, and the Curriculum** Teachers manage student learning activities in a technology-enhanced environment. (NETS · T III-D)	• Technology is often an exciting motivator for students. But it can also complicate lessons. Students need to be prepared for active engagement and hands-on activities with the technology. • Teachers need to plan for managing the classroom and the activity if all the students are to benefit. • During the activity or hands-on lesson, teachers need to assure that the environment is positive and engages students in learning.
Principle 6. Communication Skills		
Principle 6. Communication Skills Teachers use knowledge of effective verbal, nonverbal, and media communication techniques to foster active inquiry, collaboration, and supportive interaction in the classroom.	**Standard III. Teaching, Learning, and the Curriculum** Teachers implement curriculum plans that include methods and strategies for applying technology to maximize student learning. (NETS · T III) **Standard V. Productivity and Professional Practice** Teachers use technology to communicate and collaborate with peers, parents, and the larger community to nurture student learning. (NETS · T V-D)	• Implementing technology lessons requires that teachers establish a classroom conducive to learning. Communication is critical to fostering the active inquiry, collaboration, and supportive interaction in the classroom in technology lessons. Verbal, nonverbal, and media communication are essential communications needed in the lessons. • Teachers also need to use these communication skills in working with parents, peers, and others in enlisting their assistance in integrating technology in instruction.
Principle 7. Instructional Planning Skills		
Principle 7. Instructional Planning Skills Teachers plan instruction based on knowledge of subject matter, students, the community, and curriculum goals.	**Standard II. Planning and Designing Learning Environments** Teachers design developmentally appropriate learning opportunities that apply technology-enhanced instructional strategies to support the diverse needs of learners. (NETS · T II-A) **Standard III. Teaching, Learning, and the Curriculum** Teachers facilitate technology-enhanced experiences that address content standards and student technology standards. (NETS · T III-A)	**Standard V. Productivity and Professional Practice** Teachers use technology to communicate and collaborate with peers, parents, and the larger community to nurture student learning. (NETS · T V-D) • Integrating technology in instruction requires careful planning to meet the following: 1. the diverse needs of students, are planned to assure that the technology addresses the curriculum and content standards,

	2. the students are able to use the technology in support of learning the content (technology content standards), 3. the technology does not overshadow the content, and	4. the classroom management results in an environment conducive to student learning. • Planning must include a consideration of the community requiring that teachers communicate with parents and the larger community to nurture student learning.

Principle 8. Assessment of Student Learning

Principle 8. Assessment of Student Learning Teachers understand and use formal and informal assessment strategies to evaluate and ensure the continuous intellectual, social, and physical development of the learner.	**Standard IV. Assessment and Evaluation** Teachers apply technology to facilitate a variety of effective assessment and evaluation strategies. (NETS · T IV)	• In assessing student learning in a technology-enhanced environment, teachers need to use a variety of assessments — both formal and informal — to ensure the continuous development of the learners. • Some of the assessments of student learning need to incorporate student learning with the technology — both formally and informally.

Principle 9. Professional Commitment and Responsibility

Principle 9. Professional Commitment and Responsibility Teachers are reflective practitioners who continually evaluate the effects of their choices and actions on others (students, parents, and other professionals in the learning community) and who actively seek out opportunities to grow professionally.	**Standard I. Technology Operations and Concepts** Teachers demonstrate continual growth in technology knowledge and skills to stay abreast of current and emerging technologies. (NETS · T I-B) **Standard V. Productivity and Professional Practice** Teachers use technology to enhance their productivity and professional practice. (NETS · T V) **Standard VI. Social, Ethical, Legal, and Human Issues** Teachers understand the social, ethical, legal, and human issues surrounding the use of technology in preK – 12 schools and apply that understanding in practice. (NETS · T VI)	• Integrating technology in education is new – new to students, teachers, parents, and the community. Teachers need to carefully communicate with the various constituencies in order to reflect on and evaluate the result of this integration. • With the continued advancements in technology, teachers need to continue to learn about new possibilities for integrating technologies. What technologies support the learning of the content? What technologies can be used to communicate an understanding of the content? What technologies can motivate students to learn more about the content? Those are a few of the questions that teachers must constantly reflect on in order to enhance their productivity and professional practice. • Teachers must continually consider the social, ethical, legal, and human issues surrounding how their students will use the various technologies in enhancing their learning.

Principle 10. Partnerships

Principle 10. Partnerships Teachers foster relationships with school colleagues, parents, and agencies in the larger community to support students' learning and well-being.	**Standard V. Productivity and Professional Practice** Teachers use technology to enhance their productivity and professional practice. (NETS · T V)	• An important aspect of teachers' professional practice involves their relationship with school colleagues, parents, and agencies in the larger community. When teachers decide to use technology in their classrooms, they must communicate with this larger community. This community can assist teachers in obtaining more advanced technologies, assuring that students have access to the technologies, and providing on-going support for teachers as they design and implement their curriculum. • Teachers working in partnership with colleagues, parents, and agencies are able to enhance their productivity and professional practice that ultimately affects students' learning and well-being.

Aligning the English/Language Arts Standards with the National Educational Technology Standards and Performance Indicators for Students

NCTE/IRA English/Language Arts Standards	Example Curricular Performance Indicator (Grade 8)	Corresponding NETS for Students	Example NETS Performance Indicators (Grade 8)
1. Students read a wide range of print and nonprint texts to build an understanding of texts, of themselves, and of the cultures of the United States and the world; to acquire new information; to respond to the needs and demands of society and the workplace; and for personal fulfillment. Among these texts are fiction and nonfiction, classic and contemporary works.	Read familiar and independent level text at a rate that is conversational and consistent. Read instructional level text that is challenging yet manageable.	Students use technology tools to enhance learning, increase productivity, and promote creativity. (Instructional example: Students read, mark-up, and annotate electronic text published within an online repository.)	4. Use content-specific tools, software, and simulations to support learning and research.
2. Students read a wide range of literature from many periods in many genres to build an understanding of the many dimensions (e.g., philosophical, ethical, aesthetic) of human experience.	Listen to critically, read, and discuss a variety of literary texts representing diverse cultures, perspectives, ethnicities, and time periods. Listen to critically, read, and discuss a variety of literary forms and genres. Read, use, and identify the characteristics of workplace and other real-world documents. **Assessment Limits:** Job descriptions Forms Questionnaires Instructional and technical manuals Other workplace and real-world documents	Students use technology tools to enhance learning, increase productivity, and promote creativity. (Instructional example: Students use graphic organizers generated in Inspiration or Microsoft Word to create story maps, plot syntheses, or Venn diagrams to connect elements of a broad range of texts.)	4. Use content-specific tools, software, and simulations to support learning and research. 6. Design, develop, publish, and present products using technology resources that demonstrate and communicate curriculum concepts to audiences inside and outside the curriculum. 8. Select and use appropriate tools and technology resources to accomplish a variety of tasks and solve problems.
3. Students apply a wide range of strategies to comprehend, interpret, evaluate, and appreciate texts. They draw on their prior experience, their interactions with other readers and writers, their knowledge of word meaning and of other texts, their word identification strategies, and their understanding of textual features (e.g., sound–letter correspondence, sentence structure, context, graphics).	Draw inferences and/or conclusions and make generalizations. Confirm, refute, or make predictions and form new ideas. Summarize or paraphrase the text. Discuss reactions to and ideas/information gained from reading experiences with adults and peers in both formal and informal situations. Select and apply appropriate strategies to make meaning from text during reading. Analyze the relationship between the text features and the content of the text as a whole.	Students use telecommunications to collaborate, publish, and interact with peers, experts, and other audiences. (Instructional example: Students interact with peers and authors within an electronic classroom to conduct literature circles or other interpretive activities and discussions.)	7. Collaborate with peers, experts, and others using telecommunications and collaborative tools to investigate curriculum-related problems, issues, and information, and to develop solutions or products for audiences inside and outside the classroom. 8. Select and use appropriate tools and technology resources to accomplish a variety of tasks and solve problems.

(continued on next page)

NCTE/IRA English/Language Arts Standards	Example Curricular Performance Indicator (Grade 8)	Corresponding NETS for Students	Example NETS Performance Indicators (Grade 8)
4. Students adjust their use of spoken, written, and visual language (e.g., conventions, style, vocabulary) to communicate effectively with a variety of audiences and for different purposes.	Analyze specific word choice that contributes to meaning and/or creates style. Analyze the appropriateness of tone.	Students use productivity tools to collaborate in constructing technology-enhanced models, preparing publications, and producing other creative works Students use a variety of media and formats to communicate information and ideas effectively to multiple audiences. Students use technology to locate, evaluate, and collect information from a variety of sources. (Instructional example: Students use digital video or presentation software to create literacy narratives, communicate oral histories, or to present a visual think aloud.)	4. Use content-specific tools, software, and simulations to support learning and research. 5. Apply productivity/multi-media tools and peripherals to support personal productivity, group collaboration, and learning throughout the curriculum. 6. Design, develop, publish, and present products using technology resources that demonstrate and communicate curriculum concepts to audiences inside and outside the classroom.
5. Students employ a wide range of strategies as they write and use different writing process elements appropriately to communicate with different audiences for a variety of purposes.	Generate and narrow topics by considering purpose, audience, and form. Select, organize, and develop ideas by exploring and evaluating the usefulness and quality of sources, determining completeness of support, organizing information into subtopics, generating graphic organizers, outlining, and selecting and using organizational structures appropriate to topic	Students use technology tools to enhance learning, increase productivity, and promote creativity. Students use productivity tools to collaborate in constructing technology-enhanced models, preparing publications, and producing other creative works. (Instructional example: Students complete a peer review of written essays using commenting features in Microsoft Word and sharing responses by either exchanging disks or beaming if using handhelds.)	4. Use content-specific tools, software, and simulations to support learning and research. 5. Apply productivity/multi-media tools and peripherals to support personal productivity, group collaboration, and learning throughout the curriculum. 8. Select and use appropriate tools and technology resources to accomplish a variety of tasks and solve problems.
6. Students apply knowledge of language structure, language conventions (e.g., spelling and punctuation), media techniques, figurative language, and genre to create, critique, and discuss print and nonprint texts.	Identify structural, symbolic, and syntactical differences between print and nonprint texts. Evaluate a variety of media and their respective means of communicating intended meaning (i.e., advertising, visual art, film).	Students use a variety of media and formats to communicate information and ideas effectively to multiple audiences. (Instructional example: Students create multimedia presentations using tools such as PowerPoint or Flash to communicate the multiple levels of their understanding through visual and textual means.)	4. Use content-specific tools, software, and simulations to support learning and research. 6. Design, develop, publish, and present products using technology resources that demonstrate and communicate curriculum concepts to audiences inside and outside the classroom. 8. Select and use appropriate tools and technology resources to accomplish a variety of tasks and solve problems.

NCTE/IRA English/Language Arts Standards	Example Curricular Performance Indicator (Grade 8)	Corresponding NETS for Students	Example NETS Performance Indicators (Grade 8)
7. Students conduct research on issues and interests by generating ideas and questions, and by posing problems. They gather, evaluate, and synthesize data from a variety of sources (e.g., print and nonprint texts, artifacts, people) to communicate their discoveries in ways that suit their purpose and audience.	Compose for a specific audience and purpose. Make effective decisions regarding word choice, style, information provided according to analysis of audience needs and knowledge and consideration of purpose and form. Maintain organization and coherence with logic, use of transitions, and appropriate details.	Use developmentally appropriate multimedia resources to support learning. Use technology resources for problem solving, communications, and illustration of thoughts, ideas, and stories. (Instructional example: Students conduct an I-Search project using multimedia, CD-ROM, and online resources.)	3. Exhibit legal and ethical behaviors when using information and technology, and discuss consequences of misuse. 4. Use content-specific tools, software, and simulations to support learning and research. 5. Apply productivity/multimedia tools and peripherals to support personal productivity, group collaboration, and learning throughout the curriculum. 8. Select and use appropriate tools and technology resources to accomplish a variety of tasks and solve problems. 10. Research and evaluate the accuracy, relevance, appropriateness, comprehensiveness, and bias of electronic information sources concerning real-world problems.
8. Students use a variety of technological and information resources (e.g., libraries, databases, computer networks, video) to gather and synthesize information and to create and communicate knowledge.	Search for information using efficient strategies, keywords, and information resources. Synthesize findings using an organized, clear method that is maintained and developed further through the research process.	Use developmentally appropriate multimedia resources to support learning. Use technology resources for problem solving, communications, and illustration of thoughts, ideas, and stories.	3. Exhibit legal and ethical behaviors when using information and technology, and discuss consequences of misuse. 4. Use content-specific tools, software, and simulations to support learning and research. 8. Select and use appropriate tools and technology resources to accomplish a variety of tasks and solve problems. 10. Research and evaluate the accuracy, relevance, appropriateness, comprehensiveness, and bias of electronic information sources concerning real-world problems.

(continued on next page)

NCTE/IRA English/Language Arts Standards	Example Curricular Performance Indicator (Grade 8)	Corresponding NETS for Students	Example NETS Performance Indicators (Grade 8)
9. Students develop an understanding of and respect for diversity in language use, patterns, and dialects across cultures, ethnic groups, geographic regions, and social roles.	Communicate ideas clearly and concisely to a wide variety of audiences.	Students understand the ethical, cultural, and societal issues related to technology. Students use telecommunications to collaborate, publish, and interact with peers, experts, and other audiences. (Instructional example: Students correspond with e-mail pals and telementors from other cultures and geographic areas.)	7. Collaborate with peers, experts, and others using telecommunications and collaborative tools to investigate curriculum-related problems issues, and information and to develop solutions or products for audiences inside and outside the classroom. 8. Select and use appropriate tools and technology resources to accomplish a variety of tasks and solve problems.
10. Students whose first language is not English make use of their first language to develop competency in the English language arts and to develop understanding of content across the curriculum.	(See sample performance indicators by national standard.)	Students use telecommunications to collaborate, publish, and interact with peers, experts, and other audiences. (Instructional example: Students regularly use English in correspondence and dialogue with other students and telementors.)	7. Collaborate with peers, experts, and others using telecommunications and collaborative tools to investigate curriculum-related problems, issues, and information, and to develop solutions or products for audiences inside and outside the classroom.
11. Students participate as knowledgeable, reflective, creative, and critical members of a variety of literacy communities.	Analyze, interpret, and discuss texts. Critique and offer counter perspectives in an appropriate, precise manner. Participate in class discussions using a variety of formats (i.e., Socratic seminar, literature circle, kiva discussion).	Students use telecommunications to collaborate, publish, and interact with peers, experts, and other audiences. (Instructional example: Students participate in electronic discussions of literature, peer reviewed writing, film, and other class texts with a broad audience, often including authors or other experts.)	7. Collaborate with peers, experts, and others using telecommunications and collaborative tools to investigate curriculum-related problems, issues, and information, and to develop solutions, or products for audiences inside and outside the classroom.
12. Students use spoken, written, and visual language to accomplish their own purposes (e.g., for learning, enjoyment, persuasion, and the exchange of information).	Produce effective persuasive writing that establishes and maintains a clear, consistent purpose or position, builds on strategies for generating, searching, and/or gathering supporting information, results from the purposeful selection of an appropriate text structure for development, provides fully developed supporting information, maintains coherence through devices, such as transitions, parallel structures, repetitions, rhetorical questions, uses precise word choice based on audience and purpose, anticipates and answers an opposing persuasive viewpoint, directs persuasive appeals, and enhances text with graphics, such as charts and diagrams (when appropriate).	Students use productivity tools to collaborate in constructing technology-enhanced models, preparing publications, and producing other creative works. Students use a variety of media and formats to communicate information and ideas effectively to multiple audiences. Students employ technology in the development of strategies for solving problems in the real world. (Instructional example: Students create digital videos that present a persuasive argument that calls for social action or community change.)	4. Use content-specific tools, software, and simulations to support learning and research.

Curriculum Area Professional Organizations and Website Links

Curriculum Area	National Organization	Website Link
Art	National Art Education Association	http://www.naea-reston.org/
Business	National Business Education Association	http://www.nbea.org/
Health	American Association for Health Education	http://www.aahperd.org/aahe/
English/Language Arts	The National Council of Teachers of English	http://www.ncte.org/
English as a Second Language	Teachers of English to Speakers of Other Languages	http://www.tesol.org/s_tesol/index.asp
Foreign Language	American Council on the Teaching of Foreign Languages	http://www.actfl.org/
Mathematics	National Council of Teachers of Mathematics	http://www.nctm.org/
Physical Education	National Association for Sport and Physical Education	http://www.aahperd.org/naspe/
Science	National Science Teachers Association	http://www.nsta.org/
Social Science—Civics and Government	Center for Civic Education	http://www.civiced.org/
Social Science—Economics	National Council on Economic Education	http://www.ncee.net/
Social Science—History	National Center for History in the Schools	http://www.sscnet.ucla.edu/nchs/

In the Classroom Activities Matrix

The National Educational Technology Standards for Students (NETS·S) are identified in each activity in recognition of the multiple applications to these standards. The standards codes are referenced as follows:

I   Basic operations and concepts
II   Social, ethical, and human issues
III   Technology productivity tools
IV   Technology communications tools
V   Technology research tools
VI   Technology problem-solving and decision-making tools

Number	Title	Subjects	Technology	Grades
1.1	Imagine This!	• **Language Arts:** Explore the art of storytelling and the role that imagination plays. • **Social Studies:** Explore the role of culture in imagination. • **Science:** Explore the special characteristics of real versus imaginary animals. • **Mathematics:** Explore drawing to scale.	NETS·S I, III, IV, V • Concept mapping software, Internet, word processors, and drawing software: Technology as a productivity, communications, and research tool. • Develop skill with multiple technologies.	3–5
2.1	Alphabet, Animals, Computer Mice, and Hyperlinks	• **Reading:** Students identify alphabetic animal words and connect new words with their pictures.	NETS·S I, IV • PowerPoint: Technology as a communications tool. • Become familiar with hyperlinks and the computer mouse in presentation software.	K–2

(continued on next page)

Number	Title	Subjects	Technology	Grades
3.1	What Is Technology?	• **Language arts:** Develop ability to use written and visual language to communicate ideas and understandings with words and pictures with a variety of audiences and for different purposes. • **Social studies:** Identify and describe examples in which science and technology have changed the lives of people, such as at home and work.	**NETS · S I, IV, V** • Internet, digital images, and word processors: Technology as a communications and research tool. • Gather and incorporate digital images in a word-processed document.	K–2, 3–5 partners
4.1	What Did You Say and How Should I Write It?	• **Language arts:** Understand textual features for expressing language in various dialects.	**NETS · S I, III, IV** • Word processors: Technology as a communications tool and learning basic operations of technology. • Keyboarding, spelling and grammar checking, formatting tools.	5–9
4.2	Who Was Mark Twain?	• **Social studies:** Develop an interpretive description of Mark Twain, the frontier humorist who wrote *The Adventures of Huckleberry Finn*. Fit this description with information from his childhood.	**NETS · S I, II, III, IV** • Internet, word processors, and concept mapping software: Technology as a communications and productivity tool with consideration of ethical issues. • Use a Web-based search engine to locate, copy, and cite appropriately illustrations and cartoon images of Mark Twain and the times in which he lived.	6–12
4.3	Case #123: The Banning of *The Adventures of Huckleberry Finn*	• **Language arts:** Students acquire new information and respond to needs and demands of society; students use a variety of technological and information resources to gather and synthesize information and to communicate an analysis of social issues. • **Social studies:** Students construct reasoned judgments about specific cultural responses to persistent human issues; students examine persistent issues involving the rights, roles, and status of the individual in relation to the general welfare.	**NETS · S I, II, III, IV, V** • Internet, e-mail in search of supporting evidence using movie editing or presentation software: Technology as a communications, productivity, and research tool. • Use technology to search for supporting evidence for presentation at a mock trial that explores the banning of the novel.	9–12
5.1	A Picture Is Worth a Thousand Words	• **Science:** Demonstrate an understanding about science and technology, specifically that technological solutions have intended benefits and unintended consequences. • **Social studies:** Identify and describe both current and historical examples of the interaction and interdependence of science, technology, and society in a variety of cultural settings. • **Language arts:** Apply a wide range of strategies to comprehend, interpret, evaluate, and appreciate text in the form of a picture.	**NETS · S I, II, III, IV, V** • Internet, word processors: Technology as a communications, productivity, and research tool while also focusing on social, human, and ethical issues. • Use a word processor to express thinking elicited by a picture gathered electronically, appropriately referencing the picture.	6–12

(continued on next page)

Number	Title	Subjects	Technology	Grades
5.2	Are You Good at Estimation?	• **Mathematics:** Understand attributes, units, and systems of measurement and make reasonable estimates of length. • **Science:** Work with and estimate measurements in the metric system.	NETS · S I, II, III, IV, V • Word processors: Technology as a communications, productivity, and research tool. • Create a table and design worksheets that contain digital graphics.	5–9
5.3	Sharing Our Stories	• **Social studies:** Explore and describe similarities and differences in ways that groups, societies, and cultures address similar human needs and concerns.	NETS · S I, III, IV, VI • Word processors and Internet: Technology as a communications tool. • Use technology to collaborate, publish, and interact with peers, experts, and multiple audiences.	K–5
5.4	What Is Marriage?	• **Social studies:** Compare and analyze societal patterns for preserving and transmitting culture while adapting to social change. • **Language arts:** Conduct research on issues and interests by generating ideas and questions, and by posing problems. Gather, evaluate, and synthesize data from a variety of sources to communicate discoveries in ways that suit purpose and audience.	NETS · S I, II, III, IV, VI • Internet and word processors: Technology as a research tool. • Use technology to locate, evaluate, and collect information from a variety of sources. Use word processing to process the collected data and report the results.	9–12
5.5	Constructing Historical Understandings	• **Social studies:** Understand how historical understandings are constructed through the study of two letters from the past.	NETS · S I, II, III, IV, V, VI • Word processors: Technology as a problem-solving and decision-making tool. • Use technology to organize an analysis of two letters and construct comparative interpretations of the documents using formatting tools of the word processor.	9–12
6.1	Which Sample Size Best Estimates the Actual Probability?	• **Mathematics:** Analyze the effect of sample size to identify the best estimate for the actual probability.	NETS · S I, III, VI • Spreadsheets: Technology as a productivity, problem-solving, and decision-making tool while building understanding of basic concepts. • Use a spreadsheet to prepare graphical representations of data from different sample sizes of bags of M&Ms.	5–9
6.2	Target Math	• **Mathematics:** Use the order of operations to compute solutions in a problem-solving investigation.	NETS · S I, III, VI • Spreadsheets: Technology as a productivity, problem-solving, and decision-making tool while building understanding of basic concepts. • Create spreadsheet formulas referencing cells using cell names.	5–9
6.3	On An Average!	• **Mathematics:** Find the average of a set of data.	NETS · S I, III, VI • Spreadsheets: Technology as a productivity, problem-solving, and decision-making tool while building understanding of basic concepts. • Compare built-in formulas with user-defined formulas. Identify strategies for design of reliable and dependable spreadsheets.	5–9

(continued on next page)

Number	Title	Subjects	Technology	Grades
6.4	How Different Were the North and South Before the Civil War?	• **Social studies:** Challenge accepted views of the past.	NETS · S I, II, III, VI • Spreadsheets: Technology as a productivity, problem-solving, and decision-making tool while building understanding of basic concepts. • Investigate Internet data for authenticity and using spreadsheet sort and charting capabilities.	8–12
6.5	How Are My Grades Determined?	• **All subject areas:** Determine grades for a class. • **Mathematics:** Explore greater than and less than in conducting logical tests.	NETS · S I, III, VI • Spreadsheets: Technology as a productivity, problem-solving, and decision-making tool while building understanding of basic concepts. • Absolute and relative cell referencing; formatting in percentage; using the IF formula to print appropriate grade.	8–12
6.6	Is the Homicide Rate Continuing to Increase?	• **Social studies:** Determine the value of various graphical representations of data on the homicide rate in the United States.	NETS · S I, II, III, VI • Spreadsheets: Technology as a communications, problem-solving, and decision-making tool while building understanding of basic concepts and considering ethical issues in presenting data. • Consider ethical presentations of data when changing the scale on chart axes.	8–12
6.7	Have the Voting Patterns Changed?	• **Social studies:** Identify voting patterns in presidential elections from 1952 to 1976.	NETS · S I, II, III, IV,V, VI • Spreadsheets: Technology as a communications, productivity, research, and problem-solving and decision-making tool while building understanding of basic concepts. • Create and manipulate charts to communicate responses to proposed hypotheses.	8–12
6.8	Where Are These Towns in the West?	• **Science, mathematics, and geography:** Develop and evaluate inferences about U.S. towns from predictions based on data analysis.	NETS · S I, III, IV, V, VI • Spreadsheets: Technology as a research and problem-solving tool while building understanding of basic concepts. • Analyze data using averages and standard deviations to prepare charts that help in identifying mystery towns.	5–9
6.9	Satellite Movies or DVD Movies?	• **Mathematics:** Model problems using representations such as graphs, tables, and equations to draw conclusions.	NETS · S I, III, IV, VI • Spreadsheets: Technology as a problem-solving and decision-making tool while building understanding of basic concepts about dynamic spreadsheets. • Creating dynamic spreadsheets that allow for user exploration; using absolute referencing.	7–19

(continued on next page)

Number	Title	Subjects	Technology	Grades
7.1	People, Places, and Wildlife from the Atlantic to the Pacific	• **Social studies:** Study people, places, and environments across the United States. • **Science:** Develop an understanding of animal populations and ecosystems and study various landforms across the United States.	NETS · S I, II, V, VI • Navigating the Internet: Technology as a research and problem-solving tool while building understanding of basic concepts. • Navigate websites in search of valid information.	5–9
7.2	Forming the Grand Canyon	• **Science:** Students investigate the physical processes that shape the patterns of Earth's surface and expand their abilities in scientific inquiry by developing descriptions, explanations, predictions, and models based on evidence and explanations.	NETS · S I, II, III, V, VI • Internet: Technology as a productivity, research, and problem-solving tool while building understanding of basic concepts. • Navigate websites to gather information.	5–9
7.3	For or Against?	• **All subject areas:** Students organize and consolidate their thinking through written communication. They analyze and evaluate written expressions. They must express ideas precisely in writing.	NETS · S I, II, IV, V, VI • Internet: Technology as a communications, research, and problem-solving tool while building understanding of basic concepts. • Use an e-mail listserv to communicate ideas in support of or against a particular proposal.	6–12
7.4	What Will Be Remembered from 9-11?	**All subject areas:** Students organize and consolidate their thinking through written communications. They analyze and evaluate written expressions. Students express ideas precisely in writing.	NETS · S I, II, III, IV, V, VI • Internet: Technology as a communications, productivity, research, and decision-making tool while building understanding of basic concepts. • Incorporate a weblog for communicating ideas triggered by digital images.	6–12
7.5	Women in Mathematics, Science, and Technology	• **Science and mathematics:** Inquire about the role of women in science and mathematics disciplines.	NETS · S I, II, III, IV, V, VI • Internet: Technology as a communications, productivity, research, and decision-making tool while building understanding of basic concepts. • Identify valid and reliable Internet resources for use in conducting a research project.	6–12
7.6	World Hunger	• **Social studies:** Analyze the problem of world hunger and propose solutions to the problem of hunger on a local level.	NETS · S I, II, III, IV, V, VI • Internet: Technology as a research and decision-making tool while building understanding of basic concepts. • Access Internet databases about the availability of food in various places in the world.	6–12
8.1	Evidence of Change	• **Social studies:** Analyze patterns of change. • **Science:** Provide evidence of change. • **Language arts:** Study the change process.	NETS · S I, IV • Multimedia: Technology as a communications tool while building understanding of basic concepts • Morphing pictures in slide-presentation applications.	6–12

(continued on next page)

Number	Title	Subjects	Technology	Grades
8.2	Multimedia Communication—Valuing and Respecting Diversity?	• **Social studies:** Study of America's cultural diversity, explaining how information describes diverse cultural groups.	**NETS · S I, II, IV** • Multimedia: Technology as a communications tool while building understanding of social, ethical, and legal issues involved along with basic concepts of technology. • Evaluating and appreciating the capabilities of multimedia in promoting respect for diversity.	6–12
8.3	Letter or Video Story-telling?	• **Language arts:** Extend literacy skills with respect to spoken, written, and visual language to communicate effectively with different audiences and for a variety of purposes.	**NETS · S I, IV** • Multimedia: Technology as a communications tool while building understanding of basic concepts of technology. • Investigate the making of a movie for communicating a story digitally.	5–9
8.4	Why Do I Need to Learn This Stuff?	• **All subject areas:** Investigate and explain why an educated citizen needs to know the subject.	**NETS · S I, IV, V** • Multimedia: Technology as a communications and research tool while building understanding of basic concepts of creating movies with available technology. • Investigate the making of a movie.	5–9
8.5	Does Climate Identify a Town?	• **Social studies:** Identify and describe people, places, and environments. • **Language arts:** Develop an understanding of and respect for diversity in geographic regions and social roles. • **Science:** Develop descriptions analyzing data and using evidence to support explanations.	**NETS · S I, IV, V, VI** • Multimedia: Technology as a communications, research, and decision-making tool while building understanding of basic concepts of technology. • Incorporate multimedia elements in a PowerPoint presentation.	5–9
9.1	What's in the Sack?	• **Language arts:** Compare students' reading skills used in reading a sequential, linear document with their skills used in reading a hyperlinked document, navigating a nonlinear text to access relevant information or to follow the sequence cues in nonlinear documents.	**NETS · S I, IV** • Hypermedia and Web authoring: Technology as a communications tool while building understanding of basic concepts of Web technology. • Comparing communication via Web-based reading with traditional, sequential reading.	3–5
9.2	Freedom of Speech and the Web?	• **Language arts:** Evaluate the accuracy, relevance, appropriateness, comprehensiveness, and bias of electronic information sources. • **Social studies:** Analyze the influence of diverse forms of public opinion on the development of public policy and decision making. • **Science:** Scientific inquiry and using technology to enhance the gathering of data for an investigation. Challenge investigation procedures with respect to guidelines for scientific investigations.	**NETS · S I, II** • Hypermedia and Web authoring: Consider the ethical, cultural, and societal perspectives displayed by Web presentations in presenting evidence while building understanding of basic concepts of Web technology. • Engage in processes that help in the design and development of Web presentations.	5–9

(continued on next page)

Number	Title	Subjects	Technology	Grades
9.3	How Does the Weather Vary in Our Town?	• **Science:** Investigate weather patterns for specific geographic locations. • **Mathematics:** Calculate averages for data sets and present data in graphical form in a spreadsheet.	**NETS · S I, III, IV** • Hypermedia and Web authoring: Technology as a communications and productivity tool while building understanding of basic concepts of Web technology. • Web authoring and spreadsheets: Integrating, creating, and managing Web information; creating a spreadsheet graphical presentation.	5–9
9.4	What Have I Learned?	• **All subject areas:** Displaying learning outcomes across the content areas.	**NETS · S I, II, III, IV, V, VI** • Hypermedia and Web authoring: Technology as a learning tool while building understanding of basic concepts of Web technology and social, ethical, and legal considerations for Web presentations. • Integrating, creating, and managing Web information; meeting the NETS · S guidelines.	3–12
9.5	A Research Investigation	• **Science:** Understanding scientific inquiry, particularly with respect to making results of investigations public, describing the investigation in ways that enable others to repeat the investigation.	**NETS · S I, II, III, IV, V** • Hypermedia and Web authoring: Technology as a communications and research tool while building understanding of basic concepts of Web technology. • Integrating, creating, and managing Web information; investigating the use of technology tools to report results of research projects.	6–12
9.6	Where Are These Mystery Towns in the United States?	• **Social studies:** Identify towns based on data about the history, society, economy, climate, and other identifying characteristics. • **Language arts:** Develop a set of clues to guide readers in solving a mystery.	**NETS · S I, II, III, IV, V, VI** • Hypermedia and Web Authoring: Technology as a communications, research, problem-solving, and decision-making tool while building understanding of basic concepts of Web technology. • Design a Web presentation that includes a variety of media elements and incorporates hyperlinks.	5–9
10.1	• What Mathematics Did Leonardo da Vinci Use for Drawing Human Figures?	• **Art:** Consider ratios of human parts in drawings. • **Mathematics:** Solve problems involving scale factors, using ratio and proportion. • **Science:** Collecting data to develop a hypothesis about the ratio for a perfect human figure.	**NETS · S V and VI** • Graphing calculators: Technology as a research, problem-solving, and decision-making tool. • Enter data in lists in a calculator; use calculator functions to analyze data.	5–9
10.2	Effective Leads	**Language arts:** Determine the qualities of an effective lead in a piece of narrative.	**NETS · S III, IV** • Graphing calculators: Technology as a productivity and communications tool. • Use a notetaking application of the calculator with a keyboard attachment for ease in entering text information.	5–9

(continued on next page)

Number	Title	Subjects	Technology	Grades
10.3	How Healthy Is This River?	• **Science:** Make observations, gathering data over an extended period of time.	**NETS · S V, VI** • Probeware: Technology as a research, problem-solving, and decision-making tool. • Collect temperatures of water with the temperature probe; analyze the collected data.	5–9
10.4	Can You Name That Tune?	• **Mathematics:** Identify the amplitude, period, phase shift, and vertical shift in the sine function to produce a specific sound. • **Science:** Investigate the Bernoulli effect and its connection with the creation of sound.	**NETS · S V, VI** • Probeware: Technology as a research, problem-solving, and decision-making tool. • Use the probeware microphone to collect the sound waves of various notes.	9–12
10.5	Is Democracy Viewed the Same by All?	• **Social studies:** Explore the concept of democracy portrayed by news articles. Use critical thinking skills in investigating sources of articles.	**NETS · S III, IV, V** • RSS and weblogs: Technology as a productivity, communications, and research tool. • Use RSS and weblog sources to identify articles about a particular topic.	9–12
10.6	Has My Reading Improved?	• **Language arts:** Describe the growth in reading skills developed over time.	**NETS · S II, III, IV** • Podcast: Technology as a productivity and research tool and considering important human issues. • Use podcasting technologies to develop an audio program to communicate.	K–12

Technology Links Matrix

Number	Link Name	Topic
1.1	Memory	Online religious petitions collection at the Library of Congress' American Memory resource.
2.1	Animal	PowerPoint beginning for the alphabet animal presentation.
2.2	Professional Development	An online learning environment for teachers focusing on significant issues in teaching and learning and on ways that innovative uses of technologies can help address those issues.
2.3	Legal	Online resources to support appropriate legal and ethical uses of technology resources.
3.1	Book	Online word processed template for use with In the Classroom 3.1.
4.1	Library	Link to Electronic Text Center at the University of Virginia Library.
4.2	NETS	Electronic versions of the NETS student and teacher guidelines.
4.3	Standards	Electronic versions of national content standards for language arts, mathematics, science, and social studies.
5.1	Truman	The Truman Library link that contains several documents about the atomic bomb that can be retrieved by searching this site on *atomic bomb*.
5.2	Families	Connects you to the iEARN website to join and begin a classroom project among schools around the world.
6.1	Actual	An Excel spreadsheet called M&Mexperiment.xls is available at this book's website. This spreadsheet contains samples of 5 bags, 50 bags, and 100 bags to be used for In the Classroom 6.1. The link connects you to the M&Ms websites to find the actual probability for the United States and also for the United Kingdom.

(continued on next page)

Number	Link Name	Topic
6.2	Census	The best source for data concerning the economic, social, or cultural conditions in the United States is the U.S. Census. Data from historic U.S. censuses are available on various websites, but one of the best is the University of Virginia's Historical Census Browser.
6.3	Climate	The best source of data for In the Classroom 6.8 is available on the Web by searching for Regional Climate Centers. In particular, the Western Regional Climate Center provides the most complete climate data sets. Historical data are available in their Historical Climate Information section. You can download the data or use the link to download ten different mystery town data sets, both temperature and precipitation data. Change the town names to Mystery1, Mystery2, etc., and provide the data sets to your students as they work collaboratively in groups to identify all four mystery towns.
7.1	Internet Map	A visual map of the Internet. Use to connect to the Opte Project and download a graphic providing a colorful display of the millions of connections created by the Internet in one day.
7.2	Pen_pals	Find pen pals all over the world. Use the link to access sites where you can collaborate with teachers and students across the globe.
7.3	Discussion	These discussion group links provide access to interactive, threaded discussions for classroom use.
7.4	WebQuest	WebQuest, created by Bernie Dodge with Tom March at San Diego State University, is a task-oriented activity that focuses the students on using information rather than searching for it. WebQuest links you to more information about the model and to a large number of predesigned WebQuest activities.
7.5	Weblog	This link provides a free website to quickly construct your own weblog, working with online templates to support your writing.
7.6	Digital	Access the digital archives that the Smithsonian Institution is collecting to preserve and present the history of the September 11, 2001, attacks in New York, Virginia, and Pennsylvania and the public responses to them.
7.7	WIP	Access the Web Inquiry Project (WIP) model developed by Philip Molebash at San Diego State University that uses Web resources in promoting classroom inquiry.
8.1	Storyboard	A freeware package video can be downloaded for engaging students in the important preproduction phase for creating a movie. The link connects you to one possible site.
8.2	Storytelling	Investigate different online digital storytelling resources by selecting the Storytelling link.
8.3	Sounds	The link accesses free, legal sound effects to be considered when searching for audio media effects.
9.1	ICT	Connects you with the Information and Communication Technology (ICT) Literacy Maps (use the Publications link) for geography, mathematics, English, and science with additional reports and publications created by the Partnership for 21st Century Skills.

(continued on next page)

Number	Link Name	Topic
9.2	Digital Libraries	Connects you with a variety of online digital libraries for exploration of topics in various subject areas.
10.1	Networked	Connects you with the Texas Instruments activities exchange portal for sharing various content area activities to use with networked systems.
10.2	RSS	Connects you to a free Web-based news aggregator that you can use to begin your explorations of this emerging technology.
10.3	Podcast	Connects you to a free Web space for exploring podcasting as an emerging technology.
13.1	Scoring Guides	Connects you to Kathy Schrock's assessment and rubric information with multiple links to access rubrics for Web pages, PowerPoints, iMovie video projects, and other types of technologies.

Glossary

Absolute Cell Reference Cell reference technique when copying cells in a spreadsheet. When $B$3 is copied to another cell in the spreadsheet, the reference is held constant rather than referencing the particular row or column in which the copy is made. For $B3, what is held constant is the column when copying; for B$3 what is held constant is the row when copying. (Chapter 6)

Absolute Hyperlink A link from one Web page to another Web page that is stored in another computer location, thus having a different Web address. (Chapter 9)

Affective Objective (or Outcome) Statement of emotions that students are to gain from instruction. (Chapters 12 and 13)

Aggregator Software that supports the collection of a variety of news feeds. See RSS. (Chapter 10)

Anchor A Web page feature that identifies a specific location in the page so that hyperlinks may refer to the specific location. (Chapter 9)

ARPANET Created by the U.S. Department of Defense's Advanced Research Projects Agency (ARPA) to enable critical information to be distributed in multiple places and moved from one place to another in a quick and efficient manner. (Chapter 7)

Assessment A process that involves monitoring students' progress toward important learning goals and objectives. (Chapter 13)

Authoring Tools Technology tools that support users in creating presentations including movies, Web presentations, and other forms of communication. (Chapters 8 and 9)

Backbone The main network connections that compose the Internet, which may be envisioned as the trunk of the Internet tree. (Chapter 7)

Behaviorism The field of psychology that focuses on external behavior and the observable stimulus–response when discussing learning. (Chapter 3)

Blog See weblog. (Chapters 7 and 10)

Bot-Based Web Search Bot is short for robot. This technique works the same as in crawler-based searches. (Chapter 7)

Byte The amount of computer memory needed to store one character of a particular size (either 8 or 16 bits). See kilobyte, megabyte, gigabyte, and terabyte for larger storage amounts. (Chapter 1)

Calculator Based Learning (CBL) A handheld, battery-powered instrument that accepts a variety of sensors, including microphone, motion (distance, velocity, acceleration), pH, temperature, and light intensity for real-time data collection. (Chapters 2 and 10)

Calculator Based Ranger (CBR)   A handheld, battery-powered instrument that collects motion data including distance, velocity, and acceleration. (Chapters 2 and 10)

Cell   An individual location in a spreadsheet that is referenced by a row and column, such as B3 where the cell is the intersection of column B and row 3. (Chapter 6)

Channel   A news feed for a specific topic identified in an RSS news aggregator. (Chapter 10)

Chat Rooms   Real-time Internet discussion spaces supporting simultaneous conversations that appear instantly on the screen for everyone. (Chapter 7)

Cognitive Objective (or Outcome)   Statement of intellectual skills students need to gain from instruction. (Chapters 12 and 13)

Cognitive Science   The field of psychology where psychologists are focused on what happens mentally for the learner, how the learner's schema are changed as a result of learning. (Chapter 3)

Concept Map   A graphic tool that provides opportunities to organize ideas and communicate thoughts using visual graphics. (Chapter 8)

Constructivism   The view of learning that holds that the learner must engage in an active role in building understanding and making sense of information. (Chapter 3)

Crawler-Based Web Search   A Web search that relies on a "crawling" technique for collecting information about websites and storing that information in database indexes that are later used for matching words in a user's request to identify potential sources for information. (Chapter 7)

Database   A collection of information organized in fields and records that support easy retrieval. (Chapter 7)

Declarative Knowledge   The ability to present definitions, terms, facts, and descriptions. (Chapter 2)

Deep Web   A more inclusive description of the Web that considers not only the Web pages but also the many databases and nontextual files available within the entire WWW structure. (Chapter 7)

Demonstration   An instructional strategy that is typically teacher-centered with the teacher invoking either direct or inquiry type processes to involve students in thinking about their observations of the demonstration. (Chapter 11)

Dependable Spreadsheets   Spreadsheets that provide accurate results when values on which the calculations are made are changed. (Chapter 6)

Devil's Advocate   A writing strategy that challenges the logic and reasoning of the written content. (Chapter 5)

Digital Age   A term to describe the time when digital computers and related technologies were developed; often considered beginning in the latter half of the twentieth century and used synonymously with Information Age. (Chapter 1)

Digital Storytelling   Delivery of stories, events, or ideas using image and sound capabilities. (Chapter 8)

Direct Instruction   A teacher-centered instructional strategy that usually includes a presentation or demonstration accompanied by teacher explanations, examples, and opportunities for practice and feedback. (Chapter 11)

Discussion Groups   An Internet service that allows messages to be posted in a central location with a subject heading, date, time, and author's name or e-mail. Most discussion boards offer browsing and searching features to identify discussions in a particular area of interest. (Chapter 7)

Dynamic Spreadsheets   Spreadsheets designed so that the user can change the values and see the calculations and graphics changed for the different values, and thus investigate different problems. (Chapter 6)

Electronic Books (eBooks)   Digitized versions of printed books often available on the Web. (Chapter 10)

Electronic Mail (e-mail)   An Internet service that allows people to create, send, and receive messages; for received messages, people can reply, forward, save, delete, or even print. (Chapter 7)

Electronic Portfolios   Portfolios are purposeful collections of an individual's work, including best work and other items that show the growth and development over time in particular classes or activities. Often these collections are more manageable in electronic format, using Web, CD, and other media. (Chapter 5)

Field   Categories of information in each record in a database. (Chapter 7)

File Transfer Protocol (FTP)   A procedure for transferring electronic files from one computer to another, most often used to transfer Web pages to Web server computer. (Chapters 7 and 9)

Formula   Data type in a cell of a spreadsheet that is composed of either built-in formulas or user-defined formulas. The spreadsheet uses the operations and cells referenced in the spreadsheet to return a value to the cell that contains the formula. (Chapter 6)

Gigabyte   A unit of memory equal to one billion bytes, abbreviated as GB. (Chapter 1)

Grouping   A teaching technique to organize students in laboratory or hands-on activities. (Chapter 11)

Heterogeneous Grouping   A grouping strategy that varies the abilities of students in the group. (Chapter 11)

Homogeneous Grouping   A grouping strategy that purposefully arranges the groups with students of similar abilities. (Chapter 11)

Hyperlink   A graphic, icon, or word in a file that when selected automatically links to other information. Three types of links include target (link within a Web page), relative (link to another document in a similar computer location), and absolute (link to another computer). (Chapter 9)

Hypermedia   Technology applications that provide users with the ability to link media in the control of the display of a sequence of ideas. A nonsequential system similar to hypertext that uses computer technology to input, manipulate, and output graphics, sounds, text, and video in the presentation of ideas and information. (Chapters 8 and 9)

Hypertext   A nonsequential association of images, sounds, text, and actions. (Chapter 9)

Hypertext Markup Language (HTML)   An Internet protocol that enables people to create websites. (Chapters 7 and 9)

Indirect Instruction   A student-centered instructional model that includes inquiry, problem solving, and/or discovery learning. (Chapter 11)

Information Age   The term applied to the period where movement of information became faster than physical movement, more narrowly applying to the 1980s onward, sometimes considered in conjunction with the term Digital Age. (Chapter 2)

Inquiry   A teaching strategy that is typically student-centered, involving students in hands-on experiences. (Chapter 11)

International Society for Technology in Education (ISTE)   Professional society dedicated to supporting the use of information technology to aid in learning and in teaching of K–12 students and teachers. (Chapter 2)

Internet   A worldwide network of computer systems that enable users to send and receive information in a variety of formats. (Chapter 7)

Interstate New Teacher Assessment and Support Consortium (INTASC)   A professional organization that provides a framework that specifically addresses the essential knowledge, skills, and abilities of new teachers as they begin their first teaching positions. (Chapter 2)

Kilobyte   A unit of measurement of computer storage equal to 1024 bytes, abbreviated by K or kB. (Chapter 1)

Label   Data type in a cell of a spreadsheet that includes at least one nonnumeric character. If a cell contains a label, the spreadsheet assumes the cell is empty when the cell is referenced in a formula. (Chapter 6)

Laboratory   A student-centered, hands-on teaching strategy. (Chapter 11)

Listserv   Commonly thought of as a Mailing List Server, where a special e-mail delivery protocol automatically sends messages to all subscribers of the list. (Chapter 7)

Logo   A programming language created by Seymour Papert that engages students in an exploration of microworlds. (Chapter 8)

Mailing List Server   See Listserv. (Chapter 7)

Media Literacy   The critical thinking and creative production abilities that utilize an increasingly wide range of messages using images, language, and sound along with the ability to locate, access, analyze, evaluate, manipulate, and communicate information effectively in a variety of formats including printed text, graphics, animation, audio, video, and motion. (Chapter 8)

Megabyte   A unit of computer memory storage equal to one million bytes, abbreviated by MB. (Chapter 1)

Microworld   A programmable environment that supports the creation of characters, agents, worlds, universes; original microworld often thought of with the Logo Language. (Chapter 8)

Multimedia   Applications that support a combination of medias to communicate information, medias including text, still pictures, graphics, animation, sounds, motion, and video. A subset of hypermedia that offers opportunities to create graphics, describe motions, and manipulate text. (Chapters 8 and 9)

National Assessment of Educational Progress (NAEP)   Also known as "the Nation's Report Card" is the only nationally representative and continuing assessment of what America's students know and can do in various subject areas. NAEP has been used to monitor students' progress in reading, mathematics, science, writing, U.S. history, civics, geography, and the arts in grades 4, 8, and 12. (Chapter 3)

National Council for Accreditation of Teacher Education (NCATE)   A professional organization focused on promoting national standards for both the initial preparation and continued professional development of teachers. (Chapter 2)

NETS·S   The National Educational Technology Standards for Students developed by the International Society for Technology in Education. (Chapter 4)

NETS·T   The National Educational Technology Standards for Teachers developed by the International Society for Technology in Education. (Chapter 2)

News Aggregator   A software program for displaying RSS feeds, sometimes referred to as a newsreader. (Chapter 10)

Nutshelling   A writing strategy that focuses on precision of the words and sentences in communicating the author's intent. In this strategy writers examine their writing, looking for the one sentence that captures the core ideas they are trying to express. (Chapter 5)

Objective   A learning outcome for a lesson, which could be cognitive, affective, or psychomotor in nature. (Chapter 12)

Packets   A formatted block of electronic bits of information carried by a computer network that consists of a header, the information being carried, and a trailer that marks the end of the packet. (Chapter 7)

Pedagogical Content Knowledge (PCK)   Teachers' integration of their knowledge of subject matter content with their pedagogical knowledge of teaching and learning that results in the translation of ideas in a form understandable by students. (Chapter 1)

Pedagogical Reasoning   A teacher's reasoning process that begins with comprehension of the subject matter and continues with new comprehension after reflection on instruction. This self-perpetuating process is the transformation of knowledge into a form accessible by the learners. The process model includes five important subprocesses: preparation, representation, selection, adaptation, and tailoring. (Chapter 1)

Podcast   Web-based program focused on distribution of audio and/or video. (Chapter 10)

Portal   A Web display of links to specific websites that are in a common category, such as might be developed through an RSS feed. (Chapter 10)

Presentation Software   Graphics applications, such as PowerPoint, that allow for organization and presentation of ideas in slide format. (Chapter 8)

Prewriting   The first stage in writing that includes all the thinking, creation of notes, and gathering other ideas before the first draft of the writing. (Chapter 5)

Probeware   Computer-based/calculator-based laboratory equipment that combines sensors (or probes) for gathering data with software that supports the storage and analysis of the collected data. Typical sensors include motion, conductivity, temperature, pH, and force. (Chapter 10)

Problem-Based Learning (PBL)   An instructional environment focused on student engagement in a project designed to support their learning. The environment places students in the role of identifying and confronting ill-structured problems in attempting to find some meaningful real-life solution. (Chapters 2 and 7)

Procedural Knowledge   The ability to complete sequences of steps in a task or subtask. (Chapter 2)

Protocol   An Internet system for interacting with and arranging information to be sent such as HTTP for hypertext transfer protocol. (Chapter 7)

Psychomotor Objective (or Outcome)   Statement that describes the physical abilities that students are to demonstrate after instruction.(Chapters 12 and 13)

Publishing   The final stage of writing that is focused on the communication in published form where careful attention is paid to the audience and the format through the final editing process. (Chapter 5)

Questioning   A teaching strategy that is focused on engaging students in the ideas and is used to stimulate student thinking. (Chapter 11)

Record   Row of information in a database that consists of multiple fields of data. (Chapter 7)

Relative Cell Reference   Cell reference technique when copying cells in a spreadsheet. When B3 is copied to another cell in the spreadsheet, the reference is referencing the particular row or column in which the copying is made. See Absolute Cell Reference to hold references constant. (Chapter 6)

Relative Hyperlink   A link from one Web page to another Web page in the same computer location. (Chapter 9)

Revision   The editing stage of writing focused on improving a piece of writing through rethinking the ideas. (Chapter 5)

Rich Text Format (RTF)   A document file format developed and owned by Microsoft for document interchange across platforms. Most word processors are able to read and write RTF documents, indicating that RTF is useful for exchanging files among incompatible word processors. (Chapter 5)

Router   A computer networking device that acts as the junction between two or more networks to transfer data packets among the networks. (Chapter 7)

RSS Newsreader   Rich site summary or really simple syndication is a programming language that enables Web page designers to add content from various sources to their websites, sometimes referenced as an aggregator or news-feed collector. (Chapter 10)

Scaffolding   Arranging instruction to support students in building knowledge and skills with particular learning tools. (Chapter 12)

Schematic Knowledge   The ability to explain why actions are as they are by drawing on both declarative and procedural knowledge, such as principles and mental models. (Chapter 2)

Scoring Guide   Criteria planned for judging the performance and its product on a particular assessment (sometimes called scoring rubric). (Chapter 13)

Search Engine   A database-type software program that supports the location of information on the Internet.(Chapter 7)

Simple Mail Transfer Protocol (SMTP)   Protocol used for sending text messages across the Internet. (Chapter 7)

Spreadsheet   Software application that provides the user a 2 × 2 display of cells that can contain labels, values, or formulas for exploring specific problems that are considered through tables and charts. (Chapter 6)

Storyboard   A multimedia authoring technique that supports the decision-making process for determining the message along with the media to be included in displaying the message and the order and timing of the media. (Chapter 8)

Strategic Knowledge   Knowing when and where to use domain-specific knowledge and strategies, such as planning and problem solving together with monitoring progress toward a goal. (Chapters 2 and 11)

Tablet PC   Wireless electronic computer devices. (Chapter 10)

Target Hyperlink   A link to a particular part of a Web page that is within the page itself. (Chapter 9)

Technological Literacy   Knowledge about basic skills with technologies, use of technologies to search for solutions to problems, and ability to use technologies to learn. (Chapter 4)

Technology   In its broadest terms technology is an amalgamation of products, systems, and processes focused on improving the quality of life. Some think of technology as tools invented by humankind for making work easier and life better. Others think of technology from a more restricted vision, a vision that is bounded by computer-based, electronic technologies. (Chapters 1 and 2)

Technological Pedagogical Content Knowledge (TPCK)   A specialized pedagogical content knowledge (PCK) that teachers need to emphasize their growth and development for teaching with technology. TPCK is an integration of three primary domains of knowledge (subject matter content, teaching and learning, and technology) that teachers merge as they plan for teaching concepts in a form understandable by their students. TPCK is also described as a way of thinking strategically that involves planning, organizing, critiquing, and abstracting for specific content, specific student needs, and specific classroom situations. (Chapters 1 and 2)

Terabyte   A unit of storage equal to one trillion bytes or 1000 gigabytes. (Chapter 1)

Transmission Control Protocol/Internet Protocol (TCP/IP)   Protocol on which the Internet's operational system is based. This protocol specifies the rules for dividing a message into the packets, sending those packets along the best route possible, and reassembling the packets. (Chapter 7)

Uniform Resource Locator (URL)   Address for a particular website.(Chapter 7)

Value   Data type in a cell of a spreadsheet that includes only numeric characters. If a cell contains a value, the spreadsheet uses the value in the cell for any calculation in which it is referenced. (Chapter 6)

Web (World Wide Web or WWW)   A collection of pages on the Internet connected by hyperlinks that allow the user to navigate quickly among the various pages using the hypertext transfer protocol (HTTP). (Chapters 7 and 9)

Web Inquiry Project (WIP) An instructional model similar to WebQuest that encourages students to locate their own Web-based resources and allows for authentic inquiry. Developed by Philip Molebash at San Diego State University. (Chapter 7)

Weblog Online, Web-based communication tool that provides a journaling space that is public for others to read and interact with. Blog for short. (Chapters 7 and 10)

WebQuest A Web-based, six-building-block instruction model created by Bernie Dodge with Tom March to guide teachers in designing task-oriented activities that focus students on analyzing and synthesizing information (some gathered from the Web), rather than simply identifying information. (Chapter 7)

Wiki A Web technology that offers open editing of pages in a website while also archiving previous versions.(Chapters 4 and 5)

Word Processor A computer application designed for creation by input, editing, and production of documents and text. (Chapter 5)

XML (Extensible Markup Language) A language format that is used for calling on remote Web servers to deliver news headlines, summaries, and links to full stories, such as used for RSS newsreaders. (Chapter 10)

Zone of Proximal Development (ZPD) A term identified by Vygotzky (learning theorist) when referring to cognitive functioning of the learner from the point where the learner cannot solve a problem alone but can succeed with adult guidance. (Chapter 3)

References

Allen, R. M. (1999). Ordered-pair relations—a performance assessment. *Mathematics Teaching in the Middle School, 5*(3), 190–94.

Analyzing smoking & lung cancer. (n.d.). Retrieved May 14, 2005 from the University of Virginia, Center for Technology and Teacher Education Web site: http://teacherlink.org/content/math/activities/ex-smoking.

Anderson, L. W. & Krathwohl, D. R. (Eds.). (2001). *A taxonomy for learning, teaching, and assessing: A revision of Bloom's taxonomy of educational objectives.* New York: Longman.

Arter, J. A. & McTighe, J. (2001). *Scoring rubrics in the classroom: Using performance criteria for assessing and improving student performance.* Thousand Oaks, CA: Corwin Press, Inc.

Attia, T. L. (2003). Using school lunches to study proportion. *Mathematics Teaching in the Middle School, 9*(1), 17.

Atwell, N. (1998). *In the middle: New understandings about writing, reading, and learning* (2nd ed.). Portsmouth, NH:Boynton/Cook.

Ausubel, D. P. (1961). In defense of verbal learning. *Educational Theory, 11,* 15–25.

Ayers, E. L. (2002). Technological revolutions I have known. In O. V. Burton (Ed.), *Computing in the social sciences and humanities* (pp. 19–28). Urbana and Chicago: University of Illinois Press

Bangert-Drowns, R. L. (1993). The word processor as an instructional tool: A meta-analysis of word processing in writing instruction. *Review of Educational Research, 63,* 69–93.

Barrett, J. R. (2001). Indispensable inventions. *Learning and Leading with Technology, 29*(1), 22–26.

Battista, M. T. (1993). Mathematics in baseball. *Mathematics Teacher, 86*(4), 336–342.

Bell, R. L. & Garofalo, J (Ed). (2005). *Science units for grades 9–12.* Eugene,OR: International Society for Technology in Education.

Bell, R. L., Niess, M. L., & Bell, L. (2001–02). El Niño did it: Climate phenomena model integrating technology with teaching science and mathematics. *Learning and Leading with Technology, 29*(4), 18–26.

Borko, H. & Putnam, T. (1996). Learning to teach. In Berliner, D. C. & Calfee, R. C. (Eds.), *Handbook of Educational Psychology* (pp. 673–708). New York: Simon & Schuster Macmillan.

Bowen, A. & Bell, R. (2004). Winging it: Using digital imaging to investigate butterfly metamorphosis. *Learning and Leading with Technology, 31*(6), 24–27.

Brown, N. M. (1993). Writing activities. *Arithmetic Teacher 41*(1), 20–21.

Bugliarello, G. (1995). Science, technology and society. *Bulletin of Science, Technology and Society, 15*(5–6), 228–234.

Bull, G. & Bull, G. (2001). Virtual art. *Learning and Leading with Technology, 29*(3), 54–58.

Bull, G., Bull, G., & Sigmon, T. (1997b). Common protocols for shared communities. *Learning and Leading with Technology, 25*(1), 50–53.

Bull, G., Bull, G. & Walker, L. (2000). Writing with abandon. *Learning and Leading with Technology, 28*(1), 54–57.

Burns, M. (2002). Beyond show and tell: Using spreadsheets to solve problems. *Learning and Leading with Technology, 31*(2), 22–27.

Bush, V. (1945). As we may think. *The Atlantic Monthly*, 101–103.

Calkins (1994). *The art of teaching writing.* Portsmouth, NH: Heinemann.

Calkins - Lehr, F. (1995). *Revision in the writing process.* ERIC Digest. ERIC Clearinghouse on Reading English and Communication.

Cangelosi, J. S. (1990). *Designing tests for evaluating student achievement.* New York: Longman.

Carroll, J. A., Kelly, M. G., & Witherspoon, T. L. (2003). *Multidisciplinary units for prekindergarten through grade 2.* Eugene, OR: International Society for Technology in Education.

Carter, A. J. R. (1999). Using spreadsheets to model population growth, competition and predation in nature. *American Biology Teacher, 61*(4), 294–296.

Cetron, M. J. & Davies, O. (2003). *50 trends shaping the future (special report).* Bethesda, MD: World Future Society.

Chesebrough, D. (1993). Using computers: Candy calculations. *Learning, 21*(7), 40.

Chiappetta, E. L. & Koballa, T. R. (2002). *Science instruction in the middle and secondary schools* (5th ed.). Columbus, OH: Merrill Prentice Hall.

Clark, C. M. & Elmore, J. L. (1981). *Transforming curriculum in mathematics, science and writing: A case study of teacher yearly planning.* (Research Series 99). East Lansing: Michigan State University Institute for Research on Teaching.

Clark, C. M. & Peterson, P. L. (1981). Stimulated-recall. In B. R. Joyce, C. C. Brown, & L. Peck (Eds.), *Flexibility in teaching: An excursion into the nature of teaching and training.* New York: Longman.

Clark, C., & Peterson, P. (1986). Teachers' thought processes. In M. R. Wittrock (Ed.), *Handbook of research on teaching* (3rd ed.) (pp. 255–296). Upper Saddle River, NJ: Merrill/Prentice Hall.

Collecting and numerically analyzing M&Ms data. (n.d.). Retrieved May 14, 2005 from the University of Virginia, Center for Technology and Teacher Education Web site: http://teacherlink.org/content/math/activities/ex-mmnumerical.

Consortium of National Arts Education Associations (1994). *National Standards for Arts Education.* Reston, VA: Music Educators National Conference

Curtis, M., Kopera, J., Norris, C., & Soloway, E. (2004). *Palm OS® handhelds in the elementary classroom: Curriculum and strategies.* Eugene, OR: International Society for Technology in Education.

Danielson, C. (1997). *A collection of performance tasks and rubrics: Upper elementary school mathematics.* Larchmont, NY: Eye on Education.

Dede, C. (2004a). Enabling distributed learning communities via emerging technologies – part one. *T H E Journal, 32*(2), 12.

Dede, C. (2004b). Enabling distributed learning communities via emerging technologies – part two. *T H E Journal, 32*(3), 16.

Dexter, S. & Watts-Taffe, S. (2000). Processing ideas: Move beyond word processing into critical thinking. *Learning and Leading with Technology, 27*(6), 22–27.

Dodge, B. (2001). Five rules for writing a great WebQuest. *Learning and Leading with Technology, 28*(8), 6–9, 58.

Drier, H. S. (1999). Do vampires exist? *Learning and Leading with Technology 27*(1), 22–25.

Drier, H. S. (2001). Teaching and learning mathematics with interactive spreadsheets. *School Science and Mathematics, 101*(4), 170–179.

Dunham, P. H. & Dick, T. P. (1994). Connecting research to teaching: Research on graphing calculators. *The Mathematics Teacher, 87*(6), 440–445.

Eggen, P.D. & Kauchak, D. P. (1996). *Strategies for teachers: Teaching content and thinking skills.* Boston: Allyn & Bacon.

Eisner, E. W. (2003). Preparing for today and tomorrow. *Educational Leadership, 61*(4), 6.

Elfrank-Dana, J. (2001–02). Building and using a web database with FrontPage. *Learning and Leading with Technology, 29*(4), 14–17, 62–63.

Exploring sunspots. (n.d.). Retrieved May 14, 2005 from the University of Virginia, Center for Technology and Teacher Education Web site: http://teacherlink.org/content/math/activities/ex-sunspots/home.html.

Fogarty, J., Wang, M., & Creek, R. (1983). A descriptive study of experienced and novice teachers' interactive instructional thoughts and actions. *Journal of Educational Research, 77*(1), 22–32.

Francis, J. W., & Sellers, J. A. (1994). Studying amino acid sequence using word processing programs. *American Biology Teachers, 56*(8), 484–487.

Frenandez, M. L. (1999). Making music with mathematics. *Mathematics Teacher, 92*(2), 90–95.

Friedlander, A. (1998). An EXCELlent bridge to algebra. *Mathematics Teacher, 91*(5), 382.

Gastineau, J., Appel, K., Bakken, C., Sorenen, R., & Vernier, D. (2000). *Physics with calculators.* Portland, OR: Vernier Software.

Gibson, J.J. (1979). *The ecological approach to visual perception.* Boston: Houghton Mifflin.

Gillett, M., & Gall, M. (1982, March). *The effects of teacher enthusiasm on the at-task behavior of students in the elementary grades.* Paper presented at the annual meeting of the American Educational Research Association, New York.

Godsall, L., Crescimano, L., & Blair, R. (2005). Exploring tablet PCs. *Learning and Leading with Technology, 32*(8), 16–21.

Goldberg, K. P. (1992). Database programs and the study of seashells. *The Computing Teacher, 19*(7), 32–34.

Golden, J. R. (n.d.). *Child mortality in our world.* Retrieved May 14, 2005, from University of Virginia, Center for Technology and Teacher Education Web site: http://teacherlink.org/content/social/instructional/mortality/home.htm.

Golub, J. (1999 a & b). *Making learning happen.* Portsmouth: Boynton Cook.

Golub, J. (1999 a & b). Thoughts worth thinking about: Reflections, connections, projections. *The Virginia English Bulletin, 49* (2).

Good, T., & Brophy, J. (2002). *Looking in classrooms* (9th ed.). New York: Longman.

Graham, B. (n.d.). *Economic perspectives in colonial America.* Retrieved May 14, 2005 from University of Virginia, Center for Technology and Teacher Education Web site: http://teacherlink.org/content/social/instructional/ameconpop/home.html.

Graham, B. (n.d.). *Job distribution after 1945.* Retrieved May 14, 2005 from University of Virginia, Center for Technology and Teacher Education Web site: http://teacherlink.org/content/social/instructional/jdistrib/home.html.

Greeno, J. G., Collins, A. M., & Resnick, L. B. (1996). Cognition and learning. In D. Berliner & R. Calfee (Eds.), *Handbook of Educational Psychology* (pp. 15–45). New York: MacMillan.

Grimmett, P., & MacKinnon, A. M. (1992). Craft knowledge and the education of teachers. In G. Grant (Ed.). *Review of research in education* (pp. 382–456). Washington, D. C. : American Educational Research Association.

Grossman, P. L. (1989). A study in contrast: Sources of pedagogical content knowledge for secondary English. *Journal of Teacher Education, 40*(5), 24–31.

Grossman, P. L. (1990). *The making of a teacher: Teacher knowledge and teacher education.* New York: Teachers College Press.

Hagins, C., Austin, J., Jones, R., & Timmons T. (2004). Authors "in residence" making writing fun! *Learning and Leading with Technology, 31*(6), 36–30.

Hanfland, P. (1999). Electronic portfolios: Students documenting their best work. *Learning and Leading with Technology, 26*(6), 54–57.

Hannah, L., Menchaca, M., & McVicker , B. (Eds.). (2002). *Multidisciplinary Units for Grades 3–5,* Eugene, OR: International Society for Technology in Education.

Harris, J. (2000–2001). Virtual vantage points: Using webcams for teleresearch. *Learning and Leading with Technology, 28*(6), 14–17, 54–55.

Harris, J. (2003). Generative connections: An Internet-supported response to standards schizophrenia. *Learning and Leading with Technology, 30*(7), 46–49,59.

Harris, J., White, P., & Fisher, B. (2003). Helping dependent readers use the Web. *Learning and Leading with Technology, 31*(3), 40–45.

Harrow, A. J. (1972). *A taxonomy of the psychomotor domains: A guide for developing behavior objectives.* New York: David McKay.

Heard, G. (2003). *The Revision Toolbox.* Portsmouth: Heinemann.

Hemmer, J. (1998). Eduardo's year in seventh grade: A technology integration vignette: Part 2. *Learning and Leading with Technology, 25*(6), 25–29.

Hersberger, J. & Frederick, T. M. (1995). Flower beds and landscape consultants: Making connections in middle school mathematics. *Mathematics Teaching in the Middle School, 1*(5), 364–367.

Hollis, R. (1990). Database yearbooks in the second grade. *The Computing Teacher, 17*(6), 14–15.

Holmes, B. (1998). The database: America's presidents. *Learning and Leading with Technology, 25*(7), 6–11.

Holmes, E. D. (1997). The spreadsheet—absolutely elementary!. *Learning and Leading with Technology, 24*(8), 6–12.

Hooper, K. (1990). Multimedia in education. In S. Ambron, & K. Hooper (Eds.), *Interactive multimedia Redmond* (pp. 316–330). Redmond, WA: Microsoft Press.

Insinnia, E., Skaecki, E., & Tucker, J. (2000). Teach a novel without the Internet? Never again!. *Learning and Leading with Technology, 27*(8), 28–35.

International Society for Technology in Education. (2000). *National educational technology standards for students: Connecting curriculum and technology.* Eugene, OR: International Society for Technology in Education.

International Society for Technology in Education. (2002). *National educational technology standards for teachers: Preparing teachers to use technology.* Eugene, OR: International Society for Technology in Education.

Interstate New Teacher Assessment and Support Consortium. (1993). *Model standards for beginning teacher licensing and development: A resource for state dialogue.* Washington, DC: Council of Chief State School Officers.

Jankowski, L. (1998). Educational computing: Why use a computer for writing? *Learning and Leading with Technology, 25*(6), 30–33.

Johnson, R. L., DeMoss, G. S., & Sorensen, R. (2002). *Earth science with calculators*. Portland, OR: Vernier Software.

Johnson, R. L., Holman, S., & Holmquist, D. D. (1999). *Water quality with CBL*. Portland, OR: Vernier Software.

Jonassen, D.H. (1997). Instructional design models for well-structured and ill-structured problem-solving learning outcomes. *Educational Technology: Research and Development, 45*(1), 65–95.

Joyce, B., Weil, M., & Calhoun, E. (2004). *Models of teaching* (7th ed.). Boston: Pearson Education.

Kajder, S. & Bull, G. (2003). Scaffolding for struggling students: Reading and writing with Blogs. *Learning and Leading with Technology, 31*(2), p. 32–35

Kelly, M. G. & Haber, J. (2006). *Resources for student assessment*. Eugene, OR: International Society for Technology in Education.

Krathwohl, D. R., Bloom, B. S., & Masia, B. B. (1964). *Taxonomy of educational objectives. Handbook II: Affective domain*. New York: David McKay.

Kulik, J.A. (1994). Meta-analytic studies of findings on computer-based instruction. In E.L. Baker & H.F. O'Neil, Jr. (Eds.), *Technology assessment in education and training*. Hillsdale, NJ: Lawrence Erlbaum.

Lee, J. K. (n.d.). *Social demographics and election statistics*. Retrieved May 14, 2005 from University of Virginia, Center for Technology and Teacher Education Web site: http://teacherlink.org/content/social/instructional/election/home.html.

Lee, J. K. (2007). *Elementary social studies*. Hoboken, NJ: Wiley & Sons.

Lee, J. K. & Moelbash, P. (2004). Using digital history for positive change in social studies education. *Journal of Computing in Teacher Education, 20*(4), 153–157.

Lehman, J. R. & Kandle, T. M. (1995). SSMILes: Popcorn investigations for integrating mathematics, science, and technology. *School Science and Mathematics, 95*(1), 46–49.

Lewis, P. (1997 a & b). Using productivity software for beginning language learning—part 2: Spreadsheets, databases & mail merge. *Learning and Leading with Technology, 25*(1), 12–17.

Lewis, P. (1997 a & b). Using productivity software for beginning language learning—part 1. The word processor, *Learning and Leading with Technology 24*(8), 14–17.

Littlefield, H. M. (1964). The Wizard of Oz: Parable on populism. *American Quarterly* 16 (2): 47–58.

Lucas, K. B. (1994). Charting northern skies with the aid of a spreadsheet. *School Science and Mathematics, 94*(3), 151–57.

Margerum-Leys, J. & Marx, R. W. (2002). Teacher knowledge of educational technology: A study of student teacher/mentor teacher pairs. *Journal of Educational Computing Research, 26*(4), 427–462.

Martorell, P. H., Beal, C. M., & Bolick, C. M. (2006). *Teaching social studies in the middle and secondary schools*.Upper Saddle River, NJ: Person Merrill Prentice Hall.

Marzan, R. J., Pickering, D. J., & Pollock, J. E. (2001). *Classroom instruction that works: Research-based strategies for increasing student achievement*. Alexandria, VA: Association for Supervision and Curriculum Development.

McCombs, J. (2001). Coloring outside the lines. *Learning and Leading with Technology, 29*(1), 28–30, 57.

McKenzie, W. (Ed.). (2004). *Social studies units for grades 9–12*. Eugene, OR: International Society for Technology in Education.

Mishra, P. & Koehler, M. J. (2006). Technological pedagogical content knowledge: A framework for integrating technology in teacher knowledge. *Teachers College Record, 108*(6), 1017–1054.

Mittlefehldt, B. (1991). Social studies problem solving with databases. *The Computing Teacher, 18*(5), 54–55.

Molebash, P. E. (2004). Web historical inquiry projects. *Social Education, 68*(3), 226–229.

Morrison, C., Moor, D., & Numaly, D. (1999). Traversing the web up the Mississippi to Lake Itasca: An Internet experience. *Learning and Leading with Technology, 26*(7), 14–17.

Multisilta, J. (1996). *Hypermedia Learning Environment for Mathematics*.Unpublished doctoral dissertation, Tampere University of Technology, Publication 183, Finland.

Murray, D. (1982). *Learning by teaching: Selected articles on learning and teaching*. Montclair, NJ: Boynton/Cook.

Murray, D. (1994). Teach writing as process not product. In Graves, R. (Ed.) *Rhetoric and composition: A sourcebook for teachers and writers*. Upper Montclair, NJ: Boynton/Cook.

National Academy of Sciences. (1996). *National science education standards*. Washington, DC: National Academy Press.

National Board for the Professional Teaching Standards. (1994). *Toward high and rigorous standards for the teaching professional*. Arlington, VA: Author.

National Council for Accreditation of Teacher Education. (2002). *Professionals standards for the accreditation of schools, colleges, and departments of education*. Washington, DC: Author.

National Center for Study of History in the Schools (1996). *National standards for United States history*. Los Angeles: UCLA

National Council for the Social Studies. (1994). *Expectations of excellence – Curriculum standards for social studies*. Silver Spring, MD: Author.

National Council of Teachers of English. (1996). *Standard for the English language arts*. Urbana, Illinois: Author.

National Council of Teachers of Mathematics (2000). *Principles and standards for school mathematics*. NCTM, Reston, Virginia.

National Science and Technology Council. (2002). *2020 visions: Transforming education and training through advanced technologies.*http://www.visions2020.gov/Papers.htm

Nelson, T. H. (1974). *Dream machines.*Redmond, WA: Microsoft Press.

Newman, J. M. (1989). The flexible page (online). *Language Arts, 66*(4), 57–64.

Niess, M. L. (1992). Math: Winds of change. *Computing Teacher, 19*(6), 32–35.

Niess, M. L. (1992). Mathematics and M&Ms. *The Computing Teacher, 20*(1), 29–31.

Niess, M. L. (1998). Using computer spreadsheets to solve equations. *Learning and Leading with Technology, 26*(3), 22–24, 26–27.

Niess, M. L. (2005). Preparing teachers to teach science and mathematics with technology: Developing a technology pedagogical content knowledge. *Teaching and Teacher Education, 21*, 509–523.

Norton, P. & Harvey, D. (1995). Information knowledge: Using databases to explore the tragedy at Donner Pass. *Learning and Leading with Technology, 23*(1), 23–25.

O'Hara, S. & McMahon, M. (2002). Imagination. In Hannah, L., Menchaca, M., & McVicker, B. (Eds.), *Multidisciplinary units for grades 3–5*. Eugene, OR: International Society for Technology in Education.

O'Hara, S. & McMahon, M. (Eds.). (2003). *Multidisciplinary units for grades 6–8*. Eugene, OR: ISTE.

Papert, S. (1980). *Mindstorms: Children, computers, and powerful ideas*. New York: Basic Books, Inc.

Parkay, F. W. & Stanford, B. H. (1995). *Becoming a teacher* (3rd ed.). Needham Heights, MA: Allyn & Bacon.

Parker, J. & Widmer, C. (1991). Teaching mathematics with technology: How big is a million? *Arithmetic Teacher, 39*(1), 38–41.

Partnership for 21st Century Skills. (2004). *Framework for 21st Century Learning*. Retrieved September 30, 2006 from: http://www.21stcenturyskills.org/.

Pierson, M. E. (2001). Technology integration practices as function of pedagogical expertise. *Journal of Research on Computing in Education, 33*(4), 413–429.

Prensky, M. (2001). Digital natives, digital immigrants. *On the Horizon, 9*(5).

Project 2061. (1993). *Benchmarks for science literacy*. New York: Oxford University Press.

Putnam, R. T., & Borko, H. (2000). What do new views of knowledge and thinking have to say about research on teacher learning? *Educational Researcher, 29*(1), 4–15.

Ramondetta, J. (1992). Learning from lunchroom trash. *Learning, 20*(8), 59.

Reissman, R. (1991). Using computers: Movie matters. *Learning, 20*(4), 48.

Reissman, R. (1996). Computerized fortune cookies – A classroom treat. *Learning and Leading with Technology 23*(5), 25–26.

Reissman, R. (2001). Someone's in the kitchen: Multimedia activities for multidisciplinary exploration. *Learning and Leading with Technology, 28*(7), 46–49.

Richardon, W. (2004). Blogging and RSS – The "what's it?" and "how to" of powerful new Web tools for educators. *MultiMedia, 11*(1), 10.

Riggs, I. M. & Enochs, L. G. (1993). A microcomputer beliefs inventory for middle school students: Scale development and validation. *Journal of Research on Computing in Education, 25*(3), 383–391.

Rogers, E. M. (2003). *Diffusion of innovations* (5th ed.). New York: Free Press.

Ross, D. D. (1989). First steps in developing a reflective approach. *Journal of Teacher Education, 40*(2), 22–30.

Sandholtz, J., Ringstaff, C., & Dwyer, D. (1997). *Teaching with technology: Creating student-centered classrooms*. New York: Teachers College, Columbia University.

Santrock, J. W. (2006). *Educational psychology* (2nd ed.). Boston: McGraw Hill.

Shavelson, R., Ruiz-Primo, A., Li, M., & Ayala, C. (2003). *Evaluating new approaches to assessing learning* (CSE Report 604). Los Angeles: University of California, National Center for Research on Evaluation.

Shulman, L. S. (1986). Those who understand: Knowledge growth in teaching. *Educational Researcher, 15*(2), 4–14.

Silverstein, S. (1974). *Where the sidewalk ends*. New York: Harper and Row.

Simmons, J. M., Sparks, G. M., Starko, A., Pasch, M., Coloton, A., & Grinberg, J. (1989, March). *Exploring the structure of reflective pedagogical thinking in novice and expert teachers: The birth of a developmental taxonomy*. Paper presented at the annual meeting of the American Educational Research Association, San Francisco, CA.

Sims, K. C. (2001). Great US women: Student research projects with a multimedia twist. *Learning and Leading with Technology, 29*(1), 42–47.

Snyder, I. (1993). The impact of computers on students' writing: A comparative study of the effects of pens and word processors on writing context, process and product. *Australian Journal of Education, 37*(1), 5–25.

Sowell, E. J., & Casey, R. J. (1982). *Research methods in education*. Belmont, CA: Wadsworth.

Staley, D. J. (2002). *Computers, visualization, and history: How new technology will transform our understanding of the past*. Armonk, NY: M. E. Sharpe, Inc.

Stiggins, R. J. (2005). *Student-involved assessment for learning* (4th ed.). Columbus, OH: Pearson/Merrill Prentice Hall.

Strickland, J. (1997). *From disk to hard copy: Teaching writing with computers*. Portsmouth, NH: Boynton/Cook Publishers.

Strickland, A. W., & Hoffer, T. (1990–91). Integrating computer database with laboratory problems. *The Computing Teacher, 18*(4), 30–32.

Trowbridge, L. W., Bybee, R. W., & Carlson-Powell, J. (2004). *Teaching secondary school science: Strategies for developing scientific literacy* (8th ed.). Upper Saddle River, NJ: Prentice Hall.

Truett, C. (2001). Sherlock Holmes on the Internet: Language arts teams up with the computing librarian. *Learning and Leading with Technology, 29*(2), 36–41.

Tufte, E. R. (2003). *The cognitive style of Power-Point*. Cheshire, CT: Graphics Press LLC.

Twain, M. (2001). *The adventures of Huckleberry Finn*. New York: Modern Library, a division of Random House, Inc. (Original work published 1885).

uit Beijerse, R.P. (2000). Questions in knowledge management: Defining and conceptualizing a phenomenon. *Journal of Knowledge Management, 3*(2), 94–109.

U. S. Department of Commerce. (2003). *2020 visions: Transforming education and training through advanced technologies*. Washington, DC: Author.

Van de Walle, J. (2006). *Elementary and middle school mathematics: Teaching developmentally* (6th Ed.). Boston: Allyn & Bacon.

Volz, D., & Sapatka, S. (2000). *Middle school science with calculators*. Portland, OR: Vernier Software.

Vygotsky, L. S. (1962). *Thought and language*. Cambridge, MA: MIT Press.

Wang, L., Ertmer, P. A., & Newby, T. J. (2004). Increasing preservice teachers' self-efficacy beliefs for technology integration. *Journal of Research on Technology in Education, 36*(3), 231–250.

Wiebe, J. H. (1992). Word processing, desktop publishing and graphics in the mathematics classroom, *The Computing Teacher, 19*(5), 39–40.

Werner, W. (2002). Reading visual texts. *Theory and Research in Social Education, 30*(3), 401–428.

Wertsch, J. V. (1991). *Voices of the mind: A sociocultural approach to mediated action*. Cambridge, MA: Harvard University Press.

Wiggins, G., & McTighe, J. (2005). *Understanding by design.* Upper Saddle River, NJ: Pearson/Merrill Prentice Hall.

Wilson, S. M., Shulman, L. S., & Richert A. E. (1987). '150 different ways' of knowing: Representations of knowledge in teaching. In J. Calderhead (Ed.), *Exploring teachers' thinking* (pp.104–124). London: Cassell.

Wineburg, S. S. (1991). Historical problem solving: A study of cognitive processes used in the evaluation of documentary and pictorial evidence. *Journal of Educational Psychology, 83*, 73–87.

Wood, D., Bruner, J., & Ross, S. (1976). The role of tutoring in problem solving. *British Journal of Psychology, 66*, 181–191.

Woolfolk-Hoy, A. (2004). *Educational psychology* (9th ed.). Boston: Pearson Allyn & Bacon.

Zhao, Y. (2003). *What teachers should know about technology: Perspectives and practices*. Greenwich, CT: Information Age Publishing.

Name Index

Subject Index